IN SEARCH OF
MICHAEL HOWARD

IN SEARCH OF
MICHAEL HOWARD

MICHAEL CRICK

SIMON &
SCHUSTER

London · New York · Sydney · Toronto · Dublin

A VIACOM COMPANY

First published in Great Britain by Simon & Schuster UK Ltd, 2005
A Viacom Company

Copyright © 2005 by Michael Crick

The right of Michael Crick to be identified as author of this work
has been asserted in accordance with sections 77 and 78 of the
Copyright, Designs and Patents Act, 1988.

1 3 5 7 9 10 8 6 4 2

Simon & Schuster UK Ltd
Africa House
64–78 Kingsway
London WC2B 6AH

www.simonsays.co.uk

Simon & Schuster Australia
Sydney

A CIP catalogue record for this book
is available from the British Library

ISBN 0-7432-6829-6

Typeset in Bembo by M Rules
Printed and bound in Great Britain
by Mackays of Chatham plc

CONTENTS

THE HOWARD FAMILY TREE

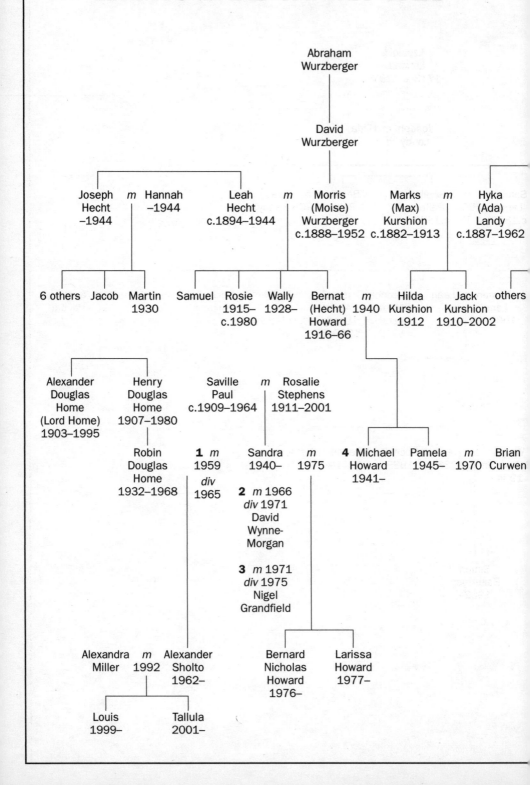

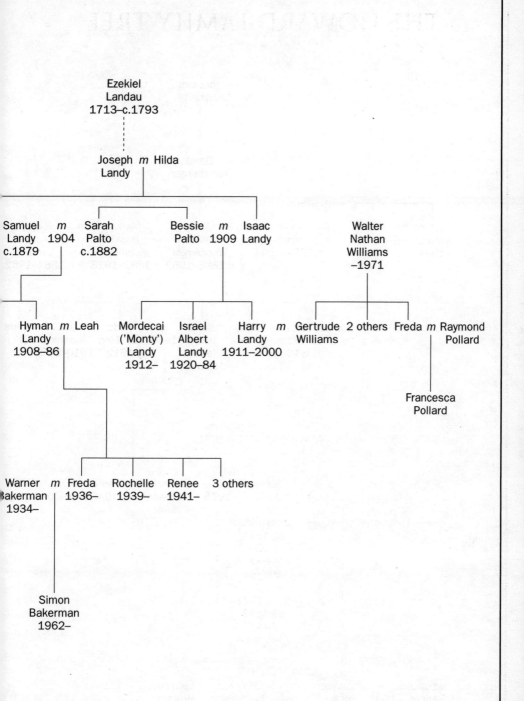

THE COWARD FAMILY TREE

INTRODUCTION

'Relaxed?' said the former Home Office official in disbelief. 'Michael Howard? *Relaxed* about you writing a book about him? You've got to be joking.'

But 'relaxed' had been the official word from the new Conservative leader's office when I wrote to him in December 2003 announcing that I had been commissioned to write this biography. I wasn't seeking Howard's approval or co-operation – that's not the way I operate; I feel more comfortable writing biographies independently of the subject. Michael Howard's response was that he wouldn't interfere: he wouldn't either encourage or discourage his friends from talking and it was up to them (and most of his closest friends subsequently did speak to me). Strangely, he was a lot more concerned about close members of his family. His 92-year-old mother, Hilda, said she wanted to help, but explained that she had been 'told' not to.

I first met Michael Howard in April 1987 in the garden of the British Embassy in Tokyo, where I had been sent as a reporter for *Channel 4 News* to cover his efforts as a junior trade minister to persuade the Japanese to open up their financial markets and telecommunications industry to British firms – what was seen as a big story at the time. We met again a few weeks later when a friend of mine bought Howard's home in Notting Hill and invited us both to his house-warming party. Howard intrigued me. Here was clearly a politician of great intelligence and potential, with an engaging smile, yet he was hard to get to know. He seemed suspicious of me as a journalist. I soon learned Michael Howard is a very private individual, which makes him all the more challenging as a biographical subject; this also explains much of his difficulty in engaging with the British electorate.

It was with some trepidation that I wrote to him at the end of 2003, for our most recent encounter, only three months earlier, had involved a heated row. It had occurred in, of all places, a Jewish old people's home in Willesden, where I was filming for BBC *Newsnight* in the Brent East by-election. After we had recorded a bit of footage with Howard, a couple of elderly women had beckoned us over to come and talk to them, and I happily did so, since I take the old-fashioned view that elections are as much about voters as politicians. Howard got extremely upset when he saw this. We should confine our filming to him, he insisted; and when we refused to comply with this condition, he threw us out. It was an interesting insight into a less attractive side of his character. Ironically, the two Jewish ladies were among the few people I met in Brent that week who said they'd be voting Conservative.

In the early 1990s, with the end of the Cold War and the election of John Major and Tony Blair as leaders of the Conservative and Labour parties, British politics entered an era in which the role of ideological and class conflict has greatly diminished. The old Left–Right battles of the post-war period – unions versus management, state control versus private enterprise, and East versus West on the international stage – are now history. Over the last decade the policy differences between the main players at Westminster have shrunk dramatically – elections are now fought over variations of a few billion pounds in tax or public spending. The differences between what the parties *end up doing* once elected are closer still, despite the efforts of politicians and many journalists to persuade us that the divisions are still great. When parties are more and more alike in terms of policy, then politicians' character, competence and integrity become much more relevant. Tony Benn may say politics should be confined to 'ishoos', but for most voters in 2005, as in 1997 and 2001, the personal traits of those seeking our support are as important as anything they promise to do if elected. Nowadays people often vote according to whether they feel comfortable with a candidate and accept his or her 'values'.

I have relied on huge help in writing this book. Mark Garnett, the author of two excellent biographies of Keith Joseph and Willie Whitelaw, has been a faithful companion and guide; quite apart from his extensive contribution in terms of knowledge and research, he prepared a preliminary draft of most of the latter half of the work. Miles Goslett did much of the work on Sandra Howard, Howard's efforts to find a seat, his record at the Bar, and Folkestone. Tom Lumley also gave valuable research help. I am grateful to my *Newsnight* colleague Louise Weston for obtaining tapes and ferreting out facts. Luke Pearce helped with transcriptions, and research in Llanelli; and my daughter Catherine copied several reams-worth of press cuttings.

Michael Jolles, the author of *A Directory of Distinguished British Jews 1830–1930*, advised me on aspects of Jewish culture and history, while Charles Tucker tried to unravel parts of the complicated Howard genealogy. In Romania I would have been lost without the help of George Iurca during my visits to Ruscova, and he and his wife provided wonderful hospitality. John Lloyd at the Home Office was patient and very responsive to my requests for access to the naturalisation files of various Howard relatives.

In Llanelli, Yvonne Jones of the local history library and Laura Grime of the *Llanelli Star* went out of their way; I was made most welcome by Eric Lewis and his colleagues at Graig School; Barrie Lewis saved much effort by putting me in touch with numerous old boys of Llanelli Grammar School; and Emyr Phillips was a regular source of advice.

For the Cambridge years I am grateful to Malcolm Balen for lending me material gathered for his biography of Ken Clarke, and to Victoria Prentis for her work on the university Conservative association. Godfrey Waller at the university library was a model of the perfect librarian. David Bailey assisted with Howard's legal career. Covering his time at Westminster, Lewis Baston, Michael Cockerell, Simon Coates, David Butler, and Sarah Knight of *Breakfast with Frost* generously gave me access to their past interviews, and Mark

Hollingsworth also copied parts of his great archive. Andrew Roth allowed me to use his amazing biographical files. Philip Cowley of Nottingham University helped with Howard's voting record and recent Conservative leadership contests. Ingrid Hassler, Susan Gray and Martin Durham also deserve praise, along with Mike Morton of Transylvania Uncovered.

The research involved interviews with several hundred people, many of whom are cited in the footnotes. Among these, I am especially grateful to John Butcher, John Entwistle, Jo Gladstone, Leslie Griffiths, Celia Haddon, Martin Hecht, Deian Hopkin, Peter Kilfoyle, Norman Lamont, Gordon McKelvie, Margaret Morgan, Ben Patterson, George Stern, Barry Sutlieff, Peter Temple-Morris, Keith Thomas, Peter Thurnham, John Toulmin, Nina Tuckman and Renee Woolf, who all went out their way to supply extra material.

Margaret Crick was immensely supportive, both with supplying ideas and in reading draft chapters. Pat Crick, Alex Millar and Lucy Oliver also commented on early versions of the manuscript. Andrew Curry, for the sixth time on one of my books, improved my prose and tidied up much of the text. Bob Davenport put in his usual brilliant performance as copy-editor, spotting mistakes and inconsistencies. Martin Soames guided me round potential legal problems. I must also thank Andrew Gordon and Ian Chapman at Simon & Schuster for taking on and nurturing the project, and my agent Bill Hamilton for arranging the terms.

If you spot any errors, blame me, but please do tell me as well. I'd also love to hear from anyone who has interesting new insights and material on the subject. You can contact me via my email address below.

Michael Crick
London
February 2005
CrickML@aol.com

1

THE HECHTS OF TRANSYLVANIA

We have a duty to give refuge to genuine refugees, but most
people claiming asylum in this country are not genuine refugees.

MICHAEL HOWARD, 2004[1]

He would have to go back, Dover officials told the tall, handsome
young man who'd just arrived on the two o'clock ferry. It didn't
matter that he had a British visa in his passport. The immigration men
did not care what letter he was carrying. It made no difference that he
might have been promised temporary work in London. The rules
were strict. Since he didn't have a work permit from the Ministry of
Labour, they couldn't let him into Britain to take up a job. The new
arrival was stuck on Admiralty Pier, where the ferry quay ran alongside the platforms of the old Dover Western Docks railway station, his
path blocked after his first few paces on British territory. He would
have to get on the boat, due to leave at 4.55 p.m., and make the three-
hour journey back to Ostend.

Michael Howard's father was being turned away.

That Sunday in March 1937 must have been a humiliating and
bewildering experience for the young Bernat Hecht. At the age of
twenty, he was more than a thousand miles from his family home in
rural Romania. Yet only a few days earlier the British embassy in
the Hungarian capital, Budapest, had seemed happy with his

arrangements when they stamped a visa in his passport. It would have taken him at least twenty-four hours to make the train journey across a continent where life was becoming increasingly difficult for people of Hecht's background and religion. His intention, if things worked out in Britain, seems to have been eventually to bring over the rest of his family.

Bernat Hecht was ambitious and determined; he was intelligent and well educated, and spoke several languages. But his broken English wasn't good enough to persuade the men from the Home Office Aliens Department. They were not impressed when he said that 'he did not know that it was necessary' to have a work permit. Nor did it help that Hecht couldn't tell the immigration men how long he planned to stay in England, 'but later [he] suggested a month'. Refused leave to land, he had no option but to re-embark on the *Prince Leopold* ferry and sail back to the Continent.[2]

Fewer than sixty years later the son of this would-be immigrant would preside over the same government department that had turned away his father. In that role he would publicly insist that Britain's immigration system needed to be much tougher.

Bernat Hecht's journey from Romania to Dover had started three weeks before with a letter from the Kehelath Moise Anshei Belz Synagogue in Fairclough Street, Whitechapel. The synagogue had invited him to come to England for a month to see if he was suited to becoming their cantor. In particular, they wanted Hecht to assist the rabbi and lead the choral activity during Passover at the end of March. On 5 March the secretary and president of the synagogue had written to say, 'We have heard favourable reports about you and if you are interested we shall be pleased to send you a ticket to London, and we are prepared to pay your expenses over the period of trial. We should consider it a special favour if you could reach London in time for us to give you a trial on the Passover Services.'[3]

Now, Hecht's high hopes seemed dashed. Passover was the following weekend, and it could take days, weeks or even months to obtain the necessary work permit. How could he arrange that in Belgium, where he had few contacts and didn't speak the language? Lesser men might have given up. And had Bernat Hecht simply stayed in Belgium, or gone back to Hungary, or even returned to his home village in Romania, then he might well have died in the coming Holocaust, along with 6 million others and many of his family.

But Hecht did not give up. Nor, to his great fortune, did the East End synagogue which wanted to employ him. Instead they quickly enlisted political help.

Two days after the deportation from Dover, the Labour MP for Whitechapel, J. H. (Jimmy) Hall, personally delivered a handwritten letter to the Home Secretary, Sir John Simon (who, despite his name, was not Jewish). Although this was an era when MPs paid little attention to constituents' casework, Hall could not afford to ignore the large Jewish population in his area. As a 'personal favour', Hall asked Simon for an 'early reply . . . because of the urgent character of the situation'. Hall explained what had happened to 'Mr Bernard Hecht of Budapest', and added, 'I have been requested to approach you in the hope that you may be willing to reconsider this matter as there is a dearth of Cantors during the Passover period. I am informed that the services of Mr Hecht would be required for only a month.'[4]

Sir John Simon did not help – at least not immediately – and some in the Home Office may have assumed that that was the end of the case. 'Reconsideration requested,' one official wrote on Hecht's file on 30 March 1937, only for a colleague to respond that 'reconsideration would do little good now that the Passover is over'.[5] But Hecht and his prospective employers persisted. The following month the Whitechapel synagogue placed a six-line advertisement in the Yiddish-language *Jewish Times* for a 'First Reader'. The ad was probably superfluous, but it supposedly came to Hecht's attention, even though he was now in Antwerp, and he applied for the job. Indeed, the synagogue was so keen to employ him – again proposing a four-week trial – that this time they arranged to seek Home Office permission through the body which supervised the appointment of Jewish clergy in Britain – the Advisory Committee for the Admission of Jewish Ecclesiastical Officers.[6] Later that month the Home Office granted Bernat Hecht a four-week entry visa, though an administrative blunder meant the permission was sent to Brussels, rather than Antwerp. So it was almost two months before he was told that he would be let into Britain after all.

Hecht returned to Dover on the *Prince Baudouin* ferry on 20 July 1937. His new work permit was valid for only twenty-eight days, but he had a toehold. He was in.

Today Whitechapel and the surrounding parts of the East End of London are home to a large Asian population, but before the Second World War the area housed by far the biggest community of Jews in Britain (150,000 out of a UK Jewish population of 350,000). The Kehelath Moise Anshei Belz Synagogue where Bernat Hecht worked – also known as the Fairclough Street Synagogue – was one of a hundred in Whitechapel, and there were another fifty elsewhere in the East End. As with the area's Asians today, much of the Jewish community remained unassimilated: there were Jewish shops, cafés and restaurants; there were several local newspapers printed in Yiddish, and even a Yiddish theatre. Around 85,000 Jews lived in Whitechapel itself, though the more prosperous had already started to move away to areas such as Stoke Newington and Golders Green in north London. During the 1930s the area saw violent confrontations as the fascist leader Sir Oswald Mosley and his notorious blackshirts demon-strated against the local Jewish population.[7]

As 1937 progressed, and despite Jimmy Hall's claim that Hecht's services would be needed by the synagogue for 'only a month', his stay was extended bit by bit. In August he was granted another two months, 'to enable the Congregation to hear him officiate during the coming Jewish High Holydays'.[8] In October he got a further two months when the Whitechapel synagogue announced that they'd like to employ him as their 'regular Reader' for the next three years, on a salary of £200. Two months at a time his stay was gradually prolonged into 1938, and then extended by a whole year. The synagogue said they were so pleased with Hecht's performance that in March 1939, only a few weeks before his visa was yet again due to expire, they offered him the job for a further five years.

Bernat Hecht was fortunate, for Britain was notoriously strict about immigration in the 1930s, partly in response to public disquiet about the threat to jobs at a time of high unemployment. Only around 90,000 refugees were allowed into the UK between 1933 and 1939, and almost nine in ten are estimated to have been Jews.[9] In many cases the Jewish community agreed terms and conditions with the government for people to be admitted, and guaranteed their upkeep.

Hecht, however, could not really be described as a refugee, even though he was part of a significant exodus of Jews from central and eastern Europe in the 1930s, at a time when the Nazis were tightening their control of Germany and sympathetic regimes were emerging in neighbouring states. In 2004 this author asked the Home Office to allow an 'accelerated opening' of Bernat Hecht's immigration file, which otherwise would have remained closed to the public until 2049. They agreed, in accord with the government's policy of greater openness, though the process took several months and formally the release had to be approved by the Lord Chancellor, Lord Falconer. When I went to Kew to examine the file at the National Archives, officials explained that, because I was getting an advance preview, I could read the papers only on condition that I was locked in a small room where I could be observed through a video camera. I never mentioned why I was interested in Hecht, nor that he was Michael Howard's father, but staff seemed to know that the papers were potentially very sensitive.

The special security at Kew only heightened the sense of drama. Bernat Hecht's file consisted of more than eighty pages, many of them handwritten notes by officials considering his case, others typed or carbon copies, all tied together with string in an old-fashioned, brown government folder. I examined each page carefully, learning of decisions made by civil servants almost seventy years ago, but nowhere in the file did I find any suggestion that Hecht had been fleeing persecution, anti-Semitism or Nazism. There was no mention of him seeking political asylum, or evidence that the British authorities treated him as a refugee. The official papers suggest instead that Hecht's repeated applications to stay in Britain were prompted by the offers of employment by the Whitechapel synagogue. In short,

Michael Howard's father seems to have come to Britain to improve his opportunities. He was what one would now call an 'economic migrant'.

For Bernat Hecht, the noise and bustle of 1930s Whitechapel must have been a world away from rural, backward Ruscova.

Bernat Hecht's home village is situated in the Maramureş region on the far north-western edge of Romania, in a remote wooded valley in the Carpathian mountains close to the border with Ukraine. The community stretches two or three miles along the two arteries of the valley: the main road which leads up to two further villages, and the cold, rushing waters of the Ruscova river.

Visit Ruscova today and you get vivid glimpses of what agrarian life was like in Europe for most of the last thousand years. The village economy is still largely self-sufficient: much of what people eat and wear is produced locally. Without piped water, citizens still draw supplies from wells, and for most homes the lavatory is a wooden hut over a hole in the backyard. Many peasants wear much the same clothes and perform the same daily tasks as their forebears in medieval times. An old woman guides her single cow along the main street; a group of young men drive a horse and cart carrying huge logs felled on the steep local hillsides. At the height of summer, peasants wearing traditional dress walk the roads carrying their haymaking tools – the men with menacing-looking curved scythes over their shoulders, the women with long rakes pegged with wooden teeth. Once cut and gathered, the hay is laid on ancient racks. In a day or two, when the harvest has dried brown, the fields appear to have been invaded by hairy mammoths.

The winters, by contrast, are severe: for almost half the year the ground is covered in snow and the sides of the river ice over, though the water runs too rapidly to freeze completely. Apart from agriculture, the other major industry is mining. The local hills contain significant seams of copper, lead, tin and gold.

While Ruscova's everyday life may be little changed, its history and politics have rarely been tranquil. To describe Ruscova as Romanian is an oversimplification. The village lies barely five miles from the

Ukrainian border, and in practice this is a Ukrainian community, where most people speak Ukrainian rather than Romanian.

People here are glad to live in Romania, which is a more advanced economy than Ukraine, but more than nine out of ten regard themselves as Ukrainian. The new mayor elected in 2004 even stood as a 'Ukrainian' candidate. Before the war, Ukrainians were also the biggest grouping, though not in such overwhelming numbers, and Ruscova's national and linguistic mix was then complicated by the presence of more than 1,000 Jews in a population of about 3,000. In Maramureş as a whole more than one person in five was Jewish.

As elsewhere, many Jews in Ruscova were traders and shopkeepers. Most of the wooden houses and shops along the main street were owned by Jews, and properties would often double up, with families running businesses from the ground floor of their homes. Ruscova's Christians, in contrast, tended to live further from the main road, on the edge of the fields.

The main street also boasted two synagogues, though neither still exists. One site is now occupied by a grocer's, and you can just spot where ancient window frames from the old structure were incorporated into the new building. But the only obvious sign that Jews ever lived in Ruscova is the Jewish cemetery, located some way from the main street and requiring a fifteen-minute walk. Beneath a steep hillside and perched above the river, most of the cemetery's 200 or so remaining gravestones are now too badly weathered to read.

The ancient Maramureş region, which straddles the corners of several neighbouring states – Romania, Ukraine, Hungary and Slovakia – was a popular destination for thousands of Jews who had been driven from Germany, Poland and Russia by persecution and violence over hundreds of years. There is hard evidence that Jews were living in Ruscova in the early 1700s, but they may have first arrived during the previous century. The name Hecht suggests Germanic origins – *hecht* is German for the pike fish – though family members believe the Hechts lived in Russia before coming to Ruscova. Hecht was also a very common name in Ruscova in the early twentieth century. Local birth records show, for example, that in the three years of 1914, 1915 and 1916 at least eight children with the name were born in the village. The last, who arrived on 13 November 1916, was Bernat Hecht.

The genealogy is not straightforward, however. Bernat took his surname from his mother, Leah Hecht (known informally as Lycha), not from his father, Morris (or Moshe or Mozes) Wurzberger, who worked as warden of one of Ruscova's two synagogues. This was because the authorities in what was then the Austro-Hungarian Empire did not recognise marriages conducted in synagogues, so unless their parents also performed a civil ceremony Jewish children were officially obliged to take their mothers' names. This official 'illegitimacy' is reflected in the handwritten registration book in the village hall (where the baby's name is spelt 'Bernarth'), and which merely records his mother as being Lea Hecht, age twenty-eight. His father is not mentioned.[10]

But Hecht was a good name to have in Ruscova. The Hechts were not poor, unlike most Jews in Eastern Europe, but one of the richest and most influential families in the village. Leah's father, David Hecht (Michael Howard's great-grandfather), was a substantial local farmer and landowner: he owned hundreds of acres in the Ruscova valley and beyond, which not only were used for the family's many hundreds of cattle and sheep, but also were rented out to local peasants and shepherds for their smaller flocks, and for growing hay to feed the livestock in winter. The Hechts also owned orchards and large parts of the hillside forests, as well as a grocer's shop, a bakery and the village watermill. They employed dozens of people, Jews and Christians, and most peasants were obliged to use their mill if they wanted an efficient way to turn their corn into flour. Even today elderly Ruscova residents recall how the family were nicknamed 'Zubrecht', or energetic. Yet, despite their economic clout, they do not appear to have been resented. 'The Hecht family was very appreciated as nice, gentle people, especially when Christians wanted to borrow money,' says Grecica Sava, who worked for the family as a teenager, and whose mother and father also worked for them, as housekeeper and gardener. 'For poor people they sold food on credit.' Sava, who later served as village mayor and still lives in Ruscova, adds that when times got hard during the Second World War the Hechts would waive their grinding charges for poorer villagers.[11]

Yet by the 1930s there was a huge disparity of wealth within the Hecht clan. Before he died, around 1940, David Hecht passed on the bulk of his property to his only son, Josef, while his four daughters received little. Leah Hecht and her husband, Morris, got a house on the main street next to Josef's much larger home, and also had a small shop opposite. 'It sold bits and pieces,' says Martin Hecht, who is Leah's nephew – 'everything and nothing.'[12] Behind the shop they also had a long, narrow strip of land, and an orchard of apple and plum trees.

Martin Hecht is Bernat Hecht's cousin, even if, as Josef's youngest son, he is closer in age to Michael Howard. Today he lives in Golders Green in north London. As a boy in Ruscova in the 1930s, in the morning he went to the main village primary school, where children were taught in Romanian, the official state language. He and his siblings would have a midday meal at home before attending the village Jewish school in the afternoon. All Jews in the village were strictly orthodox, and would attend synagogue in both the morning and the evening.

The citizens of Ruscova, like many people in central Europe, were fluent in several languages – the Jews especially so. It all depended on the context. 'At home we spoke Yiddish,' says Martin Hecht. 'On the street we spoke Ukrainian, and at school we spoke Romanian.'[13] And for religious occasions Jews also spoke Hebrew.

Indeed, in training to become a cantor, Bernat Hecht would have gone away to a religious school – a yeshiva – to learn Hebrew to a very high level. And Romanian, Ukrainian, Yiddish and Hebrew were four very different languages. Ukrainian, for instance, uses the Cyrillic alphabet and is very similar to Russian; Romanian, in contrast, is a Romance language, derived from Latin, like many languages spoken in western Europe.

The political history of Ruscova was also complex. Over past centuries the village had been part of the semi-independent state of Transylvania, subsequently ruled by Austria, and then part of the

Austro-Hungarian Empire. When the empire collapsed at the end of the First World War, Ruscova and the rest of Transylvania became part of the newly created kingdom of Greater Romania. (To many people Transylvania conjures up Dracula, Bram Stoker's fictional character based on Vlad the Impaler, but Ruscova is almost 200 miles from the acknowledged site of Dracula's castle.)

There were about 800,000 Jews in the new state, out of a total population of about 18 million. The new Romanian government which signed the Treaty of Paris in 1919 agreed to 'recognise as fully privileged Romanian subjects without any formality the Jews living in all the Romanian territories and who have no other nationality'.[14]

Compared with the violence and persecution they had suffered in the past (and with what was to follow), Romanian Jews found the 1920s and early 1930s to be a period of relative emancipation. Nevertheless there was still regular anti-Jewish agitation, encouraged by the emergence in 1927 of a strongly anti-Semitic and nationalistic fascist movement, which was originally called the Legion of the Archangel Michael, but later became known as the Iron Guard. Within the constant turmoil that characterised Romania between the wars, and where governments could not afford to crack down on them, the Iron Guard's death squads were effectively tolerated, even when they attacked and murdered people. Most of their victims were Jews, though, remarkably, they also managed to assassinate four current or former prime ministers. By 1932 the Iron Guard had 32,000 branches in Romania, with significant recruits among those in influential positions such as government officials, judges, clergymen and businessmen. Its emergence as a potent political force in Romania ran in close parallel with the success of the National Socialists in Germany, and was greatly bolstered by Hitler's coming to power in 1933. Like the Nazis, the Iron Guard were paramilitaries, with uniforms and salutes, and encouraged the glorification of their leader, but unlike German fascism the movement had strong religious and agrarian influences. In ever-closer alliance with the Nazis, the Iron Guard promised to eliminate Jews from Romanian business and culture and replace them with ethnic Romanians.

Yet the Iron Guard does not seem to have posed a very serious threat to Jews in Ruscova when Bernat lived there. The organisation was late to arrive in the village, and recruited few members. 'The Iron Guard was not big in Ruscova,' says Martin Hecht, 'although Jews were murdered in other places. In Ruscova the non-Jews relied for everything on Jewish people, especially for work. But we had no problems. There was no resentment towards us – or if there was they didn't show it.'[15] Others from Ruscova agree that there was relative harmony between the village's Jews and Christians, most of whom belonged to the Greek Orthodox Church. It is possible, in fact, that when he arrived in Whitechapel in 1937, while agitation by Mosley's blackshirts was at its peak, Bernat Hecht encountered more anti-Semitism than he had experienced at home in Ruscova.

In the 1930s Romania was a very poor country, whose people suffered from weak diet, bad sanitation and poor housing conditions. It had the worst infant mortality rate in Europe, and the worst death rate for the population as a whole. In 1940 the average life expectancy was between forty-eight and fifty.[16] Of those who died in rural areas, at least a third had had no access to a doctor or to any medicine.

It was therefore not surprising that during the 1930s several of Ruscova's more resourceful Jews left the village and emigrated overseas. There was a big response in the village when the Zionist movement sought recruits to develop the Jewish national home in Palestine, though only two or three Ruscova families were eventually chosen. It was under this scheme that, around 1935, Bernat Hecht's uncle Josef and three of his oldest children travelled to Palestine, intending to establish a family foothold in the land of Israel. Josef left two daughters there, and came back to Ruscova with his son, fully intending to sell up all his property in Romania and move the whole family permanently to the Middle East. But his plans were thwarted by the British authorities, who would not grant the necessary visas. Britain had been governing Palestine since 1922, under a mandate from the League of Nations, and after 1930 the British were much more restrictive in the number of Jews they allowed to settle there, for fear of upsetting the Arab population.

So Bernat was not the first member of the Hecht family to abandon Ruscova. But the big mystery is how such a young man managed to secure a job in London, 1,200 miles away, at a time when communications were poor, and why the synagogue were so interested in someone they had never met. Who had made the 'favourable reports' about Bernat mentioned in the letter the synagogue sent to him in March 1937? What seems to have happened is that Bernat's father, Morris Wurzberger, went to England some months before his son, hoping to build a better life for his family, although no record seems to exist of Wurzberger's arrival or initial presence in London. Nevertheless, three Hecht cousins, and two people who later worked for Bernat, all say that Morris also came to Britain in the mid-1930s.[17] It seems a reasonable presumption, then, that it was Morris who found the synagogue in Whitechapel which needed a cantor, and told them he knew somebody who would be ideal for the job (possibly without even letting on that Bernat was his son, since they had different surnames). The plan seems to have been that the two men, father and son, would then establish themselves in Britain before arranging for Leah Hecht to come over with the family's three younger children – Rosalia (known as Rosie), Samuel and Wolf (known as Wally).

The other important question is *why* members of both branches of the Hecht family chose to leave Ruscova. With hindsight it is tempting to suggest, as some commentators have done, that their decision was political: that they feared the rise of fascism and anti-Semitism in Europe, and that effectively (even if the official file doesn't say so), Bernat was an asylum seeker. Indeed, when Michael Howard became Tory leader in 2003 he spoke of how his parents 'saw Britain as a beacon in a dark and threatening world'.[18] Specifically, of his father's move from Romania, he has said, 'There were clouds on the horizon. It perhaps hadn't started raining yet, but there were lots of clouds on the horizon.'[19] In 2004 Michael Howard's son, Nick, wrote to *The Times* to object to a cartoon which, in his view, suggested his father was a 'grotesque hypocrite' on immigration. Bernat Hecht in the 1930s had, he wrote, 'fled to Britain to save his life from the fascists of

Eastern Europe . . . It is self-evidently unfair to compare this with the economic migration expected after EU enlargement.'[20] Yet in 1995 Michael Howard pointed out to David Frost that his father hadn't applied for asylum. 'He came because he had a particular job to go to.'[21]

If Bernat Hecht really was fleeing fascism or anti-Semitism, he certainly showed great foresight. Although the Romanian regime was increasingly anti-Semitic during the 1930s, the persecution did not extend to a remote northern village like Ruscova. By March 1937, when Bernat first set foot in Britain, it was not obvious that Hitler posed a serious threat to the Jews of eastern Europe, or that he intended to conquer the whole continent, although the future of Europe looked increasingly unstable. At that point the Nazis had only reoccupied the Rhineland, which had been German territory before the First World War. Even though the Nazi regime had already shown itself extremely hostile to Jews in Germany, Ruscova was more than 400 miles from Germany, and people living there were very poorly informed about developments elsewhere.

The decision by Bernat Hecht and his father to leave Ruscova was 'nothing to do with the political situation getting bad', says Bernat's cousin Martin. 'They were poor, simply trying to better themselves in going to England.'[22] The Hechts were dynamic and restless individuals, and Ruscova offered limited opportunities. 'There was no future for us there – that's the end of it,' says a more distant cousin, another Josef Hecht, who remembers seeing Bernat as he bade farewell to the village:

> He went out into the world to look for something, to learn a trade, to become somebody. He left for a better life. The kids had nothing to do in town. There was no industry. It was a farming town. I remember when he left, and I envied him that he was leaving. We knew he was going to England. We knew he had his father already there. It was a big thing. He was leaving for England, for something that was going to let him see daylight. He was going to make something out of himself.[23]

Ruscova lacked many of the amenities of modern civilisation, and was too isolated to have regular newspapers, telephone lines or even good radio reception. In winter the village might be cut off for months on end, with families confined to their homes for days by roof-high snow drifts, dependent on stores of food kept in their cellars. One can understand why ambitious people were keen to leave. And their timing was extremely fortuitous.

Bernat Hecht was clearly an able young man – bright, ambitious, adventurous, and, says Grecica Sava, 'good-looking, well respected and liked'.[24] And his choral skills and religious training provided a helpful means to get to England.

At the end of 1937, several months after either Bernat or Morris left for Britain, an anti-Semitic government came to power in Romania. It soon revised the conditions of citizenship for Jews; it suppressed the Hebrew and Yiddish press, and began to carry out ever greater discrimination. The Iron Guard then became a threat in Ruscova and Maramureş. 'We were afraid to go out on the streets,' Josef Hecht says of the period a year or two after Bernat left. 'If a Jewish person went on a train, and went from one town to another, he had problems.'[25] But none of the half-dozen survivors I have interviewed recalls anyone being murdered by fascists in Ruscova at that time.

In 1940 the Romanian regime became increasingly pro-Nazi and German troops entered the country, which meant that in much of Romania Jews began suffering on a huge scale. Tens of thousands were massacred by Romanian troops; others died of starvation, as the authorities accused the Jewish population of being Russian agents. Yet for several years Jews in Ruscova again managed to escape most of this anti-Semitism, simply because, under the 1940 Award of Vienna, the Germans and Italians agreed to hand control of Maramureş and northern Transylvania to Hungary, thus meeting the Hungarians' historic claim to the territory. Ruscova effectively became part of Hungary.

The Hungarian regime, led by the regent Admiral Nikolaus Horthy, was certainly anti-Semitic, but not on the same scale as Romania or Germany, and for economic reasons Horthy resisted Nazi pressure to deport and eliminate his Jewish population. In Ruscova the

Jewish community survived relatively unscathed for several years, though the Hungarian regime banned Jews from jobs as teachers, doctors or lawyers, and thousands of young men were conscripted into labour battalions to join the German war effort against the Soviet Union. Bit by bit, Jews were segregated from the rest of society, which meant that Leah Hecht and her children lost their home and were forced to move across the street. The Hungarians closed down all the Jewish shops in Ruscova and consolidated them into one store, which occupied the Hechts' former house.

Yet many of the 44,000 Jews in Maramureş may not have known how badly Jews were being treated in the rest of eastern and central Europe. It was a sign of how isolated the village was, and ignorant of developments elsewhere, that early in 1944, when German forces passed through the village on the way to the Russian front, it was the first time the teenage Martin Hecht had ever seen soldiers. He says his parents, Josef and Hannah, gladly let German officers occupy their yard and sleep overnight in their large home, where they laid down mattresses on the floor. The Hechts fed their German visitors without realising how hostile the Nazis were to Jews. 'We were so naive, so ignorant,' says Martin Hecht. 'In Ruscova there were no newspapers, no radio. We didn't know what was going on. It was so primitive.'[26]

The quiet life in the border backwater was to end abruptly in 1944. The Nazi leadership, increasingly obsessed with their 'Final Solution', became exasperated by Hungary's failure to deport its Jewish population, and in March, under Operation Margaret, the Germans occupied the country. Within days the notorious Adolf Eichmann arrived, and all Jews were immediately obliged to wear a yellow Star of David. Mass deportations began in May 1944, supervised by the Hungarian gendarmerie. In Ruscova, the teenage Grecica Sava watched in horror as they began at the upper end of the village, forcing Jews from their homes and then sealing off one building after another to prevent people hiding in them:

People had to leave, and after a house was emptied it was sealed with wax and rope. It all happened over about a week or ten days.

The whole village cried, because they saw how badly the Hungarian gendarmes were treating the Jewish population. Everyone was wailing – children and adults. Children were hanging on to their mothers' dresses. But the Hungarian officers took the children and threw them into the carts like sacks. Local people were beaten up if they tried to help. People realised they would be killed. 'Now we are going to die and to be burned,' they cried.[27]

Sava says he remembers the events as if they were yesterday. The village secretary was Jewish himself, and the Hungarians forced him to identify the homes of fellow Jews, deriding him while doing so. German officers were also present, but merely watched while the Hungarians did the work. 'Germans were there only to ensure that their orders were fulfilled,' says Sava. 'Even people offering food were arrested. I remember that among them was a young girl called Rita Hecht. I tried to save her by hiding her where we kept the potatoes under our house, but she was caught, and I was hit by a German soldier. I later visited her in Israel.'[28]

'There were soldiers on every bridge, and at each end of the village,' recalls another Ruscova resident, Ostas Gheorghe:

Other inhabitants were told, 'If you dare to hide Jews, you and members of your wider family will have the same fate.' The people on our neighbouring farm, who were Jews, had two girls. Their Jewish mother came to my mother and said, 'Please take our daughters.' My mother said, 'They know how many children I have. Even if I dress them in the same clothes I couldn't get away with it.' They were all confined to horse carts, two or three families per cart, depending on the number of children. Children were crying, asking their mothers, 'Where are we going?' And their mothers said, 'Don't cry. It's all right.'[29]

Several members of Bernat Hecht's immediate family were among those taken away – including his mother, Leah, and his sister, Rosie.

They were joined by Leah's brother, Josef, his wife, Hannah, their daughter, Basku, and their five sons, Abraham, Samuel, Israel, Jacob and Martin.

Ruscova's Jews were initially crowded into a temporary ghetto on the outskirts of Vişeu de Sus, about ten miles away, where they were imprisoned with others from nearby communities. 'We were only there for a few weeks, but it was horrendous,' says Jacob Hecht, who also lives in London nowadays and is another of Bernat's cousins. 'We had no food, shelter or clothes.'[30] His father, Josef, suffered the humiliation of having his beard cut off by the SS guards. Towards the end of May 1944 the Jews in the Vişeu de Sus camp were pushed on to cattle trucks. The Germans told them they were being transported for their own safety, since the Russians were advancing rapidly. When the war was over, they were told, they would be allowed to return.

The rail trucks, each crammed with up to a hundred people, were marked as holding 'German worker-resettlers'. The 200-mile rail journey took them north-west through the Carpathian mountains, first along Romania's border with Ukraine, then through Slovakia into southern Poland. 'There was no water, no food, no sanitation for two or three days until we got to Auschwitz,' says Martin Hecht. 'When we arrived there were already people dead inside the trucks.'[31] 'They were allowed only a single bucket of water and a single waste bucket to each wagon,' the historian Martin Gilbert has written. 'Hundreds died during the journey. Many committed suicide or were driven insane by confinement and fear.'[32]

Jacob Hecht recalls that:

When we got off the trains . . . Adolf Eichmann was there in front of us . . . He never spoke. All he did was wave and point his finger. Someone told us to make ourselves look taller than we were because they were sending us to a slave labour camp, and if they didn't send us there we would be taken to the gas chambers. If we looked tall that meant we might be more capable of work, so we stood on our toes. My parents were pushed to one side and my brothers and sister to another side. That was the last I saw of my parents. For no other reason than they were Jews.[33]

Leah Hecht – Michael Howard's grandmother – was among the vast majority who were taken straight to the gas chambers. She was forcibly parted from her daughter Rosie who had refused to hide with non-Jewish friends when the family was taken from Ruscova, and had insisted on staying with her mother to protect her. In later years Rosie would tell her nephew Michael Howard the incredible story of how she herself escaped death. Twice she was sent to the gas chamber, and twice she came back alive – on one occasion because they ran out of gas; the second time because of another malfunction. 'Then the third time,' says Howard, 'they came to the barracks where she lived to take everyone in it to the chamber, but she was so thin – all she was given to eat were potato peelings – she managed to hide in the chimney. They didn't find her. She, alone among that group, miraculously survived.'[35]

Meanwhile Bernat and Rosie Hecht's cousins – the five boys and a girl – were deloused, shaved, put into the notorious striped concentration camp uniforms, and placed in bunk beds in crowded barrack rooms. There was little food, and people were dying all around. The girl, Basku, was taken to a women's camp, while the boys were held at Auschwitz for roughly three weeks. Over the next nine months the boys were sent on an appalling series of forced marches from camp to camp – the so-called death marches – as the Germans tried to destroy evidence of their crimes in the face of the advancing Allied armies. They were marched first to Dornhau, a quarrying camp in Lower Silesia, where they replaced inmates who had died. Martin was forced to work in the local quarries, and then on building a railway through the mountains – an experience which he compares to scenes from the film *Bridge on the River Kwai*. He was given little to eat. 'In the morning they would say they were giving us a cup of coffee, but it was only hot water. In the evening there was meant to be soup, but it was just hot water with a bit of cabbage in it. So people were dying like flies.'[35]

'I've gone through miracles to stay alive,' Martin Hecht says. 'One day some SS guards came and said, "We are taking all the children to a children's home," and they selected five or six hundred of us. Jack (Jacob) and myself were chosen to be among them. Of all the boys in that camp I was probably the smallest, but I was also tough.' But then one of the Jewish 'capos', who supervised the camp on behalf of the Germans, took pity on Martin and Jacob and decided they shouldn't go to the 'children's home' after all. But, to account for numbers, they had to be replaced with two other children. 'Afterwards,' says Martin, 'we were told they had been sent to Auschwitz, to the gas chambers. One of the boys who replaced me was from our village.'[36]

Five or six months passed, until, towards the end of 1944, the prisoners of Dornhau were told that because of further Russian progress the whole camp would be evacuated – except those who were dying, who would be abandoned. 'We were moved on another death march, to Schotterwok. We marched for nearly a week, but on the way only about half the camp survived. People who fell were shot and simply left by the roadside.'[37] The prisoners' bodies were quickly disintegrating from the hunger, cold, exhaustion and disease. Numbers diminished by the day. Only the toughest, and the luckiest, survived.

After a brief spell in Schotterwok came yet another long march. 'One night we stayed in a forest. In the morning we were woken early and they did a selection. My two older brothers, Israel and Samuel, were in the group who were selected as no longer capable of carrying on marching. We'd gone 150 yards and heard shots and were told that all those who'd been selected were shot. That's when I lost my two brothers.'[38]

Martin and Jacob continued marching together, often at night as well as by day, until at one point in Bavaria early in 1945 they were put into open cattle trucks, only to find themselves being strafed by American planes. Unaware of the horrors being perpetrated beneath them, the pilots clearly didn't know whom they were shooting and killing.

Then came a further division into two groups, when Martin was placed on one side while his older brother Jacob was deemed fit to carry on. 'But we wouldn't separate,' says Martin. 'We were so weak. It was drenching rain, terrible weather, but Jack wouldn't let go of my hand. And I managed to get to the other group with my brother. He was holding my hand. He wouldn't let go. But those on the other side were shot. When we'd left Dornhau there must have been 10,000 people, then we picked up thousands more at Schotterwok. But now we were down to five or six hundred.'[39]

Their next destination was Flossenbürg near Weiden, by the Czech border, the third largest Nazi concentration camp of all, where German and French political prisoners were also kept and conditions were even worse. 'I saw people dying every day. There were five or six people to a bunk, and every night only two or three survived. It was horrendous, indescribable.'[40]

The Hechts' final march, from Flossenbürg to an unknown destination, involving 4,000–5,000 people, was the worst experience of all. 'People were absolutely dead. We had no food for days. People were just skeletons, and as they fell down people were just shot by the SS guards on each side. Eventually there were about 300 left.'[41] Remarkably, the Hecht brothers found themselves on the same march as their distant Ruscova cousin Josef, with whom they'd lost contact, and who'd similarly spent time in Auschwitz followed by long death marches. The German regime was disintegrating, and the Jews were forced from place to place almost aimlessly, sometimes being brought back to locations they had visited a few days before. 'They didn't know what to do with us any more,' says Josef Hecht. 'They just drove us round, marching around, from one town to another.'[42]

Then suddenly one morning they saw tanks coming from behind – American tanks. Soldiers began to jump out, shooting the Germans. 'There were Jews among the Americans who spoke Yiddish, and they said "Get behind the tanks!" They had already liberated some camps, so they knew who we were. But the first thing they started doing was throwing chocolates and sweets at us, and that was the worst thing they could have done. Some people who had survived so much died afterwards from the chocolates.'[43] Their stomachs were simply too small and too weak to absorb such rich food. 'The Americans meant well but the result was disastrous,' says Jacob Hecht.[44]

Martin and Jacob managed to find a German house. The woman occupant fled, and they stayed there a week devouring her food, sleeping and recovering. Eventually the brothers were shipped to England, where, in a refugee centre near Southampton, they were reunited with Bernat Hecht and his father, Morris Wurzberger.

Michael Howard's aunt Rosie also moved to Britain after the war. She had been badly traumatised by her time at Auschwitz, having suffered regular beatings and whippings, and was left partially bald. She weighed only seventy-six pounds – less than five and a half stone – when the camp was liberated in January 1945.[45] Her brother Wally ended up in Britain as well, having been conscripted into a labour battalion on the Russian front, doing work such as digging trenches. Wally, too, had then endured a series of death marches from camp to camp, but he likewise emerged alive. Bernat's other brother, Samuel, also survived. He had escaped across the border into Ukraine, where he was imprisoned in a Soviet prison camp for several years before being forced to join the Red Army. Samuel later settled in the Soviet Union and brought up a family. That such a high proportion of the Hechts emerged from the Holocaust alive may reflect the fact that their family had been prosperous, and they were probably better nourished and healthier than many of their fellow Jews.

It might have been different. Ruscova's Jewish community had been fortunate to survive so long unharmed, and Maramureş was liberated by the Russians only five months after their deportation. 'If we had known what was about to happen we could have gone into the forests and hid. But we knew nothing,' Martin Hecht explains.[46] 'I would have been hiding out somewhere, in the mountains,' says Josef Hecht, who today lives in New York. 'Even if I had got killed there, I wouldn't have minded getting killed there, rather than going to Auschwitz.'[47]

Of roughly 44,000 Jews in the Maramureş area before the war, only about 3,000 returned afterwards, while a further 2,000, like the Hechts, are thought to have emigrated to Israel, western Europe or America. The survivors from Maramureş included Elie Wiesel, who came from Sighet, the historic regional capital thirty miles away, and who won the Nobel peace prize in 1986 for his writings on the Holocaust.

In Ruscova the empty Jewish properties were invariably looted, and some came to be occupied by poor people. But gradually the wooden houses fell into ruin and were demolished. A new building was constructed on the site of Bernat Hecht's family home, while the land opposite, once occupied by the Hechts' shop, is now an open space next to a hardware store, with a timber yard at the rear.

Barely eighty Jews returned to Ruscova after the war, but they gradually departed again, the last one in the late 1980s. Apart from the Jewish cemetery, and the registration books of births and marriages in the village hall, there is no record of what was once a vibrant community.

Michael Howard takes surprisingly little interest in his father's background. An acquaintance who once tried to raise his Romanian roots with him was astonished at how uncomfortable Howard suddenly looked, and noted how he quickly tried to move the conversation on. Perhaps the thought was just too painful.

In the 1980s, before the fall of Communism, Wally Howard's two children, who were born in Britain, visited Romania together. Martin Hecht has been back several times, and is now engaged in a protracted legal dispute with the Romanian government, demanding the return of ninety properties in the area which he has identified as belonging to the family.

It looks unlikely, however, that Michael Howard will ever follow them, even though the mayor of Ruscova has more than once urged him to pay a visit.

'My father never felt the need to go back,' Howard once said, 'and nor have I.'[48]

2

THE LANDYS OF LLANELLI

> During his residence in this country he has not taken any interest
> in politics and he informs me that he is not and never has been
> a member of any foreign political organisation. I have no reason
> to believe that he is disloyal to this country.
>
> POLICE REPORT ON MICHAEL HOWARD'S FATHER, 1947[1]

In April 1940 the twenty-three-year-old cantor Bernat Hecht left his
well-paid job in Whitechapel and travelled 200 miles westward to
Llanelli in South Wales. He had fallen in love.

Hilda Kurshion was almost five years older than Bernat. Although
she too came from a Jewish immigrant family, Hilda spoke good
Welsh and English with a strong Welsh accent. Dark-haired and short,
she always dressed in smart, fashionable clothes. Hilda was intelligent
and astute in business matters, forceful and outgoing in her dealings
with people, yet courteous and even-tempered.

For Bernat, moving to Llanelli (which was Anglicized as 'Llanelly'
until 1966) was a wise move at a time when hundreds of thousands of
people, mostly children, were being evacuated from London because
of the threat of German air raids; the East End, of course, would suffer
the worst of the Blitz when the bombs started falling on London in
the summer of 1940. Llanelli was hit by only one bomb during the
whole of the Second World War, though in Swansea, twelve miles

south-east, 240 people were killed in the town's Three Nights' Blitz of February 1941.

'A miserable village close to the coast,' is how one visitor described Llanelli in 1727.[2] But the town was enriched by the Industrial Revolution. It was roughly halfway along the south coast of Wales, north of the Gower peninsula and at the eastern end of Carmarthen Bay. There was plenty of coal in the surrounding area, particularly the special anthracite from the western end of the South Wales coalfield, which burns with hardly any flame or smoke. But it was metal, not coal, which helped Llanelli thrive. The town's first copperworks opened in 1805, and in 1846, its first tinplate mill, which exploited the process whereby iron is coated with a layer of tin. In time Llanelli would earn the name 'Tinopolis'.

The first Jewish community in Wales had been established in nearby Swansea around 1730, when immigrants arrived from Lithuania. The nineteenth century witnessed widespread Jewish settlement throughout South Wales – not just in the large ports, but inland, up the valleys, in mining towns such as Pontypridd, Aberdare, Merthyr Tydfil and Ebbw Vale – and immigration increased following serious anti-Jewish pogroms in Russia after the assassination of Tsar Alexander II in 1881.

Relations between Jews and the indigenous Welsh population were relatively harmonious. There was a natural affinity between Judaism and Nonconformism, most obviously through their common emphasis on the Old Testament and on choral music in their services, and Wales is dotted with biblical place names, such as Bethesda, Bethlehem and Hebron. Anti-Jewish riots in Tredegar during the miners' strike of 1911, when shops and houses were looted and wrecked, were notable because they were exceptional. The Nonconformist communities of South Wales seem to have been more welcoming to the Jewish immigrants than they were to the thousands of Irish Catholics who also arrived during the second half of the nineteenth century. Unrest against Chinese or black people was also more common than against Jews. It helped that the Jewish immigrants did not compete with locals for jobs in the main industries. 'There were few Jewish seamen or dockers,' writes one leading historian of the Jews in South Wales. 'The few who went down the pits were for the most part only temporary miners, and those who stayed in the industry joined the Union, which was seen as a guarantee against undercutting wages.'[3] Instead, as in Ruscova and elsewhere, the Jews became traders and shopkeepers, or worked as pedlars, selling goods from door to door.

Hilda's family did exactly that. The Kurshions had been part of an earlier generation of Jewish emigrés from eastern Europe. Hilda had arrived in Llanelli in August 1912, when she was only eight months old, along with her older brother, Jack, and her parents, Max and Ada. They came from the town of Ostrog in the region of Volhynia, which was then in Russia. Situated about 200 miles west of Kiev, and roughly 250 miles north-east of Bernat Hecht's home village of Ruscova, Ostrog claims to be the oldest city in Ukraine. During the early decades of the twentieth century, Jews accounted for about two-thirds of its 15,000 inhabitants, many of them involved in the timber industry based on the surrounding forests. Ostrog was an important centre of Jewish teaching: it had several Jewish schools, as well as a Jewish library, hospital and old-people's home. After the First World War Volhynia was part of the territory ceded to Poland, and following the German attack on Russia in 1941 nearly all the city's Jews were exterminated, most of them shot by the SS. Today Ostrog is part of Ukraine, and only a handful of Jews remain.

Hilda's father, Max Kurshion, died of an epileptic fit at the age of thirty only five months after the family reached Britain. His widow, Ada, was left to bring up her two young children on her own.

Ada Kurshion, who was Michael Howard's maternal grandmother, had been born Ada Landy – the name Landy is derived from the more common Jewish name Landau. Her family was one of some repute, which counted amongst its ancestors one of the most distinguished leaders and theologians of European Jewry. Ezekiel Ben Judah Landau (1713–93) was chief rabbi of Prague in the late eighteenth century, and celebrated for a scholarly book called *Noda bi-Yehuda*. Landau, according to one account, had 'a commanding appearance and rare intellectual ability, was of strong character imbued with a love of truth and of his fellow men, and had considerable diplomatic skill'.[4] He was Michael Howard's six-times-great-grandfather.

Ada Landy was one of several Landy brothers and sisters who emigrated from Ostrog to South Wales in the early years of the twentieth century, joining Llanelli's rapidly growing Jewish community. One family story has it that when the first Landys left Russia by sea they were expecting to go to the United States, and that the captain landed them on the South Wales coast pretending it was America. Another version says they ended up in Llanelli 'after a shipwreck near Swansea'.[5] Whatever the truth, conditions in such immigrant ships were generally so atrocious that the first Landys were probably glad to reach dry land of any kind.

By 1912, when Ada and her husband arrived, Landys were already well established within the local Jewish community, which numbered about eighty people. An 'S. Landy' – probably Ada's brother Samuel – was one of the stewards in May 1909 when the Chief Rabbi of England and Wales, Hermann Adler, came to open the town's new synagogue in Queen Victoria Road.[6] Samuel Landy was originally a glazier and picture-framer, and owned a shop in Water Street next to a boxing booth run by a black boxer called 'Jos' Black.

Later, Samuel Landy seems to have given up his premises in the town centre and instead travelled round Llanelli and neighbouring villages selling framed pictures from door to door. His customers were mainly working-class people who paid him on credit by instalments.

To judge from the local newspaper reports, Landy was a pretty unpopular character. In the summer of 1915 the papers reported a court case in which he was accused of sexually assaulting one of his female customers in the pit village of Tumble, ten miles north of Llanelli. Rose Jones, a miner's wife who had two young children, alleged that Landy called at her home while she was sitting by the fire suckling her baby. The court was told that he 'walked up to her, behaving in an improper manner. She protested and he then made an indecent suggestion, promising to bring her a new skirt within a fortnight, but she told him to return to his wife and children.' Jones alleged that on a second visit Landy had 'made an indecent invitation to her, at the same time trying to pull her on to the bed'.[7] He then offered to obtain a dress for her baby, she claimed.

Landy (who was the future Home Secretary's great-uncle), denied the charges, protesting that because of his Jewish background he would never have committed such an act. 'That can be proved,' he said, 'because according to the Jewish law if a Jew at any time inter-feres in such a manner with a Gentile he is cast out of the Jewish tribe. That is according to the law of Moses. It is the greatest dis-grace on earth for a Jew to associate with a Gentile in such a manner.'[8]

Landy claimed that he had not even been in Tumble at the time of the first alleged incident, and he was acquitted. Rose Jones may have made her allegations against the salesman because he had threatened to take her husband to court over an unpaid bill. Press reports suggest that Samuel Landy was regularly in the civil courts, either suing others for money, or being sued himself. One paper, dated a few weeks after the assault trial, even carried the headline 'Landy Again!' above a report of an allegation that Landy had bought a house without paying for it. The court registrar observed that Landy was the 'plaintiff in an enormous number of cases in this court'.[9]

Another branch of the Landy family later owned a chemist's shop; a third would open a radio and TV store (whose premises, with the 'Landy' sign still visible, remain to this day in a small arcade in the centre of Llanelli, though nowadays no one called Landy lives in the town). But the most popular family trade was drapery, which Samuel Landy had turned to from glazing. And this was also how his sister Ada – Michael Howard's widowed grandmother – earned her living as she brought up her two children.

Ada Kurshion became a well-known figure in the Llanelli area in the inter-war years, and older residents vividly remember how she went around the community selling from door to door. Rosemary Stratton, then a young child, remembers 'Mrs Kurshion' as a short but roundish woman who used to knock at her parents' door once a

week, and spoke with a strong foreign accent. Ada would be carrying
a large package of children's clothes, wrapped in brown paper:

> It was a huge parcel. You can imagine now: she's a dumpy little
> Jewess, only about four feet tall, and this parcel on her hip, tied up
> with a bit of string and she'd come into the house and dump the
> parcel on the table. She used to open a corner of it and just pull the
> clothes out – 'What do you think of that?', 'Do you want that?' and
> 'Do you want this?' And then she used to put them back in the
> same little place from where she'd pulled them out, and nothing was
> creased. The parcel was really tidy, but it was as big as herself – just
> an extension of her really! She wouldn't undo it altogether. She just
> tied it up so that she could undo this corner. If you think about it,
> if she went from door to door opening the whole parcel each time
> she wouldn't get anywhere.

Rosemary Stratton says she and her brother had all their clothes supplied by Mrs Kurshion, who was paid at a steady, manageable rate. 'It
doesn't matter what you bought, it was a shilling a week.'[10]

Much of the time Ada Kurshion travelled on foot, but she
might take the train or bus to neighbouring communities such
as Burry Port, four miles west of Llanelli, where Vernon Haebe lived.
His recollection, from the late 1930s, a few years later than Rosemary
Stratton's, is that Ada's parcel was wrapped in black polythene. 'She'd
take everything out on the floor, and show my mother what she had
to sell. She was always talking, mostly about the weather and what was
going on in Burry Port and in Llanelli, and what she'd picked up from
gossip. She was very talkative – more talkative than Michael Howard.'
Yet she wasn't that smartly dressed, Haebe recalls. 'You can't go by
looks, but she was a very nice old lady, mind.'[11]

By the 1930s Ada Kurshion had been joined in the door-to-door
clothes business by her two children: Jack, born in 1910, and Hilda,
born the following year. Jack Kurshion's application for British citizenship in 1935 stated that he kept 'a large stock of drapery' at home,
and owned 'an Austin 7 motor car which he uses to carry on with the

business'. Unlike his uncle Samuel Landy, Kurshion had managed to avoid court disputes over debts. He had not been a bankrupt, Llanelli police reported to the Home Office, 'or been involved in any criminal or civil proceedings of any kind whatever . . . He appears to be in fairly good circumstances.'[12]

Llanelli residents recall that the Kurshions also received customers at home. Initially they lived in a small terraced property in Island Place, right in the heart of Llanelli, on a site now occupied by the bus station, before moving in 1928 to a larger house at 95 James Street, a long, narrow, curved street of attractive pastel-coloured terraced houses about a quarter of a mile away. Tony Harries, a retired teacher who has lived in James Street almost all his life, recalls as a boy being dragged along to the Kurshions' house to watch his aunt being fitted for a new dress. Two rooms on the ground floor, he recalls, had been knocked into one to make a shop.

Tony Harries's family lived further down James Street, opposite the home of Isaac Landy, who owned the electrical store. As orthodox Jews, the Landys weren't allowed to light their fires on the Jewish sabbath, so Harries's mother would cross the street every weekend to do it for them. And in turn the Landys looked after their Welsh neighbours. Once, when Harries's parents were having trouble with the TV set, his mother went to Isaac Landy's electrical shop to seek help. 'By the time she got back here,' says Harries, 'there was a repair man at the door saying, "I don't know what pull you've got with the Landys, but I was told to drop everything and come here."'[13]

As she grew older, Hilda Kurshion – Michael Howard's mother – followed Ada in touring the district with clothes for sale. At other times she sold clothes and dressmaking material from a stall in Llanelli market. There she struck up a friendship with Annie Price, a dynamic Jewish woman who was ten years her senior, and known throughout the town for her own draper's stall. Mrs Price – or Mrs P, as everyone called her (no one seemed to know her first name) – was an active local citizen, involved in a wide range of charitable and fund-raising projects. She was also a keen member of the Llanelli Labour Party, and recruited Hilda to the Labour League of Youth, the party's young section.

Llanelli was a staunch Labour town, especially in the 1930s, when thousands of local tinplate workers were unemployed because of the Depression. Conservatives and Liberals were scarcely seen: if council elections were contested then Labour's main opponents described themselves as 'Independents'. Such was the dominance of the Left in local politics that Llanelli had two Communist councillors in the 1930s, and in the 1935 general election Llanelli was one of nine seats in South Wales which were so solidly socialist that only a Labour candidate bothered to stand. In time, Llanelli's most prominent socialists included a future deputy leader of the Labour Party, Jim Griffiths (elected for Llanelli in a by-election in 1936), and a future Lord Chancellor, Elwyn Jones.

Two months after Bernat Hecht arrived in Llanelli, on 25 June 1940, he married Hilda at the local synagogue. The wedding took place during one of the darkest periods of modern British history. A week earlier, following the evacuation of Allied troops from Dunkirk, Britain's new Prime Minister, Winston Churchill, had pledged that the country would fight alone: 'If,' he famously declared, 'the British Empire and its Commonwealth lasts for a thousand years men will still say, "This was their finest hour."'[14] Three days before the wedding France surrendered to Germany.

Barely a year after they were married, on 7 July 1941, Bernat and Hilda had the baby who would become the most distinguished Conservative ever to be associated with Llanelli. He was born not in the town itself, but in Gorseinon general hospital, halfway between Llanelli and Swansea. His parents didn't bother with a middle name and called him simply Michael.

Bernat Hecht was in a very fortunate position. On the one hand, despite still being a citizen of Romania, an enemy power, he was not interned by the British authorities (the unfortunate fate of many German Jews in Britain). And yet, because he wasn't a British citizen, neither was he liable for conscription into the armed forces. Instead, Bernat was free to concentrate on establishing himself in Llanelli, which he rapidly did, though he had to abandon his religious vocation. The local Jewish community was not big enough to afford a

professional cantor or reader for its synagogue: in 1939 it had only
thirty-one members, though this figure would represent only male
adults, and with wives and children the Llanelli congregation would
probably amount to more than a hundred people. But Bernat, as a
former full-time cantor, was naturally asked to take an active role in
Jewish services. And he quickly immersed himself in his wife's drapery business, to the extent that on Michael Howard's birth certificate,
only fifteen months after moving from Whitechapel, Bernat described
himself as 'draper', with the word 'Master' in brackets preceding it. Yet
Hecht started modestly, and trade can't have been easy during wartime
clothes rationing. Martin Hecht, who visited his cousin in Llanelli just
after the war, says Bernat would go down to the market every day
with suitcases of clothes.[15]

In January 1942 the Hechts stopped living with Hilda's mother and
brother in James Street and bought their own home just round the
corner at the bottom of a hill – 15 Alban Road. This was a slightly
larger terraced house, with a small front garden, standing opposite a
large Methodist chapel. Behind the backyard was the modest ground
of Llanelli Football Club, though in Llanelli the non-league soccer
team carried far less prestige than the famous rugby side. Again the
Hechts used their home as a base for the clothes business. In 1945
their second child was born, and they gave the baby girl another very
English name, Pamela.

In 1947, having lived in the UK for almost ten years, Bernat Hecht
applied for British citizenship. It is one of the ironies of this tale that,
just as the Conservative leader's father had used one Labour MP,
Jimmy Hall, to help him enter Britain in 1937, a decade later he
employed another as his solicitor to process his application for citizenship. Barnett Janner was himself Jewish and came from South
Wales, having been born in Barry, and had made a considerable reputation as a lawyer specialising in Jewish naturalisation cases. Before
joining the Labour Party, Janner had been a Liberal MP – coincidentally for Whitechapel, until he was defeated in 1935 by Jimmy Hall.
He became a distinguished figure in Britain's Jewish community, serving as president of the Board of Deputies of British Jews and ending

up in the House of Lords. (The Janners were almost Jewish nobility, since Barnett's son, Greville, would follow a similar career path – lawyer, Board of Deputies, Labour MP and life peer.)

In applying for citizenship, Bernat Hecht was given the customary interview by the Carmarthenshire police and had to produce documentary proof of his wealth. The police reported that 'He is financially solvent. He owns the premises where he resides and values it at £2,000. He also owns a motor car valued at £425 and stock valued at £800. He has £200 in the Post Office Savings Bank and £50 in Savings Certificates.'[16]

These were impressive assets for a man who had been in business for only seven years – the equivalent today of perhaps £100,000 in strictly cash terms, though the house alone would probably be worth about that much now. 'He is hard working and industrious,' wrote Detective Inspector William Lloyd, who saw no reason to think that Hecht might be disloyal to Britain.[17] Bernat's application was backed by four Welsh neighbours – a confectioner, a greengrocer, a butcher and a labourer in the local steelworks.

Having paid the statutory £9 fee and declared an oath of allegiance, Bernat Hecht acquired citizenship in January 1948, and his wife, Hilda, became a British subject shortly afterwards on payment of a further 10 shillings (50p). Bernat then immediately applied for himself, his wife and their children, Michael and Pamela, now aged six and two, to change their surname by deed poll (and formally to change his first name to Bernard, as he had been calling himself for years). It was perhaps an understandable decision at a time when having a German name in Britain would not have been popular, and yet Bernat's cousins Martin and Jacob Hecht have lived in Britain under their given name to this day. In choosing a new surname one option would simply have been to translate the family's existing name into English, as many Jews did, and call themselves Pike. Instead, Bernat and Hilda chose the much more distinguished-sounding Howard.

Howard was also the surname of two of the most famous Hollywood stars of the 1940s, both of them English. Trevor Howard had just starred in David Lean's 1945 classic *Brief Encounter*, while Leslie Howard, who was killed in 1943, not only had been Jewish but also had Hungarian ancestry. A slightly stronger reason to have chosen the name Howard was closer to home. Martin Hecht was impressed on his visits to Carmarthenshire at how quickly his cousin Bernard had managed to assimilate himself into local middle-class society, as if he'd been living in Llanelli all his life. He remembers how Bernard Howard had joined the local golf club, for example, and acquired a fine set of irons. Hilda Howard, meanwhile, became president of the Llanelli Jewish Ladies' Guild. And what better way to attach yourself to Llanelli's elite than by adopting the same long-standing English surname as the town's highly popular aristocrats? More than thirty years earlier, in 1911, the Englishman Sir Stafford Howard, a former Liberal MP who was descended from the dukes of Norfolk, had married Catherine Stepney, the daughter of Llanelli's then leading family. The following year – around the time that Hilda Kurshion arrived in Llanelli with her family – Sir Stafford and Lady Catherine inscribed their name on the map of Llanelli by purchasing Bryncaerau Castle, which overlooked the town, and its surrounding gardens. They renamed the grounds as Parc Howard, and then agreed to let both house and gardens to Llanelli town council for a token five shillings a year, for the benefit of local citizens. Sir Stafford and his wife imposed one condition: the council had to restore the property within eight months – a proviso which was met only because a long coal strike meant that local miners badly needed other work. It was, says one historian, 'the finest present ever made to Llanelli'.[18] Lady Howard – known locally as 'Lady Bountiful' – subsequently served as mayor of Llanelli and as a county councillor for almost thirty years, and, until her death in 1952, was regarded as the town's most eminent citizen. And it is certain that the Hechts would have visited Parc Howard, especially since it was barely half a mile from their home.

Despite my questions to several different members of the Howard family, no one professes to know why the name was chosen. Perhaps it was a way for Bernat and Hilda to identify with their adopted town. Or perhaps it was simple social climbing. And of course Howard was a very *English* name, not Welsh.

A much bigger mystery surrounds the details which Bernat Hecht had given the Home Office Aliens Department about his father, Morris Wurzberger. On the application form for citizenship which he submitted in February 1947, Hecht had stated that his father, whom he called 'Morris Hecht', was dead. The subsequent two-page report compiled by the Carmarthenshire police, signed by the chief constable and based on Inspector William Lloyd's interview, shows that Bernat told the police that his father had died in Ruscova in 1939. Almost equally strange, he stated that his mother, Leah, had died in Romania in 1943, rather than at Auschwitz in 1944.[19]

That claim by Bernat Hecht in 1947 clearly does not square with what his cousins Martin and Jacob Hecht say today. Their version is that Morris Wurzberger/Hecht came to Britain from Ruscova around 1936 or 1936, paving the way for Bernat's arrival, and that Morris carried on living in north London for several years after the war. Jacob and Martin both say that they regularly met Morris after 1945, and Martin remembers Morris's presence in London in some detail. His recollection was that Morris remarried – though possibly in a common-law marriage – and that he and his wife occupied a house in Woodberry Down, a street not far from Manor House underground station in north London. It was a very happy relationship, people say, though short-lived. Martin remembers that Morris died and was buried in Willesden's Jewish cemetery. Another source thinks he was buried in Ealing.

For a while I was sceptical about what Martin and Jacob Hecht were saying, even though there appeared to be no collusion between them. Despite persistent efforts, I could find no hard evidence that Morris Wurzberger/Hecht spent almost two decades living in this country. The Jewish cemetery in Willesden had no record of his burial, and I could find no record of his death or a will. He seems not to have applied for citizenship, and so didn't appear on any electoral register. In any case, why would Bernat Hecht lie to the police about what had happened to his father – or at best mislead them – since it might endanger his chances of getting citizenship if he were caught lying?

It was all a great puzzle. Then suddenly I found very close corroboration of what Martin and Jacob Hecht said, stumbling across it by the most astonishing accident that is ever likely to befall me as a journalist.

I had been looking into a completely separate part of Michael Howard's life, examining his notable cases as a barrister. Having discovered there is another QC called Michael Howard, I though I'd better contact him to check that I hadn't got any of their court appearances mixed up, which would have been a pretty embarrassing mistake. When the other Howard assured me I was in the clear, I asked him whether he had had any dealings with his political namesake. Funnily enough, he said, there was a distant family connection. In the early 1950s his step-grandmother, who had been called Dinah Newman, had lived in north London with Michael Howard's grandfather, who was known within the family as 'uncle Morris'. Amazingly, this effectively meant that Dinah Newman had two step-grandsons called Michael Howard who both became QCs – and yet they had acquired the same surname, Howard, from totally unconnected roots. More important, it gave me, totally unsolicited, the vital proof I needed that Morris Wurzberger/Hecht had indeed lived in London after the war.

Unfortunately the other Michael Howard knew very little detail about his step-grandmother's common-law husband, Morris. He suggested I talk to his mother, Tilly Howard, who confirmed the detail about Woodberry Down. Yet she became strangely suspicious when I asked for details of where and when Morris had died. 'Why do you need to know?' she demanded, insisting it was totally irrelevant to my book. She even accused me of invading people's privacy, which seemed rather strange when Morris had died about fifty years ago, and deaths are generally a matter of public record. It was an astonishingly defensive attitude, and I got the impression I had touched on something very sensitive.

My suspicions were aroused yet further when my researcher made contact with Dinah Newman's daughter, Rose Silverstone, who is now in her nineties and lives in Southgate in north London. Rose

Silverstone's daughter Barbara Ross – Dinah's grand-daughter – inter-
cepted his approach and said they would have to seek permission
from Michael Howard (the politician) before they could respond. My
researcher had explained that his enquiry was for a book on Howard,
but it seemed strangely deferential and protective to seek Howard's
say-so when he is merely a distant cousin of Rose Silverstone (and
legally not even that).[20] Having contacted Howard, Barbara Ross said
she could say nothing about where and when Morris died. It increasingly looked as if I was on to something.

I soon discovered I was not the first to suspect that something was
wrong. Fifty years ago civil servants had been equally puzzled by the
family's conflicting stories about when and where Morris
Wurzberger/Hecht died. In 1947 Home Office officials had no reason
to know that details on Bernat Hecht's naturalisation forms were incor-
rect, but they became deeply suspicious when his brother Wally and
sister Rosie subsequently submitted their applications to become
British citizens in the early 1950s, having arrived in Britain in 1946 and
1947 respectively. They, too, claimed that their father, Morris, had died
in Romania, but whereas Bernat said that his death was in 1939, Wally
said he had died in 1943. On the other hand, Rosie said Morris had
died in 1940, adding authenticity to her claim by saying she had been
living with him in Ruscova at the time. Rosie actually claimed that
Morris was only her stepfather, and that her own surname was Hercz
not Hecht, though the Home Office was equally sceptical about this.

Home Office officials were so suspicious when they received
Rosie's form that they even constructed a table laying out the various
discrepancies between the different accounts by the three siblings.
They then asked Carmarthenshire police to reinterview her. 'The
information furnished by each of the three about their alleged father
has not always been accurate,' an official wrote to the chief constable.
'It is indeed so inconsistent as to give rise to doubt whether they have
begun to be factual about him.'[21] The police also questioned Bernard
about what he'd told them in 1947, but neither the Home Office nor
the police, nor MI5 (who also considered Rosie's application) ever got
to the bottom of the affair.

The Home Office official handling the case reported that Rosie claimed that 'sufferings during the war have affected her memory, but I am not convinced that this is so'. He concluded, however, that the 'misinformation is apparently directed to hiding . . . a question of legitimacy. It would seem likely that they did not have (or all have) a legal father, but that no more sinister motive has caused the discrepancies.' The civil servant might have taken a much less favourable attitude had he known the truth – that the father had in fact been living in England on each of the three suggested dates for his death in Romania, and was quite probably still alive at the time of the report. The official decided that, despite the factual inaccuracies, and for family consistency, Rosie should be given British citizenship. 'In the light of the fact that both brothers are now British there is some justification for granting the sister, though I am pretty certain she has furnished inaccurate information deliberately. However, in all the circumstances it may be thought right to give her the benefit of the doubt.'[22]

Only a few weeks before publication of this book, I began a wider check of the public records for details of Morris Wurzberger's existence. It was then that I suddenly found confirmation of his death, in north London in 1952 – not under that precise name, but under the slightly different spelling (and pronunciation) of Morris (or Mozes) Werczberger. The death certificate states he was 'formerly a synagogue beadle', and it was signed by his 'widow' Dinah Werczberger. Yet strangely, she merely made her mark, an 'X', rather than provide a normal signature, even though she knew how to write. Dinah's failure to sign properly suggests she was unhappy about the situation, perhaps because she had never officially been married to Morris.

It was now clear that Michael's Howard's father and his aunt Rosie both deliberately lied to the British authorities about their father's death, and it appears that his uncle Wally misled them too. Morris did not die in Romania in 1939, or in 1940, or in 1943, but in London in 1952. Put bluntly, there was a conspiracy between them to cover up the fact that Morris had been living in Britain since around 1935 or 1936 – a fact they obviously must have known, given the close relations between family members. But they botched the plot by failing to straighten out the exact details of their concocted story, perhaps because Bernard had forgotten exactly what he'd already told the authorities by the time his brother and sister applied for citizenship in the early 1950s.

The big question, of course, is *why* they felt the need effectively to kill off their father in the eyes of the state.

By far the most probable explanation is that Morris Wurzberger/Hecht had always been an illegal immigrant and that his children were simply keen to protect him. He seems to have entered Britain around 1935 or 1936 and to have survived here through the war and beyond without ever registering with the British authorities – hence the apparent lack of any official record of his existence until he died in 1952.

It seems surprising the lengths to which the Hecht/Howard family went in order to deceive the authorities. Perhaps it was a case of one lie leading to another, and a fear that if the deception was ever discovered then Morris might be deported back to Romania, which was by then under Communist control. In reality, had the family come clean and Morris owned up to his presence in the UK, it is almost certain that immigration officials would have considered his case favourably in the aftermath of the Holocaust, the war and the Soviet domination of his home country. But Bernat Hecht and his siblings may not have thought rationally, and perhaps feared that any confession might put the whole family in jeopardy. And as Bernat, Wally and Rosie each compounded the deception in their successive citizenship applications they must have felt they were digging themselves deeper and deeper into a hole.

The story worried me. Could there be some other explanation for the discrepancies in Bernat Hecht's naturalisation papers and those of his siblings? Might I have been confused by the fact that Michael Howard's grandfather went under two different names, with numerous variations in spelling? Was it possible that Morris Hecht and Morris Wurzberger were two different people? To suggest that the Leader of the Opposition's presence in Britain was originally based on his grandfather being an illegal immigrant was a fairly serious charge, especially when, at the start of 2005, Howard again began making a big issue of immigration and particularly illegal migrants. I would look very foolish if I was wrong.

Then suddenly, in late January 2005, I received an email from Howard's press secretary, Guy Black, asking whether there was anything I wanted to check with him as publication of my book must be imminent. So I took the opportunity to mention the discrepancy over Howard's grandfather, and asked if he had any explanation. Black said he would try and get a response from his boss.

For nine days I heard nothing. Then late one evening I was phoned by a *Newsnight* colleague and learned that Howard and Black had chosen to respond not in the normal manner, but on the front page of the next day's *Daily Mail*. 'HOWARD: MY GRANDFATHER THE "ILLEGAL" IMMIGRANT' the headline read. In an interview, Howard explained that as a result of learning of my inquiries into his family background, he had conducted his own investigations at the National Archives (though it's hard to believe he went there in person). He soon reached much the same conclusion as me as to why Bernat deceived the Home Office. 'I have speculated on the reason,' he told the *Mail*, 'and I suppose one possibility is that my grandfather might have entered Britain unlawfully. That may be one answer, but it will remain a mystery . . . There might have been some irregularity about his status. It came as a surprise to me. What my father did was wrong. I don't condone it. But I don't feel embarrassed, because I have done nothing wrong myself.'[23]

Michael Howard had made a pre-emptive strike. Rather than wait for me to reveal the details in this book, he had chosen a newspaper which strongly supports his immigration policies. It had taken the sting out of what was potentially quite an embarrassing revelation by releasing it on his terms, with sympathetic coverage which glossed over the obvious political implications. It was ruthless, but effective.

And as this book went to press, I still awaited a formal response from Guy Black.

3

SCHOOLBOY REBEL

He was immaculately turned out. I can remember the way
Michael walked – there was something magical about him.

EMYR PHILLIPS, SCHOOLFRIEND[1]

'I knew he was going somewhere from the very beginning,' says Jean
Pugh, who taught Michael Howard at primary school. 'He was very
bright. He had everything he needed up top. He was an extremely
nice chap – exceptionally nice. Quiet, unassuming and polite.'[2]
'Bright', 'intelligent', 'nice' and 'polite' are the words used by all four
of Michael Howard's primary-school teachers who still live in
Llanelli.

Until he was seven, Michael Howard attended Stebonheath Infants'
School, a few hundred yards up the hill from the family home, and
known to its pupils as 'Stebbo'. Then he moved to Park Street, a
junior school in the centre of the town, which had around 200 boys
(and, unusually for a primary school, it *was* all boys). It had a wider
catchment area, which made it much more working-class than
'Stebbo', and many pupils were the sons of tinplate men and workers
in the local steel foundry.

Whereas Stebonheath was relatively modern, having been built
between the wars, Park Street was Victorian, forbidding and ill-
equipped. The steps had been worn down by successive generations;

the lavatories were outside in the playground, and the classrooms were divided by partitions which rattled on windy days.

He was 'what I'd term a high-flyer', says Eiry Rees who taught Howard in his first year at Park Street:

> I remember in arithmetic, maths, I'd only have to show the class once and Michael would have grasped the basics straight away. And I'd have to give him a book for him to go off and work the sums, problems, on his own. And it was tick, tick, tick. He was what I'd call articulate. He could communicate, even then. He was a very well-behaved and well-liked pupil. I can see him now wearing short trousers. I remember Michael so well because he was what I'd call a 'pretty' boy.[3]

'One of the most intelligent boys I've ever had,' says Gerwyn Williams, Howard's next teacher, who recalls him as 'very quiet' and 'a bit of a loner'.[4] Most mornings, so Williams remembers, the young Michael would walk to school, taking a short diversion to a neighbouring street to collect his best friend, Stuart Evans, whose father was a teacher. Then at midday they'd walk back again for lunch.

Harriet Griffiths, who taught Michael at nine and ten, also says he was 'a very diligent scholar. He got on with his work, and needed very little teaching. I knew he was university material, but you never thought further than that in the junior school because other things pressed in.'[5]

The uniform at Park Street was traditional: blue or grey suits with short trousers, three-quarter socks to the knee, and shirts and ties. 'We had Welsh lessons, and he did his bit with the other children on St David's Day. And I'm quite sure he knows his Welsh anthem,' says Harriet Griffiths – 'I don't think he would have left Park Street without knowing that.'[6] The young Michael also acquired a Welsh accent.

Although the Howards were orthodox Jews, Michael's parents were clear that he should not stay out of any Christian element of the primary-school day. The same applied to the son of the local rabbi, who was also at Park Street. 'There was to be no difference,' says Harriet

Griffiths. 'We sang hymns, had assembly and so on. Their fathers were definite about them not being separated at that time.'[7] No one recalls the boys being bullied for being Jewish.

Meanwhile the Howard drapery business continued to prosper. In the 1940s the work had involved both the door-to-door sales business, inherited from the Kurshion family, and regular market stalls in Llanelli and neighbouring Swansea and Carmarthen. Bernard Howard's stall mainly sold material cut from rolls, for women who wanted to make clothes at home. Now, in the early 1950s, the family took a big step upmarket. Initially they bought a shop called The Beehive, a busy going concern which sold fabric, general haberdashery, furnishing fabrics, curtain materials, school uniforms and children's clothes. 'Everything for BABIES . . . and TINY TOTS, that's our speciality,' declared an ad for The Beehive in the *Llanelli Star*.[8] In March 1958 the couple opened a second shop selling fashionable women's clothing, which they called Howards. Both shops were on prime sites in Cowell Street, in the heart of the Llanelli shopping district. The new store was promoted with a large advertisement over two-thirds of a page in the local paper. 'Please note – We are not a Multiple Shop,' it stated. 'We give you personal and individual attention. Make a date next Thursday, and every day, and buy our Clever Clothes for personal charm at . . . Howards.'[9] 'Are you going to a party this Christmas?' asked another ad. 'We have a wonderful selection of party and evening gowns to suit all tastes. At most reasonable prices. Call now and visit our most modern showroom and choose at your leisure the gown for you.'[10]

Howards, on a corner now occupied by a café, took up two floors. In the window, mannequins displayed the latest dresses, but much of the ground floor was devoted to women's hats – in an era when women usually wore hats – and some children's items. Upstairs, overlooking the street, the shop had a bridal showroom.

Bernard Howard was skilled at the window displays, and had a flair for colour and fashion. Margaret Morgan, who worked in both Howard shops, remembers him as the business brain, while Michael's mother, Hilda, always elegantly dressed, handled customers:

She was the seller. She was the front woman, I would say. He walked round looking important, but didn't get very involved in the selling. Sometimes he would come in when you were in the bridal room and he'd make some remark: 'It looks beautiful.' It was a flourishing business, and had a bit of everything. They had a very expensive range for weddings and that, but quite a decent mix. It wasn't rubbish.[11]

If Hilda Howard spotted someone looking in the window, she would think nothing of going out on to the pavement and urging them to step in. 'It was very difficult to go into the shop without coming out having bought something,' says Vaughan Evans, whose family owned a store opposite. 'It was almost a joke among traders, because she was so persuasive and persistent.'[12] At least twice a year the Howards would travel to London for the clothes shows, spending the best part of a week watching the various fashion houses display their new seasonal ranges. Stock would be ordered for direct delivery to Llanelli.

The main shop employed four or five full-time staff – all women – and every Christmas the Howards held a dinner for the whole team. A photograph of one such celebration from the early 1960s shows a beaming Bernard Howard, in black tie, surrounded by fourteen women – his wife, sister and daughter, and eleven staff from their shops. 'They were very good to work for,' says Joan Jones, who also worked in Howards. 'They were great – like a family.'[13] Around the end of 1960 the Howards opened a third shop, behind the law courts in Carmarthen, fifteen miles away, but the distance made it difficult to run.

The shops were much smarter than the Howards' previous business, and more lucrative, if more expensive to maintain. Unlike with the door-to-door work or the market stalls, their shop customers were mostly middle-class, or working-class women who needed something for a special occasion. And, whereas the previous business was based on giving people credit and letting them pay by small weekly instalments, here their customers paid on purchase.

In 1952 the Howards moved house again, to a rather grand property not far from Parc Howard. Number 2 Ty'rfran Avenue, which they bought from a local soft-drinks manufacturer, was a detached 1930s building, much bigger than the semi-detached houses in the rest of the street, and its windows had a good view over the town. But the adjacent street, Glasfryn Terrace, led down into what's known as the Llanerch, which had a reputation as a rough council estate. 'Bernard said the house was a bit too near the Llanerch for his liking,' says John Thomas, a retired steelworker who still lives in the council house next door. 'But they were the people from whom he'd made his money.' Thomas found Hilda Howard to be an especially considerate neighbour: 'When I was working in the steelworks and not earning that much, I could take my daughter into the shop and she would let you have things on approval. Very trusting she was. "Come to the shop," she would say. "Take three or four coats. You can pay me when you bring them back."'[14]

And Michael happily mixed with people from the nearby council houses. Neighbours recall how he would often go round the corner to Mrs Jones's home and sit in her kitchen devouring Welsh cakes (a kind of flat scone). 'My mother doesn't make these,' he reportedly told her. Neighbours remember him as a very polite young man, but, like most boys, not always that talkative.

The Howards ate kosher food at home and regularly attended the local synagogue, but, although they regarded themselves as orthodox Jews, they were not always fully observant. Like most Jewish traders in Llanelli, they opened their shop on Saturdays – the Jewish sabbath – and stayed open until five o'clock on Friday evenings in the middle of winter, which meant that, contrary to orthodox practice, they didn't get home until well after dark.

Bernard Howard was not a very practical man, and employed an odd-jobber for any work around the home. Michael Howard says that, shortly after his parents were married, Bernard 'tried to fix something in the bathroom, punctured the plumbing of the entire house, caused an enormous flood, [and] used that as an excuse for the rest of his life not to do anything in the house'.[15]

After the war, Bernard Howard had arranged for his brother Wally and sister Rosie to come to Britain. Both eventually settled in Llanelli and took British citizenship, and Wally adopted the Howard name as well. Wally also worked in the drapery trade before opening a shop in Swansea. Rosie had previously been employed as a housekeeper in London, but when Michael was eleven Bernard and Hilda invited her to live with them, working as the family cook and housekeeper on a wage of £2 5s. (£2.25) a week. Rosie had been badly scarred by her time in Auschwitz, and her camp identity number, A-27879, was still visible on her forearm, tattooed in German lettering. 'It ruined her life, not surprisingly,' Michael Howard has said.[16] 'She was perfectly balanced and sane, but ruined by it. She had been married before . . . but she never married again. She never had children. My sister and I became a substitute for them . . . She was a good cook – always there when we came home from school, making the tea – and very good company. She was very special; an attractive, fair-haired woman. I was very fond of her.'[17]

In the shop, where Rosie sometimes lingered for hours, though never officially working there, she would chat away to customers and staff. At times Rosie seems to have been more of a hindrance than a help. 'If you were seeing to a customer,' says Margaret Morgan, 'she always had her full pennyworth. She would oversell. She was quite sweet.'[18] Rosie occasionally visited cousins in France and Belgium, and at one point she even went to the Soviet Union to see her brother Samuel, who now had a family, but was suffering from TB. The Howards sent him medicine, and clothes for his two daughters.

In 1952 Michael Howard took the eleven-plus exam, whose sixty-minute arithmetic paper included questions such as 'Multiply 7 gals. 2 pts, by 39' and 'Divide 74 hours 56 minutes by 8.'[19] To no one's surprise, he won a scholarship to the all-boys Llanelli Grammar School (having no doubt answered '282 gals. 6pts.' and '9 hours 22 minutes'). The 'Gram' was, in Howard's words, 'a traditional Welsh grammar school – clean, disciplined and orderly'.[20] Masters wore gowns, and the boys sat at one-piece wooden desks with inkwells. In the lower school the uniform comprised dark trousers and maroon blazers, with ties and caps in maroon and green.

The 'Gram''s most distinguished old boy, politically, was the Labour MP for West Ham South, Elwyn Jones, who during the Attlee government had served as parliamentary private secretary to the Attorney-General, Sir Hartley Shawcross. The school had just over 600 boys when Howard arrived (it had expanded to more than 800 by the time he left), and they were split into four classes in the five years to O-level. Forty-four per cent of the boys spoke Welsh as their first language, which reflected Llanelli's proximity to the Welsh-language heartland of western Wales. Two of the classes had half their lessons in Welsh, while the other two were taught in English, though they still learned Welsh as part of the curriculum for the three junior years. Each pair of classes was also streamed according to ability. Michael was placed in the all-English top stream, which was class 1A1 in his first year. He preferred arts subjects and 'wasn't brilliant on the science side', he once admitted.[21]

The school seems to have had a considerate, caring atmosphere, encouraged by the long-standing headmaster, T. V. Shaw, who was a devout Christian. The community spirit was fostered by the fact that half the masters were themselves old boys. But, judging from a school inspection conducted in the year that Howard arrived, the teaching wasn't without flaws. In history, 'the written work of the pupils throughout the school leaves much to be desired,' the inspectors declared. 'The speech of the pupils [in English lessons] is apt to be slovenly,' while in French less able pupils revealed 'a quite inadequate grasp of the language and little fluency in speech'.[22]

The school suffered from being divided between two sites, almost two miles apart. The four upper years were based at older, more cramped, buildings near the centre of Llanelli, not far from Michael Howard's former infants school. The three junior years were taught about a mile east of Llanelli, in a new building just beneath Stradey Castle and woods, not far from Stradey Park, home of the renowned Llanelli rugby team. Not surprisingly, given the fervour for the game in Llanelli, it was very much a rugby school, with no soccer teams.

Michael Howard stood out in several ways – sometimes literally. Unlike in his time at primary school, he and the one or two other

Jewish boys would usually not attend the religious part of morning assembly. 'We filed past in the corridor, and they'd be waiting to come in,' says fellow pupil Jeff Hopkins. 'After the Christian service was over they'd come in then.'[23]

'You could see even in those days that there was the proverbial "cut above the rest" in the way that Mike spoke, the way he dressed,' says Emyr Phillips, who was one of Howard's closest friends in his early years. 'Most of the boys were sons of miners, tinplate workers or people in the steel industry. Perhaps 2 per cent of parents owned their own businesses.'[24] Howard also stood out, of course, as the son of immigrants; he was middle-class, whereas most of the boys came from working-class homes; he was cleverer than most pupils; and he had asthma, which meant he often missed games in what was a very sporty school. He was also absent from school for the first few days of his first year, when his aunt Rosie took him to Switzerland to recuperate. These may seem minor details from an adult perspective, but for an adolescent they would have been significant.

Despite this, or perhaps because of it, Howard seemed to enjoy being a bit of a rebel. Emyr Phillips tells of how in the junior years he and 'Mike', as he called him, often escaped from school in the lunch hour, against the rules, and with the aid of Bernard Howard:

> Mike's father would come to the gates at the end of the drive. I'm 95 per cent sure his car was a Humber Hawk, black. We would go into Llanelli in the car. Mike had lunch with his parents and I used to go to the Savoy fish and chip shop, directly opposite their shop, and then I got a lift back . . . And when we got back we got the message 'Would these two report to T. V. Shaw, the head.' And we found a different excuse every day as to why we had to go into Llanelli. He, the future barrister, invented the excuses. It was just a way of getting out of school meals.[25]

The benign Shaw didn't believe in caning boys: their usual punishment, says Phillips, might be a hundred lines, though Howard recollects once suffering 'a ruler across the hand from the form master – but I honestly can't remember why'.[26]

Michael Howard also stood out as a keen soccer player. 'I can remember him every break time and lunchtime rushing out to play football on the school field,' says a former classmate, Gerald Ballard. Sometimes though, because of his asthma, 'after about half an hour he'd be gasping for breath, but he'd keep plugging on'.[27] Howard himself likes recounting how he upset the rugby-obsessed institution by starting a school soccer team (in which he played centre forward). 'That was quite dramatic,' he once said. 'This was one of the biggest rugby schools in one of the strongest rugby areas in Wales . . . This was definitely inspired by rebellion. The most obvious thing a rebel could do where I come from was start a soccer team.'[28] This story is greeted with scepticism by contemporaries, many of whom have no recollection of his team. John Davies, a former teacher, who claims to have started the school's first official soccer eleven in the 1960s, says, 'He might have played for some unofficial school team, but hundreds of pupils before him did that. I did that when I was a lad.'[29] The closest Howard came to any distinction at games was his service as joint secretary of the Chess Society, but he often had to miss matches against other schools when they were played on Friday nights, because he had to be home before dusk to observe the Jewish sabbath.

Yet it is perhaps not surprising that Michael Howard's soccer activity may have gone unnoticed when the school was so fanatical about rugby. Many old boys had gone on to play for Llanelli – the Scarlets, who became Welsh heroes in 1957 after their shock victory over the visiting New Zealand All Blacks – and to be picked for the Welsh national team. In his penultimate year, 1958, Llanelli Grammar School took a 'sevens' rugby side to Roehampton in south-west London and won the national Public School Sevens tournament, despite not being a public school. They won the competition twice more, in 1961 and 1962 – a remarkable run of three wins in five years.

That Howard should have bucked the trend and taken more interest in soccer may stem from his living as a young boy right next to Stebonheath Park, the home of Llanelli Football Club – the Reds.

There was a huge gulf between the standing of the local rugby and soccer teams. While Llanelli's rugby union side was historically one of the big four in South Wales – alongside Newport, Cardiff and Swansea – Llanelli's soccer team was some way outside of the Football League, the top ninety-two clubs in England and Wales. Nevertheless, it was at its peak in the late 1940s and early 1950s, playing in the Southern League, one of two leagues just below the Football League. Because the Football League imposed a maximum wage on players, Llanelli was able to sign good professionals by paying more than they were permitted to earn at League clubs. Michael Howard has said that one of his strongest memories of his Welsh boyhood is of the autumn of 1950 when Llanelli met Bristol Rovers in the first round of the FA Cup and he was among the crowd of almost 13,000 packed into the Stebonheath ground, where the two teams drew 1–1.[30] Rovers won only after a second replay on neutral territory, and went on to the quarter-finals. That season the Llanelli FC side included the legendary Jock Stein, who became captain and later manager of the great Glasgow club Celtic. But Michael Howard was never committed to one club. He would watch the nearest League side, second division Swansea Town (as it then was), and also supported Liverpool, who had won the League title in 1947, when Michael was five. There was no family connection with Merseyside, though Liverpool has always had close links with Wales. Howard says he chose the team out of admiration for its Scottish centre forward, Billy Liddell. His commitment may have been strengthened later when one of his school contemporaries, Gordon Wallace, who lived not far from Ty'rfran Avenue, briefly played for the Merseyside team.

And what of politics? Howard's cousin Renee remembers, 'He used to tell us as a young boy "I'm going to be in Parliament," and we said "Don't be ridiculous!" We used to say "Get away with you, get away with you!" We used to laugh at him.'[31] At school, he seems to have been equally interested in law. Gerald Ballard recalls a teacher in their second year, when the boys were twelve or thirteen, arranging a mock trial. Howard, he says, insisted on being the prosecution barrister. 'This was a big thing, and you ought to have heard him ripping into the witnesses – and that was as a thirteen-year-old!' When the teacher complimented him afterwards, Howard explained that this was what he wanted to do in life. 'It was more law than politics at that stage,' says Ballard.[32] Howard's cousin Renee recalls, 'He always used to say to us, "I'm going to be in Parliament. I'm going to be a judge." This was at about thirteen. He was very determined, strong willed.'[33]

Michael Howard's first real interest in political issues can be dated to 1956, when the Egyptian leader Colonel Nasser nationalised the Suez canal, which was jointly owned by Britain and France, and the two powers, operating covertly with Israel, went to war to take the canal back. The Suez Crisis was one of the critical episodes of post-war British history, but of especial interest to a Jewish family who had cousins in the young state of Israel. 'That was the first time that I can remember really having a view and saying that one thing was right and the other was wrong,' Howard later said.[34] 'I remember being most disappointed when we withdrew.'[35]

Yet, if one believes the anecdotes, others had spotted the future politician much earlier. Margaret Morgan says that the Howards' family GP, Dr Llewellyn, had been calling him 'My little prime minster' ever since the young Michael, then aged four or five, had shown he could already read Hebrew.[36] It's also said that Hilda Howard's close friend Annie Price had earmarked Michael as a future recruit to the Labour Party. But whatever sympathies Hilda or her son had for Labour seem to have disappeared with Suez, when the Labour Party, led by Hugh Gaitskell (whose deputy was then Jim Griffiths, Llanelli's MP), strongly opposed the Conservative government of Sir Anthony Eden. Howard has spoken of a home where politics was 'always discussed' but his parents were 'totally non-political and there'd been no real influence on me to be partisan'.[37]

After Suez, Howard spent more time arguing with his economics teachers, and in the sixth form he took A-level subjects that one might expect for a budding politician – English, History and Economics. He pursued equally suitable extra-curricular activities, too, and in his final year he chaired both of the main political groups. One was the Sixth Form Forum, the school's main debating society, where Howard was 'a formidable debater', says teacher Dai Smith.[38] 'He was well informed, very eloquent, very persuasive in his manner. He had definite views, and wasn't afraid of putting them forward. Confident, yes. Arrogant, no.'[39] Yet Howard admits he took the chairmanship of the debating society against the wishes of the new head, Stanley Rees:

I certainly wasn't the headmaster's choice for that. I can't remember – he had someone lined up for that, and some of the other boys said to me, 'Why don't you stand?' and I said, 'Well, you know, Stan's got his man, then let's leave it at that.' But they said, 'No. If we nominated you, would you stand?' And I said, 'All right,' and then I was elected – which was probably the first thing I was elected to.[40]

The other body which Howard chaired was the school's Council for Education in World Citizenship, part of the national organisation which promotes political interest and good international understanding among young people. Members of the CEWC that year were treated to films on how elections work in Britain, and on the life of an MP. Yet contemporaries don't recall Michael Howard as being particularly fanatical about his politics; he didn't join the Conservative Party locally, and he certainly didn't try to convert people to the cause. But he probably wouldn't have got far if he had.

To declare oneself a Conservative was a brave act in a town where Labour took two thirds of the vote in the 1955 election (won nationally by the Tories), and where almost one in ten of the workforce had no job – at a time when most of Britain enjoyed full employment. But in other ways the affiliation would have been perfectly understandable. Not only were the Howards small businessmen, but the countries from which they had escaped – Romania and Ukraine – had both been swallowed up by the Soviet empire. The year 1956 had also seen that empire crush the anti-Soviet Hungarian uprising led by Imre Nagy. What little contact the Howards had with Bernard's brother Samuel in Russia would only have underlined the limitations of the state socialism practised in the Soviet bloc, which had not yet emerged from the shadow of Stalinism and was still quite anti-Semitic.

Throughout his time in Llanelli, Michael Howard was still very much an orthodox Jew, and his family played a leading role in the town's Jewish life. His parents both served on the committee of the Llanelli synagogue, where Bernard continued to help with services. In preparation for his bar mitzvah at the age of thirteen, Howard attended weekly Hebrew classes on Sunday mornings and on weekday evenings, when he would have memorised prayers and learned to translate them.

It was almost as if he lived in two worlds. Outside school, Howard's social life revolved around Jewish friends and his extended family on his mother's side, the Landys. He saw a lot of two of his cousins, Rochelle and Renee Landy, who were a similar age. 'We were a very close family,' says Renee (now called Renee Woolf). 'We always shared Friday nights or the Jewish holidays and the families used to join in celebrating together. Mr Howard's father used to blow the shofar [a ritual ram's horn] to bring in the new year, and God, he was amazing!' The teenage Michael took part in the ritual too. 'He was very learned – he could do any service.'[41] The family would often go on Sunday afternoon outings to the Gower peninsula on the other side of the estuary, and to other spots along the South Wales coast.

Howard has mentioned how at school lunchtimes in Llanelli he might visit a snooker hall in the town, and even 'nip off a bit early' to do so in the afternoon.[42] But he spent only a limited amount of time socialising with schoolmates. He was never, for instance, a member of what his school friend Keith Marshall calls the 'Parc Howard gang', a crowd of middle-class teenagers from the boys' and girls' grammar schools who often gathered in the local park. 'We used to have great evenings in the pub, and Mike wasn't part of that. He was slightly more family-oriented and within the Jewish community . . . I certainly don't remember him in the evening with us at all. I think his parents had a very strict routine for him. It may be that they thought we were a bunch of reprobates!'[43]

As befits the son of a cantor, the teenage Howard took a keen

interest in music. Having learned the piano until he was about thirteen, he then took up the guitar. Veronica Jones, who was three years
younger than Michael, lived in the house over the road, and from her
bedroom she looked directly across on to his. She has an abiding
image, she says, of the teenage Michael framed in his bedroom
window strumming his guitar, singing the same tune incessantly – the
traditional American folk song 'It Takes a Worried Man to Sing a
Worried Song'. 'That was the only one I heard him play,' she says. 'I
don't think he could play anything else.'[44]

Howard was an early Elvis Presley fan. When a friend alerted him
that the record 'Heartbreak Hotel' was on sale, he says, he went
straight to the record shop 'and bought it immediately. I must have
been about sixteen.'[45] His cousin Renee recalls him performing like
Elvis all day. 'He wanted to be Elvis Presley,' she says. 'He used to sit
in the bath shrinking his jeans – or so I was told. I don't know if it's
true! He had a teddy boy hairstyle.'[46]

Keith Marshall, who was a more experienced musician than
Michael, and knew how to write music, recalls being recruited one
day to help Howard commit a song to paper. It was his scheme to get
rich quick.

> He wasn't a big musician, that's for sure. I remember once he said,
> 'I want to write some rock 'n' roll.' He used to think up some
> songs, and he used to sing them to me. He had this tune, and I
> remember bringing some manuscript over and jotting it down, and
> he was going to send it off to some publisher or other, and I said,
> 'OK, well I'll transpose it for you into some form so that it can be
> played by saxophones or trumpets and trombones.' He thought up
> both the words and the music. I don't think it was any cop, but we
> both did it thinking it would be. That was on the back of when Bill
> Haley and the Comets were about. He was very enterprising even
> to think about it, because, of course, that could have been a way to
> making a good fortune.[47]

Howard also formed a skiffle group with friends from school. 'I was the singer and we had sideburns and wore drainpipe trousers,' he once revealed. 'We did all the Lonnie Donegan numbers and later some Elvis Presley songs but I don't think we did many public perform-ances.'[48] He even wore fluorescent socks, but no one, not even Howard himself, can remember the group's name, and, of thirty or so former teachers and contemporaries from Llanelli Grammar School approached by this author, only one can actually recall the group – playing at a Christmas school concert. Again, this set Howard a little apart from his 1950s Llanelli contemporaries; many of them, from old-fashioned 'chapel' homes, were confined to singing songs round a piano, or learning traditional stringed instruments such as the violin. 'The skiffle group was not quite the done thing,' says Eurion John, a schoolfriend. 'Elvis, "Rock Around the Clock", Bill Haley – he was into all that. Mike had that side to him which was, by Llanelli stan-dards, rather more cosmopolitan, I suppose. He was a more rounded person.'[49]

In what were plainly sheltered times and a sheltered environment, Howard was rather more sophisticated in his knowledge of the world, suggests Keith Marshall:

> I remember once in the lobby we were talking about some chap or other, and someone mentioned the word 'homosexual', and Mike knew what that was. And I thought, 'What are we talking about, "homosexual"?' And nobody knew what the hell he was talking about. But Mike had obviously read it up in some dictionary or other, and come out with it.[50]

Perhaps because of his strict Jewish upbringing, the schoolboy Howard never showed much outward interest in sex. 'We had girl-friends while we were at school, but there were no great romances,' he says.[51] 'I never saw Michael with any girls,' says his teenage neighbour Veronica Jones.[52] But, like his father, Bernard, he was a good-looking man, and young women were starting to take an interest. Equally, at school Keith Marshall has no recollection of Howard 'attending any of the joint things with the girls' school that we used to do. We had a very active sixth-form society which was always an excuse to get down to the girls' school. I suppose you could say, yes, he was very much on his own, but not any the worse for that.'[53]

In his final year a satirical article in the school magazine suggested that 'Mr Howard . . . in his attempts to cut himself off from the rest of humanity, goes around all day in a state of trance with a blank look on his face. When roused, however, the colour rises in his cheeks and he becomes a frothy demagogue.'[54] It was intended humorously, but probably contained grains of truth. There is no suggestion that Michael Howard was actually unpopular with his contemporaries: on the contrary, he was 'well liked' says Jeff Hopkins, who now acts as agent to Llanelli's Labour MP. 'I never came across anybody who didn't like him.'[55] 'The one thing I remember,' says Eurion John, 'he had great enthusiasm. He always had a delightful personality.' He was confident and cheerful, but it's clear he was also a bit of a loner, a cat who walked by himself – somewhat independent and never really one of the crowd. Keith Marshall best sums up the consensus: 'It could be fair to say he didn't have that many close friends. He didn't have a 'buddy', let's say.'[56]

Even so, Howard does not seem to have spent every evening and weekend at home, swotting away at schoolwork. He joined the Jewish youth group in Swansea, and during the Christmas and summer holidays he went on national camps organised by the Jewish Youth Study Group, which were held at Moreton Hall near Oswestry in Shropshire. These camps, which lasted a fortnight in summer, were part religious and part social, and were aimed at brighter students between the ages of about fourteen and eighteen – boys and girls who went to grammar or public schools and hoped to go to university. The mornings were occupied with more serious work – rabbis and visiting lecturers would talk about Jewish history, culture, ethics and philosophy. In the afternoon, in contrast, the 150 or so students in each camp would organise their own social activities, with singing and dancing, and the teenagers would elect leaders from among themselves. There was also a daily religious service. And at the end of the fortnight the students might put on a concert or a play.

Michael Howard went to football matches and to the Jewish group in Swansea, and he also learned to drive at quite a young age, though he had to borrow his father's Humber Hawk. One evening, perhaps the worse for drink, he came home and parked the car outside his father's garage on Glasfryn Terrace, but failed to put on the handbrake properly. The car rolled across the road and, accelerating with the gradient, demolished part of the small front wall belonging to the house opposite. Bernard Howard was furious. 'Michael's father made him pile up the bricks neatly,' says their next-door neighbour, Ann Thomas, 'and then had to pay a man to rebuild the wall.'[57] Presumably the car needed repairing, too.

Howard's academic career suffered no such mishaps, and former teachers at the 'Gram' speak well of him. 'His face has hardly changed at all,' says the former art master John Bowen. 'It was a very smiling face – not one of those sour ones.'[58] 'He was very mature for his years,' recalls Dai Smith, who taught chemistry.[59] The French master Gwyn Evans thought him 'a very serious lad. No doubt he had a sense of humour, but he was always totally committed to his work, and you knew that as you were teaching him he was taking it in and thinking about it. He was a pleasure to teach.'[60]

The school magazine shows that in his early years Howard regularly won prizes for being among the handful of boys to average more than 75 per cent in his exams. In class, he would often be asked to read out his work. His essays were 'always correct' says one former pupil, Allan Sims – 'nothing special, but well written'.[61] Contemporaries agree that Howard was not the cleverest boy in his year, but it was a exceptionally talented year (what his headmaster Stanley Rees called his *annus mirabilis*). In 1957 Michael was surprised to get much better grades than expected in his eight O-levels (English Language, English Literature, French, Latin, History, Geography, Maths and Economics), so he and his father went to see Rees with a view to applying for Cambridge. Rees, who was a leading light in the Aberystwyth former students' association, preferred to steer his best pupils towards Welsh universities. For instance, he told the future Methodist leader and broadcaster Leslie Griffiths (now Lord Griffiths) to try for Cardiff rather than Oxbridge, saying, 'Although you're bright enough, Leslie, I don't think you could cope socially.'[62] Similarly, Rees thought Howard was being 'presumptuous' in choosing Cambridge. Try Aberystwyth first, Rees advised, adding that he could always go to Cambridge afterwards (the route taken by the politician Elwyn Jones). Howard says he thought about it for a while, 'but I decided I wanted to have a go, at any rate, at getting to Oxbridge first'.[63]

The late 1950s were the era of John Osborne, John Braine and Britain's other 'Angry Young Men', and the Cambridge examiners couldn't resist the question: 'Why I am an angry young man.' Nor could Michael Howard, though his script said nothing particularly radical, he says, but merely explained that he got upset with hypocrisy.

He almost failed to get in. Howard tried several Cambridge colleges, and, perhaps unfamiliar with the complicated admission system, was rejected by all his initial choices. Then Peterhouse suddenly accepted him to read Economics. It was his 'last shot', he claims. 'I was obviously the first person from my family to go to any university, and yes, that was a great moment.'[64]

4

CAMBRIDGE MAFIOSO

Cambridge transformed me, introduced me to a different world
which I had no knowledge of before . . . where people from very
different backgrounds mixed freely in magical surroundings.

MICHAEL HOWARD, 2004[1]

Peterhouse has long been regarded as one of Cambridge University's
more eccentric colleges – closed, cliquey, and a touch secretive.
Situated on Trumpington Street, on the edge of the city centre, it has
the distinction of being both the smallest of the ancient colleges (with
only 230 students in 1959) and the oldest, having been founded in
1284. Its reputation rests largely on its history teaching. The master of
Peterhouse when Howard arrived was Herbert Butterfield, who also
held the university posts of vice-chancellor and professor of modern
history, and once famously remarked that: 'History is one bloody
thing after another.'[2]

In recent times Peterhouse has acquired a reputation for being
right-wing, especially by Cambridge standards: it strongly resisted the
admission of women in the 1980s, and played a leading role in the
thinking which underpinned Thatcherism. The most important figures in this were the historians Maurice Cowling and Edward
Norman. The 'Peterhouse Right', as Cowling later dubbed this
group, embraced academics and journalists who had either taught or

studied at the college and held broadly similar anti-liberal if liber-tarian views, including Roger Scruton and John Vincent. Another member was Michael Portillo, who had converted from Labour to Conservatism while a history scholar at Peterhouse.[3] It is tempting to add Michael Howard to the 'Peterhouse Right'. But it would be wrong. Neither Cowling nor Norman was around when Howard was at Peterhouse. Nor did Howard experience the same student political odyssey as Portillo. Michael Howard began life in Cambridge as a rather left-wing Conservative, and moved leftward from there.

The Cambridge political grouping which included Michael Howard as a member was of a very different political hue from the Peterhouse Right. The so-called 'Cambridge Mafia' described them-selves as Conservatives, but few of them could be described as 'intellectuals'; they were propelled more by the prospect of high office than by high ideals. They were attracted to the Conservative Party in the late 1950s partly because it was the party in power, and looked like staying so for the foreseeable future. In September 1959, just before going to university, Howard had campaigned for the Tories during the general election (and questioned Llanelli's MP Jim Griffiths at a public meeting about Labour's plans to abolish grammar schools). In the very week that freshmen arrived in Cambridge, Harold Macmillan secured his party's third successive election victory. The Conservatives' increased majority of 102 made some suggest that Britain was in danger of becoming a one-party state.

'My impression of these chums,' says Peter Hill, who edited the university newspaper *Varsity*, 'is that they were greatly ambitious, but they didn't believe in anything very strongly. They wanted to become MPs rather than change society.'[4] In short, the Cambridge Mafia were young men on the make, and became highly successful at making it. Michael Howard and his student colleagues belonged to what proved to be a golden age for the Cambridge University Conservative Association, known as CUCA (it rhymes with 'puker', not 'pukka'). In the space of just five years, between 1959 and 1964, the presidency of the Cambridge Union debating society and the chairmanship of CUCA would be held by seven men who, a generation later, would sit together in the Conservative Cabinets of Margaret Thatcher and John Major. Leon Brittan (Home Secretary), Michael Howard (Home Secretary), Kenneth Clarke (Chancellor), Norman Lamont (Chancellor), John Nott (Defence) and John Gummer (Environment) all served as presidents of the Cambridge Union. Norman Fowler (Health and Social Security) was chairman of CUCA, along with Brittan, Gummer, Clarke and Lamont.

It is safe to say that no other political club at any British university has produced such an abundance of future Cabinet timber as CUCA at that time. In addition to these political stars, several other Cambridge contemporaries became Conservative junior ministers, prominent MPs or Euro-MPs – including Nicholas Budgen, Hugh Dykes, Michael Latham, Peter Lloyd, Ben Patterson, Peter Temple-Morris, Christopher Tugendhat and Peter Viggers. No one has convincingly explained why this generation proved so successful, but one factor may be the increased competition for places in the late 1950s, caused by the decision to phase out National Service. In 1957 the government had announced that any man born after September 1939 should not now expect to be called up, which meant that Howard escaped by almost two years, although the call-up process continued until the end of 1960 (for men born before 1939). Most undergraduates in the immediate post-war era had completed their two years' compulsory military training before going to university, which meant they didn't become students until they were twenty or so. So for the two years between 1959 and 1961 those who, like Howard, had been spared the rigours of National Service were competing for places at Cambridge with those who had deferred their entry to serve their time in the armed forces. Two generations overlapped, and those who were successful in getting a place were often of higher calibre. When the eighteen-year-old Howard turned up in Cambridge in the autumn of 1959, he was alongside hundreds of freshmen who were more mature and experienced after two years' military service.

What also distinguishes the Cambridge Mafia is that they were a more meritocratic group than past generations of Oxbridge Tories. At a time when Harold Macmillan's Cabinet was still full of Old Etonians and the premier's distant relations, this new influx came from middle-class backgrounds. They weren't the sons of peers, government ministers and names in *Who's Who*: in most cases their fathers did unexciting but respectable professional jobs. Instead of Eton, Harrow or Winchester, they had been educated at grammar and direct grant schools. Kenneth Clarke, the son of a jeweller, had gone to Nottingham High School; Leon Brittan, the grandson of Jews from Lithuania, was the son of a London GP, and went to Haberdashers' Aske's, a direct-grant school. Norman Fowler, the son of an engineer, went to King Edward VI School, Chelmsford; Norman Lamont, whose father was a surgeon, was educated at Loretto School in Edinburgh, while John Gummer, the son of an Anglican vicar, had been to King's School, Rochester. 'All of us came from homes where there wasn't any capital,' Gummer once said. 'If you overspent you had to save.'[5] Often, like Michael Howard, they were the first generation from their families to go to university.

This generation reflected the rapid social change that Britain was experiencing as traditional hierarchies and assumptions were challenged. The 'Angry Young Men' of the 1950s gave way to the irreverent satirists of the 1960s, and in Cambridge itself the undergraduates David Frost and Peter Cook were developing the kind of anti-establishment sketches in the Footlights Revue which led directly to the satire boom of that decade, with the show *Beyond the Fringe,* the magazine *Private Eye* and the TV programme *That Was The Week That Was.*

Michael Howard suffered none of the snobbery which Michael Heseltine, for example, endured at Oxford at the start of the 1950s, where he was derided by Tory toffs because he came from Swansea and his father managed a steel factory.

Yet in analysing the Cambridge Mafia one should not assume that they were exact contemporaries who arrived and left simultaneously; they were more a network of friends who overlapped with each other in successive years. Leon Brittan, for example, left in the summer of 1961, just as Norman Lamont arrived. Yet, while the Cambridge

Mafia had serious internal disagreements, they still showed unusual cohesion, since student politics can be more petty and bitter than the real thing. This unity remained in later life, when they maintained their friendships, acting as best men and godparents for each other, despite very public political differences. To this day they still hold regular reunions.

As undergraduates, the members of the Cambridge Mafia had a very similar political outlook. With the odd exception they were to the left of the Conservative Party, and allied with the Bow Group, the research body founded in 1951, which had become an influential party think-tank. CUCA was 'as progressive as its well-developed sense of decorum permits', declared the 1960 edition of the *Varsity Handbook*, the guide for Cambridge students.[6] 'Most leading members are moving rapidly leftwards,' the handbook claimed a year later, 'and the moving of protest motions prevails. The right wing Tory is not over popular in the Conservative Association.'[7] CUCA's magazine was called *New Radical*, and its cover was printed in a daring red and white rather than orthodox Conservative blue. 'We saw the Tories as a radical party with radical ideas and wanting to change things,' John Gummer has explained, 'and we saw the Labour Party as very reactionary. We came from backgrounds where we'd seen that "opportunity" was what it was all about, that if you had a proper opportunity then people could do what they wanted to.'[8]

The pinkishness of CUCA's leading lights showed itself most often in foreign affairs, where most were keen on joining Europe, and hostile to apartheid in South Africa – so much so that the committee even voted to boycott South African sherry. (A second vote, on whether because of Franco to ban Spanish sherry too, failed.) They favoured independence for black Africa, supporting the man who was the hero of that generation of ambitious and progressive young Tories, the Colonial Secretary Iain Macleod. Other political heroes were Macmillan's rising young ministers Edward Heath and Reginald Maudling.

In broad terms, the Cambridge Mafia was Butskellite, an expression which summed up the narrow centre-ground which dominated British politics in the 1950s, with 'Rab' Butler on the left of the Conservative Party holding similar views to Labour's right-wing leader Hugh Gaitskell. Yet CUCA also benefited in this period from the left-wing stance of the University Labour Club, which strongly disagreed with Gaitskell and backed both unilateral nuclear disarmament and further nationalisation. A Gaitskell supporter explained in *Varsity* how CUCA had prospered at the expense of the Labour Club:

> The days of . . . smooth young men of Good Family have gone. . . . From solidly right wing and upper class, CUCA has become radical and middle class . . .
>
> The tragedy for the Labour Club is that radicals who ought on any examination of their views to be active Labour Club members, are finding their way and a welcome in the Tories.
>
> They will admit that they are not Conservatives, that they find Mac[millan] repulsive, but claim that in the Tories and in the Bow Group they can find expression for radical ideas which are swamped in the Labour Party . . . a considerable and influential number of people, genuinely calling themselves radicals, are finding a not too uncomfortable niche in CUCA.[9]

CUCA was appealing to those who were interested in politics but unsure of where they stood. It is striking that not a single future Labour Cabinet minister or prominent Labour MP was active in Cambridge politics at this time, with the exception of Gareth Williams, who, as Lord Williams of Mostyn, would become Tony Blair's Leader in the Lords before his sudden death in 2003. At Cambridge, Williams was 'a wild Welsh figure with unkempt hair', according to Peter Temple-Morris.[10]

At that time, people interested in politics tended to join several of the Cambridge political clubs, whatever their personal leanings, simply to hear well-known speakers. Politics enthusiasts might also join more committed groupings such as the recently formed Campaign for Nuclear Disarmament (CND), the Gaitskellite

Campaign for Democratic Socialism (CDS) or the Conservative Party's Bow Group.

Coming from a quiet Welsh town such as Llanelli to one of the world's most vibrant universities was a huge culture shock for Michael Howard, just as his headmaster Stanley Rees had predicted. Says one contemporary, David Hacking, 'He was absolutely in a new world in Cambridge and overawed. In the Cambridge Union I remember he was quite shy, quite nervous at first.'[11] 'It took a bit of time,' Howard has said. 'I think it probably took most of my first year to find my feet.'[12]

It was during his time at Cambridge that Michael Howard ceased being an orthodox Jew. He didn't abandon Judaism altogether – he belonged to the University Jewish Society, and often attended a Jewish dining group on Friday evenings – but he seems to have kept his Jewishness very quiet. 'One of the odd things was that I was never conscious of the fact he was Jewish,' says Hugh Wilson, who was active in CUCA, 'whereas with Leon Brittan it was quite clear. And I never knew Michael was the son of immigrants.'[13]

Howard clearly felt comfortable in the meritocratic, left-leaning milieu of CUCA, which, with around 1,500 members, was as big as the Labour and Liberal clubs combined. Life in CUCA centred on Sunday-afternoon meetings held in a gloomy room at the Red Lion Hotel, next to Heffer's bookshop, where members were served tea and cake and blessed with the wisdom of Tory ministers who'd been persuaded to give up their Sunday rest and take the train to Cambridge. If the minister was willing to stay afterwards, a lucky few might get to dine with him.

In his first year, 1959–60, Howard was one of two freshmen who made an immediate impact by raising intelligent points with the Sunday guests. Leon Brittan, who was CUCA chairman at the start of 1960, 'vividly' remembers one particular meeting because of the quality of questions from two eager first-years. 'I thought from the way they were asking them that these two people will go very far indeed – not just at university level, but beyond that.' The other bushy-tailed inquisitor was Kenneth Clarke, who was reading Law at Gonville and

Caius College. 'Both Ken and Michael have been much the same ever since – in their demeanour, attitude, character and appearance they were recognisably what they have been since.'[14]

Those teatime meetings marked the start of a relationship – part friendship, but mostly rivalry – which would intrigue and amuse observers for four decades. In recalling Cambridge politics in the early 1960s, people often bracket Michael Howard and Ken Clarke together like twins. 'They both knew they were rather good and wanted to be better than the other,' says Peter Temple-Morris.[15] Having started as humble 'college reps', by their third term the pair had both been co-opted on to the CUCA committee by the chairman, Peter Viggers. Clarke was made assistant librarian, helping to look after CUCA's collection of tatty books and pamphlets, while Howard got the apparently more senior job of assistant secretary, an appointment nonetheless of such insignificance that Viggers, who is now one of Howard's backbench MPs, can't recall making it. In the following term Howard got one up on Clarke by getting elected to the committee in his own right, and was made publicity officer for the start of the following year, when Norman Fowler was chairman. Fowler's term card alerted members to a weekly event called 'Towards the Future', billed as 'a discussion with members of other political groups'. It would be held at 4.30 on Thursday afternoons in Michael Howard's room in Peterhouse, under the joint auspices, the card announced, of Howard and Clarke.[16]

At that time neither Oxford nor Cambridge had a traditional students' union along the lines of most modern universities. As a public forum, the Cambridge Union Society was the nearest equivalent. Life membership cost ten guineas (£10.50) in 1959 – a significant sum and worth about £150 today – and members enjoyed access to the bar, restaurant and library of the Union's premises behind the Round Church in the centre of Cambridge. The famous debates, where well-known guests would spar with undergraduate speakers, took place once a week.

In both CUCA and the Union, much time was spent plotting and squabbling over who would get what post. University terms lasted only eight weeks, and the convention was that no one held any office for more than a term, which meant constant electioneering for the next term's positions. At a distance of forty years, the wheeling and dealing of undergraduates may seem a trivial business. Yet in the febrile world of student life the ups and downs of who's been selected for what can take on a disproportionate degree of significance. At the same time, in the early 1960s, there were far fewer universities in the UK than there are now, and with fewer students, and the British establishment was far closer knit – and British society more deferential – than it is today. As a result, the activities of Oxbridge students were far more visible. *Varsity*, for example, was read by the news desks of the national press. A successful student career could readily open doors to a future in politics, law or the media.

Elections, therefore, took on some importance. Under the rules, contenders couldn't canvass members, or form so-called 'slates' to group candidates together. But there were always unofficial tickets, whereby candidates would privately agree to get their college votes out for each other, trading on the parochial tendency of Cambridge students to support people from their own college. Amid the horse-trading and regular votes, informal queues would be formed as it became known who was expected to get which top jobs in the coming terms. Once elected to the post of secretary in either body, the tradition was that you usually became vice-president the following term (or vice-chairman in CUCA), and then president (or chairman). It was quite common for ambitious Conservatives to use success in CUCA as a springboard for the Cambridge Union, following up the CUCA chairmanship with the Union presidency a few terms later.

CUCA's leading lights tended to dominate the Union, because the Conservatives were the popular party among Cambridge undergraduates. But many people who were active on the Left boycotted the Union because they saw it as being concerned more with form than with content. Although it was a student society, it had the trappings of a gentlemen's club, with black tie being worn by speakers, and debates apeing the conventions of the House of Commons. In 1960 it still excluded women. One exception to the left-wing boycott was Brian Pollitt, the son of the long-serving leader of the British Communist Party, Harry Pollitt. Brian had left school at sixteen and had gone to Cambridge as a mature student in his early twenties; the Cambridge party decided the Union was too good a platform to ignore and paid Pollitt's subscription for him.

Early in 1961 Leon Brittan and Norman Fowler, who had become CUCA's two grandees, came to the aid of their protégés, Howard and Clarke, who were a year their junior. Their worry was that too long a queue of hopeful CUCA chairmen was developing, including two contenders who planned to hold the job in their fourth year. 'Black is the gloom of the two best ex-future Chairmen we have, Michael Howard and Ken Clarke,' claimed the 'Napoleon Boot' gossip column in *Varsity*. Brittan and Fowler proposed that the CUCA rules should be changed to stop people becoming chairman beyond the end of their third year. 'Enter centre left two shades of yesteryear,' the paper reported: 'Loyal Leon and noble Norman are not going to let their young champions fail. If their efforts can persuade CUCA to ban fourth year Chairmen at the end of Term, Michael and Ken are safe. If not, to arms!'[17]

Unlike the more confident Clarke, Michael Howard initially kept a low profile in the Union. Remarkably, in the light of subsequent events, he didn't contribute to any debate during his entire first year. He later explained this was because debates clashed with a series of lectures on existential philosophy.[18] Ken Clarke, in contrast, began speaking there at the start of his second term.

Howard remedied his omission at the opening debate of his second year, contributing from the floor against a motion of 'no confidence in Her Majesty's Government', in front of a chamber which largely comprised excited freshmen eager to learn whether the society was worth joining. The pro-government side that night in October 1960 saw a remarkable line-up of undergraduate speakers – Leon Brittan, the Union president, followed one after another by Norman Fowler, Ken Clarke, Howard, and then John Gummer. It is doubtful whether in the history of debating at any university five consecutive student

speakers on the same side have all gone on to become Cabinet ministers. With so many Tory guns, one might have expected the evening
to have been a triumphant defence of Harold Macmillan and his ministers. In fact it was a disaster for the CUCA men. Speaking between
Brittan and Fowler, Hugh Fraser, a junior minister, had ruined the
government case by a deeply embarrassing contribution – 'the kind of
speech that is any politician's nightmare', says Fowler.[19] Fraser ludi-
crously suggested that Labour would reintroduce sweet rationing,
then compounded his gaffe by accidentally knocking his glass of water
over with a sweep of his hand; finally he dropped his entire text on to
the ground. Howard's five-minute floor speech was hardly likely to
turn matters round. The vote went heavily against the Tories, with the
Union ignoring its long-standing, if bizarre, tradition of never
denouncing a sitting government. So shaming was the event for
CUCA activists that Howard and Clarke, rather self-importantly, went
round to Fowler's rooms a few days later, 'worried', Fowler says, 'at
the damage the Union debate had done to the Conservative cause'
and insisting on 'urgent action to correct the position'.[20]

From then on Howard made regular contributions to Union
debates. His reputation as a debater was mixed, to judge from
hindsight. John Barnes, a leading CUCA member who later made his
name as a politics academic, says Howard was 'a very polished
speaker', and a better performer than Clarke, but 'clearly came from
a school debating society'.[21] 'Ken Clarke was really quite narrow
and rather dull,' says Oliver Weaver, one of the Union presidents of
the era. 'Michael Howard was not. Michael was always interesting
and entertaining and funny. He was mischievous; he was witty; he
was clever without being stylised.'[22] John Dunn, now a history
professor at Cambridge, disagrees. While he found Clarke 'warm
and buoyant', Howard was 'a stiff and deeply uncharismatic figure,
who contrived to speak at length, smoothly and with considerable
emphasis, without ever saying anything even faintly memorable'.[23]
'One thing about Michael Howard's style then which is true today is
that he was most difficult to persuade that he was wrong, although he
was always willing to argue the point,' says Colin Renfrew, who was

Union president in Howard's second year. 'He had a kind of skilful inflexibility. And he was always very well prepared.'[24] Michael Latham, who himself became an MP, likes to compare the stars of his generation:

> Michael was not in my view anything like as natural a speaker as Ken Clarke or John Gummer. John Gummer was the most fluent of them all, but his content wasn't always terribly impressive. Ken Clarke was always the most incisive and brilliant. Norman Lamont was brilliant in technique but, as someone said, his content was what he had read in *The Economist* the previous Friday. Ken Clarke always had real style but also tremendous content in his speeches. Michael Howard had good content but I didn't regard him as as fluent an orator as Ken Clarke and John Gummer, but he was still obviously capable.[25]

Norman Lamont remembers that Howard often wore a suede jacket when speaking from the floor. 'He had one hand in a pocket and gestured with the other.'[26] As one might expect, given his parents' business, 'he was carefully dressed', according to David Hacking, 'and much better tailored than Ken Clarke'.[27] Peter Fullerton, a future Union president, agrees that Howard was much less 'slovenly' than his colleagues: 'Michael tended to wear three-piece suits and a waistcoat with lapels. He was rather dapper. The rest of us weren't quite in duffel coats, but it was sports coats most of the time.'[28] Peter Temple-Morris, a CUCA chairman who also came from Wales, felt that 'even then he was perhaps a little too visibly ambitious. He was always a person of nice, soft charm, very charming. He never consciously distanced himself from his Welshness, but he was not *Welsh* Welsh. Very quickly the Welsh accent diminished.'[29]

Howard's contributions week by week provide the first clues to his early political thinking (even if undergraduates would sometimes adopt debating positions that they didn't necessarily believe in). In his first 'paper speech' – one billed in advance on the order paper – he argued that the Liberals were the 'radical party of the future', though this could be read at least two ways. He took a tough line on the Cold War, speaking against the motion that 'the West is fighting a losing battle.' He backed Britain's reliance on nuclear weapons, and, following the erection of the Berlin Wall in 1961, agreed that 'This House would fight for West Berlin' – a motion opposed by both Ken Clarke and the freshman Norman Lamont. Equally, as Harold Macmillan spoke of the 'winds of change', Howard took a progressive stance on Africa. Twelve months after the Sharpeville massacre, in which fifty-six blacks were killed in South Africa, Howard, backed by Clarke and Gummer, argued that 'South Africa's present policies are incompatible with membership of the Commonwealth.' As Southern Rhodesia and South Africa continued to deny votes to blacks, he called for an immediate system of 'One man, one vote in British Africa'.[30] Such was Howard's reputation as an opponent of apartheid that the *Varsity* gossip column suggested light-heartedly in March 1961 that in the coming Union elections 'those who loathe South African sherry will doubtless troupe [sic] behind our Pal from Peterhouse'.[31]

In their first two years Howard and Clarke had enjoyed mixed fortunes in student elections. Despite his late start as a debater, Howard was elected to the Union's governing body, the standing committee, halfway through his second year, at the end of Lent 1961 (the term from January to March), ahead of Clarke. In contrast, Clarke was far quicker to climb through the ranks of CUCA. While Howard was beaten for the job of CUCA treasurer and then secretary, Clarke was elected chairman for the Michaelmas term (October to December) of 1961. It now looked as if Clarke might be able to exploit his clout in CUCA to overtake Howard in subsequent Union polls as well.

The rivalry between Howard and Clarke, each the son of a shopkeeper, was hotting up. Yet they were also friends and got on together. When Leon Brittan left Cambridge in the summer of 1961 to go to Yale Law School, he let his two young protégés borrow his beloved car, a 1938 Morris 8 Coupé. 'It was called Fidelio – maroon I think. I bought it for £40,' Brittan recalls. 'I was very fond of it and said they could have it while I was away. Well, it wasn't a going concern when I got back.'[32]

That autumn the pair became embroiled in a public dispute which has subsequently become part of folklore. As CUCA's top man in the Michaelmas term, when hundreds of new freshmen joined the association, Ken Clarke was well placed to secure many more votes in the Union, especially if he managed to arrange a lively programme for the Cambridge Tories, since running the Union successfully requires the skills and flair of an impresario rather than a debater. Among Clarke's proposed CUCA speakers was Sir Oswald Mosley, who was then trying to make a political comeback through his British Union Movement and by advocating a federal Europe. While Clarke might have had some sympathy with the sixty-five-year-old fascist on Europe, he would have supported Mosley on little else. Yet he knew that such a historic figure was bound to attract a huge audience, and it was probably not coincidence that the Mosley meeting was scheduled for the night after the Union elections. Clarke has since admitted that he invited Mosley 'partly because he would be a good draw, and partly I suppose because it wasn't a safe thing to do. I wished to have controversial speakers.'[33] A public row would only boost Clarke's profile. Indeed, student disputes over Mosley were a recurring event at Oxford and Cambridge in the 1960s and '70s, with student organisers, protesters and Mosley himself all feeding on the publicity which such invitations inevitably brought. Yet it was only eighteen months since Mosley had last visited CUCA. In the spring of 1960 he had won sympathy from the large audience after one spectator had thrust a jelly into his face.

Michael Howard's resignation from the CUCA committee was front-page news in the student newspaper, *Varsity*, which published a photo of the couple sitting together with the caption: 'We used to be friends . . . Mosley has broken up another close partnership by splitting Howard and Clarke.' Howard explained that in quitting the CUCA committee 'I wanted to make it quite clear where I stood in this matter.'[34]

Ken Clarke was typically robust in defending his invitation. 'There is not one fascist in CUCA,' he insisted; it was simply a matter of free speech.[35] 'The fact that we invite Sir Oswald Mosley in no way means that we associate ourselves with him . . . We try to have as wide a range of guests as possible . . . Mosley is a serious political figure; racialism is rising . . . he's got to be faced.'[36]

None of CUCA's leading names seems to have shared Michael Howard's public disgust over the issue, and the officers were confident they could expose Mosley, even though he was one of the most ous- tanding British orators of the twentieth century. According to John Barnes, 'Most of us said this was somebody who was well worth hearing. And you can arrange for some very pointed questions to be asked in a public meeting if you want to make sure he is exposed for the anti-Semite he is.'[37] But, to placate his critics, Clarke pushed through a motion that CUCA 'views with alarm the manifestation of racialism in this country and deplores any attempt to exploit this and affirms its belief in a non-racial society'.[38]

Mosley's views were 'intrinsically ridiculous', Clarke declared.[39] 'If the chairman thinks our views can be dismissed so lightly let him try,' Mosley responded, no doubt glad of the attention.[40] In the Union, Howard spoke in favour of an emergency motion calling on Clarke to reverse the decision: 'The only way in which CUCA's reputation can be enhanced is to withdraw the invitation,' he said.[41] Clarke and the rest of CUCA declined to back down.

If Ken Clarke's invitation was a stunt to boost his personal standing, Howard was suspected, too, of being opportunistic in resigning from the CUCA committee; his departure was fuelled more by his Union ambitions, critics claimed, than by genuine outrage. It seemed odd, for example, that he should have resigned when Clarke invited Mosley, but not when the fascist leader came four terms earlier (though Howard was now more senior, and perhaps feared that Mosley was becoming a regular fixture). In taking his stand, Howard inevitably allied himself in the Union with Brian Pollitt and others on the Left.

'Michael had this extraordinary ability to convince himself that what he was doing was out of principle, not ambition,' says John Barnes. 'A lot of my friends saw it as a move to secure the presidency of the Union.' While Barnes believes the invitation to Mosley was a 'perfectly genuine affront' to Howard, he makes an observation which has recurred regularly throughout Howard's career: 'He could change course and convince himself absolutely that it was a totally principled decision. I think Michael used that issue as a way of distancing himself from CUCA.'[42] Peter Temple-Morris feels it was 'an excuse to leave, to cut a dash in the next election up'.[43]

No one now disputes that Michael Howard had obvious personal reasons for complaint, since many of his family had been the victims of fascism and anti-Semitism. His grandmother and cousins had died in the Holocaust, while his father had lived in the East End when the local Jewish community was besieged by Mosley's blackshirts. Yet Howard seems not to have mentioned this background during the dispute; many people in Cambridge were not even aware that he was Jewish, let alone knew the extent to which his family had suffered.

Michael Howard and Ken Clarke were regarded as the two leading contenders to become secretary of the Union. On past precedent, whoever won was likely to become president two terms later. 'The battle for Secretary will be a hot one,' suggested the obviously pro-Clarke but anonymous 'Napoleon Boot' in *Varsity*. 'Kenneth Clarke is powerfully placed with the Conservative crocodile having received its instructions. Michael Howard, having thrown over CUCA, can expect CUCA to return the compliment. After all, did he really expect it to prefer Mike to Mosley?'[44]

But Ken Clarke's invitation to Mosley backfired. He gambled and lost. 'I should have won the secretaryship. It pushed me off the queue,' he said thirty years later.[45] 'The row over my inviting Sir Oswald Mosley was tremendous. It was a huge controversy. I fell out with everybody.'[46] It was 'a reckless piece of exhibitionism,' says one of Clarke's biographers, 'which dogged him for the rest of his time at university.'[47] Howard took the post of Union secretary, while Clarke was reduced to third place among the four contenders. Clarke's loss was Howard's gain.

If Michael Howard's move *was* calculated, it showed shrewd thinking. In challenging Clarke, he would have known that in a straight fight Clarke was likely to emerge triumphant, both through holding the top job in CUCA and strong support from Caius College, which had a lot more Union members than Peterhouse. In publicly opposing the Mosley visit he perhaps judged that any Tories he alienated were likely to have voted for Clarke anyway, but he now stood to pick up votes from everyone to the left of Clarke, including most Liberal and Labour people. Although Brian Pollitt was unsuccessful in the contest for president, his prominent candidacy boosted turnout and probably brought out more left-wing voters than usual, and, as Napoleon Boot now suggested, 'the left had to vote for someone' in the contest for secretary.[48]

The Mosley meeting duly went ahead in the university examina-tion halls. Police were present, and this time the thousand-strong audience was denied either jellies or drama. With what *Varsity* called a 'display of evasion and procrastination', Mosley managed to avoid much discussion on his more contentious ideas.[49] Clarke had initially planned to deliver a detailed rebuttal of Mosley's speech, but suffered what he calls 'a rather surprising loss of confidence' and enlisted John Gummer to help him denounce Mosley's anti-Semitism.[50] They were briefed by members of the Jewish Society.

Howard was never active in CUCA again, and, although he didn't resign as a member, his departure from the committee marked the start of an eighteen-month period where his views were publicly unclear and he had private doubts about his politics. The cynical Napoleon Boot in *Varsity* suggested he now tried to be all things to all men: 'Our new [Union] secretary is nothing if not ambitious; he has set himself the task of ensuring that his attendances at CUCA and Labour Club meetings are in exact balance; that he shows at all times a keen interest in Liberal affairs; and all this whilst retaining the good-will of the CND and worse.'[51]

One should acknowledge that comments by Napoleon Boot were often tongue-in-cheek and not to be taken literally, but, like the earlier jibe in the Llanelli school magazine, this contained a shaft of insight. The charge of opportunism has dogged Howard ever since. He was indeed now seeking support in the Union from all shades of political opinion.

With Clarke seemingly out of the reckoning, Howard was now front runner, in line with Union convention, to become vice-president in the Easter term of 1962 (from April to June), and president the following Michaelmas, after completing his finals. In fact the process was then speeded up by a term, when the vice-president in Lent, John Dunn, declined to run for president; he decided to concentrate on his exams, as he hoped to become an academic. So Howard ran instead, though the election was contested by Gareth Williams. Michael invited his parents, Bernard and Hilda, to attend the presidential debate in which the two contenders staked their respective claims. The next day Howard beat his fellow Welshman by 208 votes to 158.

At the end of November 1961 Michael Howard's student career had looked to be going nowhere; less than four months later he had reached the top job in Cambridge politics. 'Fresh fearless faceless Howard amoeba like ascends his hard won throne,' declared Napoleon Boot, who reported that the new president had commiserated with Ken Clarke, who had still failed to win any post in the Union. 'Politics is easy when you've got principles,' Howard allegedly told Clarke, slapping him on the back.[52] But Howard found it hard to shake off his opportunist image, and continued to be pilloried by his *Varsity* critic: 'Step forward Michael Howard and take a bow. Show us all exactly how it should be done. First of all you run with CUCA until Ken Clarke beats you. Then Mosley gives you a few cheap votes. A loud approach to the Labour club, a public promise to speak on their platform is followed by an agonizing reappraisal . . .'[53]

When the *Llanelli Star* suggested that Michael Howard was the first old boy from Llanelli Grammar School to become president of the Union, Howard wrote to correct it. 'So far as I know, I am in fact the second, following in the footsteps of Mr F. Elwyn Jones QC MP, who was President in 1931,' he said, displaying a characteristic refusal to take undeserved accolades. But then, showing a distinct lack of calculation, he added, 'I hope we will not have to wait another 21 years [*sic*] before Mr Jones' precedent is followed for a second time.'[54]

The presidency of Michael Howard in the summer of 1962 was

undistinguished. But it's always a struggle to keep members interested in the Union at a time of year when most are revising for exams and want to spend their free time in outdoor activities such as punting on the Cam, croquet, garden parties and May balls. A good start was made with his first debate, on whether South America should look to Kennedy or Castro. 'Union debating back to sparkling form,' said the *Varsity* reviewer.[55] After that, Howard's term fizzled out, and his debates were dull and sparsely attended.

The most heated argument that term was on an internal matter which had divided the Union for years – whether to let women join the society. Howard had long aligned himself with the Left in wanting women members, and his CUCA colleague Norman Fowler backed the campaign in articles in *Varsity*. Yet several other leading Tories, including Leon Brittan, Ken Clarke and John Gummer, firmly opposed admitting women, and amending the society's constitution required a three-quarters majority. John Barnes and Norman Lamont, who were both in favour, calculated that a more fruitful strategy would be to first change the constitution to reduce the three-quarters majority to two-thirds, and they pushed this through with the help of a loophole in the Union rules and Howard's apparent connivance. He was criticised for using his power as president to let the new threshold be passed at a Union business meeting rather than hold a full ballot of members. 'It seems strange that a change involving the procedure of a poll should itself not be put to a poll,' said the former president Colin Renfrew.[56] But when the question of admitting women itself was put to a full vote it still fell short of gaining even the new two-thirds threshold, with 371 in favour and 220 against. It was a big disappointment for Howard, since it would have been, as *Varsity* suggested, 'a memorable ending to his term of office' and would have helped him leave a permanent mark on the Cambridge Union.[57] Women were eventually admitted twelve months later – ironically, during the term when Ken Clarke finally served as president.

More memorable was the moment when Howard performed the traditional ceremony of handing over the presidency to Brian Pollitt, who had been elected as his successor. ITN sent a crew to cover the advent of the Union's first Communist president, and Howard couldn't resist playing to the cameras. In what was probably his first appearance on national television, he introduced Pollitt by speaking in Russian. The hostile Napoleon Boot presented a damning verdict on his term: 'Poor old Michael! Boot's non-entity of the term; no-one's come to his debates, no-one's laughed at his jokes (no wonder if they're as puerile as that little Russian episode . . .) and now no-one will go to a May Ball with him.'[58]

In fact Michael Howard seems to have had some success with women in Cambridge, especially considering that men outnumbered women at the university many times over. Others concur with the observation made by his friend the broadcaster Anne Robinson in 2003: that at Cambridge Howard 'had a reputation of being a very fine lover', though she herself wasn't there at the time.[59] 'He was always pleasantly heterosexual,' says Oliver Walston, a friend who was active in Labour politics, 'whereas an awful lot of people were *ni l'un, ni l'autre* – myself included. We'd call them late developers now. Michael was not a late developer.'[60] The *Varsity* gossip column mentioned an occasion when Howard's eye was caught by a 'purple sweatered thespian who adorned' a Labour Club meeting, saying that he had 'been living in a world of fantasy ever since'.[61]

One girlfriend was Celia Haddon, the beautiful blonde daughter of a wealthy Exmoor farmer who, she says, would have been horrified if he'd known her boyfriend was Jewish. 'He used to make me laugh, and also he seemed terribly sophisticated,' says Haddon. 'We're very different really. It wasn't a dedicated relationship on my part or on his. I went out with other people, and he must have taken other people out too.'[62] Haddon, who now works as a kind of pets agony aunt for the *Daily Telegraph*, later wrote a book about sex and the problems of growing up as a sexually liberated woman in the 1960s, though it offers no obvious insight on her relationship with Howard.[63] In Cambridge they went to the cinema and saw horror movies such as *The Killer Shrews* and *The Blob*. Another date, in February 1963, was seeing the Beatles perform at the Regal Cinema – though only as third billing beneath a couple of American soloists, Tommy Roe and Chris Montez.

Ken Clarke, too, remembers that it was Howard who introduced him to the Merseyside band. 'I went to his room in Peterhouse one day and he was playing either "Please, Please Me" or "Love Me Do". He said, "You really must listen to this. It's a new group called the Beatles." I laughed and said that was a ridiculous name for a group.'[64]

Academically, Howard's decision to serve as Union president in his finals term didn't help. Two years earlier, in part one of the Cambridge tripos, he had achieved an upper second in Economics. It was a more creditable result than it would appear nowadays, when the grade is much more common. In 1960 only 3 of the 205 Economics candidates got firsts, and upper seconds were awarded to another 19 people. So Howard was in the top 11 per cent of his year. After his first year Howard switched to Law, even though Peterhouse had no Law dons and it meant going outside college for tutors. A schoolfriend who visited him in Cambridge, Brian Davies, recalls Howard saying he'd made the move because Law would be easier. 'He didn't say, "Law's going to give me better opportunities," but "Law's a better skive."'[65] In truth, his new subject was widely dismissed as an easy option, and Cambridge undergraduates were often warned that if they didn't do better they'd end up reading Law. But Economics was also then seen as one of the less serious degree courses, and the switch hardly paid dividends, for Howard got a lower second in the second part of his tripos. Again, this was quite respectable, since nearly half the Law candidates got lower seconds, while almost a third got thirds.

Michael Howard chose to stay on a year to do a postgraduate masters Law degree, the LLB, to help him become a barrister. He simultaneously studied for his Bar finals by correspondence course, having chosen the Inner Temple as his proposed Inn of Court. He passed his Bar finals in December 1963 with a third – the grade awarded to the overwhelming majority of candidates. He then gave his correspondence course notes to Ken Clarke – a sign perhaps that the Mosley row had not caused long-standing animosity.

His next steps politically were less clear, as Howard, like most of

Britain, went through a period of serious disillusionment with the Tories, who had been in power since 1951. 'There was wide disaffection with the Conservative Party,' says Leon Brittan. 'It looked dozy, complacent and a bit doddery. It was the end of thirteen years, after all.'[66] It was a time when the Conservative government appeared to be class-ridden, tired and decrepit, especially after the famous 'night of the long knives' in July 1962, when Macmillan sacked a third of his Cabinet. Tories were soon subject to huge ridicule by the new generation of young satirists, two of whom, Peter Cook and David Frost, had both been stars of the Footlights Revue during Howard's time at Cambridge. Labour, in contrast, had suddenly become fashionable, especially in the universities and with the election to the party leadership of the young former Oxford don Harold Wilson, whom some saw as Labour's version of John F. Kennedy.

In February 1963 *Varsity* published an article written under the names of Michael Howard and Kenneth Hyde, entitled 'Where Have All the Right Men Gone?', which suggested how disillusioned Howard had become:

> CUCA's warmest devotee could hardly claim that as an organisation it is bursting with energy or that it plays a very influential role in Cambridge politics. Almost all the political impetus in the university comes from the left . . . The CUCA bandwagon is for those who are hoping for the offer of a safe seat when they go down . . . there are, in fact, no thinking Conservatives in Cambridge.[67]

That last remark, of course, was insulting to his friends in the Cambridge Mafia, and the following week a letter appeared from Howard disassociating himself from the article and its 'grotesque conclusion that there are no thinking Conservatives in Cambridge'.[68] It was all rather puzzling, especially since his co-author seems to have been hiding behind a pseudonym.

'Michael had a brief flirtation with Labour,' confirms Leon Brittan, who was probably his closest Cambridge friend at that time, while Ken Clarke and John Gummer believe Howard actually joined the

Labour Party, albeit only briefly. Howard was undoubtedly a huge fan of the Labour leader Hugh Gaitskell, who had long been trying to take his party down the path of social democracy. He particularly admired Gaitskell for his very public confrontations with CND and Labour members who wanted Britain to renounce nuclear weapons. 'Gaitskell was his political hero,' says Norman Lamont. 'He was very upset when he died.'[69] Yet even in early 1963, when the more left-wing Harold Wilson took over from Gaitskell, Howard was clearly still toying with the idea of joining Labour.

That March, Howard twice went to London to see the Labour MP Bill Rodgers, national organiser of the Campaign for Democratic Socialism. Rodgers has a note of both meetings in his diary, on two Thursdays a fortnight apart, 7 and 21 March, though he has no record or recollection of what he and Howard spoke about. The very fact that Howard was seeing a figure as influential as Rodgers, and travelling twice from Cambridge to do so, suggests a serious degree of interest in Labour. One possibility is that Howard was sounding out Rodgers about becoming a parliamentary candidate, since the MP was then heavily involved in getting CDS supporters chosen for good seats, though Rodgers thinks it unlikely they discussed this.[70] Oliver Walston, a CDS activist who accompanied Howard to the first meeting, but can't recall the event, suspects the idea was 'for me to show Michael that there were nice chaps in the Labour Party who weren't crypto-Communists, CNDers and so on – Bill Rodgers being the sort of acceptable face of the Labour Party'. Walston doubts whether Howard went so far as actually to join the party. 'If he did join, I certainly didn't know about it, and I would have thought I probably would have done. It's not the sort of thing he would have kept private from me.'[71]

Two days after the first meeting, *Varsity*'s Napoleon Boot column, written that term by CDS member Richard Strange, acknowledged Howard's dilemma, yet also his growing taste for the smarter, more fashionable things in life:

Michael Howard has almost finished his monumental ideological rethink; however, one nagging fear still prevents him fully embracing the philosophy of democratic socialism. Will he, as a Labour MP, be able to wear a clean shirt and own an E-type Jaguar? Michael, you perceive, is a far-sighted man of vision. Boot advises him to attend the Liberal Party Assembly – they, at least, wear nice ties; perhaps a career there would be more suitable.[72]

Privately, Strange and some of his colleagues were deeply suspicious of Labour's potential new recruit. 'We thought Michael Howard was largely motivated by ambition for a government career, and that Labour was looking a better prospect at the time. Michael Howard had a smooth, even unctuous, exterior but appeared driven more by personal ambition than a principled interest in ideas and their implementation.'[73]

5

A TALE OF THREE CITIES

He was very romantic. He had fads, fancies and enthusiasms. He
was passionate about baseball, John F. Kennedy, Lotus sports cars
and about girls.

FORMER 1960s FLATMATE OF MICHAEL HOWARD

In June 1963 a million people lined the streets of West Berlin to greet
the American president John F. Kennedy. It was during one of the
bleakest periods of the Cold War, less than two years since the
Russians had divided the city by building the Berlin Wall, and only
eight months since the Cuban Missile Crisis, when Kennedy's diplomacy had helped avert nuclear world war. Hidden among the
multitude was the twenty-one-year-old Michael Howard.

The young American president marked his visit with one of the
great speeches of post-war history. 'Ich bin ein Berliner' – 'I am a
Berliner' – Kennedy declared as he stood next to the mayor of the
western sector, Willi Brandt. 'All free men,' Kennedy went on, 'wherever they may live, are citizens of Berlin.' Michael Howard watched
from a spot in front of the Rathaus Schöneberg. 'I was quite far away
from him,' he would later recall, 'but you could see in the distance this
slim, young figure on whose shoulders the burdens of the world
rested. It was an inspiring moment which obviously I shall always
remember.'[1]

Howard was in Berlin to attend a week-long youth conference organised by the Anglo-German Association. Two days later he went over to Karl Marx Platz in the Communist part of the city and saw the Soviet leader Nikita Khrushchev and his East German colleague Walter Ulbricht address a crowd of East Berliners, before the two leaders drove off in an open-topped car. 'It was a very overcast day,' Howard recently recalled, 'and almost immediately after they drove away . . . a wind blew up and blew sand into our faces, and there was the most tremendous thunder and lightning, as though it were a sign from the gods . . . It was a most dramatic afternoon.'[2]

The youth conference was an offshoot of the Königswinter gatherings, the annual get-togethers which were established after the war to promote Anglo-German understanding and further the cause of European unity. Although Howard seems to have had positive feelings about Europe at that stage, his trip to Berlin may inadvertently have contributed in the long term to his becoming a great Atlanticist, fervently pro-American in outlook, and ultimately pretty hostile to European union. President Kennedy had been gaining Michael Howard's admiration ever since his rousing inaugural address in 1961. 'He marked a new age,' Howard said in 2003. 'He was young; he was good-looking; he spoke a different language to the language his predecessors had spoken and it was exciting, it was glamorous. We hadn't really been used to hearing speeches like that . . . That made a terrific impression on a young generation that was interested in politics.'[3]

That autumn, having left Cambridge, Howard visited North America during the final weeks of the Kennedy administration. The English Speaking Union had asked the Cambridge Union to nominate people for its renowned annual debating tour in which two of Britain's top student debaters traditionally spent ten weeks travelling around the US and Canada. The list of past debaters was dominated by the two Oxbridge Unions, and included a distinguished list of politicians-in-the-making, among them 'Rab' Butler, Michael Foot, Edward Heath, Tony Benn and, two years earlier, Howard's friend Leon Brittan. After interviews at the ESU in London Howard was chosen from the Cambridge short list along with John Toulmin, a former chairman of CUCA, who went on to become a High Court judge.

The 1963 visit involved a relentless programme of thirty-nine debates in ten weeks. It started at McGill University in Montreal, but the subsequent itinerary was hardly a tour of leading US academic institutions: Howard and Toulmin didn't speak at any of America's top Ivy League universities, and San Francisco and Los Angeles were the only major cities they visited. Most of the schedule was west of the Mississippi through sparsely populated parts of the Midwest and the Rockies, then the Pacific states, followed by Texas and Louisiana in the south. Travel was by a combination of plane, train and long-distance bus, while accommodation was provided in hotels, halls of residence and sometimes with families of university staff or students. If it lacked glamorous locations, the tour undoubtedly gave Howard a glimpse of ordinary, everyday America, and an idea of what most of the States, away from the bright lights and big cities, is really like.

The host universities had to choose one motion from ten which the Cambridge team had suggested in advance. On some motions Howard and Toulmin offered to speak on just one side; in others they expressed no preference; and for a few they would speak against each other. Four of the motions were on topical Cold War subjects, such as: 'This House would rather be Red than Dead' (which the Cambridge men wanted to propose) and 'Only the USA and USSR should possess nuclear weapons,' which Howard offered to support, while Toulmin would speak against. But the British debaters were united in urging that America 'should recognise Red China now', and also in proposing perhaps the most contentious motion: that 'America's record in race relations is a blot on Western Society.' One of the most popular debates saw the pair proposing that 'The USA needs a National Health Service.'[4]

Of the six political motions where Michael Howard declared any preference, it's notable that he always came down on the more liberal side of the debate. John Toulmin says that when the team was first chosen, in the spring of 1963, he himself was a firm Conservative, while Howard was treated as a Labour supporter, even if he was perhaps not formally a party member. 'I think Michael was selected on the basis that he and I provided some kind of political balance. But I never thought Michael was very committed to Labour. I thought he was just investigating views.' On the personal CVs provided by the tour organisers, Toulmin mentioned his membership of CUCA, but Howard didn't cite a political affiliation. And, in between his selection for the tour in the spring of 1963 and their departure for America that autumn, he seems to have concluded that Labour wasn't for him, after all. 'I think he was a Conservative again by the time we got there,' says Toulmin.[5]

Shortly after arriving in North America, that October the two were upset to hear the news from home that Sir Alec Douglas-Home had been chosen as Prime Minister and Conservative leader in succession to Harold Macmillan, who had retired suddenly through ill health. Howard and Toulmin believed that the aristocratic former Earl of Home was unsuited to leading a modern party, and Howard also disapproved of what he read from London about the secretive and undemocratic way in which the leadership had been decided. Howard was so incensed that Iain Macleod had not been chosen instead that he wrote a fan letter from America expressing his dismay and sympathy.

Audiences for the American debates ranged from 80 to 2,000, with an average of about 400. Each university had paid $100 for the cost of the speakers' visit (about $1,500 today) and many were determined to get full value for money. 'Some colleges expected us to put on a travelling vaudeville act,' the pair wrote afterwards. 'Others were devoutly thankful that we didn't.'[6] In South Dakota the debate organiser cheerfully told them that, since his university had had to pay so much, they were going to 'suck them dry' with a series of events, and they even asked John Toulmin to preach a sermon.[7] The tour was a whirlwind of debates, coffee receptions, speeches, lectures, lunches, dinners, question and answer sessions, radio and TV interviews, and yet more receptions. In Missouri they had a twenty-minute audience with the former President, Harry Truman, who quizzed them on why Home had replaced Macmillan. Toulmin's scrapbook shows that the couple also watched several baseball games, played soccer, and, in a loose moment in Los Angeles, visited the Pink Pussycat College of Striptease in Santa Monica Boulevard.

But Michael Howard didn't start the tour well. His first speech 'was a good one', Toulmin subsequently wrote to his parents, 'but I learnt afterwards that it was too fast and the Welsh accent made it inaudible to a large part of the audience.'[8] Howard's speaking style seems to have improved by the time they visited the University of Missouri ten days later, where the local paper's account was headlined, 'Those Charming Englishmen':

> They come to pan America on American soil.
> Results? Charming.
> Their audience loved them . . .
> Tall, bespectacled Michael took the speaker's podium . . . Michael took a long look at the audience, touched his glasses and said, 'Ladies and gentlemen . . . You may feel that my friend John here looks a bit austere, even a bit pale and thin. It's his austerity that makes him look pale and thin. For the trip over here I came on the *Queen Elizabeth*. But John wanted to swim – so he did. That should make him quite popular with the President's physical fitness council.'
> The audience roared. And Michael continued with his witty jibes at John. Later, through the debate, both these jolly Englishmen took their debate seriously and battered hard at their opponents.
> After the debate, people crowded round them to chat. One lady beamed at Michael and said, 'Englishmen are always so charming. And you are especially so' . . . And she was right, charming was the word for the two young men.[9]

'Michael fell in love with America,' says John Toulmin:

> I would not have been surprised if he had gone there for good. We were both captivated by the States. The thing that excited us both

was the feeling of freedom. In going there for three months we were leaving behind our obligations at home. There was a feeling it was much less stuffy. The Cold War was still very much on, but the threat of the Bomb in Europe, that certainly wasn't a worry in the US, or the idea that the Russians might walk into western Europe. It was an extraordinarily liberating experience. You felt that the American Dream still existed, that anyone with talent and luck could achieve it in the US.[10]

But they would also experience the darker side of that dream.

Around mid-morning on Friday 22 November 1963, the Cambridge pair were about to check out of their hotel in Moscow, Idaho, ready to be driven to their next venue, nearby in Washington state. Howard noticed a group of people at the end of the lobby crowded round a TV set. Then someone said the President had been shot.

'I immediately thought they were referring to some South American country,' he said forty years later. 'It never crossed my mind that they should have been referring to President Kennedy.' The news clouded the rest of the tour. That night's debate was cancelled, and another one in California a week later, since it was no longer apt to debate whether JFK's 'New Frontier' had lost its way. The assassination was 'a tragic event for me', Howard has said. 'I saw President Kennedy as the leader of the Western world . . . It was the height of the Cold War, the tension was high. It was very frightening.' Howard admits that in 1960 he would probably have voted for Richard Nixon, the Republican nominee, but he now felt that Kennedy's success in handling the Cuban Missile Crisis was a 'huge turning point' in the Cold War. History, he says, 'would have been very different if it had been handled in a different way . . . The blockade option he chose wasn't necessarily the most obvious, but it was brilliantly successful. And, in my book, for that he deserves huge credit.'[11]

Three weeks later the Cambridge team arrived in Dallas itself, to debate a motion that 'The American dream has become a Nightmare.' JFK was not mentioned once: nobody thought it appropriate.

Matters had also been tense, for different reasons, earlier in the tour, when they debated their provocative race relations motion, for racial discrimination was still widespread in much of the States. John Toulmin says, 'The thing which really outraged both of us was that the people in the north felt quite superior on race, until we were in Vermillion, South Dakota, and noticed a city ordinance which said that no black people could have houses within the city limits, which we felt was absolutely outrageous.'[12] It was good ammunition for subsequent debates, of course, and Howard pointed out in Colorado that in America only 7.9 per cent of blacks went to schools with whites – 'an increase of one tenth of one per cent over the prior year'. The US Navy, he complained, employed very few blacks, and most of those were on 'food jobs'.[13]

Howard and Toulmin were clearly shocked by some of what they'd seen, and although they'd not visited the more liberal north-east, they also hadn't spent much time in the deep south, where racism was worst. Afterwards the debaters reported that 'Our basic ideas have not been radically changed and it would be surprising if they had. The force and vehemence of American conservatism in the universities we visited was much stronger than we had expected and constantly amazed us . . . It is rather important . . . for both sides to realize that conservatives in America have nothing in common with the Tory Party in Britain.'[14]

Michael Howard's most enduring memory of racial segregation came after the debating tour officially ended in December 1963 and he travelled from New Orleans by Greyhound bus to spend Christmas with friends in Kentucky. On board, he struck up a conversation with a black teacher. When they stopped for a break in Mississippi, Howard suggested they went off for a coffee. Howard recalled almost forty years later how the teacher told him they would not be allowed to sit together in the café. 'I said, 'Look, if you can't come into the white part, I'll come into the black part,' and he said, 'You can't, they'll put you in jail.' And I still find it incredible that this happened in my lifetime.'[15]

Howard had arranged to stay in America for the first half of the following year, 1964. Having written to eight leading New York law firms, and been interviewed by two, he secured an attachment with the prestigious Lord, Day and Lord, a gentlemanly, old-fashioned Ivy League institution, located on Broadway, whose partners had served the same clients for generations. The firm's most distinguished partner was Herbert Brownell, an important fixer in the Republican Party, who had been campaign manager to Thomas Dewey, the presidential candidate in 1944 and 1948. He later became a close associate of President Eisenhower, served five years as his Attorney-General, and had initiated the historic 1957 Civil Rights Act, the first legislation to help blacks in more than eighty years.

If Michael Howard loved the United States of America, he was particularly smitten by New York. It was the first time he'd lived in a big city, and New York was in vibrant mood early in 1964 as it hosted the World's Fair to commemorate the three-hundredth anniversary of the Duke of York's seizing the city from the Dutch. Howard was passionately determined to make the most of his time, to immerse himself in the culture and breathe the atmosphere.

'New York was a swinging, exciting place to be, and there was not this English class background to deal with,' says John Entwistle, a Liverpudlian lawyer whom Howard met there and who shared his interest in politics.[16] Entwistle was one of several young friends that Howard made in Manhattan legal circles in his six-month stint. Another was Robert Rubin, who had known Leon Brittan at Yale Law School and later became Treasury Secretary under Bill Clinton. A third was Jerry Zarr from New England, who worked with Entwistle at another law firm, Sherman and Sterling.

After a day of legal toil, Howard and his friends would visit night clubs such as the Five Spot Café in St Mark's Place, where they listened to the renowned jazz pianist Thelonious Monk and his quartet. 'The crowds comprised of college students . . . by the droves, especially during the holidays . . . seasoned listeners, hippies, many musicians, tourists, explorers, and a not so tiny ungroupish group of people immediately familiar to each other, if perhaps obscure to others, Monkfans.'[17] Jerry Zarr's favourite late-night haunt was the Village Vanguard on Seventh Avenue:

> New York was the kind of place where you worked very hard. I worked very late, and I know Michael did as well. There were a lot of times down at Wall Street when we'd get together and have a meal and go back to our respective firms and work some more, and sometimes we'd meet in the Village later, and it was nice if you were out at ten, ten thirty and able to go to a place until three in the morning.[18]

Howard claims at one point he was even tempted by a suggestion that he go down to Tennessee, where a friend of a friend thought it would be novel to employ a disc jockey with an English accent on his radio station (much as John Peel was employed in Dallas). 'I must admit that the prospect of being a disc jockey in Nashville did have its attractions.'[19] He also saw the Rolling Stones in New York, and met Bill Wyman, but this was really the time of frenzied Beatlemania, as the Liverpool group paid their first visit to the States that winter. Howard could impress Americans by explaining he was one of their earliest fans, having seen them perform long before they were famous.

That spring Howard also fell in love with baseball. Herbert Brownell took him to see the famous New York Yankees, but he was bored. Instead he began to watch the unfashionable New York Mets, a team which had been formed only two years before, following the departure of both the New York Giants and the Brooklyn Dodgers for California. The Mets were becoming renowned for losing more often than they won, but they tended to excel against top sides, and in the spring of 1964 they moved into the brand new Shea Stadium near LaGuardia Airport in Queens. Howard's friends were astonished at how passionate he became about the game. 'He gets terribly excited about his latest theme. It's so infectious with other people,' says John Entwistle.[20] He would happily spend a whole Saturday at a 'double header' fixture, where one match is staged immediately after another. When Zarr asked how he put up with so much baseball in one stretch,

Howard explained it was the 'spirit' of the whole experience he enjoyed.

'Enjoying the spirit' encapsulates Howard's whole approach to America. He spent one weekend with Bob Rubin in Florida; another weekend he and Jerry Zarr visited Cape Cod. 'He was game for anything,' says Zarr. 'I rented a car and drove up. And Michael was chatting up girls on the beach and going to bars and stuff like that.'[21]

In meeting Americans and making new friends Howard played the raconteur, regaling people with stories of his experiences in the US, chuckling at the outlandish and shocking aspects of American life that he'd noticed. Above all, Zarr recalls, he couldn't get over the language:

> He would love Americanisms. You'd suddenly make a statement – some kind of Americanism – and he'd say 'That's terrific!' and he'd keep on repeating it. On the weekend we went up to Cape Cod, I got lost trying to get to the New England Throughway. Finally I got a guy in a service station who was black and I said, 'Hey, I want to get to New England – how do I do it?' And he said, 'Take the third right and you're there man,' or something, and he added, 'You're on your way,' or something like that. And Michael kept repeating it – he thought that was great. He'd just pick the odd American phrase and kind of wear it to death.[22]

That year, 1964, was an important one in American politics, as the country underwent a period of intense self-examination after Kennedy's assassination. The first half of the year was dominated by civil rights. In one of his final acts, Kennedy had tabled a new Civil Rights Bill to stop the kind of discrimination in public places which had so shocked Howard earlier in his trip. The English visitor particularly admired the way that Kennedy's successor, Lyndon Johnson – probably the greatest power-broker in post-war American politics – collected every political debt and twisted every arm to ensure support for the bill on Capitol Hill. Johnson crudely exploited Kennedy's murder to shame senators into backing him. A few days before

Howard returned home that summer, the US Senate finally passed what is now regarded as the most important of all the civil rights measures of the 1950s and '60s.

It was a presidential election year, too, and, although Johnson was unopposed as the Democratic contender, Howard witnessed a fierce struggle for the Republican nomination between New York's liberal governor, Nelson Rockefeller, a supporter of civil rights, and his arch-conservative opponent, the Arizona senator Barry Goldwater. In New York, meanwhile, there was increasing speculation as to whether Bobby Kennedy would resign as Johnson's Attorney-General to run for one of the state's two Senate seats, in preparation for his own presidential bid.

Howard was particularly fascinated by American campaign techniques, in which personalities are more important than parties or policy. He was intrigued at how powerful individuals operated – from charismatic figures like the Kennedy brothers to fixers such as Lyndon Johnson and the 'Tammany Hall' bosses who still controlled many American cities through networks of patronage and corruption. Yet, because of the checks and balances of the US political system, each player operated within constraints. 'He was interested in federalism,' says Jerry Zarr, 'and how active the cities were in relationship with the states, and the way there was a lot of jostling and give and take between different branches of government.'[23]

Howard returned to England in July 1964 in time for the autumn general election. Having effectively been exiled from Tory politics for almost three years, he had little chance of becoming a parliamentary candidate. Instead he spent the campaign as unpaid personal assistant to Selwyn Lloyd, the former Foreign Secretary and Chancellor who'd been sacked by Macmillan but had returned to Cabinet under Alec Douglas-Home. Lloyd, a former president of the Cambridge Union, whom Howard had met through the Bow Group, was defending his Wirral constituency as well as playing a significant role in the Tories' national campaign. Yet it must have been frustrating, in such an intensely political year, for Howard not to be standing himself, especially when several of his Cambridge generation were taking their first steps on the political ladder. Ken Clarke was fighting Mansfield and John Gummer was standing in Greenwich, though both were hopeless prospects.

The month after Labour regained power, Michael Howard was called to the Bar. He began his twelve-month pupillage in the chambers of another former president of the Cambridge Union, Elwyn Jones, the Labour MP who was also an old boy of Llanelli Grammar School. When Jones died, in 1989, Michael Howard explained to mourners at his funeral that he had secured his pupillage through the help of Jones's elder sister, Winifred Evans, a JP and prominent figure in Llanelli in the 1950s and '60s. Elwyn Jones had a habit of appointing Welshmen to his London chambers, but his daughter claims that Howard's Jewishness would also have been an important factor. Jones liked Jews; his wife was Jewish, and he had been a leading prosecutor at the Nuremberg war crimes trials.[24] It didn't matter that Jones was a socialist MP, or that his set, Lamb Buildings in the Temple, had a reputation as a 'Labour' chambers. The future Labour Cabinet minister Harold Lever had belonged there before becoming an MP in 1964, while two London Labour MPs, Tom Williams and Sam Silkin, were also on the books. Silkin became head of chambers when Harold Wilson appointed Elwyn Jones as Attorney-General in the new government (a post Silkin later held as well).

Despite their political differences, Elwyn Jones was a big patron for Howard, and their curious relationship developed further when, only a few months into his pupillage, the trainee advocate got the chance to pursue another of his youthful ambitions. In his biographical details for the American tour he'd stated his intended career as 'possibly broadcasting' as well as 'probably barrister'.[25] At that time the relatively new medium of television was a more common route into politics and it is surprising how many politicians briefly worked as TV presenters in their youth, including Michael Heseltine, Jeffrey Archer, David Steel, Neil Kinnock and Gordon Brown. In February 1965 BBC Wales asked Howard to conduct an interview for a series of twenty-five-minute programmes called *My Time Again*, in which leading Welsh figures reflected on their careers. His subject was to be

Elwyn Jones (by then Sir Elwyn). 'Michael was so chuffed about it,' says the wife of one of his chambers colleagues.[26]

The interview, which occupied almost the whole programme, was a conversation rather than an interrogation, but it seems an odd decision for BBC producers to let Howard quiz the man who was effectively one of his bosses – albeit *in absentia* – and would therefore undoubtedly have a say in whether his pupillage in Lamb Buildings would become a permanent place. The discussion was recorded at the BBC studios in Shepherd's Bush and was broadcast in prime time, at 8.50 on a Friday evening, although only in Wales. A preview feature in *Radio Times* described the interviewer as 'a young Welsh barrister whose life so far, step by step, has matched Sir Elwyn's own', though strangely the magazine did not name Howard. Nor did it mention the chambers connection or his political ambitions.[27] He was paid twenty guineas (£21) for the job, though his broadcasting career went no further.

The fee would have been welcome, since pupil barristers earn little. But Howard had received a scholarship worth around £1,200 from the Inner Temple, and he was also lucky in finding somewhere to live. On arriving in London he had moved into a flat with a prestigious West End address – on the top two floors of 144 Harley Street, a four-storey building three minutes walk from Regent's Park and within sight of the soon-to-be completed 1960s monument the Post Office Tower. Howard was invited to live there by Peter Pagnamenta, a former editor of *Varsity*, who had just joined the BBC and who shared the flat with two BBC colleagues with even grander names, John Prescott-Thomas and Richard Somerset-Ward. When Pagnamenta left, a year later, Howard recommended that Norman Lamont, who'd just joined Rothschild's Bank, should take his place.

The flat, owned by a dentist called Lady Colwyn, was quite cheap, even for 1964, and the tenants had to pay only £18 a week between them for quite spacious accommodation. 'There was no lift,' says Norman Lamont, 'so we had to walk to the top floor. It was above doctors' consulting rooms, which made it rather gloomy, and one had this idea of Arab patients down below being told they had only ten months to live!'[28] Howard had the best bedroom – the former dining area – though it had the disadvantage of French doors which opened on to the sitting room, which made it somewhat less private. The furnishings were shabby: broken-down chintz sofas and worn carpets. The kitchen had a rather dirty sink and a gas stove which didn't look safe. The flatmates, like most young men who live together, did little to improve matters. 'It was generally pretty squalid,' says one of the tenants. 'In the fridge one of us would have a couple of fish fingers, and Michael would have a sausage.' John Prescott-Thomas, who had higher domestic standards than his colleagues, got upset with the tidemarks of scum regularly left round the bath, and arguments would erupt over why people hadn't kept to the cleaning rota. From time to time communal bottles of milk had to be poured away because they'd gone sour, and there'd be disputes over whose turn it was to carry the dozens of empties down the stairs to the street. And, says Richard Somerset-Ward, 'there was tension over getting into the bathroom in the morning. But it was really a good-tempered place.'[29]

The flat was littered with stacks of newspapers, which Howard devoured avidly for news of America and the New York Mets, as well as domestic politics. 'Norman and Michael continually discussed politics,' says John Entwistle, who often visited. 'Norman never seemed to go to bed and left getting up in the morning to the very last minute, when a whirlwind seemed to take place as he got washed and dressed and out of the house in two or three minutes.'[30] John Gummer, Leon Brittan and Ken Clarke would also come round for political meetings and chat, to the dismay of other residents who weren't Conservatives.

Everyone had his own record player, and Michael played the Beatles and the Rolling Stones, though one tenant says, 'The Kinks were on all the time.' Since the flatmates were out most evenings, they rarely ate together, except sometimes for Sunday breakfast, and they might have a drink while watching *Match of the Day* on Saturday nights. Occasionally two or three of them would go to Odin's, a restaurant about five minutes' walk away in Devonshire Street. It was a trendy place run by an eccentric character who had hung a collection of umbrellas from the ceiling.

Michael Howard's friends remember him as surprisingly fashion-conscious in his Harley Street days. 'He was very much into that glossy lifestyle stuff,' says John Prescott-Thomas, 'very much a young man about town of the sixties, very much the sharp dresser with the elastic-sided Chelsea boots, and three-piece suits and stiff collars and all that kind of thing.'[31] 'He enjoyed parties, and he certainly did get around a lot and he was a very social animal,' says Richard Somerset-Ward. 'The 'good-time guy' was the one who was the real Michael Howard, I always felt. He had a great zest for everything that he did.'[32] Before long he had acquired a white Lotus Elan sports car – the type where the lights pop up – even though he couldn't have been earning much at the Bar. One day John Prescott-Thomas, who was doing a directors training course at the BBC, persuaded Howard to use the car in a brief film without dialogue which he shot in a park in Ealing. It required a 'smart guy to drive up snappily in a posh sports car, and whisk a girl off and drive her away', he recalls. 'He was absolutely fine, took direction beautifully. It was a kind of chase thing. The people were just known as "the girl", "the villain", "the saviour" and so on, and Michael was "the saviour".'[33] The female part was played by a future Bond-girl, Caroline Munro, but unfortunately the celluloid evidence of Howard's brief turn as a film star seems no longer to exist.

And his obsession with the US grew deeper. Norman Lamont recalls how he might even debate the merits of America's most popular salad dressings: 'Was Roquefort better than Thousand Island?'[34] New York Mets pennants were pinned on his bedroom walls, and in 1969 he even travelled to Baltimore to watch his baseball team win the World Series for the first time. Howard's room was also decorated with large Kennedy posters, and he became as big a fan of the more liberal younger brothers, Bobby and Teddy, now both in the Senate, as he had been of JFK. 'I think he fell for the Camelot myth,' says Lamont, 'and he was fascinated by the dynastic element of the Kennedys.'[35] John Prescott-Thomas says Howard's teenage-like infatuation with all things American 'went along with a kind of non-enthusiasm for things European. He and I were always on opposite sides of the fence in that I loved France and Michael had no enthusiasm for France at all. I spoke the language and he didn't, and so forth. He was very much temperamentally a trans-atlanticist rather than a European.'[36]

Although Howard had missed out on being a candidate in 1964, Harold Wilson had only a tiny majority and would soon need to call another election. Now one of the friends he'd made in New York came to Howard's aid. John Entwistle's father, Sir Maxwell, was a prominent solicitor in Liverpool and a powerful figure in local Conservative circles. After six years as Tory leader on the city council, Sir Maxwell became president of the party in the Edge Hill constituency, just south of the city centre.

In late 1965 Sir Maxwell asked his son if he could recommend any promising young Tories who might make good candidates, as the Edge Hill party needed someone for the imminent election. 'I immediately thought of Michael, who told me he would very much like to be considered,' says John Entwistle, even though Howard wasn't on the official candidates list approved by Conservative Central Office in London.[37] Howard was invited to Liverpool's Adelphi Hotel to be interviewed for the short list. On such occasions outside contenders dredge up even the most tenuous local links, and Howard proudly played the football card, proclaiming his love of Liverpool, who had just won the FA Cup. 'There was then a deathly hush,' says Howard, and he learned that most of the committee supported Everton, Liverpool's local rivals. 'I thought that had absolutely done me in.'[38]

Howard was selected all the same – four weeks before Wilson called the March 1966 election – by what his agent calls an 'overwhelming' vote, having been 'head and shoulders above the other candidates'.[39] At a time when Liberals in Liverpool were almost unheard of, Edge Hill was not the lost cause for Conservatives it would be today. In 1959, when Harold Macmillan's party held six of Liverpool's nine seats, they had come within 700 votes of winning the seat. Edge Hill had lost 7,000 voters since then, as local families were moved out to overspill estates under slum clearance programmes. The

Tories optimistically assumed that these departed voters were mostly Labour.

Edge Hill's sitting MP was Arthur Irvine, another barrister, who'd been a radical Bevanite in his early career, but later drifted to the right, and had a poor reputation in Liverpool. It was rumoured that once an election was called Irvine would drive up to Crewe and park his Rolls-Royce in a garage for the duration of the campaign, before donning shabby clothes and continuing to Liverpool in a battered old car. Or so the story went.

If Michael Howard still craved life in Manhattan, the Merseyside of the mid-1960s was the next best thing – with its thriving Beatle-driven music scene, two highly successful football sides, its intense politics, and a Scouse wit which rivalled anything that brash New Yorkers could offer. As in the States, Howard had great fun repeating things he'd heard from sharp-tongued Liverpudlians. Passengers on the railway into Liverpool Lime Street often found it more convenient to alight at Edge Hill station a couple of miles from the city centre. It tickled Howard that in Liverpool the phrase 'getting off at Edge Hill' also meant coitus interruptus. Norman Lamont says it also amused him at a Liverpool game when a fan asked, 'Where's the stink?', by which he meant the gents.[40] In later years Howard loved talking about the time he gave a woman voter one of his personal leaflets. 'She looked at the photo and then me, and said, "Flattering, isn't it?"' Howard later related. 'I love that kind of thing.'[41]

Edge Hill was a poor community, where many families still slept several to a bed, and many houses had no bath. But Howard enjoyed mixing with brash, working-class Scousers, jousting with local characters. He took quickly to the rumbustious, raw style of Liverpool politics, which is similar to his own. As in America, he couldn't help but admire the political personalities, the boss figures for which Liverpool was famous – the men who acquired and held power by doling out council jobs for their supporters, or fixing them up with council flats. The young candidate grew particularly fond of Jimmy Ross, a working-class printer who was both chairman of the Edge Hill party and Tory whip on the city council, and who produced most of the Conservatives' election leaflets from his print shop on the edge of the constituency. 'Michael has always been interested in the operations of politics,' observes John Entwistle. 'Jimmy Ross was a great Tammany Hall political operator. He did a lot for Michael. Michael admired people like that who get things done. Jimmy knew everybody in the political world. Like Michael, he absolutely lived politics. It was in his blood. He enthused it.'[42]

Again as in America, politics in Merseyside was still divided by religion, and the Tories traditionally depended on thousands of working-class Protestants who wouldn't vote Labour because the party in Liverpool was historically linked with Catholicism and Irish nationalism. This largely explains why it wasn't until 1964 that Labour first won a majority of the city's seats at Westminster. Some members of the city council had even been elected on a Protestant label, and Orange lodges were a powerful force in parts of Edge Hill. While supporting Liverpool Football Club might offend half the community, the fact that Howard could say he was Jewish, and therefore be perceived as neutral on religion, was probably an advantage, though he has never been one for proclaiming his Jewish roots.

Michael Howard approached his task with gusto, and spent almost the entire campaign in Liverpool. 'He didn't have to be pushed out of the committee room to get on with canvassing like some other candidates,' says his agent, John Bosworth, a peppery character with red hair.[43] A Tory jeep toured the streets with loudspeakers blaring out the tune 'Seventy-six Trombones' to attract attention, with Howard wearing a red, white and blue rosette with the blunt slogan 'Kick 'em out'. The campaign literature for the future Tory leader's first election was printed in red, which by some historical quirk was the traditional colour of Liverpool Conservatives.

Edward Heath had now replaced Sir Alec Douglas-Home as Conservative leader, and Howard was among the Liverpool contenders who sat with him on the platform as Heath addressed 2,000 people in the city's St George's Hall. Later Howard joined Reggie Maudling in a cavalcade of cars through the city; a lorry with a placard declared, '1066, Harold defeated at Hastings. 1966, Harold defeated at hustings: Shoot your Arrow, Vote Conservative.'[44]

Despite Conservative claims, opinion polls suggested that Wilson would gain a much bigger majority at Westminster. But Howard claimed to have met many voters who'd told him they'd voted Labour in 1964 but were now switching to him. 'They were not saying it just to get rid of me,' he boasted. 'I would say to the opinion polls: "Come to Edge Hill." They might change their ideas.'[45] Selwyn Lloyd repaid Howard's help in 1964 by crossing the Mersey to address his main campaign meeting. It was the third election at which he'd spoken in Edge Hill, Lloyd proudly announced, only for a heckler to shout, 'You're a bad omen. They always lose when you come here!' 'That's a voice I have heard before,' said Lloyd. 'You will again!' the heckler shot back.[46]

When the candidate himself rose to speak, the heckler cried out, 'Make it short, brother,' for Howard to respond, 'I hope the day will come when he will call me Mike.' Reports suggest the young politician was then as aggressive in his politics as he famously would be later. With 'the lilt in his Welsh voice betraying his Welsh birth', said the local paper, Howard 'didn't take long to nettle the Socialists in the audience. There were howls of protest and a shower of questions when he spoke of the rising rents and rates, and pandemonium for a few seconds when he described what the Conservatives proposed to do with, and to, the trade unions.'[47]

On polling day Arthur Irvine was suddenly taken ill with heart problems which the hospital said were 'associated with strain from the election'.[48] This posed something of a tactical dilemma. Howard sent Irvine a telegram wishing his recovery, but his team were worried that publicising the illness might attract sympathy votes for their opponent. In the event, Irvine increased his majority from 5,886 to 7,541, a swing to Labour of 4.1 per cent – the highest in Liverpool, and well above the national average of 3.0 per cent.

If he'd been elected, Michael Howard would have been the youngest MP in the House of Commons, at the age of twenty-four. Yet he was not too distressed by the result, as throughout the contest his thoughts had often been elsewhere. Around the time he was short-listed to become a candidate, he had been told that his father was dying.

Bernard Howard, unusually for a man, had got breast cancer, and it had been diagnosed too late for him to recover. 'The last six months were pretty grisly,' Howard has said.[49]

Bernard died four months after the election, in July 1966. He was only forty-nine.

6

LOUD PROTESTS AND THUMPING

I was never actually interested in law. I was interested in advocacy.
I've earned my living as an advocate.

MICHAEL HOWARD, 1993[1]

'Apologise and withdraw!' shouted one of his many critics inside the hall. 'This man is lying,' someone else cried. 'Apologise, Mr Howard!' demanded another.[2]

Michael Howard faced this vociferous and angry onslaught not at a Conservative public meeting, or during a political debate, but at a planning inquiry held in north London during the spring and summer of 1977. For several minutes the meeting lapsed into uproar as protesters accused Howard of slandering them. Long before his election to Parliament, and almost two decades before becoming Home Secretary, Michael Howard was demonstrating his tendency to provoke and infuriate opponents, and his love of dramatic, public confrontation. But it was as a planning barrister, rather than as a politician.

Despite Howard's failure to win Edge Hill in 1966, his political ambition continued to burn fiercely, and in the late 1960s the future looked bright. Indeed, psychologically his ambition may have been boosted by the loss of his father, for history shows that an unusual number of top politicians have suffered the death of a parent early in life (including John Major, Tony Blair and Bill Clinton). At that time, however, there were far fewer ancillary jobs available in British politics: ministers and shadow ministers did not employ party advisers and researchers; nor were there many policy think-tanks to keep budding politicians occupied. While waiting for a way into Parliament Howard knew he would have to bide his time and earn a living at the Bar. Although he admits that he neglected his career as a barrister for the first five years or more,[3] the law would eventually become a substantial substitute occupation for the frustrated politician.

For most of the past two centuries a career at the British Bar has often gone hand in hand with a life in politics. Many of the men involved in passing legislation in Parliament were also active in implementing the will of MPs in the courts. Future politicians would often build up substantial practices as barristers before entering the House of Commons, where the unusual hours and long holidays enabled them to continue with their legal careers. Figures such as F. E. Smith, Edward Carson and Stafford Cripps made their names as brilliant and highly paid silks before achieving further fame at the highest levels of government. Conversely, a spell in Parliament was regarded as the quickest route to the High Court bench, and in times past many by-elections were caused by promotions to the judiciary. Nowadays, however, it's generally thought that the Bar and politics each require too much commitment for anyone to excel in both. Michael Howard, an MP who achieved the rank of Queen's Counsel on merit, is an increasingly rare creature. Even for him the dual distinction was unintended. It was only because he took longer than his contemporaries to land a safe Commons seat that his legal career progressed as far as it did.

The Bar was a much smaller profession when Howard joined his chambers in 1964. There were fewer than 2,000 barristers at that time, compared with around 14,000 today. Around half of England's barristers worked in the area of the City of London occupied by the four ancient Inns of Court, anachronistic institutions whose appearance and customs are very similar to the older public schools or Oxbridge colleges. Sets of barristers' chambers are clustered around stone staircases throughout the area. At lunchtime, or for formal evening dinners, barristers eat at long wooden tables in the Inns of Courts' huge medieval dining halls. It was a world of long-established rituals and hierarchies: snobbish, traditional and sexist. Nor was the Bar particularly well paid when Michael Howard joined it.

For a twenty-three-year-old pupil barrister in a profession where seniority and deference are important, Howard could be surprisingly assertive. On one occasion a senior colleague tried to help the pupils in his Lamb Buildings chambers by taking three or four of them to observe one of his court hearings. Afterwards Howard complained that no one could learn from the exercise when there were so many pupils present; they needed individual attention, he said. Howard later pressed his chambers clerk, Eric Cooper, to give him better cases. A colleague recalls, 'He would say to Eric that if he didn't get this brief or that brief he'd have to leave the Bar. But it's not quite "on" to try and apply pressure to the clerk.' Howard was careful not to go too far. He had quickly grasped where the real power lay in barristers' chambers, and recognised that Cooper was far more important to his prospects than the senior lawyers. 'I remember him telling me to behave well to his clerk,' says Celia Haddon, whom he still saw from time to time in the mid-60s. 'He said, "I don't mind if you are rude to the senior partners but you've got to be nice to the clerk, because he gives me the briefs."'[4]

Eric Cooper was a huge asset to Lamb Buildings. The convention then was that when a barrister was appointed Attorney-General the senior clerk from his chambers would act as the Attorney's lead clerk while continuing to organise the affairs of his chambers. As a result, Cooper became a famous figure in the Temple, holding considerable patronage, especially since he achieved what was thought to be the unique distinction of being clerk to two different Attorney-Generals, Elwyn Jones in the 1960s, and Sam Silkin in the late 1970s. Although Lamb Buildings might suffer some loss in income as a result of its clerk being distracted by government business, this was more than offset by his extra clout. It was accepted that, as an informal compensation, an Attorney's clerk was sometimes allowed to allocate government briefs to barristers from his own chambers. Cooper explains, for instance, that Lamb Buildings would often get the nod if another chambers suddenly told him that its barrister had to pull out of a government case at the last minute. 'If I got a call late in the day saying, "Sorry, my man can't do that case," then you are more likely to give it to one of your own chambers. It would be much easier for me to give it to somebody I knew was free and could cope with that particular case.'[5] Cooper's exercise of patronage in this way, over a period of more than ten years, was resented by others at the Bar. The Attorney-General's office is now run differently, and such favouritism would be regarded as a conflict of interest, but Cooper's barristers were undoubtedly the beneficiaries of an archaic but widely accepted practice. Michael Howard was among those who gained.

Howard in turn was able to bring himself and his chambers some work through his own modest connections. His mother's cousin Albert Landy ran a small two-man solicitors' practice in Great Russell Street called Landy, Laufer & Co, and the personal link helped ensure that many of its briefs – mostly landlord-and-tenant cases – came to Howard's chambers, and a good relationship was established. Stanley Laufer, Albert Landy's former partner, explains, 'They both came from Llanelli, and because he was related that's why we gave him the work – though I'm sure it wasn't the sole reason.'[6] The chambers also got occasional instructions from Albert's brother, Monty Landy, another solicitor who had moved to London.

Michael Howard's career at the Bar, like that of many barristers, began mainly with criminal cases, attending minor hearings in magistrates' courts, often for road-traffic offences. Much of the work was trivial, but Howard achieved an early reputation in chambers when his pupil-master, Peter Downe, got into a spot of trouble when someone accused his dog of biting them. The victim was applying for a court order against the animal. Downe's wife attended the hearing, and the barrister asked Michael Howard to help. 'How did it go?' Downe enquired later. 'A case of mistaken identity,' Howard proudly announced. It was one of his first successes.

His chambers colleague Gary Flather tells the story of Howard going to defend a speeding charge in Reading, only to be stopped by police on the way there for driving his Lotus too fast down the M4. He was relieved to be let off with a warning. To Howard's horror, when he arrived he found the same policeman sitting in court with the prosecution team. 'That was Michael,' Flather says. 'In spite of being wrong-footed, he carried it off with aplomb.'[7]

In July 1967, barely two and a half years after being called to the Bar, Howard was in the Court of Appeal arguing before the celebrated Master of the Rolls, Lord Denning. The case concerned a right of way in Norfolk, and a man was about to be jailed for seven days for ignoring a court order. Howard won part of his case when Denning and his two colleagues agreed that the committal order had not been written out correctly, and they lifted the jail sentence. For such an inexperienced barrister to appear before Denning was quite an achievement, and the more so to emerge partly victorious.

Years later Howard appeared again before Denning, in a famous public order dispute which became one of Denning's favourite judgements and crops up often in textbooks – the Harry Hook case. 'To some this may appear to be a small matter, but to Mr Harry Hook it is very important,' Denning explained in his beautifully crafted verdict. Hook, a trader in Barnsley market, had been caught urinating in the street after trading hours, when the public lavatories were locked. Barnsley Council responded by banning Hook for life from trading in the town market. 'All because of a trifling matter,' said Denning. Howard may have been the son of two market traders, but cases are allocated on the 'cab-rank' principle, and he was representing the council. Denning, Lord Scarman and a colleague decided against him, declaring that the council had 'taken away this man's licence to trade without justification and without having that due enquiry which the law requires'.[8] Harry Hook was allowed to reopen his stall.

In the 1960s, however, Howard's appearances in senior courts would have been rare. Road traffic and criminal cases are typically not challenging intellectually, or well paid, and in time he chose to specialise in civil cases, albeit over a wide range of law. Increasingly he concentrated on employment law, more often than not acting for employers. In 1973, in the short-lived Industrial Relations Court, he had to defend the Gestetner company against a worker who sought compensation for dismissal under a closed shop agreement with the engineering union, after he had failed to pay his union dues.

Howard also took part in a few election cases, which are something of a rarity. In 1976 a solicitor friend from his CUCA days, Martin Suthers, employed him in a special election court on behalf of the Nottingham Labour Party, which was trying to overturn the result of a council election on the grounds that an inattentive polling clerk had failed to stamp forty-three ballot papers: the case was weak, and he lost. In 1979 he appeared in a case which had echoes of his own protest against Sir Oswald Mosley. His client was the Labour MP Jim Marshall, who had refused to take part in a BBC election film on his constituency, Leicester South, if his opponent from the extreme right-wing National Front was also interviewed. When the BBC simply filmed Marshall while he was out campaigning, he sought an injunction to stop the broadcast. Lord Denning, however, ruled that Marshall had no right to 'veto' BBC coverage of the election.[9]

Howard was also involved in the public investigations into two of the major disasters of the early 1970s. The first, the 1973–4 Summerland inquiry on the Isle of Man, was a big step in his legal career. Howard was one of around thirty barristers who spent almost three months examining why fire had broken out at the large Summerland holiday complex, near Douglas, and burned fifty-three people to death. The following year he worked on the court of inquiry into the huge explosion at the Flixborough chemical plant in Lincolnshire, which killed twenty-eight workers.

Disaster inquiries tend to employ barristers from the planning Bar, where Howard increasingly worked in the early 1970s, sometimes as a junior to Sam Silkin, a planning specialist. Now it gradually became Howard's specialism too. Planning often involves highly technical work, requiring a barrister to master vast amounts of scientific material on complex and detailed issues such as geology, noise levels, pollution emissions, and traffic-flow statistics.

But the heavy workload and long hours reviewing thousands of pages of evidence can also be highly rewarding: planning is one of the most remunerative areas of the profession, after commercial law, tax and shipping. It is also an unusual branch of the law, in that the great majority of the advocacy work occurs at public inquiries which are conducted less formally than court hearings: barristers don't have to wear wigs or gowns, for example. Inquiries usually take place near the site of the proposed development, and can last for months, with hefty fees clocked up each day.

Once he has identified the crucial issues, the barrister needs the intellectual skill to regurgitate the material in court in a comprehensible form, and the agility to cross-examine technical experts. Being a successful planning barrister is more about advocacy than about understanding the law. 'Planning is the nearest thing at the Bar to politics,' Howard once observed, 'because you are arguing things like, "Here is a green field and should you have lots of houses built on it?"'[10]

Planning also involves a type of advocacy rather different from that in other branches of the law. Instead of making eloquent speeches before juries or arguing esoteric legal points before judges, one usually has to convince a planning inspector appointed by the government – most likely a planning barrister himself – about practical issues. The downside, however, is that planning inquiries can require barristers to be away from the capital for long periods, and thus absent from the public arena of the London law courts. Howard risked being forgotten by his legal colleagues, and by those in high places who decide legal promotions. It also made it hard to manage his personal commitments.

Most of Michael Howard's planning practice involved large-scale road and motorway schemes, where he generally acted for the Department of Transport (or the Environment), notably on inquiries into parts of the M25, the motorway round London, and the M23 in Surrey and Sussex. But he did sometimes act for the department's opponents, as for instance in the 1976 inquiry into the controversial scheme for the M3 to be extended through the picturesque Twyford Down near Winchester (not far from where Howard then rented a cottage), and the 1979–80 inquiry into the proposed bypass round Okehampton in Devon. Such schemes usually generated huge protests both from local citizens and also from the green movement, which was emerging as a visible political force. As a result, they often attracted great media attention locally.

Perhaps the most controversial planning inquiries of Howard's career were those into the Archway motorway scheme, conducted in three separate stages between 1974 and 1977. The Transport Department (headed latterly by Bill Rodgers, the former CDS organiser) wanted to extend the A1 southward to create a motorway through Highgate in north London, by widening the existing Archway Road. This generated a vocal alliance of middle-class residents who objected to losing their homes or feared the area would be blighted, and environmentalists who argued that, with limited oil supplies, the state should restrict road traffic, not encourage it. These disparate forces were joined by socialists such as the Lambeth councillor Ted Knight and his ally Ken Livingstone, who was hoping to become Labour MP for nearby Hampstead. These objectors argued persistently that the planning process was undemocratic and loaded against them.

The Archway hearings were among the most rowdy ever held in Britain, with lawyers, witnesses and the inspector, Ralph Rolph, having to speak against regular catcalls and interruptions from the public seats. Police would often be on standby outside. As the barrister for the Department of Transport, Howard became Public Enemy Number One for those opposed to the scheme. They would often heckle his speeches with shouts such as 'oily lawyer', though he never appeared to be rattled. Indeed, unlike most planning barristers, Howard seemed to relish such encounters, and at times he even appeared deliberately to taunt his critics. 'He certainly gave the impression of enjoying rather than being intimidated by the noise,' recollects John Adams, who gave expert evidence against the road.[11] 'We found him quite provocative,' says Peter Levin, a lay advocate for the objectors, 'as though he was actually trying to goad protesters into taking direct action, into tiring themselves out as irrational and emotional and militant.'[12]

This was most clearly illustrated during the third inquiry, held at Archway Central Hall in 1977, when hearings were held in the evenings to help objectors attend – a move which Howard had opposed. One opponent complained, for example, that Howard had denigrated John Adams's claims about traffic flows as an 'obsession'.[13] But Howard's occasional partisanship could play into the hands of the opposition. 'Our *modus operandi* was cheering people on our side and booing the others,' admits George Stern, a founder of STAMP – Stop The Archway Motorway Plan. 'What we banked on very much was hustling the inspector, booing and cheering and so on. We had a lot of scientific stuff as well, but we hadn't completely worked out a case.'[14] So when Howard chose to seize on some ill-judged comments by a railway union official, Neil Milligan, he should have foreseen the reaction. Clumsily, Milligan picked up on previous suggestions that the proposed highway would be like the Berlin Wall: 'If the Berlin Wall is offensive – and I don't necessarily accept that it is so – if it is offensive it is no more offensive than a concrete motorway that divides the communities between one side and the other, and destroys the access of both to both.'[15]

Eight days later, Howard cited these remarks to make what was essentially a debating point, designed to draw attention to the politics of some of the objectors. Milligan's 'apparent affection for the Berlin Wall', he taunted, 'and the round of applause which greeted that observation, said more about the alleged devotion to democracy, of which we have heard a good deal, of many of the people then in this room than could any words of mine'.[16]

The several dozen protesters in the hall were outraged. They reacted with what the official transcript describes as 'loud protests and thumping'.

'That is just low, common cheek,' shouted one voice. 'If we are all Communists . . .!'

'That ought not to be allowed! You have no right to,' cried another. 'It is absolutely disgusting!'

The shouting and protests continued, though the transcript obviously captures only snatches of what was said.

'What you are saying is that we are a bunch of thugs with Communist links!'

'Who is he to talk about democracy?'

'Withdraw! Withdraw!'

'I object to being slandered in this way!'

'I am no Communist.'

'He does not withdraw it,' one woman screamed. 'I think it is slander. I do not approve of the Berlin Wall.'

'It is absolutely disgraceful.'

'It is deliberate provocation on Mr Howard's part!'

'Mr Howard is just trying to provoke an adjournment!'

One leading protester, Nina Tuckman, says she waved her finger in Howard's face and accused him of 'McCarthyist' tactics. He was 'a bit taken aback', she says. But Howard made no immediate effort to withdraw or qualify what he'd said.[17]

Unable to calm the protests, the inspector summoned a senior police officer, only to be met by loud boos and taunts of 'Police state!' The row continued: 'Come on, let us have your democracy!'

As Howard tried to resume his speech, he explained that he had merely been referring to 'those people who had applauded that particular remark' of Milligan's. It did no good.

'It is a smear campaign,' one voice shouted, as the inspector desperately tried to achieve calm so that Howard could carry on.

'Most of us are not Communists,' an objector cried. 'I do not know anybody who is a Communist.'

'It is a lie!' some shouted.

The inspector again tried to get people to sit down, only to be met with more shouts, prolonged clapping and thumping.

'We demand a public apology!' a voice cried.

Eventually, after several minutes' uproar, which showed no sign of abating, Rolph adjourned the meeting. Two days later the inspector readopted a previous arrangement whereby he and the main participants in the hearing were moved to a side room from which all but one or two members of the public were excluded, to stop people interrupting again. The proceedings were relayed to the public in the main hall through loudspeakers – though the equipment did not always work – and protesters quickly dubbed the small room the 'bunker'.

One leading objector, Jane Kleiner, claimed Howard's comments about the Berlin Wall had been 'a deliberate ploy to provoke uproar which would serve as a pretext for Mr Rolph to return to the bunker. This is just the latest episode in a campaign of dirty tricks and intimidation being waged against the objectors in a bid to silence them.'[18]

When the hearing restarted, Howard admitted that his comments about the Berlin Wall had been a 'somewhat contentious observation'. He had now listened to the tape of Milligan's speech, he said, and acknowledged that there had been no applause at the relevant point in the union official's remarks. 'I therefore unreservedly withdraw the observation,' he announced, without actually apologising for it.[19]

One protester later complained to the Bar Council about Howard's original comment, though the case was rejected. Obviously he had been at fault in stating that Milligan's point had been met with applause, and it's clear he couldn't resist making a partisan jibe which had an element of a smear about it – not something one expects of a profession which is generally known for its unctuous tact. Nor can it be easily dismissed as a spur-of-the-moment comment made under pressure, since Howard had had eight days to reflect on Milligan's remarks. He also seems to have misjudged the objectors: most of them were not political activists, but middle-class residents who were angry that they might lose their homes; indeed, many were Conservative voters. On the other hand, the opposition couldn't claim complete innocence. Milligan himself, who had only just left the Communist Party, had clearly implied that he felt some sympathy towards the Berlin Wall. Nor were Howard's comments so offensive as to merit the uproar in the hall that caused the inspector to adjourn the sitting. It later became part of the mythology of the Archway campaign that Howard had accused the objectors of being Communists, though he never actually used the word. Part of the background to the highly charged situation was that many protesters believed they were under surveillance by MI5 or the Special Branch, which routinely infiltrated left-wing and dissident groups in the 1970s. The protesters suspected that Howard had been briefed by the authorities about their backgrounds, though he strongly denied this many years later.[20] On balance, it seems more likely that it was simply that his debater's instincts got the better of him.

In short, both sides were guilty of going over the top in exploiting what their opponents had said. Yet the objectors were incensed that, despite Howard's retraction, the inspector refused to return the hearing to the main hall, and at one point the audio system was sabotaged. Suddenly the so-called bunker was stormed by protesters. Accompanied by both Ken Livingstone and Ted Knight, they chased the inspector on to a high external fire escape, shouting, 'You pig, Rolph!' and 'You coward!'[21] Rolph fled, and locked himself into his room.

More than twenty years later, Ken Livingstone recalled that Michael Howard tried to come to the inspector's aid in this fracas, and he claimed that Howard had pleaded with him not to throw the inspector off what Livingstone describes as 'the roof'. Howard himself suggests that the threat was rather less dangerous, and that Livingstone may have embellished his account:

> I wouldn't say it was a roof, but it was a balcony with a substantial drop. Ken says I tried to protect Rolph by saying: 'Don't throw him over!' Well, I can't ever remember saying that. I was more worried about Ted Knight because he had raised his fist. I interposed myself between the inspector and the two demonstrators not because I thought Ken Livingstone was going to throw him off but because I thought Ted Knight might punch him.[22]

The demonstrations continued in the following days and weeks, and at one point protesters even performed a play called *Last Days in the Bunker*, in which they wore military uniforms and armbands with swastikas and portrayed several leading participants, including Howard, as Nazis.

A few months later the Archway inquiry was adjourned when

Ralph Rolph insisted the government should produce revised figures on estimated traffic use. In 1978 Bill Rodgers announced he was abandoning the scheme, and partly blamed the 'campaign of organised disruption'.[23]

Howard's belligerence, illustrated at Archway, did not always impress planning inspectors and judges, who were accustomed to a more graceful manner from barristers who appeared before them. 'He wasn't everybody's cup of tea,' says Lionel Read, a planning QC, who likens Howard's cross-examination technique as a planning advocate to the way he later confronted Tony Blair at Prime Minister's Questions. 'He's quite abrasive, and that style does not go down desperately well before a planning inspector. He wasn't very popular.'[24] But memories and opinions are mixed. David Woolley, himself a planning inspector, found Howard 'a very forceful advocate' in one inquiry he chaired, and adds that 'he wasn't difficult or quick-tempered. I didn't think much of his client's case, but he put it forward most persuasively.'[25] George Dobry, who was the inspector at one of the contentious M25 inquiries, reckons Howard had 'a marvellous ability for dealing with objectors and the public by his particularly charming and fair presentation of cases. His skill was his softness, not aggressiveness.'[26]

By all accounts, Howard worked phenomenally hard at his briefs, and there was much less time for the busy social life he had enjoyed in Cambridge, New York and London in the 1960s. Christopher Symons, a chambers colleague, recalls that Howard would often rise at 5 a.m., having got home from the inquiry at eight or nine o'clock the night before. 'He was absolutely exhausted a lot of the time.'[27]

In 1980 Howard was made a junior counsel to the Crown, one of the specialist panel of barristers from which the Treasury Solicitors' Department selects names for important cases. Places on the panel were highly sought after; the work wasn't that well paid, but there was plenty of it, and it was high profile. By then Howard was considering leaving Lamb Buildings, which was beset by internal tensions. The head of chambers, John Newey, tried to sack Eric Cooper on the grounds that he wasn't doing enough work to justify the 10 per cent

cut of the barristers' earnings he received as senior clerk, and that he
had gone on holiday without telling him. It was said that, after eleven
years working in government for Elwyn Jones and Sam Silkin, Cooper
was out of touch. And, with Labour no longer in office, there was no
extra government work to compensate. At a special chambers meeting held on a Saturday morning, Howard was one of the few barristers
to defend Cooper against Newey's attack. 'That's one of the lasting
memories I have of Michael,' says a former colleague, Leo Charles:

> Everyone else was determined that we'd had enough of Eric, and he
> was costing us far too much money for far too little work. But
> Michael had a lot of courage and I remember congratulating him
> after his little speech. I said, 'I think that was very brave of you. You
> took on the whole of chambers and spoke your mind, and well
> done.' Even if I didn't agree with a word, he did display consider-
> able confidence and courage.[28]

Others put a less charitable interpretation on Howard's support for
Cooper, and suggest it was merely returning a favour to the man
who had handed him briefs for so long. Yet the most opportunistic
political operator would surely have seen which way things were
going and kept his mouth shut.

Too many barristers in Lamb Buildings were past their prime; those
who'd stood in for Jones and Silkin as head of chambers had been less
effective, and several promising colleagues had already defected to
more dynamic sets. In 1980 Howard was approached by another
chambers, 2 Paper Buildings, which had a good specialist reputation
in planning and local government; in the past it had enjoyed a fruitful relationship with Whitehall and with local councils, and it almost
invariably played some role in any big planning case. 'Michael's other
chambers may have got government work because of successive
Labour Attorney-Generals, but they didn't get the plum planning
work,' says George Dobry, who, as a QC at Paper Buildings, played a
role in recruiting him to the new set.[29]

Dobry had just been made a judge, along with another leading planning QC at the chambers, and there were already signs that planning work might fall off because of a lack of top people. Steve Graham, then junior clerk at Paper Buildings, says, 'The big cases that always used to come our way suddenly weren't, because we hadn't got the magnets to attract them.'[30] In effect, Howard was identified as a promising future silk, and headhunted to ensure Paper Buildings maintained its reputation as the leading planning chambers.

Politically the move made sense too. If Lamb Buildings was a Labour set, 2 Paper Buildings was undoubtedly a Tory chambers, and Dobry calls it 'traditionally the most important Conservative set of chambers in history'.[31] The head of chambers was Geoffrey Rippon, who had negotiated Britain's entry to the European Community during the Heath government. Two other members had also been Tory ministers: Sir Derek Walker-Smith (who was very hostile to Europe) and Sir Frederick Corfield. The chambers enjoyed a good relationship with Conservative Central Office, which often employed them on legal matters. Moving could help Howard's career in more ways than one. But it wasn't an easy choice. 'It was quite a brave decision to switch,' says John Entwistle. 'He agonised over it.'[32]

Even if the decision kept him awake, Michael Howard's career blossomed afterwards. He joined the set on the understanding that he would now concentrate almost exclusively on planning, with the hope of soon becoming a QC. Steve Graham says his arrival made an immediate difference. 'Very quickly after that we were suddenly getting the calls we were used to,' he says. 'Michael Howard made a huge impact on the planning Bar in a very short space of time. People just don't realise how immediately successful he was.'[33] 'He was a fearsome performer,' says Christopher Lockhart-Mummery, one of his new colleagues. 'He used to work manically hard. He was working all hours.'[34] 'He was', Steve Graham adds, 'one of the chaps that, once you'd talked a solicitor into taking him, word got round: "They've got someone there who's really special." And indeed that was the case.'[35]

One of the most informed assessments of Howard's qualities as a senior planning barrister comes from a colleague who acted as his junior on more than one occasion.

He was very fluent, very clear. He had a lovely way of making light of things. He wasn't beyond pouring scorn on a witness's idea or line of argument. He used levity. He was forceful without being aggressive. He was a very skilful advocate. He had a fiery temper, a quick temper. If he felt someone was being stubborn or stupid he would spend a certain amount of time trying but he didn't suffer fools gladly. I saw him let rip. With that said, if he was in the wrong he would climb down immediately. Michael's was not a frequent temper, but it was a noticeable one. He was always quick to calm down, though.

Anne Seifert was Howard's pupil for a spell, having previously interrupted her pupillage to have children. She found Howard supportive of her personal circumstances, which were unorthodox in the very traditional world of the Bar. 'He was a wonderful, inspiring teacher, and had this fantastic charisma that infected everyone around him,' she says. 'And he gave you enormous confidence that you could actually achieve it.'[36]

It was around 1981 that Howard first applied for silk – to become a QC – though he was rejected initially. One colleague reckons he had upset too many judges with his abrasive manner, and judges are often consulted when the Lord Chancellor decides on new QCs. In April 1982 a new application was successful. He was still only forty, generally considered to be the earliest age at which one can realistically expect to take silk, though the most outstanding barristers occasionally do it in their late thirties.

For a very short spell of two or three years Michael Howard was one of the biggest names at the planning Bar, and earned very good money. As a sign of his new riches, he became a Lloyd's name in the early 1980s, underwriting about £250,000 worth of business, which would have required him at that time to have had realisable assets of around £80,000. Three of his five syndicates were particularly sought after, and would have needed some influence to join.

Had Howard stayed at the Bar, he could have earned a fortune as a planning QC, especially in the late 1980s after Margaret Thatcher's government cut taxes on high incomes. By the early 1990s he would almost certainly have been among the top five or six planning silks, earning the equivalent today of between £500,000 and £750,000 a year. Alternatively, had he wanted to, he could easily have become a senior judge, like many of his contemporaries from Cambridge and the Bar.

But Michael Howard had other plans, of course.

7

THE LOVE OF HIS LIFE

'Hmmm,' said Mark thoughtfully. 'You say that, but Michael
Howard's got an extremely attractive and intelligent wife. He must
have some sort of hidden charms.'
    'Like what, you mean?' I said, childishly, hoping he would say
something about sex.
    'Well . . .'
    'He might be a good shag, I suppose.'

HELEN FIELDING, *Bridget Jones's Diary*[1]

'I'm in love!' Michael Howard declared as he opened the door of his
London flat. 'He greeted me with arms wide, a seraphic smile and the
ecstatic announcement,' the journalist Valerie Grove recalls of her
visit that evening in late 1973. Grove had been on a few dates with
Howard – 'a drink at El Vinos, a pizza in Chelsea', she says – but was
married to someone else.[2] The new object of Michael Howard's affections was not her but a famous and beautiful model.

He'd met the thirty-three-year-old Sandra Paul one evening at
Stratton Park, a country house near Winchester which belonged to
the banker John Baring, who had allowed his home to be used for a
charity dance (in aid of local youth clubs). 'It was a strong reaction,'
Sandra says of their first meeting, though she got 'very cross' that
Michael didn't invite her on to the dance-floor.[3] 'I kept thinking,

"Why on earth doesn't he ask me to dance?" I suppose it was because he'd actually taken somebody else to the ball.'[4] Instead, Howard asked whether she'd seen the 1960s John Schlesinger film *Darling*, which is set in the world of fashion. She had, Sandra said, and had enjoyed it. He also mentioned F. Scott Fitzgerald's novel *Tender is the Night*, which Sandra admitted she hadn't read. 'He seemed appalled by this – that there was anybody in the world who hadn't read *Tender is the Night*.'[5] Interestingly, both *Darling* and *Tender is the Night* are about beautiful women who get involved in adulterous relationships.

Michael Howard had been staying that weekend with a Bow Group friend, Jennie Enfield, who subsequently married their colleague Christopher Bland. She recalls that in the car on the way home Howard announced that Sandra was the woman he was going to marry. The next day he sent Sandra a copy of *Tender is the Night*, with a note suggesting she should ring him to let him know what she thought of the book. 'It was several weeks before I got back to him,' Sandra has said. 'Then I rang and said I was taking my mother to the theatre and had a spare ticket and would he like to come. He said yes and that's how it started.'[6]

For weeks Michael Howard seemed transformed. 'He was absolutely glowing,' says Celia Haddon, who says she saw Howard the day after he met Sandra. 'I see Michael as a rather romantic, passionate person. He was just raving about her. There was a physical change in him.'[7]

Sandra was pretty keen on Michael, too. 'It's something about his way of talking to you,' she later explained – 'a sort of energy comes off him. It's very infectious . . . He's quite romantic and almost sentimentalist, I think.'[8] The only trouble was that Sandra was already married, to an advertising executive called Nigel Grandfield, who was her third husband. She also had an eleven-year-old son from her first marriage.

Michael Howard had never been short of girlfriends. The observation in 2003 by his friend the TV presenter Anne Robinson that he was known as a good lover at Cambridge chimes with other recollections from Howard's youth. The Lotus Elan and smart suits no doubt boosted his appeal to women, and he was always very careful to keep himself in trim. Although he took little exercise beyond the occasional game of tennis, he has always managed to keep his weight down. David Mellor, who joined Lamb Buildings as a young pupil barrister, and squatted for a while in his room, recalls that Howard was never tempted by the buttered crumpets at the chambers afternoon tea.

On leaving Cambridge, Michael Howard still saw Celia Haddon occasionally: they had met again while he was in New York and she was attending a summer school at Harvard, and later when she worked for the *Daily Mail* in London. Another date was Linda Seifert (a cousin of his subsequent pupil Anne), whom he met in the Inner Temple while she was going through the process of eating dinners to qualify as a barrister. Seifert achieved a brief moment of fame when she was called to the Bar at the age of only twenty, making her one of the youngest barristers of modern times (though she wasn't allowed to practise in court until she was twenty-one). As a result, she was hauled before a disciplinary committee because other barristers complained that the widespread press coverage she had received was effectively advertising, which is prohibited at the Bar. She and Howard had dinner in Harley Street on one occasion, and Seifert and her brother went with Howard and his sister, Pamela, on a double date to Odin's restaurant. But they could never be deemed girl- and boyfriend. 'He's a really, really charming man,' Linda Seifert recalls, insisting their relationship was merely a couple of dates.[9]

Women barristers were a rarity in the mid-1960s – fewer than 10 per cent of those working at the Bar, compared with around a third today. Indeed, Michael Howard seemed close to cornering the market. His relationship with Catharine Williams, an attractive redhead, was more serious. The daughter of a civil servant, and a law graduate from King's College, London, Williams was two years younger than Howard. She had been called to the Bar in 1966, having also joined the Inner Temple, and later worked for the government's newly established Law Commission. 'Catharine was gorgeous,' says John Entwistle. 'We all went to a May ball together.' Entwistle recalls that while Howard was campaigning in Liverpool he was thrilled to spot a Catharine Street in Toxteth with the same unusual spelling (with two 'a's). 'Michael liked tiny little details like that.'[10]

'They were obviously very, very keen on each other indeed,' says a friend from that period. The problem was that Catharine Williams wasn't Jewish. Howard himself might have long ceased being an orthodox Jew, but he did not want to upset his mother, especially after she was widowed following Bernard Howard's early death in 1966. Michael's flatmate Richard Somerset-Ward recalls that Michael became 'very conscious of his mother' after his father died. 'She suddenly had a position in his life that I don't think she'd had before. I don't know if "responsible" is the right word, but certainly he paid very close attention to what she said.'[11] 'He was more considerate of his family than other people of that age and stage,' says another acquaintance. 'He was very conscious in a Jewish sort of way about his family.' So concerned was Michael not to offend his mother by his relationship with Catharine that they went to some lengths to hide it from her. But the affair didn't last. At the end of 1968 she instead married Roger Henderson, who had also been to Cambridge and was an even more promising barrister than Howard. Today Henderson is one of Britain's top QCs, a specialist in public law.

Michael Howard never seemed short of female company. For summer breaks he would book singles' holidays through agencies such as Murison Small. One year he visited the Greek island of Mykonos, where he stayed in a villa with several other single holidaymakers of both sexes. One of those in the same villa recalls that Howard was always keen to go down into the town in the evenings. Years later, one of the women he met in Mykonos bumped into him in New York and reminded him of the great time they'd had together. Howard denied all knowledge of the brief friendship.

Howard's other serious relationship in his bachelor days was with another Inner Temple barrister. Ann Mallalieu joined the Lamb Buildings chambers in 1970 – only their second woman – after coming down from Cambridge, where she had achieved worldwide fame in 1967 by being the first woman president of either of the Oxbridge debating unions. Because of this, she was often asked to write for the newspapers, and was an obvious guest for radio and TV producers. Blonde, with long hair, she was the daughter of J. P. W. 'Curly' Mallalieu, a junior minister in the Wilson government, and her uncle and grandfather had also been Labour and Liberal MPs. Ann made no secret of her ambition to become the third generation in the Commons, under Labour colours, and subsequently became a parliamentary candidate. Years later she made headlines with her campaign for women barristers to be granted tax relief on their expensive legal garments.

Howard had first met Mallalieu on his visits back to Cambridge to see friends in the Union, but the relationship didn't get going until she had been in chambers for several months. They never did cases with each other, though they discussed law, and often went to the races – another growing passion for Howard. Yet, while they both enjoyed arguing, Mallalieu says they deliberately avoided talking about politics. Within Lamb Buildings they were so discreet about the affair that many colleagues weren't aware of it, though it was quite well known among Howard's Bow Group friends. 'We went out together for about six months,' Mallalieu says, 'and it was very pleasant and ended with no acrimony at all, and it wasn't of great significance in either of our lives.'[12] Some of Howard's friends disagree: 'Annie' was a serious girlfriend, they say, who was around for significantly longer than six months. She eventually married a Tory baronet, received a peerage, and became a Labour home affairs spokesman in the Lords, and so was in direct opposition to her former lover when he became Home Secretary. In 2004 she played a leading role in the Lords' efforts to stop the ban on fox-hunting.

It was while seeing Mallalieu, around 1972, that Michael Howard left Harley Street after more than seven years there. He now bought a small basement flat by the Thames, at 121 Cheyne Walk, one of the smartest streets in Chelsea. 'He fell hopelessly in love with that part of London,' says Norman Lamont, though Howard lived at the less fashionable end of Cheyne Walk, near World's End, where it was more noisy.[13] Visitors were not impressed with Howard's efforts to cook. Celia Haddon, by now a friend rather than a girlfriend, recalls him serving her duck in cherries, ready-cooked from a frozen packet.[14] 'Once,' says Lamont, 'he was trying to impress a girlfriend, and dished up some dreadful potatoes from Marks & Spencer.'[15] The flat was extremely small, and to save space, Howard's bed was above a cupboard. 'You had to climb a ladder into this shelf, and there was about four feet between the mattress and where your head would hit the ceiling,' says the journalist Richard Compton-Miller. 'I thought it was the most unsexy seduction chamber you could have. And yet it didn't obviously reduce his private life or his pulling capacity.'[16]

Howard's bed even had purple sheets. Coloured bedlinen was fashionable at that time, and the choice may have been inspired by a famous scene in one of his favourite movies, Michelangelo Antonioni's *Blow-up*, the 1966 art film in which a fashion photographer – played by David Hemmings – frolics with two nude girls on a purple backing sheet. If the scene looks mild today, it was considered risqué at the time, and very briefly contained one of the first cinema glimpses of pubic hair. The film, which also starred Vanessa Redgrave and Sarah Miles, captured the mid-sixties ambience of 'swinging London', with sex, drugs, rock 'n' roll, protests, students and some glamour. As well as reflecting the 1960s, it contributed to the cultural change of the decade by helping to liberalise what could be seen on screen. In Howard's other top film, *Darling*, released the year before, his favourite actress – Julie Christie – climbs the career and social ladders through relationships with a succession of men. That Howard should consider these to be among his favourite films, even today, seems to reflect a hankering for the glitzy lifestyle and a yearning for glamorous women.

No wonder he fell for Sandra Paul.

At the time, she was one of the best-known models in the world, the Naomi Campbell or Kate Moss of her day. At the start of 1964 she achieved the rare distinction for an Englishwoman of appearing on the cover of two consecutive issues of the American edition of *Vogue*. She was in constant demand, one of the faces of sixties fashion, along with Jean Shrimpton and Twiggy.

Sandra Clare Paul had been born in a military hospital in Malta in

1940, during the German blockade of the island. She was the daughter of Saville Paul, who was stationed there as an RAF doctor. 'When
I was almost a year old,' she says, 'we were put on a ship to go home
through the Straits. My mother said you could see the torpedoes in
the water. She very quickly had me christened.'[17] Her ancestry was
certainly mixed. Her mother, Rosie, was half Swiss; her father was of
Russian ancestry, and part Jewish, but had been born and brought up
in South Africa. Sandra once wrote that she felt a 'bit of a fraud' when
always being described as 'a typical English rose', which was 'really
rather funny since there is not a drop of English blood in my veins'.[18]

Saville Paul specialised in tropical medicine and Sandra spent much
of her childhood overseas, with spells in Rhodesia and Singapore, and
an education which involved thirteen different schools. In 1956, after
she had completed her O-levels, the family sailed home from
Singapore on a troop ship which was the first vessel to be turned back
from the Suez Canal during the Suez Crisis. 'We had to go all around
the Cape, this wonderful six-week trip with all these good-looking
young army types. I had my 16th birthday in Zanzibar,' Sandra has
recalled.[19]

While her father had studied at Guy's Hospital in London, her
mother had gone to St Hilda's College, Oxford. Sandra initially hoped
to go to Oxford too, encouraged by one of the nuns at her convent
school. Then a schoolfriend suddenly announced she was going to
London to become PA to a television producer, and suggested that
Sandra might like to share her flat. Why not try to become a model
with the famous Lucie Clayton agency? the friend suggested. Sandra
threw her A-level essays into the fire and agreed, though she now
wishes her parents had tried to restrain her from modelling: 'They
were quite intrigued by the idea. I wish that they hadn't been. I'm
cross with them . . . It [Oxford] would have been good for me. I still
feel I've got an untrained mind. I had a terrible chip about it for a long
time. I just think they had a responsibility to push me, and you'd
think, with my mother being a real bluestocking . . .'[20] 'I suppose I'm
naturally impatient and I wanted results quickly,' she said a couple of
years later.[21]

Her training at the Lucie Clayton School, overlooking Buckingham Palace, involved walking on chalk lines, wearing false eyelashes, nails, hair and breasts; and efforts to lose weight, before she was sent out to conquer the tough world of photography studios, clutching a portfolio of personal pictures. 'Your first visit to a studio in search of work is worse than sitting ten exams,' she once said. 'You can never find the studio and you get windswept and cold as you roam the streets looking. Finally, after frantically patching-up your make-up with the aid of a compact with cracked mirror in the lift, you tap nervously and are told coldly: "The photographer is busy, ill, away, or creating. Leave a picture and perhaps next time . . ."'[22]

Her big break came when a fellow model was ill and had to withdraw from a shoot with the renowned photographer Norman Parkinson. Sandra was sent instead, and the couple hit it off. 'I've got a stammer and so had his son,' she related recently. 'He kept on using me after that. So I owe my entire modelling career to the fact that Norman Parkinson liked my stammer.'[23] By 1959 Sandra was already reported to be earning £100 a week from a career which one paper then described as 'one of the biggest romances in post-war modelling . . . In little more than a year, her own combination of apparent sophistication and schoolgirlish, almost gawky, charm has brought new life to that devalued term, top model.'[24] 'She's quite bright,' says a friend. 'She has enormous style, but never had very good dress sense. The face was beautiful – the legs weren't so good. From the waist down she wasn't quite the same. She'd made the most of what she'd got.' 'I hate my legs,' Sandra once admitted. 'They are Russian peasant woman's legs.'[25]

Sandra Paul was well educated, intelligent, charming, and good fun, but it took great resolve to overcome her natural shyness and the slight stammer. Behind the beauty lay an intense ambition and steeliness. 'She's never changed,' says the model Tania Mallett (now Radcliffe), who's known Sandra since they were both about seventeen:

> She's an incredibly organised person. She's very ambitious, but she's got this doe-like quality. I've never known a woman that so many

men want to wrap their arms round and look after. She's got those brown eyes and that little stutter, and every man thinks she's the most vulnerable thing in the world, and she's not really. She knows what she's about.[26]

It was a highly glamorous lifestyle. Tania Mallett tells a story of when they went on a two-week modelling cruise around the Mediterranean, at a time when bikinis had just come into fashion. The other girls suddenly noticed that Sandra was in some distress in the swimming pool, with several passengers looking on. 'Sandra – she was so embarrassed, mortified – had pushed two "falsies" down her bikini top. They'd popped out, and there she was, desperately thrashing at the water, trying to catch these two foam things floating on the top. It was utterly excruciating for her.'[27]

The teenage Sandra Paul had a flat just off Piccadilly, and was soon a fixture on the London upper-class social scene. She was widely expected to marry Patrick Bashford, a musician and fellow model. But then she met twenty-six-year-old Robin Douglas-Home, whose uncle Lord Home held several posts in Harold Macmillan's Cabinet, including Commonwealth Secretary, and later succeeded him as Prime Minister. The relationship is said to have begun at a bus stop. Douglas-Home had noticed Sandra at a fashion show some days earlier, and when he spotted her waiting for a bus he offered her a lift. The lift was diverted to a cocktail party, then dinner, and everything flowed from that. Douglas-Home was an attractive man in many respects – highly talented, charming and witty – but he was also spoilt, and could be difficult and resentful. 'He wanted Sandra because she was the prettiest girl in London,' a friend said afterwards.[28] 'I'm shattered,' Patrick Bashford said when he heard of their engagement a few weeks later.[29]

The marriage, in July 1959, just four months after they first met, was one of the society weddings of the year. While Michael Howard was still in Llanelli, waiting to go to Cambridge, Sandra was on the society pages of the national press, wearing a diamond tiara, an heirloom of the Douglas-Home family. The ceremony took place at St

James's Church in Piccadilly, and the reception was held in the gardens of the Hyde Park home of Lady Fermoy, a distant relative of Douglas-Home. The 200 or so guests included Lord Home, the TV presenter Robin Day, and the groom's cousin Lord Althorp, the father of Princess Diana.

It was not a successful match. Sandra admits she was chosen 'a bit on the rebound' from an intense relationship that Douglas-Home had just enjoyed with Princess Margarethe of Sweden, which had generated huge coverage in the late 1950s gossip columns.[30] The Princess's family had forbidden her to marry Douglas-Home. King Gustav, her grandfather, did not think he was of sufficient social standing: Douglas-Home worked in an advertising agency, played the piano in a Mayfair hotel, and dabbled in journalism. He did not have enough money, the Swedish king thought, to look after his princess. 'I don't know what he's on about,' Douglas-Home reportedly told friends. 'My family were aristocrats in Scotland when his ancestors were still running round in woad.'[31]

Things went well for the first year as Sandra and her husband worked in London and lived in rural Hampshire. 'We commuted by train every day,' she later explained, 'and we used to meet at Smith's at Waterloo at 5.30, and go back to the cottage and watch television, and have the weekends in the garden.'[32] Before long, however, Robin got bored with the routine. He wanted to spend more time in London, not always with Sandra. She would always want to know what he had been doing.

In theory, with Sandra's income, there should no longer have been any financial difficulties, but Douglas-Home felt an old-fashioned unease at earning less than his wife. It can't have helped that even before the engagement she was quoted as saying, 'He has the same problem as most clever young musicians – no money. I could take us both out to dinner every night. But that would be wrong, embarrassing to him.'[33] Robin Douglas-Home resented the fact that, although he was one of the most talented members of his family, he was also among the least well off.

Without doubt, Douglas-Home treated Sandra badly while they

were married. 'I had a very happy first year,' she has said. 'He was unfaithful but I didn't realise. I was a schoolgirl really, in outlook. Schoolgirls have these nice dreamy fairytales . . . I remember one old roué who put his hand on my knee at a party and said, "Within a year, your husband will be unfaithful, but you must rise above it." I was fairly shocked. He had a point really.'[34]

Douglas-Home regularly told Sandra and other people that her success was down only to having married him, and to his family name. When the housekeeper of their country cottage cleaned the stove, Robin asked why his wife couldn't have done the job, and when Sandra got pregnant he warned that when the baby came 'it's going straight down the plug-hole', the housekeeper, Kathleen Wood, later revealed. 'He couldn't bear us to talk about it.'[35] Though when the baby did arrive – a boy, born in 1962 – Robin quickly came to adore him. They called him Sholto.

Douglas-Home was constantly chasing other women, and made no effort to keep his liaisons secret from Sandra. On one occasion, while they were entertaining people to lunch, she came out of the house to look for her husband and found him making love to Nicolette, Marchioness of Londonderry, on the back seat of her car. Indeed, he had a thing about sex in cars – preferably while they were moving – and was notorious for pouncing on women in taxis. 'He was capable of directing all his attention at you,' one of his many lovers said later. 'He had a weak mouth but it managed to say all the nicest things and was very good at kissing, I remember. He certainly knew where to press all the right buttons and was an excellent and imaginative lover. The only thing I found a bit off-putting was that he spoke with quite a high-pitched voice.'[36] In 1961 Nicolette Londonderry had a daughter, Cosima, by Douglas-Home, though she passed the baby off as her husband's and the truth did not emerge publicly until 1998.

But the marriage did give Sandra some extraordinary social introductions. Princess Alexandra visited their Hampshire cottage; they also got to know Kirk Douglas and Frank Sinatra. The singer had invited the couple on the inaugural tour of his personal jet, and they flew round America spending a night or two in each place, including

Sinatra's home in Palm Springs, but Sandra insists that he never tried to seduce her. Sholto Douglas-Home was actually conceived while the couple were staying with Sinatra in Palm Springs. In 1961 Robin Douglas-Home spent almost two months in America researching a short photo-biography of the singer.[37] Sinatra became Sholto's godfather, though in later years the boy had understandable difficulty in persuading schoolfriends that the latest American transistor radio he'd received was a gift from the legendary entertainer.

Sholto's godmother was equally distinguished – Sylvia Ormsby-Gore, the wife of Sir David Ormsby-Gore, the British ambassador to America during the Kennedy administration. Robin Douglas-Home was a great friend of the Ormsby-Gores, and he and Sandra often stayed at the embassy in Washington. Because Ormsby-Gore was close to the Kennedys, and distantly related by marriage, the Douglas-Homes became regular visitors to the White House living quarters. While the student Michael Howard could only observe the president from the back of the crowd in Berlin, his future wife was enjoying his personal attention across the dinner table. Remarkably, at the age of only twenty-two, Sandra was at the White House one Sunday evening in the midst of the 1962 Cuban Missile Crisis (though the outside world was not yet aware of the crisis). 'Jack Kennedy was in a very light, fresh mood, as he often was, and fooling about and joking and having fun,' Sandra related in 2003. 'It was just an overall energy that oozed out of him . . . He was a tease. He liked to flirt and chat people up.' But every now and then JFK would be 'tapped on his shoulder' and then took a call at a window seat behind a half-curtain. Sandra was astonished by 'this extraordinary ability to obviously engage when he needed to engage, but not to be totally overcome by it. I mean he could pick up a light-hearted flirtatious conversation where he'd left it off, when he was obviously talking about pretty fundamental and world-shaking things.' All this was the evening before Kennedy went on television to deliver his momentous speech warning of the risk of worldwide nuclear war if the Soviets continued stationing nuclear missiles on Cuba. 'It was quite a historic moment, to say the least.'[38] Sandra was clearly excited by being so close to a man of such power.

Forty-eight hours later the Douglas-Homes were guests at the White House again, at a black-tie dinner party in honour of some Indian friends of Jackie Kennedy. After the meal, guests gathered round as Robin Douglas-Home played at the piano, while at the other end of the room the President and his brother Bobby had grave discussions about the Cuba crisis. Robin Douglas-Home sat up well into the night talking to Jackie, and he had two more long conversations with the First Lady later that week, and even travelled to a house which the Kennedys had rented in Virginia.

Two months earlier Sandra and her husband had also been guests of Jackie Kennedy when she went on holiday, without JFK, to the coastal resort of Ravello in southern Italy, where her other guests included the Fiat boss Gianni Agnelli. Robin Douglas-Home grew extremely close to Jackie over the course of several long conversations in Ravello, and she confided in him about her problems, and the huge strains of being First Lady and First Mother. Years later he revealed that 'after a day spent swimming, sun-bathing and water ski-ing, the others went to bed early and Jacqueline Kennedy and I were left alone. We talked, and talked, and talked . . . These hours of conversation were, I think, the most immediately emotionally disturbing I have ever had.'[39]

Given the long and intense nature of these conversations, along with Robin Douglas-Home's promiscuity and the reputation of the Kennedy family, one is bound to suspect that the couple had an affair. Most of Jackie Kennedy's biographers think not.

While lending a sympathetic ear to the First Lady, Douglas-Home was less understanding of his own wife's independent and successful career (though at the time they had got engaged she had been quoted as saying that her own work would 'gradually taper off').[40] It was still an era when women were expected to concentrate on raising families, not to show the kind of driven ambition that Sandra displayed. 'I am too successful to give up work,' she said in 1962, ten weeks after Sholto was born. 'But I miss my baby terribly when I am away from him. Unfortunately, there can be no half measures. . . Modelling is an all-demanding job. To stay at the top a model must dedicate every-thing to it, should look like a model all the time.'[41] More recently she has said, 'I needed to know all the bills were going to be paid. I had a bourgeois approach. Had I been a bit more bohemian about it all it could have helped. I was a bit too tame and he liked excitement. I was pretty boring really.'[42]

It was a period when Sandra Paul's face often appeared on newsagents' shelves, her picture taken by the top names of sixties fashion photography. Primrose Hanson, a model who worked with her from around 1960, says, 'Sandra was great fun to work with. We used to work with John French – the leading photographer. To work with him you knew you'd arrived. David Bailey was his assistant at the time.'[43]

Sandra was one of a select group of about ten models who did most of the prestige assignments. And at a time when air travel was just beginning to open up – at least for the influential and the wealthy – those assignments were increasingly overseas. She visited Paris, New York, Cape Town, Majorca, the Lebanon, Greece and Italy for work during the early 1960s.

The top British models belonged to a close-knit world. Most of them socialised together, going out in the evenings to places around the Kings Road. But Sandra is recalled by contemporaries as being more distant than the rest. Primrose Hanson describes her as 'not a girl who'd completely open up during a shoot. She'd concentrate on the job. She wouldn't divulge a lot.'[44]

Sandra also found time for the odd bit of journalism, writing about both the pleasures and perils of being a leading model and on topics such as how tough a mother should be with her two-year-old child. On a visit to Downing Street, recently vacated by her uncle-in-law Alec Douglas-Home, she admitted she was 'already in trouble for voting Liberal' in 1964.[45] Today she says she thinks she 'voted Tory' at that time, and that her parents were Conservatives.[46]

Robin Douglas-Home found her lifestyle hard to take, as he later explained: 'She was incredibly beautiful; she had a tremendous quality of innocence, and she was, I thought, she was a vulnerable creature in a highly suspect world – the world of models and fashion, which I despised then and I despise even more now. And so in a sense maybe

I was trying to rescue her from what I thought was going to be a decline in her character due to her career.' And he would have liked her to have 'made it plainer that her married life, and her future family life, was more important to her than standing in front of a goddam camera being flattered by some fashion photographer'.[47]

Sandra's overseas assignments only provided opportunities for Robin to stray. By the start of 1964 she was fed up, and went off to New York with baby Sholto for a trial three-month separation (at the same time, coincidentally, as Michael Howard was working in Manhattan), only for Douglas-Home to chase after her and beg her to return. When she agreed, her husband perversely announced that he was leaving her after all.

At that time divorce was rather more difficult than it is today, and often one party had to prove adultery or cruelty by the other. Douglas-Home tried to provide the necessary evidence for the pro-ceedings by going through the ludicrous process of participating in two stage-managed adulterous incidents – what he later described as 'a very expensive and thoroughly unsavoury business, involving expensive and thoroughly unsavoury girls, in expensive and thor-oughly unsavoury hotels, and it cost me a bloody packet'.[48] The whole process degenerated into farce when the detective who had masqueraded as a waiter, supposedly to 'catch him' on the morning after the first night, failed to recognise the woman with whom he had supposedly been in bed. So Douglas-Home had to go through it all again, but couldn't afford another prostitute and another hotel, and this time got a friend to act as his supposed lover.

Robin Douglas-Home's lawyers had previously feared that Sandra might remove Sholto from the jurisdiction of the English courts, so they had applied, successfully, for the boy to be made a ward of court. While this may have seemed a clever legal move, emotionally the consequences for Douglas-Home – never the most stable of char-acters – were devastating. It greatly restricted what Sandra could do with Sholto, and her solicitors advised her that the adultery evidence was not enough: to win back custody of her son she would have to allege cruelty against her husband. This required her to set out the detail of their five-year marriage chronologically in a long petition. Douglas-Home said it was like a 'small bomb had gone off inside your head' when he received the document specifying the cruelty allegations:

> It chapterised the marriage almost day by day, and incidentally letter by letter, [copied] in the most unpleasant and vicious terms, with me as the aggressor and the cruel one. Five years of one's life, say 70 per cent of which were very happy, reduced to a great wad of foolscap, typed out by leering little clerks in solicitors' offices. Your letters from the moment you'd met, typed out, [copied] your letters to your mother, her letters to her mother, her mother's letters to me . . . I couldn't bear her to put a kind of tombstone on this marriage, reading in the way that that petition read.[49]

The fact Sandra had agreed to the petition, and helped compile it, illustrates the tough side to her character. She later explained, 'I had to be ruthless in order to be free, and because I had a child I particularly wanted to be free.'[50] When the divorce was granted, the judge did not dwell on the fact that Sandra had admitted misbehaviour herself – by implication adultery, though it was not spelled out.

Afterwards, Robin Douglas-Home fell into a quick decline, brought down by a dangerous cocktail of drink, sex and gambling, with violent men pursuing him for debts. He still kept a picture of Sandra on his dressing table, and regularly hounded his ex-wife with phone calls, demands to meet him, and pleas for help. 'He threatened to commit suicide on several occasions,' says a friend of Sandra, 'and she would go rushing down.' Yet somehow he continued to charm dozens of women into his clutches. One was the twenty-eight-year-old Elizabeth Harris, then wife of the actor Richard Harris (and later married to Rex Harrison, and currently to Jonathan Aitken). Douglas-Home had liaisons with several other women while seeing her, and would even ring them while in her company. Having never before been unfaithful to her husband, Harris later admitted, she now 'developed an intemperate passion for an entirely unsuitable man', and was persuaded into pawning much of her jewellery to pay off £2,000 of his gambling debts.[51]

Douglas-Home's most significant affair following his divorce was with Princess Margaret, for whom he had often acted as an escort in the 1950s, before her marriage to Antony Armstrong-Jones (later Lord Snowdon). By early 1967 the Snowdons' marriage was in deep trouble, and there were rumours that Margaret had attempted suicide. Her passionate affair with Douglas-Home lasted just thirty days, in February and March 1967, while Lord Snowdon was overseas, and was later substantiated publicly by two highly affectionate letters she wrote, one of them on Valentine's Day. But, facing the wrath of her husband, Margaret suddenly insisted they stop seeing each other. For the second time he had lost a princess called Margaret.

Early in 1967 Robin Douglas-Home cashed in on his past friendship with Jackie Kennedy by publishing in several different journals in Britain and America an extensive account of their encounters and conversations back in 1962 and 1963.[52] She and her friends saw it as a great betrayal. A few weeks later Douglas-Home also did a long television interview for an edition of the famous BBC series *Whicker's World*, entitled 'The Stresses of Divorce'. Millions of viewers saw him break down in tears as the presenter Alan Whicker asked him about Sandra's cruelty claims, and the programme was publicised around the world. 'It was the first time *upper class* tears had been seen on television,' Whicker later wrote.[53] It must have been hugely distressing for Sandra to see details of their marriage laid bare in such a manner, and yet she had also agreed to give her side of the story, explaining to Whicker how she'd had to point 'an accusing finger, and bring out old sordid things' against her ex-husband, because he seemed to have an 'anti-divorce phobia'.[54]

Alan Whicker says that after they filmed Sandra's interview his crew all 'agreed Robin must be a Right Bastard to have treated that lovely girl so badly – how could anyone be so Bloody Cruel?' Yet after talking to Robin Douglas-Home 'the crew all angrily wondered how that Spiteful Bitch could have been so calculating and ruthless to such a nice gentle guy'.[55]

When Whicker asked Douglas-Home what he now thought of Sandra, he said, 'I try not to think about her.'[56] The words might equally well have applied to Princess Margaret, and his depression got worse when he learned the Princess was seeing the actor Peter Sellers.

In 1968 came further humiliation when Douglas-Home fell in love, from afar, with the reigning Miss United Kingdom, Kathleen Winstanley. She was persuaded to visit his Hampshire home, on the pretext of his doing a freelance interview, whereupon, she said later, 'he started talking about his ex-wife. He seemed to want to talk about the marriage and how it had gone wrong. Then suddenly, he just looked at me and said, "I love you and I want to marry you."'[57] Winstanley rebuffed him, explaining that she already had a boyfriend back in Wigan.

There was no point in carrying on, Douglas-Home decided. 'Life has gone sour on me,' he said.[58] In October 1968, the night before he was due to enter a drugs rehabilitation clinic, he phoned four women – Elizabeth Harris, his mother, his sister, and also Sandra, who was about to leave for a business engagement with her second husband, David Wynne-Morgan. Sandra wanted to go to see Robin immediately, but Wynne-Morgan reminded her that it wasn't the first time he had threatened to commit suicide. Douglas-Home's mother was with him, and advised Sandra not to worry. 'So I didn't go, and I regret that,' she now says. 'That night he'd hidden some sleeping pills they'd given him as a sedative. His poor mother had to find him.'[59]

Robin Douglas-Home dictated a suicide note into a tape recorder: 'There comes a time when one comes to the conclusion that continuing to live is pointless.'[60] He then took an overdose of sleeping pills. They proved fatal.

He was thirty-six. It had been a short and self-destructive life. Douglas-Home had undoubted talents – as a pianist, as a photographer and as a writer – and he was starting to make money as a novelist. His second novel, *When The Sweet Talking's Done*, published a few months before he died, contains touches from his own life.[61] More autobiographical, in a rather macabre way, is *The Faint Aroma of Performing Seals*, which tells the story of a photographer who ends up murdering his son and wife.[62] Much of the detail of the novel appears to be drawn directly from his marriage to Sandra: the photographer comes from a landed family; his wife wears the family tiara at their wedding; as things turn sour they increasingly live apart; he has numerous mistresses including a married princess; his wife leaves to work in New York. Before the book's publication, three years after Douglas-Home's suicide, the publishers had publicly to assure Sandra that the wife in the story was not based on her. A fourth novel, about the Kennedys and Frank Sinatra, and entitled *Why Did I Buy Those Blue Pyjamas?*, remains unpublished. 'It's dynamite,' says Sholto Douglas-Home, who inherited the manuscript and believes it shows that his father did in fact have a sexual relationship with Jackie Kennedy.[63] When he read it, Sholto says, he realised that his father was 'telling the truth. The story recalls the relationship between an artist and an American First Lady. I'm sure all the conversations, the situations, the anecdotes are based on real facts. It was very much in my father's style to fictionalise a relationship rather than just revealing it.'[64] But Sholto says, 'Its ending is very sad, and poor compared with the quality of the rest of the writing. It's a shame, because I would like to adapt it for publication.'[65]

In 1970 Sandra took legal action on behalf of Sholto to stop Princess Margaret's letters to Douglas-Home being published in Britain. She succeeded, though they were later published abroad.

Sandra had married David Wynne-Morgan in 1966, having known him since the late 1950s. A former *Daily Express* reporter who now ran a successful London public-relations firm, he was also divorced. 'I think she married David to make some kind of home for Sholto,' says one of Sandra's closest friends, Dottie Bond.[66] The marriage did not get off to a good start. During the wedding reception Wynne-Morgan's beloved family dog ran out into the road and was killed by a car. Then, for their honeymoon, they got to Heathrow just on time, only to discover their plane was taking off from Gatwick.

Sandra helped her new husband with his business. According to Bond, who was a fellow model, 'She would sometimes turn up for work at nine o'clock practically in a cocktail dress and pearls, because she'd been hosting a breakfast meeting that morning. She was always very supportive in that way.'[67] Wynne-Morgan in turn helped Sandra do more journalism, and she wrote features for the *Sunday Express* – Sandra had 'lunched and dined regularly for several years' with the editor, John Junor, says Junor's daughter Penny.[68] For a while she also wrote a monthly column for *Harper's Bazaar* magazine; this mainly gave advice on what to wear, especially on foreign holidays. But Sandra was also determined to continue working as a model, and to stay at the top of her profession – partly to prove that Robin Douglas-Home had been wrong in claiming she succeeded only because of his family name. 'I understood that,' says Wynne-Morgan, 'but didn't want her to go on big overseas trips. She was making much more money than me. She was at the top of her profession. She was very keen on her career. I could see why.'[69]

This marriage lasted less than four years. 'I wasn't the best of husbands,' says Wynne-Morgan, who admits that he was unfaithful to her. 'It was my fault the marriage broke up. I found it difficult being at home alone when she was away on major modelling assignments.'[70] In 1970, when Wynne-Morgan returned from a trip to the Philippines, Sandra announced she was leaving, to go and live with Nigel Grandfield, the boss of an advertising business, who was also divorced. 'The next move was always in place,' Wynne-Morgan observes.[71]

In October 1971, still only thirty-one, she married for a third time. According to Dottie Bond:

> She was reasonably happy with Nigel Grandfield, but he couldn't have children – that was the position, which she didn't realise when she married him. It wasn't ideal. Her ambitions at that time – earlyish seventies – were to have more children, and she definitely wanted a good marriage. I think if she hadn't fallen in love with Michael she would have stayed with Nigel. It was an OK marriage, but Michael really swept her off her feet.[72]

When Michael Howard met Sandra in 1973, he knew that having a passionate affair with a married woman was perilous for a budding

Conservative politician, especially when the woman was a well-known public figure. 'I am very sad,' Nigel Grandfield told the *Sun* at the time. 'All our friends are upset. They thought it would be third time lucky for Sandra. I thought we had really found happiness together,' he said as she left the couple's Hampshire home to move in with Howard in Cheyne Walk.[73] 'My wife tells me she intends to marry Mr Howard. I will sue her for divorce and I intend to cite Mr Howard . . . I do feel very bitter about Mr Howard. I have met him once or twice and never imagined that this would happen. It came as rather a shock.'[74]

'I felt a huge amount of trepidation,' Sandra said recently. 'I was ending a marriage, which I hadn't really done before. I felt at fault and got into a bit of a muddle. I had a child to consider, and then there was the agony of telling my mother I was remarrying once more . . . And Michael's mother was pretty horrified that he wanted to take on someone with a past like mine, as well as a child, two cats and a dog.'[75]

She says that several of Michael's friends wrote and asked him if he was mad, suggesting he would last no longer than any of her previous husbands.

They married on the first day of August 1975, shortly after her divorce came through. It was a hot day and a quiet ceremony at Winchester Register Office. The reception was held at a small country cottage near Abbotsworthy in Hampshire, which the couple rented from Jennie Enfield, the mutual friend who'd taken Michael to the charity dance where he'd met Sandra two years earlier. Norman Lamont was best man (Howard having done the same for him four years earlier), and the guests were limited to close friends such as Leon Brittan, Peter Pagnamenta and John Entwistle. It didn't seem to matter that Sandra was not Jewish, though it perhaps helped that she boasted some Jewish ancestry.

Sandra Howard's three marriages had lasted roughly four years, three years and two years respectively. Michael Howard would joke that he'd done the arithmetic and the prospects did not look good. He knew it would take extra effort to make this one work, and it would be particularly difficult since Sandra had a twelve-year-old son.

The Howards' first child, a son, was born the following March, seven and a half months after they married. They named him after Michael's father, Bernard, though he would come to be known by his middle name, Nicholas, or Nick. 'Michael was present at the birth,' Sandra says. 'He changed smelly nappies and burped the little creature (reading *The Times* at the same time, so I was constantly having to clean up patches of sick on his shoulders).'[76]

Fourteen months later they had a girl, whom they called Larissa (named after Lara in *Doctor Zhivago*). Michael missed her birth because he was working late that night, at an evening session of the Archway inquiry.

Married and with young children, Sandra knew modelling could now only be an occasional occupation, and, not surprisingly, she was less in demand as she got older – though she aged better than many of her contemporaries.

All her former modelling colleagues are struck by how ambitious Sandra Paul was – not just for herself, but for her husbands. 'I think when she met Michael,' says one of them, 'and particularly when he went into politics, she thought, "Right, that's it." I think she had a plan.'

8

SOMEWHERE TO SIT

The Bow Group are just a bunch of arse-lickers really. Creepy little aspirant candidates who tremble at the thought . . . of someone Right Wing. And they have one other thing in common, namely that they want to enter Parliament.

ALAN CLARK, 1972[1]

The most difficult step, of all the rungs up the political ladder, is that of being picked for a winnable seat. It is the moment when the party activist turns into the professional politician. Being selected usually requires a considerable amount of persistence, and a fair amount of luck.

The outcome of the largely private selection system depends on the candidate's performance in front of a few hundred committed party members, whose political views tend to be very different from those of the electorate as a whole. Success can turn on a well-judged answer, the cut of one's suit, or the presence and presentability of one's wife or husband. Perhaps forty or fifty such selection opportunities come up for a mainstream party candidate in the four-year life of a typical British parliament.

The party selection processes are effectively Britain's hidden elections, largely unexplored by journalists or academics. In America the Democratic and Republican primary elections are high-profile events, which involve a substantial section of the electorate – those people registered as party supporters. In Britain the candidate chosen for a safe seat is lucky if his achievement gets a paragraph in the broadsheet papers. Yet in most British constituencies the private selection contest conducted by the dominant local party is much more important than the public parliamentary election which follows. Once chosen, and assuming no mishaps or boundary changes, a candidate picked for a safe seat can remain an MP for many years – until he or she retires, or dies.

For Michael Howard that critical step nearly proved beyond reach. And he had to watch as so many others achieved that goal before him.

During the early 1970s almost a dozen of his university contemporaries became MPs. Of the stars of the Cambridge Mafia, Ken Clarke, Norman Fowler and John Gummer were all elected to the Commons in 1970. Norman Lamont won a by-election two years later, while Leon Brittan was a bit of a straggler but still managed to enter the House in the election of February 1974. Less substantial figures had also been elected MPs by the middle of the decade – Christopher Tugendhat and Hugh Dykes in 1970; and Peter Temple-Morris, Peter Viggers, Nick Budgen and even the obscure Michael Latham in February 1974. Members of the Cambridge Mafia say that, in finding good seats, they were often spurred on by the success of their university colleagues. Given their record, it almost appeared as if seats could be found by anyone who cared to look. Except Michael Howard.

After 1966, the Edge Hill Conservatives had understood that he'd now want to find a seat which realistically he could win. But they felt he'd been a good candidate, and told Howard that if he failed to find a better constituency he was welcome to come back and fight Edge Hill again. It was a generous offer, and one which offered him a small chance of getting into Parliament ahead of his contemporaries. It was not the sort of thing to discuss in public, but Howard was aware, because of Arthur Irvine's illness on the eve of poll in 1966, that the sitting MP had heart problems. Edge Hill could face a by-election at any moment, and in this event Howard would almost certainly have been the Tory candidate. Given Labour's unpopularity for most of the

1966–70 parliament, and the extraordinary swings against the Wilson government in by-elections elsewhere, the Conservatives could well have won such a contest. (Labour did eventually lose Edge Hill, in a by-election in 1979, though by then the Tories were in such steep decline in Liverpool that the Liberals were the beneficiaries). For the time being, however, Irvine survived.

For the next four years Howard carried on calling himself the prospective candidate for Edge Hill, and even held regular surgeries there, while also looking for a better opportunity. His quest was unsuccessful. In the spring of 1969 he applied for the North Wales constituency of Conway, where Labour's majority was only 581. He was reasonably well qualified as a Welshman, and North Wales has close affinities with Liverpool. Conway, however, was a strong Welsh-speaking area, and its Labour MP spoke the language. Invited to the selection meeting, Howard tried to impress local Tories with a short, rehearsed passage in Welsh. This prompted one of his audience to ask a question in their native tongue. Despite having learned Welsh at school until he was fourteen, Howard was unable to answer. It was a humiliating moment – one he should have foreseen – and the Conway Tories chose the Welsh-speaking Wyn Roberts instead. A few months later Howard tried another constituency in North Wales, West Flint, which contained the seaside resorts of Rhyl and Prestatyn, and where the former minister Nigel Birch was retiring. West Flint was a much better prospect: a Tory seat which was even closer to Liverpool and contained far fewer Welsh-speakers. Howard reached the final short list, only to be beaten by Sir Anthony Meyer, who had previously been MP for Eton and Slough, and later achieved brief fame as the 'stalking horse' who challenged Margaret Thatcher in 1989. These were probably not the only constituencies for which Howard applied in the late 1960s, but his efforts were to no avail. After losing in West Flint, he decided his chances of a better seat at the next election were negligible; a few weeks later the Edge Hill Tories formally reconfirmed him as their candidate.

It must have been a demoralising experience fighting an even bigger majority in the same seat. By an amusing twist, his adversary in

Edge Hill had become deputy to Howard's boss. In 1967 Harold Wilson had appointed Irvine as Solicitor-General (whereby he became 'Sir Arthur'), under the Attorney-General Sir Elwyn Jones. But Howard treated the rematch seriously. He took a postal subscription to one of the Liverpool papers; he regularly drove up to visit the constituency (timing his trips to coincide with fixtures at Anfield); and he enjoyed the social scene on Merseyside and in north Cheshire. John Entwistle, who stood against Harold Wilson in nearby Huyton in the June 1970 election, recalls that they got publicity out of persuading the Mecca group to think again about closing the city's only skating rink, which involved them going down to London to see the Mecca boss, Eric Morley, who was himself a committed Conservative. A picture of the three men appeared in the Liverpool press, though the rink's closure was merely delayed until a few weeks after polling.

Halfway through the campaign Howard got so frustrated that he abandoned traditional door-to-door canvassing and adopted a more American style of electioneering. Michael Latham, who fought the neighbouring seat of Liverpool West Derby, recalls, 'He said to me he was absolutely fed up with just knocking on doors and people saying they wouldn't vote for him, or "I don't know," or whatever. He felt it was a waste of time and he was going to do a much more lively campaign. He would turn up in the streets, use a loudspeaker and say, "Here I am. Come and talk to me." Actually he did well.'[2] In 1966 Howard had suffered the worst anti-Tory swing in Liverpool, but this time Edge Hill was by far the best result for the Conservatives in the city, with a swing to the party of 5.8 per cent – above the national average. However, it wasn't enough to make Howard MP for Edge Hill, even if the Conservatives, under Edward Heath, did take power nationally.

Howard's prospects of persuading a Tory seat to adopt him in the near future had been boosted that spring by his election to the chairmanship of the Bow Group. The organisation took its name from the East End location where it had been founded in 1950 by Geoffrey Howe and others, with the aim of giving the Conservative Party more intellectual input, and to counter the image of the 'stupid party'.

It was conceived as the Tory equivalent of the Fabian Society, whose ideas had made a huge contribution to the 1945–51 Labour government. The Bow Group was not meant to represent any particular view within the party, though in time its leading members tended to be left-wing Conservatives, if keen on the free market. The right-wing Monday Club was founded in 1960 to redress the left-wing influence which the Bow Group was increasingly perceived to exert on Conservative ministers.

Members of the group also earned a reputation as careerists. A novel called *The Short List*, published in 1964 by the Conservative MP David Walder, features the loosely disguised 'Stepney Group'. 'Look my dear chap,' says Walder's fictional minister, when asked about the Stepney Group, 'all ginger groups are useful at first, then they start to die. The first signs of death are when the members start getting into the House of Commons. Then the rest of the Group becomes pompous and opinionated and people start to join who regard the Group as useful as an avenue to the House.'[3]

Michael Howard had belonged to the Bow Group since 1961, when he'd organised meetings of the Cambridge University branch. He was first elected to the Group's council – its governing body – in 1965, and thereafter he gradually rose though its network of committees and study groups to the leading posts of secretary and then political officer. There was an upper age limit of thirty-five on officer posts and, as in the Cambridge Union, people were usually not expected to hold the same office twice, and there was a gentlemanly atmosphere that often meant that people moved from one post to the next unopposed. Indeed, at times the Bow Group began to look like the Cambridge Union, with Leon Brittan, Norman Lamont, Hugh Dykes and Peter Lloyd among its other officers, and Ken Clarke playing a leading role in the Birmingham branch.

As chairman during the year which saw a new Conservative government, Howard was suddenly in a position to influence ministers, though he didn't always behave tactfully. Howard has told of how, in the summer of 1970, he drove the new Employment Secretary, Robert Carr, to a Bow Group meeting in central London. Unable to find a proper parking place, Howard left his car in a dubious spot in the middle of the wide road. 'Are you sure this is a good idea?' Carr asked nervously. 'Oh, don't worry,' Howard replied, 'no one will recognise you.' Then, realising his blunder, he added, 'Not this early in the term.'[4]

The Bow Group was a research body, and could have been expected to come up with ideas for the new government, but Howard seems to have taken little interest in such work. His only significant output was a handful of briefing papers, and these were no more than a few duplicated sheets. In every case he wrote them with other people. *Through a Glass Darkly*, written in 1968 with Norman Lamont, analysed Labour's policies. *The Greatest Claim*, published in July 1970, addressed the question of British Asian passport holders in Africa who wanted to come to Britain. It was Howard's first public pronouncement on immigration, though by no means his last, and he took a liberal line at a time when it was a highly charged issue in Tory politics; all four of his co-authors were left-of-centre Conservative MPs – Julian Critchley, Sir Anthony Meyer, Timothy Raison and David Walder. The party was still smarting from Enoch Powell's notorious 1968 'Rivers of Blood' speech (Howard had been 'amazed' at Powell's 'inflammatory' remarks, says John Entwistle, and backed Heath's decision to sack him from the Shadow Cabinet).[5] Tory MPs had split three ways over how to vote on Labour's Commonwealth Immigrants Act, which became law the same year. The act restricted immigration from Asian British passport-holders in Africa to a quota of 1,500 entries a year. Howard and his colleagues were not in favour of repealing the 1968 legislation, because this would cause an outcry; the 'social consequences of such a controversy would be too high a price to pay'.[6] However, they argued that the current 1,500 quota 'must be raised', and they proposed a clever measure to enable a lot more East African Asians to come to the UK. Under the 1962 Immigration Act, 8,500 work vouchers had been allocated to Commonwealth citizens who had jobs arranged in Britain and skills which were needed. But in 1969, the authors said, only 4,100 of these 8,500 work vouchers had been taken up. So why not reassign the rest to Asians who were being persecuted in Kenya and Uganda, even though strictly they might not qualify?

In both Kenya and Uganda British Asians were forbidden from running shops unless they were in prescribed urban areas, and even then they were restricted to certain goods – quite similar discrimination, in fact, to that which Jews had once suffered in eastern Europe. And all non-citizens in the two countries needed permits to take employment.

In 1971 Howard went further, accusing Conservative ministers of ignoring the plight of East African Asians in their proposed immigration bill. 'The Government has now had eight months to take action . . . The fact is that there are thousands of British citizens in East Africa suffering real hardship because they are British citizens.'[7] A year later the debate was overtaken by events, when the despotic Idi Amin expelled 50,000 Asians from Uganda, and Britain agreed to take more than half of them.

Howard's third publication, *A Tax on Inflation*, written with Julian Critchley, was only four pages long. It attempted to help the government confront the growing problem of inflation, at a time, the authors said, when it was 'generally agreed that it is incomes and their translation into costs which is the engine driving our inflation'.[8] In the era before monetarism became fashionable, ministers were pledged not to impose controls on wages and prices, but it didn't look as if voluntary restraint would work either. With the benefit of hindsight the paper has the hallmarks of the classic think-tank proposal: clever, but too complicated ever to get adopted by ministers. Inspired by the work of an American professor, Howard and Critchley proposed an Excess Wage Settlement Tax on firms which awarded wage increases beyond a percentage laid down by Whitehall. The authors argued that:

What is needed is a tax on inflation at source to make it more expensive for industrialists to yield to excessive wage demands. And by universality of application it would remove from firms the fear of being outflanked. Their competitors would all be in the same boat . . . Every conventional 'remedy' has been tried and failed. The method we suggest might work; it would limit the increases in costs which push prices upwards, and would control the income purchasing power which pulls prices higher. It's worth a try.[9]

In the autumn of 1970, in his capacity as Bow Group chairman, Howard wrote a rather belated public letter to Edward Heath congratulating him on 'a famous victory. It was to a very considerable extent a personal triumph and we are all greatly in your debt.' Although Howard warned, 'We shall be watching the Government carefully over the next few years,' he was careful also to compliment his party leader.[10] 'It is surprising', he told Heath, 'how some people have yet to grasp that the lack of hasty deeds from your Government is indicative of the fact that it is a Government which to an almost unprecedented extent is eschewing the shadow of gesture for the substance of premeditated action.'[11]

His letter focused on industrial relations – a professional interest of Howard's, of course, as well as being a huge political issue at the time – and the employment barrister caused headlines in broadsheet papers by suggesting that the government should withdraw state benefits from strikers, and not give them special treatment on tax rebates. 'Employees,' he said, 'no longer suffer various hardships when they withdraw their labour. Their strikes, both official and unofficial, are subsidised by the state. If workers wish to strike, let them do so at their own cost unaided by the state.'[12] It was a theme pursued in Howard's first speech to the Conservative Party conference a few days later. 'The immediate preferential payment of income tax rebates to strikers is a pernicious piece of nonsense, and it should stop,' he told representatives. There seemed to be 'what amounts to a conspiracy', he said, to speed up the payment of tax rebates to strikers so that they can get them immediately they go on strike. 'The rest of us have to wait for our rebates: strikers do not.'[13] His suggestions were ignored by the Heath government, though later adopted by Margaret Thatcher.

The period 1970–71 was also marked by the Tory government's renewed application for Britain to join the Common Market. The historian of the Bow Group, James Barr, has pointed out how committed the organisation was to the European cause during the late 1960s and early 1970s, including Howard's term as chairman.[14] Howard was to the fore in supporting Heath and his negotiator Geoffrey Rippon, though technically the Bow Group was not meant to take a 'corporate view' on policy matters. He invited two leading Europeans, Franz Josef Strauss of the Christian Social Union in Bavaria and the future French president Valéry Giscard d'Estaing, to speak at Bow Group meetings, though neither accepted. Howard and his friend Christopher Bland edited the Group journal *Crossbow*, and ensured that it took a strong pro-Common Market view. The Bow Group had strong ties with two pro-Europe bodies, the European Forum (which later became the Conservative Group for Europe) and the cross-party European Movement, which even subsidised the Bow Group's spring conference towards the end of Michael Howard's year. When the Bow Group published its pamphlet *Our Future in Europe*, putting the case for entry to the Common Market, there was no publication putting the counter view, in contrast to the time of the Macmillan government's European negotiations, a decade before, when the Group had published separate pamphlets from both viewpoints.

Between 1970 and 1973 Howard served on the committees of both the European Movement and the Conservative Group for Europe. He supported the 'Yes' campaign in the 1975 referendum on Europe, and Norman Lamont recalls Sandra wearing a pro-Europe T-shirt. But Lamont, who would later become a more fervent Euro-sceptic even than Howard, insists that their position then was not incompatible with their subsequent views. 'We thought Europe was purely an economic venture.'[15]

In 1971 Howard was part of a Bow Group party which visited their sister organisation, the Konrad Adenauer Stiftung in Germany. Another member of the group, John Butcher, recalls that 'We were collected in the evening by bus from Cologne/Bonn airport, and suddenly and mysteriously it turned off somewhere and stopped in this side road in the dark in the middle of nowhere. And we were all wondering what was happening. And this voice chirped up: "And

now we are all going to get shot!" It was Michael Howard. We all
laughed.'[16]

Later in the trip, the Bow Groupers visited Cologne cathedral
where, Butcher recollects, they saw an old woman lighting candles
and saying prayers: 'I indicated to Michael, "Isn't that pathetic?" And
he said, "But it means a lot to her." That made me think he was right,
and showed the kind of considerate person he is.' Butcher also recalls
that when he had been ill in Westminster Hospital a couple of years
before, Howard had been the only Bow Group colleague to go out of
his way to visit him.[17]

Despite being strongly pro-Common Market, and despite his Bow
Group activity, Howard had moved somewhat to the right since the
time at Cambridge when he couldn't decide if he was a Conservative
or a social democrat. His girlfriend from around 1971, Ann Mallalieu,
who had always seen herself as being on the right of the Labour Party,
says there was a huge gulf between their views. And whereas in the
1960s Howard had been a great admirer of the liberal Bobby Kennedy,
a 1971 analysis he wrote for *Crossbow* of the American political scene
suggested enthusiasm for President Nixon's tough views on welfare
reform, and an identification with Republicans in general – though
preferably liberal Republicans.[18] But he still kept pictures of the two
assassinated Kennedys on his wall.

Membership of the Bow Group reached 1,170 in 1971, its highest-
ever level, and Eric Koops, the treasurer that year, credits Howard with
a 'certain courage in getting to grips' with the Group's poor financial
situation. 'He was prepared to deal with it in a way his predecessors
were not.'[19] Yet Howard's term saw significant internal unease at the
way the Group was being run, and several critics circulated an anonymous letter entitled 'Crisis at the Bow Group?'. There was no
ideology involved, since the overwhelming majority of Bow Group
activists were on the left of the party, in line with Conservatives generally at that time, and could be termed Heathites. 'We identified very
much with Heath, and his meritocratic, efficient style of politics,' says
Norman Lamont.[20]

The dissidents felt, however, that the Bow Group's policy work had markedly declined, both in quality and in quantity. 'Neither journalists nor the Conservative Party are waiting with bated breath for definitive Bow Group statements,' one critic, David Weeks, observed in *Crossbow*, explaining that the Group preferred to exert influence by entertaining junior ministers in gentlemen's clubs. 'Many members have a strong feeling that the lunches with under secretaries are being used less to promote well-researched policies and more to oil political escalators for the Group's leading lights to climb to power.'[21]

The dissidents tended to be from red-brick universities and lived outside London. 'There was a sort of Cambridge clique who were running it,' says Weeks, 'of whom the two key figures were Howard and Lamont.'[22] Together with a few friends from Oxford and London, Cambridge men appeared to have carved up the leadership between them, and seemed always to nominate each other for the top jobs. It was widely understood that Howard would hand over the chairmanship to his flatmate Lamont, and that's what happened. There was also resentment over the way in which Howard used his office to speak for the whole organisation on policy matters when officially the Bow Group had no collective view.

The row came to a head at the Bow Group annual general meeting in April 1971 – the last event of Michael Howard's term of office – where, in order to block two critical motions, the council had to promise to improve the Group's public relations. Dissatisfaction with the leadership was also shown by the AGM's rejection of their proposals to raise subscriptions by almost 100 per cent over the next two years; they agreed to a 50 per cent increase instead.

The small dissident group were astonished, however, at the way in which Howard rounded on them. 'Rather than give the Bow Group annual general meeting a report on the Group for the previous year, he spent most of his time just attacking us,' says one critic, Pam Dyas. 'Looking at the man now, it is hard to believe that he should be so politically inexperienced as to give people so much importance. He was incensed that anybody should dare to stand up against him. By doing so he actually made himself considerably small. He didn't have a very wide view of what the Bow Group should be doing.'[23]

Leading the Bow Group for twelve months had undoubtedly raised Michael Howard's personal profile – though this may have been double-edged, since many Tory activists saw the Group as elitist, London-based intellectuals. 'Many think of the Group as an effete left-wing organisation whose members do academic research on political topics, but who do not like sullying their hands with canvassing,' David Weeks had commented.[24] Nor, around this time, would it have helped Howard in his quest for a seat if local Conservative associations had known that his girlfriend was Ann Mallalieu, the daughter of a socialist politician, who was looking to become a Labour candidate at the same time as he was trying to become a Conservative MP. She eventually stood in Hitchin in 1974. Had the couple remained together and Howard found a seat himself, it would have provided a great media story.

His search continued, with depressing results. In May 1972 he tried for Plymouth Sutton, where the other contenders at an early selection meeting included Alan Clark. 'I recognised Michael Howard,' Clark wrote in his famous diary, 'much plugged in the broadsheet press as *thrusting*, a barrister, a high-flier certain to enter the new Parliament, etc.' As Howard left the gathering, Clark says, a local party 'bigwig held him in "politician's grip"; one hand holding his, the other on Howard's elbow. Not necessarily a good sign, more usually an indicator of impending betrayal of some kind. However – "Well done," I overheard. "You'll be hearing from us very shortly . . ."'[25]

It was indeed a bad sign for Howard, and it was Alan Clark himself who triumphed from a short list which also included both David Hunt and his future Cabinet colleague Norman Fowler, who needed a new seat because of boundary changes. That summer it seems that Howard also applied to contest Gosport in Hampshire, but failed to reach the final short list. His CUCA colleague Peter Viggers got the nomination instead, and it must have been galling to learn that it was the first seat for which Viggers had applied. In December Howard reached the final three in the constituency of Thanet East in Kent (along with the future Chief Whip John Wakeham), only for Jonathan

Aitken to emerge triumphant. At least Howard admired Aitken, having predicted in the 1960s that he would one day lead the party.

Some suspect that being Jewish may have harmed Michael Howard's chances. This could also explain why Leon Brittan didn't get a good seat until 1974, for in those days contenders had to state their religion on the application form. Yet that should have been no problem in Brent North, in north-west London, which had a substantial Jewish population. In his CV for the contest, Howard mentioned making several appearances on TV – notably in a debate on pornography, where he spoke against the publisher of *Oz* magazine, Richard Neville, and the barrister John Mortimer. Howard stated his special interests as 'housing, Anglo–American relations, foreign affairs, industrial relations, [and] the environment with special reference to town and country planning'.[26]

At the February 1973 selection for Brent North, Howard was up against the elderly sitting MPs for the two old Wembley seats, Sir Eric Bullus and Sir Ronald Russell, in a fight for the single constituency created by the recent boundary review. Howard made it to the last four, but got only 54 votes compared with 204 gained by the victor, Rhodes Boyson, the eccentric Lancastrian headmaster of an inner-London comprehensive school, who was making waves as a right-wing maverick on education matters.

Towards the end of 1973, with an election likely during the following year, Howard's political prospects were not looking good. His great Cambridge rival Ken Clarke was already a member of the Heath government, albeit as a lowly junior whip, yet Howard was not close even to being an MP. Norman Fowler, meanwhile, had found himself a second seat – rock-solid Tory Sutton Coldfield. But Howard refused to give up.

Suddenly, in December 1973, a promising chance appeared. The sitting Tory MP for Tonbridge, Richard Hornby, unexpectedly announced that he'd got a new job, and so he couldn't fight his seat, now reorganised as Royal Tunbridge Wells, at the coming election. Central Office urged local Conservatives to find a new candidate quickly. The country was in crisis. The government was about to institute a three-day week because of the miners' strike, and Heath was contemplating a quick election on the question of who ran the country – the unions or elected politicians?

Howard applied immediately, though he knew the selection process might be difficult since he was busy on the Isle of Man working on the long Summerland inquiry. It was also possible that details of the affair he had just started with Sandra Paul might soon seep out. Yet, since many of the strongest names on the Conservative candidates list had already found seats, Howard surely had a fair chance. And what was a more typical Conservative seat than Royal Tunbridge Wells?

The selection took only a few days in mid-January. On a Monday and Tuesday evening fourteen people were interviewed at the local Spa Hotel. Howard was one of three who were invited back to the local Conservative offices on the Wednesday, when the party would make its choice. At least now the fact that he was a London barrister could hardly be a handicap, since each of the three finalists practised at the London bar (all eventually became QCs). His rivals were Anthony Lloyd, who later became an Appeal Court Judge; and the future Northern Ireland Secretary Patrick Mayhew, who hadn't even been on the party's long list – his name had been added only when some-body else dropped out.

According to the minutes, Howard was thrown some tricky ques-tions – on the policies of Enoch Powell (who was about to leave the Tories), on how Britain should handle its rebel colony of Rhodesia, and on the fruit industry, which was an important part of the local economy.[27] Lloyd was eliminated in the first ballot, leaving a contest between Mayhew and Howard. Mayhew had the advantages of both living in the constituency and being accompanied by his wife, and Howard could hardly take Sandra as his escort since she was married to someone else. The margin of Mayhew's victory was never formally made public. All officials would say was that the contest had been extremely close. In fact the two candidates had tied among the seventy-strong selection committee, and the chairman cast his deciding vote for Mayhew.

Had Howard persuaded just one more member of the Tunbridge

Wells Conservatives, he would probably have been elected MP for the
Kent constituency at the general election six weeks later. If so, he
could reasonably have expected to have become a junior minister
when the Conservatives returned to power under Margaret Thatcher
in 1979, as Clarke, Brittan, Fowler and Lamont all did, as well as
Patrick Mayhew himself. (Indeed, Clarke and Mayhew were among
only five people to hold office throughout the whole eighteen years of
Thatcher and John Major, along with Malcolm Rifkind, Tony
Newton and Lynda Chalker.)

Although Royal Tunbridge Wells was a solidly safe seat, it is only
probable that Howard would have become its MP had he been selected.
Only three weeks later – and two days before Heath called the election – details of his relationship with Sandra Paul emerged in the
Sun, along with Nigel Grandfield's bitter accusations of adultery. In an
election campaign, the story of the Conservative candidate for
Tunbridge Wells having an affair with a famous, glamorous married
model would have been too good for the tabloids to resist. Howard's
political aspirations could well have been derailed. One can imagine
that the Tories of Royal Tunbridge Wells would have been dismayed,
if not disgusted.

The public exposure of his relationship with Sandra Paul certainly
scotched any hope of standing in the second general election of 1974,
or in any of the few seats that became available between the two polls
of February and October that year. He would have to wait until he
and Sandra were happily married and Nigel Grandfield had calmed
down.

Michael Howard's close friends often claim that for a long period
after marrying Sandra he withdrew altogether from the process of
trying to find a parliamentary seat. Instead, they say, he put all his
effort into making sure that this time Sandra's marriage worked, into
looking after his two young children and his teenage stepson,
Sholto, and into developing his practice at the Bar. This is a bit of an
exaggeration. True, Howard did devote a lot of time to his marriage
and family. He regularly took Sholto to the races, and also to football.
(Unlike Howard, Sholto is a Manchester United fan, partly because he

got to know George Best, a friend of his mother during the swinging sixties. Howard treated him like his own son. Sholto says:

> He would always take a close interest in what I was doing. He'd say, 'Where do you want to go to dinner on your birthday?' He was very sensitive to seeing how to be a stepfather, and doing the right thing. I would play football with him, and he would take me to see my team, Manchester United, whenever they were playing nearby. He was very, very good at disengaging from his work and playing things like Subbuteo and backgammon for an hour or so. He would use me as a healthy distraction from his work. We used to book the public courts in Winchester to go and play tennis on Sunday mornings. Then after that you wouldn't see him for hours. But Michael could also work in the same room while the football was on TV, or racing, and he would carry on with his legal work, despite the TV being loud in the background. Then he would break away and watch the 2.40 from Newbury – not least because he would probably have had a bet.[28]

Sholto admits that his stepfather could have a 'volatile temper over seemingly insignificant issues', though it quickly subsided. He learned to ignore 'short-lived eruptions over such minor matters as a door being left open or the TV not being turned off when coming to the dinner table'.[29] Howard could be a stickler for rules – the car-parking incident with Robert Carr notwithstanding. He wouldn't take Sholto to *Saturday Night Fever,* he said, as it had an 'X' certificate – adults only. 'So Mum said, "I'll take you, and we'll tell him we went to something else." Michael is always very proper.'[30]

But politics was never far from Howard's thoughts. During a summer break in the Balearic Islands in 1976, Sholto Douglas-Home says, 'The whole holiday was dominated by "Do I, Don't I?" over whether my stepfather should again go for a parliamentary seat.' Howard pointed out that being an MP would mean he would make a lot less money. 'There are pros and cons – would you support me?' Sholto recalls him asking. 'He involved me as much as my mother in the discussion about whether to become an MP. I remember I was quite touched by that discussion. It showed how thoroughly he had thought it through.'[31] They agreed he should try again.

In the autumn of 1976, barely a year after his marriage to Sandra, and six months since the birth of his son, Nicholas, he applied for Huntingdon, one of the safest Tory seats in Britain. Howard sailed through the first two rounds, but failed to make the final short list of four. He was in good company, since Chris Patten and Peter Lilley were also rejected. Huntingdon Tories eventually chose a thirty-three-year-old PR man with a City bank called John Major.

Howard's lack of progress began to look worrying. 'If you'd asked me in about 1976 or 1977 whether I'd get there, I'd have answered probably not,' he later revealed.[32] In the past, Wyn Roberts, Sir Anthony Meyer, Alan Clark, Rhodes Boyson and Patrick Mayhew had all been at least a dozen years older than him; now he was starting to lose to contenders who were younger, and who on paper looked less impressive. John Major was two years his junior, and, while Howard had been starring in Cambridge politics and touring America as one of Britain's top debaters, the young Major had been unemployed and drifting, with just a few O-levels to his name.

The next evidence of Howard seeking a seat comes just over two years later, during the 1979 'winter of discontent'. This time, in West Derbyshire, he made the three-man short list only to be beaten by Matthew Parris, who was then an aide to the Conservative leader, Margaret Thatcher, and who had been invited only because another contender, Peter Lilley, was excluded after a bureaucratic blunder. It was probably Howard's last chance of a seat before the 1979 general election, and his failure was a blow, especially since Parris was eight years his junior. Nor can it have helped Howard's self-confidence to see the election to Parliament that year of David Mellor, even though he was a good friend. Like Parris, Mellor belonged to a later generation at Cambridge, and as a young barrister he had even squatted at a small desk in Howard's room in Lamb Buildings after the chambers refused to award him a permanent place.

There were only two years between the selections in Huntingdon
and West Derbyshire, which suggests that if, as his friends claim,
Howard gave up looking for a while, he did not do so for long. It is
quite probable that he applied for other seats in between these two
contests. Nevertheless, it may be that Howard's quest for a seat was less
wholehearted during this period. Perhaps because of his new family,
and the pressure of work, and growing demoralisation with each failure, he applied for fewer seats, or did not put in enough effort each
time. 'I wasn't exactly single-minded about politics at that time,' he
subsequently admitted.[33]

The fascinating question is *why* Howard was failing so repeatedly.
He clearly had many good qualities. At the same time, such contests
are always something of a lottery, and selection committees can be
capricious. Matthew Parris says that in West Derbyshire 'by common
assent' Howard made the best speech:

> He was charming and fluent. He was obviously extremely clever.
> He had gone to some trouble to brief himself about the con-
> stituency and its special problems. The skill with which he answered
> questions was little short of dazzling – but in a barristerial sort of
> way. His wife, Sandra, wowed the association. But a minority
> thought that he sounded rather too much the London lawyer;
> while a handful (no more) had been muttering about his being
> Jewish.[34]

Parris says that some party officials later admitted to him that they
didn't vote for Howard because he was Jewish. But while this could be
taken as evidence of anti-Semitism harming him, several other Jews
had been selected for winnable seats – most notably Nigel Lawson and
Malcolm Rifkind – even if anti-Semitism was probably greater in the
rural Midlands than it would have been in a major city or the south-
east. What's more, Howard was never noticeably Jewish anyway.
While in private he observed the Jewish high holy days and lit a
candle on the anniversary of his father's death, it is striking how often
people who dealt with him didn't even know he was Jewish.

As for the barrister image, that problem too was probably confined to the more agricultural seats. Parris was hardly a tractor-driving rustic, even if the West Derbyshire Tories would almost certainly have rejected him had they known he was homosexual. Perhaps Howard suffered, unlike the dishevelled Ken Clarke for example, for *looking* too much like the clever London barrister, dressed in his black pinstripe suit and the shirts with fashionably wide stripes which he liked at that time. Matthew Parris adds, 'I think it is this almost unnatural fluency – this lawyerliness about him – that people react against. They don't like someone to sound like a lawyer . . . People think that he's slippery . . . because he talks like a lawyer . . . but he's not slippery. He's remarkably straight for a politician.'[35]

So Howard had to sit out the May 1979 election – his third in a row. As Margaret Thatcher reached Downing Street, it was almost nine years, and three changes of government, since Howard had even been a candidate. The Edge Hill campaigns on his CV were starting to look like history. Nor had Howard been active politically in other ways since stepping down as Bow Group chairman in 1971. He had not produced any further pamphlets for the Group, or for the Conservative Research Department. He hadn't written newspaper articles; he did not craft speeches for Mrs Thatcher or other senior Tories; and he hadn't spoken at the party conference since 1970. Nor, unlike some aspiring politicians, had he served as a Conservative councillor, and he seemed unlikely to. The only other political lines on his CV for the 1970s were the chairmanship in 1972–3 of the Coningsby Club, a dining group for Conservative Oxbridge graduates which holds regular black-tie dinners at Westminster, and membership of the political committee of the upmarket Carlton Club, which involved raising money for the party and arranging programmes of lunchtime speakers. To the local Conservative associations who actually chose the party's candidates, it must have begun to appear that Howard's only political activity was his opportunistic hunt for a safe seat. It almost looked as if he were sulking, suggesting that if no one was going to select him he didn't see why he should help the party in other ways.

This meant that Michael Howard was on the sidelines during the party's radical transformation of the late 1970s. 'He wasn't there in the early days of Margaret,' says the former treasurer of the Bow Group, Eric Koops. 'Michael Howard never played a major role in the mainstream of the new thinking of the Conservative Party.' Howard was not one of Thatcher's early foot soldiers, and did no work for Thatcherite think-tanks such as the Centre for Policy Studies or the Institute for Economic Affairs. 'He didn't have any relationship with Margaret,' adds Koops, who briefly worked for Thatcher during that period. 'He was never "one of us". I know he was quite a loner.'[36]

Yet Howard continued pursuing his Westminster ambitions, and during the 1979–83 parliament he applied to fight at least two by-elections. Trying for selection as a by-election candidate is a gamble: it has the advantage of being quick, since one can become an MP within a few weeks; on the other hand it is also extremely risky, since by-election votes are very unpredictable. In Crosby on Merseyside, where the Tory majority was 19,272, he was not even considered by the local party, despite the fact that the seat was only a few miles from Edge Hill. Instead they chose his Bow Group colleague John Butcher, who acknowledges that Howard would have been a stronger candidate. But not fighting Crosby for the Conservatives was fortunate. Despite their huge majority, the Tories lost the November 1981 by-election to the newly formed Social Democratic Party (SDP). Given his past interest in the Campaign for Democratic Socialism, it is perhaps not surprising that around this time Howard should have been asked to join the fledgling SDP. 'I was approached,' he admitted years later, but he replied that he was still firmly a Conservative.[37] The fact that Howard was even considered by the party of Roy Jenkins and Shirley Williams suggests he was not seen at that time as quite the full-blooded Thatcherite he later became.

Crosby occurred during a period of Thatcher's unpopularity and of public support for the SDP, whose candidate, Shirley Williams, was hugely popular; any Conservative was likely to have lost, no matter how talented. If Howard had fought the seat he might have been ir-retrievably labelled as a 'loser'; Butcher certainly never fought another one. Politics is cruel, and candidates who unexpectedly lose safe seats in by-elections are rarely given another chance.

Howard didn't see it that way, of course. 'I would have given my eye-teeth to be selected there,' Butcher recalls him saying afterwards.[38] 'I would have won that seat,' he later told another aspiring MP.[39] It was now so long since Howard had been a candidate that this was becoming a handicap in itself, rather like houses which have been on the market for so long that potential buyers begin to ask *why* they haven't sold. He was so disheartened not even to be considered in Crosby that Norman Lamont tried to help him out by going to see the newly appointed Conservative Party chairman, Cecil Parkinson. Parkinson recollects Lamont explaining why Howard hadn't fought a seat since 1970:

> He had married a beautiful woman and he had wanted to make the relationship work. Michael Howard had been acutely aware that Sandra's previous husbands had all fallen by the wayside one way or another, and he didn't want to risk having the same experience. He had been well aware that his Cambridge friends were getting ahead of him on the ladder, but his private life was more important to him.[40]

If Parkinson is correct, then Lamont's account was plainly an over-simplification of what had happened, as the Tory chairman would have seen had he consulted Howard's Central Office candidate file and noticed his many failed applications. Lamont confirms that he did meet Parkinson, but he seems to have been badly briefed about Howard's history, for he was later surprised to learn how many times his friend had applied for selection since 1970. Parkinson told Lamont that he 'could help in a background way', but said that any suggestion that Howard was a 'favoured Central Office candidate . . . was likely to rebound against him'.[41]

In Beaconsfield in Buckinghamshire, where Howard applied for the 1982 by-election, he failed again to secure even a place on the local party's long list of forty names, let alone an interview. Tim Smith was chosen as the candidate instead. By then the SDP bubble had burst; Britain was in the midst of the Falklands War, and Smith was easily elected. Had Howard been picked as the Tory nominee it would have provided a foretaste of battles to come, since Labour's man in Beaconsfield was the thirty-year-old Tony Blair, fighting his first campaign. Tim Smith eventually had to give up politics in 1997 over the 'cash for questions' affair, but he could console himself with the distinction of having brushed aside both Michael Howard and Tony Blair to win his place in Parliament.

Simultaneously with Beaconsfield, a contest also took place in the Kent constituency of Folkestone and Hythe, where the MP, Sir Albert Costain, was retiring. For Michael Howard the seat had several attractions. Costain's 16,020 majority made it safe. The area also had historic Jewish ties: when the constituency was known simply as Hythe it had elected three MPs who were Jews, including the Conservatives Sir Edward Sassoon (1899–1912) and his son Sir Philip (1912–39).

While the ferry terminal of Folkestone was pretty unattractive, the seat had other features to commend it: the chalk cliffs above the Channel; the ancient town of Hythe, which, along with Romney, was one of the medieval Cinque Ports; the Romney Marsh of *Great Expectations* fame, and its Norman flint churches; the narrow-gauge Romney, Hythe and Dymchurch Railway; the beautiful Elham valley, and some of England's most glorious rolling grassland. The constituency also contained Saltwood Castle, the moated home of Alan Clark, who'd had his eye on the seat for years. Much of Clark's diaries from 1974 to 1982 are taken up with his ambition to ditch his Plymouth seat in favour of Folkestone; he didn't get on with his constituency activists, and was fed up with the long journeys. Clark lobbied hard and formally applied for Folkestone and Hythe, but eventually realised that it would be almost impossible to switch seats without offending people in both places, as well as attracting disapproval in Westminster.

Folkestone party officials whittled down 252 applicants to 25, who were invited for interviews. The second stage involved six contenders, all of whom later became MPs. Tim Smith (who was about to be chosen for Beaconsfield anyway) was eliminated, along with Robert Atkins and Bill Cash, leaving Howard to compete with Marion Roe, a member of the Greater London Council, and Michael Lord, who made his living as an expert on trees and landscaping.

Sir Albert Costain, whose family owned the Costain construction firm, had been a popular, avuncular MP, but was a poor speaker who rarely said anything in the Commons, and lacked ambition. 'He was quite content to be a backbencher – almost like a pre-war-type phenomenon,' says Peter Rees, the neighbouring member.[42] He'd been selected twenty-five years earlier precisely because he clearly wasn't interested in ministerial office, and would devote himself to Folkestone. Michael Howard could hardly take that approach. Local activists could see he would go far, and some worried that he might neglect them. Did they really want an MP who was going to be in the Cabinet? Wouldn't it be better to have someone like Sir Albert again? But the prevailing mood was for a change of style: to opt for an MP who might make a name for himself, and put Folkestone on the map.

The final selection, involving more than 400 party members, took place at Folkestone School for Girls on 4 June 1982. It was a hot Friday evening – 'about eighty degrees', says the agent George Bunting: 'one of the hottest days of that summer'.[43] In the South Atlantic, British troops were pushing for victory in the Falklands. At home it was only eight weeks since Michael Howard had been made a QC. Could he finally add two more initials as well?

Marion Roe was favourite. She'd been down to Folkestone and Hythe to speak to party members long before the selection process began, and had got to know the area. Roe had also polled strongly in the early rounds. 'There was a lot of lobbying going on for her from the Young Conservatives,' says David Crowthorn, a former party official who later joined Labour. But Howard performed better on the night, he says:

> I do remember he was very pro-Europe, because the constituency
> depended on quotas and Romney Marsh is a big farming area, and

they rely on fishermen in Hythe and Folkestone. He didn't take a very right-wing stance. It was all quite 'consensus'. He didn't attack the Labour Party, whereas Marion Roe was a lot more attacking of what would happen if Labour got back in. And also everyone liked Mr Howard's wife. I think she won a few of the army majors over. Mrs Roe's husband was quite a bigwig with Rothschild's and I think that put off quite a few of the rural types – he was there in his pinstripe suit. But none of the spouses spoke.[44]

'Sandra was looking absolutely fabulous,' says another activist, John Palmer, who thinks Michael Howard captured people's imagination. 'I think everyone realised we were starting a new era with a new MP. He was very fluent. I think there was this atmosphere that he was a very clever chap and we were going to have a different style to Albert Costain.'[45]

While Marion Roe had strong support among members from Hythe, she seems to have been less popular in Folkestone. 'Folkestone was full of a lot of old fuddy-duddies, who lived in the smarter part of town – most of them were colonels or had double-barrelled names. I think the thought of a woman being selected for Folkestone and Hythe was a bit abhorrent to them.'[46] 'There was an anti-women feeling at that time,' agrees party member Eileen Bailey, 'and it seemed to come from the other women. Some of the queen bees said, "Oh, we couldn't possibly have her – she wears high heels."'[47]

Having suffered occasionally from anti-Semitism in the past, Michael Howard now benefited from grass-roots sexism. He won on the first ballot, with what George Bunting reckons was 'well in advance of 60 per cent of the vote'. And sexual discrimination of a different kind gave his candidacy an extra glitter. 'It was rather strange,' says Bunting. 'On the day before, a couple of elderly ladies, who had kept magazines for some years, suddenly rooted them out and brought in photographs of Sandra Howard.'[48]

Howard's success may have come just in time. 'He'd practically given up,' says his close friend Christopher Bland. 'I would guess if he hadn't got Folkestone he would have called it a day, and he'd been close to doing that before. I remember him saying he was not going to go on much longer.'[49] It's hard to believe that Howard would have continued his search beyond the 1983 election and into another parliament, especially when he was now suddenly earning so much as a planning silk.

The quest had taken Michael Howard sixteen years. Since the Edge Hill Tories first advised him to look for somewhere better, he'd tried more than forty winnable seats. He'd enlisted the help of friends, visited places throughout England and Wales, researched their histories and topography, and had his hopes raised, and then dashed. It must have seemed so unfair. As the loyal Jewish son, he had delayed getting married but had then been the victim of anti-Semitism; he was a devoted husband but had been tainted by scandal; he'd worked hard to become a successful lawyer, but lost votes because of his image as a slick London barrister. He was intelligent, eloquent and witty, but perhaps too clever, too articulate and too inclined to put people down with a sarcastic, cutting remark. On at least one occasion he'd lost by a single tantalizing vote.

Now – if elected, which seemed almost certain – he would be representing a stretch of England only a few miles from the spot where, less than half a century before, his father had first set foot in this country.

Persistence had finally paid off.

9

IN AT LAST

Michael was a formidable opponent, an intelligent man with a
barrister's ability to master a brief.

BRYAN GOULD, FORMER LABOUR SPOKESMAN[1]

'I was sitting on the floor, leaning on Michael's knee,' recalls Vivaria
Gover. The Folkestone activist had invited Tory colleagues back to her
home to celebrate the election result with champagne, but had run
out of chairs for her guests. 'All of a sudden he clenched his fist and
bashed it on the arm of the chair, and said, "I'm in! I'm in!"' That
night, 9 June 1983, Michael Howard had finally been elected to the
House of Commons. 'No one else registered it,' Gover says, 'but I
thought it was rather sweet – like a small boy who's won the prize.'[2]

On a night of national success for the Conservatives, Michael
Howard had won more votes than his predecessor, Sir Albert Costain,
and a larger share of the poll, even if the Conservative majority in
Folkestone of 11,670 was down by more than 4,000. Many Labour
voters had switched to the Liberals, who had fought that election in
alliance with the SDP. Nationally, Margaret Thatcher had been re-
elected with an overall majority of 144. The result was regarded as a
personal triumph for the Prime Minister, and set the tone for Michael
Howard's first parliament.

Until the Falklands War, there had been good reason for ambitious

MPs to hedge their ideological bets, unless they were genuinely committed to the principles of 'Thatcherism'. In its early years, her government had been hugely unpopular, as its monetarist policies had caused recession and unemployment. But any Tory elected for the first time in 1983 had a strong incentive to accept the leadership line on all the main issues of British politics. Howard was now almost forty-two. The years spent searching for a seat left him hurrying to catch up with his Cambridge peers. For any new and ambitious MP, the only career path was to sign up to full-blooded Thatcherism, and to keep quiet about any misgivings.

Years later Howard remembered during his first few days in the Commons 'looking round the lobby at all these new members – most of whom were younger than I was – and thinking, "It's going to be jolly difficult to make much of an impression here."'[3] He was one of 101 new Conservative MPs in 1983, but as a QC, and a known member of the Cambridge Mafia, he was immediately identified as 'one to watch'. Roger King, the new MP for Birmingham Northfield, remembers that during that hot summer new members sat on the Commons terrace 'eyeing the potential runners and riders'.[4] Howard was seen as a safe bet for early promotion. 'There was a general acceptance amongst the new intake that he was incredibly able,' says Robert Hayward, who, like King, later became Howard's parliamentary private secretary (PPS). 'He had the assurance of somebody who was going to make progress.'[5] King observed that the class of 1983 quickly divided into cliques. When they were not in the chamber, he and his friends were to be found in the Commons tearoom. Howard, on the other hand, was definitely a member of the more exclusive dining-room set. This informal segregation was partly a matter of financial resources, but it also reflected ambition. In the dining room, a new MP was far more likely to catch a minister's eye.

In this respect, Howard was off to a flying start. Most of the other members of the Cambridge Mafia were already ministers. Two of them, Norman Fowler and Leon Brittan, were in the Cabinet, and Brittan, in particular, looked a promising patron, since he had just succeeded William Whitelaw as Home Secretary. But relying on his

Cambridge friends for promotion would only cause resentment. Howard would have to prove himself as a parliamentary performer in his own right, and he took the first opportunity to do so – in the debate on the Queen's Speech. He referred to the tradition that a maiden speech should steer away from party controversy, but also reminded MPs that 'as a practising barrister of nearly twenty years' standing I cannot pretend to be a stranger to controversy'.[6] The content tested the limits of parliamentary etiquette.

His main demand was for further trade union reform, specifically to outlaw the closed shop. Although, he said, the Conservative Party had taken big steps to redress the balance of power in the workplace, it was still possible for workers to lose their jobs if they refused to take part in a strike, without 'any of the compensation or other remedies generally available at law for a worker who is unfairly dismissed'. His remarks were bound to provoke Labour MPs. He then attacked the Liberal leader David Steel for having expressed sympathy with 'the creation of a federal European state', and hoped that the voters of Folkestone and Hythe would continue to return him to a Commons that 'has not been shorn of its powers'. In closing, he quoted from a speech by Lord Denning which had appealed for greater clarity in legislative language.[7]

As a piece of self-promotion, Howard's maiden speech could hardly have been better judged. He managed to agree with Margaret Thatcher on important questions such as Europe and the unions, while advertising himself as an experienced lawyer who could scrutinise every line of a bill before it went through.

One test of a maiden speech is the number of complimentary remarks by MPs in the subsequent debate. Judged by that standard, Howard's effort was far from a classic. Labour's Jim Craigen complimented the delivery, if not the content, but Howard was not singled out for praise by any other speaker.

Howard had been quicker off the mark than another of the 1983 newcomers. The thirty-year-old Labour MP for Sedgefield said nothing in the Queen's Speech debate. Tony Blair didn't make his maiden contribution until a few days later, by which time Howard had already spoken a second time. But before long the pair would regularly be confronting each other across the chamber.

In November 1983 Tony Blair launched a fierce attack on the government's new Trade Union Bill. Even though he was later to accept the Conservative union reforms almost in their entirety, Blair claimed that the second part of the bill elevated 'hypocrisy into an art form'. There was 'an overt and blatant political bias', he declared, because unions would be forced to hold a ballot before they gave money to the Labour Party, while no restrictions whatsoever were placed on company donations to the Conservatives. It was a 'scandalous and undemocratic measure', Blair said, and a 'shabby, partisan stratagem'.[8]

As yet, no one had challenged Blair during a debate. But this was too contentious to go unanswered, and the Employment Secretary, Tom King, intervened halfway through Blair's speech. The Labour tyro brushed him aside, telling him that before he interrupted 'he should at least have the courtesy to read his bill properly'. At this point Michael Howard jumped to his feet with a further objection, whereupon Blair coolly claimed that Howard and King had made contradictory points. He implied that Howard at least understood the bill, though this compliment was somewhat backhanded, since it was made at the expense of a senior minister.

Less than half an hour later Howard spoke in the same debate, expressing disappointment that the bill did not abolish the closed shop. By a neat piece of symmetry, the first backbench Labour MP to intervene in a Michael Howard speech in the Commons was Tony Blair – the shape of things to come. Sadly, the Commons was not yet televised, so no film exists of these early clashes between tomorrow's men. The printed account of the debate suggests that they saw themselves as the leading advocates for their different positions – that these two barristers (both employment specialists) were the only MPs who really understood the issues at stake and had enough wit to express their views.[9] Their impatience to interrupt each other suggests a desire to clear the arena of mediocrities and begin the real battle in earnest.

The sparring freshmen had much in common. Each might easily

have ended up in the opposite party, and had parents who had once been active on the other side – one might say they had both betrayed their backgrounds. They each had dynamic high-powered wives; they shared a love of popular music, and had each entertained the teenage dream of being a pop singer and guitar-player. They'd both read Law at university, but each expressed regret at not reading History.[10] Not only had they both been employment barristers, by a strange quirk they had been the protégés of heads of chambers who went on to become successive Labour Lord Chancellors – Elwyn Jones and Derry Irvine.

Despite their political differences, Michael Howard wanted to meet his youthful opponent in a less confrontational setting, and he and Sandra invited Tony and Cherie Blair to dinner at their home in Notting Hill, along with Norman Lamont and his wife, Rosemary. One of Blair's biographers, John Rentoul, dates the occasion to around 1990; Lamont, in contrast, is adamant that it was within a few months of the 1983 election, and his former wife agrees.[11] Howard suggested the idea, Lamont says, 'because he was anxious to try to ascertain why on earth Tony, all appearances to the contrary, claimed to be a socialist'. After the meal – which the three husbands, at least, enjoyed – Lamont and Howard decided that Cherie was the reason for Blair's commitment to Labour: 'She was rather more severe than she is today and also more left-wing than Tony.'[12] Howard's stepson, Sholto, who popped in towards the end, recalled that she said little, but 'the moment Tony Blair had put his coffee cup down, Cherie said, "Right, we're off."'[13]

Howard was never likely to become a favourite with Blair's Labour colleagues. Ten days after their duel over trade-union policy, he spoke in a debate on a backbench bill on sickness and disability. The Opposition was convinced that the government whips had organised an attempt to kill the bill, and the mood in the chamber was ugly. Howard made the last speech from the government benches, and ran into a barrage of hostile comments. Before he had even got into his stride, Merlyn Rees, the former Labour Home Secretary, muttered, 'This is the worst speech I have heard in twenty years.'[14] In a later debate, Labour's John Fraser dubbed Howard 'Creep of the Year'.[15] Howard was not afraid to mix it with Labour's big-hitters, clashing in his first few months with Denis Healey and John Smith, who denounced him as a government 'apologist' in a debate on union rights at the spy communications centre, GCHQ.[16]

Riling senior Opposition figures was unlikely to harm Howard's prospects. His interest in unions was topical, and about to become more so because of the 1984–5 miners' strike, which dominated that period. It won him an early appointment as vice-chairman of the Conservative backbench committee on employment, and he also became joint secretary of the party's legal committee.

In February 1984, after just eight months as an MP, he was appointed PPS to the Solicitor-General, Sir Patrick Mayhew. It was not the most onerous of jobs – the government's law officers rarely need much help in the Commons, or reports on how MPs are thinking – but Howard was one of the first of the 1983 intake to be made a PPS. Mayhew, who had beaten him so narrowly in the selection for Tunbridge Wells a decade before, was pleased to have the services of 'a sound lawyer as well as a sensible politician'. Howard was 'clever; he was nice; he had good judgement', he says.[17] Mayhew was a good spotter of high-flyers: before 1983 his PPS had been John Major.

It was just as well it was not an onerous job. At the end of 1982, before his election to Parliament, Howard had been appointed as one of the leading counsel on the planning inquiry into the government's proposed new nuclear power station at Sizewell on the Suffolk coast, known as Sizewell B. The inquiry was an enormous operation, largely because the power station was seen as marking a new phase in the development of nuclear energy in Britain, and Sizewell B would be the UK's first pressurised water reactor. It turned out to be the longest public inquiry ever held; it lasted two and a quarter years, sat for 340 days, and heard from 195 witnesses, and the resulting report by the inspector Sir Frank Layfield ran to eight volumes.

Although no one foresaw that the inquiry would be quite so extensive, Howard must have realised when it began at the start of 1983 that it would clash with his future duties as an MP. He was keen, however, to pick up the large fees. He knew that politics would be far less remunerative than the Bar, and he had had only a few months to exploit his recently acquired status as a QC, which entailed much higher earnings.

Howard was acting for the Nuclear Installations Inspectorate (NII), the government watchdog which legally is required to approve all stages in the building of a nuclear site, and then agree to its operations. In fact most of the inquiry's first year was taken up with economic issues, but Howard still had to work hard preparing for the safety section; this meant long hours not in the hearing itself, but in the NII office at the inquiry, digesting vast amounts of material. It was a heavy undertaking and Howard had to master some incredibly complicated issues of nuclear physics. There were also geographical difficulties; the hearings were held close to the proposed Sizewell site, at Snape Maltings near Aldeburgh, a hundred miles north-east of London. The Howards were living full-time in his constituency at this time, renting a cottage, having let their home in Notting Hill to an American journalist for a year. The journey from Folkestone to Snape was almost 200 miles by car, and travelling by train was often impractical because of the bulk of documentation to be carried.

People at the inquiry would see the more abrasive side of Howard when he felt the NII was being criticised unfairly. 'Michael made a very punchy statement to Sir Frank Layfield,' says one of the barristers present, 'and afterwards you could have heard a pin drop. He was a fearless advocate in that respect. Once he had made his mind up about something, that was it. He had guts.' Another lawyer thinks it was a mistake for the NII to have employed him: 'It was a fairly sensitive role, as it transpired, and Michael Howard was not known for delicacy. He started coming out fighting and being aggressive and telling the inspector he didn't like the way he was behaving, and with a degree of prickly hostility.'

Sir Patrick Mayhew was happy for Howard to combine his parliamentary duties with his continuing brief at Sizewell. But, even for someone with Howard's capacity for work, something had to give. A month after his appointment as Mayhew's PPS it was announced that he was standing down from Sizewell. Nevertheless, they had been fourteen very lucrative months.

People who knew Michael and Sandra Howard during the early 1980s often remark that they seemed short of money. As a well-paid model, Sandra had been accustomed to a fairly expensive lifestyle, and both her second and third husbands, David Wynne-Morgan and Nigel Grandfield, had enjoyed high incomes. The Howards also planned to send Nicholas and Larissa to fee-paying schools. (Sholto had reached twenty-one in 1983, and was about to start work in marketing.) They reoccupied their London home at the end of 1983, and Sandra became a shrewd player in the property game, buying cheap, renovating, and selling more expensively, before repeating the cycle. For much of the 1980s the Howards had a lodger in their London home, and for summer holidays they would sometimes do house-swaps with Americans. In 1984 they swapped with the New York writer Robert Caro, whose outstanding multi-volume biography of Lyndon Johnson has achieved a cult following among ambitious British politicians. *The Years of Lyndon Johnson* is probably the finest political biography ever written. It is an incredibly detailed work (2,300 pages so far, covering LBJ up to 1960, before he even became vice-president), and is essentially a study of power.[18] Caro recalls that, when he arrived in Notting Hill, Michael Howard had stayed behind for a night and took the opportunity to discuss the first volume at length with the author. 'I was tired from the flight,' says Caro, 'but I woke up during the conversation because he had really studied that first volume. I was struck by how much he understood the book.'[19] While Howard must have despised the racism and dishonesty of the young Lyndon Johnson, he would have been struck by how much LBJ was able to achieve through ambition, energy and persistence, by his appreciation of where power lies and how it can be manipulated, and by his understanding that, without power, principles and policies mean little. In 2004, like William Hague before him, Howard would choose LBJ's biography as his book for *Desert Island Discs*.[20]

Michael Howard could not match LBJ's energy and capacity for relentless, exhausting work – though at times he came close. Despite giving up the Sizewell inquiry, he did not abandon his legal practice completely, and continued to juggle the Bar with Westminster. Howard's junior chambers colleague Christopher Katkowski remembers doing a planning inquiry in Surrey with Howard during the week of the 1984 Conservative Party conference in Brighton. Howard didn't want to miss either, and his schedule was planned with military precision, enabling him to squeeze the most from each day, and attend conference events each evening (though his legal work meant he was already in bed at his own hotel by the time the IRA bomb exploded at the Grand Hotel in the early hours of the Friday morning). Sandra acted as their chauffeur, and fortunately Katkowski lived in the town. 'The routine,' he says:

> was that each morning Mrs Howard would arrive outside my door at my terraced house in Brighton, knock on the door, I'd come out, hop in the car. Michael would be in the back of the car fast asleep. We'd drive over to Guildford, Michael fast asleep all the time. We'd stop just outside Guildford at a Little Chef, wake him up, get him out of the car, give him his breakfast, get him back in the car, he'd then fall asleep for the remaining few minutes to Guildford. We'd wake him up outside the venue, get him in, and he'd then be absolutely brilliant during the course of the day – absolutely marvellous. Michael must have been on his feet for at least half the inquiry, either cross-examining or calling his own witnesses.[21]

Howard could always return to the law if things didn't work at Westminster; indeed, in March 1986 he received further legal recognition, being selected as a recorder for the South-Eastern Circuit, though in practice this was an honorary appointment (he seems never to have sat in court before the title lapsed in 1994). But, despite the financial sacrifice, he would soon see himself as a full-time politician.

In May 1985, after less than two years in the House, Howard was named by Harold Wilson's former secretary Marcia Falkender in her column in the *Mail on Sunday* as one of three Tory newcomers to watch (along with Richard Ryder and George Walden).[22] In the

September reshuffle he became the first of the 1983 intake to join the government, being appointed junior minister for corporate and consumer affairs in the Department of Trade and Industry (DTI).

Years later, Howard related that at his home in Kent he had received a phone call from Downing Street asking him to come up to London to see the Prime Minister. According to his account, Sandra had asked why Thatcher wanted to see him. Their eight-year-old daughter, Larissa, he says, suggested that the Prime Minister's phone must be out of order.[23]

No one could accuse Howard of having accepted a government sinecure. As a parliament under-secretary – known as a PUS, or Pussy – he was on the lowest rung of the ministerial ladder, but in practice his responsibilities were greater than many of those who were ministers of state, the next rank up. Howard was probably just glad to be a minister. As well as being the most demanding under-secretaryship in the government, his was also potentially the most rewarding, and if its official ranking had been higher it was unlikely that it would have been given to a new MP. One Cambridge friend recalled a conversation around this time when Howard suggested that he'd been very lucky even to get a junior minister's job. 'He still felt he was way behind his contemporaries from Cambridge,' says David Hacking, 'and didn't think he'd ever catch them up.'[24]

Howard's appointment meant that he was now working for Leon Brittan, who had become Secretary of State for Trade and Industry on the same day that Howard joined the DTI, having been demoted from Home Secretary. Their working relationship lasted for barely four months, however. In January 1986 Brittan was forced to resign over the Westland affair, which also saw Michael Heseltine make a dramatic exit from the Cabinet in protest at Margaret Thatcher's style of government. Westland was the last remaining British military helicopter manufacturer, and had been forced by financial difficulties to seek a takeover by a foreign company. Heseltine, then Defence Secretary, preferred a European solution; Thatcher and Brittan both backed the US company Sikorsky. During the Cabinet infighting that followed, Brittan tried to discredit Heseltine by leaking to the press legal advice given to the Cabinet by Sir Patrick Mayhew. 'I don't understand why he resigned on the narrow issue that he did resign,' said Howard, adding that it 'could have been avoided, it was completely unnecessary'.[25] On the day of his resignation Brittan spent much of his time closeted with Howard and Norman Lamont (at that time a junior minister in Heseltine's department). There was a general feeling within the DTI – shared by Howard – that Brittan would have to go. Although he was personally supportive of Brittan – and their friendship remained strong – Howard argued that he had no choice but to quit.

Howard's main task at the DTI was to steer through Parliament a new bill to regulate the financial-services industry. This complex legislation would have been a challenge even for an experienced minister with intimate knowledge of the City of London; when finally enacted in 1986 it ran to 278 pages. 'I'm not pretending that the man on the Clapham omnibus can pick up the Financial Services Bill and read it like a novel,' Howard admitted, seeming to forget his pleas in his maiden speech for laws to be written in more accessible language. His own explanation of the principles behind the bill would not have satisfied the Plain English Campaign: 'The basic concept of a statutory framework conferring powers on the Secretary of State for Trade and Industry which he then transfers to an organisation, which in turn supervises self-regulating organisations, is well understood,' he claimed, unconvincingly.[26]

Howard must have realised that the Financial Services Bill was unlikely to make him many friends, or enhance his public profile. Its origins lay in the decision by Cecil Parkinson, a previous Trade Secretary, to exempt the London Stock Exchange from the terms of the Restrictive Practices Act. Since the late 1970s the Office of Fair Trading (OFT) had been investigating certain business practices in the City of London, such as the division between the roles of brokers and jobbers, the sellers and buyers of stocks and shares. Each took a cut of the transaction price and increased costs for the owners of the shares. If the OFT had taken legal action over these restrictive practices there would have been a protracted and damaging court case. With the support of the Chancellor, Nigel Lawson, Parkinson argued that the City should be freed from this threat and instead be encouraged to put its own house in order. A number of changes to deregulate the financial markets were eventually introduced on a single day, 27 October 1986, which became known as 'Big Bang'.

The difficulty, as Lawson anticipated, was that Labour accused the government of relaxing its grip on its friends in the City while at the same time tightening laws on trade unions. The Financial Services Bill proposed a new Securities and Investment Board (SIB) to oversee the various City regulatory organisations, but most of the members of these institutions would still be City people. Labour claimed that the bill was only window dressing, and that the financial markets would continue to be supervised by nothing more rigorous than nods and winks in a private, tightly connected social network.

The collapse of Johnson Matthey Bank in the autumn of 1984, amid allegations of fraud, revealed how necessary reform was. The arrest in America of the international financier Ivan Boesky drew attention to the rather tougher regulatory regime across the Atlantic, and the US investigation seemed likely to uncover evidence of malpractice in Britain. Yet the whole purpose of Big Bang and the Financial Services Bill was to make London a more attractive place for financiers to secure international investment and maintain the City of London's position as the leading financial centre in Europe. There was an obvious tension between giving the City freedom to make money and ensuring that the markets were supervised properly to prevent fraud and to give investors and consumers confidence.

If the workings of City institutions had been a high priority for British voters, the government might have been in trouble. City fraud was a major theme for Labour during Margaret Thatcher's second term, and leading figures in government spent much time worrying about financial scandals. But, whereas the unions were very visible quarry for the Conservatives, capable of affecting the daily lives of most Britons, the City fox spent most of its time out of sight, and it was easy for voters to imagine that it preyed only upon *other* people's chickens. Labour MPs such as the indefatigable Brian Sedgemore, who was constantly trying to expose City malpractice, were seen as obsessives even by some on their own side. Their only chance of landing a serious blow was to implicate a government minister in shady practice.

In December 1985, just a few days before the publication of the bill, Labour's trade spokesman, Bryan Gould, wrote to the Prime Minister calling for Michael Howard to be replaced. There was, Gould claimed, a serious conflict of interest, because the minister was a member of the world's leading insurance market, Lloyd's of London. In response, Howard said that Lloyd's fell outside the scope of his bill, because it had been operating its own system of self-regulation since 1982. It was too early to tell whether this would work: any fraud cases relating to Lloyd's at that time were relics of the previous regulatory regime. But Howard promised that he would be ready to take action if necessary.

A week after Gould's letter, Labour tried to embarrass the government by calling a debate on City fraud. Inevitably, Howard's position came up. He told the Commons that he had resigned as a Lloyd's underwriter on the day of his appointment, as ministerial convention required. 'I have no further business there save for the running off of my pre-existing contracts,' he explained. Although he would continue to accrue profits – or suffer losses – as a result of trading after his appointment to the DTI, his financial prospects, he insisted, could not be affected by any decisions he took as a minister.[27]

Howard had behaved with propriety, but one could question the judgement of those who had appointed him. Labour could see no good reason why Lloyd's had been excluded from the bill; indeed, Howard's ministerial predecessor, Alex Fletcher, had threatened to include it if Lloyd's did not put its house in order. Some people believed that Fletcher's tough stance was connected with his un-expected departure from office. In order to persuade the government to bring Lloyd's within the scope of the legislation, the Opposition would also have to persuade Margaret Thatcher to sack a minister, or move him to another post. The affair, pursued energetically by Brian Sedgemore and Bryan Gould, managed to draw attention to the intimate links between leading institutions and the people who were legislating for them. There were, after all, at least fifty Tory members with significant interests in Lloyd's. Misgivings were not confined to the Labour benches: *The Times* reported that 'a number of Conservative MPs' also questioned Howard's position.[28]

One might even suggest that Michael Howard's nascent ministerial career was rescued by Westland. If there had been no other political stories at the end of 1985, his membership of Lloyd's would undoubtedly have received more publicity as the second reading of the bill approached. As it was, by the day of the debate, 14 January 1986, Labour was hunting more senior scalps; and, by the same token, Margaret Thatcher was not in the mood for resignations at the DTI, or anywhere else, unless they became absolutely necessary. During the debate, Howard was constantly interrupted by Labour MPs, and refused to say how much money he had invested in Lloyd's. But he got through his speech, and of course the government won the vote, with a majority of 130.

When the bill went into committee, in late January, Gould repeated his charge that Howard should not be handling it because of Lloyd's. Howard provided some more details about his membership, explaining that, although he had ceased trading, the results from his syndicates would not be known until 1987. Gould thought there was more mileage in the issue. After all, back in September the *Financial Times* had noted that the newly appointed minister had enjoyed 'overall an above-average return in the last underwriting account'.[29] Howard was believed at the time to be a member of four or five Lloyd's syndicates (it was five in fact), so Gould speculated during the committee hearings that 'The scale of the Minister's interest in these matters probably runs into several hundreds of thousands of pounds.' 'I wish it did,' Howard replied. When the Labour MP Dale Campbell-Savours intervened to suggest his total commitment was £500,000, Howard retorted, 'Certainly not!'[30] The true amount he had underwritten, though not reported at the time, was about half of that. Labour MPs let the matter rest, hoping that Howard's replies might cause him problems later. In fact the Lloyd's issue never resurfaced.

By the end of the bill's committee stage the Opposition may have judged that it had actually gained from Howard's continued steward-ship. Any new minister entrusted with his first bill would have been rattled if the opening discussions were dominated by his personal finances. Howard did well to recover his composure as much as he did. But he did not recover it entirely. Whatever the merits of self-regulation in the City, Howard needed to improve the regula-tion of his own temper. Some Conservative members of the standing committee complained of his 'bullying' manner.[31] Bryan Gould later reflected, 'He knew his stuff and was not above putting the boot in if he thought he saw a chance to do so. But (at that stage, at least) he was politically inexperienced and was perhaps a little short of the skills one needs to handle one's own supporters and to keep them a united team.'[32]

One of his first newspaper profiles noted that he had 'exasperated several of his backbenchers by putting them down too readily in debate'. 'He's not one of us. He's not one of the boys,' one MP com-mented. 'He's pretty right-wing, isn't he?' suggested another. When Howard himself was asked about his tendency to be 'very brutal' in debate, he seemed surprised and said, 'I'm the last person able to judge my behaviour.'[33]

His PPS, Robert Hayward, remembers that Howard took to the legislative process 'incredibly well – he was just a natural'. DTI civil servants enjoyed working with Howard on the committee of the Financial Services Bill, he says, because he genuinely 'revelled' in the arcane detail of drafting – whether, for example, the word 'and' should be inserted in a particular clause or not. Howard worked immensely hard on the bill, attending lunches in the City to gather the opinions of leading businessmen, and rising at four o'clock on the day of a par-liamentary session to study departmental briefings. This committee was particularly memorable because Gould and Howard were impres-sive and well-matched adversaries. 'If you heard both of these two,' says Hayward, 'then people were left thinking "We are not quite ade-quate."'[34]

Yet Howard's poor man-management undoubtedly hampered his cause. As he'd shown in the Bow Group, Howard finds it hard to accept internal dissent. He was defeated on three amendments during the committee stage, and it seems that Conservative colleagues rebelled the more easily because they had been roughed up by their own front man. 'His reaction actually made my task easier,' said Gould.[35] The thrust of the rebel proposals was to toughen the regulatory framework. This was certainly not the bill's intention, and at the end of the process Howard was grudging in his thanks to the committee, while Gould was fulsome. Asked afterwards if he was satisfied, Howard pondered for a while before saying, 'I don't suppose satisfaction is something I should confess to.'[36]

The Financial Services Bill was the kind of measure that matched Michael Howard's free-market principles. On this view, the market could mostly be trusted to regulate itself. But there was always the possibility of market failure, in which case the state should have powers to intervene. This was a common enough approach on the centre-right of the Conservative Party in the mid-1980s; it was also well-suited to lawyers used to working under the auspices of the Law Society and the Bar Council. The problem with self-regulation, as Nigel Lawson later lamented in relation to Howard's Financial Services Act, was that 'most of the ablest practitioners are too busy making money to be able to devote adequate time to the task of regulation'.[37] A less generous view would be that without independent scrutiny there are insufficient incentives for the practitioners to protect their customers' interests when these clashes with their own profitability. Before the next election the government had established the Serious Fraud Office because, for all its ideological commitment to the market in practice, it knew that some of its financier friends were not entirely reliable.

According to Howard's critics, the Financial Services Act was directly responsible for one of the worst scandals of the whole period of Conservative government. They argue that it left those consumers unprotected who exchanged their earnings-related employers' pensions for private provision, under legislation introduced at almost the same time as Howard's bill. But, while it is true that the Financial Services Act failed to prevent the widespread mis-selling of pensions, the main problem was caused by the SIB's decision not to make it compulsory for insurance companies to disclose the level of commission being charged. Howard had nothing to do with this decision, which could have happened only in the mid-eighties climate of optimism about the functioning of the market.

It was also said of Howard that his new Secretary of State, Paul Channon, had frequently overruled him during the Financial Services Bill's passage through Parliament. Channon's stewardship of the DTI is often criticised, and he had an uneasy relationship with his junior ministers, who included (after January 1986) Alan Clark. But this was a difficult time for Channon, whose daughter had recently died of a drugs overdose. Channon's family connections also meant that he ceded responsibility to Howard in a matter which, almost two decades later, still rouses strong feelings.

In the December 1985 debate on fraud in the City of London, Howard had been forced to admit that a 'lamentably small number of successful prosecutions' had been brought under the government's laws on insider trading. But at least the Thatcher government had been the first to act against the practice of using privileged information to manipulate share prices, in the 1980 Companies Act.

For many years afterwards Michael Howard would be dogged by his role in the examination of two of the major takeovers of the period. The first problem occurred when Paul Channon rightly decided that, as a member of the Guinness family, he had to exclude himself from any consideration of the brewing firm's bid for the Distillers company. It was therefore Michael Howard who ordered DTI inspectors to investigate the deal. Thus he triggered a saga which lasted many years, featuring four successful prosecutions for insider dealing, appeals that went as far as the European Court of Human Rights, and even a rare case of Alzheimer's disease going into remission. This was a City scandal which escaped from the business pages to the front page, and Howard was recognised as the leading player on the government side. One profile even positioned him as 'the man who set the dogs on Guinness'.[38]

Michael Howard had a duty to be guided by DTI officials on such matters. There was no way that he could initiate an investigation and drive it through to a successful prosecution on a personal whim. However, the profile headline reflected a widespread feeling that the decision to appoint a team of inspectors to investigate Guinness – and the subsequent course of the inquiry – was motivated by something more than a concern for fair dealing. It has been suggested that the Conservatives needed an example to show that they were capable of taking tough action against financial fraud, to spike Labour's guns. The timing of the Guinness affair was perfect; an inquiry could be ordered immediately, while with deft management the final report could be delayed until after the next general election. (In the end, the trial of Ernest Saunders, Sir Jack Lyons and the four other defendants did not open until 1990; six years later the European Court ruled that evidence given at the trial had been inadmissible because the DTI inspectors had not respected the accused's right to silence.)

On this interpretation, Howard pushed for an investigation of the Guinness takeover to serve the Conservatives' political interests. But, in the face of allegations of a rushed and mismanaged inquiry, there is an alternative explanation. Unusual share dealings in advance of the Distillers bid were uncovered by American investigators. The affair thus threatened not just the prospects of the Conservative Party, but also the integrity of Britain's financial institutions and the resilience of the City's regime of self-regulation. As it was, revelations from the Boesky affair led to the introduction of further legislation against insider dealing in November 1986. Thus the urge for tough action was not confined to Howard himself, or to his fellow ministers. Ernest Saunders tried to enlist the help of Margaret Thatcher's friend Woodrow Wyatt, and told him that the 'City establishment' was 'terrified' of the Guinness affair and just wanted a few scapegoats.[39] Saunders also attributed Howard's tough line to his ambition.

Michael Howard had entered a world full of dangerous associations, from which inventive minds could weave intriguing tales. Ernest Saunders later claimed that the Conservative deputy chairman, Jeffrey Archer, had brought up the subject of political donations at the time of the takeover. Howard's predecessor at the DTI, Alex Fletcher, had become an adviser to the Argyll Group, which had just lost the Distillers takeover to Guinness. Saunders later became an associate of Tiny Rowland – another businessman who claimed that he had been approached about a donation to the Conservatives while he was involved in an unsuccessful takeover.

In 1985 Rowland, the chairman of the secretive conglomerate Lonrho, had finally lost a long and acrimonious takeover battle for the store group House of Fraser, which owned Harrods. The successful bidders were the Fayed brothers, Mohamed and Ali. Mohamed Fayed was to become a central figure in the 'sleaze' scandals which troubled the Conservative Party for much of the 1990s, and he acquired his lasting dislike for Michael Howard from this time.

On one level the DTI's decision to order an inquiry into the Fayeds' 1985 takeover of Harrods could be filed alongside Guinness in that it was possible to construct a political motive. According to this theory, senior Conservatives were anxious to appease Rowland. Having been outmanoeuvred in the bidding for Harrods, Rowland embarked on a prolonged vendetta against the government in which no tactic was regarded as too devious, and no bribe too big. Lonrho also owned the *Observer* newspaper, and the conspiracy theorists argued that unless Rowland was silenced he would publish discrediting stories about Margaret Thatcher and her family. One costless way of achieving this goal would be to announce an inquiry into the Harrods takeover, then wait until after the next election before deciding whether further action was needed.

But Michael Howard could hardly have guessed the trouble that the affair would cause him a decade later (see Chapter 16).

At the beginning of 1987, the respected *Observer* columnist Alan Watkins picked out Howard, along with Kenneth Baker, as a minister who had recently enhanced his reputation.[40] (Fayed would no doubt have read special significance into the fact that Howard was praised in an *Observer* piece.) He was being tipped for promotion – although he would not have been pleased at the suggestion that he might become Welsh Secretary, which is traditionally a graveyard job which rarely leads to greater things. He was more attracted by the idea of succeeding

Sir Patrick Mayhew as Solicitor-General, another move mooted at the time. 'He was very keen on this,' says his friend David Mellor, who was an equally ambitious junior minister. 'I said to him, "No, go into the mainstream." He said, "But I'm late. I'll have no opportunity." I said, "No, you've got to believe in yourself more."'[41] Solicitor-General was well below the Cabinet, but, rather like the hierarchies of the Cambridge Union and the Bow Group, was sometimes a first step towards Attorney-General and even Lord Chancellor. In the end Howard did well to avoid either avenue at a time when the Tory ranks at Westminster were increasingly depleted of either Welshmen or QCs.

For someone so ambitious, Michael Howard spent surprisingly little time making new friends at Westminster. Apart from Mellor, there were his chums from Cambridge and the Bow Group, but they were by no means all political soulmates. He didn't belong to any Tory dining groups. Although Robert Hayward acted as Howard's PPS for almost two years, he never felt that he got that close to him. Nor did Howard build up extensive contacts among the Westminster press corps, though he knew some journalists from Cambridge, and the political editor of *The Times*, Robin Oakley, was an acquaintance from their days in Liverpool. People who attended parties at the Howards' home in Notting Hill were surprised at how few Westminster faces they saw there. Robert Hayward did his best to help him develop new links, but it was a struggle. The BBC correspondent Mike Baker, who then covered politics, was surprised in July 1986 to find himself in a restaurant with about twelve other people celebrating Howard's forty-fifth birthday. 'It was a bit strange, because I didn't really know Howard,' he says, 'but Rob Hayward, whom I knew, said, "Will you come along, because he doesn't know many people?"'[42]

The fact was that Howard was simply too busy to have much time to make friends and allies. His DTI brief was extensive, detailed and technical, in an area where Labour was on the watch for the slightest mistake. His long-standing friend Celia Haddon noticed the toll it took. 'When he was first a junior minister what struck me was how incredibly tired he looked – just exhausted,' she recalls. 'He had four boxes a night. It was impossible.'[43]

Just before the 1987 election Howard left on a long-scheduled ministerial trip to Japan, to discuss how to cooperate against fraud. What should have been a fairly routine series of meetings abruptly took on new importance because of increasing trade disagreements between the two countries. In particular, Cable & Wireless was being prevented from competing within the Japanese telecommunications market, and British firms wanted better access to the Tokyo stock exchange. The status of the visit was increased without warning by the Prime Minister, who unexpectedly announced at Question Time that a DTI minister was about to fly to Japan to deal with the looming crisis. It became a big story for several days, though in retrospect it's hard to see why.

This was good evidence of Margaret Thatcher's high regard for someone so new to ministerial office (and indeed Parliament). A few months before, she had told Woodrow Wyatt, 'He is very good. A very acute silk.'[44] But the Tokyo mission was a demonstration of faith which Howard could have done without. For example, her intervention required an immediate change of travel plans. He was scheduled to fly on a foreign airline, reflecting the original low-key nature of the trip and civil-service parsimony. This was no longer politically wise. There was no suitable British Airways flight, but if he went by Japanese Airlines he would undermine the new purpose of his visit, which was to talk tough about trading conditions in Japan for British firms. In the end he flew by Cathay Pacific, via Hong Kong.

But these were trivial problems when set alongside his new brief in Tokyo. How far could he go in threatening sanctions against the Japanese if they did not cooperate? Such a delicate mission required careful preparation, good practical instincts, and a large degree of tact. At this stage in his political career, when it came to international negotiations, Howard could be sure only of the first. At a press conference in Tokyo he did his best to sound upbeat, but he could not help betraying his irritation with his negotiating partners. The

Japanese, he felt, were incapable of showing their usual 'integrity and resourcefulness' when it came to removing trade barriers.[45]

For the first time, the tabloid press began to notice Howard. Because of Thatcher's intervention, the visit attracted a media circus (which included this author, then reporting for *Channel 4 News*, and his producer, the future Tory Shadow Cabinet member Damian Green). The press comment was not flattering. The *Sun* devoted editorials to the subject on consecutive days. Their primary purpose seemed to be to whip up jingoistic antagonism towards the Japanese, and Howard was the victim of this unfriendly fire. 'How much longer will we go on kow-towing to the Japs?' the paper asked. 'They marched Trade Minister Michael Howard round a circuit of ministerial offices then gave him a lot of gobbledegook about how much they would like to help us export more but "*Velly solly we can't.*" So poor Mike is coming home empty-handed.'[46] Howard was also a victim of his low ranking: in a country which is acutely sensitive to hierarchy and status, the Japanese wouldn't pay much attention to the views of a junior minister. Had the issue been important, the Japanese would have reasoned, the British government would have sent a member of the Cabinet. Given the tabloid headlines, it was not much consolation that when the dust settled Howard was recognised as having performed a thankless task with some dignity. And he was now better known than some Cabinet ministers.

Three hours after 'Mike' had returned from the Far East he was in Folkestone at a surgery for constituents. He could easily have cancelled it; but a general election was imminent.

Howard was terrified that he might lose Folkestone, and warned Sandra to expect the worst. That May's council results persuaded Margaret Thatcher to call the election almost immediately. This was worrying news for Howard, since the Liberal Alliance had triumphed in Shepway, the council area which exactly matched his seat, having taken a lead of almost 2 per cent in votes and returned one more councillor than the Tories. The opposition parties were bound to dwell on the relatively high unemployment in the area – more than 15 per cent.

Despite the distractions of his first parliament – the Sizewell inquiry, being Mayhew's PPS, and the complexities of the Financial Services Act – Howard was no slouch as a constituency MP. He was a robust defender of local interests, trying to encourage small businesses, tackling ministers over plans to cut civil-service posts, supporting a bird sanctuary, and defending the fishing industry. He even announced that voters should invite him into their homes if they had anything to discuss. He was 'rather amazed' by the response, and had to accept that it was an inefficient use of his time away from Westminster.[47]

If Howard was slow to develop journalistic contacts in London, he had realised that in the constituency it was vital to establish a good relationship with his local newspaper. David Gemmell, the editor of the *Folkestone Herald* from 1984 to 1986, remembers Howard's 'massive personal charm'. Most of the newspaper's staff were idealistic and left-wing, he says, 'but they all really liked Howard. They thought he was an excellent constituency MP.' He was clearly aware that small personal touches can be as important as popular local campaigns: 'He would come along to events or parties, chat to people, remember their names. It's always baffled me that he doesn't come across well on television because he is brilliant at putting people at ease and saying, "It's wonderful to see you."'[48]

Thanks to Howard's charm, the *Herald* was usually sympathetic. His attempts to help on local issues were invariably noted, especially his concerns about crime. For example, he favoured compulsory minimum sentences without parole for some offences, and on one occasion he criticised local magistrates for being too soft.[49] He also won coverage for his attempt to attract cross-party support for an amendment to the Criminal Justice Act which would have outlawed kerb-crawling.[50]

In Folkestone, as previously in Edge Hill, Howard was always keen to talk tough on law and order. In his 1983 election address, capital punishment had been one of only three issues highlighted in bold (the others were the economy and pensions). 'I do not believe the increase in the use of firearms can be halted unless capital punishment is restored for some categories of murder. I would vote for its restoration,' he said.[51] When it came to a vote in 1983, however, Howard must have disappointed some constituents, since he supported the death penalty only for killing on-duty police and prison officers, and for murderers who used bombs or guns. Even these measures were rejected by MPs. 'I think innocent lives will be lost as a result of this vote,' he said afterwards.[52] Yet he had abstained on murder by terrorists, murder in the course of a theft, and murder in any other circumstances.

But locally Michael Howard's first term as an MP was dominated by one issue which he feared might bring his love affair with Folkestone and Hythe to an abrupt halt.

Back in 1981 Margaret Thatcher and the new French President, François Mitterrand, had spoken of reviving the long-term idea of a tunnel between the two countries. Although Thatcher had supported the idea as a member of the Heath government, it looked initially as if she had made nothing more than a cost-free oral commitment to Mitterrand. The government was not going to pay for a tunnel, and recession meant that the private sector could not generate funds for such a large-scale investment. Before the 1983 general election the Prime Minister gave Conservative candidates in Kent every reason to suppose that the idea would come to nothing.

By December 1984, however, with the British economy picking up, Thatcher's scepticism was transformed into messianic support for the project (encouraged perhaps by her gratitude to Mitterand for offering to find her son, Mark, when he was lost in the Sahara desert). The official announcement was not made until January 1986, but as soon as the tunnel became a realistic possibility Howard knew that he was in serious trouble. For Folkestone and Hythe the project was a double-whammy. There was sure to be damage to the area's environment, and serious disruption during construction of the tunnel itself, an extension of the M20 to get to the tunnel, and a large terminal to transfer cars on to trains. Then, once the tunnel opened, the ferry companies would suffer from competition. Even if they weren't driven out of business, jobs would almost certainly be lost, with a resulting knock-on effect throughout the vicinity. The benefits were less to Kent than to the British economy as a whole, and if any Kent community were to gain it would be the area around Ashford, where the main railway station was planned, some distance outside Howard's constituency. Folkestone, once a major staging post between London and the Continent, was about to be bypassed.

There was an immediate impact on Howard's relationship with the *Folkestone Herald*. When the tunnel was confirmed, the paper asked its readers to submit their views on forms printed in the paper. 'We had sacks and sacks of the things,' David Gemmell recalls. 'We had to hire people to come in and do the counts. People were furious about the tunnel proposals.' Well over 80 per cent were opposed, he says.[53]

When Gemmell next had lunch with Howard they had their first row. The editor hoped that, having built him up as a dynamic, crusading constituency MP with growing influence at Westminster, Howard might raise the tunnel in the Commons. 'David, you're being very naive,' the MP reportedly replied. 'And I said, "Really? Sorry, in what way?" And he said, "Margaret wants it."' In Gemmell's words, the pair had 'a small sort of stand-off'. The editor suddenly realised the situation: 'The moment he said "Margaret wants it" was the moment I realised that he couldn't give two tosses if every person in Folkestone didn't want the Channel Tunnel. There was no way he was going to go against Mrs Thatcher, because he had a career and he didn't want to jeopardise it.'[54]

David Gemmell acknowledges that he had unrealistic expectations of Howard. It was not the last time that the MP would say 'Margaret wants it', to end an awkward discussion. But Gemmell was indeed being naive. If Thatcher wanted something, especially given her majority and authority at that time, it would happen whether or not Kent MPs organised a rebellion. When some in Folkestone suggested that he should resign from the government to fight the tunnel, Howard replied that he could 'do far more for my constituents by remaining within the Government; resigning would be a futile gesture'.[55] Howard had to operate behind the scenes, trying to minimise the environmental damage and pressing Folkestone's claims for any economic benefits. He even arranged for Leon Brittan, who was now on the backbenches, to propose a successful Commons motion extending the deadline for petitioners. He could not publicise his activities without appearing disloyal, and he had to hope that others would make gentle reference to his role. He must have been grateful that Jonathan Aitken, who was also a Kent MP (and who knew he was unlikely to secure office under Thatcher), felt free to campaign energetically against the tunnel. Howard's 1987 election address cited Aitken as 'perhaps the most prominent opponent' of the tunnel, and quoted him as saying that Howard had fought 'behind the scenes just as effectively, if not more so, than those of us who have the privilege of the freedom of the back benches to fight our battles up front'.[56]

Michael Howard balanced conflicting forces over the Channel Tunnel with a skill which would have impressed even Lyndon Johnson. According to Sir John Grugeon, the Conservative leader of Kent County Council, he achieved a 'remarkable balance of what was good for the country and what was best for his constituents'.[57] But the tunnel caused Howard genuinely to fear he might lose his seat. The Conservative constituency chairman for Folkestone and Hythe, Sally Ridley-Day, remembers some 'quite raucous' meetings, and some personal abuse for Howard himself.[58] One Tory thinks Howard may even have considered standing down.[59] 'Press, council, local people, ferry companies, environmental groups, he had them coming at him from every direction,' remembers David Crowthorn, a former chairman of the Folkestone Young Conservatives, who eventually left the party over the issue.[60] In September 1986 the Commons Transport Select Committee held three days of public hearings in the area, but the eloquent testimony of local people couldn't shift the committee's view that the overall benefit to the country outweighed the possible economic damage on the Kentish coast.

Jonathan Sloggett, who was then chief executive of Dover Harbour Board, thought that 'To an extent, Howard tried to have it both ways. But if you'd asked him he'd probably have said that he was pro-tunnel.'[61] George Pepper, who succeeded Gemmell as editor of the *Herald* in 1986, explains that 'Folkestone was a pretty dead town in those days. It lost its way. It has lost its ferry service, and the Channel Tunnel came along and it put it back on the centre stage.'[62] Howard concluded that the tunnel could help to revive the area, although this would take time. But that would be small comfort in the short term if his constituents chose a new MP. Yet he was always highly sensitive to the suggestion that his constituency was struggling economically. At one party conference he is reported to have complained about a stall which included Folkestone and Hythe as an example of one of Britain's deprived areas.

If Howard found it prudent to keep his feelings to himself, Sandra faced no such restrictions. David Gemmell recalls that Howard himself would never have anything but praise for Margaret Thatcher, but he relates a fascinating incident which occurred just after he had rowed with the MP over the Channel Tunnel. Gemmell was invited to lunch at the Howards' home, along with his wife, Valerie, and their children. In the afternoon Michael left to watch the local non-League football team in Folkestone, while the others went for a walk together. Gemmell asked Sandra if her husband was enjoying life in politics. She reportedly said, 'Oh yes, Michael loves it – well, apart from that dreadful woman!' When Gemmell asked which 'dreadful woman' she meant, Sandra replied, 'That Thatcher woman. Michael loathes her.'[63] Valerie Gemmell, who is now separated from her husband, confirms his account. 'I remember her reference to Margaret Thatcher as being "that awful woman". If it wasn't exactly those words, that was the inference. It was very clear.'[64]

The editor decided not to use the story: he had, after all, just enjoyed Howard's hospitality. In hindsight he thought he had missed an important scoop of how a new, supposedly Thatcherite minister actually couldn't stand his boss.

Until that time there had been little personal contact between Howard and Thatcher, and maybe when he got to know her better his feelings changed. One possible explanation for Sandra's outburst is that Howard was annoyed with Margaret Thatcher because of her personal involvement in the Channel Tunnel, and that Sandra took the risk of confiding in Gemmell – in Michael's absence – to show that her husband secretly shared the feelings of *Herald* readers. Perhaps she hoped the paper would then cause the minimum of embarrassment to their local MP. If Gemmell had repeated her revelation the immediate political consequences for Howard could have been fatal. Equally, had the paper turned against Howard on this crucial issue he could easily have lost his seat, making his reputation in Downing Street inconsequential. As it was, in April 1985 the *Herald* reported that Howard had rejected a challenge to a public debate from John Macdonald, the Liberal candidate, on the grounds that the tunnel was 'too important to be a vehicle for political confrontation'.[65] It infuriated Howard that his local opponent opposed the project whilst nationally the Liberals were in favour.

Howard's jitters in Folkestone were misplaced. Labour support could scarcely be squeezed further by tactical voting and he would lose only if his own supporters stayed away. At the election on 11 June 1987 there was a 3 per cent swing from Howard to the Liberal Alliance candidate, but that was nowhere near enough to unseat him. He was back for his second term, with a majority of 9,126 (down from 11,670 in 1983).

After the count, Howard congratulated the Labour candidate, Vidya Anand, who had won fewer than 4,000 votes. But he was far from magnanimous towards the Liberal Alliance. Their campaign, he said, had, 'from top to bottom, from the leader of the party to the canvassers on the doorsteps, been a disgrace'. Later Howard claimed that Liberal canvassers had been saying that he never visited the constituency, which would have baffled anyone who had opened a copy of the *Folkestone Herald* during the previous four years. John Macdonald called the election night speech an 'amazing outburst', and other Liberals were furious.[66]

It showed how rattled Michael Howard had been by the Channel Tunnel – and how badly he would have been hit by defeat.

10

MR POLL TAX

I didn't know anything about it. If I had I might have been a lot less happy, because I don't think I realised when Margaret Thatcher asked me to do the job quite how poisoned a chalice it would prove to be.

MICHAEL HOWARD ON THE POLL TAX, 2005[1]

It sparked some of the most violent and bloody scenes witnessed on the streets of London since the Second World War. One Saturday in March 1990 at least 50,000 people marched through the capital to protest against the government's new poll tax. It was only when the demonstrators reached Whitehall and the bottom of Downing Street that things turned ugly. The trouble began with people throwing a few bottles and stones. Then, as the police were pushed back and lost control, shops were looted and vehicles overturned. In Trafalgar Square, protesters bombarded police and their horses with bricks, scaffolding poles and oil drums. By the end of the day much of London's West End was strewn with broken glass and burnt-out cars. The figures were stark: almost 500 injured; more than 300 arrests; 250 reports of damage to property.

The pictures were transmitted around the globe, and were all the more shocking for their familiar, touristic backdrop – Nelson's Column and Big Ben. The violence had been encouraged by a small anarchist and revolutionary element, and most demonstrators had come with peaceful intent, but it reflected strong popular feeling. That Saturday would come to mark the beginning of the end for Margaret Thatcher's government, and the poll tax would prove to be her greatest political blunder. Seven months after the first bills went through letter boxes, she was ousted from office by Tory MPs who feared losing their seats. But the man who pushed the controversial measure through Parliament would emerge almost unscathed – just as Michael Howard survived his role in introducing Section 28, another measure which brought protesters on to the streets and came to symbolise the Thatcher years.

Howard's promotion after the June 1987 election was the highest compliment that the Prime Minister could have paid. After just four years in the Commons he became Minister of State at the Department of the Environment (DoE), with responsibility for local government – one of the most important posts outside Cabinet. It coupled good prospects with a high turnover: between 1984 and 1990 the incumbent changed every year, but seven of the nine men who held the post under Margaret Thatcher were subsequently promoted to Cabinet. Michael Howard himself held the job for less than fourteen months, but the measures he championed during that time still haunt him and his party, cited by critics as examples of Conservative injustice and intolerance.

Michael Howard's primary new task was plain – to promote what Margaret Thatcher described as the 'flagship' policy of her third term, the community charge, or what became better known as the poll tax. Some think he even angled for the job, and it was reported that Margaret Thatcher had 'overruled' Howard's new boss, the Environment Secretary Nicholas Ridley, who had wanted to put him in charge of housing instead.[2] It gave Howard the chance to prove that, in addition to the forensic skills which he had already demonstrated at Trade and Industry, he had the charisma to sell a policy to the public. If he made a success of this brief, it would show that he could make it to the very top in politics.

The significance of Michael Howard's appointment was not lost on the press. The well-connected Trevor Kavanagh of the *Sun* called him a 'whizzkid'; Howard had 'performed brilliantly' at the DTI, he wrote, and he was even described as a possible successor to Thatcher.[3] The *Daily Express* carried an interview with Howard under the prophetic headline: 'He's the man with the most thankless task in Britain'; and the paper said that Thatcher had marked him as a man of 'infinite tact'.[4] But there were critical judgements too, including a perceptive profile by Edward Pearce, who wrote in the *Sunday Times* of 'a hint of self-doubt' about Howard, and of the 'lack of a sharply defined political profile . . . He is not unprincipled, but he is a professional advocate; and if there was a way of getting Jack the Ripper off, this good lawyer would loyally take the brief.'[5]

Howard himself claimed that 'the job is the most exciting anybody could be given'. The existing property tax, the rating system, was 'desperately unfair', he said. It meant that a widow living on her own paid the same as a family of four or five adults next door. The system was also complicated, so that 'the rates you pay bear absolutely no relation to the area you live in or the service your council provides.'[6]

In later years a large number of leading Cabinet ministers would be tarnished one way or another by their role in introducing the poll tax, including Kenneth Baker, William Waldegrave, Nicholas Ridley, Michael Portillo, David Hunt, John Redwood and Michael Forsyth. Michael Howard was among them, though he could not be classed as one of the inventors of the community charge. Among ministers, that accolade goes to Baker and Waldegrave, aided from the Downing Street Policy Unit by Oliver Letwin. Long before the 1987 election, all had worked on an alternative to the rates which would satisfy Margaret Thatcher. Back in 1974, as Shadow Environment Secretary, she had pledged that the Tories would abolish the rating system – though, contrary to popular myth, she had been sceptical, at least initially, that the poll tax was the answer.[7]

Michael Howard's job was to bring the measure into effect. Although he played a part in deciding how quickly the poll tax would be introduced, he had simply been assigned another difficult brief. Unlike the Financial Services Bill, it became notoriously unpopular.

Edward Pearce, with a rich cocktail of metaphors, saw the perils of Howard's latest task:

> Howard will not be a brake on the natural imperiousness of his boss, that autistic personality, Nicholas Ridley, still less upon Mrs Thatcher. If they resist the substantial amendments necessary to make the Poll Tax half-way equitable, Howard is the sort of loyal ploughman willing to drive his furrow through the landmines . . . Howard is clever. He is also, in my view, rather nice. But is he smart? It just could be his misfortune to be the ambitious laboratory mouse who volunteered for the wrong experiment.[8]

Howard and his colleagues believed that accountability was the main argument for using the number of adult occupiers, rather than property values, as the basis for local taxation. In many areas, people who contributed towards council budgets through their rates could be outvoted by those who paid nothing. In those circumstances, he said, 'it is not surprising that we get local authorities who are irresponsible, who engage in behaviour that everybody now describes as loony'.[9] Once everyone paid something towards the cost of local services, there would be an incentive to elect parties which offered better value for money, and so high-spending councils would lose out. Greater accountability would bring political gains for the government, but this could be presented as a side effect which reflected the fact that Labour councils spent more money. The community charge would 'become the real scourge of the hard left', Michael Howard told the Conservative conference that autumn. 'Almost every voter will have to pay it,' and it offered 'the prospect of a return to good, honest, old-fashioned local government, concerned not with playing politics but with serving communities efficiently and well.'[10]

Yet opponents of the community charge could deploy an emotive illustration which was more than a match for the metaphorical single widow. Under the new system a dustman would pay the same as a duke; indeed, on the government's own calculations, Prince Philip would pay the same as the live-in servants at Buckingham Palace

(£396 per year), while Howard himself, in the borough of Kensington, would be £470 better off than before. This seemed to be even less 'fair' than the rates. In any case, critics suggested to Howard, surely a government which believed in market forces should encourage widows to sell up if they couldn't meet their bills?

With an overall majority of 100, ministers could expect to pass the legislation. The issue was more about potential political damage. A big parliamentary rebellion would both harm the government and encourage a campaign of non-payment. Howard also had to reassure those Tory MPs who were worried about losing their seats at the next election. In turn, this meant persuading the public that the charge was unlikely to be high – or that, if it was, their councils were to blame, not the government. Part of his work involved convincing national newspaper editors of the virtues of the poll tax, and a nationwide tour to meet provincial editors. This kind of direct personal approach to the media – or 'spinning' – would become an important feature of his ministerial style.

When Michael Howard accepted his new job he could be fairly confident of success. In June 1987 the Department of the Environment estimated that the average bill would have been £172 per year if local councils had been operating the poll tax then. Howard was happy to quote this figure, which suggested that even those who lost out as a result of the reform would not be hit too badly, and he believed that the final sum would be lower. He saw the community charge as a clever mechanism – akin to the market – which would drive prices down as inefficient councillors were put out of business by bargain-hunting voters. A system of concessions and exemptions would relieve the burden on those who were genuinely unable to pay.

Another reason for quiet confidence was that the community charge had hardly featured during the June 1987 election. Since 1983 the new Opposition leader, Neil Kinnock, had been fighting an internal battle to bring Labour's more left-wing councils into line, and party strategists had been keen to keep local government off the agenda, fearful that the Tories would play the 'loony left' card. At the time of the election an opinion poll found that, while 39 per cent of those asked were opposed to the proposed tax, 43 per cent actually supported it.[11]

So the risks in June 1987 would have seemed acceptable even to a more cautious man than Michael Howard. But the position rapidly changed over the summer. In July, Howard and Ridley faced more than two hours of critical questioning from Tory backbenchers, and MPs later voiced their misgivings privately to Howard rather than to the Secretary of State. 'Ridley will simply not listen to argument,' one would-be rebel complained.[12]

Despite their very different characters, Michael Howard seems to have developed a genuine affection for his boss, and invited him to stay at his home in Kent. A languid Old Etonian with a feverish belief in the free market, Nicholas Ridley was a gifted amateur artist who preferred a broad brush in politics. He would arrive late for meetings at the department's offices in Marsham Street, airily explaining that he had been finishing a painting. Howard's PPS, Roger King, remembers that the reaction was amusement rather than irritation.[13]

The two ministers complemented each other. Ridley was the original thinker, the ideas man, worried about the big picture, constantly questioning officials and chewing over the effect the poll tax would have on different groups of people. As a former civil engineer, Ridley wanted to know the overall figures, and would sit calculating the sums for himself. How many billions would it cost? Which groups would be the winners, and which the losers? Howard, meanwhile, mastered obscure and often technical details of the legislation. He was never a numbers man (at the Bar he'd sometimes struggled with calculating his VAT returns); civil servants did not mark him down as a future Chancellor.

Nicholas Ridley eventually left the government in July 1990 – between the implementation of the new tax and the fall of Thatcher – after some crass comments about the Germans. Howard would later be identified as Ridley's 'last real chum in the Government', and he later attended a dining club named in his old boss's honour.[14] Howard's admiration might not have been reciprocated – Ridley refers to him only once in his memoirs[15] – but there is something apt about the idea of a friendship between two men who could be warm and witty in private, yet publicly were among the most unsympathetic of Margaret Thatcher's ministers.

In her autobiography Thatcher praised Ridley's 'clarity of thought, political courage and imagination' in his approach to local government.[16] But her close personal and political relationship with Ridley made life more difficult for Howard. Although he sincerely believed in the principles behind the community charge, he was to some extent the prisoner of his superiors when it came to the details. He could not hope to appeal over Ridley's head to the Prime Minister if backbenchers or representatives of local government raised constructive objections. Like Margaret Thatcher, Ridley was impatient with pressure groups and vested interests of all kinds; when the Confederation of British Industry (CBI) withdrew its support from the government's proposed uniform business rate, there was no chance that either Ridley or Thatcher would listen. Their most likely response to criticism was to dig in their heels and tough it out.

By the end of July 1987 it looked as if the ideological allies would have to curb their radical instincts. Thatcher met Ridley and Howard for an hour and a half to discuss the idea known as 'dual running'. Under this arrangement – accepted before the election by Kenneth Baker, the previous Environment Secretary – the rates would be retained for a transitional period after the planned starting date of April 1990, while the community charge would year by year account for an increasing proportion of the money raised locally. Baker had originally envisaged it would need ten years to switch to the new tax; the Chancellor, Nigel Lawson, hoped the transition would take five years, but Ridley wanted the charge to be introduced in one go, and senior DoE officials supported him.

In his battle against Lawson and the Treasury, Ridley's position was weakened by an opinion poll suggesting that opposition to the tax had mushroomed in the few weeks since the election. More than half of voters were now against it. Howard commented that a single poll was hardly representative, but ministers were also aware of misgivings in the Conservative ranks. The whips reported that nearly 100

backbench MPs were unhappy, and two dozen were outright opponents. It was this which originally scuppered Ridley's first attempt to
introduce the tax in one move. Initially, it was agreed that the transitional period should last four years.

When the decision to persevere with dual running was announced,
Howard put on a brave face. He denied that it would have been politically more courageous to scrap the transitional period, although he
admitted that it would have been cheaper, and simpler administra-
tively.

The tone of Howard's remarks implied that he shared Ridley's disappointment at the outcome of the discussions, and Nigel Lawson says
that Howard was active in stirring up backbench opposition to dual
running. As it turned out, the battle was not lost. The legislation was
scheduled to be introduced after that year's Conservative conference in
October. Lawson later thought that during the conference debate
Ridley and Howard had 'contrived a succession of speakers from the
floor' to urge the abandonment of the transitional period, among
them Gerry Malone, who had just lost his Scottish seat at the election.[17] This apparent show of feeling impressed Thatcher, who told
Ridley that dual running should be reviewed. With the Prime
Minister's open support, the Environment ministers triumphed over
Lawson five weeks later. The poll tax would arrive in one go – what
became known as the 'Big Bang' policy: the second time that a job of
Howard's had been linked to the phrase.

Some observers suggest that this was the moment when supporters
of the poll tax effectively killed it through their eagerness. On the
other hand, a transitional period might have turned the difference
inside the party into a even longer-running open sore. It is one of the
great 'what-ifs' of recent British politics. Ministers had been aware
before the election that radical reform of local-government finance
was a complex issue, and always controversial. The arguments for
going ahead immediately, however, extended beyond cost and sim-
plicity. As Thatcher put it, a delay 'would have postponed the very
accountability our reforms were about'.[18] But, after so many years of
what she saw as irresponsible spending by local councils, could the

government not wait a little longer to ensure that it ended this once and for all? Back in July, even Howard had acknowledged the force of this argument when he said, 'This is a very radical change and people do not like change very much.'[19]

Margaret Thatcher's impatience is understandable. She had spent well over a decade trying to find an alternative to the rates. If the measure could be carried through in full before the next election – which could be no later than 1992 – her chances of securing an unprecedented fourth term would, as she saw it, be greatly improved. Howard had his own motives for gambling on early implementation. The sooner the tax came in, the more likely it was that he would secure the PM's lasting approval.

When the Local Government Finance Bill was given its second reading in December 1987, after a two-day debate, seventeen Tory MPs rebelled and a similar number abstained. The government, nevertheless, had a majority of seventy-two. But serious damage was inflicted by the former Environment Secretary, Michael Heseltine. He warned that the government would be saddled with the blame, not high-spending local authorities, if the tax turned out to be higher than official estimates. While Heseltine prudently abstained, the former Prime Minister Edward Heath voted against the bill.

The bill was sent to be scrutinised in committee. Ridley attended some of the sessions in person – an unusual step – but the main responsibility for managing this stage of the process fell to Howard. Proceedings began on 11 January 1988, and eventually stretched over 35 meetings and 120 hours of discussion before they ended 11 weeks later. It was gruelling work; local government finance was just as complicated as Sizewell or the Financial Services Act.

Opponents of the tax failed to make much impact during the committee stage, even though the committee itself was larger than usual, to allow Tory critics to have their say. But outside Westminster things were looking ominous, and polls suggested that public opposition was growing. Howard denounced 'scare propaganda' and insisted that more than half of households would actually benefit from the change.[20] His department predicted that 80 per cent of single pensioners would be better off. Howard also claimed that the 1987 election gave the government a mandate to introduce the tax, even though it had never been a significant campaign issue.

In fact the government had already lost the propaganda war, as Heseltine had predicted. The press had quickly labelled the community charge as the 'poll tax', and even if the public did not know the chequered history of flat-rate charges – stretching back to the levy which provoked the Peasants' Revolt of 1381 – they seemed to recoil from this phrase. In an interview in the summer of 1987 Howard himself even referred to the 'poll tax', though he quickly reverted, even in private, to Margaret Thatcher's practice of using its official name.[21]

It was too late. The crisper title proved so popular with sub-editors that even sympathetic newspapers used it in headlines. When ministers persisted in talking about the 'community charge' this only drew attention to their sensitivity on this point. In committee, Labour's Jeff Rooker asked Howard when the government had stopped referring to a poll tax, despite having used the phrase freely in earlier official documents. Howard replied that the term was no longer applicable, because the original idea of tying the tax to the 'eligibility to vote' had been dropped.[22] This cut no ice with Labour members of the committee, who argued that there was indeed a link with voting: they predicted, correctly, that many people would stop registering to vote so as to make them harder to track down if they didn't pay the tax.

It was beginning to look as if the government could save the day only with significant concessions. But in committee Howard insisted that nothing should undermine the precious principle of 'accountability'. His hands were tied. His PPS, Roger King, remembers urging him to look again at the position of students, who were likely to suffer hardship even though they were eligible for an 80 per cent discount. 'I think the problem is that Margaret wants them included,' Howard reportedly replied.[23] In February 1988 he saw at first hand how damaging the tax would be with young people, when the Young Conservative conference passed a critical motion, despite his grandiose claim that the community charge could be compared to the 'great reform bills of the nineteenth century'.[24]

Although the Commons committee stage had been negotiated, Howard knew that the parliamentary battle was far from over. Heseltine's ally Michael Mates had supported the bill on its second reading, but only on the understanding that the government would later look sympathetically at modifications. But ministers drew the line at what became known as 'the Mates amendment', debated in the Commons in April 1988. Mates wanted to relate the tax to the ability to pay, so that those who paid no income tax would pay only half the community charge, while higher-rate income tax payers would be liable for 150 per cent.

In the month before the debate on Mates's proposal, Nigel Lawson had slashed the top rate of income tax, provoking open gloating from some affluent Conservative MPs. Since the same people also stood to gain most from the poll tax, the government was looking more vulnerable than ever on the question of fairness. Tension was high before the debate, as wavering Tories were pressurised by the whips. The ill-feeling spilled into the chamber. Howard interrupted Michael Heseltine's speech to ask why previously he had 'voted for its introduction in Scotland', where the measure had been brought in earlier.[25] Heseltine could not produce a convincing reply, which was some compensation for Howard's own discomfort when he wound up for the government. Mates had been given access to DoE officials to check that his alternative proposal really would be fairer than the poll tax. When Howard claimed that the Mates amendment would make some people worse off, the MP intervened and revealed that his sums had been endorsed by the department. Mates also disclosed that a senior civil servant had told him that the objections to his scheme were 'political' rather than financial. Howard chose to regard this as a breach of confidence, and could not contain his anger.

The government might have lost the argument, but it won the vote with a majority of twenty-five. It had been the most serious rebellion of the Thatcher period. On 25 April the third reading of the bill saw a more comfortable majority. Howard had a relatively easy time disposing of Labour's objections; after all, the Opposition had still not come up with its own alternative to the rates. But in this debate Jeff

Rooker was able to claim with some justice that the measure would not have passed through the Commons if MPs had been allowed 'a free or secret vote'.[26] The impression that the tax was being hustled through without the proper consent of Parliament was reinforced when the bill moved to the Lords, and government whips ensured the attendance of numerous Conservative 'backwoodsmen', who rarely turned up for debates, to push it through. Although some of the poll tax rebels were already regarded as professional dissidents with grudges against Margaret Thatcher, there was still room for revenge once the voting was over. Mates was deprived of the chairmanship of the back-bench Conservative home affairs committee in retaliation for his well-intentioned initiative. He was likely to remember his brush with Howard, and was still an MP when Howard became leader of his party fifteen years later.

The third Commons reading marked the end of Michael Howard's direct involvement with the poll tax. In July 1988 his responsibilities for local government passed to his Cambridge colleague John Gummer (a sign of how much Howard had caught up), and by the time the first poll tax bills duly arrived, in April 1990, he was in the Cabinet as Employment Secretary. Once the full extent of the fiasco became clear, and Margaret Thatcher herself had been forced to resign by MPs who saw the tax as a fatal liability, it was possible to identify a wide range of ministerial culprits. But no one can seriously suppose that the tax would ever have been implemented under a different Prime Minister. Thatcher and Ridley needed a more junior figure to carry out their orders. Michael Howard was glad to perform this task. And if the strategic responsibility lies with Thatcher and Ridley, Howard shares the blame for poor tactics.

It was during this first spell at Environment that Howard developed a reputation within Whitehall for his brusque dealings with civil servants. Early on, he effectively got rid of his opposite number in the civil-service machine – the deputy secretary at the DoE in charge of local government finance, Ken Ennals, who was persuaded to take early retirement at the age of fifty-five. Ennals was liked by colleagues, who saw his departure as an abrupt end to a civil service career which

stretched over thirty-five years. Howard felt that Ennals wasn't effective or forceful enough, or sufficiently versed in the complexities of
local-government finance, one of the most arcane subjects in
Whitehall. But, above all, Ennals wasn't keen on the poll tax, and had
made it perfectly clear among DoE colleagues that he didn't think the
measure would work.

'They didn't see eye to eye,' says a close friend of Ennals, who died
in 1995. 'It was basically the poll tax, and Michael Howard was new
to the job. Ken thought Michael Howard was very clever and could
master a brief quite quickly, but that Howard was also rather insecure
and a bit nit-picky. Ken was fed up about it, because he was doing a
job he enjoyed.'

It's not unknown for Cabinet ministers to ease out officials they
don't like, but it was considered unusual for a middle-ranking minister who had been in government for only a couple of years. Other
ministers simply learn to work with officials they don't care for;
Howard, in contrast, is never comfortable unless he has complete
confidence in those around him, and will change his team if necessary.

He had also earned a reputation for his fierce grilling of departmental officials, testing them in great detail, as if they were criminal
suspects rather than colleagues. 'Michael Howard had the capacity for
making those he questioned feel a bit stupid,' says one DoE official,
though like Margaret Thatcher he often had more respect for those
who were willing to stand up to him. Civil servants quickly learned
the body language. 'You could see from the way he moved about in
his chair being restless and irritable about things, so you had to be on
edge to cope with whatever it was biting him.' On one occasion
Howard was visited by a delegation proposing various schemes to
clean up Britain's streets, but grew increasingly exasperated when
most of his officials sat silently, offering no arguments as to why the
anti-litter proposals might not work. 'Only one of us spoke up,' a
former colleague recalls, 'and Howard said afterwards, "Why on earth
did those people not intervene, and just sit there like dummies?" He
was very impatient about that sort of thing.'

Ken Ennals's replacement as deputy secretary was Derek Osborn, who had a much more substantial record in local-government finance. He found a minister who knew what he wanted. 'Michael Howard didn't much like open-ended discussion,' says Osborn. 'He knew his own mind, and liked to come swiftly to closure. His relationship with me was like with a chief of staff: "I want us to do this, this and this, Derek. See to it."' A small but characteristic example, says Osborn, was Howard's attitude to a DoE working party involving councillors and official from local government together with Whitehall civil servants. This group had been asked to examine various constitutional aspects of local-authority organisation, such as the statutory role of specific committees and officials in different councils, and what should be required by law and what left to local descretion. The working party, Osborn recalls, had come up with a 'consensus package' of proposals:

> Michael Howard ignored the consensus and overnight went through each detailed issue on his own, sometimes agreeing with the working group, but deciding several points differently. I remonstrated and suggested that there was some value in supporting a complete package that had been thoroughly worked over by a well-informed group, and had achieved a measure of consensual agreement between central and local government. He said, 'No, I'm the minister. There are my reasons for deciding each of these issues. Now let it be done as I have decided.' He backed his own judgement – as he was perfectly entitled to do – and was not very interested in the consensual view of things.[27]

Howard certainly won respect for hard work. Papers did not sit around waiting for decisions. While some ministers ignore their red ministerial boxes for days on end, the contents of Howard's box generally came back the following morning having all been dealt with. 'Some ministers take for ever,' says Osborn.

> Other people often think discursively – 'I wonder how this relates to something else, or perhaps we should look at that before we do

this,' whereas he wouldn't do that. He would deal with his papers briskly and efficiently, one issue at a time. But in backing his own judgement he sometimes gave short shrift to the views of others and seemed to have little interest or patience with trying to achieve a consensual view. He did not therefore achieve a wide personal loyalty. Many people felt used or dominated by him rather than valued in their own right or for their own options.[28]

The poll tax received the royal assent in July 1988, but the government's favourite gunslinger had yet to win his sheriff's badge. He had still to prove himself by performing another difficult task as Ridley's deputy. But, while everyone knew that he had suffered some flesh wounds in the poll tax fight, even he probably did not realise just how bad a long-term injury he caused himself on a separate assignment.

An essential part of Michael Howard's brief at Environment was to discredit Labour councils, and he performed this task with enthusiasm. For many Conservatives, and many in the tabloid press, the hallmark of a 'loony' left-wing council was its campaigning on behalf of lesbians and gays. At the October 1987 party conference, for instance, Howard took a swipe at Ealing Council in west London for spending £2,000 'on public meetings for gays and lesbians' that month. 'They voted to allow gays and lesbians to adopt children,' he charged, and then challenged the Labour leader Neil Kinnock who was a resident in the borough: 'Does he agree that schoolchildren in Ealing should be taught that a homosexual lifestyle is equally as valid as a heterosexual one?'[29] This theme was picked up by Thatcher herself in her conference address.

In fact few councils spent more than trivial sums on homosexual issues. Perhaps Howard thought that his rhetoric would have no direct practical effect: the community charge would be enough to stop authorities spending on non-essential matters, of which the campaign for homosexual rights was merely the most eye-catching example. If so, he had made a serious misjudgement. For one thing, throughout 1987 part of the government machine had been forced to take a more careful attitude to homosexuality, running an expensive advertising campaign which warned against the dangers of AIDS. The leading message was 'Don't die of ignorance.' Yet at the same time Howard was attacking councils which tried to raise public consciousness of homosexuality, and exploiting for personal and partisan advantage the public prejudice which had been fuelled by the AIDS crisis.

Howard's rhetoric could only encourage these elements within the Conservative Party who wanted to tackle this 'menace' to family values. Towards the end of the previous parliament the Earl of Halsbury, an elderly computer expert and long-standing campaigner against homosexuality, had introduced a bill to restrain councils from 'promoting' homosexuality as an acceptable family relationship, and to give parents the right to sue any authority which did so. The government minister in the upper house, Lord Skelmersdale, was personally sympathetic to Halsbury's crusade, as was the Prime Minister. But after a debate in which the former Master of the Rolls Lord Denning compared Haringey Council to Sodom and Gomorrah, Skelmersdale assured peers that the measure was unnecessary. The government, the minister said, would have powers to prevent homosexual propaganda in schools under the terms of its new Education Act. Skelmersdale also advised fellow peers that such legislation as Halsbury proposed would be hard to operate, since its imprecise wording would open it to legal challenge.[30]

Nevertheless, Halsbury thought that the depth of feeling in the Lords was too great to drop his bill. It proceeded to the Commons, where it was promoted by the Conservative backbencher Jill Knight, only for Labour to kill the measure through lack of a quorum – much to Margaret Thatcher's dismay.

Opposition to the poll tax had been a long-running affair, so that sceptics could predict a policy disaster even before the legislation had been debated. By contrast, people were caught unawares in December 1987 when the Commons committee discussing a new Local Government Bill was suddenly invited to consider a new, last-minute clause which was virtually identical to Lord Halsbury's bill. It originally said that:

A local authority shall not –

(a) promote homosexuality or publish material for the promotion of homosexuality;

(b) promote the teaching in any maintained school of the acceptability of homosexuality as a pretended family relationship by the publication of such material or otherwise;

(c) give financial or other assistance to any person for either of the purposes referred to . . . above.[31]

Clause 28, as it was later named, was originally a backbench amendment, formally tabled by Jill Knight but proposed in committee by David Wilshire, who had only just been elected to the Commons. Wilshire cannot recall any discussion with Michael Howard beforehand; indeed, he was so new to the House that he didn't know that it was normal practice for government backbenchers to discuss their suggested amendments with ministers. Wilshire presumed that his proposal would get nowhere, and that in committee Howard would express sympathy but then come up with an excuse as to why it couldn't be included. 'I was flabbergasted when it made the statute book,' he says. 'I was gobsmacked.'[32]

On the face of it, given his fond feelings for the swinging sixties and his sexually liberal past, Michael Howard was an unlikely promoter of Clause 28. Yet his voting record over his four and a half years as an MP suggested he was a conservative on most social issues. In addition to supporting a limited return of capital punishment in 1983, Howard had voted for the Obscene Publications (Protection of Children) Bill, and had also promoted his own backbench bill against kerb-crawling. But he had not supported Clare Short's famous attempts to ban pictures of topless women in newspapers. On divorce – an area where Sandra had considerable personal experience – he had in 1984 supported amendments which would introduce a period of reflection before the final separation, but he had opposed the idea of preventing divorce within two years of marriage (instead of one), and another amendment which reasserted the idea of 'fault' in divorce. In short, he wanted to make divorce only a little harder. In

1985 Howard supported Enoch Powell's attempt to prevent research on embryos (though five years later he supported such work). There was nothing remarkable about this record; it was broadly in line with that of most Conservative MPs.

But Clause 28 wasn't just a matter of social conscience; it was also about party politics. Michael Howard undoubtedly bears much responsibility for the controversial law. He may not formally have proposed it, or even have been in cahoots with David Wilshire, but he relished the debate, and he certainly came to it well prepared, brandishing extracts from publications such as *Gay, Young and Proud*, and the story *The Milkman's on His Way*, both of which were being promoted by Haringey Council as suitable reading for young people below the homosexual age of consent. Howard declined to 'offend the ears of the committee' by quoting from the latter book. 'It glorifies in a detailed description of homosexual practices,' he said, and contained 'revolting descriptions of the homosexual act'.[33]

Everything about the debate in committee points to an ambush with ministerial connivance. It was the last day of committee deliberation on the bill, the perfect opportunity to smuggle in clauses which were of no direct relevance. In fact the main purpose of the Local Government Bill – drawn up before Howard went to Environment – was to enforce 'compulsory competitive tendering' on local councils, effectively privatising such services as school meals and waste collection. It was much of a piece with the poll tax, which followed it in the parliamentary schedule.

But the legislation also included an attempt to curtail council campaigns on broader political issues. Howard had already provoked a row by claiming that councillors had no right to use taxpayers' money to support anti-apartheid groups in South Africa. Labour's spokesman Allan Roberts had called his intervention 'one of the most disgraceful ministerial replies that I have ever heard' in eight years as an MP.[34]

When the committee debated Wilshire's unexpected new clause on homosexuality, Howard agreed that it was no 'part of a local authority's duty to glorify homosexuality or to encourage youngsters to believe that it is on an equal footing with a heterosexual way of life'.

He did, however, add an amendment specifying that the clause should not 'prohibit the doing of anything for the purposes of treating or preventing the spread of disease'.[35]

Labour's main spokesman, Jack Cunningham, was handicapped by his party's reluctance to defend councils which were tarred as 'loony left', and actually said that he and other Labour MPs would vote for the new clause. As it turned out, there was no vote in the committee stage, because nobody pressed for one – no Labour member; nor the Liberal MP on the committee, Simon Hughes; nor the two members of the committee later known to be gay, Allan Roberts (Labour) and Michael Brown (Conservative). Indeed, given the subsequent notoriety of Clause 28, it was an astonishingly low-key debate, though at one point Cunningham did shout, 'Shut up, fathead!' to a Tory backbencher.[36]

Only the left-wing Labour MP for Tottenham, Bernie Grant, recently elected as one of Britain's first black MPs, caused a fuss, saying that the promoters of the amendment made his 'blood run cold'.[37] In substance, Grant's case was the same as that made against Lord Halsbury's bill by the Conservative minister Lord Skelmersdale earlier that year – that it would prove impossible to define what counted as the promotion of homosexuality. Howard responded with undisguised glee, calling Grant's speech 'disgraceful'. 'It is not possible for the Labour Party to disassociate itself from that hon. gentleman [Grant] and his observations,' he claimed. 'His continued membership of the Labour Party is a badge of shame for the Opposition to wear.' Cunningham condemned Howard's onslaught as a 'pathetic, puerile little attack' on Grant's honour.[38]

In denouncing Bernie Grant, Howard had exposed the true motives for his enthusiastic involvement in Clause 28. For some Conservative MPs the targets were homosexuality, local government and the Labour Party, in that order. In Howard's mind, this order appeared to be reversed. As an experienced barrister, he would have known that the clause was unlikely to lead to a single prosecution. But the timing of the debate is crucial to understanding his support for the measure. Parliament was about to rise for the Christmas recess. When it returned, the committee stage of the poll-tax legislation would begin. With no sign of an upturn in public opinion, and dissident backbenchers proving resistant to ministerial charm, Howard needed every weapon in his fight to discredit the rates, and by implication Labour councils which he felt spent too much. In October he had expressed the hope that the poll tax would stop councillors from promoting minority causes. Two months later he had identified a minority cause which he hoped would help the government case for the poll tax.

By the time the bill reached the full House a huge campaign by gay-rights groups was under way. Opposition parties were now better prepared to limit the clause with amendments. Labour wanted to require councils to discourage discrimination against homosexuality and to protect civil rights. The Liberals wanted to permit sex education in which children would be taught about different sexual orientations. Howard dismissed both amendments as 'a Trojan horse' which would negate the measure.[39]

When the gay actor Ian McKellen visited Howard to lobby in support of amendments, he was told that the objection was not homosexuality as such: Howard simply did not want councils to promote it with ratepayers' money. Before McKellen left, Howard asked him for an autograph to give to his son. The actor told reporters that 'The minister did not seem aware that Clause 28 would affect the lives of individual gays.'[40]

With Clause 28, Howard established a dogmatic public reputation, even within a party which had entered the penultimate, 'triumphalist', phase of Thatcherism. He had cut away his last moorings to the social liberalism of the Bow Group. Already identified with the Tory Right on economic issues, he was now seen as a fellow-traveller on social questions. He required only a more Euro-sceptic profile to complete the outfit.

Clause 28 would taint Howard's public image for years, particularly once he became Conservative leader. But the short-term reaction was not entirely unhelpful for someone who would need the support of right-wing tabloids if he was ever to run for the leadership. When the Lords debated the Local Government Bill in February 1988, a group of lesbians abseiled into the chamber shouting slogans. A few insubstantial Lords amendments required a further Commons debate, in which only three Conservative MPs voted against the government whip. They didn't include Howard's former PPS Robert Hayward, who later came out as homosexual and became chairman of the gay rights group Stonewall, which emerged from the campaign against Clause 28. Hayward had declined the invitation to follow Howard to the DoE as his PPS, and felt 'a sense of relief' not to have done so when the row over Clause 28 blew up.[41] It is possible that, had he stayed with him, Hayward would have persuaded Howard to drop the measure, but unlikely given the Conservative mood of the time. The day before Clause 28 became law (and officially became *Section* 28), the BBC's *Six O'Clock News* was interrupted by four lesbians who had invaded the studio to protest.

Although no one was ever prosecuted under Section 28, it certainly acted as a deterrent within local government. Despite Labour's later commitment to abolish the legislation, it was not removed from the statute book until 2003, six years after the party returned to power. Social attitudes towards homosexuality had changed radically in the intervening period. Whereas in 1988 the Tories had used Section 28 to embarrass Labour, by the new century the positions were starkly reversed, and Labour could use the controversial law to depict the Tories as outdated and intolerant.

Although the history of the DoE during the late 1980s was thus dominated by two of the most controversial policies of modern British history – and Michael Howard was intimately involved in both – the department also had to handle what, at the time, was an even more unpopular measure – the privatisation of the state-owned water industry. A *Times* survey in January 1988 found that only 22 per cent of voters supported this policy, 1 per cent fewer than favoured the poll tax.[42] There could only be one man up to the task of transforming opinion, and in a reshuffle of responsibilities within the DoE in July 1988 Howard was duly put in charge of water.

When the poll tax was entrusted to Howard the year before, he had good reasons for confidence. There were few reasons to be confident about water privatisation, however. Previous state sell-offs had been very unpopular when they were announced, but the public tended to come round in the end. Thatcherites hailed the emergence of a 'share-owning democracy' as profit-seekers rushed to pick up underpriced stock in British Telecom and British Gas.

Water was very different. This really could be seen as a shared national asset – a freely available, God-given resource from the heavens. It was also a natural monopoly, so it was harder to justify the sale on competition grounds. The best reason for taking the industry into the private sector was also slightly discreditable to Thatcherites. Heavy investment was needed to bring British drinking water up to European Community standards, and to clean up Britain's rivers and beaches. But, as Kenneth Baker once observed, the water industry's capital programmes were always 'the first thing offered up' whenever the Treasury sought spending cuts.[43] Given the state of the infrastructure, modernisation could not be deferred for ever; better to have private water companies increase bills than restrict the government's room for further tax cuts.

Michael Howard decided to concentrate his argument for privatisation on the environmental question. Skilfully tapping into rising public interest in green issues, he argued that if consumers wanted cleaner water they would have to pay for it. To back up his claim that water would be purer if it were privatised, there would be an independent regulatory body – the National Rivers Authority (NRA) – to police standards. Previously the water industry had regulated itself, so this was certainly a step forward, though regulation could have been introduced without privatisation.

In fact the British water industry had never been wholly nationalised. There were ten state-owned companies, covering different regions, but several smaller private water companies remained, serving 12 million consumers. It was from this unlikely source that Howard received his first serious blow. During the second reading of the Water Bill the private firms began pressing for significant price increases. One of them, West Kent Water, wanted customers to pay an additional 42 per cent. It was partly French-owned, yet Howard had just denounced people who 'gasp with xenophobic horror' at the thought of Britain's water being bought up by 'French or other overseas investors'.[44]

Howard called on the private water companies to reconsider. At the end of February 1989 he tried to talk them round, but they were unmoved. To make matters worse, an opinion survey conducted by the DoE itself confirmed that around 70 per cent of voters were still opposed to privatisation, and nine out of ten thought that it was unnecessary.[45] By now the bill was in its committee stage, where Howard was his usual combative self. But in early March his position was further undermined when Thatcher declared in a speech that 'The subject of the privatisation of water has not in fact been handled well or accurately.'[46]

Twelve days later the BBC Six O'Clock News led with a story saying that Thatcher saw Michael Howard as the culprit for this failure. The BBC correspondent Martin Dowle said that Downing Street thought Howard had not 'shown a good political touch in defusing misgivings among grass-roots Tories'. There was also 'considerable annoyance', Dowle reported, at the way the day before – Budget Day – Howard had finally confirmed price rises of 22 per cent by the existing private companies.[47] Thatcher was 'so unhappy' about the way privatisation was going, declared the Nine O'Clock News headline, that she was 'going to put the case herself'.[48] This was potentially disastrous for Michael Howard.

It quickly emerged that Dowle's story came from the Prime Minister's press secretary, Bernard Ingham, whom he had taken out to lunch that day, accompanied by Lance Price, a fellow BBC political correspondent. Price, who later worked in Downing Street for Tony Blair, confirms that their source was Ingham, though water had only come up as an afterthought at lunch, when the conversation reached a lull and the two BBC reporters were desperately trying to think of something else to discuss. 'I asked him who Thatcher had really meant when she said water privatisation hadn't been well-handled,' says Price. 'He offered Michael Howard as the answer and went on to say that while he was no doubt a good barrister his political skills had been lacking. He was so clear about it, and so firm in his views, that Martin and I clearly knew we had a good story.'[49]

Ingham later denied telling the BBC journalists that Howard was to blame. 'I told them that Mrs Thatcher was criticising the government collectively,' he wrote in his memoirs two years later. 'I told them [Howard] was doing a remarkable job (brilliant might have been a better word) in processing the legislation through the Commons.' Ingham rather undermined the force of his recollection, however, by getting the name of one of the BBC reporters wrong.[50] There seems little doubt that Ingham had fingered Howard. But it was never completely clear whether Thatcher herself really was upset with him – though it seems likely, since Ingham was known closely to reflect her views. The only other possible target for Thatcher's ire would have been Nicholas Ridley, yet she had said just the week before that Ridley was 'the best Environment Secretary we have ever had'.[51]

In the hours following the BBC story Michael Howard made every effort to defend his reputation, visiting radio and TV studios to denounce the BBC reports as 'absolute nonsense'.[52] He was upset by Thatcher's remarks, and understandably so. It was a public relations disaster, caused entirely by the Prime Minister's firm belief that any political problems were always caused by bad presentation. But, whatever his personal feelings about Ingham's remarks, the bill had to get through Parliament.

Between the committee stage of the Water Bill and the actual share flotation in November 1989, Howard showed how much he had learned as Minister for Controversial Subjects. He faced down the private water companies by warning them that the government would be able to regulate their prices in the following year, and would take previous increases into account. It was announced that 42,000 water workers would be given free shares, or allowed to buy at knockdown prices. Promotional packages were sent to Tory backbenchers, who were invited to add their names to pre-written articles for publication in their local newspapers. To prevent the privatised companies from simply selling off their property assets to the highest bidder, conservation bodies like the National Trust would be given first refusal on any disposal. And, to ensure that private investors were not deterred by the threat of tough regulation, the guidelines on the discharge of effluent into rivers would be relaxed temporarily.

Even so, there is some evidence that water was not Michael Howard's finest performance. A couple of other reporters recall that when interviewing Howard at that time he seemed ignorant of the details, despite his widespread reputation for mastering briefs. In one case, talking to a specialist journal, Howard appeared unsure about what role local government would play in the industry after privatisation. Equally, John Penycate, then a reporter for the *Money Programme* on BBC2, was surprised at how little Howard seemed to understand the complex formula the government was proposing for calculating water bills: 'He didn't seem to be terribly well briefed about it, and kind of lost his temper and got extremely cross. He obviously found the whole experience very uncomfortable. Every time I said to him, "By how much is water going to go up?" he'd evade the question. And I'd ask him two or three times, and this is part of his act – evading the same question over and over.'[53]

On another occasion, having argued that Britain's beaches were safe for bathers and that they had nothing to worry about from sea water, a reporter from the *Today* newspaper asked him to drink from a bottle of water which had just been collected from Brighton beach. 'No, no, no,' Howard insisted, 'I'm not going to be part of a stunt.' He claimed that he hated the taste of sea water, even if there would be no adverse effect on his health.[54] Fortunately for him, it seems that he was never asked the obvious question of why privatisation was necessary if environmental standards were improving anyway. But it was not the end of his ordeal. After frequent reports of sewage on beaches around Folkestone, he felt obliged to accept his local paper's challenge to take part in a stunt after all. The Howard family went for a dip near Folkestone, and were rewarded by helpful press coverage and pictures which showed that Sandra was still shapely. Howard angrily denied suggestions that his office had asked the local water company whether it really was safe to bathe in the area.[55]

As the water flotation loomed, it became clear that the government would again ensure the success of a privatisation launch by under-valuing the shares.

The stock market was rising sharply, and the issue was heavily oversubscribed. What had seemed at one time potentially to be an aquatic version of the poll tax was now reckoned, at least by the City, to be the third most popular privatisation of the Thatcher years. A handsome premium was expected for anyone who acquired shares and immediately sold them. No wonder that on the day of issue the queue at the NatWest Bank in the City stretched for about 250 yards. An elated Howard hailed 'a reaffirmation of popular capitalism'.[56] On the opening day of trading shares sold at almost 44p higher than the 240p offer price – an instant gain of almost 20 per cent.

From a personal and political point of view, it was a triumph for Michael Howard. The *Guardian* introduced a more sombre note. In an editorial, it accepted that the sale would raise about £5.3 billion. Against this, however, the government had sweetened the prospectus by writing off £5 billion of debts, and had given the privatised indus-try a 'green dowry' of £1.6 billion for environmental improvements. Thus the taxpayer was 'actually £1.3 billion worse off', the paper said, for selling what most people still regarded as a natural state asset.[57] Such arguments would hardly worry Downing Street.

Financial services, the poll tax, Section 28 and water had all helped Michael Howard win his spurs as a hard-nosed Thatcherite. An opportunity to show a more caring, sympathetic side of his character came at the end of 1989, when Chris Patten took over the DoE and Howard briefly became his housing minister. Nick Hardwick, the head of the Centrepoint charity for the homeless, persuaded Howard and Patten to come and witness for themselves the growing problem of people – especially the young – sleeping rough on the streets of central London. Late one cold evening the two ministers walked through Soho and along the Strand talking to the homeless, before crossing the Thames to visit the notorious 'bullring'. Beneath a roundabout near Waterloo station the ministers saw the frightening subterranean community of two or three hundred people, many of them with mental problems, living in cardboard boxes and huddling round fires fuelled by discarded wood and plastic. 'He was shocked at what he saw,' says Hardwick, who gives Howard considerable credit for immediately laying the groundwork for what became the Rough Sleepers' Initiative to build shelters for the homeless. 'The big Whitehall battles', Hardwick believes, were 'fought and won by Michael Howard with a degree of personal commitment'.[58] When the initiative came to fruition after 1990, however, it was Michael Howard's successors who mainly got the credit.

At least by then Howard was in Cabinet.

11

ME AND MY SHADOW

He once did say to me that he thought that Labour wouldn't win again until Tony [Blair] became leader, 'because' – and I think these were his words – 'because he looks and sounds like a Tory'.

ALASTAIR CAMPBELL ON MICHAEL HOWARD[1]

In July 1991 Matthew Parris, the former MP who had become a parliamentary sketch-writer for *The Times*, peered down from the gallery of the House of Commons on what he called 'an entertaining battle between two rising stars':

Both are young, both good-looking. Both are barristers, both articulate. And both are very, very bright. Each speaks for his party on employment. Each is tipped as a possible PM. Neither is wedded to dogma, for these men are not crusaders or class-warriors: political pragmatism is another thing they share. Little comes between them: little except ambition, and party.[2]

On this occasion Parris thought that Tony Blair had got the better of Michael Howard. Blair had been covering Employment since October 1989, a crucial stage in his journey to the party leadership and to Downing Street. A month before Howard was appointed Employment Secretary in January 1990, Blair had endorsed in full the

EC's proposed Social Charter, which guaranteed the right of workers to join a union but also allowed them *not* to join. This meant that Labour was no longer committed to the trade-union closed shop. It was a significant and controversial change, which established Blair's reputation as a politician who was prepared to risk his career to force through reforms to make the party more electable.

If Margaret Thatcher had got her way, however, Michael Howard's clashes with Blair might never have occurred. His predecessor, Norman Fowler, had recommended Howard as his successor towards the end of 1989, when he first informed the Prime Minister of his intention to stand down, for 'family reasons', as Employment Secretary. Thatcher initially saw the unexpected vacancy as a chance to promote her young favourite Michael Portillo. Fowler agreed to delay his departure for a few weeks, and recalls that when he went to Downing Street for a formal farewell on his final day in office 'She said that she'd taken advice and I was right, and Michael Howard should be my successor. Obviously she'd been talking to the whips. I think she said words to the effect that "You've won."'[3]

Michael Howard thus became the first of the 1983 intake of MPs to reach the Cabinet, while Portillo would have to wait another two years. It had taken him just six and a half years since his election to Parliament – the fastest climb to Cabinet in two decades (though Gillian Shephard would subsequently manage it in less than five years). He had also leapfrogged two of the brightest names from the 1979 entry – William Waldegrave and John Patten, who were both handi-capped by being considered 'Wets' by Margaret Thatcher.

As Sandra Howard enthused to their local paper, reaching the Cabinet was the 'realisation of an ambition', though Michael himself insisted, 'I don't want to be Prime Minister – there are half a dozen people who are better qualified than me.'[4] The workload would not cause the Howards the domestic problems with which Fowler had explained his resignation; their children were older, and had always been used to their father working all hours.

Howard had long-standing interests, both professional and political, in trade-union reform, an important element of his new job. The defeat of the miners' union in the 1984–5 strike and the subsequent failure of print workers to prevent Rupert Murdoch's News International from moving to a new plant at Wapping suggested that the Conservatives had already solved the union problem. The political benefits of attacking the unions were also diminishing. As their powers were progressively eroded and membership declined (to below 10 million in 1991, the lowest figure since the early 1960s), the unions had become more popular. In 1979 more than a third of voters thought them a 'bad thing'; by 1987 almost three-quarters expressed positive views about them.

Although the third Thatcher government had passed legislation in both 1988 and 1989 to curb remaining union powers, the issue was no longer a priority for most Tories, and many neutral observers (and even the Conservative Trade Unionists group) felt that the balance of power in industrial relations had swung too far towards employers. In 1991, while Howard was Employment Secretary, the number of working days lost through industrial action fell below 1 million for the first time since 1940. This landmark received little attention.

Howard's first major task as Employment Secretary was to pilot through the Commons yet another piece of union legislation – the 1990 Employment Act, which removed union immunity from claims for damages arising from secondary disputes, and also banned the closed shop. Although Howard had inherited the bill from Norman Fowler, it was one of the political issues about which he felt most passionately. As a barrister, he had defended at least one closed-shop victim; the issue had been the subject of one of Howard's few public pronouncements during the 'wilderness' years he spent looking for a seat (in a letter to *The Times* in 1980), and it featured again in his Commons maiden speech in 1983.[5] It also meant that, by a quirk, both Michael Howard and Tony Blair were involved in significant moves against the closed shop within only a few weeks of each other. But even Howard acknowledged that this sixth major change to industrial relations law within a decade was likely to be the last.

If there was little political benefit to be gained from adding new constraints to the heavily restrained labour movement, Howard was under pressure from the outset on unemployment. During 1989 the much-disputed official unemployment figure dipped below 2 million for the first time since 1980. When Fowler left office, just over 1.6 million people were unemployed – fewer than half the post-war peak of 3.4 million reached in 1986. December 1989 was the forty-first month in a row to see a drop, but it was the smallest fall for three years – an early sign that the 'Lawson boom' was turning into a recession which threatened to drag unemployment back to the forefront of politics. Norman Lamont's claim that rising unemployment was 'a price well worth paying' to contain inflation compounded the damage.

According to Roger King, who had been Howard's PPS since 1987 and followed him to his new job, the employment statistics did not cause too much dejection within the department: the Conservatives knew that they had survived bad times before.[6] Even so, an ambitious minister would have hoped to start his Cabinet career in a more promising climate. At least Tony Blair was less likely than his predecessors to exploit this issue, having virtually abandoned Labour's goal of full employment. But Blair's flexibility was itself a new source of difficulty for Howard. He could no longer rely on the standard Conservative responses, because Blair represented a moving target.

In the first exchange between Howard and Blair, at Employment questions in January 1990, the Labour man gave the briefest of welcomes to his new opposite number before attacking the government's record on training. In return, Howard accused Blair of 'routine party political criticism'.[7] Less than a fortnight later, when the sparring partners faced each other during the second reading of the Employment Bill, Blair lambasted the measure as 'shabby, ill-thought-out and bigoted'.[8] Before both men moved elsewhere after the 1992 general election, the rhetoric became sharper. There were no direct personal attacks, but even without the benefit of hindsight there was a detectable edge to their exchanges. In Howard's case, the determination to demonstrate that Blair had not made progress in moving Labour away from its socialist roots seems to have been motivated at least in part by a fear that the venture might succeed, making Labour more like the Gaitskellite party that he had once thought of joining.

Tony Blair, for his part, certainly made an astute tactical choice by concentrating his attack on training. It was the ideal theme for a pro-European 'moderniser' with little ideological baggage, allowing him to suggest that Britain could lose out to better-equipped competitors when the European Single Market came into force in 1992. Only 38 per cent of the workforce had a vocational qualification; in France the proportion was 80 per cent. Seven out of ten in the existing British workforce had left school at the first legal opportunity. With declining numbers of school leavers, there was a need to retrain older workers to meet skills shortages in an increasingly sophisticated economy. Howard's inheritance helped Blair here, too. While unemployment had been falling, the Employment budget had been a prime candidate for spending cuts, especially since take-up of the various Conservative schemes for reducing the dole queues had proved disappointing. Howard took over a department which had been targeted by the Treasury for savings at exactly the time that the case for extra cash was becoming stronger. If this had been a courtroom duel, there would be no doubt which counsel had the better brief.

In the eyes of Sarah Baxter in the *New Statesman,* Howard was no match for Blair because 'he's bland, he's boring and he's a Thatcherite.'[9] But more objective observers recognised that Howard suffered handicaps which were not of his making yet still managed to score points against his nimble opponent. His stock in the Commons certainly increased while he was at Employment. This partly reflected the quality of the competition. In a *Guardian* profile of October 1991, Michael White quoted a 'Tory insider' who thought that 'he's doing very well when a lot of other people aren't.' But White's source also suggested why this relative success might not register beyond Westminster: 'He's a lawyer and he's Welsh. He's Jewish and he doesn't look very lovely on TV. People aren't sure what he stands for.'[10] In the same month the *Sun* reported that only 7 per cent of British voters recognised Howard from his picture, while his approval rating was a dismal 13 per cent.[11] Six months after his promotion it was reported that Howard had approached Martin Sorrell, who ran the world's biggest advertising group, WPP, to ask him to recommend an adviser to improve his department's communications and image, though nothing came of it. Howard did, however, employ Roger Rosewell, a former Trotskyist who had become a *Daily Mail* leader-writer, to help with ideas and speeches.

Within the department itself, Howard earned mixed reviews. His successor, Gillian Shephard, recalls that he was 'very, very popular and charming in the private office. They loved his decisiveness, his clarity and quickness. They appreciated his fierce defence of his position.'[12] Some saw him as demanding, liable to complain when he thought that he was being poorly served, but not one to bear a grudge. He was regarded as an intellectual, but better at asking questions than suggesting policies of his own. Unlike one of his predecessors, Lord Young, Howard didn't bubble with new policies; instead he was adept at picking up colleagues' proposals and developing them. More than a year into the job, Howard publicly admitted he wasn't an original thinker: 'I'm not sure you would find all that many practising politicians who can lay claim to original ideas. I think the art of politics is selecting the best of the ideas which originally were thought of by those not active in politics and making an assessment whether they will work and achieve the result you wish to achieve.'[13] It was an extraordinarily honest admission for a politician to say he couldn't come up with his own ideas.

It was soon no secret within Whitehall that Howard did not get on with his Permanent Secretary, Sir Geoffrey Holland, who hated the partisan way in which the Secretary of State used his position. Holland was not a typical civil-service mandarin, having spent all his thirty years in government working on employment matters, much of it at the Manpower Services Commission, where he had enjoyed devising new jobs schemes and training projects. Many staff at the department found Howard unusually challenging and aggressive for a minister. 'Because he was so keen to get at the heart of an issue he would interrogate people,' says his information director Barry Sutlieff. 'Sometimes you did feel you were in the witness box at the Old Bailey under cross-examination. Some officials didn't like him, but he commanded a deep respect among others for his ability to get things done.[14] Yet he always listened to officials, and always said 'thank you'.

Although Howard struggled to transmit his human qualities during the course of his official duties and on television, he was good at expressing his gratitude to those who shared his burdens. Twice a year he invited key members of the departmental team – including his ministerial driver – for dinner at his London home. On these occasions, Roger King remembers, the Employment Secretary and his wife refused offers of help with the catering, and Howard would greet guests in his apron. He also took personal care in giving Christmas presents. More practically, he encouraged the development of childcare facilities for his staff.

Nevertheless, Michael Howard's Cabinet career was almost curtailed before it had really begun – and for reasons which were only partly of his own making. By November 1990 the rumbling discontent within the party both about the poll tax and more generally about Margaret Thatcher's increasingly remote style of leadership finally persuaded Conservative MPs that she had to go. Even if Howard was not one of the main architects of the poll tax, he had served as a chief foreman and had brought it on to the statute book, missing no opportunity to defend it robustly or to belittle its opponents both inside and outside the party. Furthermore, whether by conviction or convenience, his strategy since his election as an MP had been to identify closely with Margaret Thatcher and her views.

On Tuesday 20 November 1990, Conservative MPs voted in the ballot triggered by Michael Heseltine's challenge to her leadership. After the first vote proved inconclusive, Thatcher consulted Cabinet colleagues one by one amid rumours that support for her was crumbling. Howard was the fifth minister to see her, having canvassed his junior ministers, who included Robert Jackson. 'I thought she was sure to lose,' says Jackson. 'I knew a lot of people who would switch the next time round. I don't think he liked what I was saying.'[15] Howard seemed to panic when the true gravity of the situation became clear; he gave his Cabinet colleague Cecil Parkinson a list of those who were likely to vote against Thatcher, although Parkinson says this included people from his own department (Energy) who had pledged to stand firm.[16]

By the time that Michael Howard entered the Prime Minister's study she had already been informed bluntly by Ken Clarke that if she contested the second ballot she would lose, and her defeat would split the party. Howard's interview was none the less painful. She had not expected much support from her first three visitors – Clarke, Peter Lilley and Malcolm Rifkind – but the fourth, Peter Brooke, had been more positive. If Thatcher was hoping that Howard would continue the momentum in her favour, she was soon disappointed, and instead he helped persuade her that her time was up. According to one authoritative account, Howard described her as looking 'like a wounded bird'. He reportedly told her, 'I wish to God I didn't have to say this . . . I don't think you're going to win. I fear there is a danger that the margin against you could be quite big.' MPs with marginal seats, he said, felt they could no longer sell her on the doorstep. Some felt their obligation to vote for her in the first round did not extend to the second ballot. Some MPs would want to be on the winning side, he warned, so as more declared for Heseltine, others too would soon desert.[17] Thatcher recalled him promising he 'would not only support me but would campaign vigorously for me'.[18] But if she did step down, he said, John Major was best placed to defeat Heseltine.

Howard's anxiety about a Heseltine premiership was understandable, even though on a personal level the two Michaels had much in common. They came from the same area of south-west Wales (Heseltine is from Swansea), but had quickly shed their Welsh roots. At Oxbridge they'd become star debaters, but had fallen out with their university Conservative associations. In the 1960s they'd both been active in the Bow Group, leaned to the left on Europe and race, and driven smart cars before they could really afford to. Both had successful careers outside politics; both had dabbled in the public arena of being TV presenters, yet were private individuals who found it hard to suck up to backbenchers. Both had glamorous wives. Both had fallen in love with Liverpool. And both were hugely ambitious. Above all, they were political professionals.

But Michael Heseltine's main attraction to uncommitted MPs was his promise to abolish the poll tax. Howard's robust advocacy of this measure, and his Commons attacks on Heseltine and his chief lieutenant Michael Mates, might make him an obvious victim in a Cabinet reshuffle if 'Hezza' took over. Howard had burned any remaining bridges with the Heseltine camp by branding the former Defence Secretary as 'the most divisive figure in the party for the past five years', so if he hadn't been sacked he might have felt obliged to resign anyway.[19] And, even if Heseltine's bid failed, Howard would still be vulnerable after a change of leadership because it looked unlikely that the poll tax would survive no matter which candidate won. His best chance of staying in office was to make an early declaration of support to the contender who looked most likely to beat Heseltine.

Although Michael Howard had earned respect from his parliamentary colleagues, he had built few personal ties which would have persuaded colleagues to help save his career. Robert Jackson recalls that Howard had few friends in the House, while Roger King recollects that when Howard recruited him as his PPS they had never met before.[20] Fortunately for Howard, the depth of his personal support was never put to the test. Circumstances suddenly made his longest-standing political friend, Norman Lamont, an invaluable ally. Although John Major initially declined to appoint an official campaign manager on declaring his candidacy, Lamont had been a prominent supporter from the start and soon assumed the role. It was equally natural for Lamont to ask Howard to play a leading part in Major's team, although Howard and Major had not been close nor worked together. Howard reportedly shed tears (along with John Gummer and the Home Secretary, David Waddington) during Thatcher's final Cabinet meeting, but Lamont also remembers exchanging impatient glances with his friend as ministers tried to dispose of routine business. They were both anxious to close the meeting, for nominations for the leadership closed at noon. They had different motives. For Lamont, a

Major victory would lead to promotion within Cabinet; for Howard, it might be a political lifeline.

So Michael Howard emerged from Thatcher's downfall not as a minister in danger of dismissal, but as a valued member of the winning team. At one stage it even looked as if he would be chosen to nominate John Major, along with Lamont; but after some discussion John Gummer replaced Howard as Major's seconder, because a Lamont–Howard line-up was regarded as too right-wing and anti-Europe. There were, however, some awkward moments during the campaign. In his memoirs, Major recalled that Howard 'pressed for a fundamental review of the role and financing of local government, thus outbidding Heseltine'.[21] It would be interesting to know what Howard had in mind; perhaps he felt that the promise of a 'fundamental review' would bury the issue for the time being, but that it would eventually conclude that the poll tax was the best solution after all. It was a hazardous issue for Major, since he had to convince Thatcher's supporters that he would be a safer custodian of her legacy than either Heseltine or the Foreign Secretary, Douglas Hurd (who also contested the second ballot). Howard's idea was rejected, and not for the first time in his career he found himself labelled as an opportunist. The *Guardian* noted that he had 'just distinguished himself by vowing undying loyalty to the old Prime Minister and undying loyalty to the new boy in two [consecutive] *Newsnights*, with all the fervent sincerity of a tired barrister shuffling briefs'.[22]

In March 1991, in the wake of Major's victory, Michael Howard delivered a speech to the Conservative spring conference which argued that the change of leadership would make no difference to the government's purpose. It was later published by the Conservative Political Centre as a short pamphlet, *Consistency and Change*, his first published policy statement since his days in the Bow Group twenty years before. Howard used the rhetorical trick of juxtaposing quotations from Thatcher and Major, inviting his audience to spot the difference. Both of them had been inspired by a vision of a dynamic 'opportunity society' in which the individual enjoyed the maximum freedom of choice. But this prompted the obvious question: if Major and Thatcher had the same convictions, why change leader? For some Conservatives the answer was that Major was a less divisive figure, who would consolidate Thatcher's achievements following the radicalism of the 1980s. But Howard explicitly rejected the charge that the party had been too radical. 'Perhaps we have talked too grandiosely about encouraging enterprise and devolving power,' he mused. But there was 'one simple test' of a government's policies – 'do they contribute to the well-being of the ordinary man or woman in the street?' Judged by that standard, there could be no doubt that things should continue as before, since the Conservative 'formula' of the 1980s had 'brought our Party and our country unparalleled success'.[23]

There was, it seemed, no need to say sorry for anything – not even the poll tax, whose abolition had been announced by the new Environment Secretary, Michael Heseltine, shortly after the budget in March. In his diary, Woodrow Wyatt reported Howard as saying 'he had been alone in the Cabinet in resisting' the replacement measure, the council tax, which reintroduced the principle that local taxation should bear some relationship to property values.[24]

Unfortunately for Howard, the job of Employment Secretary during the early 1990s was largely unsuited to applying Thatcherism. There were some exceptions: he oversaw the privatisation of the Skills Training Agency, involving the loss of more than 400 jobs, and proposed the scrapping of the few wages councils which had eluded previous culls. Howard had inherited from Norman Fowler a scheme to cover the whole of England and Wales with new Training and Enterprise Councils – TECs. Inspired by West Germany, Fowler thought that training should be devolved to local level, and run by local businessmen rather than bureaucrats or elected councillors. In a form of partial privatisation, the businessmen would be responsible for managing state initiatives such as the Youth and Employment Training Scheme, and they would also encourage employers to develop their own in-house training. The Employment Department's role would be limited to supervision.

Thus Howard took over an idea which already had much to recommend it from the Thatcherite perspective; indeed, Margaret

Thatcher had given it her approval. The difficulty was that it still depended on central-government money; and, as unemployment rose, so did the case for more cash. The businessmen themselves wanted bigger budgets, while the Treasury pointed out that the various schemes were performing badly, with many trainees failing to complete their courses and fewer people than expected enrolling in the first place.

In public, Howard talked up the eighty-two English TECs as much as possible, claiming that 'the TEC movement has caught the imagination of the business world.'[25] But this was ministerial flannel. In June 1990 Howard had told an interviewer that the businessmen were 'averse to being told what to do by me', but they were certainly not 'averse' to barking orders at the minister.[26] Towards the end of 1990, minutes of two meetings between Howard and TEC leaders were leaked to the press. On the first occasion, Howard had been warned that swingeing cuts in the training budget would undermine the vision which had encouraged the businessmen to volunteer their services. In December, after the Treasury axe had duly fallen, ten senior TEC chairmen told him to offer more resistance in future, and to consult more widely before announcing new training initiatives. Howard's minuted response was remarkably meek. 'The TEC chairmen are treating him like a poodle, and he's taking it,' said Labour's junior employment spokesman, Henry McLeish.[27]

In fact Howard had fought hard to preserve his budget in 1990, when negotiations between spending ministers and the Treasury took place at the Bournemouth party conference. Margaret Thatcher had already let it be known that those who resisted too much would be punished with additional cuts. Howard decided to settle without taking the matter to the 'Star Chamber', the committee of final appeal against the Treasury. After a battle with Thatcher's Chief Secretary, his friend Norman Lamont, he had been obliged to swallow a £300 million cut in training.

However much they opposed high public spending in theory, Thatcherite ministers naturally resented budget cuts in their own departments, not least because they were seen as a test of political muscle.

Everyone remembered the unfortunate fate of John Moore, the Health Secretary whose career had been destroyed by his failure in negotiations with the Treasury. In Howard's case there was a genuine argument for minimising cuts at a time of growing unemployment. In the following year's spending round he fought even harder. Lamont was now Chancellor, with more authority to confer the benefit of any doubt, and Lamont's replacement as Chief Secretary was another personal chum, David Mellor. Sparring began in earnest in September 1991, with a leaked memo from Mellor which argued for a £1 billion cut in the training budget over the next three years. Mellor cast doubt on the work of employment as a whole by emphasising once again the mixed fortunes of its initiatives, and his negotiations with Howard took six weeks to resolve. Far from agreeing to a cut, Howard had actually demanded a £700 million increase. Under the Major regime such defiance could pay off. Howard ended up pocketing an extra £470 million, but Mellor never 'felt Michael's conduct of public expenditure negotiations was anything to write home about'. Mellor concluded that Howard wasn't in the same league as a negotiator as Ken Clarke, then at Education, and that he let himself down by proposing measures without costing them properly.

It was a time of momentous change globally. The Berlin Wall had fallen only a few weeks before Howard arrived at Employment, and he seized the opportunity to make trips to Czechoslovakia, Poland and Russia to distribute 'Know How' funds to encourage a market economy. He got on well with the former dissident Jacek Kurón, who was now Polish labour minister, and also with the Czech economics minister, a former blacksmith. 'Helping these countries was very close to his heart,' says Barry Sutlieff.

He genuinely wanted to help in Eastern Europe, and I think he drove it within the department. On those trips we saw a different Michael Howard – one who was clearly moved by what he heard and saw. He had a sense of a huge cloud being lifted from the people of those countries, and was treated with a great deal of warmth. For me, the enduring memory is of the suave, Cambridge-educated barrister getting on so famously with the denim-clad, smoky-voiced Kurón, who'd suffered in Gulags.[28]

This Howard passion to help the former Communist bloc perhaps stemmed in part from his own ancestry, yet he never mentioned his background. Nor did he discuss with his colleagues a personal trip he made one day to Auschwitz, where his grandmother had been murdered by the Nazis. 'It was an absolutely desolate experience,' he said in 2005. 'There were shoes that were taken from the people there . . . There was human hair because everyone was made to shave their heads. I thought, that could have been my grandmother's shoe, her hair.'[29]

If he felt excited by an Eastern Europe which had finally been liberated from totalitarianism, he became increasingly depressed by the European Community, then limited to twelve members from the western side of the old 'iron curtain'. Michael Howard's dealings with the EC while at Employment were dominated by a fraught relationship with the Commissioner for Social Affairs and Employment, Vasso Papandreou. On the European stage, the Greek Papandreou was the Left's answer to Margaret Thatcher. At the Madrid summit in June 1989 she had proposed a Social Charter which would prevent Britain from using its veto to block regulations on conditions at work, but Thatcher had condemned the Charter as a 'socialist' initiative.

Michael Howard's fear was that Papandreou would use the decision-making processes set up under the Single European Act to push through on a majority vote measures which would otherwise require the agreement of all twelve member states. In June 1990 he expressed outrage that Papandreou had backed proposals to give part-time workers the same rights on sickness, maternity, redundancy and pensions as their full-time counterparts, arguing that it would discourage employers from recruiting part-time staff.

Howard faced a battering of social legislation coming out of the European Commission, including an early draft of the Working Time Directive, which proposed strict limits on hours of work. He never seemed comfortable at the numerous gatherings of social-affairs and employment ministers in Luxembourg and Brussels. Such trips were often a waste of time, he thought, but he felt it was an 'evil necessity' to go and defend the British economy against what he saw as damaging restrictions. 'He didn't make many friends in Europe, and didn't really seem to want to,' says Barry Sutlieff. 'I think he saw the Commission at that time as being driven by a bunch of socialists. He had difficulty with the formalised style of meetings, and found it very difficult to allow assertions made by Vasso Papandreou to go unchallenged. But interventions at such meetings were not the done thing. The relationship between the two can best be described as "icy".'[30]

After Major replaced Thatcher, some observers detected a more conciliatory tone in Howard's remarks, to match the new Prime Minister's own approach. In January 1991 he noted that the UK had implemented all eighteen of the agreed directives on social affairs – a record of compliance superior to that of Germany and France. In a letter to *The Times* he promised that 'The government will continue to take an active, constructive part in the discussions on EC social affairs.'[31] He had, in fact, just met Papandreou in London, and had identified twenty proposals – including those on health and safety, the movement of workers, and an action programme for women – where agreement might be possible. But he had already confirmed that Britain would block any attempt to impose the terms of the Social Charter as a whole.

In some quarters the Conservative opposition to the Social Charter – which was due to become the Social *Chapter* of the Maastricht Treaty – was dismissed as a sop to appease hardline Eurosceptics within the party and the press. Howard's own position may have been affected by tactical considerations; after all, it was an issue on which he could delineate clear differences between himself and Tony Blair, with some reason to hope that the electorate would support his position. Yet no one who had pinned his colours so firmly to the free-market mast could preside as the responsible Secretary of State and be happy with the proposed Chapter. In the days before the final showdown at the Maastricht summit in December 1991 Howard deliberately echoed Margaret Thatcher's 1988 Bruges speech, arguing that 'We did not remove unnecessary British bureaucratic controls only to see them replaced by European ones.'[32] He had recently irritated his Continental colleagues by brandishing a letter from a British lorry driver who said that he was quite content to work for sixty-two hours a week. The maximum working week proposed by Britain's partners was forty-eight hours. A few days before Maastricht, Howard met John Major and the Foreign Secretary Douglas Hurd and confirmed his adamant opposition to the Chapter. The *Sun* even reported that Howard and Peter Lilley were both on the 'brink' of resigning over the issue.[33]

Michael Howard did not attend the two-day Maastricht conference himself, but he remained in regular phone contact with several leading players who were present – the head of Major's policy unit, Sarah Hogg; the British ambassador to the European Community, Sir John Kerr; and Norman Lamont, who as Chancellor was primarily involved in the Maastricht negotiations on the single European currency.

While Major continued to resist the Social Chapter, he came under strong pressure from other European leaders; it was even suggested that the whole treaty could collapse if Britain did not sign up. Hogg says that Michael Howard offered suggestions for an alternative, 'cosmetic Social Chapter', which Major presented at Maastricht 'knowing that it would be unacceptable to other governments' and 'an empty gesture'.[34] In his memoirs, Major says that Howard supplied 'useful ammunition against seductive offers' by other European leaders. 'Michael, I think, feared we would reach an unsatisfactory fudge, but it was never likely: I disliked the Social Chapter intensely, and knew well enough the necessity of rejecting it if I wished to obtain approval in Parliament of the treaty as a whole.'[35]

In a famous episode of diplomacy John Major held out, and European leaders agreed that the Social Chapter would become a protocol outside the main Maastricht Treaty. The other eleven countries could then agree to abide by this without Britain's support.

Ever since Maastricht there has been disagreement over how influential Howard's role was in ensuring that Britain remained outside the

Social Chapter. In 1999 the former Prime Minister wrote to the *Daily Telegraph* to correct a suggestion that he had insisted on the opt-out from the Social Chapter only because Howard had threatened to quit. This was 'simply not true', Major said. 'Michael . . . never approached me to indicate that he would resign if I agreed to the Social Chapter. . . There was never any chance of it being signed by [me].'[36]

Yet Major's approved biographer, Anthony Seldon, who interviewed most of the key participants, suggests that the Prime Minister's opposition to the Chapter was less than steadfast. Seldon says that Norman Lamont and Sir John Kerr, 'on Major's instructions, telephoned Howard in London on Monday to see if he would yield in his opposition to the Social Chapter, even in a very heavily watered-down form, which would enhance their bargaining power elsewhere. But Howard was adamant. He told friends privately that he would consider resigning if Britain signed up to the Social Chapter.'[37] It seems, however, that Howard never conveyed that resignation threat to Major himself.

The late journalist Hugo Young even suggested that Major was glad of the role played back in London by 'uncompromising forces' such as Howard, 'whom he seemed almost to beg to apply their pressure . . . This early version of a Major tactic – "the more you pressure me, the more readily I will agree with you" – had the desired effect.'[38]

Although Howard was always loyal to John Major in public, he clearly retained doubts about the Euro-sceptic (or Thatcherite) credentials of the man he had supported in the leadership election. These misgivings must have been present from the start. It was Major, after all, who had coaxed Margaret Thatcher into signing up to the European Exchange Rate Mechanism (ERM) a few weeks before her downfall, though Howard as Employment Secretary was then obliged to play a prominent role in defending ERM membership publicly.

On balance, it seems that Michael Howard's threat of resignation if Major signed was implied rather than explicit, and perhaps conveyed to others rather than to Major himself. But Norman Lamont certainly believes that Howard was instrumental in ensuring that Britain stayed out of the Social Chapter. Howard himself pronounced it an 'excellent outcome'.[39] But, for the Major government, it was not the end of the matter.

For the next six years Labour promised to sign up to the Social Chapter if returned to power, and it promptly did so in 1997. Just as horrific in Howard's eyes was Labour's pledge to introduce a national minimum wage. Howard saw the policy as both an affront to the free market and also an excellent way of embarrassing Tony Blair. He was encouraged to exploit the issue by his bright young special adviser Tim Collins, an LSE graduate who brought a sharper political edge to the Employment Secretary's work. They identified the minimum wage as potentially a serious weakness in Labour's programme, but it was one of the few positive policies on offer from the Labour modernisers. Howard pummelled away at it with some success.

The minimum wage was a relatively simple issue for the public to understand, and it divided the unions. Despite its obvious appeal for those with a concern for social justice, for the unions it was a major departure from the traditional collective bargaining, on which Old Labour's instincts were probably closer to Howard than to Blair. Many on the Labour Left felt that strong unions were the real answer to low pay, while right-wing trade unionists representing skilled workers worried about the erosion of their members' pay differentials.

Yet voters were strongly in favour of a minimum wage. Even two-thirds of Conservative supporters thought it was a good idea. But Howard took the issue head on, and fought a classic tactical campaign. His trick was to grab the headlines with dramatic claims about the likely impact on employment. His argument was that the minimum wage would destroy jobs immediately, because it would raise employers' costs, and that there would also be a knock-on effect as better-paid workers demanded increases to restore pay differentials. This was a clever strategy, as it reminded voters of the leapfrogging wage demands which had made unions unpopular in the 1970s. It also reminded trade unionists of why many of them had resisted the minimum wage before Labour adopted the policy in 1986.

Howard was reckless in his use of statistics; officials in the Employment Department also queried whether it was proper for civil-service economists to analyse the effects of a minimum wage when the results were clearly intended for party purposes. Even staff at Conservative Central Office had misgivings about Howard's use of figures. He seized on estimates from sources which would be regarded as friendly to Labour, such as the Keynesian National Institute of Economic and Social Research (NIESR), and even the Fabian Society, to claim that his views represented the consensus among experts. This kept the minimum wage in the headlines, but at a cost: both NIESR and the Fabians rebuked Howard for distorting their work. Yet such skirmishes were unlikely to influence the public much; and only the most dedicated observer would notice that Howard's predictions changed to suit his audience. His original claim, based on work by statisticians in the Employment Department, was that un-employment would rise by 1.25 million under Labour's minimum wage.

Blair did his best to rebuff the statistical onslaught. When an aca-demic study came up with a tally of just 100,000 lost jobs, he expressed the hope that this would be 'the final nail in the coffin of government propaganda over the minimum wage'. It wasn't, of course. Howard coolly suggested that Labour should drop this 'alba-tross', knowing full well that the public would be perplexed if the Opposition discarded one of its best-known policies.[40] In February 1992 Howard said that economists in his department reckoned 'between 100,000 and 1.5 million jobs could be destroyed' under Labour's minimum wage, depending on what happened to pay differ-entials, and that 'up to three million jobs could be under threat' from Labour's employment proposals as a whole.[41] For the minimum wage, this actually represented a fall from the previous month, when he had claimed 'it has been calculated' that the policy would throw up to 2 million people out of work.[42] He could continue this game indefi-nitely, and there was clear evidence that Blair had been rattled by academic research which indicated that, although Howard's figures were wildly exaggerated, there would indeed be a significant loss of jobs unless the wage was reduced from the planned £3.40 an hour to

£3. Blair refused to accept that the policy would cost jobs, but his agreement in June 1991 'that econometric models indicate a potential jobs impact' sounded very lame. Howard had clearly touched a raw nerve, and later told one of Blair's early biographers, 'He [Blair] was very uncomfortable on that issue. Either it is so low that it doesn't make a difference, or it is so high that it costs jobs. If it means that employers are going to have to pay more than they would otherwise pay, there will be some employers who will not be able to afford to pay that, and they won't offer the jobs.'[43]

Almost fifteen years later, knowing more now about the dynamics of high-wage economies, and when Michael Howard has promised that the Conservatives would not abolish the minimum wage if elected, it's hard to appreciate the difficulties his attacks must have caused Tony Blair. One suspects Blair even shared some of Howard's doubts. The BBC's John Fryer, who discussed the matter with Blair regularly as the 1992 election approached, said that 'when you looked into the whites of his eyes you detected a lack of true conviction' in his answers. On a phone-in show on Sky Television during the campaign itself, Labour's Transport spokesman, John Prescott, even admitted that 'there may be some shake-out in some of the jobs in certain areas'. It was a potentially dangerous admission, but Blair managed to persuade the BBC not to give it coverage.[44]

Michael Howard's bruising tactics were beginning to attract attention among political commentators. Bruce Anderson, a seasoned Tory-watcher, said in June 1991 that it was the right time to 'buy shares' in Howard's career, because he had 'chopped his opponent off at the knees' over the minimum wage.[45] The following month Andrew Grice of the *Sunday Times* noted that Howard was 'scoring lots of points in the Tory hierarchy for his aggressive stance'.[46] In September, Donald Macintyre remarked that Howard 'enjoys Major's increasing confidence', and the *Guardian*'s Michael White described Howard as 'the nearest thing the Cabinet now has to a Tebbit, to chill the voters' spines about TUC paymasters'.[47] Like Norman Tebbit, one of his predecessors, Howard roused the fury of the Labour movement. During the TUC conference the Scottish engineering workers' leader

Jimmy Airlie went beyond the usual rhetoric in saying that he had 'never seen a more nauseating, smarmy and hypocritical figure'.[48] To the Labour MP Andrew Faulds – no stranger to parliamentary pugilism – he was simply the 'nastiest man in the government'.[49]

These judgements show that Michael Howard didn't adopt a new more abrasive persona when he became Home Secretary. As a junior minister, or indeed as a planning barrister, he had never flinched from bruising encounters with opponents. With the two main parties neck and neck in the polls from the spring of 1991, and the government's record on employment vulnerable to attack, it made sense to carry the fight to the Opposition. And he wasn't content to counter-attack on one flank. Hoping to portray Labour as the puppet of the unions, he rethought his position on further labour legislation.

But Howard faced the same difficulty which had threatened to undermine his campaign on the minimum wage. Opinion polls suggested that the public was against further union curbs. Matters were further complicated by one idea which was mooted: of introducing a compulsory 'cooling off' period before strikes in the public sector. While this policy was popular among Conservative voters, a vocal element wanted to go even further than Howard, and favoured a more prolonged delay before any industrial action could start. Some even wanted a complete ban on disputes in key services. In the past senior officials at the Employment Department had persuaded ministers to drop the idea, arguing that new legislation would be of little practical value.

Undeterred, Howard published a consultative Green Paper, which proposed that unions should keep their members fully informed and that there should be postal ballots for the election of union officials, a seven-day notice period for public sector strikes, and legally binding agreements between workers and employers unless both parties decided against them. Workers would be able to join any union, even if it was not represented locally; this was obviously designed to deepen divisions by stirring union rivalry for members. Yet Howard acknowledged that legislation was unlikely before the next election, which laid him open to the charge of partisan posturing. The organisation of

Conservative Trade Unionists told Howard that he had gone too far. Tony Blair dismissed his proposals as 'scandalous and undemocratic'.[50]

When the Green Paper led to Howard's White Paper, *People, Jobs and Opportunity*, and a Commons debate, some Tory backbenchers seemed uneasy, as if the 'people' were them, the 'jobs' were theirs, and the 'opportunity' was Howard's. The former Conservative MP Matthew Parris called Howard's speech 'a party political broadcast'.[51] The *Guardian's* Andrew Rawnsley jeered that the White Paper was like 'a first draft of a few pages of the Tory manifesto. He used the despatch box not so much to detail his proposals but as a platform for a party conference-style speech attacking Labour'.[52] At the time of the White Paper debate an election was only a few weeks away.

The previous year's local election results suggested that Michael Howard could have difficulty in keeping his seat, and things looked even worse for him in Folkestone than they had in 1987. In 1991, for the first time, the Liberal Democrats had won outright control of Shepway Council (whose boundaries matched his seat exactly, despite the different name). The Lib Dems won 33 of the 56 seats and 46.6 per cent of the vote, compared with only 40.5 per cent for the Conservatives. In September 1991 Howard boasted in his local paper that unemployment in the Folkestone area had fallen by nearly a third since 1987, from almost 5,000 to 3,334.[53] But competition from the Channel Tunnel forced Sealink ferries to shed more than 500 jobs.

Michael Howard's Cabinet position, the regular ding-dongs with Blair, and the fight against the Social Chapter had all raised his national profile, and this was likely to have a favourable impact in Folkestone during the April 1992 election – some voters enjoy having a famous MP. Yet equally, his higher status meant that he was more likely to be diverted by the national election battle. During the campaign itself he spoke in more than one Tory constituency that was safer than his own. He spent some time on the road with the party chairman, Chris Patten, a very different character, who had serious reservations about Thatcherism. But they formed a reasonable working relationship, per- haps out of mutual sympathy: Patten's seat in Bath was even more

Michael Howard's cousins, the Hecht family, in Ruscova, Romania c.1938–39. L–R: Jacob, Israel, Hannah, Basku, Joseph, Abraham and Martin. Hannah, Joseph and Israel died in the Holocaust. Jacob and Martin survived long Nazi death marches and now live in London.

Advertisement in the *Llanelli Star*, March 1958, for the opening of the Howards' second shop in the town. They already owned the Beehive and later opened a third shop in Carmarthen.

Howard (centre) in the fourth
year at Llanelli Grammar School.

Michael's father, Bernard Howard, surrounded by fourteen women at a Christmas dinner for the
family's shop employees in the early 1960s. Michael's mother Hilda and his sister Pamela are just
to the left of Bernard, while his aunt Rosie, who survived Auschwitz, is on the immediate right.

Howard, third from the right, watching rugby at Llanelli's ground, Stradey Park, in 1961. Howard was, in fact, much more of a soccer fan. He rebelled at his rugby-dominated school by starting an informal soccer eleven, and nowadays shares his affections between the football clubs of Llanelli, Swansea, Liverpool, Folkestone, and Hythe. [Dragon Pictures]

Sandra Paul with Frank Sinatra in 1961. Sandra and her first husband, Robin Douglas-Home, stayed at the singer's home in Palm Springs while Robin was writing a book on Sinatra. [Rex Features]

In the early 1960s Sandra Paul was one of the most famous and best-paid models in the world. *[Rex Features]*

Below: Sandra Paul on the front covers of *Vogue*, photographed by Peter Rand in June 1963 (left) and David Bailey in 1964 (right). At the start of 1964 she also achieved what was said to be a unique distinction for an English model of being the cover picture for two successive American editions of *Vogue*. *[Condé Nast Publications Ltd.]*

THE
NEW
BIG
VOGUE

...at makes Britain wear well?

VOGUE

E LOOKS IN
GUE NOW
VE CAR
LL TOUR
ANCIS BACON
R JOHN ROTHENSTEIN

Sandra on a visit to 10 Downing Street in March 1965. She admitted she was 'already in trouble for voting Liberal' the previous October, when her husband's uncle, the Conservative Prime Minister Sir Alec Douglas-Home, lost office. *[Associated Newspapers]*

"We used to be friends . . ." 'Varsity' files are full of pictures like this, but Mosley has broken up yet another close partnership by splitting Howard and Clarke.

Michael Howard and his life-long rival Ken Clarke, as portrayed in the Cambridge University newspaper *Varsity* in 1961. Howard resigned from the Conservative Association committee in protest at Clarke's decision to invite the former fascist leader Oswald Mosley.

Howard in Regency dress at the Cambridge Union in March 1962 for the farewell debate for his predecessor John Gummer (wearing the hat).

Five future Cabinet ministers among the Cambridge Mafia at Ken Clarke's wedding in 1964. L–R: Peter Fullerton, Howard, John Gummer, Clarke, Leon Brittan, Christopher Mason and Norman Lamont.

Conservative candidate for Liverpool Edge Hill in 1966. After losing, Howard tried to get a better seat elsewhere but failed, so he fought Edge Hill again in 1970. *[Liverpool Post & Echo]*

Howard on holiday in Menorca in 1976.
[Rex Features]

With Sandra in Menorca, a year after they married.
[Rex Features]

Howard with his daughter, Larissa (born in 1977), and son, Nicholas (born in 1976). *[Rex Features]*

Michael Howard with his son, Nicholas, who inherited his father's devotion to Liverpool and also his politics. [Rex Features]

Howard campaigning with Jeffrey Archer in the 1987 general election only a few weeks before the libel trial at which Archer committed the perjury which eventually sent him to jail. Howard was always close to Archer and supported his successful bid in 1999 to become Conservative candidate for Mayor of London, though Archer was later forced to step down when his perjury was exposed. [Mike Griggs]

The Howards in their constituency home. Howard admits he is hopeless at cooking and DIY, but does make his wife an early morning cup of tea. [*Associated Newspapers*]

Table-tennis is Howard's main form of exercise, along with tennis in summer. [*Kent Regional Newspapers/Folkestone Herald*]

Howard with Derek Lewis, the Director General of the Prison Service in 1993. Lewis, who had been appointed by Ken Clarke, says their first meeting was 'devoid of warmth' and Howard showed 'no spark of interest' in prisons. *[Daily Telegraph]*

Howard in 1996, not plotting his leadership bid, but visiting Belgravia police station to promote a weapons amnesty. *[PA/EMPICS]*

Howard and William Hague appearing on *Breakfast with Frost* in May 1997, the weekend after the collapse of their leadership pact. Hague pulled out because he thought Howard was unlikely to win. He won the leadership while Howard finished fifth out of the five candidates. *[Times Newspapers]*

Howard with his former prisons minister Ann Widdecombe, whose 'something of the night' comment in May 1997 ruined his leadership campaign. *[Bob Johns/Peter Orme]*

The *Newsnight* interview of May 1997, in which Jeremy Paxman asked thirteen times whether he had threatened to overrule Derek Lewis. The story was that Paxman kept asking the same question because the next item on *Newsnight* wasn't ready, but the presenter had a hunch that the question was likely to embarrass Howard. *[BBC]*

Howard visited his friend Jonathan Aitken in prison in 1999, but in 2004 firmly blocked Aitken's plans to return as a Conservative candidate. *[Mike Gunnill]*

Howard and the Conservative Party chairman Theresa May standing by Iain Duncan Smith on the day in October 2003 when IDS announced a leadership ballot had been triggered. Howard remained loyal to IDS until the end, though his friends had been preparing for his succession.
[Associated Newspapers]

Howard with his closest aide Rachel Whetstone watching his local football team Folkestone Invicta the weekend he took over as Conservative leader. *[Chris Laurens]*

Howard's second cousin Simon Bakerman, who was released from prison on the day Howard became Conservative leader in 2003, after serving one year of a three-year sentence for drugs offences. Bakerman was also an associate of John Haase and Paul Bennett, the Liverpool gangsters to whom Howard controversially granted royal pardons in 1996. *[Mirrorpix]*

As Leader of the Opposition, Howard made an immediate impact in the Commons, but this had little effect on the polls which suggested the Conservatives were even more unpopular at the end of 2004 than during the last weeks of IDS. *[PA/EMPICS]*

The Howards with Margaret Thatcher at a reception in 2004 to mark the 25th anniversary of her premiership. Howard is always regarded as a strong Thatcherite, but a former editor of the *Folkestone Herald* recalls Sandra saying in the late 1980s that Michael loathed Thatcher. *[Rex Features]*

Howard and his front-bench team in June 2004. He initially halved the Shadow Cabinet to twelve members, though it later crept back up to seventeen. *[Daily Telegraph]*

Venturing into solid Labour territory, Howard is presented with a special edition of the *Weatherfield Gazette* by *Coronation Street* star Barbara Knox. *[PA/EMPICS]*

vulnerable to the Liberal Democrats than Folkestone (and he ended up losing it).

During the campaign, Howard's special adviser Iain Wilton (who had temporarily replaced Tim Collins) mused about him succeeding Patten as Conservative chairman. After all, he was seen as the new Norman Tebbit, and the latter had also served at Employment before running the party machine (even if Tory chairmen are by tradition more junior figures during the first half of a parliament). And Howard had some bruising Tebbit-like encounters with the BBC in the closing months of the parliament. In October 1991 he pulled out of a live interview with the *On the Record* programme just before transmission, when producers refused to break precedent by letting him see their introductory film in advance. Even more tetchy was his behaviour when BBC's *Panorama* tried to film him during a visit to Tyneside for a programme on inner-city policy. He barred the programme's crew from filming his visit to the local TEC, and then walked out of a chamber-of-commerce lunch at a nearby hotel when he spotted that the persistent *Panorama* team were present. Howard was furious with government press officers for telling *Panorama* they could film freely, and refused to return to the lunch until the BBC crew left. The programme's reporter, Jane Corbin, was allowed into the subsequent press conference only on condition that she asked no questions.

Radio 4 incurred his wrath when he was asked questions about training when he had agreed only to discuss unemployment, and he also protested to the Director General, John Birt, when the BBC correspondent Nicholas Jones broadcast details of supposedly leaked Employment Department documents, supplied to him by Labour, which Jones suggested showed divisions between Howard and Sir Geoffrey Holland over TECs. In his memoirs Birt says that Howard 'wrote long, involved, lawyerly letters of complaint', though not always, it seems, with the full support of his officials. 'When Howard moved from the Department of Employment,' recalls Birt, 'a senior civil servant rang me up and said: "I shouldn't say this – but the patience and care with which you dealt with Michael Howard was remarkable. I couldn't believe your forbearance!"'[54] Such pressure sometimes worked, however. On Nicholas Jones's report Birt told Howard, 'I regret the terms in which the BBC reported this story and have informed those concerned that I do.'[55]

Howard may have appeared excessively keen to control coverage, but he was only emulating the tactics which had increasingly been adopted by Labour under their then communications director, Peter Mandelson. Nicholas Jones would later say that Howard had a 'machiavellian talent for media management. To my mind he was their answer to Peter Mandelson.'[56] But unlike Tony Blair and Gordon Brown, the Labour modernisers whom Mandelson promoted on television, Michael Howard did not come across well on screen. Despite an engaging smile and the occasional twinkle in his eye, he was too belligerent and pedantic, too partisan and unsympathetic.

The most spectacular example of this was actually on radio, five weeks before the April 1992 election, when Howard was invited to debate with Labour's Jack Cunningham on the *Today* programme. Before the discussion, conducted by Sue MacGregor, the pair had an amiable conversation, and Howard even offered Cunningham a lift back to Westminster. On air, however, the atmosphere quickly turned sour. Howard took the offensive, claiming that Labour would cripple Britain's competitive position with 'the sharpest ever peacetime tax increase . . . interest rates higher by two and a half points . . . a public-sector pay explosion as the public-sector unions cash in on the debts the Labour Party's incurred to them' and 'attempts to maintain differentials' because of the minimum wage. 'If you sat down and drew up a blueprint to damage the economy of this country you couldn't do it more effectively than what would happen in the first few months of a Labour government,' he said. Cunningham deplored what he said was Howard's 'misrepresentation of our position', and charged him with 'absurd nonsense'. Howard accused Cunningham of 'hysteria'. Cunningham accused Howard of shouting him down. The men kept interrupting each other, ignoring MacGregor's pleas for calm, and at times it was hard for listeners to hear what anyone was saying.[57] Of the two, Howard had been more effective in getting across his basic message, yet both politicians must have lost votes that morning. This time the great complainer was complained about, and several dozen listeners phoned the BBC, some saying the protagonists should have been cut off much earlier. A *Times* leader called the exchanges 'infantile', and Ken Clarke was overheard telling Radio 4 executives that the incident had done nothing to improve the image of politicians.[58]

Nor were viewers impressed by Michael Howard's constant refusal in interviews to tackle difficult questions – a habit for which he would become notorious. The BBC correspondent Peter Smith, who had often interviewed him when the monthly jobs statistics were issued, described him as the 'Cabinet's Geoffrey Boycott'. 'No matter what question I threw at him each month about the unemployment figures, he just stonewalled. I could never catch him out.'[59]

The only time Howard slipped up – and badly – was during a regional TV interview in Kent, when he claimed that unemployment around Folkestone was below the national average. In fact the 9.0 per cent local jobless figure that month was half of a per cent *higher* than for the UK as a whole. For an ordinary MP this would have been a significant gaffe, but for the minister responsible for employment statistics it was a huge blunder. Howard should have noticed when they showed his own seat was doing worse than the rest of the country.

It did Howard little harm. On election night, 8 April 1992, he strolled into the count in Folkestone, arm in arm with Sandra, less than an hour before the result was announced. Despite his previous nerves, his majority over the Liberal Democrats was cut by little more than 200 votes, to 8,910. The national result was a historic fourth term for the Conservatives. The party's majority fell to just twenty-one, though in the overall vote they had a comfortable lead over Labour of more than 7 per cent. Howard had been among those Cabinet members the year before who had urged John Major to delay the poll to await Norman Lamont's 'green shoots of recovery'. Now his judgement had been vindicated.

The upturn had not yet filtered through into jobs, however. The Tories entered the 1992 election with unemployment having risen for twenty-two months in a row: it stood at 2.67 million in January 1992, the highest figure for four years. The number out of work had gone up by more than 1 million during Michael Howard's twenty-seven months at the department. It would eventually peak, nine months later, at around 3 million.

A year before, Michael Howard had told his friend Woodrow Wyatt that 'unemployment never matters' when it comes to votes in elections.[60] Both in Folkestone and across the UK as a whole, he seemed to be right about that too.

12

GREEN HOWARD

I was responsible for the fact that the United States went to the
Rio conference.

MICHAEL HOWARD, 1999[1]

When Norman Lamont emerged from the Treasury to tell the assembled journalists that Britain had suspended its membership of the
European Exchange Rate Mechanism, it produced one of the most
memorable political images of the 1990s. The lights were dazzling,
which made him look shaken rather than just exhausted as he spoke
of 'an extremely difficult and turbulent day'.[2] It had seen interest rates
soar from 10 to 15 per cent as the Bank of England desperately tried
to stop the value of sterling falling below the limits of the ERM; but
the battle was lost. Wednesday 16 September 1992 would soon be
named 'Black Wednesday', although Euro-sceptics thought it a day for
celebration. Lamont's political career was all but over, though he
stayed in office for eight more months, and the Major Government
never recovered its reputation for economic competence. Having
beaten Labour comfortably in the popular vote in April's general election, it was 21 per cent behind in the polls by November.

The Conservative Party was still feeling the effects of Black
Wednesday when Michael Howard became leader more than eleven
years later. In 1992 the impact on him had been mixed. When

Lamont asked him whether he ought to resign, Howard said he shouldn't. 'Much later,' says Lamont, 'he told me that on reflection his advice had been wrong. I thought it was a bit late to say so!'[3] But, in the inevitable speculation about a change of Chancellor, Howard was named as a front runner, along with his long-standing Cambridge rival Ken Clarke (with John MacGregor as a possible compromise).

Immediately after the 1992 election Michael Howard's stock continued to rise. He returned to the Department of the Environment – the scene of his bruising battles over the poll tax, Section 28 and water privatisation – as Secretary of State. It was a sign of his current prestige that he should be regarded as an appropriate successor to Michael Heseltine (who had moved to the DTI). But it seemed strange that the man who had killed off the poll tax should be replaced by one of its most vocal advocates. Howard was an unlikely choice to champion Heseltine's replacement measure, the council tax, when the first bills were falling due – especially since he claimed to have conducted a lonely rearguard against it in Cabinet. His previous record at the DoE was also likely to hinder good relations with local authorities, whose cooperation was essential.

Howard's move was well timed, however. Local government had changed since 1990. Councils were all realists now. The majority of Labour authorities had adopted an attitude which reflected both their modest constitutional status and the desire of many in the Labour movement to ensure the party got back into power. During Howard's previous stint many Labour councils portrayed themselves as small-scale demonstrations of how a socialist party could govern, notwithstanding Thatcherite dominance at the national level. Councils had now become much more focused on providing local services, employing the best-value contractors, thanks to the Tory policy of compulsory competitive tendering, even if there were significant differences of approach between Labour and Conservative authorities.

Just before he left Environment, fourteen months later, Michael Howard could say with truth (and a little retrospective self-criticism) that 'We have taken local government with us all the way on the mechanics [of the council tax], which was not the case on the community charge.'[4] But in one respect this new sense of responsibility was bad news for Howard and his party. 'Loony-left' councils had served a valuable political purpose for the Tories, but this time he would find it harder to find suitable bogeymen to cheer party loyalists and scare voters. In fact Labour had been changing, internally and externally, since Neil Kinnock had become leader almost a decade earlier: the party was now more effective, more pragmatic, and hungrier for power. Kinnock had stepped down after the party's fourth successive election defeat. His replacement, the Shadow Chancellor John Smith, was a party loyalist who had declined to join the SDP in the early 1980s despite his dismay at Labour's hostile attitude to Europe. There was something of 'Old Labour' in Smith, and some blamed the party's election defeat on his tax-raising policies. But his public persona was that of a shrewd and sympathetic bank manager. Like Howard, he was one of the dwindling band of Commons QCs who'd earned the title on merit, and in debate he was just as incisive.

Labour opposed the council tax, pledging to replace it with a fairer system. But the issue had scarcely registered during the April 1992 election. And the local-election results a month later marked a significant recovery for Conservative councillors. The party still controlled only one metropolitan district, but its total number of seats returned to the same level as before the advent of the poll tax.

Once elected party leader, in 2003, Michael Howard would suddenly become converted to the virtues of decentralisation. At Environment, however, he took a very different view of the relationship between central and local government. Although most councils set their council tax at levels which were acceptable to Whitehall, Howard used the DoE's powers to 'cap' the tax, picking ten offenders in 1992–3 to discourage others. The reintroduction of property values as the chief element in local taxation hit hardest the people who had benefited most from the poll tax. The predictable result was a new list of antagonists, creating risks for an ambitious minister in a government with a precarious majority. Terry Dicks and Michael Shersby, Tory MPs whose constituencies straddled the capped London borough of

Hillingdon, were outraged when Howard refused to change his decision. Dicks regarded the cap as a 'disgraceful insult' to his constituents.[5] Another capped council was Basildon, so recently the cause of rejoicing in Central Office when its early declaration on election night signalled that the Major government would be re-elected. Howard and his junior minister, John Redwood, responded with a 'charm offensive' among aggrieved MPs. Before long, 'Whitehall sources' were suggesting that Howard and Redwood were keen to assign responsibility where they felt it was due: apparently they were telling some MPs that the council tax was 'full of flaws', that mistakes were made in valuations, and that Heseltine was to blame.[6]

In September 1992 Michael Howard predicted, without obvious regret, that the power to cap budgets was here to stay. The Labour leader of the metropolitan authorities, Jeremy Beecham, observed that 'Even Nicholas Ridley said he was philosophically opposed to permanent capping.'[7] For Howard, the matter was not about philosophy, but about funding. After the subsidies to cushion the blow of the poll tax, and despite its replacement with the council tax, Whitehall now contributed 80 per cent of local budgets, and Howard planned to increase that share further. He was asking the Treasury for an additional £2 billion, mostly for the 'transitional relief' which would be required to manage the shift from poll tax to council tax in the Conservative heartlands of the south and south-east, where up to 70 per cent of householders could lose out. If the Treasury was being asked to pay the piper, it made little sense for Howard to speak of a day when Whitehall would lose the power to call the tune. The new Chief Secretary, Michael Portillo, might be sympathetic, since he had been at Environment under Heseltine, helping to devise the new tax. But Treasury ministers got few points for leniency in the Whitehall spending round, and Portillo was taking a hard line. Unlike David Mellor, he found Howard to be a 'tough negotiator', and he met his demands more than halfway.[8] In the end Howard got £1.3 billion, although only £350 million was allocated for transitional relief.

While promoting the case for council-tax subsidy, Howard had no intention of earning himself a reputation for reckless spending. The power to control local budgets ensured that the government could tell councils and their staffs that they had to choose between wage restraint and job losses. Howard fought off a threatened 50 per cent cut in the City Challenge urban regeneration programme – the Heseltine scheme which satisfied Thatcherite criteria by distributing funds on the basis of competition between councils. But when political considerations coincided with the opportunity to restrict spending he acted without hesitation. In July 1992 he blocked grants worth £56,000 to two London housing charities which had advertised specifically for black and lesbian employees, which Howard thought was 'offensive'.[9] He also used cost as the pretext for rowing back from Heseltine's plans for single-tier local government and elected mayors, although he decided not to scrap the Banham Commision, which Heseltine had set up to rethink the structure of local government area by area.

While local councils' finances remained a critical domestic issue, Howard's second stint in Marsham Street was dominated by one of the most urgent of global problems – climate change. Environmental issues had risen up the political agenda since the 1989 elections to the European Parliament, when the Green Party took third place in Britain with 15 per cent of the vote. In response, even Margaret Thatcher had tried to convince voters that the Conservatives were the true party of conservation.

For the green movement, it looked like a backward step to swap the tree-loving Michael Heseltine for a Thatcherite QC who had usually acted on the side of developers in planning inquiries. If sustainability begins at home, Howard was hardly impressive: eight months into the job he could boast only a few energy-saving light bulbs in his house in Notting Hill, and some lagging in the roof.

Howard had inherited from Michael Heseltine as his special adviser on environmental matters Tom Burke, a former director of Friends of the Earth, who was by no means a Conservative. 'Michael Howard had no instincts or knowledge about green issues,' says Burke, 'but he knew it was quite high profile.'[10] Yet, against expectations, the issue of climate change engaged both Howard's intellect and his emotions. It also broadened his horizons. His previous experience of international diplomacy, over the Social Chapter and the Maastricht Treaty, had only confirmed his dislike of the European Community. At Environment he was acting on a bigger stage, and relished the experience. One of his early official duties, in June 1992, was to attend the historic first Earth Summit in Rio de Janeiro, the biggest conference the UN had ever held, with representatives from 178 countries, including more than 100 heads of state.

Howard remains proud of his contribution to the 1992 Rio summit – formally called the UN Conference on Environment and Development. Even if, as critics would suggest, the long-term, practical results of the international agreement were limited, the real achievement was to create a precedent for such gatherings, which so many countries with diverging priorities allowed their representatives to attend, and where they committed to some form of agreement on the environment, even if it was diluted. Michael Howard's diplomacy behind the scenes played a significant part.

Getting the Americans to participate was the key to making the Earth Summit a success. The administration of the senior George Bush was divided, and some advisers argued against involvement. The controversial area was the suggestion that countries should reduce greenhouse-gas emissions to avert catastrophic change in the world's climate. The European Community, and Germany in particular, was keen for a legally binding agreement to reduce greenhouse emissions to the levels of 1990 by the year 2000. America was sceptical about this, partly for business reasons. And some figures in the administration of George Bush senior weren't convinced that global warming was happening – notably the White House chief of staff, John Sununu, who had personally analysed the meteorological data on his computer. British officials still smarted from the occasion a year earlier when Michael Heseltine had visited the White House. Ill prepared for Sununu's onslaught, he was left badly bruised.

The Rio summit was due to take place only two months after Howard took office, but Europe and America – the important players – had still not decided the text of the proposed agreement, the

Framework Convention on Climate Change. The EC wanted a legally binding commitment and timetable, but everyone knew the Americans were unlikely to support this. And, unless the Americans were happy with the document being prepared for signature in Rio, there was a serious possibility that George Bush simply wouldn't attend, which would undermine the status of the whole event. The European presidency was held during the first six months of 1992 by the Portuguese, who were doing the job for the first time and were inexperienced negotiators. 'There was a real danger that Rio could be spoiled by Portuguese incompetence,' says one official. DoE officials suggested to Howard that he might try to break the deadlock in Washington by brokering a deal he knew would be acceptable to both America and Europe, in advance of a UN meeting in New York which would, in the custom of international conferences, agree the final wording ahead of Rio. 'When I said to him that there was an impasse, and suggested that a trip to Washington was needed, his eyes lit up,' says Derek Osborn, the deputy secretary in charge of green issues. 'It was a situation in which Michael Howard's legally-honed negotiating skills and his strong network of contacts in Washington could be used to good advantage.'[11] Howard saw it as an opportunity to make an impact on the global stage. It might also show the Europeans how negotiations could be conducted when one didn't have to secure the agreement of twelve different countries. EC leaders were not pleased with his planned mission.

Today, Michael Howard's work in Washington that day features strongly on his official CV.[12] Howard regards it as one of his biggest achievements in twelve years as a minister: 'The whole participation at presidential level was in doubt, and I spent the most fascinating single day of my entire time in government wandering around the six departments of state in Washington that had a view on this and persuading them all that it was essential Bush went to Rio.'[13]

Constitutionally, any breakthrough in Washington required the approval of several domestic departments, since restrictions on emissions would have a big impact within US borders. The crucial talks were those at the State Department towards the end of his day. The problem came down to a few words, and the placing of a single comma, and Howard suggested a way through. 'It was just to find that compromise that balanced the two positions – between Europe and America,' says a British official who sat in with him. 'What came across to me as I sat there was: "This is what a really good British legal mind can do face to face with American negotiators."' 'With his silken pen he came out with a form of words to which we could all rally,' says Christopher Meyer, who accompanied him from the British embassy.[14] The agreed text was signed off at the White House that evening.

It had helped that John Sununu was no longer Bush's chief of staff. Also, Michael Howard was not seen in Washington as being pro-European like Michael Heseltine (or indeed Howard's successor, John Gummer). Part of his task was, of course, to explain to Washington what Europe would ultimately accept – to act in Britain's traditional role as a transatlantic bridge – but given his personal history he could not be suspected of promoting the European position.

A few days later in New York the text brokered by Howard was agreed by 143 countries at the United Nations. But bringing the Americans on board had come at a price. Instead of being legally binding, the idea of cutting greenhouse gases to 1990 levels by 2000 had now merely become an 'aim'. The Worldwatch Institute, an environmental group based in Washington, claimed that the framework convention was now 'so vague to be meaningless'.[15] Some European ministers – especially the Germans, the Dutch and the Danes – thought Howard had been used by the US. Their view was reflected in the Commons by Labour's Bryan Gould: 'The new Secretary of State has concentrated not on persuading the Americans to recognise their responsibility but on making common cause with them in frustrating the world's environmental agenda. It has been a disreputable collusion which does this country no credit.'[16]

One should be careful not to exaggerate. It had not been a dramatic intervention. The Americans would have had to move on the issue very soon, regardless of Howard's involvement. But he brought the Bush administration as far as it was willing to go, and ensured that Rio was seen, for all its limitations, as a success and not another missed opportunity. Without Howard's work the Americans might never have agreed the text of the climate-change convention. Without a text agreed in advance, Bush and the Americans might not have gone to Rio. Without Bush, the Rio agreement would have been far less effective in the long term. In practice only Britain and Germany succeeded by 2000 in cutting emissions down to 1990 levels, but Rio at least put climate on to the mainstream international agenda and prompted the Americans to start programmes which cut emissions. It brought the United States into a continuing discussion, even if Congress and George Bush's son rejected the subsequent 1997 Kyoto Protocol which set out in detail how countries should reduce greenhouse gases. This remains a live issue in US politics, and globally of course.

Michael Howard's role in Rio was not confined to his trip to Washington. Shortly afterwards Bob Zoellick, an under-secretary in the US State Department, rang the Environment Secretary in London to find out whether Britain really was committed to an agreement. Howard's special adviser Tom Burke recalls that Zoellick received a firm response when the American hinted that the US government might back away from the convention: 'Zoellick did not directly say, "I want to take it back," and Howard was not saying, "I won't let you." But I'm absolutely confident Zoellick would have gone back and said, "It will be OK with the Brits that we don't sign" if Howard hadn't held firm. You could pin it down to Howard that he stopped the US backing off. It was a tough forensic discussion with Zoellick.'[17]

Up to this stage Howard had been using his persuasive powers for fairly narrow political ends. He knew that the credibility of the government was at stake. Britain had been the first of the Group of Seven (G7) governments to commit itself to attending the summit. John Major strongly supported the green argument; after the summit itself he said that environmentalists 'were right fifteen years ago, when nobody else was', which implied that governments still had a great deal of catching up to do.[18]

But Michael Howard's experience during his visit to Brazil created an emotional commitment to another green issue – the preservation of biodiversity. Before the summit he visited the inland river port of Manaus, at the heart of the Brazilian rainforest. There he was confronted with an environmental protester of an unexpected kind. The governor of the state of Amazonas was a determined *opponent* of conservation, and had organised a media 'ambush' in which he sought Howard's help in scotching some of the myths about the area. 'I hope to have you as one more ally to demystify the Amazon. We want to develop our livelihoods.'[19] The governor then asked Howard whether he had seen any deforestation during his flight to Manaus. Howard diplomatically sidestepped the question by saying that it had been too cloudy to see very much, though in fact he had just flown over large areas of forest clearance. He later went to a biological institute deep in the jungle, where he climbed a ladder up a swaying tower of scaffolding which was about 150 feet high, part of an environmental research project which was half funded by Britain. It took him right up to the top of the jungle canopy, where looking out over thousands of square miles of rainforest made a lasting impression. 'He had quite an epiphany,' says Tom Burke. 'It had a real impact which was quite visible to his staff. For several days afterwards he couldn't stop talking about it.'[20]

This first-hand research proved invaluable to Howard, who spent much of his time at the Rio summit itself negotiating on how to preserve the rainforests. His legal background helped draft the conference agreements; but his contribution seems to have gone deeper. According to John Major, he 'showed a commitment to Rio that surprised those who knew the image of a dry-as-dust right-of-centre lawyer, but did not know the man. He was immensely energetic and supportive of the environmental case.'[21] Some of the ideas announced by Major in Rio, including the offer of British expertise to other countries interested in conservation, had been prompted by Howard.

In the course of just seven months Michael Howard had played a leading role in the outcome of two of the most important international agreements signed by the UK during the 1990s – Maastricht and Rio. On the latter, it was remarkable that he should have done so working in a department which was not traditionally associated with foreign relations. Yet Howard soon recognised that 'an increasing amount of international diplomacy is environmental diplomacy. This is an international department in a way which would have been regarded as inconceivable a very few years ago.'[22]

Howard was surprised at how big a role the EC now played in environmental matters, and at how much Europe spoke for Britain in this area. Yet he was often impatient at how the EC operated, with its slow consensus-based approach to policy. 'What struck him vividly,' says one former senior official, 'and he had not appreciated, is how we had committed ourselves to acting together in Europe on so many issues. In international places where there are no community competences, Europe nevertheless seeks to speak with one voice. He was sort of restive about that.'

During the second half of 1992 Britain took over the presidency of the European Council from Portugal, which meant that Howard had to chair meetings of EC environment ministers. He did not enjoy the experience, and his body language made it obvious. 'He didn't like the feeling that you didn't have the authority to impose a view, and had to do things you didn't want to agree to,' says one former colleague. Howard's experiences undoubtedly contributed to a hardening of his attitude towards Europe. That summer one of his duties was to host an informal gathering of European environment ministers at Gleneagles in Scotland. 'Michael was conspicuously bad at it,' says one official. Rather than take part in the festivities, which involved Highland dancing and bagpipes, he spent most of the occasion in his room, working on government papers, leaving his minister of state, David Maclean, to act as host. 'My impression', the official says, 'is that it was not his cup of tea and that he wished it was all over as soon as possible. A more extrovert politician would be in his element and create a real friendliness. John Gummer was a master at that kind of thing.'

After Rio, Britain was now committed to reducing greenhouse-gas emissions to the 1990 level by the year 2000 – a target which Norman Lamont, for one, thought 'had gone too far'.[23] Howard's new knowledge of climate change produced an unexpected outcome. In October 1992, with the government already reeling from the fiasco of its abrupt departure from the European Exchange Rate Mechanism, Michael Heseltine announced a programme to shrink further the state-owned coal industry, which had already halved in size since the year-long miners' strike of 1984–5. Heseltine wanted to cut the number of working mines from 50 to 19, with the loss of up to 30,000 jobs. Having prised £1 billion from Michael Portillo for redundancy payments, Heseltine failed to anticipate the likely response, both from the general public and also from Conservative MPs. Even Cabinet colleagues, including Howard's successor as Employment Secretary, Gillian Shephard, had been kept in the dark about the plan. Heseltine was forced to promise a review of the industry. Howard was prominent among the ministers who resisted the idea of reprieving some of the pits, and it was widely presumed that he was objecting on the familiar Thatcherite ground of respecting the market. But his main concern, it transpired, was the impact on the environment, and on keeping the Rio pledge, if Britain remained reliant on coal-fired electricity generators. His arguments, backed by expert submissions from his department, helped to strengthen the government's resolve. Perhaps there was also some shrewd politics at play: supporting the closures for green reasons was bound to cause disarray among the government's opponents. The five-month review took the sting out of the crisis, and Heseltine's original programme was eventually carried out with only minor modifications.

The fate of the mines was an instance where Howard thought that policy decisions could be driven by a convergence of environmental imperatives and market forces. This was typical of his approach at the DoE. Although he decided in 1992 to incorporate the National Rivers Authority, local-authority waste regulators and Her Majesty's Inspectorate of Pollution into a majestic new quango, the Environment Agency, his instinct was to use the market in preference to regulation. His department advised the Treasury on a carbon tax, which was introduced in Norman Lamont's last budget, and Howard advocated a further increase in the higher duty paid on leaded petrol.

In February of that year he returned to America to investigate California's efforts to reduce traffic pollution, and met Bill Clinton's green-friendly Democratic Vice-President, Al Gore. Working with John MacGregor at the Department of Transport, Howard also examined the possibility of toll roads and congestion charges.

Michael Howard's contribution to the pit-closure controversy reflected his increasing stature within the government, where he was emerging as the leader of the Euro-sceptic forces in Cabinet. Norman Lamont says that Howard 'expressed the strongest opposition to any idea of rejoining the ERM. In fact, I think he considered resigning on this point.'[24] This was in contrast to John Major, who had said that Britain should rejoin when conditions were right, and Howard came close to breaching collective Cabinet responsibility towards the end of September 1992 when he said that Britain's departure from the ERM had provided an 'additional opportunity' which meant the government could now 'set our economic policy exclusively by reference to British interests. We are no longer constrained in the same way by the actions of the [German] Bundesbank.'[25] Conservative Euro-sceptics were delighted with this intervention. In early November, in an interview on Channel 4, he remarked that the sceptics were voicing 'a legitimate concern' over Maastricht, and described the treaty as 'certainly the last move I would tolerate so far ahead as I can foresee'. In the *Independent*, Colin Brown speculated that Howard might be a right-wing candidate for the leadership if Major were to fall: 'He is not an ideological Thatcherite, but Maastricht has forced him out into the open.'[26]

Howard's public comments were not helpful to John Major at a time when he was under political pressure. Privately the Prime Minister conceded that he might have to resign over Maastricht, or call a general election. When the Danes rejected Maastricht in a referendum, Howard and Peter Lilley had argued in Cabinet that consideration of the treaty should be held over until the new year. They were overruled, although Major agreed that the legislation should proceed through the Commons in stages, after stern warnings from the backbench 1922 Committee.

In the early part of 1993, however, the tone of Howard's pronouncements changed markedly. Whereas the previous autumn he
had said that the Maastricht Treaty needed to be made 'more acceptable' to the British people, by February he was calling it 'a very
acceptable price to pay for a continued place at the European table'.[27]
When the news leaked out that Peter Lilley and Michael Portillo had
lunched with the irreconcilable Lady Thatcher, Howard began to
look like an honourable minister who might disagree with his leader
but would not stoop to undermining him. It was later reported that
Howard had also recently lunched with his former leader, but just for
social reasons; in other words, Howard was a friend of Thatcher's
rather than a follower. This leak was so helpful to his image that some
suspected him of being its author. The emerging impression of
Howard as a bridge between factions rather than a fomenter of them
was reinforced by his public call for an end to party divisions as
Thatcher and her predecessor, Edward Heath, squabbled over Europe.
At the Conservative Central Council at Harrogate he heaped praise on
Major, calling him 'a Leader any party would be proud of. A leader
any country would be proud of.'[28] At the same gathering Howard also
tried to rally Tories by referring to the Ian Dury hit song 'Reasons to
be Cheerful', though this allusion may have been lost on most of his
audience.

In hindsight, this was the guise in which Cabinet colleagues tended
to remember Michael Howard – forceful, even 'obdurate', in private
discussions on Europe, but steadfastly loyal.[29] But his rash public statements in the autumn of 1992 suggest that this was not his instinctive
position. There are three plausible explanations for the later shift of
emphasis: that initially Howard had now realised the extent of the
government's peril, and decided to retreat from the brink; that he
acquiesced after Major had 'read the riot act' to his leaky colleagues in
January 1993; or that Howard had decided that some loyal noises
would best suit his own career prospects. It may have been a mixture
of all three, but the third is the most likely single explanation. Even a
despondent prime minister is a potent source of patronage – and in a
tight spot he is likely to give preferment to reliable supporters rather

than candid critics. In the first few months of 1993 it looked as if there would soon be a significant promotion for Major to make. If the vultures had begun to hover over the Prime Minister himself, they were already pecking at the body of his Chancellor of the Exchequer, Norman Lamont, whose departure now looked inevitable.

The personal rivalries of Cambridge University politics of thirty years previously were replayed in speculation about the succession at the Treasury. In February 1993 it was reported that Howard's office had telephoned the BBC to request a transcript every time his main rival for the job, Ken Clarke, talked about the economy.[30] Lamont had noticed how often his two Cambridge friends had been doing interviews and pronouncing on Treasury matters. 'I was irritated by Michael Howard's speeches on the economy at the time when there was speculation about my position as Chancellor,' he says, though he acknowledges that John Major had asked Cabinet colleagues publicly to back the government's economic policy. 'I told Michael Howard quite bluntly that I would like him to desist, and he did so.'[31] To underline the point, Howard also dismissed gossip connecting him to Lamont's current post as 'ridiculous'.[32] But Howard's aides acknowledge that they were pressing his claims in the face of a widespread assumption at Westminster that Ken Clarke would succeed Lamont. David Cameron, who was then a special adviser for Lamont, but later worked for Howard, recalls, 'Those close to Michael felt it was worth reminding the world that there were other candidates.'[33]

Yet socially there was no change in the cordial relations between Howard and Lamont. Just after Black Wednesday both were guests at the marriage of Howard's stepson, Sholto, to Alexandra Miller (held at Weston Park in Shropshire, the stately home of the Earl of Bradford, the bride's brother-in-law). On New Year's Day 1993 Woodrow Wyatt phoned Lamont and interrupted him while he was playing table tennis with Howard, who complained that the call was giving the Chancellor a 'breather'.[34] From a professional perspective it was only natural that Howard should take an interest in the possibility of replacing his friend, given the widespread understanding that a change at the Treasury was only a matter of time.

In February, the best-informed punters gave Howard little chance: out of a panel of economists, almost half supported Portillo, more than a quarter backed Clarke, and only 4 per cent had bought shares in Howard. The same proportion favoured another member of the Cambridge Mafia, Norman Fowler, who had returned from his brief family break to become Conservative Party chairman.[35] Everyone knew that the appointment of either Clarke or Howard would be seen as a significant victory for one side or the other in the Cabinet debate on Europe. But, if Howard could beat Ken Clarke to that job, a bigger prize beckoned. In early May 1993 the bookmakers William Hill made Howard second favourite to succeed John Major, at 4–1.[36] Unfortunately Clarke was ahead of him, as the evens favourite. (Heseltine had fallen back because of the mining fiasco.)

To improve his odds, Howard seems to have adopted two chief tactics. The first was slightly to reposition himself on the European debate, but this risked losing friends among the Euro-sceptics, while gaining few new allies in the pro-European camp. Bill Walker, a backbench rebel in the battle of Maastricht, remembers that the rebels were pleased to have a sympathiser like Howard in the Cabinet.[37] Others seem to have taken a less charitable view of his manoeuvres. Teresa Gorman, for example, includes only one (critical) reference to Howard in the whole of her memoirs.[38] The second move was as risky. Anonymous 'friends' of Howard briefed against Clarke to the media.

With Cabinet discipline breaking down, the two sides were drawn towards open combat. In March 1993 a well-informed piece in *The Times* considered the qualities of the two men. Clarke was reported to think that the kind of energy taxes being proposed by Howard would endanger Britain's economic recovery and cost up to 3 million jobs – the kind of numbers game that Howard had played over the minimum wage. It was suggested that Howard had 'gone native' at Environment and become the prisoner of green pressure groups.[39] The two ministers were also at loggerheads over the pleas by Clarke, who was now Home Secretary, to reduce local-authority influence over the police, which Howard regarded as both an infringement of council powers and an intrusion on to his patch. It was a classic instance of a Whitehall turf war, and before long – when he reached the Home Office – Howard himself would try to take central control of police authorities even further than Clarke had planned.

Michael Howard's DoE responsibilites also encompassed housing, where again his more pragmatic side emerged, and he channelled billions of pounds of public money into the new Housing Action Trusts (HATs), which were expected to rely on private capital for further investment in their public-housing programmes. One housing expert, writing recently for the Labour-affiliated Fabian Society, says, 'Howard performed a remarkable political trick for a Conservative,' and he praises HATs as 'the most successful housing-based regeneration programme since the war'.[40]

Opinions of Michael Howard within the Department of Environment were mixed this time round. Hostility may have been worsened by plans to move 2,000 civil servants from Marsham Street to the less-accessible Canary Wharf – one of Michael Heseltine's ideas – which had already caused unrest inside the DoE before Howard provoked further problems by dithering over the issue. But Tom Burke, who had previously worked for Michael Heseltine, and later worked for a third Environment Secretary, John Gummer, says that Howard had 'good relations with his personal staff. He was very considerate, and has a fabulous sense of humour. On television he undersells himself, and there's a little bit where he's brittle and it shows. He thought of Christmas cards, birthday presents and so on. There is a bit of him that seeks affection.'[41] Despite Howard's right-wing reputation, Burke found him to be a pragmatist whose positive views were unclear, even if his dislikes were fairly plain.[42]

Howard's previous PPS at Employment, Roger King, had lost his seat in 1992, and as a replacement Howard appointed Peter Thurnham, who had done the job for other ministers and had been an exact contemporary at Peterhouse, though not active in Cambridge politics. Normally PPSs act as the minister's friend within the department, and his eyes and ears at Westminster, assessing political feeling. Perhaps Howard felt some unease with Thurnham, since he was percieved to be on the left of the party, and later joined the Liberal Democrats. Thurnham found it difficult to establish the same kind of relationship he'd enjoyed with previous ministers.

> Although I admired his ability, he wasn't able to spend much time with me. Michael is a withdrawn, very remote, very reserved person. When I was his PPS he didn't confide in me at all. I'd never know what he was thinking. I suppose 'cold' is the word to use for him. He didn't want to open up to me in any shape or form. He cultivates considerable remoteness. He is a totally committed politician with his eye on the top job. I wouldn't say it was an unhappy experience working for him, but it wasn't exactly inspiring. Michael is out for himself, and would use me to help his own ends. He wasn't particularly bothered about my progress.[43]

Eventually, Thurnham decided to give up the unpaid position to concentrate on his marginal constituency in Bolton. Howard reacted as if Thurnham had somehow rejected him, and demanded to know whether there was any unspoken reason behind the decision. 'He couldn't conceive of somebody stepping off the ladder without a motive,' says Thurnham. Howard even visited his flat to ask whether there was any problem. 'It wasn't just concern for me: he was concerned for himself as well.'[44] As a parting gift, Howard gave Thurnham a book of fairy tales.

Another observer, Lord Crickhowell of the National Rivers Authority – the former Welsh Secretary Nicholas Edwards – remarked that he knew Howard 'far less well than any of his predecessors' at the start, 'and a year later I knew him little better. When we met . . . Michael listened attentively to what was said, but he had very little to say himself and gave little indication of whether he agreed or disagreed. It was hard to read his mind.' Crickhowell describes a meeting with Howard where his board outlined their concerns for the NRA. 'It was obvious that the Secretary of State had not been adequately briefed, or, if he had, that he had failed to comprehend the scale of the problem or anticipate the strength of feeling of the board. Afterwards, we heard that officials had received a severe dressing-down.'[45]

Michael Howard's second stint at the DoE lasted little more than a year. In May 1993, following a disastrous by-election in Newbury (which the Conservatives lost to the Liberal Democrats on a record swing), John Major implemented a Cabinet reshuffle which was dominated by the Cambridge Mafia. The Prime Minister finally decided that Norman Lamont should leave the Treasury, but wanted him to remain in office. Having summoned the Chancellor to Number 10, Major asked if he would move to Howard's job at Environment. Lamont viewed this as a demotion, refused the offer, and resigned from the government. Another Cambridge man, John Gummer, took the DoE instead.

Norman Lamont records that following his resignation he received almost 2,000 letters, mostly supportive, and that among the sympathisers were Ken Clarke and Norman Fowler. He also received a note from his old friend Michael Howard. 'He had addressed it in his own hand,' says Lamont, 'but rather bizarrely he hadn't finished the message. It read something like: "Dear Norman, I am very sorry about . . ."'[46]

Perhaps Howard broke off when he heard his own summons to Number 10, distracted by the prospect of at last landing one of the great offices of state.

13

CRIME MINISTER

He has to know he's in control and making the difference. He's
a fighter. He thinks, 'Don't leave it to anybody else. Trust nobody,
or trust just a few people.' God knows what it does to his
constitution.

FORMER HOME OFFICE OFFICIAL

'Michael,' Jeffrey Archer cried to cheering Tories gathered in the
Winter Gardens in Blackpool, 'Stand and deliver!'[1]

The millionaire novelist was acting as warm-up man for the most
memorable speech of Michael Howard's career, though it was perhaps
unfortunate that, during a debate on law and order, Archer should
have used the challenge of that eighteenth-century mugger, the high-
wayman. Four and a half months into his appointment as Home
Secretary, Michael Howard would certainly deliver, promising his
party conference twenty-seven measures to assist the police, to help
victims, to improve the chances of getting convictions, and to expand
the prison system. Perhaps the most controversial of Howard's proposals was ending the right to silence of the accused, allowing jurors
to draw conclusions from defendants' refusal to explain themselves. By
a huge irony, Jeffrey Archer, once a policeman, would himself fall
victim to Howard's 'delivering'. In 2001 the novelist was sentenced to
four years in jail for perjury, after the judge had allowed the jury to

take note of Archer's decision not to appear in the witness box or to answer police questions.

'At last we've got a Home Secretary who is on the public's side,' declared a *Sun* editorial, less than three weeks after Michael Howard had been named as the seventh occupant of the office since 1979, and the fifth in five years.[2] It must have been heartening to have gained such approval from the most widely read newspaper in Britain – the paper 'wot won' the 1992 election for Howard's party. A subsequent editorial went further: 'If the *Sun* could choose the next Prime Minister – which sadly we can't – Michael Howard might well be the man.' In contrast, the paper said John Major was a 'pygmy'.[3]

If Howard had known how quickly he would make his mark in his new job he might have felt happier when he took over on 27 May 1993. It was no secret that he had wanted to succeed Norman Lamont as Chancellor: the press had carried regular reports on the scrap for the post. However, Howard had lost out to his long-standing rival Kenneth Clarke. As consolation he got the post which Clarke had just left. 'Michael had never contemplated the Home Office,' says a close adviser, who says it was a moment of some 'crisis' for him. 'He said privately that he never wanted to go there.'

The fact that Howard could feel disappointed after taking one of the top jobs in government was a sign of both his ambition and his progress since 1983. If he was still one step behind Clarke, he had made up most of a thirteen-year gap. Yet it still might be a case of 'so near, so far'. Howard had reason to suppose that Clarke would be a success at the Treasury, since he believed that Britain's departure from the ERM the previous autumn offered a marvellous economic opportunity. Clarke would take all the credit for the favourable economic trends he had inherited from Lamont – inflation and interest rates low and falling further, unemployment on its way down, and even the balance of payments moving in Britain's favour. Whatever the *Sun* might say, Clarke was likely to be in a strong position to succeed John Major when the time came.

Howard consulted his family briefly about the security implications of being Home Secretary, and the need for twenty-four-hour

protection which went with the position. He also knew it was a notorious graveyard for political aspirations. Soon after he took the job,
one of the party's 'elder statesmen' told him that no Conservative
Home Secretary had ever become Prime Minister. He later recalled
that 'For a minute he looked shocked.' Howard might have been
trying to remember from his own study of history whether Sir Robert
Peel or Winston Churchill had been exceptions to this rule (the party
was not called 'Conservative' when Peel was Home Secretary, while
Churchill held the post as a Liberal). Labour's James Callaghan had
more recently made the transition, so there was no curse on the office
itself. It was just that so much more was expected of the Home
Secretary of the 'party of law and order'.

At least that was how the Conservatives traditionally saw themselves. It was a perception which had been challenged directly by
Labour since July 1992, when Tony Blair had become Labour
spokesman on home affairs. His predecessor, Roy Hattersley, had
advised Blair that it was a much better job to take on in Opposition:
'In government you're waiting for somebody to break out of prison
every day. In opposition you're hoping that somebody will break out
of prison so you can complain about it.'[4] Or, as Howard himself put
it after he had learned from experience, the Home Office is 'not a
place where you can keep your mistakes secret . . . The spotlight
shines brightly on almost everything that goes on there.'[5] A day
assigned to one subject would suddenly be overtaken by some unfore-
seen crisis. But Tony Blair was not content to wait for events to
strengthen his hand. In January 1993 he had given the first airing to
one of the most effective slogans of post-war British politics – 'tough
on crime, tough on the causes of crime'. His words struck a chord
when, only a few weeks later, the nation was shocked by the abduc-
tion and murder on Merseyside of two-year-old James Bulger by two
boys who were only ten years old.

With a single phrase, promoted by the party's most acceptable face
(though devised by Gordon Brown), Labour addressed one of its most
serious weaknesses. After the 1992 election, Gallup had found that the
Tories were more than twenty points ahead of Labour on law and

order.[6] Yet between 1980 and 1993 recorded crime had more than doubled, from 2.5 million to 5.6 million.[7] Even this record figure fell short of the actual tally: the British Crime Survey indicated that many crimes were never notified to the police. Fear of crime was also rising. The proportion of people afraid of burglary rose from 60 per cent to over three-quarters between 1987 and 1994. More than half the population was frightened of being mugged. Four in ten were afraid to go out alone at night.[8] For a party which had been in government for well over a decade, this should have been a big handicap, not a strength.

So when Howard became Home Secretary the Tories were suffering both from the crime figures and from the new-found willingness of the Labour Party to use the area to attack the government. There were only two ways of retrieving the situation. The first was to improve the figures, so that a reduction in crime was matched by a fall in the fear of crime. The second was to show that Blair's rhetoric was hollow. If he could be provoked into opposing tough anti-crime proposals, Labour's position would be exposed as being no more than party posturing.

On its own, Tony Blair's challenge on crime was serious enough to dictate a hard-line policy even from a liberal-minded Home Secretary. Other factors also pointed the same way. If Howard wanted to lead his party, he had – at the least – to convince the Conservative rank and file that he was taking decisive action to deal with crime. And if the crime figures also started to fall, so much the better: some whip-cracking speeches at party conferences would ensure that he was personally identified with the success. It might even help him to overhaul Ken Clarke on the last lap.

These factors explain why Howard was such a self-publicising populist as Home Secretary. But they do not provide a complete picture. This was one of those happy circumstances when the pressure of events propels a minister towards policies which chime with his personal instincts. Crime had always featured strongly in Howard's election campaigns, and in Folkestone he had encouraged Neighbourhood Watch schemes and criticised lenient magistrates.

His genuine sympathy for the victims of crime, mirrored by an unremitting hostility towards the perpetrators, might have arisen from experiences at the Bar, or even from his exposure to the deprived living conditions in parts of Edge Hill. And within hours of Howard's appointment as Home Secretary his son, Nick (then at Eton), was pushed, jostled and chased by an aggressive beggar at Windsor station. Howard was also convinced that crime was a matter of individual responsibility. Those who blamed 'society' were avoiding the issue; those who excused criminals because of their poverty were slandering the law-abiding majority among the poor.

On his first day at the Home Office, Howard held the customary photo-call, though, unlike most of his predecessors, who had usually wanted to read themselves in first, he happily briefed lobby corre-spondents as well. 'His reaction was to get stuck in there,' says a close colleague, 'and get a grip on things, so that it would not be a "crisis" for him any more.' He wanted to master his new brief as quickly as possible, and he spent much time closeted with his Permanent Secretary. Sir Clive Whitmore told him, Howard said later, that 'the Home Office only works well if there is strong political leadership from the Home Secretary'.[9] Other officials were called in, including Derek Lewis, the Director General of the Prison Service, who com-pared the experience unfavourably with that of Howard's predecessor: 'He said "Good morning" and smiled formally. He made no ice-breaking small-talk about my background, nor did he ask about the state of the prisons. There was no hostility, but the meeting was devoid of warmth. He just sat and waited impassively. What a contrast with the genial Clarke!'[10]

Lesser officials were worried too. 'You could say there was an audi-ble groan around the Home Office at the time,' says one former civil servant, 'because his reputation had preceded him. However, a mes-sage then came through that "actually he's probably not quite as bad as people think he might be. He's actually grown up since his days at Environment when he introduced the poll tax."'

When Howard was visited by the Lord Chief Justice, Lord Taylor of Gosforth, it was taken as a sign that he wanted to establish a good working relationship with the judges. In view of later events, one might think instead that Howard was sizing up the opposition.

Certainly he felt he was entering hostile territory when he first went to the Home Office, situated in a large modern building in Queen Anne's Gate, close to New Scotland Yard. It was not part of Howard's plan to provoke dangerous opposition if he could avoid it, and he tried hard not to blame any of his six Tory predecessors for the situation he had inherited. The Home Office itself acted as a surrogate. Howard's new policy line implied that the department had 'captured' people like David Waddington (1989–90) and Kenneth Baker (1990–92). In Howard's view it was almost the last relic in Whitehall of the post-war consensus, packed with defeatist liberals. This impression was confirmed to Howard soon after his arrival, when he was shown graphs which illustrated the rise in crime. Civil servants insisted to him that nothing could be done about it.

> The officials actually said to me, 'This is the pattern of rising crime. It's gone on, with one or two small and inconsequential blips, like this for most of this century. It is going to continue to go up, and the first thing, Home Secretary, that you have to understand is that there is nothing you can do about it. Your job is to manage public expectations, and to make the public understand that there is nothing that can be done about it.' That was not advice I accepted.[11]

Howard saw the Home Office as one of the few departments to have escaped the Thatcher Revolution, and he felt that it was 'deeply imbued' with the culture of what he called the 'criminal-justice establishment'. He wanted to challenge its existing assumptions. 'The prevailing philosophy was heavily orientated towards the criminal rather than the victim.'[12] Howard was suspicious of his officials, and feared being thwarted by the Home Office machine. One of his junior ministers, Michael Forsyth, later told the MP Gyles Brandreth that 'he and Howard used to pass papers to one another personally, to keep the diluting influence of the civil servants at bay.'[13] Leon Brittan, who had endured an unhappy spell at the Home Office (1983–5), thought that his friend had taken a 'draconian' view of the whole department.[14] Little wonder that the *Sun* should beam so brightly on the man who seemed set to avenge the deeds of 'do-gooders' such as Willie Whitelaw (1979–83) and Douglas Hurd (1985–9).

There was only one change to the existing ministerial team at the Home Office, but it gave a strong indication of Howard's intentions. David Maclean had taken over Whitelaw's Cumbrian constituency in 1983, but this was rather like John Wayne taking over a film role from James Stewart. On crime, Maclean represented the type of Tory who had heckled Whitelaw at party conferences. A vocal supporter of capital punishment, he regarded criminals as 'vermin' who should be driven from the streets, and thought the law sided with the criminal. The draft of a speech in which Maclean put forward this opinion was leaked to the journalist Nick Cohen. When Cohen gave this information to Tony Blair, he found that Labour's spokesman was hesitant to use it against Maclean. 'A lot of *Daily Mail* readers would agree with him,' Blair pointed out.[15] It was an early sign of a different political consensus on Home Office matters. Howard's relationship with Maclean, with whom he had worked closely at the DoE, prospered during his Home Office years, and Maclean would play a pivotal role in events when Howard eventually became Tory leader in 2003. 'He had a manner with Michael that didn't rub him up the wrong way,' says the former prisons' director Derek Lewis. 'David's a good listener, and I suspect if he disagrees with Michael he doesn't go in with a full-frontal attack and say, "You're wrong!"'[16]

Howard secured another supporter from the Right in Liam Fox, a young GP who'd just been elected to Parliament, and replaced Peter Thurnham as his PPS. Howard also kept Patrick Rock, who'd been his special adviser at the DoE. At forty-two, Rock was a lot older than most special advisers, and he had done the same job for Tories as diverse as Nick Ridley and Chris Patten. His own hopes of being an MP had been dashed by losing the Tory seat of Portsmouth South in a by-election in 1984. Officials noticed that he spent much of his time on the phone briefing journalists, and he courted controversy – 'Radio Rock' they called him in Downing Street, reflecting his tendency to sound off too much. 'He invented spinning before Alastair Campbell was out of bed,' says a former colleague. 'But Patrick had occasions when he overdid it a bit, and this would become a major story the next day.' 'A political Rottweiler with a grating bark,' says Derek Lewis, 'he was quick in the expression of his views, which appeared to be somewhere to the right of Attila the Hun's, and slow to hear the ideas and opinions of anyone else . . . Howard frequently tired of his fourth-form interjections, issuing curt instructions for him to keep quiet: but Rock was quite oblivious to his irritation, and merely came back for more.'[17] As a second adviser Howard took on the twenty-seven-year-old David Cameron, a bright Old Etonian who'd previously advised Norman Lamont at the Treasury, and had spoken as a schoolboy of becoming Prime Minister.

The rest of the ministerial team, which Howard acquired from Ken Clarke, was a mixed bag. The spokesman in the House of Lords, Earl Ferrers, showed no sign of dissenting from the Howard line. Peter Lloyd, the prisons minister, had known his boss in both CUCA and the Bow Group, and spiritually had remained in the latter while Howard moved to the right. Lloyd was more in line with the Home Office orthodoxy on penal policy and the need for rehabilitation, and when he spoke at policy meetings, says Derek Lewis, 'Howard's eyes glazed over in barely concealed contempt.'[18] After Lloyd left the Home Office, in July 1994, he made many criticisms of his former colleague which might have been more damaging had Lloyd been as media-conscious as Howard.

The new Home Secretary managed to impress the *Sun* even before his first appearance at the dispatch box. He had expressed concern about the case of two vigilantes from Norfolk who had been given five-year prison sentences. His own favourite sound-bite at this time was that he favoured vigilance rather than vigilantes, but he retained some sympathy for those who chose to fight back. No crime could be condoned, but sometimes it could be understood; and Howard felt that the rise of the vigilante reflected a decline of confidence in the criminal-justice system.

Other views which attracted the *Sun*'s support were equally sound indicators of his approach. He had refused to condemn the newspaper for publishing the photograph of a sixteen-year-old murder suspect. Nor did it do Howard any harm with the paper when he had serious doubts about introducing a law against press intrusion, which had been recommended by a Home Office committee chaired by Sir David Calcutt.[19]

Howard also delighted both the *Sun* and the police with his decision to allow trials of the side-handled extendable baton, which critics thought was too dangerous. This reversed a ruling by Clarke, whose relations with the police had almost reached breaking point in the weeks before the reshuffle. At the annual conference of the Police Federation he had been heckled, and the chairman of the Metropolitan Police Federation called him 'an arrogant, rude, social snob'. Howard was by contrast 'a good listener'.[20]

Policemen had much they wanted to tell him. They frequently advised Howard that they knew who was committing much of the crime in their areas, and if only these people were jailed then the figures would drop. 'I took the view that they were right,' Howard later explained, 'and that if we could get to a point where those career criminals were being locked up, then the public would be protected; there would be an impact on the crime figures; the country would become a safer place in which to live.'[21] Howard's problem was that Home Office officials did not agree, nor the probation service, nor the judiciary. It also perplexed Howard that sentences barely seemed to increase with second and subsequent convictions. Burglars, he felt, made the calculation that prison was simply a hazard of the job.

The main police grievance, however, was the inquiry which Clarke had set up under the businessman Sir Patrick Sheehy to study pay and conditions in the force. The relentless rise in crime had exposed the police to the kinds of reform which were, by the early 1990s, familiar to other public servants. Spending on the police had risen by almost three-quarters in real terms since 1979. Pay had increased by 44 per cent, and numbers by 15 per cent. But over the same period the crime clear-up rate had fallen from 38 per cent to 29 per cent.[22] Sheehy's proposals, unveiled at the end of June 1993, were correspondingly radical. He wanted to end the 'jobs for life' culture, to introduce performance-related pay and restrict certain police benefits, and to cut starting salaries by £2,000 per year. Middle-management ranks would be trimmed, and a new disciplinary procedure would make it easier to sack officers who failed.

If Howard had any doubts about the depth of feeling in the force, he would have been disabused by a rally of almost 20,000 policemen at Wembley that July, and by the commissioner of the Metropolitan Police, Sir Paul Condon, who said his own position might be untenable if Sheehy's recommendations were implemented in full.

Against this agitated background, Michael Howard's response to Sheehy was an exemplary compromise. Implementation of the full recommendations would have damaged morale at a time when the Home Office needed police cooperation. A considered selection from the various options would reassure the police that the Home Secretary was on their side, but at the same time he gave notice that he was concerned about police performance. When Howard announced his official response to Sheehy in October, Tory MPs who had been troubled by Sheehy's full recommendations lined up to applaud him. Fixed-term contracts (below the rank of superintendent) and the cut in starting pay were dropped, and the performance-related element was diluted. But the posts of chief superintendent and chief inspector would be abolished to streamline police management. Howard predicted that the changes would save enough money to fund 3,000 more front-line officers. In the meantime, he had also accepted sixteen proposals to cut police paperwork.

October 1993 also saw Howard travel to Blackpool to face his first Conservative conference as Home Secretary. The outlook seemed ominous, judging from some of the press previews. Tony Blair had kept up the pressure with a speech to his own conference in which he boasted of Labour's progress on law and order. Howard was painfully conscious of the threat which Blair represented. In a sign of increasing indiscretion at the Home Office, one official claimed that policy-making was now being driven by the hope of provoking the Opposition spokesman.[23] The *News of the World* suggested that

Howard's honeymoon with the right-wing press was over. 'Wake up, Michael,' it thundered in an editorial. 'No amount of glib oratory to the squires from the shires in Blackpool will make a jot of difference.'[24] Two hundred and forty-four motions on law and order had been submitted by the party rank and file.

Howard arrived in Blackpool armed with two crowd-pleasing orations. The first, delivered to the Conservative Political Centre (CPC) on the Tuesday, was influenced by his spiritual home across the Atlantic. His love affair had deepened during a visit to the United States that summer, when he discovered that being a British Home Secretary, and married to a once-famous model, opened some exclusive doors. In California, Michael and Sandra dined with Michael Caine and Sidney Poitier, among others, at a £100-a-head restaurant. On another evening he ate with Charlton Heston, a more predictable showbiz icon for a man of his views.

But Howard saw the US as more than a source of autographs. He told the CPC that Britain could learn from various policies being tested in each of the fifty American states. The Home Office and its agencies, he said, were often 'picking up the pieces' for the failures of others. These included the 'failure of some schools to insist on effective discipline', and the 'failure of some churches to foster moral values'.

> So called 'Progressive' theories in the '60s and '70s made excuses for crime and seemed to blame everyone apart from the criminal. Some parents neglected the difference between right and wrong. In many cases discipline lapsed in our schools. Television helped to make violence and loutish behaviour more acceptable. And part of this story has been the decline of the traditional two-parent family.

With the growing prevalence of divorce, absent fathers, and single mothers who relied on state support, his eye had been caught by an experiment in New Jersey, where single mothers were denied benefits for any children beyond their first. 'We can and must examine all our policies to ensure that we are reinforcing, rather than weakening, a sense of responsibility.'[25] His views chimed with the main theme of the Blackpool gathering.

John Major, in his speech, urged that Britain should go 'back to basics'. When this ill-considered slogan duly rebounded on a party which was becoming increasingly identified with sleaze, Major's supporters claimed that he had not meant sexual morality. He called for a return to 'self-discipline' and 'consideration for others' – standards which were ignored by many of his colleagues, and which (as Edwina Currie later revealed) he had failed to follow himself. Like Howard he believed in individual responsibility, and thought that anyone who blamed social pressures was making excuses.

The Home Secretary had helped to create a revivalist atmosphere at the conference in advance of his main address. Like many of the things he did between 1993 and 1997, Michael Howard's speech divided informed observers. Yet any connoisseur of conference oratory had to accept that it was a noteworthy effort. Its dominant feature was the twenty-seven-point programme, which he boasted was 'the most comprehensive programme of action against crime that has ever been announced by any Home Secretary. Action to prevent crime; action to help the police to catch criminals; action to make it easier to convict the guilty; action to punish them once they are found guilty. And this is just the first instalment.'[26] The speech had been strongly influenced by his junior minister David Maclean.

On most subjects, Howard's oration would have been a little *too* comprehensive for a party conference. But on law and order, the party faithful would have stayed and cheered through 270 points. And, by explaining his strategy in such lavish detail, Howard managed to shift the ground in his favour. Even if crime was still rising at the same time next year, he could be deemed to have 'delivered' provided that the majority of his measures had been put in place.

His twenty-seven points were wide-ranging. They included new offences, new means of detection, new court procedures, and new help for victims and witnesses. Meanwhile, squatters, new-age travellers, hunt protesters, juvenile offenders, bail bandits and terrorists would all face a crackdown. He would introduce DNA testing for all crimes, and bring in new rules on evidence in rape trials. Some measures – such as his promise to build six new private prisons – could be implemented without legislation. But the majority would have to go through Parliament. This was likely to prove contentious, not least because Howard planned to curtail the traditional right to silence. This had particularly been exploited by terrorists, he said. 'What fools they must think we are. It is time to call a halt to this charade. The innocent have nothing to hide and that is exactly the point the prosecution will be able to make in future.'[27]

An accused person might remain silent for many reasons, however, and Howard's proposal was difficult to square with the key principle of British justice – the presumption of innocence until guilt is proven. Although some of Howard's measures had been recommended by a recent Royal Commission on the criminal justice system, headed by Lord Runciman, this idea had been rejected.

Howard's most notable passage, however, was on the value of locking up criminals. 'Prison works,' he declared. 'It ensures that we are protected from murderers, muggers and rapists – and it makes many who are tempted to commit crime think twice.'[28]

The speech was rewarded with a standing ovation of almost two minutes, and hearty pats on the back from a beaming John Major. The *Sun* thought that Howard deserved 'ONE HUNDRED AND THREE' cheers. 'What a great day for people power!' it gushed.[29] (Oddly enough, Howard's 'prison works' phrase – perhaps the most famous quote of his career – got very little coverage in the next day press; it took time to gain wide circulation.)

The hero of the hour had even got away with a stinging attack on his own party. 'In the last thirty years,' Howard declared, 'the balance of the criminal justice system has been tilted too far in favour of the criminal and against the protection of the public.'[30] Yet the Conservatives had held power for nineteen of those previous thirty years, and some of the most liberal changes to the criminal justice system had been made during John Major's premiership. The 1991 Criminal Justice Act had limited the extent to which judges could take previous convictions into account when passing sentence, and also promoted non-custodial penalties. It had been designed to cut the prison population, and had succeeded.

Before Howard's own Criminal Justice Bill was published, in December 1993, it was clear that his populist measures would not prevail unopposed. The Bar Council and the Law Society both came out against curtailing the right to silence. Correspondence in the broadsheets suggested that the plan was unnecessary, immoral or unworkable. Attacks in the liberal *Guardian* would have been welcome to Howard, but the most deadly arguments appeared in *The Times*.[31] Almost the only lawyer who seemed able to give the proposals a cautious welcome was Tony Blair, who had been expected to make the loudest criticisms. Closer to home, there were serious stirrings of revolt among Home Office civil servants, with complaints that the department was being turned into 'a PR machine for Mr Howard'.[32] By this time some officials had established a rival publicity operation, taking every opportunity to leak damaging material to the press. It was rumoured that a round robin of protest had been sent to Clive Whitmore. The Permanent Secretary himself was said to be disgusted by Howard's 'sound-bite' approach to policy-making, and was preparing for early retirement.[33]

These troubles should have been more than enough for any Home Secretary, but Howard added to his own difficulties. In November the official crime figures showed a further increase, to 5.7 million. Howard could not be held responsible when he had been in the job for only six months, yet his response sounded like a traditional Home Office view: 'Nobody knows how to prevent crime – it's rising all over the world. If anyone had the answer, the world would be a different place.'[34]

If Howard had given the impression at the Conservative conference that the war on crime was the government's top priority, the spending round now made it clear that it came second behind the control of public expenditure. Police recruitment was effectively to be frozen for the second year running, and a new rigid scale of payments under the Criminal Injuries Compensation Scheme meant that many victims would be worse off.

The Chief Secretary to the Treasury, Michael Portillo, had been astonished that autumn at Howard's insistence on having twenty-seven initiatives, some of which required extra money. The two had met in Blackpool at the start of conference week, Portillo recalls. 'I said, "Forget it! Twenty-seven is mad. Why not just one or two?" I said, "You can't have twenty-seven initiatives."' But Howard was willing to agree to a zero increase in his department's budget in return for the twenty-seven points, Portillo recollects. 'I remember ringing my private secretary in London and saying, "You know what? He's agreed to zero increase for the next two years." I was cock-a-hoop! But it showed how important his twenty-seven initiatives were to him.'[35]

The second reading of Howard's Criminal Justice Bill, in January 1994, was supposed to be a tactical triumph. The intention was that Blair would be exposed as the criminal's chum, resisting the will of the people by speaking and voting against the government. He did speak against, and proposed an amendment criticising Howard for ignoring the causes of crime. But Labour abstained in the vote on the overall bill. Blair regretted that Conservative backbenchers had not been present to see Howard's 'face drop about six inches' when he learned that he'd been outmanoeuvred. The Home Secretary also had to drop his prepared speech. When Blair tried to intervene just before his closing remarks, Howard snapped 'Sit down' at his tormentor. In his own contribution, Blair mocked Howard for having joined the campaign to release from prison a fictional character in the radio series *The Archers*. (Howard is an *Archers* addict, and officials soon learned not to ring him during the Sunday morning omnibus edition.) As Prime Minister, Blair would happily lend his name to such protests, but back in January 1994 he twisted the knife by quoting a *Daily Express* report that Home Office officials had been 'stunned' by Howard's intervention.[36]

Worse followed a week later. The Criminal Justice Bill was not the only piece of Home Office business before Parliament – Howard had also published a Police and Magistrates' Courts Bill, inherited from Ken Clarke. When at Environment, Howard had opposed the main proposals, which had fallen within his area of responsibility because they affected local government. These would allow the Home

Secretary to nominate five 'independent' members of the sixteen-strong police committees which oversaw each of the forty-three local forces in England and Wales (outside London). Three of the other members would be drawn from the magistrates' bench, leaving the remaining eight posts for local councillors. This arrangement would make it unlikely that Labour supporters would control many police authorities – particularly since another departmental leak had revealed that Howard wanted all Home Office appointees to be vetted by the Conservative whips. Just to make sure, the committees would be chaired by another Home Office nominee, so the Secretary of State would be responsible for appointing a third of the membership.

Even the most corrupt police districts in America might have blushed at this spectacular piece of gerrymandering. After the 1993 local elections, the Conservatives no longer had control of a single police authority in England. The party which bragged about 'rolling back the frontiers of the state' was using the power of Parliament to redress the inconvenient verdict of the ballot box. The most breath-taking aspect of the proposal was its implicit assumption, at a time when the party had only a small majority, of permanent Conservative rule. If Howard had considered the prospect of a future Labour gov-ernment, he might have thought twice before bequeathing so much power to a possible left-wing successor. But opposition to the bill went beyond party politics. It was seen as a constitutional issue. The bill had been introduced in the Lords, so critics could not be accused of going against the will of the elected chamber. Peers from all sides lined up to savage the legislation and its chief sponsor, who sat on the steps of the throne to hear the early stages. He did not stay long enough to discover that twenty-two of the first twenty-four speakers had been critical of his plans. Howard's critics included his former girlfriend Ann Mallalieu, who was now a Labour spokesman on home affairs in the Lords.

The press, however, focused on the deep misgivings expressed by the former Deputy Prime Minister Willie Whitelaw, who regarded the bill as the final straw after nearly two decades of reluctant compli-ance with Thatcherism. But he was joined by three other former

Home Secretaries now sitting in the Lords – Jim Callaghan, Roy Jenkins and the Conservative Robert Carr – in one of the most brutal parliamentary ambushes of modern times. Carr said he would have resigned as Home Secretary rather than accept powers of this kind, but Callaghan's criticisms were the deadliest. Deploring a general tendency for the government to present the Lords with 'second-rate legislation', he condemned 'a wilful and ambitious group of young ministers who flit across the political scene from department to department, supping the honey as they go and moving on quickly before their misdeeds find them out'.[37]

An assault from Callaghan and Jenkins might have been manageable for Howard. But when Whitelaw and Carr broke ranks from his own party he knew that the game was up. 'He is a pragmatist and is not going to go to the stake on this one,' one minister conceded, perhaps with a hint of glee at Howard's plight. 'It may be that Willie is a bigger warhorse than anyone in the Cabinet.'[38] Howard's first attempt to appease the vengeful veterans misfired badly. He proposed that the independent members of police authorities would be nominated from a list drawn up by local worthies, including lords lieutenant. However, he did this without consulting those august figures, who promptly announced that they would have nothing to do with such a scheme. After discussions with Whitelaw, Howard climbed down, conceding that chairmen of police authorities would continue to be elected by the other members, more than half of whom would be councillors.

Roy Jenkins described it as 'a classic example of how not to legislate', while Blair spoke of 'a total and abject shambles' which had arisen from ministers' failure to listen.[39] It was reported that Clive Whitmore had warned Howard that his bill would end in tears, and he now chose this moment to confirm his departure for the private sector. Appearing before the Home Affairs Select Committee, Whitmore denied that he was leaving early 'because there has been, in any way, a deterioration in my relations with the Home Secretary' – which only left people wondering if they had disliked each other from the start.[40]

The favourite to succeed was Sir John Chilcot, who was Permanent Secretary at the Northern Ireland Office, but had spent most of his career in the Home Office. He had the backing of both Whitmore and the Cabinet Secretary, Sir Robin Butler, but 'Howard resisted his appointment tooth and nail,' says Derek Lewis, 'the last thing he wanted was another Home Office traditionalist, more loyal to the department than to its Secretary of State.'[41] One close observer thinks Howard may have been suspicious of Chilcot's success, working with Patrick Mayhew, in the Northern Ireland peace process, about which Howard was sceptical. Howard eventually persuaded John Major to let him have his former Permanent Secretary Sir Richard Wilson, with whom he'd worked well at the DoE, even though Wilson had no experience of the Home Office. Howard also brought in the DoE communications chief, Mike Granatt, who'd previously worked for the Metropolitan Police. It was a sign of the way Howard prefers to surround himself with a team of congenial, like-minded colleagues, running his department as if it were a barristers' chambers. But it also showed skill in spotting talent. Wilson later succeeded Robin Butler as Cabinet Secretary, while Granatt subsequently became head of the Government Communication and Information Service.

News of Clive Whitmore's defection came after another unseemly episode, when the Home Office was accused of leaking details of private talks with Labour on the Prevention of Terrorism Act. This legislation had to be renewed every year, and Conservatives always tried to exploit Labour's annual attempts to water down the act as proof that the Opposition was soft on terrorists. Howard firmly denied that either he or his two political advisers, Patrick Rock and David Cameron, had been involved in 'planting the story'.[42] No one was convinced.

Certainly the Home Office became much more media-driven during Howard's reign. Everything was assessed in terms of its impact in the press and on radio and television. Early on, Howard insisted that all submissions to his office had first to be considered by the communications directorate, otherwise he refused to read them. And the press office was expected to play a much more active role in talking to journalists. This meant developing closer relations not just with home-affairs and legal specialists, but also with those who wrote newspaper editorials, even contacting them to suggest subjects for their leader columns. Sometimes Howard himself would phone them out of the blue – 'the first time I'd ever experienced a Cabinet minister ring leader-writers directly', says one seasoned press officer. 'He seemed to revel in it. He quite enjoyed trying to put across his views. He never did it an aggressive way.' Sometimes Howard might ring eight or ten journalists in a morning, one after the other. Melanie McDonagh, who then wrote editorials for the *Evening Standard*, agrees it was previously unheard of. 'You'd be hammering away at your leader, and then have the Home Secretary on the phone. It was rather engaging actually that he took so much trouble.'[43] Howard enjoyed especially good relations with Stewart Steven, the editor of the *Evening Standard*, with the precocious Matthew d'Ancona of the *Sunday Telegraph*, and with Jonathan Holborow, the editor of the *Mail on Sunday*. Repeating the technique he'd used in trying to sell the poll tax, he'd spend a week in September doing a regional tour, meeting local editors, and lunching and dining them. 'They'd be quite flattered with that,' says a Home Office official. 'They certainly didn't get the opportunity to meet Cabinet ministers very often.'

Looking forward, Howard instituted a grid system, setting out all the key events in the calendar for the next two years. Home Office staff had not been required to plan ahead so carefully before, and it bore obvious similarities to the new techniques being developed by the Labour opposition. According to one senior official, 'Those who were working in the Home Office in 1997 said that the best preparation for New Labour was working for Michael Howard.'

Equally, Howard was quick to react to unfavourable broadcasts on radio or television. One of his senior press officers, Bob Thomas, says that if Howard was at home in the morning and didn't like what he'd heard on the 7 a.m. news on *Today*, he'd ring his private secretary, who in turn would contact the duty press officer at the Home Office, who would be expected to remedy matters before the 7.30 bulletin. 'None of this "immediate rebuttal" is new, what's gone on since

Alastair Campbell,' says Thomas. 'We were doing it before, mainly at Howard's behest.'[44]

Out on the road, Howard would keep a constant eye on any accompanying TV cameras. Meeting police officers, for instance, he would be 'smiling and chatting', says a former colleague, so long as the red camera light was on.

> It was quite an experience. One minute, smiley, chatty and so on, and the next minute, as soon as the camera went off, he couldn't care less. I think these little insights give you some idea about the degree of control he wanted, but also how nervous he was, and how he wanted to ensure that all of this went absolutely right so that the correct image of him appeared as he wanted it to appear.

In this respect he was very like Tony Blair, says a senior official who has worked with both men. 'Michael Howard doesn't like unscripted events. He really envies and despises the ability of people like Ken Clarke to wing it. He hates informality, though he can do it when he's forced to. He likes structure, so he can go in there with a brief. Blair is very similar. There is no spontaneity in their souls.' Howard particularly tried to avoid being ambushed by reporters. The former BBC correspondent Nicholas Jones says that before any live broadcast the Home Secretary would insist on being told about any report which went beforehand, the names of other studio guests, and the detailed running order. 'Invariably there would have to be an undertaking that he would have the last word,' says Jones. Then Howard made sure he arrived early to listen to the preceding reports, so as to plan for any obvious questions, to rebut what others had said, or to correct any inaccuracies.[45]

When attending specific events away from the office, Howard would often refuse to take questions on other subjects. It was the job of his press officers, he insisted, to make sure broadcasters did not slip in prohibited questions. It wasn't always possible, of course. They could hardly put a hand over a TV lens, but Howard would be furious with his press minders if journalists did not obey his rules.

He was equally hardline over interviews in his office, or after press conferences. Only one reporter was allowed into his room at any one time, to prevent anyone picking up on a weak line of argument, or a tricky line of questioning. And Jones says that Howard was as effective as Labour's Peter Mandelson in one of his 'most menacing attributes: a deadly accuracy when making complaints'. Among programme editors, 'the Home Secretary was the minister they feared most: if he was dissatisfied with the way he had been treated, the production staff were told to make immediate amends.'[46] 'He'd never let anything rest,' says a senior adviser. 'When he went to America, he was taken by their determination, their ruthless campaigns, and their attention to detail. Somebody told him never to let a lie rest. We'd advise him that he was devaluing the currency of complaints. He bombarded the BBC with complaints.'

Occasionally the control slipped. Ben Stewart, a student who lived in his Folkestone constituency, secured an interview for his university newspaper for which he was later proclaimed *Guardian* 'Student Journalist of the Year'. They got into a long argument about Howard's measures to restrict loud music 'with a repetitive beat' being played at parties and outdoor raves. 'Many people believe it to be unfair that one type of music is prohibited whilst another is not,' Stewart complained. 'The point is, you have imposed upon everyone your own subjective view of what frightening and unenjoyable music is, have you not?'[47] At this, the Home Secretary got angry, and jumped up from his seat. 'He went absolutely nuts and completely lost it,' Stewart says. 'He was thrashing about, waving his arms about like a windmill. I don't know whether he had had a bad morning, but it seemed way overboard. It was startling and intimidating. He just wasn't in control.'[48] 'This is ridiculous,' Howard exclaimed. 'I think I'm going to terminate this interview. I'm not prepared to have a great argument about this.' Afterwards Howard calmed down and agreed to have his picture taken with Stewart. Then, characteristically, he apologised. 'It was not the proper way to act,' Howard admitted.[49]

Yet on another occasion, on the same issue, Howard showed the other side of his character. After addressing the AGM of the

Centrepoint charity for the homeless, he came down from the platform to argue with youngsters in the audience who were deeply upset about his anti-rave measures. Centrepoint's former director Nick Hardwick recalls, 'It was different from the public persona of Howard the scary figure. I thought the fact the Home Secretary was willing to mix it with people and defend his policies was interesting. He was not standing on his dignity, and able to mix it with kids off the streets. He wasn't patronising. He didn't talk down to them. He did it with good humour.'[50]

By the spring of 1994, many of Howard's twenty-seven points were under serious fire. Conservative MPs could not help wondering why in just six months, as *The Times* put it, 'the headlines proclaiming "Howard cracks down" have turned to "Howard climbs down."'[51] Yet, with the leadership in prospect, Howard now understood the importance of keeping in favour with backbenchers, visiting the members' dining room at least once a week – 'without fail – you must', he told Gyles Brandreth.[52]

Even the Home Secretary's 'friends' began to spice their supportive remarks with barbs. An *Observer* profile quoted one unnamed 'admirer' as saying, 'He's a bit too glib. He's a bit too sleek . . . And, I know I shouldn't say this, but I will, because it is true: he's a bit too Jewish.' 'What does Michael Howard fundamentally believe in?' wondered a right-wing MP. 'He believes fundamentally in Michael Howard.'[53] The *Sunday Times*, whose editor, Andrew Neil, had already shown his independence from the Murdoch papers on this subject, castigated Howard in April 1994 as 'a pathetic figure . . . a serial bungler . . . damaged goods . . . the Home Secretary's days are surely numbered and we must have a new one. The sooner the better.'[54] Even the *Sun* admitted that Howard's 'thoroughbred reputation is tarnished'.[55]

When the much-mangled Police and Magistrates' Courts Bill came to the Commons for its second reading, Blair concentrated his attack on the complicated arrangements to reduce the Home Secretary's influence over the choice of independent authority members. This 'extraordinary rigmarole' would never have been necessary, he said, if the government had not been suffering from 'an aversion, bordering on paranoia, to local government'. If any official in the Home Office had suggested the plan, Blair jeered, would he not be consigned to 'a padded cell with his arms stuck behind his back while he was examined by a range of psychoanalysts'?[56]

Less than three weeks after these exchanges, fate stopped the fight with Michael Howard's challenger well ahead on points. When John Smith suddenly died on 12 May 1994, Tony Blair quickly emerged as the favourite to succeed him as Labour leader. For three of the past four years Blair had displayed his talents in facing Howard as his opposite number, embarrassing the government first on Employment and then on home affairs. His performances against one of the most formidable Tory ministers helped explain why it was Tony Blair, rather than his friend Gordon Brown, who succeeded Smith, and ultimately became Prime Minister.

14

ESCAPES AND SCAPEGOATS

I was probably the last ever liberal Home Secretary – or possibly
Douglas Hurd.

KENNETH CLARKE[1]

Michael Howard's speech to the 1993 party conference was remembered not for his twenty-seven points, but for just two words. By
proclaiming that 'prison works' the Home Secretary had declared
war on liberals within his so-called 'criminal justice establishment'. By
the end of Howard's four-year stretch at the Home Office many of
those most involved in administering criminal justice were engaged in
a fight against him. This level of opposition would have deterred
most Home Secretaries. In Howard's case it seemed to make him
more determined.

Until Michael Howard went to the Home Office, British penal
policy was dominated by an unusual coalition of the well meaning and
the penny-pinching. The 1991 Criminal Justice Act, passed while
Kenneth Baker was Home Secretary, was designed to reduce custodial
sentences in favour of community sentences, and the act also introduced the idea of 'unit fines', which meant that financial penalties
would be calculated according to the declared resources of the
offender. For liberals, prison would 'work' only if it helped people
overcome the misfortunes which had caused them to commit crime in

the first place. Generally speaking, existing research supported the view that, regardless of moral views on the value of rehabilitation, this approach reduced the long-term cost of imprisonment. In contrast, Michael Howard believed that prison worked because it kept offenders off the streets; and, if the regime was sufficiently tough, it might also deter criminals from doing anything which might book a return visit.

Howard had signalled his intentions even before his 1993 conference speech. A report by Lord Justice (Harry) Woolf into the 1990 riot at Strangeways Prison in Manchester had made more than 200 recommendations, based on the principle that prisoners should be treated with dignity and respect. His proposals formed the basis of a White Paper, *Custody, Care and Justice*, and Kenneth Baker's 1991 Criminal Justice Act. Baker's successor, Kenneth Clarke, had been happy to endorse the Woolf agenda, which included replacing the long-standing practice of 'slopping out' by the provision of proper lavatory facilities, and a new code of standards setting out how inmates could expect to be treated within Her Majesty's prisons. Howard's profound disagreement was detailed in a leaked Home Office memorandum, dated August 1993. Many prisons, he felt, were 'too comfortable' and 'too lax'. The Home Secretary wanted to cut back on privileges, such as home visits and leisure activities, and he thought prisoners should do more useful work. He wanted jail to be 'a more austere experience', arguing that a large number of 'prisoners enjoy standards of comfort which many taxpayers would find it hard to understand'. The memo continued, 'Mr Howard would also like some assessment of the savings that could be made from a change in policy, recognising that this represents quite a departure from some of the commitments set out post-Woolf.'[2] Television sets ought to be a privilege which should be earned, Howard thought, and he was in no hurry to end slopping out. 'Soft-touch jails,' he said, 'are an insult to victims.'[3]

Within a week of his appointment Michael Howard visited Brixton Prison, the scene of a spectacular escape by two armed IRA prisoners in July 1991. 'He was uncomfortable throughout,' Derek Lewis, the head of the Prison Service, later recalled. 'Some VIP visitors have a natural ability to walk into a prison and be at ease, while others are on edge and tense. Howard was one of the latter. It was a very brief visit.' The Prison Officers' Association refused to meet him, in protest against the threat of job losses. But one prisoner on a balcony above greeted him by slopping out a chamber pot in his direction. Howard escaped it, unlike the ITN reporter who accompanied him.[4] The experience was unlikely to convince him that prison discipline was sufficiently strict.

Of all the hazards in a Home Secretary's life, prisons are among the most worrying and unpredictable. Prison riots and escapes are considered more damaging to ministers than bad crime figures or even acts of terrorism. Although no minister in living memory has ever resigned over a prison incident, the failure to keep control of Britain's worst criminals suggests a lack of authority. Derek Lewis was the man Ken Clarke had chosen to stop such mishaps, as the Director General of the Prison Service. Lewis's disagreements with Michael Howard would do lasting damage to the latter's career. Indeed, Howard has still has not fully recovered from them.

Derek Lewis was not a civil servant, but a successful businessman. A graduate of the London Business School, he'd gone on to become finance director of Ford Europe and then chief executive of the Granada Group, and certainly had no experience of running jails. Lewis was known to be a workaholic, but he perhaps lacked an understanding of the ways of politicians. If some found him rather cold, he had a strong sense of propriety. Like Howard he was single-minded, and good at marshalling his facts and arguments. But the two men never saw eye to eye. The very fact that he had been appointed by Ken Clarke meant, says one senior official, that 'he was suspect in Michael Howard's eyes'.

As early as August 1993, only eleven weeks after Howard took over, *Private Eye* presciently reported that Lewis 'is not expected to last very long in his present job'.[5] And that was before the trouble started. Michael Howard preferred colleagues who would support his own views on law and order, and preferably were not contaminated by previous acquaintance with the Home Office. Howard decided not to renew the contract of the former judge Stephen Tumim, the controversial Chief Inspector of Prisons, though he promptly fell out with Tumim's successor, General Sir David Ramsbotham. And when he was presented with three liberal-leaning candidates for the new post of Prison Ombudsman, he rejected all of them. Instead he chose Sir Peter Woodhead, a former admiral, who subsequently proved to have a mind of his own, and had to be 'carpeted' by Howard in 1996 for questioning ministerial decisions.

In theory, Derek Lewis should have been an ally to the new Home Secretary. He had been in post for only a few weeks when Howard arrived, and therefore should have been relatively 'uninfected' by the Home Office culture. He had been headhunted to make the Prison Service more businesslike. He agreed with Howard that the system needed shaking up, and shared some of his concern that the existing culture was too liberal. Lewis was also keen to take on the Prison Officers' Association, the union which had often blocked reforms in the past, though he found Howard reluctant to join him in this, perhaps out of a legalistic respect for the service's existing agreements with staff. 'I was surprised,' says Lewis. 'For a time this seemed more like a liberal lawyer, until the political opportunity became obvious.'[6]

Lewis certainly found it hard to develop a working rapport with Howard. Perhaps his expectations were unreasonable, after working closely with the gregarious Clarke. Howard, he felt, was not interested in establishing good relations, or in understanding the Prison Service. 'It was surprising that he appeared to attach so little importance to getting to know those who were working for him,' Lewis said later. 'I told him I thought he would get more out of his Home Office civil servants, who were by nature hostile to his views, if he did more to get them on side. They needed to feel they were being involved rather than distrusted.' Howard disagreed. 'He did not think that was necessary,' Lewis said. 'All he needed to do was to state the direction clearly and be consistent about it. Eventually people would follow.'[7] In his dealings with Lewis, Howard faced the additional complication that the rules of engagement had just been altered. The new Director General was no ordinary civil service underling.

The Major government was in the process of dispersing substantial parts of government to semi-autonomous agencies, under the 'Next Steps' programme begun during the final years of Margaret Thatcher. It was designed to bring some of the benefits of private enterprise into government, without selling off the activities concerned. The theory was that if officials were granted greater independence from politicians to run state organisations, and given their own budgets, they would show more initiative and such agencies would work more efficiently. The Prison Service had achieved 'agency status' only eight weeks before Michael Howard moved to the Home Office. Under the new framework document agreed by Ken Clarke, the Home Secretary was deemed responsible for overall prisons 'policy', while the Director General of the service was accountable for day-to-day 'operational' matters. But the Home Secretary was entitled to be consulted on any matters of concern to the public or Parliament.

In theory this should have been good news for Howard, since it would now be harder to blame him personally for prison escapes or security lapses. In practice it was unlikely to work in that way, since he would still have to answer to MPs and the media if things went wrong. It was not a situation in which Michael Howard would ever feel comfortable, especially if his reputation could be threatened by a problem in the prisons at any time. Even if the 'Next Steps' plan was a Thatcherite initiative, Howard has never been a natural delegator. He likes to exert control. He is a centraliser. The relaxed, languid Ken Clarke might have been happy to let the Prison Service get on with things, but that has never been Howard's way. In practice, Howard ended up interfering with the Prison Service more than any Home Secretary did in the days before it was an agency. According to one official of the service, 'He made clear at some meetings, "It may be your Prison Service, but you do what *I* say."' Says another adviser, 'Michael Howard took the view that "If I'm going to get shit in Parliament then I'm going to have some say on this."'

This problem of responsibility first surfaced in September 1993, after a riot at Wymott Prison, near Leyland in Lancashire. More than 700 inmates were involved, and caused more than £20 million worth of damage. Stephen Tumim had earlier drawn attention to a drug culture at Wymott, and a subsequent snap inspection showed a prison which was largely under the control of inmates, particularly at night. 'It is hard to imagine a more corrupting environment in which to place an offender, and one less likely to influence him towards non-delinquent activities,' said Tumim. The impression of a shockingly lax regime was reinforced by the revelation that prisoners had used billiard tables, provided for leisure purposes, as battering rams.[8] But there was another side to the story. Tumim's report after the riot noted the problem of overcrowding. Britain's overall prison population was increasing at a rate of 200 per month, and Wymott was particularly stretched because nearby Strangeways was still being renovated after the 1990 riot. Although the upward trend in prison numbers pre-dated Howard, his preference for custodial sentences was likely to make things increasingly difficult. That was plainly a matter of 'policy'.

The Wymott incident also illustrated the Home Secretary's inclination to get involved in operational matters. When Howard first learned of the riot, he suggested to Derek Lewis that troops should be called in. 'Absolutely not,' Lewis reportedly told him. 'Bringing in the army is the last thing we want.' The unrest was put down by prison officers in riot gear. The Director General also rejected the suggestion that Howard should visit Wymott once peace had been restored.[9]

Howard's 'prison works' speech, a month later, provoked a head-on clash with Lord Woolf (whom he'd occasionally encountered in court in his days at the Bar). Woolf had previously described Howard's attitude to prisons as 'short-sighted and irresponsible', and now said that the new emphasis on custodial sentences was likely to spark more riots. It represented a 'shocking waste of resources', he added. Howard's advisers said he had anticipated such criticism; but, instead of withdrawing 'from the fray', he intended 'to stay in there pitching toe to toe'.[10] John Major backed him.

Ultimately, Michael Howard's defence was based on the fact that he had the public behind him, whereas detractors like Harry Woolf were unelected. But these exchanges with Woolf only encouraged more critics. When seven senior judges made their concerns public, it became clear that the opposition to Howard extended beyond liberals whose protests he could comfortably disregard. His tough crime policies were 'largely an irrelevance' said Lord Ackner, a law lord who also felt that Howard was encroaching on the role of the judiciary. 'It's not the Home Secretary's job to say what punishment should be imposed.'[11] Even worse was the release of the Home Office's own research which suggested that to cut crime by just 1 per cent would require an increase of more than 20 per cent in the prison population (which was then about 47,000). 'Research suggests this is not a cost-effective solution,' the report said. A previous exercise in 1986 had produced similar findings, and had prompted the less custodial approach seen in Kenneth Baker's 1991 Criminal Justice Act. 'Prison is an expensive way of making bad people worse,' the earlier survey had concluded.[12]

When Michael Howard heard that Derek Lewis had expressed sympathy with Woolf's views in a radio interview, the prisons' boss was summoned to Queen Anne's Gate to confront a 'grim-faced' Home Secretary. 'Apoplexy quickly turned to embarrassment,' says Lewis when the transcript of the radio interview showed he had tried to strike a balance between Howard and Woolf, and the meeting ended with 'mumbled apologies'.[13] Howard had more reason for complaint a few weeks later, when the Director General addressed the annual Prison Service conference. Lewis had agreed to make some changes in advance, but the final version of his speech still sounded like a thinly coded criticism of the new drive for 'austerity' in jails.

> There has been much comment in the media about being harsher to prisoners – abusing them, providing deliberately degrading conditions or treatment, often in the name of retribution . . . We know such philosophies do not work. There is no need for anxiety on this matter; and there should be no doubt where we stand. I, the [Prison Service] board and the Home Secretary are at one on this.[14]

At the start of 1994 it was reported that Howard had quashed a suggestion by his first prisons minister, Peter Lloyd, that the assisted prison visitors' scheme might be extended to homosexuals hoping to visit their partners behind bars.[15] Howard was less discriminating on the subject of home visits: he wanted to scrap them in all but the most exceptional circumstances. His problems grew when Sandra revealed in a magazine interview that her husband's favourite meal was duck à l'orange and crème brûlée, although she had initially been reluctant to say so, it was reported, because 'Michael is cutting back on food in prisons at the moment.'[16] When this story was repeated in the *Evening Standard*, she phoned the paper to deny any such comment.[17]

Derek Lewis felt that Howard was not particularly interested in what punishment might be for – it was more a matter of how things played in the media, and whether he'd be seen as tough. The Home Secretary worried that the code of standards which emerged from the Woolf report would be seen as a prisoners' charter. He was keen on boot camps, insisting there should be an element of 'drill' in them. 'Meetings,' says Lewis, 'tended to be driven by what had been or might be in the press. There was a big debate about home leave. But none of it was about the *role* of home leave – did it reduce reoffending, or help prisoners to find work? It was all about public perceptions, suggesting that he cared much less about prison as a way of reducing crime.'[18]

In March 1994 came news that Howard had hoped for – and which discomfited his critics. The official crime statistics for 1992–3 showed a fall of just under 1 per cent. When more detailed data was released it emerged that the figure for the final quarter of 1993 marked a record drop of 9 per cent. Howard's public response was cautious, since it was too early to hail a trend, and as ever the British Crime Survey painted a less rosy picture. But the figures suggested that prison *might* work, after all. By March 1995, as judges and magistrates responded to the new climate, the number of inmates rose to more than 51,000 – an all-time high. It would climb by another 10,000 before Howard was finished.

Then struck the kind of thunderbolt which Howard had been

dreading. On 9 September 1994 six prisoners – five IRA men and an armed robber – broke out of Whitemoor Prison in Cambridgeshire after shooting a guard. The fugitives were quickly recaptured, but that was where the good news ended. The prisoners, held within a special secure unit, had constructed a jail-breaking kit which included two handguns, improvised ladders, ropes, grappling irons and wire-cutters, much of it made in the unit's hobby area. Their audacious escape had been spotted by closed-circuit TV cameras, but unnoticed by the guards in the Whitemoor control room, some of whom were playing Scrabble – more interested, it seems, in completing short words than in their prisoners fulfilling long sentences.

Howard rejected the inevitable calls to resign, and Downing Street offered full support. But it was a bad blow. According to one senior civil servant, he spent the week after the escape 'running about like a headless chicken, apparently making policy on the basis of whatever was in that afternoon's *Evening Standard* editorial'.[19] A week after the escape a small amount of Semtex explosive was found inside the prison. Howard later said it was one of his worst moments: 'That was obviously a dreadful thing.'[20]

In the circumstances, his speech a month later to the 1994 Conservative conference could never match his success of the year before. Ominously, an ICM opinion poll published that October showed just how far the Tories had fallen on law and order. In 1983 the party had had a lead over Labour on the issue of 31 per cent. Now it trailed by 14 per cent.[21] Howard also had his detractors among Tory MPs, for, as one senior figure noted, he enjoyed 'no deep reservoir of support in the party'.[22]

Howard won a two-minute standing ovation for promising 'punishment with a purpose', and for attacks on the 'woolly-headed brigade'. But he was heckled during part of his speech, which he must have seen originally as a likely crowd-pleaser. Cabinet colleagues had agreed that he could talk about the possibility of introducing identity cards, but, because there had been strong opposition to the idea of a compulsory scheme, Howard could promise only a Green Paper, talking up the prospects of a voluntary approach. Most of the party faithful, however,

wanted compulsory ID cards. 'No!', 'Rubbish!', 'Now!' people heckled
from the floor. 'Wait a minute,' insisted the flustered Home Secretary,
as he explained that three-quarters of the population would use the
cards as a driving licence or to claim benefits. 'No one else would be
forced to get one, but I believe that in time the vast majority would.'[23]
In his diary, the MP Gyles Brandreth later wrote of the ID card policy,
'Privately Michael Howard acknowledges it isn't practical and it won't
happen. Publicly we're still flirting with it . . . but we're rousing the
rabble *knowing* that in due course we're going to have to disappoint
them. Madness.'[24]

By the end of 1994 Michael Howard's political future rested partly
on the official inquiry into the Whitemoor breakout conducted by Sir
John Woodcock, a former chief constable. Woodcock's ninety-five-
page report, delivered in December, condemned the regime in the
prison as 'dangerous, unprofessional, confused and outrageous'. The
breakout had been a 'disaster waiting to happen', he said.[25] Inmates
had been pampered, with officers making twenty-five-mile trips to
collect food which prisoners had ordered by telephone. Howard had
an uncomfortable time when he gave his response in the Commons.
'I'd prefer to forget it,' he later confessed. 'It was a pretty miserable
occasion . . . I certainly couldn't defend the state of affairs which the
report disclosed.'[26] It helped that it was the last day of the session, and
many MPs had already gone home for Christmas. Howard also dis-
armed some critics by accepting all sixty-four of Woodcock's
recommendations, even though this would require a significant
increase in the prison budget. He also announced a more general
review of the prison system, headed by General Sir John Learmont, a
former chief quartermaster at the Ministry of Defence.

In the early days of 1995, Britain's growing number of prisoners
seemed hell-bent on proving that – as alleged by the Shadow Home
Secretary, Jack Straw – the system was lurching out of control. On 1
January the notorious Fred West committed suicide in his prison cell
in Birmingham while awaiting trial for mass murder. The following
day saw the start of two nights of rioting at Everthorpe jail on
Humberside. Then on the third day of the new year three 'lifers'

escaped from Parkhurst Prison on the Isle of Wight, though they were recaptured a few days later. The prisoners had escaped by forging a master key and constructing a twenty-five-foot ladder, which had been hidden in sections around the prison workshop. With the Whitemoor inquiry barely closed, this was all Howard needed, especially since he had been assured by Derek Lewis and his Prison Service colleagues that security was now under control. He felt badly let down by Lewis; he was quickly losing confidence in him.

After Whitemoor, Howard had asked his officials to check the historic precedents on whether ministers should resign after major prison escapes. They looked, for instance, at what Roy Jenkins had said after the spy George Blake escaped from jail in 1966, but particularly alighted on the explanation given in 1983 by the then Northern Ireland Secretary, Jim Prior, after thirty-eight Republicans broke out of the Maze prison, among them several dangerous IRA men. Margaret Thatcher refused Prior's resignation and, having pondered the matter, he subsequently told MPs that: 'It would be a matter for resignation if . . . what happened was the result of some act of policy that was my responsibility, or that I failed to implement something that I had been asked to implement, or should have implemented. In that case, I should resign.'[27] When the subsequent Hennessy inquiry found that Prior's policies were not to blame, but detailed security lapses inside the Maze, the minister sacked the governor rather than quit himself. Michael Howard seized on this precedent. He found it 'very neat' says a colleague, and used it to bolster the distinction between policy – his responsibility – and operational matters, which he maintained were the concern of Lewis and the Prison Service. For weeks Howard's private secretary carried round in her bag the relevant page of Hansard with Jim Prior's explanation. But Patrick Rock warned his boss not to rely too heavily on this formula – there might be times when he *needed* to intervene in operational matters. By placing such emphasis on this distinction, Howard would cause himself endless trouble.

Echoing Jim Prior, Michael Howard told the BBC's *Today* programme that 'If my policies were found to be responsible for any such

event, or if I had failed to implement anything I should have implemented, then of course I would resign without hesitation.'[28] Yet there
was a strong case for saying that Howard's policies *were* responsible at
least for the Everthorpe incident. The board of prison visitors had
protested that, because of excessive demands on the system, unsuitable
prisoners were being kept in the low-security jail. When the riots
began, 230 inmates were occupying buildings designed for barely half
that number.

On Tuesday 10 January 1995 Howard was due to make a
Commons statement about the various prison problems, after MPs
returned from their Christmas break. The day before, Richard Tilt,
the director of security for the Prison Service, produced a preliminary
report on the Parkhurst escape. It was highly critical of the prison
governor, John Marriott, accusing him of taking insufficient action in
response to a damning report on the prison by Stephen Tumim the
previous October. Supported by Tilt and two other senior officials,
Tony Butler and Philippa Drew, Derek Lewis decided that Marriott
could not stay in his current post. However, they wanted an orderly
transfer of responsibilities. It was agreed that Drew would travel to
Parkhurst the next morning to inform the governor that he was being
moved to a desk job elsewhere in the service.

Derek Lewis believed that Marriott's transfer was a purely 'operational' matter, and he did not consult Howard or tell him about the
decision until the next morning – the day Howard was due to address
MPs. Lewis was summoned to see Howard urgently in his large room
on the top floor of Queen Anne's Gate. This was the encounter
which would be the subject of much dispute over the next two and a
half years, culminating in Jeremy Paxman's famous much-repeated
question on *Newsnight*: 'Did you threaten to overrule him?' Derek
Lewis's account is that Howard 'exploded' when he heard that
Marriott was merely being transfered to office duties, rather than
being sacked outright. 'Simply moving the governor was politically
unpalatable. It sounded indecisive.'[29] 'It will be seen publicly as a
fudge,' a private secretary's note recorded Howard as saying, before
adding: 'I don't want to intervene formally.'[30] For his statement to the

Commons a few hours later, the Home Secretary felt he needed the appearance of resolution; and Lewis's plan was far from resolute enough.

According to Lewis, Howard's message was stark. 'The Home Secretary was thinking of his personal safety that afternoon, and he remained adamant. If I did not change my mind and suspend Marriott, he would have to consider overruling me. His tone was menacing and I was left with no illusions about the possible implications for me.' Howard gave Lewis an hour to rethink. Lewis then met the Permanent Secretary, Sir Richard Wilson, who 'looked grim-faced, and said that things were getting "white hot" and "in danger of going nuclear". Later he told me that Howard had said that if I did not suspend Marriott he would go down to the House that afternoon and announce that he had sacked me.'[31]

Despite the subsequent controversy over what happened at the 10 January meeting, Derek Lewis was not sacked; he largely succeeded in facing down the Home Secretary. In line with the Prison Service Code of Discipline, Marriott was moved to other duties, rather than being suspended or dismissed. But, when he saw the Home Secretary's draft Commons statement about Marriott, Lewis noticed that the change at Parkhurst was promised for 'today'. Through skilful drafting, it also gave the impression that Marriott would never run another prison, which would have prejudiced the findings of any inquiry. When the minutes of the 10 January meeting later emerged, it was discovered that Richard Wilson had asked Lewis whether the words 'is today being removed as governor' were acceptable, to which Lewis added 'or tomorrow', since he wanted to leave the precise timing to the colleague who was going down to Parkhurst to speak to Marriott. At this Howard interjected and said, 'No, no, no. I want to say "is today being removed".' Repeating the word 'No' is a common Howard habit when under pressure, and it confirms how heated the exchanges were.[32] Lewis found himself overruled: Marriott's move would be immediate.

In the House, Howard was able to announce John Marriott's departure from Parkhurst with what Lewis calls 'considerable venom'. It was enough to satisfy Tory backbenchers. 'Someone, presumably Howard's special advisers, had been briefing the lobby correspondents. The result was a rash of headlines which talked of "dismissal", "sacking", "firing", and "axing". No mention was made of suspension, still less of his being moved to other duties. It was an outrageous misrepresentation which had staff in the Prison Service up in arms.'[33]

Lewis has frequently suggested that the 10 January meeting was highly charged, and said he felt in peril of being sacked if he did not comply with the Home Secretary's wishes. But ten months later, in a Commons debate, Michael Howard would describe their discussions that day in very different terms, insisting that he had not told Lewis to do anything, merely proffered suggestions, as if it were a friendly discussion. Howard cited the official minute of the meeting, which, he said, recorded that:

> I agreed with Mr Lewis's analysis that Mr Marriott could not stay as governor of Parkhurst. I asked, as I was perfectly entitled to, if it was right for him to be moved to other duties as distinct from being suspended from duty. Mr Lewis explained why he thought that that would not be appropriate, and reaffirmed his decision not to suspend Mr Marriott but to move him to another job elsewhere in the Prison Service.
>
> I was entitled to be consulted by Mr Lewis about that important matter, and I was. I was entitled to discuss the action that it was proposed to take, and I did. I was not entitled to give instructions: I did not. It was the Director General who decided the governor should be moved: he was.[34]

Whatever the Home Office account, some Labour MPs were immediately suspicious about Michael Howard's role at the January meeting. When Derek Lewis attended the Home Affairs Select Committee a few days later, Chris Mullin and Gerry Bermingham questioned him about the events leading to Marriott's removal. 'Did the Home Secretary tell you to make sure Mr Marriott was off the premises by the afternoon?' asked Mullin. 'No he did not,' Lewis replied. Bermingham suggested to Lewis 'that a politician interfered with the operational matters on 10 January and that is why Mr Marriott was treated in the disgraceful way he has been treated.' 'No, that is not the case,' said Lewis.[35] Lewis felt himself bound by civil service rules which advise officials, when addressing Commons committees, not to expand their answer beyond what they are strictly asked. His answers were precise and truthful, but they gave no indication of the arguments which had raged that day, and Howard would subsequently use the Director General's limited account to defend himself against Lewis and other critics. Had either MP pressed the issue more forcefully, or even asked less specific questions, Derek Lewis might have been obliged to reveal more about the actual nature of his encounter with Howard.

General Learmont's prison review was not due until September 1995, but in the meantime, there had been an ominous development for Lewis. His contract had been due to expire at the end of that year, but Howard agreed to extend it by twelve months, which would then be rolled forward a month at a time. This made it appear as if Lewis was on a month's notice, when it was in fact a year. Nevertheless, he *was* effectively being put on notice.

Just before the appearance of Learmont's report, Lewis was shown a draft and was asked to respond. Learmont had highlighted widespread failings at Parkhurst, where the Prison Service's own security manual had often been ignored and basic security procedures had not been observed. He had also identified severe management failures in the service as a whole, including weaknesses in leadership and communications. In preparing his reply, Lewis had assistance from an unexpected quarter: Ann Widdecombe, who in July 1995 had joined the Home Office as the new prisons minister. She had been warned about the friction between Howard and Lewis, and later observed that 'Within a couple of days I realised just what had been going on for some time.' At her first meeting with Howard she was pointedly asked her opinion of Lewis.[36] When she had seen some of the prisons for herself (she eventually visited every one), she concluded that Lewis had made significant progress. By contrast, she was deeply unimpressed by Learmont's report when she read it that September.

Ann Widdecombe had always been an admirer of Michael Howard; they shared broadly similar views on most issues, and she had no personal interest in rocking the boat. But in this case she believed that Howard was picking on Derek Lewis to save his own skin, and once she had made up her mind to defend Lewis the water became choppy. Coached by Widdecombe – not herself the most tactful of operators – Lewis concealed his feelings about Learmont and tried to present a reasoned defence. He argued that the two headline-grabbing incidents at Whitemoor and Parkhurst were not representative of more positive trends. Escapes were actually down by 80 per cent in two years. The service was on course, despite the fact that the prison population had risen by a quarter since Howard had become Home Secretary. Miraculously, overcrowding had been reduced at the same time, if an 'overcrowded' cell was defined as one which contained three prisoners rather than two.

Learmont's report had arrived on what was otherwise a good day for the Home Secretary. He was able to announce that crime had fallen again, albeit very slightly, and this was beginning to look like a virtuous trend. Howard hailed 'a real turning point in the fight against crime', the development being trumpeted under the headline 'The evidence that proves prison really does work'.[37] But the reasons for the fall may not just have been related to sentencing policy. The largest drop had been in property crime, reflecting the fact that householders were installing security equipment as a do-it-yourself deterrent. It was also likely that part of the explanation was demographic in that the number of ten-to-twenty-year-olds – the age group responsible for most crimes – had fallen by 10 per cent since 1987. But it was still a fillip for the Home Secretary in the weeks before the party conference in Blackpool. He was likely to emerge stronger than ever – but the effect would be spoilt unless he could be seen to have taken tough decisions on the Prison Service. Learmont's report was the weapon he needed to dispatch Derek Lewis, since it contained severe criticisms.

While Howard was preparing to swing the axe, his junior minister tried to prise it out of his hands. Ann Widdecombe requested a full hour meeting with Howard and Richard Wilson, who had also given Lewis some advice on his defence document. Widdecombe felt that no progress was made, but afterwards Howard decided to give the Director General another chance to account for himself. At a meeting just before the Home Secretary left for Blackpool, Howard told Lewis that his defence had been unsatisfactory and he wanted a more detailed response to Learmont's criticisms by the end of the week. 'You heard the nails going into the coffin,' says a senior official who supported the Home Secretary's stance. 'Howard behaved immensely properly,' he says. 'Lewis was a twit. He misunderstood the relationship. Howard had had enough. Howard was aware that *his* was the authority and the accountability.'

In hindsight, it looks as if Michael Howard was just marking time. Lewis and Widdecombe probably suspected as much, but they persevered. Howard learned that Lewis was planning to meet Widdecombe at Blackpool, and told her that this was 'completely inappropriate'. But she refused to call off the meeting.[38]

It took place in a conference room at Widdecombe's hotel, a modest venue round the corner from Blackpool's traditional conference establishment, the Imperial. Suddenly, as in a scene from a second-rate thriller, Widdecombe and Lewis spotted Howard's two special advisers Patrick Rock and Rachel Whetstone (who had replaced David Cameron a year before). They seemed to be hanging round the hotel, taking glances through the glass door of their meeting room. 'It was pure farce,' Widdecombe later said. 'To this day, I think how can grown-up people be so daft?' Lewis recalls, 'They were continually walking in and out and around this place observing what was going on. We could see them walking past. Ann wasn't fazed at all.'[39] Rock and Whetstone subsequently denied it was a spying mission and insisted that their presence was purely coincidental, since they were both staying at the same hotel. They had agreed to meet in the lobby that morning, but both had apparently mislaid their keys to the front door.

When Howard returned from Blackpool, buoyed by a successful

speech, everything was set for a final showdown. On the morning of Sunday 15 October Widdecombe went to see the Home Secretary in his room in Queen Anne's Gate. She unleashed a barrage of arguments to defend the Director General, including the pertinent prediction that a forced resignation would make it very difficult for Howard to replace Lewis with another 'outsider' from the private sector. Howard was immovable. As Widdecombe became increasingly upset, Lewis waited elsewhere in the building. When his turn came to see Howard, Widdecombe's grimace signalled that they had lost the battle, and the Home Secretary duly announced that Learmont's report had made Lewis's position untenable. He had had to decide which of the two accounts he preferred, and it wasn't Lewis's. Howard said he wanted the parting to be amicable, and proposed that he should tell the Commons the following day that Lewis's term would end two months later. But he wanted his resignation within two hours. The Director General asked for time to think.

While he was doing so, Widdecombe first wrote to John Major, then poured out her profound distress at what was happening in a telephone conversation with the Prime Minister. Although she later denied threatening to resign, it was an option she considered. Major offered comfort, but he could not afford to overrule his Home Secretary. 'Michael was the Secretary of State,' he later explained. 'If Ann had been the Secretary of State, unless it was a clear-cut case – and I didn't think it was in that case – I would have invariably supported the person responsible for running the department.'[40] Others in Number 10 had severe misgivings, and felt that Major had been bulldozed by Howard into accepting Lewis's sacking as a 'fait accompli'.

Lewis refused to quit. The Prison Service board demanded to see Howard to express their unanimous disapproval of what he intended. But, after another meeting with Widdecombe and Howard, Lewis was sacked the next day. He left Michael Howard's room to find Widdecombe in tears. 'I was a bit touched,' he said later. 'I appreciated that it was bizarre to be sitting in the Home Office having just been fired, effectively, with the prisons minister in the room in tears, and me not knowing quite what to say.'[41] Ann Widdecombe sent Lewis's wife, Louise, a bunch of flowers – 'for which kindly thought', she subsequently said, 'I was bawled out by Michael Howard.'[42] She also wrote another letter to John Major. 'I said, "I can't justify what we're doing in any terms at all – ministerial, human, Christian, any terms you can mention. I can't justify this decision."'[43]

Michael Howard later admitted it 'was a pretty miserable occasion' that Monday afternoon when he delivered a Commons statement on Lewis and the Learmont findings. 'I certainly couldn't defend the state of affairs which the report disclosed. It was indefensible. It was quite appalling.'[44] He paid 'tribute' to Lewis 'for what he has achieved', but announced that he had decided 'with some sadness' that there would have to be 'a change of leadership at the top of the Prison Service' in order to implement Learmont's 127 recommendations.[45]

That evening, both Michael Howard and Derek Lewis appeared on the BBC's *Newsnight*, from separate studios. The presenter, Jeremy Paxman, asked Howard if Kenneth Clarke had made a 'serious error of judgement' in appointing Lewis. The Home Secretary obligingly stepped into the trap, by acknowledging that Lewis had 'achieved a great deal in his time in the Prison Service'. 'That rather begs the question of why you are sacking him, doesn't it?' Paxman responded. Unconvinced by Howard's faltering responses, the *Newsnight* presenter suggested, 'He's been sacked to save your skin, hasn't he?' Despite further probing by Paxman, Howard merely repeated that he was 'responsible for policy and the Director General is responsible for operational matters'.[46]

Most media comment agreed with the thrust of Paxman's question. There were blistering assaults on Howard in *The Times* from Simon Jenkins (an old Bow Group colleague), and from Andrew Marr in the *Independent*. 'One is reminded of the *Blackadder* scene in the First World War when the officer decides that it is time for a pointless sacrifice,' wrote Marr, who suggested that the Home Secretary's reputation might prove a liability to Major in the next election.[47] On the *Today* programme Stephen Tumim remarked that a 'bogus distinction' between policy and operational matters meant that 'the

Home Secretary is not responsible for anything at all'.[48] But these critics did not bother Howard. He was familiar with their views, and had
long ago decided to disregard them. Instead, he was more concerned
about the opinions of MPs. When their judgement came to be made,
the main prosecutor would not be Paxman, Marr, Jenkins or Tumim,
but Jack Straw, the Shadow Home Secretary.

Straw was unlikely to get a better opportunity to damage the reputation of his opposite number, and arranged an emergency
Commons debate for Thursday 19 October, three days after Howard's
ministerial statement. Howard knew he was skating on thin ice, and
he asked Ann Widdecombe for support. It was 'mortal combat,
mortal combat', he reportedly told her. 'It's mortal combat between
me and Derek. I need your help.'[49] Hints of the ministerial rift over
Lewis had already reached journalists. If Widdecombe went public,
Howard knew he was probably finished.

Emphasising the seriousness of the Commons debate, Sandra
Howard watched from the public gallery. Her husband was fighting to
preserve his political career. John Marriott, too, was in the gallery, like
Danton's ghost turning up to watch the guillotine claim Robespierre.
But, by the end of the debate, Jack Straw was more bloodied than
Howard.

The Shadow Home Secretary had been well briefed by Derek
Lewis, who showed him plenty of paperwork, but he failed to master
the subject in the way Howard did. According to a vivid account by
the Tory MP Gyles Brandreth, Straw was 'woolly and plodding, easily
confused, thrown by the interventions and virtually sunk, only five
minutes in, by a beautifully judged question from Bernard Jenkin'.[50]
'Does he think that the Director General of the Prison Service should
have been dismissed?' asked the Conservative backbencher.[51] 'It was a
little hand-grenade lightly lobbed,' Brandreth recorded, 'but its effect
was devastating. Straw hesitated. For a second the wretched creature
couldn't think what to say. He didn't have an answer.'[52] It transpired
that Straw hadn't been able to hear Jenkin's question properly because
he suffers from tinnitus, which causes slight deafness. His humiliation
was far from over.

It was the kind of occasion that gives the lie to those who suggest that parliamentary debates no longer matter. Howard showed a remarkable sense of occasion: 'I shall deal in due course, closely and with relish, with each of the allegations put by the Labour Party,' he declared, conciously echoing Iain Macleod's famous 1952 attack on Nye Bevan.[53] And, in flooring Straw, Howard summoned as his star defence witness Derek Lewis.

Lewis now had reason to regret his sophistry during his appearance before the Home Affairs Select Committee the previous January. The Director General had then told MPs that it had been 'essential for operational reasons that the change of governor at Parkhurst took place immediately', as well as denying Chris Mullin's suggestion that Howard had wanted Marriott 'off the premises by the afternoon'.[54] The Home Secretary now made the fullest possible use of these partial truths. He also produced the official minute of the critical January meeting about Marriott, which omitted Lewis's protest against the use of the word 'today' in Howard's draft statement to the Commons. Earlier in the debate the Labour front-bencher John Reid had asked, 'At the meeting on 10 January did he [Howard] insist that the governor of Parkhurst be removed that very day?' Howard tried to skirt around the question, but under further pressure from Reid he said, 'The answer is no because all the decisions that were made that day were made by the Director General of the Prison Service.'[55] This was clearly a highly misleading answer – a mixture of mendacity and evasion. But the documentary evidence presented during the debate seemed to support Howard's case. Labour's frustration spilled over when Gerald Kaufman said that the House had heard 'a shyster lawyer defending a shifty client, with the Home Secretary being the shyster lawyer and the shifty client. What we have here is a system of scapegoats.'[56]

Kaufman was rebuked by the Speaker for using insulting language, but he wasn't the only Labour MP to let his frustration get the better of him. Conservative MPs noticed that Tony Blair, perhaps recalling his own days as Howard's shadow, kept prompting Straw to ask questions. Goaded by Howard to say something, Blair took the bait and made an intervention of his own. For the Home Secretary this was the crème brûlée served up to follow the duck à l'orange. It is highly unusual for a party leader to push aside his official spokesman in a Commons debate, and it was embarrassing for Straw as it implied that he wasn't up to the job himself. Seeing Labour's chance slip away, Blair was exasperated. His two questions made no impact, though, and Howard scored an immediate party point, claiming that Blair's intervention cast serious doubt on his judgement.

Michael Howard had transformed the spirits of Conservative MPs. Gyles Brandreth captured the excitement in his diary:

> It was an electric ninety minutes and when Michael finished and sat back triumphant, the roar from our side was incredible. We cheered and cheered, we waved our order papers, those of us sitting right behind him lent forward to pat him – to touch his garb. Thanks to Straw's ineptitude and Michael's nerveless bravura performance, whatever the rights and wrongs of the case, Michael has set himself free. Amazing.[57]

'It's not surprising . . . that I was able to defeat Straw in that debate,' Howard said later. 'I hadn't, in any way, acted improperly or dishonourably.'[58] Yet it was a remarkable turnaround, which clinched him that year's *Spectator* award for parliamentary debating. Patrick Rock later admitted that: 'If he had made a dreadful speech and flopped, to jeers from the Labour side, he might have had to go. It was high noon!'[59] Instead of struggling for survival, Michael Howard ended up reasserting his leadership credentials. MPs could hardly avoid comparing his display at the dispatch box with John Major's hesitant performances.

Immediately afterwards Michael Howard and his junior ministers went to the Prime Minister's room for a celebratory drink. But Ann Widdecombe was far from jubilant. Few noticed at the time, but she'd wound up the debate by heaping praise on Derek Lewis's tenure at the Prison Service and saying little which could be construed as favourable to Howard. She was not the only member of the Home Office delegation with mixed emotions: Major's friend Baroness

Emily Blatch also supported the former prisons director. And, when Howard started talking about how to continue the fight against Lewis, Widdecombe stormed off. 'This is the most disgraceful episode I have ever been involved with,' she told Major when they met again later that evening. 'Now that Michael thinks he's won, he's going to be vindictive.'[60] With his hand on her knee, Major assured her that he would restrain the Home Secretary.

Over the weekend, Howard phoned Widdecombe to assure her that he saw the affair as closed. Widdecombe told him that she had just spoken to Derek Lewis and he thought the same, whereupon the Home Secretary became angry again and questioned the propriety of her talking to the former Director General at all. It can't have calmed Howard when Widdecombe explained that she trusted Lewis.

Ann Widdecombe would later tell MPs she 'should have resigned at the time' and regretted not having done so.[61] She'd come close, but ultimately didn't want to embarrass John Major with another ministerial resignation from his much-troubled administration. It would have done more harm to the party, and to her own career. What's more, she calculated, it was unlikely that Lewis would have got his job back – at the very least, that would have needed Howard to quit as well. And that would only have deepened the party's woes.

If Tony Blair regretted his intervention in the debate, it did not damage his chances of becoming Prime Minister. Even Jack Straw dusted himself down, and went on to show that two could play the populist on law and order. Howard's triumph was more apparent than real. Indeed, his success in the Commons appears only to have encouraged dissidents elsewhere. Unnamed sources within the Prison Service continued to complain to journalists about his incessant involvement in their affairs. One official told the *Observer*, 'We deal with ministerial demands for information from early morning until night. After Parkhurst, Howard sent over nine civil servants, just to keep an eye on what we are doing . . . Never mind agency status, he is the most interventionist Home Secretary in living memory.'[62] The prison governors pointedly wrote to him asking for an end to interference in operational matters. 'The idea that Howard has not been meddling is just nonsense,' one governor was quoted as saying. 'We all know that he's been messing everywhere.'[63]

Seven months later, Derek Lewis appeared before the Public Service Select Committee and provided much more detail on the events leading to John Marriott's departure from Parkhurst than he'd previously given their home-affairs colleagues. 'What I did not go on to explain at that Committee, and I was not asked to explain it, was whether pressure had been put on me to take more severe action in relation to Mr Marriott, as indeed was the case, because the Home Secretary put me under considerable pressure not simply to move Mr Marriott at the time but to suspend him.'[64]

Yet this development won less publicity than the Home Office's agreement of a £260,000 package to settle Lewis's claim for unfair dismissal. Even the pro-Howard *Sun* presented this as a 'grovelling apology', an 'astonishing climbdown' and an admission that the Home Secretary had been wrong to sack Lewis.[65] The size of the settlement drew attention to the fact that Lewis had been the best-paid official in Whitehall, earning twice as much as Howard himself.

In February 1997 Lewis published a book, *Hidden Agendas*, accompanied by both newspaper serialisation and a *World in Action* TV programme. The press focused on his allegation that even Sandra Howard had interfered in the running of Britain's prisons. Lewis claimed that Howard's adviser David Cameron told him that Sandra thought the new code of standards was 'too generous for prisoners' in requiring 'a balanced and nutritious diet'.[66] 'With evident embarrassment,' Lewis recalls, 'Cameron said the Home Secretary had passed the draft code of standards to Mrs Howard, and she had made some comments which he had been asked to pass on to me. Cameron read from the notes as he gave me the comments. I went straight back to the Prison Service and briefed my colleagues.'[67]

The Howards denied the story, and consulted the City lawyers Linklaters. They tried to stop the allegation being broadcast, and threatened to sue. Some bookshops declined to stock Lewis's book because of the possibility of legal action. But the couple took matters no further.

It did seem out of character for Sandra, who has always been well to the left of Michael on criminal-justice issues and had expressed her dismay at his saying 'prison works' – 'You can't, it sounds too harsh,' she had told him.[68] Indeed, Sandra later joined the board of the charity Addaction which helps rehabilitate drug users in prison. 'She believes very strongly in rehabilitation,' says a friend. 'She would want to see people in prisons come off drugs, learn to read and write and add up – which many of them can't – and learn practical skills to stay on the straight and narrow.'

Despite the departure of Derek Lewis, Michael Howard's prison problems were far from over. It took five months to appoint a new director general – the Prison Service security director Richard Tilt – and then in August 1996 Howard got into a major public row with him. The episode was almost comic. For almost thirty years there had been confusion within the service over prisoners given consecutive jail terms: should time spent in custody before trial be deducted from one sentence or from all of them? Now the service had decided that time on remand should count against each sentence, and had just released 541 prisoners as a result.

The first Michael Howard knew of it was when he was suddenly ambushed at the end of an interview on a totally different subject for *Channel 4 News* (whose presenter, Jon Snow, was well informed on penal affairs as chairman of the Prison Reform Trust). Howard was furious. He'd agreed to meet his private secretary, David Redhouse, on Blackfriars Bridge that evening to collect his red box before travelling down to Kent for the weekend. Redhouse got 'absolutely crucified' for not telling Howard about the new policy, says a colleague. The QC David Pannick was immediately engaged to review matters, and concluded almost at once that the Prison Service had got it wrong. When Howard subsequently appeared on *Newsnight* he told Jon Snow's cousin Peter that he'd reversed the policy that evening. Richard Tilt was then dragged back from holiday for a dressing-down from Howard. 'Richard came out completely ashen,' says one official, 'like I'd never seen him before.' Tilt could hardly be sacked – dismissing two director generals within twelve months would have been damning – but he was forced to deliver a public apology to the Home Secretary. The 541 ex-inmates, meanwhile, were allowed to keep their freedom.

The one area of penal policy where Michael Howard might have won respect from liberal opinion was in his attitude to hanging, where he went against the wishes of most of his party. In the Commons in 1994 he explained that he had been shocked by several notorious miscarriages of justice in recent years. These included the case of Stephen Kiszko, who spent sixteen years in prison having been wrongly convicted of murdering a schoolgirl when forensic tests later showed he couldn't have killed her. 'Miscarriages of justice are a blot on a civilised society,' Howard said. 'When we consider the plight of those who have been wrongly convicted, we cannot but be relieved that the death penalty was not available. We should not fail to consider the irreparable damage that would have been inflicted on the criminal justice system had innocent people been executed.'[69]

Although he had changed his mind, Howard still thought that the killers of policemen and prison officers deserved stiffer punishment. In March 1994 the Cabinet home affairs committee discussed his proposal for an amendment to the Criminal Justice Bill which would ensure that a life sentence for such offenders could be imposed without any prospect of remission – 'life means life'. Before the meeting, he had written to the Prime Minister to press his case. The letter was promptly leaked, infuriating Major, who suspected underhand tactics from the Howard camp. The Home Secretary was overruled by his colleagues, but henceforth he would instead consider release dates for police murderers 'very, very carefully', and ensure that such prisoners were old and infirm before being set free.[70]

Yet Michael Howard's attitude to possible miscarriages of justice was inconsistent. For example, until August 1996 he refused to allow appeals against the four convictions for the 1978 murder of the newspaper boy Carl Bridgewater. The original verdicts were then overturned in February 1997, confirming the view of most people who had studied the case in any detail. And when asked to look again at Sara Thornton's conviction for the murder of her abusive husband,

Howard was reported to have scrawled 'I am not inclined to do this' over the papers.[71] In May 1995 the threat of a judicial review forced him to relent, and a year later Thornton was released, having been convicted on the lesser charge of manslaughter.

Unfortunately for Howard, the impression that his decisions were driven by populist concerns, rather than the principles of justice, left him open to challenge in the European courts. The most sensational case in this category was his decision in July 1994 to set a 'tariff' of fifteen years for the juvenile killers of the two-year-old boy James Bulger – when the judge had recommended eight years and the Lord Chief Justice, Lord Lane, had opted for ten. Howard also decided that the 'Moors murderer' Myra Hindley should be kept in prison until she died, although technically her case should have been considered by an impartial review board every five years.

Of all Howard's controversies over penal issues, the Parkhurst/Lewis affair was to have the greatest long-term repercussions. John Marriott himself never recovered from his public denunciation over the Parkhurst escape, and he left the Prison Service shortly afterwards. He was particularly upset by the vituperative and personal nature of Howard's attacks. On one occasion, for instance, the Home Secretary had told MPs, 'I find it hard to understand how anyone could question the decision to remove Mr Marriott from his duties at Parkhurst without delay, or to suggest that he has been used as a scapegoat.' Then, pointing towards the Labour benches, as if Marriott were a criminal rather than a public servant, Howard taunted aggressively, 'That is the man on whose behalf the Leader of the Opposition has chosen to take up the cudgels.'[72] Marriott couldn't understand why he had been attacked so forcefully. 'Why did he need to denigrate me?' he said two years later. 'If you actually listen to what he says, it's full of venom . . . I went through an extremely difficult time after that. I felt bruised and battered. I felt that – at one stage, only once, very briefly – I felt like committing suicide. I . . . felt that my whole world had fallen apart.'[73]

John Marriott's criticism became more pertinent with hindsight when Michael Howard attacked the Blair government for the way it had put huge public pressure on the civil servant David Kelly, who famously did commit suicide in 2003. By then Marriott, too, was dead, having suffered a heart attack in 1998, at the age of only fifty-one.

Ann Widdecombe publicly supported Michael Howard for the rest of the Conservatives' time in office. When she came under public fire in 1996 over the shackling of pregnant prisoners, the Home Secretary returned her loyalty by defending her publicly. Neverthless, her decision not to resign 'plagued her', according to Widdecombe's approved biographer, Nicholas Kochan.[74] She still nursed a sense of injustice about what she saw as Howard's ruthless determination to protect himself at the expense of Derek Lewis.

If Michael Howard thought that the matter was over, he had misjudged Ann Widdecombe.

15

THE FOURTH BASTARD

Michael Howard was more awkward on Europe than the rest of
us. He would not put the subject to rest.

MICHAEL PORTILLO[1]

One weekend in July 1993, Michael Portillo was staying in a small
Edinburgh hotel to attend a family wedding. Early in the morning, he
was summoned downstairs to take a phone call. It was from the Home
Secretary. 'Have you seen the papers?' Portillo recalls Michael Howard
asking. 'It appears the Prime Minister has called us bastards!'[2]

A few days before, after doing an interview with Michael Brunson,
the political editor of ITN, John Major had carried on discussing his
many predicaments, unaware that his voice was still being recorded.
His government had just survived a vote of confidence on the
Maastricht Treaty, and he was exhausted. Brunson asked Major about
reported divisions within the Cabinet, and observed that three ministers were supposed to have threatened resignation over European
policy. Major explained that it would be counter-productive to sack
them: 'You can think of ex-ministers who are going around causing all
sorts of trouble. We don't want another three more of the bastards out
there.'[3]

There was immediate speculation about the identities of the three.
The favourites were Portillo himself, John Redwood and Peter Lilley;

Michael Howard was a fourth possibility. Major later claimed in his memoirs – implausibly – that he was not referring to 'existing Cabinet ministers'. His colourful language was, he said, directed towards former ministers who, in his eyes, had *already* proved themselves to be 'bastards'.[4]

Even so, Michael Howard had good reason to think that Major might have had him in mind. He had, it seems, threatened to resign over the Social Chapter. And his closest political friend, Norman Lamont, who would soon be seen on the front page of what *Private Eye* called Major's 'Bastards Book', had been causing trouble since his departure – not least in his resignation speech, in which he said the Conservatives gave 'the impression of being in office but not in power'.[5] Their friendship notwithstanding, Howard subsequently went on television to defend the government against Lamont's attack. 'I was very sad,' he said, 'that he made the speech that he did. I much regret it. I disagreed with almost everything he said.' That included Lamont's view that Britain needed an independent central bank along the lines of those in Germany and other European states.[6] 'It's just politics. It isn't worth destroying a friendship,' Sandra Howard assured the distressed Rosemary Lamont, whose husband never actually discussed the matter with Howard.[7] Worse followed eighteen months later when Howard responded publicly to speculation that Lamont might challenge Major for the leadership. 'He would cut an absolutely ridiculous figure if he were to do anything of the kind . . . it would be a grave mistake, I think, for anyone to play any part in such a venture.'[8] Their friendship survived, and Lamont later defended Howard's record at the Home Office.

On balance, Michael Howard was probably not regarded as a 'bastard' by Major, given his frequent expressions of loyalty to the PM. Even so, the agitated phone call to Portillo suggests that Howard worried that he didn't enjoy the full trust of the Prime Minister. Yet two years later, in June 1995, Howard was among the first to be informed when Major suddenly submitted himself for re-election as Conservative leader, in an attempt to make his critics 'put up or shut up'. Major even asked Howard to convey the news to the Welsh Secretary, John Redwood.

Choosing Howard as messenger, rather than telling Redwood in person, was a foolish move, especially since Redwood had hated Howard's 'obsessiveness and secrecy' since their time together at the DoE, according to Redwood's adviser Hywel Williams. 'There were few colleagues for whom Redwood felt a greater contempt.'[9] This, together with Redwood's anger at being one of the last in the Cabinet to hear the news, fuelled his subsequent decision to stand against Major.

Howard was sceptical about whether Major had made a wise move, but the Scottish Secretary, Ian Lang, noted in his diary that he 'pressed' for inclusion in the Prime Minister's campaign team.[10] It was a good time to be loyal, for an important Cabinet post was up for grabs. Douglas Hurd had announced at the start of the leadership contest that he would step down as Foreign Secretary once it was over, regardless of the result. It was natural for Howard to think that he could make the same transition that Hurd had made six years before, from the Home Office to the Foreign Office. Having lost to Clarke in the battle for the Treasury, he would expect to be a leading contender for the only other job (apart from the premiership) appropriate to his seniority.

In the event, although John Major beat off Redwood's challenge, more than a third of the parliamentary party – 111 MPs – failed to vote for him. Redwood received 89 votes – a remarkable tally, given the attempts of the Major camp to portray him as a fanatic – while another 22 MPs abstained. Major's allies valiantly presented the outcome as a ringing endorsement, but it was obvious that his position had been weakened.

On the day after his re-election, however, Major promoted the Defence Secretary, Malcolm Rifkind, and not Michael Howard. Rifkind was well qualified, having compiled an impressive list of contacts on both sides of the Atlantic during three years at Defence. But the Euro-sceptics regarded him with deep suspicion, and Rifkind's appointment looked even more provocative in the context of the reshuffle as a whole, because Major also decided to make Michael Heseltine his Deputy Prime Minister (a post unfilled before). As

Major admitted in his memoirs, the two appointments 'caused anguish and dissent among those who wanted a harder line on Europe'.[11]

Howard's 'anguish' at being passed over for a second time was increased by his dismay at Heseltine's appointment. He felt the Right had been betrayed, after Major had assured them during his campaign that he was solid on Europe. Howard later admitted that he was 'not very enthusiastic' about Heseltine's appointment, and that he told Major of his 'grave doubts about whether it would work'.[12] Particularly irksome were Heseltine's new powers to intervene across government, and the new Deputy Prime Minister rubbed the point home by inviting Howard's Permanent Secretary, Richard Wilson, to see him. One of Howard's friends recalled that this incident left the Home Secretary 'white and almost trembling' with fury at the breach of ministerial etiquette, at a time when relations had still not recovered from Heseltine's role in the fall of Margaret Thatcher. The previous year, when Howard was asked four times by David Frost if he now forgave Heseltine, he had evaded the question. 'We've moved on since then,' Howard blustered. 'We work very closely together as Cabinet colleagues.'[13]

With hindsight, it seems clear that the politics of the moment would have ensured that the Foreign Office went to a more pro-European minister no matter what the outcome of the leadership vote. In the unlikely event that Major's position had been strengthened by the vote, he would have felt no need to appoint someone from the Euro-sceptic wing of the party. In the weakened position in which he now found himself, to have appointed Howard would have sent a clear message that Major was now a 'lame-duck' prime minister, held captive by his critics within the party. He had begun his premiership by promising to keep Britain 'at the heart of Europe'. Moving a man to the Foreign Office who disagreed so fundamentally with this view would have been read – by British voters and Britain's partners – as a signal of how little control Major now had over his government.

Howard's views on Europe had been made very clear, publicly and privately. During the leadership campaign he had joined Major's manager, Lord Cranborne, in urging the Prime Minister to rule out membership of the proposed European single currency, for both the present parliament and the next one. In the previous year, during the run-up to the European parliamentary elections, Howard had attacked the President of the European Commission, Jacques Delors, and dismissed the prospects for the proposed euro: 'I very, very much doubt if there will be any significant move towards a single currency in my political lifetime. I don't think it's going to happen.'[14] His alternative vision drew on his family background in the fashion trade: 'What we need is a made-to-measure Europe in which the institutional arrangements comfortably fit national interests, not an off-the-peg standard-size Europe, ill-fitting and splintering at the seams.'[15] He would be still advocating the same approach a decade later.

Howard was upset not to get the Foreign Office, especially after people close to Major had plainly been telling journalists he was likely to get the job. 'I was a little bit surprised,' he admitted later, 'because I assumed that these many stories, which seemed to be very well sourced, had some substance to them. But I'd never been given any assurances of any kind.'[16] Howard had probably been used. The stories of him becoming Foreign Secretary looked like a ploy to reassure Euro-sceptics that, if Major was allowed to stay, Howard would be there to protect their interests.

If he was disappointed not to get the new position, the Home Office remained a hugely demanding portfolio. Few Cabinet ministers have withstood as much pressure as Michael Howard did in the years from 1993 to 1997. There were personal dangers, too. In 1994 hundreds of demonstrators invaded his garden in Kent to protest about his law to crack down on raves, though the family were away at the time. The following year Howard received a telephone threat from a man who threatened to 'kill' him.[17] Yet there were some perks. In 1995 he was an official guest at the Football League Cup final. 'There's only one Michael Howard,' chanted Liverpool fans as his car arrived at Wembley, whereupon he got out and started shaking their hands. He was also responsible for the regulation of gambling, which brought him into contact with horse racing, which he enjoyed as much as football. He relaxed the restrictions on betting shops, and presided over the introduction of off-course betting on Sundays, which made Sunday race meetings financially viable. His relations with the state-run Tote were more fraught. In February 1995 he agreed a two-year extension to the contract of the seventy-six-year-old Tote chairman Lord (Woodrow) Wyatt, who also wrote a column for the *News of the World*. Initially the Thatcherite Wyatt had nothing but praise for Howard in his column, and he even asked him to present the trophy for a major race at Sandown sponsored by the Tote.

Howard and Wyatt often saw each other socially, and were supposedly friends – though one wouldn't think so on reading the comments in the peer's diary. Howard was 'a despicable little man', Wyatt wrote, a 'ghastly swine' and 'spiteful' – though such opinions may have been influenced by Howard's reluctance to extend Wyatt's Tote contract much further. 'I can see now why he is so hopeless at man management,' Wyatt said. 'He is aggressive, unfriendly when he thinks he has a little power . . . I am beginning to wonder whether he is any good as Home Secretary because he rubs so many people up the wrong way.' Wyatt chose not to air these views in the *News of the World*, although he had sent John Major a private note advising him not to promote Howard further. 'Comes over badly,' it read. 'It would be dangerous to make him Foreign Secretary though his views are sound.'[18]

Woodrow Wyatt may have been part buffoon and part incorrigible social climber, but Howard couldn't afford to offend him too much. As well as writing a column for Britain's best-selling Sunday paper, he was also close to its owner, the media tycoon Rupert Murdoch, and his chief lieutenant in Britain, Les Hinton. Wyatt's diaries reveal that, only two days after the Home Secretary and his wife visited their home for dinner, his wife, Verushka, phoned Howard at the Home Office seeking a quick replacement passport for their daughter, Petronella, who had lost her original one when her bag was stolen. 'Are you actually ringing the Home Secretary, telling him to get a passport for your daughter?' asked Hinton, who overheard her while visiting the Wyatts and was astonished. 'Yes, why not?' Lady Wyatt replied. 'He was here to dinner the other night. He was very friendly.

Why shouldn't I?'[19] With Michael Howard's help, according to Wyatt, a new passport was soon available. Howard vehemently denies this.

But the bulk of Howard's work as Home Secretary was still on law and order, and in 1995 he announced dramatic new proposals. He promised that before the next election he would follow the example of California in adopting a policy of 'three strikes and you're out', under which burglars and hard drug dealers got automatic minimum prison sentences if they were convicted three times. Serious violent offenders, including murderers, would receive a mandatory life sentence on the second conviction. Ever one for the conference soundbite, Howard warned, 'If you don't want the time, don't do the crime. No half-time sentences for full-time crimes.'[20] Automatic parole would cease, and only model prisoners would be released early. Prisoners serving less than a year in jail would serve the full sentence. The maximum remission for longer-term prisoners would be 15 per cent, instead of the existing practice of releases on licence after either three-quarters or two-thirds of the term (depending on its length). Howard told the 1995 party conference that his plans would 'send shock waves throughout the criminal community', and put honesty back at the heart of sentencing policy. He also hoped that they would discomfit the new Labour leader. 'Tony Blair – tough on crime, tough on the victims of crime,' he sneered. For Conservatives in Blackpool, this rhetoric was sufficient to compensate for some less comfortable remarks from the Home Secretary. Although he promised that Britain would keep control of its borders and beat off any attempt by the European Union to relax its immigration laws. 'There must be no quarter, no hiding place, and no mercy for those who make the lives of other British citizens a misery because of the colour of their skin,' he warned. 'There will never be room for racists in this party.'[21]

Howard won a four-minute ovation this time, and his proposals were backed enthusiastically by John Major, but they had been opposed in Cabinet by his old Tunbridge Wells adversary, the former Attorney-General Sir Patrick Mayhew. As Howard probably anticipated, the cheers of his Blackpool audience had scarcely died away before he encountered the first public resistance from the legal establishment. The Lord Chief Justice, Peter Taylor, issued an unprecedented formal statement of rebuke. 'Minimum sentences are inconsistent with doing justice according to the circumstances of each case,' Taylor argued, explaining that judges 'must be free to fit the particular punishment to the particular crime if justice is to be done'.[22] By this time the prison population had climbed to over 52,000. The new proposals would add an estimated 15,000, at a cost of around £700 million for the extra prison accommodation.

A few weeks after the 1995 party conference, Howard responded to a critical editorial in the *Daily Telegraph*. 'Nothing could be more dangerous', he wrote, 'than the opening up of a large gap between the criminal justice system and the public it serves. That really would be the road to lynch law and the vigilante.'[23] That was Howard's defence against the familiar charge of populism; he had to take public opinion into account, because if popular feeling was ignored it would bring the whole judicial system into disrepute.

But Howard seemed not to consider that public opinion might itself have been distorted by what he said, and by his supporters in the press. An opinion survey of May 1996 showed the extent of public ignorance about sentencing policy. A majority thought that only one in two convicted rapists was jailed, when the actual proportion was 91 per cent. When asked how many muggers went to prison, most opted for 20 per cent instead of over half.[24]

In other words, when judges took up the cudgels against Howard they were not just complaining about his attempts to force them into a sentencing straitjacket. Some sentences were too lenient. But by giving the impression that the punishment *never* fitted the crime, Howard may have been bringing closer the 'lynch law' which he feared. In turn, he used the threat of vigilantes to justify new measures which eroded the historic independence of the judiciary from the executive. It was hardly surprising that the maverick former Master of the Rolls Lord Denning – himself a great populist – predicted 'a contest between Parliament and the courts which would be most undesirable'.[25] In the new year, Margaret Thatcher's first Lord Chancellor, Quintin Hailsham, warned, 'This business about mandatory sentences must be held in very great suspicion.'[26] Even the Archbishop of Canterbury, George Carey, intervened, saying that that revenge-driven punishment was 'what we see in wild frontier societies which have no settled legal system . . . If you treat people like animals they will respond like animals.'[27]

As if to confirm the views of Howard's critics that his policies were largely media-driven, the publication of *Protecting the Public,* his 1996 White Paper on sentencing, was delayed for a fortnight to allow for the media preoccupation with 'mad cow disease'. The former Master of the Rolls Lord Donaldson appealed to Parliament for 'second and wiser thoughts' on the measures.[28] But Labour had already signalled that worried judges could expect no help from them. The Howard camp was reported to be 'amazed' when Blair and Straw decided to support the principle of minimum sentences.[29]

'No, no,' Howard told Boris Johnson, then a reporter on the *Daily Telegraph*, 'I don't give a damn what the Labour Party do. I'm doing things that I believe to be right.'[30] Thanks to the journalistic efforts of his son, Nick – then in the sixth form at Eton – we have a more accurate picture. Breakfast in the Howard household was 'a cast-iron family engagement', to compensate for all the other disruptions, the younger Howard wrote in *The Times*. But his father demanded silence when a particularly pertinent item came up on the *Today* programme. 'It is rare for any of our times together to pass without a measure of concern, fury or delight at the tactics of the other parties.'[31]

When Straw and Blair deprived Howard of a tactical triumph over what became the Crime (Sentences) Bill, 'fury' was probably the dominant emotion. Debate on British penal policy descended into a policy auction, as Straw and Howard competed to convince the public that each would do more than the other to stamp out anti-social behaviour (such as so-called 'squeegee merchants') and be tougher in imposing curfews on young people. By the end of Howard's time at the Home Office their bitter duel had turned into a blissful duet. *The Economist* depicted the conciliatory couple with a cover headline 'Partners in crime – the threat to Britain's liberties'.[32] In February 1997 Labour let Howard go ahead with the second reading of a new bill giving the police more powers of surveillance, in the face of protests from MPs on all sides that the legislation had not been properly scrutinised. A few dissidents joined the Liberal Democrats in voting against. Even Norman Lamont described the proposals as 'somewhat alarming'.[33] Howard's law-and-order policies were, he says, 'one of the very few subjects on which we don't coincide'.[34]

If Howard had built a consensus with his shadow, former Home Secretaries were queuing up to criticise. Douglas Hurd and Kenneth Baker expressed strong reservations during the second reading of the Crime (Sentences) Bill. Howard had decided that the 'three strikes' punishment for burglary should be three years, with seven years for drug traffickers. Hurd spoke of 'a desperate race for votes', adding that the Home Secretary could not 'enter such a race in such crude terms'.[35] Damaging criticism also came from Peter Lloyd and from Howard's former Cabinet colleague Peter Brooke. The Lords undermined Howard's intention by reinforcing the element of discretion which had been left to judges by the original bill, which said that 'exceptional circumstances' could be taken into account in passing sentence, and the government had to accept their amendments in order to get the bill through before the end of the parliamentary session.

Guns were another problem, especially after a horrific incident in March 1996 in the small Scottish town of Dunblane, when a madman called Thomas Hamilton walked into a primary school and shot dead sixteen children and their teacher before turning his gun on himself. Officially, of course, Howard was not responsible for law-and-order issues in Scotland, but such was the public revulsion throughout the United Kingdom that he immediately knew he would have to take the lead in confronting the gun lobby and tightening controls. Yet Howard wanted to be measured in his restrictions. His former junior minister Michael Forsyth, who was now Scottish Secretary as well as being the highly vulnerable MP for Dunblane, thought Howard should go further. Forsyth threatened to resign, and won the backing of the Prime Minister.

The populist Howard faced a dilemma. On one side was the 'Snowdrop' petition, signed by 750,000 people, calling for an outright ban on handguns, and normally such public concern, backed by a vociferous press, would be important for Howard. On the other were around fifty Tory MPs who would not countenance what they saw as a knee-jerk reaction from the government. The Sportsman's Association was threatening to put up candidates against any MP who supported a tough line. But Howard did not have to impose his view on the party. As Jack Straw pointed out, if he wanted an outright ban he needed only to allow a free vote in the Commons. Howard opted not to offend his backbenchers, perhaps thinking ahead to a future leadership election, and the government decided merely to stop people keeping handguns at home. He told *Sun* readers that, if gun clubs were closed down, then shooting – 'which has always been an Olympic sport' – might go underground.[36]

Howard's calculations over handguns cost him support on both sides of the party. David Mellor, a strong advocate of an outright ban, was outraged that Howard refused to tell him what ministers had decided, even though as a former Cabinet member he could expect to be briefed on 'Privy Council terms'.[37] But Howard's reputation also fell among the gun lobby, even though they were promised financial compensation. In 1996 there were between 160,000 and 200,000 legal owners of handguns over .22 calibre, the category marked down for destruction under the proposed law. Howard's compensation offers increased as the important vote approached, and by early December the estimated bill to the taxpayer had reached £150 million. But this was still not enough for sixty-three Tory rebels, one of whom described the measure as 'nothing short of legalised robbery'.[38]

There was still a final flurry of crime legislation to come, although Howard had already used up much parliamentary time. He gave government backing to a private member's bill to outlaw the practice of 'stalking', although earlier he had blocked a similar proposal by a Labour MP. And in February 1997 he unveiled new proposals to limit the right to jury trial. This was intended as a cost-cutting exercise, saving up to £55 million a year, but it would also have the effect – contrary to much of his rhetoric – of reducing sentences, since many cases previously heard in Crown Courts would now be handled by

magistrates, who could not impose more than six months' imprisonment. Even Straw raised an eyebrow at the abolition of a right dating
back to Magna Carta, but he willingly endorsed other ideas, notably
the proposed reduction of the minimum age for appearance in adult
courts from eighteen to seventeen.

These plans were part of the pre-election skirmishing between the
parties, since an election had to take place that spring and there was no
time in the parliamentary timetable left to enact them. The same was
true of identity cards, although there was some progress on the design
and likely cost ($£$15) of a voluntary card. There would have been
more of a stir had the system looked likely to go ahead, and Lord
Cranborne wrote to Howard to warn him that the necessary legislation would face 'trouble' in the Lords even if the Tories won the
election.[39]

While Howard still received a warm reception at the 1996
Conservative conference – his last as Home Secretary – the spark was
missing. The magic had certainly worn thin with some Cabinet colleagues. One commented, off the record, that 'It's all done for image,
but little of it gets enacted.' Another gloated at the latest disappointing crime figures.[40] Against this background, Howard had to milk his
Euro-scepticism to win his customary ovation. 'This country's sovereignty, this country's democracy, this country's independence are at
stake,' he declared. 'They are sacred trusts. They are vital to our future.
And, under the Conservatives they are not negotiable.' Howard could
argue that Europe was relevant to his job, because he promised that
Britain would veto any attempt to remove its frontier controls.
'Immigration policy belongs in Britain, not in Brussels. And that is
where it's going to stay.'[41]

Home Secretaries possess one of the most potent but dangerous
weapons in British politics – the so-called 'race card'. During
Howard's term of office the issue of immigration threatened again to
become a central election issue, after a gap of more than a decade. The
development which brought it back was asylum.

The opposition parties first accused Howard of playing politics
with immigration during the 1994 European election, when he

alleged that Labour and the Liberal Democrats would allow more than 6 million non-EU citizens to live, work and claim welfare benefits in Britain. 'Labour's proposals would blow a massive hole in our firm immigration policies,' he warned. 'They would extend the right to live and work in this country to millions of foreign nationals now living within the European Union. This would be folly of the first order and put our excellent race relations at grave risk.'[42]

In March 1995, under pressure from Tory MPs, he promised a tough new bill on asylum and illegal immigration. The bill introduced a 'white list' of states where there was considered not to be a serious risk of persecution. Applications for asylum from those countries would still be considered, but with a truncated appeals procedure. This would enable Home Office staff to process applications more quickly, sorting out what Howard called 'bogus' asylum seekers from truly deserving cases. There would be new penalties for 'racketeers' who brought illegal immigrants into the UK, and employers would be fined for giving such immigrants work. There would also be restrictions on their access to housing and child benefit.

In the Commons, Howard reeled off the statistics. In November 1995 there were 4,700 asylum applications, compared to 2,500 in January 1994. Sixty thousand applicants were waiting for an adjudication. While the figures for Britain were rising fast, those for the rest of Western Europe were falling, because of tighter procedures elsewhere. Britain, Howard declared, should be 'a haven, not a honeypot'.[43] Since only 4 per cent of applicants were judged to be genuine victims of persecution, the system, he said, was clearly being clogged up by unwanted and undeserving guests.

Apart from asylum, Howard's other big immigration headache was caused by the forthcoming handover of Hong Kong to China in 1997. Here he came up against Chris Patten, one of John Major's closest friends, who had become Governor of the colony after losing his seat in Bath in 1992. In September 1995 Patten suggested in a radio programme that more than 3 million Hong Kong Chinese should be given the right to live in Britain after the handover. Jack Straw joined Howard in rebuffing this proposal. They stuck to the line established in the 1990 British Nationalities (Hong Kong) Act, which restricted the right of abode to 50,000 people.

But this was only the start of the contest between Patten and his former junior at the DoE. If it was unrealistic to expect ministers to let 3 million Hong Kongers settle in the UK – as even Patten recognised – there was at least a chance of letting them travel to Britain without visas. Patten knew that Howard was 'implacably opposed to making any change'. When they met, it was 'not remotely acrimonious', Patten says, but he noted Howard's 'slightly annoying barrister's habit of merely repeating his best point, while arguments you advance yourself are allowed to whizz overhead'. Howard argued that the Hong Kong Chinese already needed a visa to enter Britain, and he could not see why their rights should be improved when British rule ended – an argument that Patten found 'intellectually logical' but 'morally wrong'.[44] The Home Secretary's real fear was probably that a change would provoke a right-wing tabloid campaign about the country being 'swamped' by Chinese who hoped to stay indefinitely.

Chris Patten conducted a skilful lobbying operation, drawing on support from sympathetic colleagues. By January 1996 the Governor had secured the backing of Malcolm Rifkind, who returned from a visit to Hong Kong espousing Patten's arguments. And Patten had been astute enough to hold his biggest gun in reserve: his close friend John Major, who announced the concession granting visa-free access during a visit to the colony in March 1996. The government also gave the right of abode to twenty-nine widows of Chinese subjects who had fought for Britain in the Second World War. Howard had resisted this, too, on the grounds that it set a precedent for other groups with special claims.

A third contentious issue over Hong Kong ought to have been a sharper reminder to Howard of his own past. There were around 5,000 British non-Chinese subjects in the colony, mainly of Indian origin. A few of these had been given the right to settle in Britain under the 1990 act, but the remainder were effectively likely to become 'stateless' after the handover. Their situation was comparable with the plight of the East African Asians whom Howard had once championed so eloquently. But Howard was no longer the earnest Bow Group member of the early 1970s. More than twenty years on, he was opposed to making concessions to the Indians in Hong Kong. But he was outflanked by his Cabinet colleagues.

In the hours before Major arrived for his March 1996 visit to Hong Kong, Malcolm Rifkind was joined by Michael Heseltine in a three-way telephone call with the Home Secretary. Under their combined pressure, Howard agreed that the 'stateless' subjects should have the option to settle in Britain if they ever came under pressure to leave Hong Kong, although they would not be issued with British passports. Patten and Rifkind were still not satisfied with this. In December 1996 the Governor had further talks with Howard, demanding the right of abode in Britain and the option of citizenship after five years' residence in the UK. Howard rejected this, but the following month the Lords gave strong cross-party backing to a bill along the lines proposed by Patten. Even Baroness Blatch, who resisted the bill on behalf of the Home Office, now felt that the position was indefensible. After talking to Major, Howard caved in.

Michael Howard's tough stance on immigration may in part have been influenced by the situation in his constituency. Both Folkestone and the neighbouring Channel port of Dover were frequent entry points for asylum seekers arriving by ferry or through the new tunnel, which finally opened in 1994. On the other hand, whatever his constituents may have thought, his own father had arrived at Dover fifty years before and had benefited and prospered – as had Howard's mother and her family – from Britain's traditional willingness to take in people from abroad. There was also the mystery of Howard's grandfather Morris Wurzberger, who seems to have lived illegally in Britain for the last two decades of his life. Had Howard's ancestors applied for admission to live in Britain in the late 1990s, it is very unlikely, given their family circumstances, that they would have been admitted. They would have been regarded, in all probability, as 'economic migrants'. Even if Bernat Hecht, Morris Wurzberger or the Kurshion family had come to Britain claiming political asylum, arguing that they faced discrimination and persecution in their home countries, they would probably have been rebuffed – especially under the tougher rules proposed by Michael Howard. Yet, in all the debates and media coverage of his immigration policies, the Home Secretary's family history and the possible hypocrisy of his position were hardly raised. Rare exceptions were articles by the journalist Nick Cohen towards the end of 1995. 'The spectacle of a man who cannot see his father in the faces of the Bosnians and Nigerians his department rejects, is risible and repellent,' Cohen wrote in *Jewish Quarterly*.[45] David Frost also asked about Bernat Hecht on his Sunday breakfast programme. 'Under our rules today he would not have achieved asylum,' Frost suggested. 'Is that true?' Howard didn't deny it, but pointed out – quite correctly – that Bernat had not applied for asylum, but had come because he had a job to go to. Frost chose not to press him.[46]

Immigration and asylum also featured prominently in another theme of the Howard years at the Home Office – his regular defeats in the courts, in both Britain and Europe. His most publicised reversal concerned the Saudi dissident Professor Mohammed al-Mas'ari, whose deportation to the Caribbean island of Dominica he had ordered. The Chief Immigration Adjudicator ruled in March 1996 that Howard had not taken sufficient steps to ensure that al-Mas'ari would be safe in his involuntary exile. The decision was especially embarrassing for Howard since the Tory government had long-standing and controversial links with the Saudis.

Michael Howard's tenure at the Home Office coincided with a general rise in judicial activism, as judges grew restive about the government's refusal to incorporate into British law the European Convention on Human Rights.[47] Nevertheless, most of Howard's defeats arose from judicial reviews of his compliance with laws laid down by Parliament. The al-Mas'ari case was one of several which showed that the way to beat the former barrister at the Home Office was to show that he had acted with 'procedural unfairness'. The law lords ruled that Howard's money-saving Criminal Injuries Compensation Scheme was illegal, because it had been introduced while the earlier, more generous system was still in place. A few days later, with great chutzpah, Howard published an article promoting his

Criminal Justice Bill, entitled 'Our first duty must always be to the victims.'[48]

In November 1995 the Revd Sun Myung Moon, a favourite tabloid target in the 1970s for the alleged 'brainwashing' techniques of his Unification Church, also won a High Court victory on the grounds of 'procedural unfairness'. His ban from the UK was 'unlawful', the judges said, because he had not been given the chance to defend himself.[49] Almost exactly a year later came a ruling by the European Court of Human Rights which freed a Sikh activist who had been in prison in Britain for six years, awaiting deportation.

Home Secretaries are inevitably the subject of frequent legal challenges, some of which they are bound to lose; and in many of Howard's cases judges were not criticising *personal* actions by him, but departmental decisions taken in his name. However, the crowning judicial disaster for Howard involved a case where he had personally intervened. In May 1996 the High Court decided that the Home Secretary had been wrong to increase the sentence on the schoolboy killers of James Bulger from ten years to fifteen. Following the lines of earlier rulings by the European Court of Human Rights, Lord Justice Pill said that Howard should not have treated the convicted boys as if they had been adults. Although Pill understood the extent of public revulsion, there was a special requirement to keep sentences under review in the case of juveniles, and to promote rehabilitation rather than retribution.

Yet liberals could applaud some things Michael Howard did as Home Secretary. He voted to lower the homosexual age of consent to eighteen – though not sixteen as some wanted – at a time when many Tories wanted to keep the existing age of twenty-one. (His Home Office colleague David Maclean called it the 'buggery amendment'.)[50] Howard also attacked the right of rapists to cross-examine their victims in court, and his establishing of the first national DNA database would help secure more convictions in rape cases. The Green Paper *Preventing Children Offending*, which was issued in March 1997 to show that the Tories still had plenty of ideas on crime, was described by one civil servant as 'a last ditch attempt to make the

Home Office look human before the election'. The headlines focused on the punitive proposals: parents would have to pay compensation for crimes committed by their children, and the favoured deterrent of a lost driving licence awaited those who failed to comply. But the real story was that Howard had accepted the influence of environmental factors on offending. 'Our strategy is to tackle crime at its roots and to give children the best chance of growing up as law-abiding adults,' he announced.[51] Or, as someone else might have put it, there was no point in being tough on criminals unless one also addressed the causes of crime.

Headlines charting his legal setbacks, and almost weekly calls by Labour for his resignation, seemed only to improve Howard's reputation with the Conservative rank and file. In April 1996 the *Mail on Sunday's* resident political soothsayer noted that the Home Secretary's stock was rising. The odds against his becoming Tory leader had been slashed from 20–1 to 10–1, after a mystery punter had placed £750 on him. Whether it was a well-known gambler from Queen Anne's Gate who was backing his ambitions with his cash was not discovered. By January 1997 he was down to 6–1, behind only the two Michaels, Heseltine and Portillo.

Howard had to tread carefully, and in 1996 he was embarrassed when a letter surfaced which his wife, Sandra, apparently unbeknown to him, had written to Peter Thurnham. His former PPS had just resigned the Conservative whip, reducing the government's already slender majority to just two. Thurnham was aggrieved because he had hoped to leave his highly vulnerable seat in Bolton and fight instead the far safer Westmorland and Lonsdale, where he lived. He wasn't even given a selection interview, and the local party chose Howard's former adviser Tim Collins instead.

Sandra's gesture showed that she shared her husband's habit of sending considerate, handwritten notes. She wrote that she and Michael both had 'a bottomless well of admiration' for Thurnham. 'I know how poorly you've been treated. It's monstrous but it's not the fault of the whole body of Conservatives, sensible and honest and caring as the vast majority are.'[52] On receiving the letter Thurnham had tried to fax it to his wife, but accidentally it was transmitted to his local paper in Bolton instead. They couldn't resist printing it.

Michael Howard was so angry when he heard that Sandra's comments were about to be made public that he employed solicitors to try to stop them. When he was working so assiduously to improve his leadership chances, it did not look good to be sympathising with an MP whom many Tories considered a traitor. A survey in December 1996 revealed the extent of his schmoozing of local Conservative activists. He had visited twenty-four party associations since October, trailing only John Redwood in his attention to the grass roots. His work rate on behalf of the party was calculated to have doubled compared to the previous year. In sharp contrast, only two constituencies had hosted the Chancellor, Kenneth Clarke.[53] Howard also began inviting candidates in winnable seats for chats at the Home Office – purely to discuss policy, of course.

At the start of 1997, the well-informed Peter Riddell was asking in *The Times*, 'Can anyone stop Michael Howard?'[54] An informal leadership-campaign team was developing, with supporters such as the Foreign Office minister Nicholas Bonsor, John Greenway and Sir Michael Spicer quietly working behind the scenes, sounding out MPs. Bonsor says he was earmarked to serve as Howard's campaign manager:

> Michael and I chatted about it, probably for a few months before the election. Somebody leaked something to the press, picking it up, which was embarrassing. We did not have a regular election caucus. It was not a plot to get rid of John Major. It was all done on a very loose basis. Michael Spicer, and also Rachel Whetstone and Tim Collins, were involved. We did take the view that we were bound to lose an election and John Major would in due course go, and so certainly we were speculating about those circumstances and trying to see who might support him.[55]

The arch-Euro-sceptic Christopher Gill indicates that Spicer had been 'in overdrive promoting Michael Howard' as early as 1994, but Gill and his fellow Maastricht rebel James Cran had rejected him as an alternative leader, 'not being persuaded that he is truly "one of us"'.[56] The hardline Euro-sceptics had become more suspicious of Howard after November 1994, when he took part in a meeting of seven senior ministers which decided that on the forthcoming European Communities (Finance) Bill a potential Euro-sceptic revolt could be crushed by treating the vote as matter of confidence in the government.

The whip was withdrawn from nine MPs who rebelled nevertheless, and the episode did much to tarnish Howard's credibility among the most passionate Euro-sceptics. Yet, within Cabinet, Howard was far more vocal in pursuing a tough line on Europe than the two remaining 'bastards', Michael Portillo and Peter Lilley – John Redwood being confined to the backbenches after his 1995 challenge to Major. It was a case, on the whole, of public loyalty and private dissent, which the Prime Minister respected more than the behaviour of Howard's Euro-sceptic colleagues. 'He tended to be more outspoken than others who were actually briefing against John Major,' says Ken Clarke.[57] Portillo agrees that Howard 'was very brave over Europe, even when the Prime Minister did not want the wretched subject to be discussed'. He looked to Howard as the leading Euro-sceptic in Cabinet, who was expected to open for their side of the argument in ministerial debates on the subject, generally followed by Peter Lilley and then Portillo himself. 'He was the senior figure in the Cabinet amongst us,' says Portillo, 'and more so as time went on. I always regarded Michael as having several years' seniority on me. He was a veteran of Maastricht, where he'd had a great success, and so he very much led the debate on Europe.'[58]

By the late autumn of 1996, with an election less than six months away, John Major would have preferred his Cabinet not to discuss Europe at all. But Howard, with backing from Peter Lilley, and without warning the Prime Minister, got a Cabinet majority requiring Ken Clarke to produce a Treasury paper outlining Britain's options on the forthcoming European single currency. Howard related his achievement to an impressed Alan Clark, who recorded in his diary, 'Somewhat disingenuously (more likely hyper-shrewdly) Michael claimed that he had not warned the PM so that he (PM) could say to Ken and Hes[eltine] afterwards, "I had no idea that this was going to happen"; also, of course, because five or six people in Cabinet who "take PM's orders" . . . would, if alerted, have talked it down.'[59] After several weeks of debate, the Cabinet slightly hardened its 'wait and see' position on the proposed euro.

By now the Home Secretary's loyalty to the Prime Minister was questionable. As Major relates in his memoirs: 'As Christmas neared, "friends" of Michael Howard . . . provocatively suggested that he had "no problem" with the idea of withdrawal from the European Union.' Major describes Howard as 'a sceptic in the best and most honourable sense', but it seems curious that he did not insist that Howard get his 'friends' to shut up.[60]

Europe, of course, was one way for Howard to advertise his credentials at a time when the party was growing ever more hostile to the EU. In an article in the *Sun,* he spoke of his readiness to 'stand up and fight Europe', though most of the article was an attack on Blair for hoping that Britain would never become isolated within the EU.[61] Since this was the very position from which Major had begun his premiership, the Prime Minister's friends were unlikely to enjoy this tacit reminder of early hopes. Howard naturally explained that his intention was to help his party win the next election, rather than to advance his own prospects. His dislike for the EU had increased while he was at the Home Office; he had abandoned his previous neutrality towards the European Court of Justice (not to be confused with the Court of Human Rights, which is not an EU institution). More open Eurosceptic noises might also help counter the electoral challenge from James Goldsmith's new Referendum Party, which wanted a plebiscite on whether Britain should remain in the EU. Despite Howard's well-known views on Europe, the colourful local socialite and zoo-owner John Aspinall chose to stand against him in Folkestone. Aspinall was a next-door neighbour of Howard's in the village of Lympne, and was also meant to be a friend. Having never felt secure in Folkestone, Howard could sympathise with other Tory MPs who feared the new party could spell doom.

Certainly by the time the public gave their verdict on the battered Major administration, on 1 May 1997, the jockeying had become very public. Halfway through the campaign the Prime Minister made a dramatic public plea for colleagues not to tie his hands ahead of future European negotiations. It had no effect. Only a few days later the Howard–Clarke split on Europe was aired openly when the Home Secretary claimed that 'the agenda for the Amsterdam [European] summit is so far-reaching that it would put our survival as a nation state in question'. Five hours later Clarke said he didn't agree: 'We should not be imagining plots against us . . . I don't think the survival of Britain as a nation state is at risk because of our membership of the European Union.'[62] Howard said there was no problem with Tory candidates who made clear their disagreement with John Major's 'wait and see' policy towards the euro; he also backed the 200 or more MPs who had accepted campaign funding from the Euro-sceptic Yorkshire businessman Paul Sykes.

Unlike John Major, Howard thought it was still possible that the Tories could win the election, if only they pointed up where they disagreed with Labour on Europe. 'We never exploited that difference,' he said later. 'We never campaigned on that issue, and to the world at large it appeared that there were no real differences on policy on Europe between the two parties. I think that was a great mistake.'[63]

On the campaign trail, Howard found time to help Norman Lamont, who was fighting Harrogate, which should have been a safe Tory seat. Gyles Brandreth in Chester was also blessed with a visit, and in his diary the MP records how a 'bearded lady' kept telling Howard, 'You're the best Home Secretary we've ever had. You should be PM.' Howard 'beamed and beamed', says Brandreth, 'and revealed brown teeth which I'd not noticed before'.[64]

The visits did no good. Both Lamont and Brandreth suffered resounding defeats, so neither man was able to help much in Michael Howard's next campaign.

16

CRIMINAL COUSINS

I am the person who knows exactly how it happened – a million
pounds and half a million. He was paid through his uncle Harry
Landy, who is a crook. I have challenged Mr Howard to sue me.
I have called him a crook. If he had any dignity or honour and
knows he hasn't committed a crime, he would sue me.

MOHAMED FAYED IN *Hamilton v. Fayed*, NOVEMBER 1999[1]

One of the ironies of Michael Howard's career is that, while he is
famously tough on law and order issues, he is also distantly related to
two men who have been accused of fairly serious crimes and spent
time in prison. These unfortunate relatives have dogged Howard
almost throughout his years in front-line politics, but his own actions
have made difficult situations worse. And both cases raise genuine
questions about his own judgement.

In both affairs, unscrupulous individuals exaggerated the strength of
family connections, and invented facts to cause trouble for Howard
publicly and serve their own personal ends. In one case he fell prey to
the desperation of one of Britain's most violent and unpleasant gangsters. In the other he became one more target of the flamboyant
Egyptian businessman Mohamed Fayed.

Fayed had an extraordinary impact on British public life during the
1990s. His son Dodi became a lover of the Princess of Wales, and died

alongside Diana when their car crashed in Paris in 1997. And Fayed did more than anyone to paint the Conservatives as the party of 'sleaze', causing the downfall of three different ministers, and playing a part in exposing several other MPs. Fayed saw Michael Howard as potentially the biggest prize of all – a senior Cabinet minister – and became obsessed by him. He never succeeded in bringing Howard down, but he caused him endless anxiety.

Fayed's vendetta stemmed from the DTI's decision, back in April 1987 when Howard was a minister there, to appoint inspectors to investigate the 1985 takeover by Fayed and his brother Ali of House of Fraser, the company which owns Harrods and several other department stores. The takeover had involved a long and bitter battle with 'Tiny' Rowland, the controversial boss of Lonrho, who subsequently pressed ministers to investigate the Fayeds' behaviour during the affair. The DTI's decision was taken by the then Trade Secretary Paul Channon, but Fayed became convinced that Michael Howard was the driving force behind it, in his capacity as the junior DTI minister for corporate affairs. In 1988 the DTI inspectors concluded that the Fayeds had 'dishonestly misrepresented their origins, their wealth, their business interests and their resources' during the takeover bid.[2] This had no effect on the ownership of House of Fraser, but it prompted an inconclusive inquiry by the Serious Fraud Office and severely damaged Mohamed Fayed's ambitions to acquire British citizenship.

Within days of the DTI inspectors being appointed, Fayed was approached by a woman he knew called Francesca Pollard. She told him that Michael Howard was 'a very close nephew' of Harry Landy, one of Rowland's business associates, and that Landy was also her uncle. For an excitable conspiracy theorist such as Fayed, this was tantamount to proof that he was the victim of a political stitch-up. Before long Fayed would start asserting that Rowland, through Landy, had bribed Michael Howard to bring in the DTI inspectors. Certainly Rowland and Landy had enough in their backgrounds to suggest they were quite capable of such a criminal act, for the Lonrho boss had a reputation for achieving his business objectives around the world through bribery and corruption.

The connections between Harry Landy and Michael Howard must have looked promising to Fayed. Landy had been born in 1911 at 31 James Street, Llanelli, where he lived until his mid-twenties. The address was on the same side of the very street where, in 1941, Michael Howard spent the first few months of his life. Harry Landy and Hilda Howard were first cousins, with two grandparents in common. Michael was actually Harry Landy's second cousin, or first cousin once removed, not a nephew as Pollard had said. The extensive Landy family were leading members of the town's Jewish community, and as a boy Michael Howard saw much of his maternal relations. Because of the close-knit nature of the family, and the lack of relatives of his age on his father's side, he seems to have spent more time with his mothers' cousins than many children might do. They were almost like brothers and sisters.

But Harry Landy had left Llanelli in 1935 – five years before Bernat Hecht arrived, and six years before Howard was born. Landy had moved to London and married the daughter of a wealthy banker called Walter Nathan Williams, and became rich himself through his involvement in many of Williams's businesses. These included the London subsidiary of the Israel British Bank, of which Williams was chairman and Landy became deputy chairman and then chairman himself when Williams died in 1971. Three years later the bank was wound up after the Israeli parent company collapsed. In 1979 Landy was tried at the Old Bailey, accused of conspiring to defraud lenders and depositors in the bank of more than £27 million. It was described as 'the biggest fraud ever investigated in the City of London', and the prosecuting counsel said Landy and four other defendants had used the bank as their 'crock of gold', siphoning off funds to businesses they owned in Liechtenstein, though it was suspected that much of the money ultimately went to finance political parties in Israel.[3] Landy was convicted on three counts of fraud and issuing forged documents, sentenced to five years in jail, and fined £350,000.

In 1981, however, Landy's conviction was quashed by the Court of Appeal on the grounds that the trial judge had overloaded the jury with detail, and had failed to instruct them on what the word 'defraud' meant.

Landy might have been acquitted, but it was on a legal technicality and his reputation was ruined. He was rescued by Tiny Rowland, who had partly made his fortune through corrupt dealings in Africa, and had enjoyed extensive involvement in the Israel British Bank. Rowland had visited Landy in prison, and helped fund his appeal. Afterwards he gave Landy a job, and appointed him director of several Lonrho subsidiaries.

Francesca Pollard was Walter Nathan Williams's granddaughter, and the niece by marriage of Harry Landy (and therefore also a distant relative of Michael Howard). She believed – perhaps with good reason – that Landy and Rowland had conspired to cheat her out of the inheritance she had expected from her grandfather. Landy had been one of the executors of her grandfather's estate, and, unusually, probate on the will hadn't been settled for five years – until 1976, two years after the Israel British Bank collapsed. She was a determined woman, though often wrong with her facts. In the mid-1980s she began a vociferous, single-handed campaign which included regular demonstrations outside Lonrho's offices in the City, where she distributed leaflets and harangued Tiny Rowland though a loud hailer. A sign on her van denounced him as a 'Nazi rat'. Pollard even tried to make a citizen's arrest of Rowland outside the Lonrho AGM, and issued a relentless stream of hostile literature to company shareholders, MPs and other influential people. She later claimed that much of this work was secretly aided by Fayed, who paid her £2,000 a month, and supplied her with the van and a driver-cum-bodyguard; Fayed later told a parliamentary inquiry that he reimbursed some of her legal expenses and paid for a security consultant to help her.

The family connection between Michael Howard and Harry Landy first came to public attention in April 1989. The Labour MP Dale Campbell-Savours, who'd previously taken an interest in Howard's membership of Lloyd's, tabled two early day motions (EDMs) in Parliament. The first drew attention to Howard's 'close family links' with Landy, and to Landy's directorship of a Lonrho property company;

it also stated that 'six other members of the Landy family are also shareholders in Lonrho'. While there was, 'at present, no evidence' that Howard had ever been 'improperly influenced by the Landy family', the EDM said, the links provided 'legitimate cause for public concern'.[4] Campbell-Savours's second EDM pointed out that during Howard's two years as minister for corporate affairs, between 1985 and 1987, he had answered more than a dozen questions on Lonrho, House of Fraser, and various aspects of the takeover and the decision to appoint DTI inspectors. The MP asked 'whether it was appropriate for a Minister with unpublished family interest in Lonrho to take responsibility for these matters'.[5] At the same time Campbell-Savours submitted a formal written question asking 'on what dates since 1979' ministers had met Harry Landy to 'discuss the case for an inquiry'. The DTI minister Francis Maude gave a one-word reply: 'None.'[6]

Campbell-Savours had been briefed by an intermediary representing Francesca Pollard, and later that year she increased her pressure on Howard. In June 1989 Pollard wrote to him, 'As a Rowland "victim" I appeal to you to put politics behind you. Rise to the occasion and show Rowland that you will not be an unwitting pawn in his corrupt games.'[7] At the start of 1990, barely three weeks after Howard became Employment Secretary, she wrote a six-page letter to Margaret Thatcher, in which she claimed that Howard had colluded with Landy:

> To have now actually *promoted* him to Cabinet level, and made him a Privy Counsellor, is simply staggering. Rewarding deception with promotion, rather than censorship [sic], has been more normally associated with sinister eastern bloc regimes!! . . . If my allegations are not correct, why has he not 'come clean' or challenged me? His continued silence condemns him. Why is it allowed?[8]

Pollard also wrote a two-page document entitled *20 Things You Ought to Know about Michael Howard MP.* This alleged that Howard had acted as a legal adviser to Harry Landy, and had told him of 'the best way to escape justice' over the Israel British Bank case, though there is no evidence he ever did so.[9] Much of the document was complete fabrication; one claim in particular came to contaminate media coverage, and has been recycled regularly ever since, unchecked by journalists. Pollard alleged that Harry Landy had helped Michael Howard's father, Bernat Hecht, come to Britain before the war and to acquire his citizenship. This seems unlikely. No one has ever provided any evidence of this; nor does Landy's name crop up anywhere in Hecht's extensive Home Office naturalisation papers.

At one point Francesca Pollard and her family even went round Folkestone and the neighbouring town of Ashford distributing her *Things You Ought to Know* report to shops and businesses. 'It is littered with untruths and I'm not going to dignify this document by going through it point by point,' said Howard, who refused to discuss his relationship with Landy with the local paper. 'Nobody takes it seriously.' Howard declined to issue a libel writ against Pollard. 'There is no point in suing. She is not a woman of means.' Pollard said she wouldn't leave Howard alone, and even promised to protest outside his constituency home.[10] Then suddenly, in 1991, the protests stopped. Pollard mysteriously switched sides and issued an apology for her past campaign against Tiny Rowland.

Michael Howard might have been relieved, especially when in 1993 Fayed and Rowland had a remarkable 'reconciliation' which saw the two old enemies photographed together beneath a menacing-looking fish in the Harrods food hall. But Howard's move to the Home Office that year exacerbated his difficulties with Mohamed Fayed. The Egyptian businessman and his brother Ali were planning to apply for UK citizenship. They had already lived in Britain for more than twenty years – twice as long as Howard's father (also a shopkeeper) had done when he applied in 1947; the Fayeds had owned Harrods for almost a decade and all their children had been born in Britain. Now Hecht's son was in charge of the ministry which had to approve their applications. It was a recipe for grief. The issue would both worsen Howard's dispute with Mohamed Fayed, and also cause long-term acrimony with his junior minister at the Home Office,

Charles Wardle, who handled nationality issues on a day-to-day basis.

Ali Fayed applied for citizenship first, in January 1993, but it was clear that his brother Mohamed would soon follow. Eleven months later, two days before Christmas, the Home Office immigration division B4, based in Liverpool, recommended that Ali Fayed's application should be rejected for lack of 'good character'. By law, officials were obliged to carry out character checks on applicants, and B4 officials said they were governed by the 1988 DTI inspectors' report which had exposed the dishonesty of both Fayed brothers during the Harrods takeover. Mohamed Fayed's pending application would clearly be rejected for the same reason. Charles Wardle was content to accept B4's recommendation (though he later told Parliament that the Fayeds had been 'stitched up' by the DTI report, and subsequently he even worked for the brothers).[11]

Early in January 1994, Wardle says, Michael Howard asked him to stay behind for an informal word after a departmental meeting in the Home Secretary's office. Howard mentioned that he'd heard that Ali Fayed's application had been rejected, and Wardle indicated that he had accepted B4's decision. Then, Wardle says, Howard mentioned that the issue was difficult for him personally because of his family's connection with Rowland, and Mohamed Fayed's persistent efforts over the years to discredit him. Howard feared that if the Fayeds' applications were rejected the public sniping would intensify. 'He said it would be in everybody's interests to see if we could give them citizenship,' Wardle recalls. 'I said the findings of the DTI inquiry had been published. "They can't be expunged." What we had here was a cut-and-dried report from another government department saying these people's characters are flawed, and you had the Home Secretary saying to the junior minister, "Please understand I am likely to suffer embarrassment if this goes ahead" – there could be no other interpretation of what he was saying.'[12]

The two ministers had several more conversations about the matter between January and April 1994. At one point, according to Wardle, the Home Secretary suggested that officials should approach the Bank of England for references, since it had previously investigated the Fayeds' background. This, Howard said, might enable B4's recommendation to be reversed. Wardle recalls, 'That is what sticks in my mind – he said, "No, can't we go to the Bank of England?" I replied, "If that's your instruction, we can approach the Bank of England. But we're going to come back to the roadblock of the DTI report."'[13] Wardle later told MPs that he had been 'instructed to pursue further references that might be favourable to Ali Fayed'.[14] The junior minister relayed the conversation to his own private office, and asked them to carry out Howard's instructions by writing to the Bank.

Charles Wardle felt uncomfortable, however. Officials couldn't 'simply turn a blind eye to the [DTI] report if more favourable references were to be found', he later explained to the Commons. 'Not only would that have been unlawful and have offended the high standards of civil servants at the nationality division of the Home Office, but it would have left the law open for all manner of future abuses of the British Nationality Act. It simply would not have done.'[15] It was almost unknown – at least then – for a Home Secretary to intervene in a citizenship application in this way. Wardle felt Howard's behaviour was wrong.

The process dragged on for months, and by the time the Bank responded Charles Wardle had been transferred to the DTI. His successor, Nicholas Baker, again advised Howard to abide by B4 and Wardle's original recommendation that Ali Fayed's application should be rejected on the grounds of the DTI report.

Over the summer of 1994, however, as it was leaked to the media that Mohamed Fayed's citizenship application was likely to fail, the businessman stepped up his efforts to expose various Conservative MPs as open to bribes. Simultaneously, and encouraged by Fayed, the *Sunday Times* reported that some Tory MPs were willing to ask parliamentary questions for £1,000. 'This shows they're all fuggin' corrupt,' an excited Fayed reportedly told his aides. 'I'm going to get Michael Howard. I'm fuggin' going to get all of them.'[16]

Fayed now decided to use his new friendship with Rowland to try to overturn the DTI inspectors' report and take revenge on those he felt had helped Lonrho against him. During 1994 and 1995 Fayed and his associates held numerous meetings with Rowland and his aides, in which he tried to get the Lonrho boss to admit that he had used Landy to bribe Howard to initiate the DTI inquiry (which Howard has always strongly denied). Fayed recorded these meetings secretly on videotape, but, despite persistent questioning, nothing conclusive emerged. Rowland seemed to tease Fayed and string him along by pretending to accept his conviction that Howard had been bribed, without ever saying anything sufficiently substantial to confirm it. The unlikely allies first discussed Howard on 26 September 1994, when Rowland accepted an invitation to lunch in Fayed's private dining room on the fifth floor at Harrods. The transcript – which was later reproduced in a parliamentary inquiry by Sir Gordon Downey – shows that after discussing sex, and the extraordinary possibility of Fayed getting a penis transplant, they got down to serious business – Rowland's relationship with Harry Landy, and Landy's relationship with Howard. Rowland admitted he had helped Landy get out of jail, and then, as the Downey report recorded, hinted that Landy had indeed bribed Howard in the way Fayed seemed to believe.

'I worked on Harry Landy very hard in order to persuade Harry Landy to help,' said Rowland, 'and what Harry Landy gave Michael Howard, I don't know how much.'

'He gave him £1 million,' Fayed suggested.

'That's possible,' said Rowland.

'£1 million,' Fayed repeated.

'Well, that's half a million or £1 million,' said Rowland. 'I don't know what it was.'[17]

Mohamed Fayed interpreted these words as confirmation of his belief that Rowland had used Landy to bribe Howard.

The two men returned to the subject the following day, when Rowland came back to Harrods for afternoon tea. He was again recorded by Fayed's hidden camera in words set out in the Downey report, saying, 'Michael Howard's got a million, a million and a half or whatever it is.'

'Million and a half!' exclaimed Fayed, who was clearly surprised that the pay-off might have been even higher than he imagined. 'Now he's got another half million.'

'Whatever the bugger's got, I'll find out from Harry Landy,' Rowland promised.[18]

For the next six months Rowland prevaricated, always promising to help Fayed with proof, but never providing it. The following spring Rowland told Fayed, 'Harry Landy obviously discussed it . . . I knew that Harry Landy was well connected, had connections and so forth, and I appealed to [him] to do everything possible to help.'[19]

A desperate Fayed – whom Rowland called 'Tootsie' – more than once asked him to sign a statement confirming that Landy had paid bribes to Howard. Rowland declined. 'Sign it for me,' said Fayed, 'and I shall go to any lengths for you, as far as Australia even. Afterwards, I shall not run away. It will be Tiny and Tootsie for ever . . . Together we shall prevail.'[20]

The two tycoons met five times in all. On every occasion Fayed pressed his former rival to provide facts and evidence about bribing Howard, but the transcripts of the secret recordings show that Tiny Rowland continued to string Fayed along. The Lonrho boss seemed to enjoy it. He hinted that Landy might have bribed Howard, and frequently seemed to agree with Fayed's suggestions, but was careful never to provide real confirmation.

Fayed summoned four QCs and several other lawyers to Harrods to watch edited videos of his conversations, but they told him Rowland's words were nothing like hard evidence of misbehaviour. It was naive, perhaps, for Fayed to think Rowland would ever provide evidence of bribery, even if it were true.

Fayed went to extraordinary lengths in his attempts to 'get' Michael Howard. Rowland later alleged in a series of High Court writs that the Egyptian businessman even broke into his safe-deposit box at Harrods, and copied documents in an effort to find evidence which would force Rowland to admit publicly that he had indeed corrupted the minister. In addition, the Lonrho boss claimed that Fayed offered him £10 million and the ownership of the shirt-maker Turnbull &

Asser if he cooperated, along with the return of an envelope of papers taken from the Harrods safe-deposit box, which Fayed claimed were potentially damaging.

Beginning in 1988, Mohamed Fayed also used private investigators against Michael Howard. Fayed's former director of security, Bob Loftus, would later claim, 'I know for certain that the whole of Mr Howard's background and lifestyle were looked at by a series of people who were paid by Harrods.' Fayed's investigators followed Howard on a motorbike to find out where he lived, and then put his home under twenty-four-hour surveillance to check on comings and goings and to see if he ever met Harry Landy, and they obtained valuations on his properties in London and Kent. But Loftus denied any knowledge of a mysterious incident in December 1988 when Michael Howard's house was burgled and various personal items were stolen, including some relating to his father, Bernard.[21]

The pressure on Howard must have been enormous, and one close Home Office colleague reckons the case was taking between 5 and 10 per cent of the Home Secretary's time. Things came to a head during September and October 1994, when Howard already had plenty of other urgent problems on his plate, including the recent IRA escapes from Whitemoor, and mounting opposition to his criminal justice measures. It must have seemed, at times, as if the whole world was out to get him.

The government was suffering a frenzy of sleaze allegations in the media, many of them fuelled by Fayed, who soon began scattering tit-bits from his conversations with Rowland to the press. Extracts from one of the meetings appeared in *Today*, while Fayed boasted to the *Financial Times* that he had a video recording of Rowland saying how he had bribed a minister with £1 million or possibly £1.5 million. 'We had a BBC cameraman,' Fayed reportedly claimed. 'I interviewed him like David Frost.'[22]

In the *Guardian* Peter Preston raised the question of whether Howard had had a 'conflict of interest' over the DTI inquiry.[23] Dale Campbell-Savours revisited the points in his 1989 EDMs by writing to John Major, while it was revealed that during one recent lunch between Mohamed Fayed and Tiny Rowland, Howard's name had cropped up fifteen times.

If this wasn't bad enough for Michael Howard, that autumn the story of him asking Charles Wardle to reconsider the Fayed citizenship application appeared in print for the first time, published in the *Mail on Sunday*. The paper had clearly been briefed by Wardle himself, who by then had been moved to the DTI.[24] A beleaguered Howard drafted a rebuttal, but Wardle later told MPs he thought this contained 'factual inaccuracies.'[25] He threatened to resign as a minister and denounce Howard publicly if the statement as drafted was released to the press. The row was resolved only when the Permanent Secretary at the Home Office, Sir Richard Wilson, visited Wardle at the DTI to agree a new form of words. His trip was the sign of the intensity of the crisis, since protocol would dictate that normally Wardle should go to see Wilson, not the reverse.

The agreed statement said that Howard had made it plain 'from the outset' that it was up to the junior minister to decide on Ali Fayed's application, and the Home Secretary had reiterated this three times. During their third meeting in April, according to Howard, 'I made it clear that the decision was to be taken by Mr Wardle, but suggested further inquiries should be made before a final decision was reached.'[26]

Charles Wardle resigned from the government in 1995 over another issue – European border controls – but did not forget the Fayed passport episode. Like Ann Widdecombe over the Derek Lewis affair, he felt Howard had behaved improperly. As with Lewis, Howard insisted he had delegated responsibility, though even by his own account he suggested to Wardle how it should be dealt with.[27] And, like Widdecombe, Charles Wardle would eventually air his concerns publicly at a particularly unhelpful moment for Howard.

At the end of September 1994, Mohamed Fayed had persuaded the editor of the *Sunday Express*, Brian Hitchen, to visit John Major in Downing Street to pass on his complaints about Howard and three other ministers whose careers would all eventually be ended by Fayed – Neil Hamilton, Tim Smith, and Jonathan Aitken. Hitchen didn't convey any evidence but made it clear that Fayed wanted the

DTI inspectors' report withdrawn or reviewed. 'I had to act,' says Major, who asked the Cabinet Secretary, Sir Robin Butler, to investigate.[28] Howard overreacted, as he often does when under pressure. The *Financial Times* – which is hardly a scandal sheet – rang Downing Street to ask if Michael Howard was being investigated by Butler, whereupon the Home Secretary immediately applied that evening to a judge in chambers for an injunction against the *FT*. The political correspondent David Owen was astonished when he found next morning that his 'fairly banal' story had been blocked. 'It was a complete misunderstanding. It was a totally innocuous story. I was just totally gobsmacked by the whole thing.'[29]

Butler's investigations were superficial, and while he interviewed all four ministers, including Howard, he did not talk to Mohamed Fayed. His inquiry took less than three weeks, and dismissed every one of Fayed's charges. 'I am confident that the allegations either are demonstrably false,' Butler declared, 'or, so far as I have been able to establish, are entirely unsubstantiated as well as being denied by the ministers concerned.'[30] Smith and Hamilton soon resigned anyway, but in the case of Aitken, Butler had blundered. The Cabinet Secretary had been gullible in accepting these ministers' explanations at face value and giving them the benefit of the doubt.

Butler's verdict eased the pressure for a while. It also helped that Harry Landy issued a supportive statement about his relations with Howard:

> We may be second cousins, but we are not exactly close. We don't even send each other Christmas cards. I haven't seen him for two years. The last time was at a public meeting he addressed in London. We had a brief chat afterwards and that was that . . . I left Llanelli in 1935 before Michael Howard was even born. There is a 30-year age gap. It's not as if we used to play hopscotch together . . . I never spoke to him once either by telephone or face to face during the Harrods takeover inquiry. Why would I? It is muckraking if anyone suggests anything else. . . Michael Howard's mother is my cousin and I keep in touch with her but that is it.[31]

If he had bribed Howard, however, he too would hardly have admitted it.

Having failed with Downing Street, in 1995 Fayed took his allegations against Tory MPs – including the conflict of interest and bribery charge against Howard – to the House of Commons Privileges Committee. The committee passed them on to be investigated by the recently appointed Parliamentary Commissioner for Standards, Sir Gordon Downey. In August 1996 Fayed told Downey that, through Harry Landy, Rowland may have paid Howard between £1 million and £1.5 million as an inducement or reward for appointing the inspectors. This, Fayed argued, explained why the DTI had suddenly acted back in 1987, even though two previous trade secretaries, Norman Tebbit and Leon Brittan, had decided, despite lobbying from Rowland, that there was no reason to investigate the Fayeds' acquisition of House of Fraser. Indeed, the inspectors themselves had acknowledged that they had eventually been appointed as a result of Rowland's 'two years of unrelenting pressure'.[32] Fayed also alleged that he himself had known that inspectors would brought in three months before it was announced publicly, having been told, he said, that Howard had discussed the matter with Margaret Thatcher. 'I am not going to rest until I see Michael Howard being tried,' Fayed told the commissioner when he was interviewed.[33]

Sir Gordon Downey spent four months examining the Landy affair in great detail. He took evidence from twenty-seven witnesses – five of them, including Howard and Fayed, in oral hearings – and received 189 documents, totalling 1,600 pages. Fayed supplied copies of the secretly recorded tapes of his meetings with Rowland. He also claimed that Francesca Pollard had 'definitely' told him that money was paid, though later he modified this to 'an assumption based on [her] knowledge of the people involved, rather than on hard evidence'.[34]

Michael Howard's counter-evidence was much more substantial. To show he had not received any large, unusual sums of money during the relevant period, he supplied the commissioner with detailed information about his personal finances between 1980 and 1990, including bank statements, his underwriting accounts with Lloyd's of London, and a list of his house purchases and sales. Howard took the commissioner through every property transaction, explaining how each had been financed. Downey found no evidence of Howard receiving payments as alleged by Fayed, and saw no need further to investigate the Home Secretary's lifestyle.

Howard was also assisted by a letter which Tiny Rowland sent Downey asserting that there was 'no truth whatsoever in the allegation made by Mr Fayed that Mr Michael Howard accepted payments from Lonrho, or agents acting on its behalf'. What Rowland said in Fayed's recorded conversations was, he claimed, merely a 'tease', partly for entertainment purposes, and partly to get the Egyptian himself to reveal information. 'I thought that is what Tootsie [Fayed] wanted to hear and that would please him, to tease him in the same way that he teases me.' Rowland also supplied a recent letter, written in 1995, in which he had told Fayed: 'I know nothing of any dealings between the two people you name. One [Howard] is absolutely unknown to me, apart from what I have read in the newspapers. There is nothing in it, and it would be a major error for you to go down that path.'[35]

Harry Landy himself was said to be too ill to give evidence, but his wife told the commissioner that 'he categorically denies that any payment was ever made through him to Mr Howard. He also states that no such matter was ever raised, proposed or discussed with him.'[36]

Gordon Downey's 118-page report was published in March 1997, a few days before the start of the election campaign. He concluded that there were 'no grounds' for believing that Howard had been bribed over the appointment of DTI inspectors to examine the Harrods takeover. It had been Paul Channon who took that decision in 1987, Downey explained, not Howard. While Howard had attended some, but not all, of the relevant meetings at the DTI, and 'made the occasional contribution to the debate', the minutes showed that 'his comments did not appear to favour Lonrho – indeed some could be construed as marginally unhelpful to them'. Although Howard had supported the idea of appointing inspectors, Downey declared that his role in the decision 'was not significant'.[37]

As for what Rowland said on Fayed's tapes, Sir Gordon Downey concluded that: 'At no point did Mr Rowland quite confirm unambiguously that illicit payments had been made to Mr Howard (or to Mr Landy).'[38]

Michael Howard had told Downey that his contact with Harry Landy had been 'intermittent and occasional. Over the last 30 years I do not think I have met him on more than half-a-dozen occasions which have all been family or charitable in nature.' Howard denied any business dealings with Landy, and could recall no contact with him in the twelve months leading up to the appointment of inspectors. Howard did, however, recall Landy ringing him, probably just after he went to the DTI in 1985, and in his recollection Landy had raised Fayed's unsuitability to be a company director because he held 'anti-Semitic views'. Howard denied taking any action on this, or even making a note of it. Downey decided, on the basis of Howard's evidence to him, that the minister's personal links with Landy were extremely limited.

The report does not show whether Michael Howard told the commissioner that during his early years as a barrister he had enjoyed more substantial dealings with Landy's brothers Albert and Monty. As London solicitors, both men had provided work for Howard's chambers, and the family connection undoubtedly played a role in this (see Chapter 6). It is perhaps surprising that this Landy link was not uncovered by Mohamed Fayed's extensive investigations. It is unlikely, however, that it would have made a difference to Downey's final verdict. The minister had been correct, he felt, not to disclose his relationship with Landy on the MPs' register of interest, since it 'created no obligation or conflict of interest'.[39]

Plainly, Downey had not been impressed by Mohamed Fayed. Fayed's case had been 'distorted by emotion'; he had a 'burning obsession', and he believed 'what he wants to believe'. In summarising, the commissioner could not have gone further to clear Michael Howard. He ended his report by saying:

> Mr Howard did *not* play a significant role in the decision to appoint inspectors; the decision itself was reached rationally and on its merits; and Mr Howard's relationship with Mr Landy has never

been close enough to bear the sinister interpretation placed upon it by Mr Al Fayed . . .

Several newspapers have carried detailed accounts of the allegations, focusing on Mr Howard's supposed conflict of interest, but hinting that something much more unsavoury is involved. Unchecked, the rumours will, I believe, continue to ferment.

I consider that in the public interest – and in the interests of fairness to all those who have been implicated – these allegations should, so far as possible, be authoritatively and *publicly* dismissed.[40]

Downey may have established Howard's innocence to the satisfaction of everyone in politics and the media, but Mohamed Fayed would not let the matter rest. It was particularly unfortunate for Howard that in 1996 Fayed had won an Appeal Court ruling that the Home Secretary had handled his citizenship application unfairly, because he had not supplied reasons for turning it down. The triumphant Fayed suggested that Howard had personally intervened against him. 'Does he have a prejudice against me and is it because of his close family ties with Lonrho's former chief executive Tiny Rowland?' Fayed demanded outside the court.[41] Unusually Lord Justice Woolf and his colleagues issued a press statement saying the ruling did 'not involve any criticism of the Home Secretary or his department'.[42] In fact, according to Charles Wardle, the Home Secretary had if anything bent over backwards to *help* Fayed.

When Fayed's son Dodi was killed with the Princess of Wales in 1997, Michael Howard sent the Harrods owner a handwritten letter of condolence. Yet Fayed kept up his campaign, and only a few weeks later he wrote to Lonrho directors asking whether they had evidence of the company paying Howard. When Fayed was unsuccessfully sued for libel by Neil Hamilton in 1999, Fayed brought the Landy bribe allegation up once more, along with several other outlandish allegations he made in court, such as his claim that Prince Philip and MI5 were behind the death of Princess Diana.

Meanwhile, in 1996, a second story broke in which Michael Howard would be embarrassed by a member of the Landy clan.

The previous year, two notorious Liverpool gangsters, John Haase and his nephew Paul Bennett, had been jailed for eighteen years for organising a smuggling ring which imported heroin from Turkey, while six accomplices got various sentences up to that length. The case arose from the police seizure in 1993 of 190 pounds of heroin, worth £18 million – one of the biggest drug hauls ever made in Britain. 'It is rare,' said the judge, David Lynch, 'that courts deal with somebody so high up the ladder as you are, and it must be marked by a heavy sentence.'[43] Yet only eleven months later Michael Howard granted both Haase and Bennett a pardon – the 'royal prerogative of mercy'. They were quietly released from prison, having served a total of about three years (including two years on remand).

Michael Howard had been told by the judge that the two gangsters had provided Customs and Excise with information which had led to a series of police raids which found a total of 150 high-powered firearms, including Armalites, Uzis and Kalashnikovs. The police had also uncovered ammunition and drugs, as well as a gun which had been smuggled into Strangeways Prison in Manchester.

When the drug traffickers' release came to light a few weeks later people in Liverpool were horrified. The decision seemed to run completely counter to what Michael Howard had said and stood for during his three years as Home Secretary. It was only five months since he had issued a White Paper promising tougher action against drug dealers. He had long argued for stiffer penalties for drugs offences, and that the time should fit the crime – 'No more half-time sentences for full-time crimes.'[44] Howard had also stressed the need for greater honesty in sentencing, so that in the case of life, for instance, this should mean life.

When the media tried to report the case, Michael Howard himself intervened to limit coverage. Peter Kilfoyle, the Labour MP for Liverpool Walton, was planning to do a live interview for Sky News on the affair, from a satellite link not far from his Merseyside home. 'Twenty minutes before I was due to go on air,' Kilfoyle recalls, 'I got a phone call from Michael Howard asking me in person not to do the interview. The clinching argument was that people's lives were at stake. He was the Home Secretary and I took his advice and didn't do the interview. It was highly unusual for the Home Secretary to phone a backbencher at home.'[45] Kilfoyle was puzzled, because the two men had been seen publicly around Liverpool. 'The two villains were on the streets, bold as brass, and back up to their old tricks almost straight away. I deferred, nevertheless, to the privileged information and advice of the then Home Secretary and did not publicise what was happening.'[46] The *Observer* and the *Sunday Mirror* also came under Home Office pressure not to run the story.

It had all the hallmarks of trying to kill a story without producing any compelling information as to why we should do that,' says Paul Connew, who was then the editor of the *Sunday Mirror*, and recalls how, unusually, the requests were made in the name of the Home Secretary. 'We regarded it as a self-serving attempt to kill a story. There seemed to be an underlying, desperate desire by Michael Howard to keep this one out.' When Connew asked Home Office officials to explain in strict confidence *whose* lives might be endangered, they declined to do so, he says.[47] Both the *Sunday Mirror* and the *Observer* ignored their pleas, and Connew's paper splashed with the front-page headline 'TWO FACED HOWARD.'[48]

After these newspaper reports, Howard felt obliged to go public. Having previously persuaded Peter Kilfoyle *not* to talk about the case, the Home Secretary now took to the airwaves himself to defend his decision. He told BBC radio that he had merely put right what the judge, David Lynch, had not been able to do. 'I acted at the specific request of the trial judge,' he said. 'We have to look at this in the real world. . . This was a wholly exceptional case . . . I was faced with a specific request from the judge and frankly it was inconceivable that I could have ignored it. If I had taken any other decision in this case I would have been open to the most serious criticism.'[49] Howard told a local Labour MP, George Howarth, that the information that Haase and Bennett provided 'had proved to offer quite enormous and unique assistance to the law enforcement agencies'.[50] Howarth, a Labour spokesman on home affairs, had said, 'Given the recent history on Merseyside of armed violence, which is closely associated with the drug barons, I find the decision surprising to say the least. Understandably, local people are dismayed.'[51] Five years later Howard would claim, 'This was not a matter in which I had a choice.'[52]

An official source familiar with the background to the judge's decision confirms that David Lynch had indeed originally wanted to sentence Haase and Bennett to five years rather than eighteen, to reflect the 'enormously valuable information' they had given the police, and the Court of Appeal had said that in such cases judges were allowed to made a considerable reduction in sentence. But privately both the defence and the prosecution teams 'begged' Lynch not to give the defendants a lesser sentence at the end of the trial. This would 'give the game away – it would have alerted people', especially in comparison to the long sentences given to other members of the gang. This could have put at risk not just the lives of Haase and Bennett, but also undercover officers working for the police and Customs, and their work would be compromised. 'It was very, very sensitive,' the source adds. So Lynch agreed that instead he would write to Howard and point out that had he been free to do so he would have given the two men only five years. He recommended that Howard take that into account and cut their sentences, though it was only a recommendation. The judge understood that to protect both criminals from reprisals they would be given new identities and helped to move abroad. Howard complied fully with Lynch's recommendation, although royal pardons are confined to a handful of cases each year.

Yet once the two men were released things began to unravel. Haase and Bennett made no attempt to hide, disguise themselves or go abroad. When people spotted them walking around Liverpool, it was assumed they must have escaped from jail. Then it emerged publicly that they had told the authorities about the substantial caches of arms and drugs. So why did they not act as if their lives were in danger? It didn't take long for people to suspect that the arms had been deliberately planted by friends of Haase and Bennett to secure their early release. In short, Howard and the authorities had been tricked. Privately, many police on Merseyside were furious.

The police had carried out nineteen different raids to find the various collections of arms and drugs, many of them hidden in empty cars and deserted buildings. Surprisingly, however, there had been no significant arrests as a result of Haase and Bennett's tip-offs, and they never provided evidence in any prosecution. It is 'absolutely clear what happened', says a lawyer familiar with the case, who has examined much of the background:

> What Haase had done was that he'd arranged for his minions to leave guns under floorboards and this sort of thing, and then had made up the story. And the police at the time, and in the end Howard, acting on advice, fell for it hook, line and sinker, and Haase was let out, and there wasn't a single life saved. There wasn't a single worthwhile criminal caught as a result of that material, and it's now being used as an object lesson in how not to deal with these things.

In 2001 a notorious Scottish gangster who had moved to Manchester, Paul Ferris, claimed in a book written from jail that he and a colleague, Rab Carruthers, had sold many of the guns to Haase: 'A guy from Liverpool visited Rab on behalf of John Haase . . . Haase was on remand accused of dealing in a large quantity of heroin and set to go down for a very long time if found guilty. His friend reckoned he could have his sentence reduced in return for a consignment of illegal weapons.' Ferris claims that he and Carruthers had some qualms about the deal, but eventually decided that no one would lose from it. 'The people selling the guns would get paid top dollar, the police could kid the public they were getting guns off the street, no-one was arrested or jailed and Haase would get better treatment.'[53]

In 1998 Haase and Bennett's 'handler' as Customs and Excise informants, Paul Cook, received a memo from his boss telling him to have no more dealings with the two criminals or their representatives. 'As you know there is a sustained political interest in the activities of Haase and Bennett,' the memo said. 'In order to safeguard our position we must maintain our distance.'[54]

Howard's decision to release Haase and Bennett looked like an astonishing misjudgement, from the perspective of his stated tough approach to serious crime. He was fortunate that it did not generate more media attention – thanks, in part, to his own efforts in dampening coverage. Both men were notorious, violent criminals; John Haase was one of Britain's most feared gangsters. In 1973 he'd been given seven years in jail for taking part in five armed raids on post offices and betting shops, and two attacks on police. In 1982 he got a fourteen-year term for two armed robberies carried out by a ruthless gang called the Transit mob. By the early 1990s Haase was one of the biggest drugs traffickers in Britain, if not *the* biggest. When two *Daily Mirror* reporters tracked him down after his release in 1996 the gangster threatened them abusively.[55]

Michael Howard said he was obliged to take the advice of the trial judge, David Lynch, who had himself been advised by the police and other enforcement bodies. The Customs and Excise 'handler', Paul Cook, had told Lynch that it was 'highly unlikely that they would revert to a life of crime upon their ultimate release'.[56] On the contrary, however, they behaved worse than ever, and Haase even slit the throat of a gangland rival. In 2001 he was jailed for thirteen years for gun running and money laundering, while Paul Bennett was later sought by police for questioning over drugs matters. Yet Howard could have ignored David Lynch's recommendation altogether; he could also have reduced their sentences to, say, ten years rather than five. He had, after all, a reputation as Home Secretary for standing up to and even overruling judges. It was only two years since he had intervened over the sentence for an even more notorious crime in Liverpool, when he insisted that the young Bulger killers should serve at least fifteen years, not ten. He had also ordered that Myra Hindley should remain in jail, when she was likely to do far less harm, if released, than either John Haase or Paul Bennett.

The Haase and Bennett case has embarrassed Michael Howard ever since, though he has had support from unexpected places. In 2001, when Peter Kilfoyle initiated a Commons debate on the issue, the minister responsible for Customs and Excise, Dawn Primarolo, told MPs they should be in no doubt that 'the impetus for the reduction in sentence came entirely and properly from the trial judge'.[57] A few days before the debate, Howard even asked his Labour successor as Home Secretary, Jack Straw, to conduct a personal review of the relevant paperwork. 'I would have come to the same decision as you in these cases,' Straw wrote to Howard. 'In my view, in any event, you had little practical choice but to agree to the request of the trial judge.'[58]

What made the Haase and Bennett affair particularly embarrassing for Michael Howard was the extra ingredient of a personal family connection. Another of his Landy cousins from Llanelli, Freda Landy, had moved to Liverpool and in 1960 married an accountant called Warner Bakerman. Their son Simon grew up to become a significant criminal. In 1985 he received a suspended six-month prison sentence for obtaining money by deception. He had inflicted injuries on himself to persuade his parents that he had been attacked over a debt for £2,700. Then, to obtain money from them, he phoned his mother to say he was being held hostage in a warehouse. Peter Kilfoyle told the Commons that Simon's father, Warner Bakerman, had come to police attention, too, having once been 'arrested on drug-related charges'.[59] This concerned the seizure of a lorryload of oranges which was found to contain cannabis, though the case against him was dropped.

Michael Howard has been known to visit Warner and Freda Bakerman at their home in Liverpool when he goes to watch football at Anfield, and Freda has confirmed that she keeps in touch with him. 'We're a very close family. I speak to my aunt, Michael's mother, three or four times a week.' Simon Bakerman is even said to carry a picture of his famous politician relative in his wallet, and in 1997 he claimed, 'I last saw Michael when he came to my mum and dad's house for tea after Chelsea played at Liverpool last season.'[60]

In 2002 Simon Bakerman was jailed for three years for his role in a £20 million scheme to supply amphetamines after police had seized drugs and drug-making equipment from a Liverpool warehouse. After serving twelve months, Bakerman was released with an electronic tag from Kirkham open prison near Preston. By coincidence, it was on the very day that Michael Howard became leader of the Conservative Party.

More embarrassing still for Howard have been Bakerman's links with John Haase and Paul Bennett. In May 1997 the *Sunday Mirror* claimed that Bakerman had twice been in touch with Haase within days of the latter's release from jail the summer before, though it's thought that Bakerman is actually much closer to Paul Bennett.[61]

John Haase subsequently tried to persuade his QC, the Liberal Democrat peer Alex Carlile, of this version of events, hoping some-how to use the tale in his defence in his 2001 trial for arms dealing. But Carlile dismissed his claim as mischief, and saw it as exploiting Howard's unfortunate family connection; he insisted there was no way professionally as a barrister that he could support it in court. Indeed, for about twenty-four hours Carlile refused to represent Haase, though they were reconciled when Haase dropped the story. 'Michael Howard's involvement is not wholly clear from your instruc-tions,' Carlile wrote to Haase in 2000, 'but apparently includes his alleged connection with a supposed relative of his who has a criminal record . . . In my professional judgment there is absolutely no basis of evidence and therefore no reasonable grounds to justify the Michael Howard conspiracy allegation.'[62]

As in the case of Harry Landy (who died in 2000), Michael Howard appeared to have been the victim of his relative's wrong-doing and of people's ruthlessness in exploiting the slightest links with his cousins. Yet the case also raised questions about Howard's judge-ment, and about the conduct of his department while he was Home Secretary. As the MP Peter Kilfoyle told the Commons in a second debate on Haase and Bennett in 2004:

To a simple-minded lay person like myself, there can be only two possible conclusions. The first is that Customs and Excise, the Prison Service, the police, the judiciary and the Home Office were all duped by Haase and Bennett. The alternative is that there was, at some stage, some truth in the allegations that bribery played a part in securing Haase and Bennett's release. I do not want to believe that. All of my instincts say that that is not possible. Yet I also find it difficult to believe that no one within the system smelt a rat in the way in which the gun stashes were set up.[63]

Both cases – Harry Landy's, and Haase and Bennett's – have similar features. A huge bribe is alleged to explain an unusual ministerial decision. In both sets of claims the alleged conduit is a distant cousin who has been accused of fairly serious crimes. No one seriously believes that Michael Howard was ever offered a bribe, let alone accepted one or that he took action to favour any relative. Yet in both affairs Howard fuelled the controversy by being oversensitive. This is perhaps understandable given the huge public pressure he was under as Home Secretary on a wide range of issues, combined with the obvious unease he feels about his foreign background and family roots. His request to Charles Wardle over the Fayeds' naturalisation applications seemed partly designed to placate Mohamed Fayed, but would prolong the controversy beyond the time he was exonerated by Sir Gordon Downey, and opened Howard to further charges of abusing his position as Home Secretary which he denied. Equally, his unusual personal intervention in 1996 in asking Peter Kilfoyle and two national newspapers not to go public on his concerns about the release of Haase and Bennett only fuelled suspicions that Howard was guilty, at least, of a serious misjudgement.

And in 1997 both cases came back to haunt him when he least needed it.

17

SOMETHING OF A NIGHTMARE

I want to wreck his chances of leading the Tory party.

ANN WIDDECOMBE, MAY 1997[1]

The TV presenter Peter Snow prides himself on producing irreverent computer graphics to spice up the BBC's overnight election programmes. In May 1997 the nation was treated to Snow's 'Dicey Dozen', a list of prominent Tories who could lose their seats in a Labour landslide. Twelve cut-out figures were lined up next to a cliff which was set to crumble on top of them according to the extent of Labour's victory. The likely victims for burial included the Foreign Secretary, Malcolm Rifkind, and fellow Cabinet ministers Michael Forsyth, Ian Lang and William Waldegrave. There were also the former ministers David Mellor and Edwina Currie, and the Olympic gold-medallist Sebastian Coe. Last in line, at number twelve, was Michael Howard.

Eleven of the twelve lost their seats, along with other big names such as Jonathan Aitken, as Tony Blair became Prime Minister with an overall majority of 179. And Michael Portillo lost Enfield Southgate on a spectacular swing to Labour of more than 17 per cent. Michael Howard was the only one of Snow's 'Dicey Dozen' to hold his seat. When he appeared on TV after his victory in Folkestone and Hythe, said one commentator, 'he looked more like a man who had lost a close relative than one who was rejoicing in a lucky escape'.[2]

Four days before polling, Howard's constituency had been listed by the *Observer* as one where tactical voting could be decisive if Labour supporters switched to the Liberal Democrats. The coastal seats either side of Howard both went to Blair's party: while Dover had been Labour before, the result in Hastings and Rye was a real shock, as Labour triumphed after coming a poor third in 1992, when the distribution of votes had been similar to Folkestone's. Bizarrely, in an election where voters resoundingly rejected the Conservatives, one of their most controversial ministers, Michael Howard, survived with only a modest swing, of 2.4 per cent, against him. His majority over the Lib Dems was cut by just over 2,500, down to 6,332. There's some evidence that the opposition parties in Folkestone didn't really expect to unseat Howard, and that their campaigns were half-hearted. An *Observer* poll predicted his success, in contrast to other Tories cited as being in danger, and the paper noted that, among voters surveyed in Folkestone, significantly more had been contacted by Howard's campaign than by the other main parties.[3] His achievement was all the more creditable given that John Aspinall performed better than most Referendum Party candidates, gaining 8 per cent of the vote.

Michael Howard had benefited from a tacit alliance with his Labour opponent, Peter Doherty, against the Liberal Democrat, David Laws. At one point Doherty sent a critical letter about the Lib Dems to the *Folkestone Herald*. When it failed to appear, Howard raised the matter with the paper's editor, whereupon David Laws wondered how the Conservatives had heard about it. According to Doherty, he didn't actively cooperate with Howard. 'There wasn't an open sense of unity between the Tories and ourselves,' he says, 'but it was an underlying ripple. I suppose I was his "mate" in a way, and to be fair he's always treated me as such.'[4] 'Michael Howard was assiduous in working with Labour to try to undermine me,' says Laws. 'He's always understood that if he could split the opposition vote he could stay in power.'[5]

John Major announced his resignation as Conservative leader on Friday 2 May, the morning after the election. His party had been reduced to 165 MPs. It had lost more than half the seats won in 1992. Yet the cull of Conservatives was in one way a lucky stroke for Howard, since it removed from the field two of his biggest rivals for the leadership. Although Michael Portillo had been damaged in the eyes of some by his decision not to stand against Major in 1995, he had similar Euro-sceptic credentials to Howard, was twelve years younger, and enjoyed a much larger personal following. Malcolm Rifkind might have been an even greater threat. Before he became Foreign Secretary he had been widely regarded as pro-European, and as 'wet' on domestic issues. Since 1995 he had ditched much of this baggage, and would have stood a good chance of winning on a 'unity' ticket.

The other important withdrawal was Michael Heseltine. He had held his seat easily, but then suffered a mild angina attack on the day after Major's resignation, and his wife, Anne, announced that he would not stand for the leadership. This was less favourable for Howard. If Heseltine had stood, he would have taken votes from the other heavy-hitting Europhile of the Conservative high command, Kenneth Clarke, who was the first candidate to declare. Neither Clarke nor Heseltine could ultimately triumph, given the complexion of the parliamentary party, unless they made significant concessions to the Euro-sceptics, and since Heseltine was more likely than Clarke to do this, he would have been the more dangerous rival.

Certainly Howard would have preferred a rerun of Cambridge politics of thirty-five years before – a final showdown with Clarke – provided he could get through to the last ballot. He knew that he was unlikely to be acclaimed as the Euro-sceptic standard-bearer without a fight. In a party whose grass-roots members still valued loyalty to an incumbent leader, Howard was confident of beating John Redwood, the man who had challenged John Major in 1995. But Peter Lilley muddied the picture by standing as a third contender from the Right.

Peter Lilley, like the absent Michael Portillo, combined fervent belief in the free market with a 'libertarian' outlook on social questions. Publicly his credentials as a leadership contender looked similar to Howard's, though Lilley observed privately that, Europe aside, there was no one in the Major Cabinet with whom he had disagreed more often than with Howard. In age and Cabinet ranking Howard was the senior, and better equipped than Lilley to challenge Tony Blair in the House of Commons. Nor did Lilley convey the impression of unquenchable ambition.

Michael Howard had a plan which would, he thought, outflank his two Euro-sceptic rivals, Redwood and Lilley. On the Saturday after the election he phoned another former Cabinet colleague who had been mooted as a possible 'unity' candidate. By Tory standards the former Welsh Secretary William Hague was a moderate Euro-sceptic, but when he had taken sides in Cabinet discussions he had followed Howard's lead, and he also admired his hard line on law and order. They shared common backgrounds, having been brought up in strong Labour areas – Hague in South Yorkshire – and both had gone to state schools before political success at Oxbridge. Hague was a quick-witted debater with few personal enemies, and knew his own attractions as a replacement for Major. But at thirty-six he was young enough to wait, and on the face of it had every reason to support a fifty-six-year-old who would keep the seat warm until New Labour got into trouble. And the fact that he was about to get married weighed heavily with him: Hague felt he needed to 'get a life' and that it would be unfair to his fiancée, Ffion Jenkins, to plunge their marriage straight away into such a high-profile job.

The outlines of a pact were secretly thrashed out in calls between the pair during the course of the weekend. On the afternoon of the Monday bank holiday Hague rang Howard to announce, 'I've made up my mind, I'm coming with you.'[6] The leadership was now 'in the bag', thought one of Howard's campaign team.

That evening William Hague flew down to London from Teesside and, accompanied by Ffion Jenkins, went to South Eaton Place in Belgravia, where Howard was still living in the heavily fortified government house he'd been provided with as Home Secretary. The Howards were due to hand over the property to Mo Mowlam, the incoming Northern Ireland Secretary, and the packing cases in the elegant drawing room gave the occasion an informal atmosphere (though Mowlam says Howard 'took ages to vacate that house').[7] Earlier in the evening Howard had hosted a small supper party with a few political friends, including his adviser Rachel Whetstone and Norman Lamont, who were both kept in the dark about the proposed deal (even though Lamont was also friendly with Hague). 'He didn't mention it at all,' says Lamont. 'That's one of Michael's traits – he can be unnecessarily and irritatingly secretive at times.'[8] Suddenly, around nine o'clock, Howard started ushering most of his guests out – which they thought very odd, since they'd turned up expecting to spend the whole evening discussing how they could help his effort.

The only guest remaining when Hague and his fiancée arrived was Howard's campaign manager, Sir Michael Spicer. The bargaining had already been done; the terms were agreed. Once Howard had won the leadership, William Hague would become his deputy, and also party chairman. Their meeting, which lasted just over an hour, was taken up mainly with arranging a press conference for the following afternoon and drafting a joint statement. The two men did not shake hands, but they toasted the agreement with Bollinger champagne.

Within hours the pact collapsed. As Hague walked home from Belgravia with Ffion Jenkins, he started to have second thoughts. He felt that Howard would probably lose to Ken Clarke, with or without his backing; nor could he be sure that his own supporters would switch to Howard even if he advised them to.

One of Hague's closest political allies, Alan Duncan, had been urging him to stand for the leadership himself, as had another friend from Oxford, Brooks Newmark, who'd just been an unsuccessful Tory candidate. As Hague's two friends consulted each other that Monday evening, they were worried he might not go for the job; they'd heard an inkling about a possible deal with Howard, but neither knew it had actually been agreed. Nor could either of them contact Hague, as calls were being diverted. Duncan was in his Rutland constituency, but argued that if they couldn't get Hague on the phone then Newmark would have to go round and see him that night at his flat in Dolphin Square. 'Get in your car,' Duncan recalls saying to Newmark, who protested that he had already gone to bed, and that it was cold and raining outside. Nor did Newmark know the number of Hague's flat. 'Get – in – your – car,' Duncan repeated.[9] 'He literally spent ten minutes trying to persuade me to go over,' Newmark recalls. 'I chucked on my jeans and sweater above my pyjamas.'[10]

Walking the floors of the Dolphin Square complex, Newmark suddenly heard a familiar burst of laughter. It was clearly William Hague. He pinpointed the noise and rang the bell. 'William opened the door, and he looked at me, and he said, "So you've heard." I think I said, "Heard what?"'[11] And so Hague explained the deal he'd done.

Michael Howard had apparently persuaded Hague that it would be a struggle for the Tories to get back to office in just one parliament. It would be best, he suggested, if an experienced figure like himself did the spadework in opposing Blair during a first term, which would give Hague the chance to become leader later on. Newmark told him the deal was unwise. 'Very few times in life does a great opportunity come along,' he recalls saying. By the time the job came up again, both Michael Portillo and Chris Patten might well be back as MPs, and both had strong followings in the party. 'You don't know who you're going to be up against the next time round, and you can't calculate those things,' Newmark remembers saying.[12]

After a sleepless night William Hague rang Howard at 6 a.m. – a reasonable hour, if the latter was following his usual routine – to tell him that the deal was off. Howard rang back an hour later and Hague confirmed that the decision was final.

Howard and Hague's original plan had been to keep news of the deal secret until the press conference to launch Howard's bid, when the pair were to make a dramatic entrance together. Instead, by the time Howard turned up alone at the room he'd booked in the Institution of Civil Engineers, the whole press corps knew about the on/off pact. Hague was said to be 'irritated' about the leak, which spared none of the details. The *Daily Telegraph* had learned that Howard had been wearing 'a brown sweater and trousers' as they sipped Bollinger together, while Sandra was 'sporting a cardigan'.[13] As he faced reporters at his campaign launch, Howard was asked if there had been a deal, and if Hague had broken it off. 'Yes and yes,' he replied, crisply and honestly.[14]

It seems that someone in the Howard camp had spread the pact story hoping to discredit Hague, but subsequent stories of the 'champagne pact' did nothing for Howard's image, and probably boosted the younger contender, suggesting a previously unnoticed steeliness to his character. It took nerve to jilt the hatchet man of the Home Office, a seasoned politician who had fought his first election around the time Hague was starting infants school.

Howard's camp described Hague's defection as no more than a hiccup. Howard still had other senior supporters. His press conference was attended by the ex-ministers Francis Maude and David Davis, as well as David Maclean, who had served with him in government since April 1992. Among prominent younger MPs, he was backed by Liam Fox, Andrew Lansley and Tim Collins. Margaret Thatcher, the ghost of past glories, was said to be backing him, albeit discreetly, while her aide Robin Harris would help write Howard's speeches and press articles.

The Howard campaign found a base close to the Commons, in Jonathan Aitken's house on Lord North Street, just off Smith Square, while Aitken moved into a hotel. It was a risky choice by Howard, since a libel action by Aitken against the *Guardian* and Granada TV was due to open six days before the first ballot, and a thoughtless offer by Aitken, since he knew that his court action was based on lies. Aitken 'kept pretty well out of it', according to one Howard volunteer, Nicky Morgan. 'He was very generous in allowing people to rampage through what was a beautiful house.'[15] They had unrestricted access to two rooms on the ground floor and a kitchen. While the MPs canvassed their colleagues, a group of twenty or so young volunteers contacted local party activists and constituency chairmen. Only Conservative MPs had a vote in the leadership contest, but they might take the views of their local associations into consideration while deciding whom to back. Howard's team also drafted press releases, organised interviews, ran a website, and arranged nationwide tours for the candidate.

One of the main organisers was Rachel Whetstone, who'd been Howard's special adviser at the Home Office. Whetstone comes from a upper-class, 'country-set' background in Sussex, and has long been a keen huntswoman. Her grandfather was Anthony Fisher, a businessman who founded and funded the free-market Institute of Economic Affairs. Educated at Benenden and Bristol University, Whetstone worked at Conservative Central Office for five years, but didn't know Howard until joining him at the Home Office in 1994. No one over the past decade has been a more important confidante and adviser. One of Whetstone's earliest moves in his 1997 campaign was to do a discount deal with a friend who worked for Laurent-Perrier, obtaining enough cases of champagne to hold three parties in Aitken's back garden to entertain MPs and other influential figures.

The other need was money. In the subsequent House of Commons *Register of Members' Interests* Michael Howard declared that he raised £49,000 for the contest – less than half as much as William Hague, and £6,000 less than John Redwood. It included £5,000 from Algy Cluff, a friend and former owner of the *Spectator*, who lived near Howard in Kent. The late industrialist Sir Emmanuel Kaye gave the same amount, though he seemed to be hedging his bets politically, since he had previously donated around £50,000 to Tony Blair's office as Opposition leader. But Howard's largest donation, according to the Commons register, was £23,500 in the name of Alan Hagdrup, a Surrey solicitor. Hagdrup had never met Howard. 'I was the front man,' Hagdrup admits, 'acting for a client.'[16] The client was in fact Lord (James) Hanson, one of the best-known capitalists of the Thatcher years, whose Hanson Trust had been heavily involved in the privatisation programme. Hanson did know Howard, but wasn't a close friend. 'I just admired him as a politician from afar,' he said shortly before his death in 2004. This was despite the fact that on the one occasion when Hanson visited Howard at the Home Office, to try to stop the traditional dark-blue British passport being replaced by the new maroon European edition, he was 'disappointed' that the Home Secretary sat 'completely mute', while his officials said it 'couldn't be done'.[17]

Members of Howard's campaign team knew that Hanson was their principal donor, and it is highly unlikely that the candidate didn't know himself, but if he did know he failed in his duty to declare it publicly. To submit such a misleading entry to the register was an odd lapse for a politician who prides himself on acting honourably, and is often pedantic about sticking to the rules. The *Code of Conduct for MPs*, agreed by the Commons in 1995, states that they should be 'as open as possible about all the decisions and actions that they take'. One wonders about the point of having a register of interests if a donor's true identity can be concealed. Howard was fortunate that no one complained.

A Howard victory would take more than organisation and money. At a time when Tories were reeling from the scale of their defeat, he needed to develop themes to convince fellow MPs that he could spearhead a Conservative revival. Before launching his candidacy, he had set out his stall in the *Sunday Telegraph*, where he claimed that, despite Labour's resounding victory, the Tories could recover for the next election.[18] Most of Howard's article was devoted to constitutional matters. He attacked Labour's devolution proposals because they would 'weaken the ties that bind the peoples of these islands together'. He also wanted a referendum on the changes which were likely to emerge from the forthcoming EU summit in Amsterdam. 'Labour's twin plans for devolution and European integration threaten, like millstones, to grind our nationhood to dust between them,' he warned.[19] Surprisingly, there was no mention of the single currency in Howard's article, though he later confirmed that he would resign from any government which tried to get rid of sterling. On this he agreed with Redwood, while Lilley and Hague prevaricated.

Howard maintained the stance on Europe which he had set out in 1994, and the Centre for Policy Studies published a pamphlet, *The Future of Europe,* based on what he'd said three years before. Britain, Howard argued, could 'retrieve key powers from Brussels while remaining a committed and valued member of the European Union'. Members who wanted to go along with the 'federal' project would be free to do so, but other countries should be allowed to 'pick and choose the policies which they wish to administer jointly'. It was another version of his 'made to measure' speech. Though Europhiles scoffed that Howard would never be able to negotiate this *à la carte* relationship with the EU, he nevertheless laid out his approach in some detail.[20] During the leadership campaign he was even more specific, suggesting that the Common Agricultural Policy might be scrapped.[21] In an obvious dig at Clarke, he said Tories should not follow 'One Nation' politics, but 'One *British* Nation' politics. 'I acquired my love of and loyalty to our country on my father's knee,' he said in a rare reference to his background. 'He was not born here but he was particularly well-placed to appreciate the glories of Britain and being British.'[22]

Howard needed every vote, and then some luck. Though he was a politician who'd often been fortunate, it seemed that his luck now deserted him. Just after Howard entered the race, Sir Michael Shersby, who'd been about to declare for him, died suddenly. Presciently, a poll of eighty-five Tory MPs showed Howard joint bottom of the six declared candidates, who initially included Stephen Dorrell. Only four of the MPs surveyed admitted to supporting Howard, while Hague topped the poll with sixteen. And, however bad these figures, things were about to get much worse.

Ann Widdecombe had stayed as a Home Office minister right up until the election, feeling increasingly guilty about her failure to resign over the sacking of Derek Lewis, the Prison Service director. Michael Howard's emergence as a leadership contender gave her a chance to atone for what she now regarded as her earlier cowardice, and she planned to take her opportunity in some style. Twice she consulted her priest about denouncing Howard. 'I have a strong sense of injustice and a wish to see a wicked man get his comeuppance,' she claimed to have told him.[23]

Her intentions first emerged in the *Sunday Times*, which reported that Widdecombe had 'told friends' that Howard had misled the Commons over Derek Lewis's sacking. 'Under pressure he says and does things which are not always sustainable,' she said. Widdecombe was quoted as saying that Howard was 'dangerous stuff', and that there was 'something of the night' in his character. Rather like 'prison works' – the other phrase that's associated with Michael Howard – 'something of the night' was underplayed at first, and the paper headlined only the word 'dangerous'. She was also planning to write to John Major (still the acting party leader for the duration of the contest) with detailed allegations about her former boss.[24]

'Something of the night' won Widdecombe a place in *The Oxford Dictionary of Political Quotations* (an honour yet to be accorded to Howard).[25] She had been mulling over the phrase for months, and later explained that it had been taken from the title of a 1980 murder mystery by an American writer, Mary McMullen. It reflected her view, as a committed Catholic, that Howard had a bit of the Devil in him. The phrase seemed immediately to chime, capturing the view held by many parliamentary colleagues and the wider public, who had come to regard Howard as a stern and sinister figure. One of his campaign team observed that at one level it summed up the flaws in his appearance – the five o'clock shadow, the pinstripe suit, and the 'forced smile which was meant to look friendly but that came across as a smirk'.

Some thought the phrase was anti-Semitic, though there is no evidence that Widdecombe intended it as such, and she had once belonged to the Conservative Friends of Israel. It certainly carried undertones of Count Dracula and Howard's ancestry in Transylvania. To some it simply conveyed Howard's abrasive character, his temper and his remote and forbidding image. A former colleague from the Bar says that when he heard the words they reminded him immediately of the Michael Howard he'd observed at a social occasion a year or so before. Howard had reduced the lawyer's wife to tears when he responded with surprising vehemence after she criticised a particular Home Office measure. The policy was the shackling of pregnant prisoners, and Howard was defending Ann Widdecombe. 'He couldn't stand the woman,' the lawyer says, 'and she was making life absolute hell for him, but he wasn't going to have any criticism of her, even at a social event.'

Her appearance in the *Sunday Times* was only the start of

Widdecombe's campaign against Howard. A Commons debate was scheduled on home affairs for Monday 19 May, which would give her the opportunity to speak out publicly. Friends, including John Major and Peter Lilley, appealed to Widdecombe to call off her crusade in the interests of party unity. When she refused, Lilley disowned her as one of his campaign backers. Rachel Whetstone also had several unproductive conversations with her.

Howard prepared a counter-offensive. Helped by Robin Harris, he produced a defiant article for the *Spectator*. Widdecombe's remarks had left him perplexed, he said, because she had not felt strongly enough after Lewis's sacking to resign at the time. Joking that Widdecombe had pierced the 'diabolic darkness of my own inner soul', Howard tried to turn her remarks around; yes, he was 'dangerous stuff', because he could be tough if necessary. 'The next party leader must be prepared to take decisions which ruffle a few feathers and provoke the occasional tantrum when the situation requires.'[26]

Under the circumstances, Howard could scarcely have done better. Although he could not avoid mentioning 'something of the night', it was clever to place more emphasis on the less ominous 'dangerous stuff'. The problem was that, while Widdecombe promised new revelations, Howard could only repeat the defence he'd successfully deployed in 1995 against Jack Straw.

Even before the *Spectator* article appeared, a Howard supporter decided to play dirty, as Widdecombe had expected. On Tuesday 13 May the *Daily Mail* quoted an 'insider' who said that Derek Lewis had 'wooed' Widdecombe with flowers, chocolates and intimate dinner dates. 'I think she fell in love with him. He flattered her vanity,' the *Mail* was told. 'I don't think she was used to that, poor girl. I'm not sure he didn't do it deliberately because she was a useful ally. In the end it clouded her judgement.'[27]

Howard claimed to be appalled, and no one ever admitted to being the 'insider'. The prime suspects, Tim Collins and Patrick Rock, both denied it, although *The Times* pointed a finger at Collins, who had just been elected an MP and had been seen talking to the *Mail* reporter Paul Eastham the day before. Howard's response to seeing the story about Collins in the first edition of *The Times* was to ring the paper to try to get it pulled from the later editions – without success. The belittling of Widdecombe was a foolish misjudgement. It provoked her to speak out openly; she put the 'something of the night' quote on record, and contacted journalists to insist that the *Mail* story was a 'disgusting lie' and a 'demonstrable smear'. She had lunched with Lewis four times, she acknowledged, but only since his resignation. There had been flowers, but only a £30 Interflora bouquet which she herself had sent to Lewis's wife on the day of his sacking. As for chocolates, she said, 'nobody, especially my friends, woos me with chocolate. They have too much respect for the width of my figure.' ITN asked her if Howard was 'dangerous'. 'Very,' she replied.[28]

Now Howard had no alternative but to follow Widdecombe to try to limit the damage, as she rampaged through the broadcasting studios. Interviews for *Channel 4 News* were conducted separately, and Howard acquitted himself fairly well. But *Newsnight* was a very different matter. After Howard had insisted that the *Mail* quotes had 'not come from my campaign team', Jeremy Paxman began asking about the disputed meeting in January 1995 at which Derek Lewis had said Howard put him under pressure to suspend John Marriott and threatened to overrule him. 'Are you saying Mr Lewis is lying?' asked Paxman. Howard began by reiterating – almost word for word – his statements to the Commons in October 1995.

> HOWARD: Let me tell you exactly what the position is. I was entitled to be consulted, and I was consulted. I was entitled to express an opinion. I did express an opinion. I was not entitled to instruct Derek Lewis what to do, and I did not instruct him what to do. And you will understand and recall that Mr Marriott was not suspended. He was moved, and Derek Lewis told the select committee of the House of Commons that it was his opinion – Derek Lewis's opinion – that he should be moved immediately. That is what happened.
>
> PAXMAN: Mr Lewis says, 'I' – that is Mr Lewis – 'told him what we

had decided about Marriott and why. He' – that is you –
'exploded. Simply moving the governor was politically unpalatable, it sounded indecisive, it would be seen as a fudge. If I did
not change my mind and suspend Marriott he would have to
consider overruling me.' You can't both be right.

HOWARD: Mr Marriott was not suspended. I was entitled to express
my views. I was entitled to be consulted.

PAXMAN: Did you threaten to overrule him?

HOWARD: I was not entitled to instruct Derek Lewis, and I did not
instruct him. And the truth –

PAXMAN: Did you threaten to overrule him?

HOWARD: The truth of the matter is that Mr Marriott was not suspended. I did not –

PAXMAN: Did you threaten to overrule him?

HOWARD: I did not overrule Derek Lewis.

PAXMAN: Did you threaten to overrule him?

HOWARD: I took advice on what I could or could not do –

PAXMAN: Did you threaten to overrule him, Mr Howard?

HOWARD: – and I acted scrupulously in accordance with that advice.
I did not overrule Derek Lewis –

PAXMAN: Did you *threaten* to overrule him?

HOWARD: Mr Marriott was not suspended.[29]

By now Jeremy Paxman had effectively asked the same question
seven times. Ann Widdecombe, meanwhile, was watching from the
BBC studios in Westminster, providing a running commentary to
those around her. 'She was rowdily egging Jeremy on,' says one witness. '"Go on Jeremy, get him! Get him!"' Normally when an
interviewee fails to answer a question even three or four times, the
presenter will move on to another issue, or end the interview. Paxman
later revealed that he couldn't do this because behind the scenes
Newsnight was in some crisis that night. Just as the Howard interview
began, the Sinn Fein MP Martin McGuinness had walked out of the
BBC studio in Londonderry, from where, in the programme's next
item, he had been due to debate with the Conservative MP Michael

Mates. Producers needed extra time to try to persuade McGuinness back, and things were so frantic they hardly had time to watch the duel between Paxman and Howard. *Newsnight's* problems were all the greater because the film due after the Ireland debate still wasn't ready for transmission.

So Paxman was told through his earpiece to keep the interview going, and that he had plenty of time. 'I'm afraid I couldn't think of anything else to ask you,' the presenter told Howard a couple of years later.[30] It's a nice, self-deprecating story, but in truth Paxman had calculated that the 'threaten to overrule' question was likely to embarrass Howard, who had refused to answer similar questions from the *Newsnight* presenter two years earlier when Lewis was sacked. So he persisted:

PAXMAN: Did you *threaten* to overrule him?

HOWARD: I have accounted for my decision to dismiss Derek Lewis in great detail –

PAXMAN: Did you threaten to overrule him?

HOWARD: – before the House of Commons.

PAXMAN: I note you're not answering the question, whether you threatened to overrule him.

HOWARD: Well the important aspect of this, which it's very clear to bear in mind –

PAXMAN: I'm sorry, I'm going to be frightfully rude but, I am sorry, it's a straight yes or no answer.

HOWARD: You put the question and I will give you an answer.

PAXMAN: Did you threaten to overrule him?

HOWARD: I discussed this matter with Derek Lewis. I gave him the benefit of my opinion. I gave him the benefit of my opinion in strong language. But I did not instruct him, because I was not entitled to instruct him. I was entitled to express my opinion, and that is what I did.

PAXMAN: With respect, that is not answering the question of whether you threatened to overrule him.

HOWARD: It's dealing with the relevant point, which is what I was entitled to do, and what I was not entitled to do. And I have dealt with this in detail before the House of Commons and before the select committee.

PAXMAN: But with respect you haven't answered the question of whether you threatened to overrule him.

HOWARD: Well you see the question is, what was I entitled to do, and what I was not entitled to do? I was not entitled to instruct him, and I did not do that.[31]

Thirteen times Jeremy Paxman had asked virtually the same question, and thirteen times Howard had failed to answer. The next item still wasn't ready, but eventually Paxman did move on, asking whether Howard could unify the party when he had so little support from former ministerial colleagues. 'That's it. You've got him!' Widdecombe reportedly said when he'd finished. Afterwards she sent Paxman a note of appreciation. 'For a while,' says a former *Newsnight* colleague, 'Jeremy affected to be quite alarmed by the fondness of her attentions.' The next day Ann Widdecombe also left a message on her answering machine: 'For anybody tempted to vote for Michael Howard, last night's *Newsnight* should be compulsory viewing.'[32]

Immediately after the interview Paxman asked Howard if everything was OK. 'What do you think?' Howard shot back, as he tore off his microphone. And he could hardly complain to the BBC this time, as he often had in the past. 'It hadn't been the best interview I'd ever given,' Howard would confess when he discussed the incident with Paxman on a programme to celebrate *Newsnight's* twentieth birthday in 2000.[33]

'I couldn't remember, I couldn't remember,' a distraught Howard was overheard saying afterwards. His official line the next day was that he needed to refresh his memory by looking at the relevant papers, but, as *The Economist* put it, his refusal to answer was 'a strange lapse for a high powered lawyer who had been challenged many times before on this precise point'.[34] Howard's stepson, Sholto Douglas-Home, remembers that 'It was a very busy day. Michael had come back from Wales. He had a nap in the car, and he then remembered one of the lawyers saying to him that "You can't say X for some legal reason." So when Paxman asked him the question he just had to keep saying what he had been saying. He didn't want to say the wrong thing, and his brain was saying to him, "You can't deviate from this."[35]

It is difficult to see how a straightforward reply to Paxman's question could have had a bearing on any legal question. Maybe Howard was being excessively cautious and feared that if he was more definite he might contradict something he had said in the past, or that Paxman would use it to lead him into even more difficult areas. Tired after a long day, perhaps, and unable to remember the events, and what he'd said in 1995, he feared a trap. He was also keen not to get drawn into a slanging match with Widdecombe, who had been live on *Newsnight* just before him.

What is extraordinary is the way that Howard got so exercised about an issue which few viewers would have cared about. A more relaxed politician, such as Ken Clarke, would probably have laughed it off and told Paxman that, much though he would have liked to have overruled Lewis, and things did get a bit heated, he wasn't allowed to overrule him, and so didn't threaten to do so. Howard's problems stemmed in part from his ultra-legalistic caution, and from originally emphasising the distinction between 'policy' and 'operational' matters.

The interview was recognised as one of the most memorable moments in television history, ranked twenty-second in a Channel 4 poll in 1999 – just behind the Monty Python 'Parrot Sketch', and comfortably ahead of the wedding of Prince Charles and Lady Diana Spencer. It won Jeremy Paxman an award from the Royal Television Society, and the exchange even formed the centrepiece of a musical, *Newsnight – The Opera*, performed in London in 2003, in which video clips of the antagonists were set to music.

Yet the Paxman interview was not quite the 'tipping point' in the leadership contest which it has been portrayed as subsequently. It received little coverage in the next day's press, largely because *Newsnight* goes out so late, although accounts quickly entered the Westminster discourse. Its fame has grown over recent years, partly because it epitomised the tendency of politicians to answer the question they want to answer, rather than the one that is put to them. And no politician is better at evading questions than Michael Howard.

Over the coming days Ann Widdecombe enjoyed more positive publicity than any of the leadership candidates. Even the *Mirror*, which had once dubbed her 'Doris Karloff', published a flattering interview, in which she attacked Howard yet again:

> If he were ever to move to Number 10, the reactions I saw from him at the Home Office could had left the party in a massive mess . . . He panics a great deal. Officials will have seen it. I have certainly seen it. He was my fifth secretary of state. The others were safe hands. His first reaction if anything, however minor, goes wrong, is to ask who is to blame. People are afraid of him, and it's not a good way to get the best out of people.[36]

It emerged that Widdecombe had compiled a file of misleading statements which Howard had made to the Commons, having quietly been gathering material from inside the Home Office since Lewis was sacked. Sandra Howard suggested that Widdecombe's remarks were 'a little bit un-Christian'.[37] This was unlikely to defuse the situation, since Widdecombe's greatest claim to public attention before joining the Home Office team had been her conversion to Catholicism. In happier circumstances the interview with Sandra would have been helpful to Howard. It was illustrated with a photograph of the couple at home, stroking their two cats.

Michael Howard kept up his campaign for the leadership. On the evening after the Paxman grilling he addressed around fifty MPs and the champagne continued to flow at a party in Lord North Street which was officially hosted by Lord Hanson. He and his team must have been relieved that the Widdecombe affair was not mentioned by any questioners, though the MPs were probably too polite to raise such a difficult subject after enjoying Howard's hospitality. Now everyone awaited Ann Widdecombe's speech in the Commons home-affairs debate.

She faxed Michael Howard an advance copy of what she planned to say, though this act of courtesy may have been diminished by the fact that the fax was sent from Derek Lewis's home, where she had been consulting his archives. Her forty-minute speech began with a tribute to Howard's achievements, but then she urged the Commons 'to restore its reputation with the nation'. In Widdecombe's eyes, Howard's conduct towards Lewis and John Marriott symbolised a wider decline of standards in political life. 'Regularly to protect and excuse ourselves while visiting serious vengeance on others corrupts justice and demeans office.' Howard had 'a problem', she declared, 'in that his first reaction to attack is denial and refuge in semantic prestidigitation'. She presented him with five questions:

> Why did he say that he had not personally told Mr Lewis that Mr Marriott should be suspended immediately, when he had? Why did he say that there was no question of overruling Mr Lewis, when the question had been pursued as far as consulting the Cabinet Office and legal advisers? Why did he say that he could not recall at that distance in time why Mr Lewis had been asked to leave the meeting, when he had received only the previous day an account of that meeting, which showed that Mr Lewis had been asked to reconsider his decision?
>
> Why did he say that he was giving the House a full account, when he well knows that important issues that were discussed in the House were in fact omitted from the minutes that he laid before it as a full account?[38]

Widdecombe also challenged Howard to authorise the release of Home Office officials' 'full transcript' of the famous January 1995 meeting with Lewis.[39] Howard had released the official formal minute of the meeting during the October 1995 debate, but Widdecombe argued that the verbatim notes were likely to produce a more complete account of what had been said. (She hadn't attended the meeting herself, since she wasn't yet a Home Office minister at the time.)

Michael Howard and the new Home Secretary, Jack Straw, agreed to her request so quickly that the transcript was made public even before the debate was over. This confirmed that Howard had, indeed, forcibly expressed his view that Marriott should be removed from Parkhurst without delay, when Lewis said he should have the option of not doing so until the next day. 'No, no, no. I want to say "is today being removed"', Howard had exclaimed. 'I can't conceive of a clearer case for suspension,' he had said. 'It is inconceivable that he should not be suspended.'[40] Earlier in the debate Widdecombe had alleged that Howard had consulted government lawyers about whether he was entitled to overrule Lewis (they had told him he couldn't) and that he had also spoken about the possibility of sacking Lewis. Whether or not the threat of being overruled was made directly to him, Widdecombe said, Lewis was well aware throughout their conversations about Marriott that the Home Secretary could apply the ultimate sanction of dismissal if Lewis persisted in taking a different view of what he thought was an 'operational' matter. It was the speech that Jack Straw should have delivered back in October 1995.

In response, speaking four hours after Widdecombe, Howard denied misleading the House. Even when Widdecombe intervened, he merely repeated almost word for word his answer to Jeremy Paxman the week before: 'I was entitled to be consulted, and I was. I was entitled to express an opinion, and I did. However, I was not entitled to tell the former Director General what to do, and I did not.'[41] Now, though, he finally got round to answering Paxman's question, claiming that 'at no time did I threaten to overrule Mr Lewis'.[42] Yet even under pressure Howard showed his other side, with a good joke about his own problems which also mocked Jack Straw for copying his policies:

> It has been suggested that I have something of the night about my character. It is, of course, well known in folklore that creatures of the night have no reflection, so hon. Members will understand my relief as I look across the Dispatch Box and see my reflection smiling back at me.[43]

Few members of the public – and not even many Conservative MPs – would have been aware that Howard was capable of such self-deprecation. But these revelations of Howard's personal qualities were overwhelmed by Widdecombe's apparent suggestion that he was a direct descendant of Count Dracula.

The next day the *Sun* headlined Widdecombe's speech as the 'most savage attack ever seen in the Commons'.[44] In fact the exchange was something of an anticlimax. Widdecombe had said that the injustice of the Lewis affair had made her 'wild at the time and I'm wild now'.[45] But her 'wildness' was constrained by parliamentary etiquette, so she merely said that Howard had made statements which were 'unsustainable', rather than 'untrue'.[46] There were no baying back-benchers on either side, just polite silence. It lacked the high drama of the October 1995 debate, which might have forced the resignation of a holder of one of the great offices of state. The Commons was being used to play out a matter which, in May 1997, had become an internal Conservative Party dispute. Less than three weeks after Labour's landslide, the question of the leadership of the Opposition was more of a sideshow.

The Howard campaign team tried to shrug off the predictions of disaster which followed Widdecombe's attack. Before the end of that week they were claiming, with some chutzpah, that five new MPs had contacted them with promises of support. Two days after the Widdecombe speech, Howard was able to display his debating skills while leading for the Opposition against the government's proposals to hold referendums on devolution for both Scotland and Wales, and showed that 'Dracula' was no stranger to popular culture. Howard argued that the legislation would leave the Cabinet's Scottish and Welsh Secretaries with little to do: 'Will they make the tea or do some photocopying, or will they just sit sniggering together like middle-aged versions of Beavis and Butthead?'[47]

But Michael Howard's critics weren't finished. On 25 May the *Sunday Mirror* revived the story of the Liverpool gangsters John Haase and Paul Bennett, adding for the first time the extra ingredient of Howard's second cousin Simon Bakerman. 'As a credible contender for the leadership of the Conservative Party,' the paper stressed, 'Mr Howard cannot afford to have the smallest question hanging over his judgement.'[48]

Howard's own fortitude was a tribute to his ambition, but also to his political courage. On 27 May Alan Clark visited him at his home in the constituency, to find Norman Lamont offering to canvass his remaining friends in the Commons. Clark thought Howard 'alert, and full of life-force, although he knows he's "up against it"'. Yet in Clark's safe new constituency of Kensington and Chelsea, where Howard had lived before becoming Home Secretary, none of the eighty people surveyed at one Conservative meeting wanted him as leader. Ken Clarke topped that poll with thirty-five votes, followed by Hague and Lilley.[49] In Ludlow, where the Euro-sceptic Christopher Gill was MP, and Howard had recently been guest of honour at the association's annual dinner, he mustered two votes out of sixteen among activists.[50]

And if the collapse of the Hague pact, the Widdecombe intervention, the Paxman interview and the Bakerman story weren't enough to make the Howard camp fear disaster when MPs cast their votes, another ghost now also resurfaced from Howard's past – Charles Wardle.

The first hint had been in Andrew Alexander's column in the *Daily Mail*, which outlined Wardle's story more explicitly than ever before, and warned that the MP soon hoped to strike with his account of Howard putting improper pressure on him to help with the Fayeds' citizenship applications. 'Just squeeze the trigger, Wardle,' begged the veteran columnist, a Redwood supporter. 'Save the Tory Party.'[51] Nine days later came a full-page feature on Fayed, Landy, Howard and Wardle in the *Independent on Sunday*.[52]

On the morning of 4 June, Charles Wardle was allowed a short Commons debate on DTI inquiries, and in particular the Fayed and Guinness cases. Wardle claimed that the timing was accidental because he had applied for the debate 'every week since the new year'. Less convincingly, he insisted that his speech should not be 'construed as an attack on any colleague'.[53] While clearly not as vengeful as Widdecombe, Wardle could easily have delayed the debate until after the leadership election, or made his valid criticisms of DTI inquiries without any link to Howard.

This time Michael Howard was not even present. To have attended the debate (let alone responded) would have been to destroy Wardle's elaborate charade, in which he refused directly to identify his target even though any political audience would know immediately whom he was talking about, especially when he said that he had never believed 'the defamatory stories that surfaced in the press about a minister and a million pounds in a suitcase'.[54]

Wardle claimed he wanted the procedures of the DTI to be tightened, which gave him the excuse to raise the Fayed citizenship affair from three years earlier. He described how he had been put under pressure to reconsider the Fayeds' case, but then suggested to MPs that to have gone along with the advice he had received – to 'turn a blind eye' to the DTI report on the Fayeds – would have been 'unlawful'.[55] That advice, Wardle hinted but didn't say, had come from Howard.

Charles Wardle believes his speech was crucial in ruining Howard's campaign, and he says he was told by a senior member of the Howard team that it did more damage than the Widdecombe intervention. This is doubtful. No one else has cited Wardle's speech as a decisive factor in Howard losing votes in 1997, and it received only limited media coverage. But it may have added to the general unease. Although Wardle was seen as a maverick by fellow Tories, his intervention also emphasised Howard's difficulties in getting on with people.

On the evening after Wardle's speech, Howard joined the other candidates in addressing the 1922 Committee of backbench Tory MPs. Alan Clark thought Howard was 'white as a sheet, but was still impressive'.[56] By now Howard's odds had stretched to 16–1. Yet right until the day of the first vote he was still talking up his chances. 'I confidently expect to finish in the first three,' he declared. 'I would then expect those who came fourth and fifth to withdraw.'[57] On polling day The Times predicted that he would get 34 votes, which would comfortably have been enough, in an electorate of 165 MPs, for the third place which had now become his target in the first ballot.[58] Other papers had also forecast better figures than he eventually received. The Observer and Guardian each predicted 28 votes, and the

Independent 30, and those numbers didn't include three or four dozen MPs whose preferences were unknown.[59] Thirty-six MPs had been named publicly at one time or another as Howard supporters.

It was a tribute to Michael Howard's team that right up until the end they managed to persuade the press that their man was doing better than he really was. It helped, of course, that the tiny electorate was so volatile, and intoxicated by the atmosphere of intrigue. In fact, the result on 10 June was:

Kenneth Clarke	49
William Hague	41
John Redwood	27
Peter Lilley	24
Michael Howard	23

On hearing the news Ann Widdecombe sent a brief message to Derek Lewis: 'Mission accomplished.'[60]

It was a humiliation. In coming last, Michael Howard had been outpolled even by his former junior at the DoE, John Redwood. He'd received barely half the votes of William Hague, the man he'd almost persuaded to run as his deputy, who was twenty years his junior and had been in Parliament barely eight years, and in Cabinet for less than two.

But perhaps it was understandable. With the possible exception of Michael Portillo, Michael Howard had been the most unpopular member of what had been one of the most unpopular – if not *the* most unpopular – governments of the twentieth century. In the circumstances of the party's devastating election defeat, it made little sense for Tory MPs to pick someone so strongly associated with their recent past. The interventions by Widdecombe and Wardle had illustrated to parliamentary colleagues that Howard was not a good 'team player'. His adviser Patrick Rock said of the Widdecombe outburst, 'It rebounded on Michael in the sense that if he was going to be the leader of the party, the question would arise: "Is he good at getting on with colleagues?" That led to subliminal worries in some of the constituencies.'[61] Of nine MPs still in the Commons who had served in the government under Howard since 1990, only two had come out in his favour – David Maclean and Patrick Nicholls (who was briefly with him at Employment). While he had managed to fall out publicly with Widdecombe and Wardle, privately four other ministers from his Home Office days – Peter Lloyd, Michael Forsyth, Emily Blatch and Tom Sackville – weren't great fans either (though none was now an MP).

Howard supporters still maintain it could have been different. More compellingly, a leading academic analyst of leadership elections, Philip Cowley, has pointed out that if Howard had won over just two Redwood MPs and one Lilley supporter then the first-round figures would have been Howard 26, Redwood 25, and Lilley 23. 'Presumably,' says Cowley, 'Howard and not Redwood would then have entered the second round, quite possibly with the endorsement of the other two right-wing candidates. This may not have been enough to have enabled him to overtake either Clarke or Hague but it would have been a close run thing. He may even have won.'[62] In the event, however, three-quarters of the Howard and Lilley votes switched not to Redwood, but to Hague and Clarke in the second ballot. This may suggest that there was little ideological solidarity on the right of the Conservative Party.

According to a key campaign worker, Howard and Francis Maude were 'stunned' by the outcome. Michael Spicer, who had been crunching the numbers for so long, was less surprised. One can name with some certainly eighteen MPs who voted for Howard, largely because most of them were also active in his campaign team. They were, in alphabetical order, Graham Brady, Simon Burns, Christopher Chope, Alan Clark, Tim Collins, David Davis, David Faber, Liam Fox, Christopher Fraser, Archie Hamilton, Oliver Heald, Andrew Lansley, David Maclean, Francis Maude, Patrick Nicholls, Michael Spicer, Desmond Swayne and, of course, Howard himself. Constituency parties didn't have a vote at that time, but a survey by the 1922 Committee of grass-roots activists released on the day of the ballot showed him gaining just 26 votes out of 1,045 people asked –

less than 3 per cent – and fewer than 2 per cent of constituency chairmen.[63] The Howard camp believed such constituency opinion had a telling influence on MPs, especially new members.

Perhaps Howard had got his tactics wrong. Members of his entourage were reportedly frustrated at their candidate's refusal to take a more hardline position to beat off John Redwood's challenge. 'Michael seemed reluctant to chase the votes of the parliamentary Right before the first round,' says a leading member of his team:

> He was convinced his appeal rested on being a moderate figure, a unifier, just on the inside-right of John Redwood and Peter Lilley . . . We used to tear our hair out in frustration trying to get him to change tack. We had gone through the figures minutely, and knew that he was only one or two votes short of coming third – which was, of course, our target. We felt that his only chance was to pick up more support from within the Right. Yet Michael Howard simply wouldn't see it. On one occasion, for example, he pulled out of a meeting with Richard Body, who could well have been won over, to see a group of Clarke supporters who would never have voted for him in a million years.

'There was a lot of naivety,' says another member of the campaign staff. 'People were trusting of others too much, and let down by promises and pledges. I don't think anybody had really worked on a leadership campaign before.'

After the result, John Redwood contacted both Lilley and Howard to ask for backing in the next round. Both decided to support Hague, and Howard's decision was endorsed overwhelmingly by a meeting of his supporters. Redwood said that he expected better of Lilley, but was unsurprised by Howard. Each of the right-wing candidates had hoped to win the backing of his defeated rivals after the first ballot, but there was never any agreement. Lilley pointed out to Redwood that the party could never unite under his leadership. Hague was not an ideologue, but was still certain to take the party in a more Euro-sceptic direction. He also offered the best chance of stopping Clarke.

From Michael Howard's point of view, there was the additional complication that just a few short (if action-packed) weeks ago he had considered Hague to be the perfect running mate.

In the final ballot William Hague beat Ken Clarke comfortably, by 92 votes to 70. It showed that once Hague decided to break his pact with Howard he gained the magic political ingredient of 'momentum'. The history of leadership elections in all the main British parties suggests that, in contests which don't involve an incumbent, the winner is nearly always the youngest candidate or the contender with the least experience in Parliament. There are exceptions, but usually MPs go for the freshest face.

In losing early, Michael Howard had at least escaped one further disaster. Jonathan Aitken's libel trial collapsed on 19 June – the very day that William Hague was elected Tory leader. A media scrum gathered in Lord North Street that evening, awaiting the return of the disgraced Aitken rather than the victorious Michael Howard. The next day Aitken fled Britain through the Channel Tunnel he had vehemently opposed, and within days he was being investigated by the police for perjury. After years of allegations of Tory sleaze, it would have been the worst of all starts to a Michael Howard leadership to have run his campaign from the house of a man who was about to spend eighteen months in jail. It would certainly have raised yet more questions about his judgement.

In anticipation of a long campaign – and ultimate victory – Howard's staff still had a large stock of Laurent-Perrier in Lord North Street. In the closing days, volunteers drank little else, though the attraction began to pale. Years later, one of his leading workers still found it difficult to face a glass of champagne.

Privately, Michael Howard hadn't lost all his fizz, and those who helped his campaign received another memento. Showing generosity and good humour, the defeated candidate gave them signed copies of Bram Stoker's *Dracula*.

18

IN THE SHADOWS

Who can predict the future? The unexpected can happen. Politics
is full of tremendous uncertainties.

MICHAEL HOWARD, 1998[1]

'I don't want to go through that again,' Norman Lamont recalls
Michael Howard saying several times.[2] It had been the worst experience of his political life. As far as he was concerned, the party's
decision was final. 'I have had one shot at leadership and that's it,'
Howard told an interviewer seven months later. 'I can still play my
part without being leader.'[3] Indeed, as the years passed, Howard would
even say that the party might have come to 'the right decision' in
choosing William Hague. 'It was probably a good thing to sort of
strike out in a completely new direction with someone who wasn't as
closely associated with the previous government as I was.'[4]

His chances of winning the leadership seemed gone for ever. In
choosing Hague the party had skipped not one political generation,
but two, and the new leader had also promised to extend the franchise
for future contests to include party members as well as MPs. Despite
his constituency charm-offensive in the months before and during the
1997 election, Michael Howard's support among activists throughout
the leadership campaign had been even weaker than at Westminster.
Even if Hague's leadership proved to be short-lived, another young,

charismatic champion might well emerge. And by the next contest party heavyweights such as Michael Portillo, Chris Patten and Malcolm Rifkind could be back in Parliament and back in contention.

Howard's relief at Hague's victory over Clarke was followed by a Shadow Cabinet appointment which suggested that his party status had not been damaged by his poor showing. Ken Clarke moved to the backbenches, but the other three unsuccessful leadership candidates all took senior jobs. Peter Lilley became Shadow Chancellor, while John Redwood acquired the Trade and Industry portfolio. Howard was lined up against another sharp debater, Robin Cook, as Shadow Foreign Secretary. There was a nod towards party unity with the inclusion of Clarke's friends David Curry and Ian Taylor in the Shadow Cabinet, and Gillian Shephard, who had emerged untarnished from the Major years, also agreed to serve. Even so, Hague's team was hardly a Shadow Ministry of All the Talents. Portillo, Rifkind and Patten were outside the Commons and could not join the Shadow Cabinet, while Major, Heseltine and Clarke all preferred the backbenches and making money to continuing in the political front line.

Howard would have been reassured, however, by the absence of another well-known figure from the Shadow Cabinet. It was reported that he had blackballed Ann Widdecombe in exchange for agreeing to back Hague in the later rounds of the leadership contest. 'I'm not surprised Michael did this,' she said. 'It was quite inevitable. It's also in character.'[5]

Despite his new front-bench role, Michael Howard found it hard to adjust to the change in routine imposed by opposition. Like a long-term prisoner suddenly released, he had become institutionalised by ministerial life. Interviewed for the *New Statesman* after a year in opposition, he admitted his frustration: 'As somebody once said, in government you wake up and wonder what to do; in opposition you wake up and wonder what to say . . . You go into politics to govern, to do things.' His secretary was more forthcoming, confiding, 'He found it more painful than most of them, switching to opposition. He had been a senior minister for so long.'[6] It probably just *felt* like that: in terms of Cabinet service he was some years behind ex-colleagues like Clarke and Heseltine, but they both had previous experience of life in opposition.

Free from red boxes, his government car and the constant demands of journalists and civil servants, the former Home Secretary could now see a lot more of his family. The Howards had bought a house in Pimlico, about a mile from Parliament. 'A shadow minister about the house can take up quite a lot of time,' Sandra wrote in the *Spectator*. Michael, it seemed, was at home too much. 'I cannot, on occasion, find a quarter of an hour to call my own: "my" fax is in constant use as 27-page speeches coil their way in or out of it, looking like an Andrex advertisement without a puppy; "my" telephone is constantly busy, my friends bemoan how long "I" have been talking; my coffee-making skills are well honed and my little routines go out of the window.'[7]

The Howards had also lost Michael's ministerial income. Sandra revived her career as a model, at the age of fifty-six, and did shoots for Marks & Spencer and British Home Stores. In fact she had never entirely given up modelling, even though it could prove perilous now that Michael was so well known. On one occasion she'd done a series of stock photos for a German agency, one of which showed a male model of indeterminate age nuzzling her ear. The picture turned up in the UK in *Woman's Weekly* magazine, illustrating an item on the dangers of middle-aged people having heart attacks during intercourse and headlined 'Make sex even safer.'[8] Sandra seemed almost as busy as Michael. As well as regular work for a cancer charity, she'd kept up her journalism, producing a regular column for a French magazine on fashion, theatre and exhibitions in London, as well as occasional articles and book reviews for British publications. She'd also begun work on a book, which she described as being 'like a female version of Alan Clark'.[9] Rather than a racy diary, the project became a novel called *Love in High Profile*, which she was still writing at the start of 2005.

Michael Howard's new-found freedom was a little late for him as a father. His two children, Nick and Larissa (known to her family as 'Rissy'), were both now grown-up and away at university. After Eton, Nick Howard had, during a gap year, briefly worked in Washington for Bill Clinton's former Treasury Secretary (and the 1988 vice-presidential candidate) Lloyd Bentsen. He then went to study English at St Catherine's College, Oxford, where he caused a stir in the university and outside by trying to persuade Jews of the virtues of Christianity. Although Nick had had a formal bar mitzvah at thirteen – 'not full blown – mainly for his grandmother', Sandra says[10] – he'd converted to Christianity a couple of years later under the influence of his housemaster at Eton, and had become evangelical. Speaking at a meeting of the university Christian Union, OICCU, in 1998, and wearing a Jewish yarmulke on his head, Nick Howard argued that Jesus Christ was the Jewish Messiah. 'As Christians it is our duty to reach Jews, who are the priority in our evangelism,' he said. 'It is a process of reasoning, persuading them to become Christians. Christianity is fulfilled Judaism.'[11] According to a memo leaked to the Oxford student newspaper Cherwell, Howard and his colleagues in OICCU were deliberately targeting Jews. An Oxford rabbi, Shmuley Boteach, accused the young Howard and his colleagues of being 'small-minded bigots' and of practising 'spiritual Nazism' by specifically seeking Jews for conversion rather than non-Christians in general.[12] 'The attitudes of OICCU are not benign – they culminated in the chimneys of Auschwitz.' Howard pointed out that some of his ancestors had died in concentration camps. 'I find the claim of "spiritual Nazism" extremely hurtful,' he said. 'Hurtful isn't the word – it's horrifying.'[13] Boteach challenged Howard to a debate, which lasted more than two hours and – perhaps an indication of the scale of the controversy within town and university – attracted more than 400 people. 'He was a pleasant young man,' Boteach recalls, 'extremely sincere, godly and spiritual. But misguided. He seemed utterly ignorant – certainly of Judaism, but also of Christian Scripture. My purpose in the debate was to show that Nick had converted to Christianity not out of conviction, but, sadly, from a total lack of knowledge of his own faith.'[14]

The rest of the family made no public comment. To say it was embarrassing is probably an understatement. Nick told people he had become something of a family 'outcast', and that his grandmother would no longer talk to him. Hilda Howard, now in her late eighties, was still practising as an orthodox Jew in Stanmore in north-west London, and was active in several Jewish organisations. She was deeply upset. Michael and Sandra were sufficiently concerned to consult their rabbi, David Goldberg of the Liberal synagogue in St John's Wood, which Howard still attended on Jewish high holidays. Although Nick Howard's remarks might seem like undergraduate posturing, he should have been aware of how provocative they would be. Many Jews, even those who aren't especially religious, regard converting to Christianity as much worse than marrying outside the community. Trying to convert other Jews is seen as worse still. 'Jews have been targeted for massacre for thousands of years because we wouldn't become Christian,' says Shmuley Boteach. 'Millions died as Jews rather than live as Christians. They would not be severed from the faith of their ancestors.'[15]

Religion was perhaps the only significant area where Michael Howard and his son differed. To some, Nick looks just like his father. He can be as pedantic, often about grammar; he is a more fervent Liverpool supporter; and if anything he is more right-wing than Michael. Although Nick wasn't involved in politics at university, he feels as passionately about political affairs as he does about religion – especially on law and order and on Ireland, where he takes a strong pro-Unionist line. 'He made Ian Paisley look like some kind of wishy-washy cotton-woolled apologist,' says a former acquaintance, who remembers him expressing disapproval of the conciliatory Unionist leader David Trimble.

As a student Howard had dabbled in journalism – including one famous occasion when the *Evening Standard* published one of his unsolicited articles attacking Tony Blair under the byline of the former Labour front-bencher Bryan Gould, thanks to a mix-up over incoming faxes. After Oxford, Nick worked as a Christian youth worker in the city, and helped organise mission holidays for teenagers. There followed a job at Westminster working for the Parliamentary Resources Unit, a body which supplies Conservative MPs with background information; he proved to be an excellent researcher. He then announced he was going into the Church, and went to St John's College at Durham University to study theology. 'It's my calling,' he told friends.

Michael Howard would refer half-jokingly to Nick's 'wayward-ness', and it was clear that he thought his son could make more of his life. Ideally, Howard would have preferred him to take up one of his own professions, politics or law. 'Had Nick been going down the Anglican High Church Christian route, he and Sandra would have been more happy,' says a friend.

Both Nick and his sister, Larissa, are 'easy-going, charming, yet quite complex people', says their half-brother Sholto. 'They are not usually the life and souls of the party, as they are both quite gentle and discreet – I'm more gregarious and talkative. Although both are intel-lectually formidable, I doubt if either of them will go into politics.' Whereas Nick Howard got only a lower second in his degree at Oxford, Larissa Howard was academically brilliant, and achieved a double first at St Catharine's College, Cambridge. Unlike her father and brother, Larissa is left-of-centre in her political outlook, in the way of most students who do Social and Political Sciences at Cambridge. 'Larissa will have hammer and tongs debates with Michael,' says Sholto – 'good, hard-fought intellectual debates about politics.'[16] At one time there were thoughts of joining the left-leaning think-tank Demos, but instead she found a job with a consultancy, the Henley Centre, where she was quickly promoted from an analyst to being a consultant. Clients who might have had doubts about her age or inexperience soon had them dispelled by the quality of her contri-butions. In September 2003, with what turned out to be immaculate timing, she moved to Tokyo to work for Ogilvy, the advertising agency, and to be with her American boyfriend.

Back in 1997, given his expectations about New Labour policy towards Europe, Michael Howard must have felt initially that he'd landed one of the plum Opposition jobs. He had predicted that Britain would concede yet further sovereignty at the Amsterdam summit of June 1997. But, not for the first time in his career, Blair disappointed him, lining up with Germany's Helmut Kohl to water down proposals for a deeper 'social dimension' to EU policy. The new Prime Minister proved to have serious differences even with Europe's social democrats, and, sounding like a Thatcherite, Blair boasted to his fellow leaders about the superiority of the 'flexible' UK job market. Howard continued to press for a referendum on the Amsterdam agreement, but the summit was nothing like as important as Maastricht, and a national vote would hardly have been justified.

Before the election the Conservatives had been confident both that Blair would surrender British sovereignty and that Labour's latent divisions on European integration would be exposed if the party ever returned to government. Instead, it was the Conservatives who continued to look divided. On the single currency, Blair adopted Major's 'wait and see' policy, even if he was clearly waiting with more enthusiasm. With the Labour Party having stolen the Conservatives' clothes, William Hague had to find an alternative policy that would satisfy the sceptics without driving the pro-Europe Clarke supporters out of the Shadow Cabinet.

Hague's preferred line was to rule out the single currency 'for the foreseeable future', but a more precise timescale was needed for the 1997 Conservative conference. The official definition of 'the foreseeable future' turned out to be the present parliament and the one following – a maximum period just short of ten years, though likely to be closer to eight years. Even the most sanguine Conservative accepted, given the size of the majority, that Labour was likely to win a second term, whenever the next election was called. So in practice the Hague formula committed his party to oppose Labour if it recommended joining the euro up to the time when the Conservatives would have their first realistic chance of forming another government. But this still implied that the party might accept the euro when it returned to power, which was obviously not enough for the sceptics. They wanted to rule out the single currency for ever, as a matter of principle. On the other flank, the Europhiles derided a policy which forced the party to oppose the euro for two parliaments even if it proved to be a success in the meantime. Ian Taylor, David Curry and Stephen Dorrell found the new position unacceptable, and all eventually resigned from the Shadow Cabinet.

Michael Howard went along with Hague's attempts to find a compromise 'for the sake of unity'.[17] On the face of it, it looked as if he was planning to repeat the role of candid loyalist that he had played under Major. But the differences between Hague and Major would make this more complicated than it had been the first time round. Major had had enough experience to have confidence in his own judgement, and, if he had his disagreements with Howard, there was always an underlying mutual respect.

In contrast, William Hague seemed from the start to be ill at ease with senior party figures, preferring the advice of people who were even less experienced than himself. Hague's circle behaved as if their main task was to defend their boss against anyone with expertise. In addition, Howard was obviously suspect as a result of the aborted pact. At the time, Howard had implied that, while Hague was bound to be leader one day, it would be a mistake to run too soon. Hague's subsequent treatment of senior colleagues, having won the leadership, suggests that he feared that Howard's prognosis had been correct. Howard's presence at Shadow Cabinet meetings was a constant reminder of this anxiety.

Trouble between Howard and the Hague entourage surfaced only a few months after Howard became Shadow Foreign Secretary, when he made one of his congenial trips to America. Howard irritated Hague's circle by telling Americans it would be 'stupidity' for the Conservatives to challenge Labour for the centre ground in Britain.[18] Their reaction to his remarks suggested that Hague's allies had been looking for an opportunity to rein Howard in. On his return he was challenged during a Shadow Cabinet discussion about the forthcoming party conference and told not to answer questions at a fringe meeting on Europe. Howard duly toed the collective line of appeasement, telling angry activists that 'It was not your fault we lost. It was ours.'[19] Yet hints emerged that Howard had wanted Hague to rule out the single currency for ever. 'Nobody trusts Howard,' one Shadow Cabinet source told the *Sunday Times*.[20] It was as if he had finally been singled out as a 'bastard' under a regime which was supposedly more sympathetic to his views.

If Howard hoped to spend as little time as possible apologising for the Thatcher–Major years, he encountered unwelcome reminders at every turn. For example, the personal travails of Robin Cook – who left his wife for his secretary – could not be exploited because of the Conservatives' ill-fated 'Back to Basics' campaign, even though it was perfectly proper for Howard to ask, in February 1998, whether Cook had sacked his diary secretary, Anne Bullen, in the hope of creating a vacancy for his new partner. The trouble was that Howard's own record on personnel issues was hardly spotless, if for different reasons. More than any other Conservative minister, he had sacked or blocked officials in the hope of surrounding himself with people who would help his interests – Sir John Chilcot and Derek Lewis were just two of the better-known victims. 'The man who, when Home Secretary, sacked the Director General of the Prison Service to cover his back and was successfully sued for damages has taken to his high horse on personnel matters,' jeered Peter Mandelson, who was now a Labour minister.[21] When Howard raised the Bullen case in the Commons, he was shouted down by Labour MPs.

Howard was also handicapped on the 'Sandline' affair, which involved the exporting of arms to Sierra Leone with Foreign Office approval, in defiance of UN sanctions which Britain had supported. An official report uncovered considerable disorder within the Foreign Office, and Robin Cook appeared either incompetent or complicit. But the whole episode reminded people of the Arms to Iraq scandal of the Major years – with the significant difference that, on this occasion, as Tony Blair said, 'For God's sake, the good guys won' because of the clandestine arms traffic.[22] Cook reminded Labour backbenchers of a further parallel when the report was debated in July 1998. Under Major, he had been given just three hours to master the details of the five-volume Scott Report into Arms for Iraq, before the full Commons debate. Howard had been allowed twice that time to study the Legg Report, and yet, Cook taunted, 'He could find only five questions.'[23]

Wherever Howard turned, ghosts seemed to appear. When the former Chilean dictator Augusto Pinochet was arrested in London with a view to extradition and trial in Spain, his greatest champions were Margaret Thatcher and Howard's great friend Norman Lamont. Howard was 'extremely unsympathetic initially', says Lamont. 'He said he wanted nothing to do with it. He said the Conservative Party is not the party of Pinochet.'[24] As the affair dragged on, Howard became more critical of the Blair government, arguing that the Chileans should be left to deal with Pinochet 'free from the interference of a blundering overseas Government in pursuit of a much-needed boost to their ethical foreign policy'.[25]

The main foreign issues while Howard shadowed Cook were Kosovo and Iraq. But his room for manoeuvre was limited in both cases because he broadly agreed with the government. When he accused the NATO allies of 'gross incompetence' for bombing the Chinese embassy in Belgrade in May 1999, he laid himself open to the charge of being happy to will the end without accepting the means.[26] His main objection to the government's approach was 'the number of times when Robin Cook uttered some dire threat and final warning to Milosevic, without following through with any action'. This 'sent all the wrong signals', and thereby worsened the crisis, Howard said.[27]

In response to the Kosovo crisis Howard laid down some principles which informed his conduct five years later, when he was accused of contradictions over the 2003 war on Iraq. 'From the start,' he wrote, 'the British people have been fully aware of the justice of our cause [over Kosovo]. In return, ministers should come clean. They should let the nation into their confidence and trust the people with the facts.'[28] He adopted this approach in a debate on Kosovo on 18 May 1999. Matthew Parris of *The Times* thought that 'This was counsel for the prosecution at its best,' and that Cook was discomfited by Howard's intensive questioning. 'If Howard continues to shine like this . . . he may wipe from many minds the bad memories of his time in Government.'[29] It should have been enough to make the Conservatives regret that they would soon lose his services from the front bench.

The background whispers from those around Hague had become more noisy in May 1998, when they started to suggest – commentators like Matthew Parris notwithstanding – that Howard had done badly over Sandline and Sierra Leone. His position within the Shadow Cabinet had become less comfortable in March that year with the arrival of Ann Widdecombe as front-bench spokesman on health. Howard maintained that he was happy to see her there because she was so good at attacking the government. With what might be regarded as a backhanded compliment he observed, 'While some of us have not found it easy to adapt to Opposition, Ann has been particularly effective.'[30] Her 'something of the night' intervention had made her one of the Tories' biggest stars, and perhaps the party's most popular MP. Widdecombe had reassured Hague – at the leader's prompting – that she would not revive the Lewis affair, but that did not stop her undermining Howard in other ways. Declaring that she was 'very tired of this Mills and Boon kiss-and-make-up nonsense', she resorted to her well-practised tactic of grumbling to the press through 'friends'. 'This is the man who last week cut me dead in front of witnesses,' she was said to have responded to reports that Howard had forgiven her. Any idea of a rapprochement was 'rot', and when she heard him speak in praise of her 'I was reaching for the sick bag. Michael knows I am coming back. He has been told it is going to happen, so he can approach it in one of two ways. He can either sulk his way through it, or he can launch a pre-emptive strike, show himself in a good light and take the credit for my promotion and thus secure his own position.' This contrasted sharply with what Widdecombe said for direct attribution: 'He has made some very kind remarks about me. Time moves on. We have a task in common.'[31]

Norman Lamont says that Michael Howard would have liked to have been a Willie Whitelaw-style mentor to his young leader, 'but Hague didn't want him to be his "Willie". Michael just felt there was no special role for him.'[31] Before Christmas 1998 Howard told Hague privately that he wanted to return to the backbenches. In the new year, well-sourced reports emerged that he faced the axe, along with

John Redwood, Gillian Shephard and Norman Fowler. 'They are figures from the past,' said a 'senior Tory official'.[33] The public announcement did not come until March, when some papers gave the impression that Howard had decided to jump before he was pushed, though in fact Hague had asked Howard to reconsider. After fourteen years on the front bench, it had lost its allure. The lack of power was compounded by the constant sniping from members of Hague's inner circle. 'I had had enough,' he explained later. 'I wanted a new life. I wanted a rest.'[34] If he was stepping down from the Shadow Cabinet, he made it clear that he wasn't leaving the Commons. He still planned to contest Folkestone at the next election.

Although the political obituaries had started to appear, he remained as foreign-affairs spokesman until June 1999. The Kosovo debate in May 1999 showed that even as a lame duck he could still be dangerous on the Conservative front bench.

There was one last episode in his service under Hague. As Shadow Chancellor, Peter Lilley had made little impact on Gordon Brown inside the Commons or outside, and had been withdrawn to a policy-making role. In April 1999 Lilley made a speech questioning the party's Thatcherite legacy. It was a thoughtful performance, delivered with Hague's endorsement. But Shadow Cabinet hardliners – Howard, the social-security spokesman Iain Duncan Smith, and especially Ann Widdecombe – were outraged. They said that Margaret Thatcher's legacy was the main factor which kept the party together, and an angry Howard protested that the speech had impugned his reputation as a minister who had served under Thatcher. The Conservatives had already conceded too much, he said, in apologising for the past.

The leadership beat a hasty retreat, though the incident did not improve relations between Howard and Widdecombe. In September 2000 she made it clear that she had not forgotten or forgiven him when Nicholas Kochan published an approved biography of her. At the Conservative conference a year later Howard turned up at the BBC studio for a live broadcast, but refused to enter when he spotted Ann Widdecombe sitting inside. Peter Lilley's reward for his revisionism was to be thrown out of the Shadow Cabinet and fired as deputy leader in the same reshuffle in which Howard departed. It meant that only Hague, of the 1997 leadership contenders, was still on the Opposition front bench.

After his departure Howard enjoyed his new freedom of speech. He showed particular interest in Northern Ireland, which he had visited during the leadership contest. In April 1998 he had given a cautious welcome to the Good Friday Agreement, expressing concern about the decommissioning of weapons and the early release of imprisoned terrorists. As Home Secretary he'd served on the Cabinet Northern Ireland Committee and had visited both London's Docklands and Manchester in the aftermath of bombings. And one of his biggest clashes with Derek Lewis had been over the transfer of IRA prisoners from Britain to jails in Northern Ireland, in order to help family visits. From the backbenches he expressed strong opposition to anything which might weaken the Unionist cause, and in July 1999 he voted against the third reading of the bill which established a devolved Northern Ireland executive, because there was insufficient progress on decommissioning weapons. Only fifteen other Tories joined him, including David Maclean and David Davis.

This was one of only two occasions on which Michael Howard has ever defied his party's whip (but then he has served only three years as a backbencher). The other also related to Ireland, when later that year he joined five other Conservative MPs in voting against the Police (Northern Ireland) Bill, when the instruction was to abstain. Howard criticised as 'fatally flawed' the approach to the Royal Ulster Constabulary proposed by a review conducted by Chris Patten, his sometime antagonist on Hong Kong. Many of Patten's extensive recommendations were 'naive', he said. 'And many betray evidence of surrender to political correctness of the most insidious kind.'[35] Howard also spoke against the Disqualifications Bill, which ended the anomaly whereby a member of the Irish Senate could serve in the Northern Ireland Assembly but not in any other British legislature, though he followed the party line in abstaining when it came to the vote. Ireland was a frequent area for Tory dissent, however, and fifty-one MPs defied the whip over the issue at one time or another during the 1997–2001 parliament – almost a third of the parliamentary party.[36]

Howard's other interventions mainly covered home affairs and Europe. Some of them could be seen as self-serving: he stressed that crime rates had fallen 18 per cent during his time as Home Secretary, while asylum applications had risen sharply since Labour took over. His speeches on asylum became increasingly frequent – partly because of the constituency interest – and he also raised the state of the NHS in East Kent. He spoke and voted to keep hunting, without giving a ringing endorsement to 'country sports': it was more that the anti-hunting lobby had failed to prove its case.

One of the reasons for giving up the front bench was to spread his wings outside parliament and earn a lot more money. Other former Cabinet colleagues had found lucrative niches outside politics. For Howard, the most obvious option was to return to the Bar. Still not sixty, on the face of it he might expect another ten or fifteen years as a top-level QC, and planning was even more highly paid than when he'd left it in the early 1980s. Sandra was especially keen for him to resume his legal career, says a friend, and 'to get a job which meant he'd be out of the house by ten o'clock in the morning, and to get him out of her hair'. Howard had been assiduous in keeping in touch with his former clerk Steve Graham: even when he was Home Secretary they had met once a year for a drink. But both men knew it wouldn't work. There had been too long a gap for him to pick up where he'd left off fifteen years before. It wasn't just that his absence in the Commons had made him rusty. He'd also offended many people in his profession during his years as Home Secretary. Solicitors might find it difficult to recommend him as a barrister when he had publicly upset so many judges.

Nor was there a flood of lucrative speaking offers of the sort later enjoyed by William Hague – let alone an appearance on *Have I Got News For You?* Never a prolific wordsmith, Howard wrote sparingly for the newspapers. Most of his contributions were letters, although he still produced a regular (unpaid) column for the *Folkestone Herald*. At times his attempts to prove to his constituents that his interests still ranged from the global to the local verged on the surreal. In April 1999, for example, he previewed the clash between Folkestone and Margate in the southern division of the Doc Marten's League. 'I certainly hope that Folkestone will triumph and go from strength to strength,' he enthused. 'Meanwhile, alas, the bombing of Yugoslavia continues. The refugees continue to flee.'[37]

The other obvious option was a directorship in the City, or in industry. His friend Christopher Bland, now chairman of several companies (and the BBC), urged him to give up politics and follow John Nott and Nigel Lawson into merchant banking. The Tories were bound to be out of office for at least ten years, Bland warned. Ken Clarke had become deputy chairman of British American Tobacco, earning £100,000 a year; Douglas Hurd had secured a high-paid place in the boardroom of the NatWest Group; Norman Fowler, too, had built up a string of valuable directorships. Howard tried, but failed miserably. He contacted John Viney, the chairman of the headhunters Heidrick & Struggles, but Viney found the former Home Secretary to be surprisingly unpopular in business circles. It is possible that Howard's combative style counted against him in the business world, but there remains an intriguing 'what if?'. Had a substantial job come up, then Michael Howard's subsequent career might have been very different. He might easily have given up his seat, suggests one political friend. 'If he had been made a decent offer of another career outside politics I honestly believe that he would not be leader of the Conservative Party today.'

Even without a substantial outside job, it would not have been completely surprising had Michael Howard stepped down as an MP. He told Norman Lamont he was 'looking forward' to retiring, but he'd already promised Folkestone's Tories that he'd fight the next election, due in 2001 or 2002.[38] Howard felt obliged to keep his word, though politics in his local party was almost as fraught as it was nationally. 'People were whingeing to him all the time,' says a former aide. 'There were times when rows within the local party were driving him up the wall.'

Despite John Viney's failure to land him a high-powered City post,

Howard had picked up a couple of minor boardroom appointments after the 1997 election. One was with Finex PLC, which specialises in business communications; the other was with a printing and medical-equipment business run by David Instance, a neighbour in Kent who had contributed £1,000 to Howard's 1997 leadership attempt. He also became a paid adviser to Consort Resources, a firm involved in the North Sea gas industry, and chaired by Lord (Colin) Moynihan. As sports minister under Margaret Thatcher in the late 1980s, Moynihan had been a colleague of Howard's at the DoE, and he also lived in the Folkestone constituency.

Howard also teamed up with David Maclean to form a company called Crime Reduction International Ltd. It had been Nick Howard's idea – he had suggested his father should market to other countries his expertise and track record in this field. Michael Howard brought in Maclean, his closest ministerial colleague at the Home Office, and Jenny Ungless, who had connections to all three men, not least because she had been Maclean's mistress for several years. She had worked for both ministers as a civil servant at the Home Office, and had later been Nick Howard's boss at the Parliamentary Resources Unit. All four had shares in the company, though Michael Howard owned the majority. Their main focus would be on countries which were about to join the EU, or states which required World Bank sponsorship, where there was a clear need for more robust law and order and criminal justice structures. Howard aroused some interest from the Polish government during a lecture trip to Warsaw, but the business never got off the ground.

After 1997 Howard briefly served, too, as a non-executive director of an American company called Impac, a management consultancy firm which is best known in Europe for its sponsorship of the annual Dublin Literary Award, the world's most valuable prize for fiction. Howard almost certainly got this appointment through Jeffrey Archer, who was close to Impac's chairman, James Irwin, himself a contro-versial character. In 1999 the *Mail on Sunday* revealed that Irwin had tried to silence Archer's former aide Michael Stacpoole by buying the literary rights to his life story for £1 in addition to agreeing to buy his house, which Stacpoole had found hard to sell – a ruse which was clearly intended to stop Stacpoole telling the world what he knew about the novelist's past, and particularly his extramarital sex life.[39]

Michael Howard helped Archer secure an appearance in a television ad for BT, for whom his stepson, Sholto Douglas-Home, was then head of advertising. Howard had long been a friend of Archer, who had occasionally come to campaign for him in Folkestone. When the novelist ran for mayor of London in 1999, Howard supported his bid for the Conservative nomination, and signed a letter to the *Daily Telegraph* claiming that Archer had the 'vision, the energy and the commitment to be an outstanding mayor of London'.[40] He wasn't alone in this misjudgement, for the letter was also signed by Cecil Parkinson, Malcolm Rifkind, Norman Fowler, Tom King, Peter Lilley, Norman Lamont and Brian Mawhinney, while Margaret Thatcher, John Major and Gillian Shephard backed the Archer campaign as well.

When the novelist was jailed in 2001 for perjury, Howard visited him in prison, having previously been to see his other convicted perjurer friend, Jonathan Aitken. According to Sholto Douglas-Home, 'He would say, "Just because they are in prison, that doesn't mean I shouldn't see them." He would have that sense of fair play and support.'[41] Like Aitken, the man who had introduced Howard's famous 'prison works' speech emerged from jail in 2003 as a convert to a more liberal approach to penal policy. Archer was particularly upset that 'D' category prisoners such as himself weren't allowed out over Christmas. 'Michael Howard put a stop to that when he became Home Secretary,' he complained in his prison diary.[42]

If neither his friends nor headhunters had managed to generate lucrative business work, Howard did find a new outlet for his time and energy. He had long been thinking of a new political institute to reflect his admiration for America. Hence the Atlantic Partnership, a charitable body which Howard officially launched in February 2001. It was not a think-tank, nor involved in research or policy formulation, but then Michael Howard has never been that interested in generating ideas and policy. It was more a 'ginger group', says

Margaret Thatcher's former foreign-policy adviser Charles Powell, who was a co-founder and succeeded Howard as chairman.[43] Nor was it intended to bolster the 'special relationship' between Britain and America. Instead, it was designed as a bridge between Europe and the US, both to fight the anti-Americanism of many in the EU, and to remind Americans of the importance of Europe at a time when Washington was increasingly focusing on Asia and the Pacific. The body had an impressive roll of supporters. Official American associates included Henry Kissinger, the former National Security Adviser Brent Scowcroft, and the Democratic senator Joe Biden, while an eclectic cross-party group of British backers included John Major, David Owen and the Labour MP Frank Field. The Partnership held regular breakfast meetings in London, Europe and America, where prominent guests would address fifty or sixty opinion-formers – including politicians, diplomats, academics, newspaper columnists and editors. It was not a right-of-centre project: guest speakers included senior members of the Labour government, such as Jack Straw and Gordon Brown. The organiser was Catherine Fall, the daughter of the former British ambassador to Moscow Sir Brian Fall, who was herself half-American and had been Howard's special adviser when he was Shadow Foreign Secretary.

During the June 2001 election Howard again faced a challenge from the Liberal Democrats in Folkestone, and did his best to play off the two opposition parties against each other. If the Referendum Party was dead, its place had been taken by the UK Independence Party. The Campaign for Racial Equality asked candidates to sign a pledge promising not to exploit race in the election, but Howard refused (unlike his leader, William Hague). Instead, Folkestone Conservatives published an advertisement asking voters, 'What matters most to you? Bogus asylum seekers?' When challenged, Howard strongly defended the ad: 'The government has completely failed to deal with this problem and it's an entirely legitimate matter of public debate,' he said. 'Very large numbers are being picked up on the Eurotunnel terminal which is in my constituency.'[44] At the time there were about 600 asylum seekers in Folkestone, though the problem was less serious than it had been. 'We have to have a proper system of immigration control on this small and crowded island,' Howard insisted.[45] Not for the first time, most critics were too polite to raise the contradiction between his attitude to modern would-be immigrants and the way his own parents and grandparents had left eastern Europe for Britain.

Howard achieved a satisfying election result. While the Conservatives gained only one seat nationally, Folkestone saw a small swing from the Lib Dems to the Tories, and Howard's overall vote rose slightly despite the significantly lower turnout. Howard could feel more comfortable in Folkestone and Hythe than at any time in the past two decades.

Following his failure in the general election, William Hague stepped down immediately. Under the complex new voting system for leadership elections, MPs would now take part in a series of ballots to whittle down the candidates until only two remained. Then a vote of all Conservative Party members would decide between the final pair. This time Howard stayed out of the contest. The five contenders who went into the first ballot on 10 July were Michael Portillo, Kenneth Clarke, Michael Ancram, David Davis and Iain Duncan Smith; Michael Howard never revealed for whom he voted. Portillo, now back in the Commons, was the initial front runner, but he ran out of momentum. After a second ballot a week later it was Duncan Smith who emerged – just one vote ahead of Portillo – as Ken Clarke's challenger in the final run-off among party members. The success of Duncan Smith – known as IDS – was a measure of the depth of the Conservatives' problems. He'd been an MP for only nine years, and he'd never served as a minister. But for Howard, like many in the party, Iain Duncan Smith had one essential quality, which outweighed all of Ken Clarke's experience, intelligence and popular appeal. Duncan Smith was a Euro-sceptic, who had made his name as a Maastricht rebel under Major.

The line-up for the membership ballot exposed the personal and ideological divide within the post-Thatcher party. Margaret Thatcher endorsed Duncan Smith, while John Major reminded party members that IDS had worked tirelessly to undermine his government. Michael Howard now felt obliged to intervene, and wrote an article for the *Sunday Telegraph* explaining why he couldn't support Clarke and was instead backing IDS. He praised Clarke's ministerial record, and conceded that he was 'exceptionally likeable'. The problem, of course, was Europe. '[Ken] has told us that his views on Europe are "indistinguishable from Tony Blair's". But most Conservatives do not share these views,' Howard wrote. 'More stories on Tory splits would dominate the headlines in the run-up to the election,' he warned. Like Clarke, Duncan Smith had 'honesty and integrity', he said, but also 'clear vision, fresh views and a readiness to find imaginative new policies'.[46] (Vision, of course, was an attribute he'd praised in Jeffrey Archer two years before.)

Iain Duncan Smith comfortably beat Ken Clarke, by 155,933 votes to 100,864, and then suddenly announced Howard's appointment as his Shadow Chancellor. Howard, explained the Duncan Smith camp, was 'a major hitter who will give Gordon Brown a run for his money'.[47] The scale of his task was emphasised by the fact that Howard was the fifth person to try his luck against Brown in five years (following Clarke, briefly, then Peter Lilley, Francis Maude and Michael Portillo). Just four years after the Tories left office, he was now the only member of Duncan Smith's new front-bench team to have served in Cabinet.

Howard's return was met with surprise. He was now sixty, and it had been widely assumed – and even by himself – that his front-bench career was over. Howard would later claim that he'd come back out of concern for the state of the health service, particularly in his constituency. This concern was also personal. He had been shocked by the death in 2001 of Sandra's mother, Rosie Paul, at the age of eighty-nine, from an infection – possibly MRSA – which she'd picked up while being treated in a hospital in Surrey, part of a growing problem in the NHS.

Howard and his opposite number, Gordon Brown, were both serious political power-brokers. The two sons of clerics had been elected to Parliament together in 1983, and were quickly identified as the front runners of their generation, before being overtaken by younger, more telegenic rivals. They were powerful debaters, and boasted phenomenal work rates, yet each insisted on total control, and was easily angered when people failed to meet his exacting demands. In 1997 Gordon Brown had revolutionised the Treasury in much the way as Michael Howard had transformed the Home Office four years before, removing staff who obstructed his plans, and upsetting traditional civil servants with his autocratic insistence that politics, power and public relations were all-important. Brown, like Howard, was an admirer of Robert Caro's epic biography of Lyndon Johnson, the ultimate study in the exercise of power. Indeed, both preferred America to Europe. Yet Brown, like Howard, also had the political handicap of appearing cold and forbidding to the public, failing to convey the warmer and more personable side which is familiar to friends.

In the early 1990s the two up-and-coming front-benchers had met on a train from Swansea to London. As they chatted, Howard had presented Brown with a close analysis of where he thought Neil Kinnock's party was going wrong. Labour needed to overcome the anxiety of middle-class people on issues such as tax and education, Howard said, rather than concentrating on a socialist message. Brown had been coming to the same view, of course. Even so, Howard later wondered whether his advice contributed to Labour making itself electable again.[48]

Although Howard had wanted to succeed Norman Lamont as Chancellor back in 1993, his ambition had not arisen from any special knowledge of economics. He's 'nervous about figures' says a former adviser, while Lamont himself describes Howard as 'not naturally a financial person'.[49] He would have been a political Chancellor, not a technical wizard like Nigel Lawson. Between 1997 and 2001 there had been little scope for political attacks on the 'Iron Chancellor' Gordon Brown, since he stuck rigidly to Ken Clarke's spending plans and regarded 'prudence' as his guardian angel. After 2001, however, Brown began to loosen these self-imposed chains. The government's preference for raising indirect taxes, rather than increasing income tax,

provided some ammunition, and Howard was always ready to highlight any gap between Brown's forecasts and the performance of the
economy. The government, he jeered, was obsessed with targets.
Why, then, did Brown not punish the Treasury for being so far out
with its predictions and failing to cut its own running costs?

The best way to get under Brown's skin was to mock the well-
documented tensions between him and his neighbour in 10 Downing
Street. In one of their first exchanges, Howard lived up to his billing
as a political heavyweight. He began by congratulating Brown:

> We welcome many of his announcements. I am sure that these
> warm words will come as no surprise to him. Praise from his polit-
> ical enemies is nothing new to him. After all, only last week, the
> Prime Minister let it be known that the Chancellor was probably
> the best Chancellor in the world. To the Prime Minister, he is the
> Carlsberg Chancellor. True to form, the Chancellor returned the
> compliment, saying that the Prime Minister was the best friend that
> he had had in politics. The Prime Minister knows that with this
> Chancellor one has to read the small print: the Chancellor used the
> past tense. It seems to me that his phrase has something of
> 'Goodnight' about it.[50]

Tory MPs were bound to contrast such well-crafted sallies with the
blustering performances of their new party leader, Iain Duncan Smith.

The Chancellor's best counter-attack was to quote back to Howard
remarks he had made in 1997 saying that his party's 'aim should be to
reduce the proportion of national output taken by the state towards 35
per cent'.[51] When Howard took up his new portfolio some Tories had
been worried about these Thatcherite predilections. Howard would
'put spending cuts before peoples' needs and services', complained a
member of the party's dwindling 'One Nation' tendency.[52] This was
Howard's biggest tactical problem, since he understood that the electorate distrusted Tory intentions towards public services such as the
NHS. But even while attempting to reassure voters, he told the party
faithful that 'Other things being equal, we would like lower taxes.'[53] It

looked as if he was promising everyone the thing they wanted to hear. Nevertheless, his relative success as Shadow Chancellor – certainly in contrast to his four Tory predecessors – was shown by the fact that in February 2003 the Tories felt confident enough to call their first Commons debate on the economy since they had lost office.

Yet the Conservatives were as far from returning to office as ever. When asked by the *Guardian* whether he thought his party could form a government after the next election, Howard replied haltingly, 'I think it, I think it – could be.'[54] In November 2001 Howard was dismissive of a suggestion that he might run for the leadership again. 'No, the torch has been passed to another generation,' he told Petronella Wyatt, echoing John F. Kennedy's famous inaugural address – though one can't imagine he saw IDS as a latter-day JFK.[55] Indeed the torch looked like being extinguished altogether if it remained in Duncan Smith's hands. A year later, by the autumn of 2002, Tory MPs were increasingly alarmed by this possibility; and Michael Howard played a significant part in the new crisis.

When it was first drafted, the Adoption and Children Bill looked unlikely to cause problems for the Tories, but it was amended in committee to allow adoption by unmarried couples. This raised the possibility that children might be adopted by gay partners. For the government, the amended bill was an issue of 'conscience', and there was no question of applying the party whip. Many Tories felt differently, and after heated discussions in the Shadow Cabinet a three-line whip was announced instructing Conservative MPs to vote against the amended bill at its second reading in May 2002. Howard, David Davis and Liam Fox were reported to be the main backers of the move. However, faced by furious opposition from a minority of MPs, Howard's ally David Maclean announced in his new role as Chief Whip that, despite the three-line whip, the leadership would not crack down on anyone who didn't bother to vote. The result was a farce: four Tories openly defied the whip, and several Shadow Cabinet members deliberately abstained. It made the party leadership look foolish, for the purpose of the whip system is to enforce discipline, especially on important or contentious matters.

The Lords amended the bill and sent it back to the Commons, which was due to consider it on 4 November 2002. In the meantime, Duncan Smith had told the Conservative conference not to under-estimate the determination of 'a quiet man'. The three-line whip was imposed once again, and the number of outright rebels now doubled, to eight. One of them, the Portillo supporter John Bercow, resigned from the Shadow Cabinet to speak in favour of the bill. The numbers were less important than the people involved: Portillo voted in favour, too, along with Ken Clarke, David Curry, Julie Kirkbride, and Howard's allies Francis Maude and Andrew Lansley. The three-line whip had made the leadership look both intolerant and incompetent.

Michael Howard himself was unable to vote this time, having flown to Singapore for a long-arranged speaking engagement. It was an opportune absence, for rumours had already started that Howard would be an ideal alternative to lead the party to the next election. At the end of 2002 it was reported that he was 'positioning himself in the expectation that there is going to be a vacancy' when a row between Howard and IDS erupted publicly after the Tory leader attempted to reassert his authority by telling the Sunday Times that tax cuts were back on the Conservative agenda.[56] Howard, in contrast, had been stressing that improvements in public services should take priority over cutting tax, and 'was not amused by IDS trampling on his turf', says Duncan Smith's press officer, Nick Wood.[57] Howard also clashed several times with Oliver Letwin, who, as Shadow Home Secretary, was taking a markedly more liberal approach to crime and asylum. Howard was par-ticularly upset when Letwin publicly suggested that the Major government had been too tough on asylum. Understandably, Howard took this as a personal attack on his record as Home Secretary.

Michael Howard's relations with Iain Duncan Smith were polite but never easy. 'IDS was scared of Michael's intellect,' says one of Duncan Smith's former aides, 'so he would never enter into discus-sions with Michael. He wouldn't draw him in. So they didn't have a particularly close relationship.' Although Howard was totally loyal in public, in private he could not hide his disdain for IDS's personal ini-tiative to assist the needy in society, entitled 'Helping the Vulnerable'.

When the Tory leader demanded that each of his front-bench teams come up with some example to take the theme forward, Howard, who had been an adviser to Colin Moynihan's gas exploration firm Consort Resources, suggested they highlight the problems of off-shore oil and gas workers who would suffer from Labour's stringent tax regime. Colleagues gently pointed out that workers in the North Sea were not really the kind of 'vulnerable' people whom IDS had in mind. No, it was an excellent example, Howard insisted. If people were subject to a draconian tax grab, then they were vulnerable. Workers would lose their jobs, and there would be less investment in the continental shelf. 'He was able to adjust a party message he didn't really believe in anyway,' says a colleague. 'It was preposterous. It undermined Helping the Vulnerable. Workers in the continental shelf don't fall into that category – they're not single mums or people on the street.' Nor did Howard impress IDS or the modernisers when he publicly asserted that the 'vulnerable' included constituents of his in Folkestone who were suffering from asylum seekers.

Michael Howard's great achievement under IDS was to show that Gordon Brown could be bettered in debate. In 2003 he won the *Spectator*'s Parliamentarian of the Year award for his Commons performances as Shadow Chancellor (having won its 'debater' award in 1995). One of his best efforts came in response to the Chancellor's pre-budget statement in November 2002, when Brown announced that that year's deficit would be £9 billion worse than previously forecast. This was 'a moment of humiliation' for Brown, said Howard, scoffing at the 'downgraded forecasts of a downgraded Chancellor'.[58] Howard's speech was described by the *Guardian* columnist Simon Hoggart as the 'biggest spanking' Brown had endured 'since becoming Chancellor'.[59]

He was on equally good form the following June, when the Chancellor announced that Britain had not yet passed his five tests for entering the euro. Brown's statement, said Howard, was

a result of the frantic efforts by the Chancellor and the Prime Minister to cover up their differences. After all, that is why the five tests were thought up in the first place. We all know that they were written on the back of an envelope in the back of a taxi to fix the damage done by the Chancellor's spin doctor in the back of the Red Lion pub. It was a four-pint briefing, which led to a five-point plan that has just given us a six-year runaround.[60]

In March 2003 Tom Baldwin of *The Times* had renewed speculation that Howard might soon become leader. In response, the Shadow Chancellor was more emphatic than ever: 'I stood for the Tory leadership once. I did not find it an agreeable experience. And I have no desire to repeat it.'[61] 'It would be madness to change leadership again,' he said later.[62] 'I've said many times I'm not going to run for the leadership of the Conservative Party,' he told David Frost.[63]

By this time attention was focused on Iraq, where British troops had joined the Americans in launching a war to topple Saddam Hussein. Like Duncan Smith, Howard was an enthusiastic supporter of the action, and in March 2002 he had been one of sixty-five Tory MPs to sign a motion put down by Michael Ancram, congratulating Blair on his resolute backing of President Bush.[64]

Howard's only criticism of the war was that it had been so long delayed; as in the case of Kosovo, the Blair government had for too long relied on threats without backing them up with action. This delay, Howard felt, had given Saddam Hussein the chance to build up his weapons of mass destruction (WMDs). When the successful invasion failed to uncover any WMDs, Howard quickly turned this to political advantage. If ministers had engaged in deception in order to gain public support, he argued, it would go to the heart of the government's integrity.

This was a tenable position, but only because Howard had thought that the war had been necessary whether or not Saddam possessed WMDs. At the same time he was beginning to think that the government had misled people to justify the conflict. He had made his doubts public before the suicide of the weapons inspector Dr David Kelly, which turned the government's existing difficulties into a full-scale crisis.

Even before normal politics was suspended by the Iraq War, it was clear that the Conservatives were heading for a third disaster if they fought the next election under Iain Duncan Smith. Tory MPs began to fear that they might do even worse than last time, which would entail more of them – perhaps even Howard himself – losing their seats. Interviewed on *Breakfast with Frost* in August 2003, Howard admitted that the party's modest lead in polls wasn't nearly adequate if they were to mount a serious challenge. 'We need to be further ahead, there's no doubt about that. Our present lead isn't anything like enough,' he admitted. 'We've got more work to do.'[65]

But if he was beginning to think that a change of leader might not be such madness after all, he gave no sign of it.

'He genuinely didn't want to succeed Iain Duncan Smith,' Norman Lamont insists. 'Once or twice I said to him, "I don't think IDS will survive." He would just say: "I don't want anything to do with it."'[66]

19

THE COUP

I will lead this party from its centre . . . We will offer a new kind
of politics.

MICHAEL HOWARD, OCTOBER 2003[1]

Iain Duncan Smith spoke in an atmosphere of near-hysteria. His
address to the 2003 Conservative conference in Blackpool was punc-
tuated by no fewer than seventeen standing ovations; if they were
instigated by party staff, they also reflected IDS's continuing support
from right-wing activists in the hall who remained loyal to a leader
they themselves had chosen. During the conference the year before
IDS had been ridiculed for describing himself as the 'quiet man'.
Now the Conservative leader tried to face down his critics by sig-
nalling a new tough image – apparently inspired by Arnold
Schwarzenegger's election as Governor of California three days before.
'The Quiet Man is here to stay, and he is turning up the volume,' he
declared.[2] Many MPs were horrified by his performance, and concluded that instead it was time to press the 'off' switch.

Throughout 2003 the Conservatives had made little impact in the
opinion polls. Although they had been level-pegging with Labour for
most of the summer, the conventional wisdom is that halfway through
a parliament an Opposition needs a strong lead in the polls if it is to
have any chance of winning the next election. What's more,

psephologists calculated that, because of the way votes were now distributed, the Tories would need to be at least 7 per cent ahead of Labour at the next election to win an outright majority of MPs. In September, three weeks before the party conference, a by-election in the north-west London constituency of Brent East had dramatically illustrated the scale of the party's problems. Brent East was not natural Conservative territory, but back in 1987 the party had come within 1,700 votes of winning the seat, and in 2001 it had still been a comfortable second ahead of the Liberal Democrats. But in 2003 the Lib Dems won the by-election with an extraordinary swing of 29 per cent – one of the biggest in modern times – while the Tory vote fell to 16 per cent, less than half of Labour's total. Iain Duncan Smith's press officer later admitted that the party had run 'a spectacularly incompetent campaign'.[3] The result raised new fears in the minds of the dozens of Tory MPs who could be challenged by the Lib Dems – including Michael Howard in Folkestone.

Iain Duncan Smith and the Conservatives were then dogged by what became known as 'Betsygate', in which this author played a small part. With hindsight, Betsygate was a clear sign that IDS was losing control of his party. In May 2003, as I subsequently explained to a parliamentary inquiry, I had been approached by a senior Conservative who told me that for the first year or more of his leadership Iain Duncan Smith had been paying his wife, Betsy, a salary from his parliamentary staffing allowance. However, there was no evidence, my contact alleged, that Betsy did any work for this. It was a serious allegation, since MPs' allowances are public money, and there were already reasons to believe that IDS could be less than scrupulously honest. The previous December I had made a film for the BBC's *Newsnight* which drew attention to questionable aspects of his CV, including his claim to have attended the University of Perugia when in fact he had merely spent a few months in the Italian city at an upmarket language school called the Università per Stranieri (the University for Foreigners) and certainly didn't get a degree there. I decided to explore the allegations about Betsy for *Newsnight*, and, as I later told the Parliamentary Commissioner for Standards, Sir Philip

Mawer, I found three other senior Conservatives who confirmed the original claim that she had done little or no work for her salary. The BBC was slow to address the story, largely because it was overwhelmed by the Andrew Gilligan affair and the Hutton inquiry, but by the time of the Conservative conference in October it was widely known that *Newsnight* might broadcast a damaging investigation. IDS threatened legal action, and the BBC prevaricated, concerned that there wasn't yet enough evidence to prove the allegations conclusively. In mid-October I concluded that the BBC would never run the story, but personally felt that the charges were sufficiently serious that I should present them to the Parliamentary Commissioner so he could resolve the matter. By then the details had become public, and it emerged that Vanessa Gearson, the former head of IDS's office, had refused to give evidence on his behalf. Gearson later testified against Duncan Smith to the standards' commissioner. She and Mark MacGregor, who had been chief executive of the Conservative Party under IDS, each told Mawer that they had seen no evidence of Betsy doing parliamentary work for her husband. Both witnesses should have known if she had. Nevertheless, in March 2004 Mawer dismissed most of the allegations, and decided that IDS's wife had done sufficient work to justify her salary.

But during October 2003, amid Betsygate and with disquiet among backbenchers, the Conservative Party suffered a frenzy of intrigue. Iain Duncan Smith's leadership hung by a thread. Under the new leadership rules, however, he could be deposed only if 15 per cent of the parliamentary party – twenty-five MPs – wrote to the chairman of the 1922 Committee – Howard's former campaign manager Sir Michael Spicer – asking for a vote of confidence, and if that vote then went against him.

If Duncan Smith was forced to step down, Michael Howard was widely expected to stand for the vacant position. Yet it was by no means certain that Howard would win. And Howard was sufficiently scarred by his experience of coming last in the 1997 poll not to want to run unless he thought he had an extremely strong chance of winning. Among possible rivals, Michael Portillo had grown tired of politics and was unlikely to stand, but others had their virtues. Michael Ancram might offer a safe, if uninspiring, pair of hands. Tim Yeo, the shadow industry spokesman, might push forward a modernising agenda, while David Davis would send the party in the opposite direction. Oliver Letwin was intelligent and refreshingly honest, if relatively untried. Ken Clarke, the runner-up in both 1997 and 2001, might run again. And Howard's chances were also vulnerable to a new onslaught from Ann Widdecombe, or the emergence, as in 1997, of other skeletons from his past. On top of all these uncertainties, the leadership election system, in which MPs narrowed the selection but party members made the final decision from the two strongest contenders, made the whole process extremely unpredictable, as IDS had demonstrated in 2001, when he had won with the votes of less than a third of the parliamentary party. In short, it was a game for people with strong nerves and a shrewd understanding of the party mood.

By the weekend of 25–26 October, it was clear that a change of leadership was likely, whether or not Howard was going to run. Several top Conservative donors, most notably the spread-betting millionaire Stuart Wheeler, said they would refuse the party further funds while Duncan Smith remained in place. Howard promptly wrote an article for the *Sunday Telegraph*, arguing in defence of IDS that he had 'earned the right to lead our campaign for victory at the next election'. The Conservatives, he claimed, were 'in the process of setting out the most exciting policy programme seen from any opposition party in more than two decades'. The 'first phase of Iain's leadership' had been occupied with the development of these policies, he said. Now Duncan Smith had the perfect platform to move on to phase two, selling the ideas to the electorate.[4]

Despite this public display of loyalty, Howard received several calls over that weekend from people urging him to stand when – not if – the vacancy arose. But when he returned to Westminster, on Monday 27 October, he was still not totally committed to the idea. The former party chairman Sir Brian Mawhinney sounded Howard out in the Churchill Room at the Commons. Mawhinney was reasonably representative of the views of what could still be called the party faithful at Westminster, and – perhaps significantly – had not been a Howard supporter in the past. Howard told Mawhinney that he was still not sure about standing, but nevertheless later that day he asked his former PPS Liam Fox to be his campaign manager should the need arise.

If Michael Howard was careful never to do anything which might be construed as undermining IDS, or to be seen campaigning for the leader's job, his supporters were undoubtedly working on his behalf. They did not discuss their actions with him, but then they didn't need to. And perhaps the most influential role in the events of 2003 was that played by the Conservative Chief Whip, David Maclean.

In the 2001 contest – when Howard didn't stand – Maclean had initially backed David Davis, before switching to Iain Duncan Smith on the second ballot, whereafter he played a leading part in securing IDS's election. His reward was the post of Chief Whip, a job which is almost as important in opposition as in government. David Maclean is immediately identifiable in political circles, since he walks with the aid of a shepherd's crook to cope with the multiple sclerosis from which he suffers. He requires a cocktail of drugs to keep going, and sometimes loses all feeling below the waist. Maclean loves the intrigue of politics, and is a political fixer of the type caricatured by the fictional Francis Urquhart, the sinister Chief Whip in *House of Cards* and other thrillers by the former Conservative deputy chairman Michael Dobbs. Having served two and a half years as a government whip under Margaret Thatcher, Maclean was well qualified. Under IDS he quickly earned a reputation as a good tactician and as one of the best chief whips in Conservative history.

Yet Maclean is modest, especially for a politician: he avoids the limelight, rarely does media interviews, and his entry in *Who's Who* occupies less than five lines. He has never been ambitious, and once declined a Cabinet post – as Agriculture Minister – from John Major because he preferred to remain at the Home Office with Michael Howard. Staying there also made it easier to pursue his affair with the civil servant Jenny Ungless. While their relationship ended in 2000, after Maclean refused to leave his wife, Jay, he and Ungless remained close friends and he helped her secure the post of chief of staff in Iain Duncan Smith's office in 2001.

But after just ten months in the job, in July 2002, Jenny Ungless resigned in despair at the disorganised way in which Duncan Smith operated. By then Maclean had realised his terrible mistake in promoting IDS for the leadership. Apart from his poor performances in the Commons, and the adverse reports the Tory whips were getting from MPs, Duncan Smith's shortcomings as a party leader could be observed at first hand in Shadow Cabinet meetings. Ungless told Maclean of the chaos within Duncan Smith's high command. 'I really just got to the point where I couldn't take it any more,' she revealed when she later gave evidence to the Betsygate inquiry. 'The office was chaotic despite my best efforts . . . I think Iain suffered a bit from the fact that he had never been in government . . . so he had never become accustomed to things like the discipline of clearing boxes at night which . . . is critical to allowing things to work.'[5] (Ungless also told Sir Philip Mawer's inquiry that she 'did not see any work from Betsy [Duncan-Smith] at all but I have to qualify that by saying I may not have been in the position to see it.' IDS himself told Mawer that Betsy worked from their Buckinghamshire home and so Ungless had 'no professional reasons to contact or deal with her and would have seen little or no sign of her work'.[6])

The loyalties of chief whips are inevitably divided. On the one hand they have a commitment to their leader, and yet they are also regarded as custodians of the health of the wider party. When a party is under pressure, chief whips have to balance these competing claims. Things had got so bad, however, that Maclean no longer felt bound by loyalty to IDS. He decided he had a moral duty to resign, but was persuaded by friends that his higher obligation was to help resolve the party's troubles. He would therefore use his position to remedy the huge error that he and the party had made in electing Duncan Smith. 'He had decided enough was enough,' says a friend, who explains that from then on Maclean was driven by 'guilt that he supported and ran his campaign in the first place'.

But Maclean had also grown disillusioned with the man he had originally backed for leader in 2001 – David Davis – and in the summer of 2002 he played a leading role as Chief Whip in Duncan Smith's decision to sack Davis because of his performance as party chairman. Maclean now decided the party would be better off led by Michael Howard, his former ministerial colleague, friend and one-time business partner, whom he had supported in the 1997 leadership contest. 'Maclean saw one of his tasks as being regime change,' says a former whip. 'I think he decided the candidate most likely to rally round the parliamentary party and persuade other candidates not to stand, and most acceptable to local associations, was Michael Howard.' One of Maclean's friends recalls him later confessing, 'There's stuff that can only come out when I'm not here – stuff that will blow the minds of people.'

When MPs returned to Westminster in October 2003 it was certainly clear that some of David Maclean's team of whips were doing little either to support the leader or to prevent letters going to Michael Spicer calling for a confidence vote. Some seemed to encourage a change at the top. 'Towards the end of the period,' says one of IDS's biggest Westminster critics, 'somebody in the Whips' Office said to me, "Listen, you guys, for Christ's sake, get on with it. If you're going to do it, get on with it." And so I think they'd realised this was unsustainable. The lurch of discontent was not containable. After a couple of weeks of attrition their collective Whips' Office view was "Let's have it," almost "Let's get it over with."'

One particular whip seemed actively to be urging MPs to write to Spicer, by enquiring if they had done so yet. It was time to bring matters to a head, he suggested. 'There is no way that he was doing that without Maclean's knowledge,' says one dissident whom the whip approached. 'He asked me whether I'd done that. It was a roll-call, and he was encouraging people to write.' In his recent history of parliamentary whipping, Margaret Thatcher's former Chief Whip Tim Renton implies that Maclean's deputy, Patrick McLoughlin, stirred up dissent by going round asking MPs with small majorities about their chances at the next election: 'When he got the answer that they could not possibly hold their seats with Duncan Smith as their leader, his typical reply was, "May I tell that to the Chief Whip?"[7]

David Maclean had to act carefully. Whatever his personal views, loyalty lies at the heart of the party system, and the Chief Whip couldn't be seen to encourage dissent in any way, or do anything which might suggest disloyalty. The situation required the utmost dexterity. In normal circumstances the leader would have been able to rely on the Chief Whip and his team to discourage would-be rebels. After IDS's speech to the Blackpool conference, Maclean had taken the rare – perhaps unprecedented – step of going on television to tell potential rebels to put up or shut up. He also announced that the following week he would be summoning suspected plotters to meet him privately, while reminding them that the Whips' Office drew up annual reports and career assessments on all members of the parliamentary party. 'I will be asking if they want to be hard-working MPs who get behind the leader or not. Because if they don't they should go and work in industry,' he warned.[8] Privately, though, he was rather less combative, if still circumspect. According to one MP who met Maclean to discuss his concerns about IDS, 'He wasn't standing at the bottom of the Iain Duncan Smith statue and saluting. He was listening to what I said. I thought it was going to be much nastier. He wasn't arguing, "This guy, he's wonderful. You've got it completely wrong." But he wasn't encouraging me to make more difficulties either.'

And even Maclean's television performance might have been deceptive. For, though he appeared to be enforcing party discipline, IDS's critics took a different message from it. 'Nothing could have been more calculated to provoke us into action,' says one of IDS's leading opponents. A year later this author reminded Maclean of his unusual TV intervention of the year before. 'It worked, didn't it?' he replied.

As Iain Duncan Smith's position became ever weaker, some of Michael Howard's closest advisers, among them Rachel Whetstone, Liam Fox and the Shadow Home Secretary, Oliver Letwin, tried to discuss with him whether he would consider the leadership. 'He wouldn't let us do anything,' says one of his backers. 'He would say, "I don't want to discuss this. I want Iain to carry on."' No one could accuse Michael Howard of being disloyal. Even on Wednesday 22 October, as David Maclean told IDS that his support was ebbing away and he should step down, Howard was actually at the forefront in urging the Tory leader to keep up the fight. Howard's supporters realised they would instead have to plan for the eventuality themselves.

After IDS rejected David Maclean's advice, party discipline fell apart. 'Towards the end,' says one whip, Robert Syms, the Whips' Office 'almost shut down'. Syms had decided it was time for IDS to go, and made his feelings plain to MPs who approached him. 'My advice to them was, "Do what you think is best for the party." Over that weekend there was a strong feeling that we had to get out of a hole and the only way that we could do that was to get a ballot, and even if the ballot had supported Iain that would have closed the situation down, at least for a while.'[9]

Howard understood that – as with Michael Heseltine and the fall of Margaret Thatcher – 'he who wields the dagger never wears the crown': the senior party figure who topples the leader rarely gets to win the succession. This was politics as poker. But Howard's attitude may also have reflected an underlying ambivalence about whether he now wanted the opportunity that seemed to be presenting itself.

For most of the 1990s Michael Howard had been desperately keen to become Conservative leader; now, when it seemed a real possibility, he appeared to have lost all enthusiasm for the job. He was worried about the possibility of a rerun of his disastrous leadership bid of 1997, this time with a twist: any contest could drag on for months, as the need to ballot party members under the rules that William Hague had introduced made the process more protracted than when the choice was limited to MPs, as it had been six years before. Howard 'also wondered if the Conservative Party was still governable', says a close political friend who discussed the matter with him. At the same time, like David Maclean, he was anxious about who might become leader if he decided not to stand. In particular, he was worried about David Davis. Davis had been a leading member of Howard's campaign team in 1997, but over the past twelve months, according to a former ministerial colleague, Howard had grown 'disgusted' with Davis and felt he had 'behaved in a dishonourable way'. Since his sacking as party chairman in 2002, Davis had made no secret of his contempt for IDS, and clearly intended to succeed him. Howard feared that if he didn't try to pick up the crown then Davis would almost certainly do so.

Then, in the final days of October, the dam burst. Things moved so quickly that Michael Howard barely had time to think.

On the morning of Tuesday 28 October, Francis Maude announced on the *Today* programme that he had written to Michael Spicer to ask for a confidence motion. Maude was a former Shadow Chancellor and had played a leading role in Howard's 1997 campaign, but was now on the backbenches. Maude's letter to Spicer was more symbolic than significant, for it seems that the magic total of those calling for a vote had already been reached by the time it arrived. Around 10.15 that morning, the chairman of the 1922 Committee told IDS that the fateful figure had been passed. By then the tally was already at least twenty-nine letters – and some reports put the subsequent total closer to forty. At 2.15 p.m. the leader appeared outside Conservative Central Office in Smith Square, flanked by Michael Howard and other senior colleagues, to announce that MPs would vote on his future the following day.

Once the vote was triggered, it was clear both that Iain Duncan Smith was doomed and that Michael Howard had become the overwhelming favourite to succeed him. There was still a big question mark over Ann Widdecombe, and whether her enduring hostility towards Howard might prompt further attacks. But Widdecombe quickly decided that, while she didn't regret what she had done six years before, once was enough. 'I certainly *did* stand by what I had said,' she insists, 'and wasn't going to retract my remarks, but didn't intend to repeat them.'[10]

Ann Widdecombe had yet to announce her position in public, despite frequent media requests. She decided to talk to Howard directly, rather than have him hear a garbled version of her position from a third party such as a journalist. When she phoned him, 'You could almost hear the relief at the end of the line,' she said later.[11] He suggested they meet in his room at the Commons on the Tuesday evening, and Widdecombe then restated her position. Howard was charming and courteous. 'He said he was very grateful, and asked if I wanted to support his campaign,' says Widdecombe. 'I said I didn't, as I had made the mistake before, in 2001, of pledging myself to Michael Ancram before I knew Ken Clarke was going to stand.'[12] She urged Howard, if he became leader, to sort out the infighting within Central Office, and to reform the leadership rules to avoid a repeat of the party's existing troubles. It was the first time they had met privately since 1997.

More important than Ann Widdecombe was David Davis. An obvious candidate in any leadership election, Davis had spent the previous weekend mulling over the likely outcome, drawing up a 'logic tree' of the various scenarios that might unfold. He also consulted his closest supporters by phone. They were confident of a strong showing if he reached the final ballot of party members, since Davis had visited numerous constituencies during his year-long stint as party chairman. However, he might not survive that far, as the 2001 poll of Tory MPs had seen him come joint bottom out of five names on the first ballot, with only twenty-one votes – barely one in eight of the parliamentary party. And it seemed unlikely that Davis would be allowed a straight run against Howard. Tim Yeo had been discussing tactics with supporters for several weeks, and had decided that, if Davis stood, he would run too – not in any expectation of winning, but simply to give the party a wider choice than just two right-wingers.

Some MPs thought Davis was ineffective and were not impressed with his record as party chairman or by his obvious disloyalty to IDS. Indeed, it was possible that, if Davis stood, other candidates might enter the fray just to scupper his chances of qualifying for the final ballot. And even if Davis did reach the stage of the membership vote, he still might not beat Howard. On the Wednesday morning, as MPs began voting in the confidence ballot on IDS's leadership, Davis discussed the situation briefly with Howard in a quiet moment before the regular Shadow Cabinet strategy meeting. According to an ally, Howard 'was clear he was not going to offer any deal; no jobs, no promises'.[13] Howard had discussed the question of deals with his advisers. MPs on his team tended to favour the idea as a way of keeping Davis, and perhaps also Tim Yeo, out of the race. Others felt such pacts were undignified and would undermine his position if he were to become leader. Howard was by far the most senior member of the Shadow Cabinet; if Tories wanted him to rescue the party, it would have to be on his terms, without being bound by promises of jobs or other conditions.

Perhaps late in the day, Michael Howard started to realise that his reputation among colleagues had been transformed by his regular Commons successes against Gordon Brown. Instead of being the authoritarian Home Secretary, the 'control freak' who operated better away from the light, after the failures of William Hague and latterly IDS Howard had come to be seen by the Conservative parliamentary party as a one-man 'dream ticket'. Paradoxically, his reputation had been improved by the performance of the two Labour Home Secretaries who had succeeded him. Both Jack Straw and David Blunkett had demonstrated that they could be every bit as authoritarian as Howard, and willing to curtail civil liberties in the fight against crime (a picture reinforced in 2004 when Stephen Pollard's biography showed Blunkett to be a great admirer of Howard's record at the Home Office).[14]

Early on the Wednesday evening, forty-five minutes before the result of the confidence vote was announced, David Davis told Howard that he would not stand. 'The future of the party matters more than the future of an individual,' he was reported as saying.[15] His decision caused consternation among Davis loyalists such as Greg Knight, Derek Conway and particularly Eric Forth, the shadow leader of the Commons. Indeed, Forth was so angry that for a time it seemed that he might stand instead. Davis had decided to act the statesman, perhaps realising that his support among MPs was weak, in the hope that the party would be grateful for not prolonging its agony. Francis Maude had warned Davis that if he won with minority support from MPs, but with a majority of votes of constituency activists – the only way Davis probably *could* win – he would find himself isolated as leader. It would be another IDS situation, only worse. 'I thought through all the options,' Davis later said, 'and they were all awful because a contest would be divisive. It suddenly occurred to me that I was probably the only person that could prevent that from happening.'[16]

Both Michael Howard and David Davis claimed to have supported IDS in the confidence ballot, but it made no difference. Duncan Smith lost by 90 votes to 75. Neither Howard nor Davis, nor many of IDS's other supporters, can have voted for him out of enthusiasm either for his record as leader or for his future prospects.

Howard stood alongside him as Iain Duncan Smith delivered a dignified farewell speech outside Central Office. Yet behind the scene Howard's campaign team was already formed. His campaign manager, Liam Fox, had recruited a group of 'shadow' whips, led by the Hertfordshire MP Oliver Heald, who were ready to canvass MPs. Tim Collins and David Cameron, now both MPs, were to the fore, while another of Howard's former special advisers, Rachel Whetstone, had immediately resigned her job with Portland PR (a company owned by Tony Blair's former deputy press secretary Tim Allan) to work full-time for him. The campaign was also joined by Will Harris, head of marketing for BT's mobile-phone system O_2. They started work openly as soon as the vote against IDS was announced, though it was quickly clear that there was little for them to do. Within minutes of Michael Spicer declaring the result in Committee Room 14 of the Commons, David Davis appeared at the St Stephen's entrance to announce formally, as he had already told Howard, that he would not be a contender and would back the Shadow Chancellor. Now it was Howard's turn, six years on, to have the momentum in a leadership bid. This time other candidates would be on the back foot, and the complexity of the election rules, which Howard had seen as a barrier to his leadership prospects in 2001, now worked in his favour. Any candidate who opposed Howard risked being blamed for preventing a quick succession, and for landing the party with an unnecessary contest which could deepen the Tories' woes. On hearing that Davis had withdrawn, Tim Yeo phoned Howard to say that he, too, would not be standing.

Later that evening Liam Fox, Oliver Letwin and Stephen Dorrell – a deliberate combination of right-winger, moderniser and left-winger – issued a joint statement in support of Howard, while the man himself was sufficiently relaxed about developments to spend much of the evening watching Liverpool beat Blackburn 4–3 in the League Cup on television. Letwin, Fox and Oliver Heald subsequently arrived at his house in Pimlico to draft a public declaration for the next day.

There had been some debate among Howard's supporters about whether formally to declare his candidacy at once or, out of respect for IDS, to wait until the following Monday. They had decided to go straight away, and the morning after IDS's defeat Rachel Whetstone hunted for a venue for the official launch. She and Will Harris visited the Institution of Civil Engineers building next to the Treasury, but felt it had bad 'vibes'. It had been the venue for John Smith's disastrous shadow budget in 1992, and was also where Howard had launched his unfortunate campaign in 1997. Instead they alighted on the new Saatchi Gallery in the former County Hall building on the other side of Westminster Bridge. The name recalled the Saatchi brothers' role in Thatcher's 1979 election triumph, while the location conveyed a much-needed air of modernity. But first Whetstone had to cover up a couple of exhibits which were obvious fuel for mischievous journalists: one was a collection of dead rats; the other a heart with a dagger through its middle. Unfortunately she missed a nearby sculpture called 'Two-faced Cunt', spotted later that afternoon by Simon Hoggart of the *Guardian*.[17]

The panelled room overlooking the Thames was packed with journalists, television crews and their equipment. Gallery staff tried to restrain reporters from clambering on to the wide window sills to get a better view, while scores of Tory MPs tripped over camera wires and crouched beneath lenses in their anxiety to be seen on the Howard bandwagon. Sandra Howard, dressed in an elegant trouser suit, watched her husband speak from a lectern in front of a navy-blue backdrop with his name on placards in bold letters. (Originally they had said 'Michael Howard Campaign', but the third word was dropped once it was clear that no campaign would be necessary.) Word got out that much of his speech had been drafted by Francis Maude. This was seen as significant, not only because of Maude's role in the downfall of IDS two days before, but also because he was a leading moderniser who had run Michael Portillo's unsuccessful campaign in 2001.

Speaking with enough authority to deter any undeclared challengers, Michael Howard did his best to be all things to all Tories. After a token tribute to Iain Duncan Smith, he promised to run the party from its centre, but expected the wholehearted support of every colleague with usable talents. In case Ann Widdecombe was having second thoughts, he promised that 'there will be no place for ancient feuds or rankling discords'.[18]

Under his leadership, Howard said, the party would recover the vitality which had swept it to power in 1979. It would appeal to youth without 'trying to be hip or cool', and would reclaim inner-city constituencies. 'There can be no no-go areas for a modern Conservative Party,' he declared. In more personal passages he mentioned his family background. He had *chosen* the Conservative Party, rather than being born into it, because it offered freedom and opportunity. He had been the child of 'immigrants' who 'saw Britain as a beacon in a dark and threatening world', and he would ensure that the party was 'internationalist in outlook': it would be Euro-sceptic, but not insular. It would welcome new talent, whatever its origins – after all, Britain was a country of 'splendid diversity'.[19]

More important, Howard also claimed to have learned from the recent past, suggesting that, like Michael Portillo, he had undergone something of a personal conversion. The implication was that he had mellowed into a more 'touchy-feely' Michael Howard: 'I've learnt that if we want to persuade people, we need to preach a bit less and listen a bit more. I've learnt that just winning an argument doesn't on its own win hearts and minds. I've learnt that politicians won't be respected by the public unless they respect each other and that people won't trust us unless we trust them.'[20]

Above all, Howard pledged not to be opportunistic: 'We won't hesitate to give credit to the Government when it gets things right. We won't oppose for opposition's sake. People want better than that.' He could claim to have put this into action already, by admitting that his party had been wrong initially to oppose Gordon Brown's decision to give independence to the Bank of England. This new candid approach, he suggested, would usher in 'a new kind of politics'.[21]

It sounded like a presidential candidate accepting the nomination at an American convention; it was more a coronation than a campaign launch. But, just in case there was to be a contest, Colin Moynihan was quietly tapping supporters for funds. In just a few days the former sports minister raised £75,000, compared with just £49,000 gathered by the Howard campaign in 1997. Contributions in 2003 were limited to £5,000, so this time there was no dominant benefactor like James Hanson, who had accounted for almost half the total last time round. Hanson again contributed (this time openly), along with Algy Cluff (another second-time donor); the businessman Stanley Kalms; the sports tycoon Johann Eliasch; the chairman of Southampton Football Club, Rupert Lowe; and the public relations boss Peter Gummer (Lord Chadlington). Two donors, Maurice Saatchi and a businessman, Jonathan Marland, would get important roles in the new regime, along with Moynihan himself.

The money was hardly needed. By the evening of the Saatchi Gallery event, ninety-two MPs – well over half the parliamentary party – had pledged themselves to Howard. Yet one man was conspicuously missing from the stampede to acclaim the leader-in-waiting. Having come close to winning twice before, and with nominations open for another week, Kenneth Clarke thought things over. It was almost certainly his last chance. Having discussed it with Westminster colleagues, and activists in his Nottingham constituency, Clarke announced his decision on the morning after the Saatchi Gallery speech. 'I'm not going to give up any of my other bad habits,' he joked, 'but coming second in Conservative leadership elections is something I don't intend to do.'[22]

Clarke visited Howard, and expressed hopes that his Shadow Cabinet would be balanced politically. 'There wasn't a deal of any kind,' Clarke says. 'We talked about what needed to be done to make us electable again – how to stop being so right-wing.'[23]

By the weekend, barely a week since the Conservative Party donors had issued their ultimatums about IDS's continued leadership, Duncan Smith was gone and Howard had become the only credible replacement. Two left-leaning papers made a half-hearted attempt to discredit him by republishing the Bennett, Haase and Bakerman story, with as additional embarrassing ingredient: Howard's cousin Simon Bakerman was due to be released from prison on licence on the same day that nominations for the leadership closed.[24]

Despite their efforts, Michael Howard was the only nomination received by Sir Michael Spicer by the deadline of Thursday 6 November. Just after midday, speaking in Committee Room 14 at the Commons, Spicer announced him as the new leader, and Tory MPs expressed their approval in the traditional manner, by banging their desks. He was the fourth man to lead the Conservative Party in less than seven years. For the first time in modern history a major British party had elected a new leader unopposed.

Michael Howard's success was confirmation of the observation once made by Ken Clarke that those who become leaders are rarely considered likely to get the job only a year or two beforehand. For a man who seemed to be on his way out of politics after the humiliation of 1997, it was an extraordinary comeback.

But engineering a similar turnaround in Conservative fortunes was a far tougher proposition.

20

LEADING QUESTIONS

> It's not enough just for people to lose faith in their government –
> they also have to have faith in the alternative. And we have not yet
> done everything we need to do in order to get to that point.
>
> MICHAEL HOWARD, JULY 2004[1]

After a long period in which the main British political parties had
been choosing ever-younger leaders, Michael Howard was a stark
contrast. First John Major and then William Hague had set new
records for youth at the top of the Conservative Party, while both Neil
Kinnock and then Tony Blair had been the youngest men ever to lead
Labour. At the age of sixty-two, Howard was the oldest person to take
command of the Tories since Harold Macmillan (who had been a few
months older in 1957). It was a sign of how desperate the
Conservatives were that they should have chosen a man who was
older than each of his three predecessors – John Major, William
Hague and Iain Duncan Smith.

Few party leaders can have got off to a better start. For two months
the Conservative Party felt liberated and reborn. Iain Duncan Smith
was soon a distant memory, almost airbrushed from history. And the
Michael Howard who now led the Tories seemed rather different
from the uptight, demonic figure who had antagonised so many
people during his years in government. He appeared more relaxed,

more at ease with himself, more willing to admit past mistakes, and determined to revamp his party. And his parliamentary performances also cheered the troops, with bravura displays at Prime Minister's Questions as the long-standing antagonists resumed their duels after a break of nine years.

Michael Howard was the first practising Jew to lead either of the two main British political parties. (Benjamin Disraeli, though born Jewish, had become a Christian; and the Liberals were already the third party when the Jewish Herbert Samuel led them in the early 1930s.) Nor was Howard's Welsh background the subject of much comment. Plenty of Welshmen have come close to the premiership, including Roy Jenkins, Michael Heseltine, Neil Kinnock and Geoffrey Howe, but it's a remarkable fact that, in almost 300 years since the post was established, no one born in Wales has ever reached Number 10. (Lloyd George was born in Manchester.)

Howard had promised a 'new kind of politics', but his most radical move as leader was to cut the Shadow Cabinet to just twelve members, compared with more than two dozen who had sat round IDS's top table. Several figures, including Bernard Jenkin, Caroline Spelman, Howard's former adviser Tim Collins, and his neighbour in Kent Damian Green, were ejected from the Shadow Cabinet while being retained on the front bench. Others, in contrast, were given much wider portfolios. Tim Yeo was put in charge of health and education, while David Davis was required to shadow both the Home Office and also the newly created Department of Legal and Constitutional Affairs. If Davis's promotion was surprising, given Howard's worries about his past loyalty, perhaps he had got the job on the Lyndon Johnson principle that it's better to have someone pissing out of the tent rather than pissing in. Oliver Letwin took Howard's place as Shadow Chancellor, despite past differences over asylum and law and order.

But there was no return for Francis Maude, even if he had written much of the Saatchi Gallery speech: as a gesture to IDS, Howard decided against bringing back a man who had played such a visible role in the departure of the former leader. And, while Howard had called for all 'talents' to come forward, several leading Tories declined the invitation. The most prominent was Michael Portillo, who met Howard and told him that he had all but decided to quit Parliament at the next election, though he hadn't yet announced this publicly. 'The decision took him by surprise,' says Portillo. 'He asked me to think it through overnight and said, "Would another position make a difference?" and I said "No."'[2]

Nor, despite her diplomatic silence, did Ann Widdecombe join the new team. She was offered a job, though not by Howard himself. The Deputy Chief Whip Patrick McLoughlin approached her about becoming the Shadow International Development Secretary, but told her the post would be outside Howard's new slimline Shadow Cabinet. 'I wasn't going to take that when I had been Shadow Home Secretary,' Widdecombe says, though she knew the decision would probably mark the end of her front-bench career. Widdecombe suspects that Howard knew she would not be able to take the job, since she was now looking after her widowed mother, who was in her nineties, and it would have been almost impossible to combine her domestic responsibilities with the necessary overseas travel.[3]

William Hague, too, declined a job – probably home affairs – though he agreed to sit with Ken Clarke, IDS and John Major on a team of 'wise men' who would meet every few weeks to offer Howard the benefit of their experience. This arrangement had an advantage for Howard beyond their wisdom, for it would also make it harder for Clarke and the former leaders to criticise him publicly if they had misgivings about Howard's performance. Ken Clarke was invited to speak from the front bench in one debate, and Howard made the parliamentary party more inclusive by giving jobs to a lot more of his MPs, thereby buying off potential dissenters by making them feel they belonged. Given the party's small tally of MPs, this inclusivity stretched a long way; almost 100 of the 165-strong parliamentary party were either shadow ministers or had jobs in the Conservative hierarchy.

At Central Office, Howard appointed two co-chairmen. One was Liam Fox, his never-really-needed campaign manager; the other was Lord (Maurice) Saatchi, who had impressed Howard over the past two years as a member of the Tories' shadow Treasury team and as their economics spokesman in the Lords. David Maclean returned as Chief Whip, having resigned the post on principle just a week before, when MPs ousted Iain Duncan Smith. His rapid return left IDS's closest supporters seething at what they felt had been the whips' treachery in the dying days of the old regime.

Nearly all IDS's staff were cleared out of the Leader of the Opposition's office, and Rachel Whetstone, now Howard's political secretary, was put in charge of his new team, along with Stephen Sherbourne as his chief-of-staff. Sherbourne was an old hand, having spent five years as Margaret Thatcher's political secretary in Downing Street and having then worked as a political consultant for fifteen years. Such was the status of Whetstone and Sherbourne in the new administration that when Howard addressed his first meeting of the 1922 Committee in November 2003 he told Conservative MPs that in future they should regard what the two advisers said as if Howard was talking to them. 'Rachel is absolutely key,' says the former Education Secretary Gillian Shephard, who joined Howard's office to handle 'knotty correspondence' and to act as a political trouble-shooter. 'She has an immense grip, terrier-like propensities, and knows Michael's mind. She's a political animal, but interested when the organisation goes wrong, and has her eyes on everything. Stephen Sherbourne is much older, and of a calm disposition. Rachel is tough and fiery.'[4] One Shadow Cabinet member says Whetstone is the only one who dares tell Howard to his face in meetings when she thinks he is wrong.

Ed Vaizey, a bright former barrister and parliamentary candidate, signed up as Howard's chief speech-writer, but perhaps Howard's most imaginative move was to bring in Guy Black, who combined the post of the leader's press secretary with the post of being Conservative Party director of communications. Black was well connected with the media, having served as director of the Press Complaints Commission. More significantly, in a party trying to project a modern, youthful image, and for a leader handicapped by his role in promoting Section 28, Black is openly gay.

Howard began 2004 by publishing what was described as a personal manifesto, entitled 'I Believe' – a set of sixteen core beliefs which were emailed to 100,000 party members and printed in a series of two-page newspaper advertisements. There were obvious influences from the American Declaration of Independence. It contained five references to people's 'happiness' or being 'happy', and was part of a deliberate strategy to portray the party as being more forward-looking and optimistic, in contrast to the Tories' negative and reactionary image of recent years. Most of the points could have been endorsed by Tony Blair, or indeed any politician, such as 'I believe that every child wants security for their parents in their old age,' or 'I believe in equality of opportunity. Injustice makes us angry.' Their overriding theme was that the role of government should be reduced – 'That the people should be big. That the state should be small' – and the only international dimension to the 'manifesto' was that 'Britain should defend her freedom at any time, against all comers, however mighty.' While Howard's credo attacked 'red tape, bureaucracy' and 'armies of interferers', there was no specific reference to improving public services, or reducing taxes.[5] He also avoided issues which a modernising Conservative such as Michael Portillo might have included, such as the treatment of gays and ethnic minorities.

Howard's attempts to reposition the Conservative Party continued a month later with his 'British Dream' speech in London, which again reflected his admiration for the United States as he expanded on his core beliefs to present a positive and upbeat vision. In a rare excursion into his family background, he presented himself as an example of how British citizens could fulfil their own version of the so-called American Dream. Here he was, the son of immigrants who had built their clothes shop from nothing, now leading a political party. But this time he advanced a more modern and more tolerant outlook. Discrimination was 'one of the worst ways in which people are denied control over their own lives', he said. 'I loathe it. Everyone should be given the same opportunities that I was given – those who are born in Britain and those who settle here as immigrants. Discrimination against people because of their origins, their colour, their beliefs or their sexuality must become a thing of the past.'[6]

More specifically, Howard promised personally to support the government's Civil Partnerships Bill, which would give same-sex partners the right to register their relationships and secure many of the rights enjoyed by married couples. He also backtracked on other political positions from his past. The man who as Employment Secretary had opposed EC plans to limit the working week and improve maternity benefits now pledged that the Tories would help families achieve a better balance between work and life, and introduce measures to improve childcare. The speech was, as Ann Treneman remarked in *The Times*, Howard's attempt 'to relaunch himself as a human being'.[7] Shortly afterwards the Tories held a 'gay summit' at Westminster with lesbian and homosexual groups. Howard himself did not attend – which was perhaps just as well, since many of those who came to it had been vehement critics of his role in introducing Section 28.

In fact Michael Howard's attempt to break with the past and present himself as a more caring and more tolerant, modern Conservative sat uneasily with both his reputation in government and his recent record as an MP and a Shadow Cabinet member under William Hague and IDS. This was the man who had attacked Peter Lilley for his efforts to break with Thatcherism, who had clashed with Oliver Letwin over asylum, and who had derided IDS's Helping the Vulnerable initiative. On gay rights Howard had been among those pushing for a three-line whip to vote against homosexual adoptions barely a year before. And in 2003, when Labour finally got round to abolishing Section 28, Howard was among Tory MPs who made a concerted effort to reinstate the measure. There were huge inconsistencies.

This gave Tony Blair and his colleagues an obvious strategy. First, it was easy to denounce Howard as a figure of the past – the man of the poll tax and high unemployment. And, as he tried to move from his previous record, he could then be tarred as a political opportunist. In their first encounter at Prime Minister's Questions (PMQs), Blair taunted Howard for the 'million extra unemployed' during his time as Employment Secretary. 'Whatever we have done, none of us has introduced anything as bad as the poll tax,' Blair continued, 'as well as giving us 15 per cent interest rates and opposing the minimum wage. Same old people, same old policies, same old Tories.' Howard's reply was deft, however. He exploited Blair's current embarrassment over the notorious government dossiers which had exaggerated the dangers of Saddam Hussein's weaponry. 'I am happy to debate the past with the Prime Minister any day he likes. I have a big dossier on his past,' he jeered, waving a file across the Commons dispatch boxes. 'And I did not even have to sex it up!'[8]

The Commons was Michael Howard's first battleground as leader and for several weeks he got the better of Tony Blair. This was hardly surprising, however. The government was probably in its weakest position for seven years, and it later emerged that during this period the Labour leader was privately contemplating stepping down in favour of Gordon Brown. Labour backbenchers were unhappy about plans to introduce university top-up fees, a measure which the Tories also opposed (without offering any alternative means of increasing funding for higher education). Fees were needed for wider access, explained Blair. 'This grammar school boy,' thundered Howard, 'will take no lessons from that public school boy on the importance of children from less privileged backgrounds gaining access to university. If the case for top-up fees is so overwhelming, why, only two years ago, did the Prime Minister promise in his manifesto not to impose them?'[9] As Howard enjoyed his honeymoon period, and most of the Westminster village seemed delighted that the government had credible opposition at last, it hardly mattered that he'd sent his own children to Eton and St Paul's, two of Britain's more expensive public schools. He even got away with taunting Blair for stonewalling questions, despite his own reputation for not giving answers. 'Two questions asked and neither answered – not a very good start,' Howard jeered in their first weekly exchange.[10] 'Three questions have been asked,' he said three weeks later, 'and none answered. Let us try again.'[11]

Yet the public was perhaps less impressed by the way in which both Blair and Howard seemed to regard it all as a student debate, grinning at each other too much and showing obvious admiration when the other made a clever point. William Hague had also been an impressive Commons performer, but he never transformed his parliamentary mastery into votes. Howard seemed to have forgotten the desire expressed at the Saatchi Gallery about making politics more relevant to the wider electorate.

For eight months, between May 2003 and January 2004, British politics was gripped by the David Kelly affair, and the Hutton inquiry into the apparent suicide of the government scientist. The Blair government appeared to be in severe trouble. Andrew Gilligan, a BBC radio reporter, had alleged that the government had 'sexed up' its 2002 dossier on Iraq's weapons of mass destruction, including details which it knew were probably wrong. It was also alleged that the government had deliberately exposed Kelly as Gilligan's source, and that the resulting pressure on the civil servant had caused him to take his life. The Hutton report had the potential to damage the Prime Minister and his colleagues, with consequent gains for the Opposition, and Howard, with his reputation for mastering detail and forensic analysis, was seen as the ideal person to exploit this. However, no one knew how hard Lord Hutton would be on the government. Although the former law lord was regarded as an establishment figure, so much damaging material had emerged during the course of his inquiry that it seemed inconceivable that Blair could survive unscathed.

The new Leader of the Opposition decided to attack early, several weeks before Hutton reported, at the first Prime Minister's Questions of 2004. Howard pressed Blair on whether he stood by his statements from the previous July denying that he had authorised anyone to release Kelly's name. Three times Blair declared that he stood by the 'totality' of what he had said in the summer. The Conservative leader then pointed out that the Permanent Secretary at the Ministry of Defence had told Hutton that the decision to disclose Kelly's name was taken at a meeting chaired by Blair. 'Is not it clear that either the Permanent Secretary or the Prime Minister is not telling the truth?' Howard insisted. 'No, it is not,' Blair replied, and he suggested that Howard should cross-examine him 'on the day the report is published – according to what it says, not according to what he says'. 'I can assure the Prime Minister that I am looking forward to that,' a grinning Howard shot back.[12]

It was a highly effective performance by the Conservative leader, which discomfited Blair, and Howard returned to the Kelly affair at PMQs a week later, while the Conservative Party published a fifty-page document on important issues arising from the Hutton inquiry. Although some observers questioned the tactics of trying to pre-empt the official report, Howard's advisers reasonably feared that Hutton would be favourable to the government. It was already clear from analysing Hutton's work that he was unlikely to comment on what Tony Blair had told journalists on a plane to Hong Kong on the day Kelly was found dead. Asked on the flight, 'Why did you authorise the naming of David Kelly?' the Prime Minister had replied, 'That is completely untrue.'[13]

If Hutton was not going to denounce Blair for this apparent lie, Howard felt he should do so instead. And, even if Hutton did deal with the matter, it was well worth setting out in advance the anti-government case in the starkest terms possible, to aid public understanding. Howard knew this was his first significant chance to land blows on Labour and in preparation he assembled a Hutton team which included Peter Lilley, the former Cabinet Office minister David Hunt, and David Cameron, whom Howard had just appointed to the front bench and who was earmarked as a rising star. Howard told Cameron to become a Hutton expert, and the MP spent almost two months reading thousands of pages of evidence. He compiled a manual on the key aspects of the affair, both preparing for what Hutton was likely to say and anticipating how ministers might react. Howard also took advice from his 'wise men' and from the former Defence Secretary Michael Portillo.

Lord Hutton's report was published on Wednesday 28 January, but Howard and his team knew their opportunity was probably lost when, the night before, *Newsnight* reported a leaked story in the *Sun* that Blair and his colleagues would be exonerated. The next morning Howard was invited to the Cabinet Office for a preview, accompanied by David Cameron (who had stayed overnight with the Howards in

Pimlico), and also David Hunt. When they arrived at the Cabinet Office just before 6 a.m. they were treated to croissants, bacon sandwiches and sausage rolls. But it quickly became clear this was the only meat on offer when the three Tories began scouring the report for particular points they wanted. Once they'd all read the introduction, Cameron and Howard set to work on a statement, leaving Hunt to skim the rest. They found hardly any ammunition. The Ulster judge had exonerated Blair to a degree that surprised almost everyone, while also being strongly critical of the BBC.

'We accept his conclusions,' Howard told the Commons that afternoon, before he attacked Blair over various insubstantial points raised by Hutton. At one point Howard even denounced Blair's former press secretary Alastair Campbell for using the word 'fuck' in his private diary. It was a limp response, but the Conservative leader had been presented with weak material on a day which was bound to be seen as a triumph for the Prime Minister, whatever Michael Howard said. Blair was careful not to gloat, but insisted that Howard should have the 'decency' to 'withdraw the allegation' that he had lied to MPs.[14]

'The Prime Minister wiped the floor with Mr Howard,' wrote Alice Miles in *The Times*. 'Mr Blair was putting *him* on the spot about Hutton, not the other way around.'[15] 'It was pitiful watching poor Mr Howard trying to squeeze poison from some parenthesis in paragraph 947b (or wherever),' said Charles Moore in the *Daily Telegraph*. 'Mr Blair pointed out that the Leader of the Opposition had denied himself the chance to respond to the report in a "sensible and measured way". [It was] odious and priggish, but devastating.'[16]

Howard now called for a wider inquiry into the long-running controversy over whether Iraq had ever possessed weapons of mass destruction, similar to the Thatcher government's 1982 examination of the background to the Falklands War. But this only highlighted the Tories' weakness: it was difficult to attack the government over its decision to go to war when the Conservatives, and Howard himself, had endorsed it.

Indeed, it was a hugely disappointing week for Howard. The

previous weekend there seemed to be a real possibility that Blair could be seriously, if not mortally, wounded, not just over Hutton but also over university fees. Yet the night before the Hutton report the government, with substantial arm-twisting by the whips, had scraped home by just five votes on the bill introducing top-up charges. After all the anticipation built up over the government's severe problems, and the high hopes raised among Tories by the arrival of their new leader, it was hugely deflating – rather like losing a football match 4–3 after being 3–0 ahead with only twenty minutes to go. Howard had played his part in cranking up expectations by making such an issue of Blair's honesty earlier in the month and by publicly suggesting that the Prime Minister had lied (though he never used that word, of course). Michael Howard's leadership would never look so threatening to the government again. The week of the Hutton report was when many Tories realised that Howard might not be their salvation.

Even so, the business of party leadership continued. In Berlin, he reiterated his à la carte or 'made to measure' philosophy on Europe: that Britain should be allowed to select the areas where it wanted to combine with the rest of the EU. Under this, he said:

> Those member states which wish to integrate more closely would be free to do so. It would not be necessary for them to drag Britain, and quite possibly some other member states, kicking and scream-ing in their wake. We would say to our partners: 'We don't want to stop you doing what you want to do, as long as you don't make us do what we don't want to do.'[17]

At home, he promised to freeze civil-service recruitment and announced that the City troubleshooter David James would conduct an audit of government to find areas for substantial savings. Cheekily, the Tories placed an ad in the 'Society' section of the *Guardian* urging public-sector workers to write to James with examples of waste and inefficiency.

The most controversial move was Michael Howard's trip to Burnley in Lancashire, where eight members of the far-right British National Party (BNP) had been elected as local councillors. Denouncing the BNP was the 'specific reason' he had come to Burnley, he declared, and he rejected the idea that doing so would give them 'the oxygen of publicity'. It was the duty of the 'mainstream parties' to face up to 'extremists' of every kind:

> Let's not mince our words. The policies of the British National Party are based on bigotry and hatred. Its approach is entirely alien to our political traditions. Their leader, Nick Griffin . . . denies the existence of Nazi death camps and has written that he has 'reached the conclusion that the "extermination" tale is a mixture of Allied wartime propaganda, extremely profitable lie, and latter day witch-hysteria'. I happen to know that he is wrong about that. My grandmother was one of the millions of people who died in those camps.

Detailing the criminal convictions of Griffin and other BNP activists, he twice described them as 'a bunch of thugs dressed up as a political party'.[18]

It was a courageous intervention, but also risky. Burnley had suffered serious riots and racial tension three years before, and Howard would have been severely criticised had his trip sparked more trouble on the streets. Fortunately it passed off peacefully. It was a clear attempt to soften Howard's image among those who might have been alienated by his stance on immigration as Home Secretary. 'Britain has welcomed energetic, ambitious and optimistic people from every part of the world,' he said in Burnley.

> My father was one of them. We are a stronger and better country, rich in our cultural diversity, because of the immigrant communities that have settled here . . . But people want to know that immigration is controlled. They want to know that the asylum system is being used to protect those genuinely fleeing persecution, and not abused by those seeking a back door into Britain.[19]

The real right-wing threat to the Conservatives in Howard's first year came not from the BNP, but from the UK Independence Party (UKIP), whose profile had recently been boosted by the recruitment of the TV presenter and former Labour MP Robert Kilroy-Silk.

After Hutton, the Tories saw the June elections to the European Parliament as the next obvious opportunity of Michael Howard's first year. The minimum target should have been to do as well as William Hague in 1999, when the Tories had enjoyed a lead of more than 7 per cent over Labour.

Howard fought an energetic campaign in the European elections – unlike Tony Blair, who was barely visible. (Blair's absence was a stark contrast to 1999, when the Prime Minister was all over election literature; this time his face and name were nowhere to be seen on Labour leaflets – a clear sign that his party now saw him as more of a liability than an asset.) The Tory leader seemed to enjoy electioneering, presenting his more personable side as he alighted from his blue battlebus to chat to voters in his shirtsleeves and deliver short speeches in shopping centres. His campaign even included a day trip to Gibraltar, whose 18,000 voters had been included in a British Euro-constituency for the first time.

But Labour had already shot one of the Tories' best European foxes in the spring, when Blair had made a dramatic U-turn and, after months of insisting that a referendum wasn't necessary on the proposed new European constitution, suddenly announced that he *would* eventually put it to a vote of the British people. It was an uncomfortable moment for the Prime Minister, since Howard had long been demanding such a vote, but his change of heart did little for the Tories' election effort. Even though they beat Labour in terms of both seats and votes in the European elections, the Conservatives share of the vote slipped from more than a third in 1999 to just over a quarter this time. Part of the reason for this was the performance of UKIP, who picked up 16 per cent of the vote, and twelve seats, and pushed the Liberal Democrats into fourth place. The Tories had 27 per cent and twenty-seven MEPs.

Although UKIP were unlikely to have the same success in a general election – not least because they had gained considerably from the proportional-representation system used in the European elections – it was a sign of the Conservatives' weakness that UKIP should perform so well when Howard's views on Europe were both hardline and well known. In a general election, UKIP could damage Tory prospects by taking Euro-sceptic votes which might normally go to Conservative candidates.

The Conservatives' performance was stronger in the local council elections held on the same day – though not by enough to suggest that Howard was heading for Downing Street. The journalist Robert Peston would later claim in his book *Brown's Britain* that Howard's failure to make an impact in the June elections largely caused Tony Blair not to go through with the offer he had previously made to Gordon Brown to step down as PM before the next general election.[20]

And the gloomy news from the June poll was reinforced a few weeks later in two by-elections, held in Birmingham Hodge Hill and Leicester South. The Tories had been second in both constituencies in 2001, and Howard was determined that these by-elections would not be a similar debacle to Brent East. These were just the kind of inner-city neighbourhoods which he had said should not be treated as 'no-go areas', and the party would need to start making significant progress in the major cities, where Tory support had been evaporating over recent decades, if it were to return to power.

The Conservatives mounted a huge effort in both Birmingham and Leicester, and Howard took the unprecedented step of sending the Chief Whip, David Maclean, to the Midlands to organise the two campaigns on the ground. Maclean's presence in turn ensured an excellent turnout from Tory MPs, who were bombarded with text messages urging them to travel up from Westminster, while candidates for other parliamentary seats were expected to spend at least ten hours in the two constituencies – though such demands partly reflected the party's shortage of volunteers. Michael Howard visited both seats and even Sandra went canvassing with each candidate. Despite these extensive efforts by the Howards, the results were almost as bad as in Brent East. While the swings in both seats were lower than they had

been in north-west London the previous September, the Tory share of
the vote fell in both by-elections, and the party again dropped to third
place. The outcome was all the more depressing for MPs and Tory
activists because Howard had raised the stakes by taking the campaigns
so seriously. At least Brent East could be excused by poor organisation
and lack of effort. There were no such excuses this time, and David
Maclean left MPs with the barely comforting thought that 'If we had
not done it, then we would have been humiliated . . . and pushed into
a poor fourth place.'[21]

The by-election defeats had come despite renewed efforts by
Howard to present himself as a rounded personality through interviews about the personal side of his character. Such attempts could
backfire, as when Howard suggested that his beloved Liverpool football club should sack its manager, Gérard Houllier, and replace him
with the Celtic boss Martin O'Neill. Though Howard was only
reflecting the views of most Liverpool fans, he realised what offence
he'd caused, apologised, and later admitted it was 'one of the most
stupid things I've ever said'.[22] More often, though, journalists were
served up the same anecdotes repeated almost word for word. On
Desert Island Discs in July, however, he spoke for the first time of how
his aunt had three times escaped death at Auschwitz.

He made a largely unsophisticated, sentimental selection of records,
which included the Beatles' 'All You Need is Love', 'Cwm Rhondda'
by the Morriston Orpheus Choir; 'Blue Monk' by Thelonious Monk,
Mozart's Piano Concerto No. 21, and '(Everything I Do) I Do It For
You' by Bryan Adams, which he dedicated to Sandra. The inclusion
of the Liverpool football anthem 'You'll Never Walk Alone', by Gerry
and the Pacemakers, was perhaps an attempt to show that, unlike
Tony Blair, he was a genuine football fan.[23]

The campaign to present the personal face of Michael Howard
reached its nadir on the ITV daytime show *This Morning* in July,
where Sandra joined him in the studio. Neither of the Howards managed to relax, and the interviewers seemed to do most of the talking.

'He's not much of a domestic god. You'd be the first to admit that,'
the presenter Phillip Schofield suggested.

'Absolutely,' the Tory leader admitted.

'Not so good at DIY,' Schofield continued.

'Hopeless,' said Howard.

'The cooking and stuff like that,' said Schofield.

'No,' said Howard.

'He does make me a morning cup of tea,' Sandra said. 'But cooking is not going to ever be his strong suit, I think.'[24]

Their performance was panned. 'Dumbing down is not exactly the problem here,' wrote Oliver Burkeman in the *Guardian*. 'It was painfully obvious the Howards did not want to be there.'[25]

Michael Howard had perhaps been poorly advised. He would have been wary of appearing on such an unfamiliar platform, for, unlike news and current-affairs programmes, it was not somewhere he could feel in command. With his wife and two non-political presenters, the potential for mishaps was huge – whether from unexpected, off-beam questions or from a gaffe by Sandra.

Sandra Howard was especially nervous on ITV's *This Morning*: she spoke quietly, and her first answer had been to concede that it was a 'fairly terrifying' experience. 'I'm certainly not born to it, and there's only one speaker in the family and it's not me,'[26] she admitted. Yet Sandra was speaking publicly in support of her husband far more than any party leader's spouse in recent political history (and possibly ever before). Apart from her canvassing in the summer by-elections (for which she admitted she had to 'psych' herself up), she also addressed a small fringe meeting organised by her drugs charity, Addaction, at the Conservative Party conference.[27] Although Denis Thatcher, Norma Major, Ffion Hague and Betsy Duncan Smith were often *seen* at their partners' sides, they were careful not to answer reporters' questions, and spoke rarely. The same has been true of Labour wives – including Cherie Blair, whose occasional public pronouncements are almost entirely related to her legal work rather than her husband's political life. Sandra Howard, who had spent her early adult life under the spotlight, did several press interviews, and these were often quite revealing.

'Words can wound,' she told *The Lady*. 'Michael is pretty resilient, but I have been known to fire injured letters off to journalists in his defence. It used to release the frustrations I felt, but I don't do that any more. Now I just spend every spare minute writing my novel.'[28] The family seemed more relaxed about their son Nick's Christian evangelism. 'He'll try and convert anyone. If we have a Catholic help he'll try and convert her,' said Sandra, though apparently he had 'given up on his dad'.[29] Sandra also revealed that she was 'a bit' to the left of Michael –

> but not to the point where we could ever be in different parties. And he is not to the right as much as he is thought to be. I couldn't be married to him if he were. He's a lot more soft-centred than people assume, otherwise I couldn't be comfortable around him . . . Ninety nine per cent of the time I think he's more correct than me. Mine would be a wishy-washy over-sentimentality, and he's a realist.[30]

Sandra also caused a stir when, in an interview with *Scotland on Sunday*, she defended the swinging sixties. To many Conservatives, of course – including her husband in the past – the sixties had been the era when it all started to go wrong. On the contrary, said Sandra, it was a 'wonderful' time, when people's 'natural talents were given a chance' to blossom. 'That sense of freedom had a place and I don't think you can blame the sixties for what we are like nowadays . . . Some things may have got out of hand but it was a time when people became more liberated. It is not true to say it was a time of hedonism.'[31]

Michael Howard, meanwhile, accepted past policy errors. 'There's no government that doesn't make mistakes,' he admitted. 'Of course we made mistakes. The poll tax was one of them. No government is perfect.'[32] Nor would he reverse some of the major measures of the Blair government, despite his deeply felt opposition in the past to the minimum wage, devolution for Scotland and Wales, and independence for the Bank of England.

The most difficult area for Howard was the 2003 Iraq War, at a time when increasing numbers of voters thought it had been a terrible error, and that Tony Blair and his colleagues had deceived the country over the extent of the threat posed by Saddam Hussein and in persuading Parliament to vote for war. In July 2004 Howard gave an interview to the *Sunday Times*. 'If I knew then what I know now that would have caused a difficulty. I couldn't have voted for that resolution,' he said:

> If you look at the terms of the motion put to the House of Commons on March 18 [2003], it placed very heavy emphasis on the presence of weapons of mass destruction in Iraq. So I think it is difficult for someone, knowing everything we know now, to have voted for that resolution. I think I would have voted for a differently worded resolution that would have authorised the war . . . I am still in favour of the war . . . I think Saddam Hussein was a threat to the peace of the region. I think it is a good thing that he is no longer there. I would have done things very differently.[33]

His words were clear, but the overall message appeared confused. He had made a basic political mistake by failing to sum up his position in a simple, pithy phrase such as that suggested by his friend the journalist Bruce Anderson: 'right to fight, wrong to lie'.[34] His remarks to the *Sunday Times* made Howard look opportunistic, and in the view of one sympathetic ally they were the 'low point' of his first year as leader: 'It was an error. I was very angry when he said that.' The interview was also badly timed, coming just two days before the Commons debated the report by Lord (Robin) Butler which had made severe criticisms of the way that Blair and his colleagues had handled intelligence in the run-up to war, and the way the whole government was run. The debate should have been another opportunity to press the Prime Minister. Instead, Blair used Howard's interview to put the Opposition leader on the back foot, taunting Howard over past reasons he had given for going to war, and contrasting them with what he had just told the *Sunday Times*. 'Shabby opportunism is not the solution to his problem: it is his problem,' Blair told MPs. 'The public will respect people who were honestly for the war and they will respect people who were honestly against the war: they will not respect a politician who says that he is for and against the war in the same newspaper article.'[35] The commentator Michael Brown, a former Tory MP, described the debate as marking 'the day when Mr Howard's credibility as Tory leader was first challenged by some in his own party'.[36] The long-standing backbencher Patrick Cormack made it clear he was still glad to have voted for war.[37]

Howard's attacks on Tony Blair over Iraq had long been causing annoyance in Washington, where George's Bush's political adviser Karl Rove made it clear that Howard would not be welcome at the White House if he sought to make the traditional visit of a Leader of the Opposition. 'You can forget about meeting the President,' Rove reportedly told Howard's office in February 2004. 'Don't bother coming. You are not meeting him.'[38] It was a humiliating moment, especially since Howard – the founder of the Atlantic Partnership – had such a long history of being passionately pro-American. The Bush administration took Howard's attacks on the Blair government to be attacks on US policy as well, and its fury with him was perhaps understandable at a time when some members of the Conservative front bench, such as Alan Duncan, were openly expressing the hope that the Democrat John Kerry would beat Bush in the presidential election in November. It was a sign of Howard's anger with the Bush camp that, when the President subsequently beat Kerry, Howard refused to congratulate him publicly, though he did sent a private message. It was 'not appropriate to express a view', was Howard's response when asked about Bush's re-election.[39] It seemed to reflect how bruised Howard still felt, though there were attempts to repair relations with Washington, and Liam Fox led a delegation to study Republican campaign methods.

If the summer had been grim, things had got worse in the autumn, with another by-election in a potential Conservative 'no-go area', Hartlepool, which had just been vacated by Peter Mandelson. This time Howard made strenuous efforts to secure a popular candidate, and tried personally to recruit Ray Mallon, the mayor of nearby

Middlesbrough. Howard had got to know Mallon while Home Secretary, when Mallon had made his name as the first police chief in Britain to adopt the American 'zero tolerance' policy towards crime. Mallon decided, despite his personal admiration for the Tory leader, that he could make more impact as an elected mayor than as an MP. Howard's forlorn hope that Mallon might stand delayed the Tories' selection of a candidate, giving their rivals a big head start, and the situation became even more embarrassing when Howard's overtures to the former policeman seeped into the press. Worse still, Mallon then publicly backed Labour in Hartlepool.

Again David Maclean effectively ran the campaign, and scores of MPs were bussed in, but it proved to be a bigger by-election humiliation than even Brent East. In a seat which the Tories had once held (between 1959 and 1964), and where they had been runners-up in 2001, they were now beaten into fourth place by UKIP. Not since the war had the Opposition party ever come fourth in an English by-election. Fortunately for Howard the result was overshadowed by Tony Blair's unexpected announcement that he planned to serve just one more parliamentary term as Prime Minister.

The Hartlepool result was all the more unwelcome because it came only three days before Michael Howard's first Conservative conference as leader. That week's slogan in Bournemouth – 'Timetable for Action' – will surely go down as one of the least inspiring rallying cries in modern politics, though Howard did better by producing in his main speech an eleven-word summary of what the Conservatives stood for: 'School discipline. More police. Cleaner hospitals. Lower taxes. Controlled immigration. Ten words to address the problems that are worrying people today. Remember those words. And remember one more: accountability.'[40] Howard's five pairs of words were very similar to the five basic pledges successfully trumpeted by Tony Blair before the 1997 election, and the Tories even copied Labour's idea of pledge cards, though Labour's promises had been more specific. But what people most remembered from his Bournemouth speech was the personal element, as Howard referred more intimately than ever before to his family's experience of the Holocaust. 'Everything I have, and everything I am, I owe to this country,' he declared. This appeared to ignore his rich cultural and religious inheritance from overseas, but then Howard often acts as if he has no such ancestry. He went on:

I was born in July 1941, two weeks after Hitler invaded Russia. Those were very dark days. In the next four years millions of people were killed. Many lost their lives on the battlefield, at sea and in the air. Many lost their lives in cities blitzed from the air. And many lost their lives in the concentration camps set up by one of the cruellest tyrannies the world has ever known. My grandmother was one of those killed in the concentration camps. If it hadn't been for Winston Churchill, and if it hadn't been for Britain, I would have been one of them too. That's why when I say I owe everything I am to this country, I really do mean it. I owe my life to it. My father told me Britain was the best country in the world. I think it was. And I think it still is. But I know we could be doing so much better. And it's because I think I can help make things better that I am standing before you today. Put simply, I'm here so I can give back to Britain a tiny fraction of what Britain has given to me.[41]

Although the words were Howard's own, his aides had found it difficult to persuade him to talk so personally. 'The words "blood" and "stone" come to mind,' his press secretary, Guy Black, said afterwards. A key role had been played by the Conservative co-Treasurer Lord (Alexander) Hesketh, who had served with Howard at the DoE. There had also been much debate among his team over whether it was accurate to say that Howard owed his life to Britain and Winston Churchill; Howard insisted that it was, since if Germany had invaded Britain he and other British Jews would probably have been exterminated, just like most of the Jewish population in occupied France.

All year, Tory officials had been trying to get across to voters the Michael Howard that the public didn't know: rather than the sinister stage villain, they wanted to project the relaxed family man with hobbies and interests in sport, books, TV and films. On the final morning of the conference, Howard was given a second platform, and a chance to explore his human side, when he was interviewed on stage by the former ITN political editor Michael Brunson. 'Sandra thinks I spend too much time watching football,' he revealed, explaining that he subscribed to Sky TV at only one home – his house in Kent – to prevent him watching too many games. And every New Year's Eve he and Sandra watched a video of *Brideshead Revisited*, though there was always an argument 'about which bits to watch'.[42] (Perhaps their affection for the series stemmed from its having been filmed at Castle Howard.)

Conservative activists loved it, but privately many party staff and MPs had become disenchanted. It was a recognition that things were badly wrong when in October 2004 Howard brought in Lynton Crosby, who had run the Australian Liberal Party's campaign which, only a few days before, had delivered a fourth successive election victory for their Prime Minister John Howard – no relation, but a similar client to Michael Howard: an uncharismatic, elderly politician, who was known for being blunt and hardline on immigration and asylum. Crosby, who had a reputation for his aggressive style, had been involved in all four of the Liberals' recent triumphs, and was in overall charge of the last three. Recognised as an expert on polling and campaign techniques, he specialises in what is known as 'below the radar' campaigning – the quiet work of identifying swing voters in marginal seats and contacting them with messages tailored to their concerns, sometimes by phoning them. But his appointment was also tacit acknowledgement that the double-chairmanship of Liam Fox and Maurice Saatchi at Conservative headquarters had not worked. When *The Times* reported that Crosby had told Howard that Saatchi was 'twenty years out of date', the Conservative co-chairman was so angry that he sent out an email to party staff.[43] 'Lynton is apologetic for the remarks attributed to him and we have accepted that,' wrote Saatchi. '. . . it is never a good idea to bad-mouth your colleagues, so if you do harbour unkind thoughts about others – which I hope you don't – please keep them to yourselves.'[44]

Nor were the headquarters in Central Office any longer. One of the most symbolic acts of Michael Howard's leadership had been to move the party from its old-fashioned building in Smith Square to a suite of offices to be known as Conservative Campaign Headquarters in much more modern premises above a Starbucks coffee shop in Victoria Street, Westminster. The former Central Office building was regarded as physically unsuitable for a modern hi-tech operation, and it was also associated with the years of intrigue which had culminated in the downfall of Iain Duncan Smith. The move made little difference. Behind the scenes, younger staff and modernisers were grumbling almost as much as they had under IDS, only this time they knew there was little that could be done about the party's plight. There was also growing resentment towards the so-called Notting Hill Set, a group of Howard advisers who were friends of each other and lived in the same area of west London. The set was said to centre on Rachel Whetstone, Ed Vaizey, David Cameron and another rising star whom Howard was increasingly relying upon, George Osborne, the MP for Tatton. Older MPs were upset by suggestions from Howard's advisers that some of them were 'bed-blockers' – MPs who contributed little in Parliament and who should therefore step down in favour of younger, more energetic, candidates.

Michael Howard's reaction to the advances made by UKIP was to reshuffle his front-bench team. The Shadow Cabinet crept up to seventeen members, and the diehard right-winger John Redwood was brought back as industry spokesman – or Shadow Secretary of State for Deregulation as Howard officially called the job. This was seen as a lurch to the right by some, and John Bercow and Damian Green both resigned from the front bench after being offered lesser posts. Bercow was told he would lose his position as shadow international-development spokesman, but he refused to take another job and so effectively quit. He told Howard bluntly that he now understood why people were so critical of his man-management failings. Howard was a 'control freak', Bercow said, and there was something 'sinister' about his character; the leader was not 'attractive' to the public, or able to 'empathise with people'. Howard accused Bercow of failing to be a team player, and was especially annoyed that the MP had praised Tony Blair's statesmanship during the Iraq War.

The Conservative Party knew that, for the time being, Michael Howard was the last card in its hand. Few Conservatives spoke with conviction about winning the next election. It would, instead, be an exercise in damage limitation, in which the Tories tried to recoup as many seats as they could from Labour. The party's failure to exploit the government's persistent troubles and the ever-growing public hostilities between Tony Blair and Gordon Brown only underlined the scale of its weakness.

Labour Party leaders in opposition have often made an impact on the polls with dramatic efforts to distance themselves from publicly unpopular elements of their party or its traditions. Good examples were Neil Kinnock's attacks on Militant, Arthur Scargill and the other left-wingers; Tony Blair's axing of Labour's Clause 4; and the efforts by Kinnock, Blair and John Smith to reduce their dependence on the unions. Such confrontations, though risky, were almost deliberately overplayed by Labour strategists to give Kinnock, Smith and Blair chances to show passion, strength and leadership. But there were few obvious dragons for Michael Howard to slay. He had stopped his old friend the former convict Jonathan Aitken standing again as a Conservative candidate, but the move hardly made big headlines.

Howard had warned during the Bournemouth conference that ministers who failed to perform would be sacked, though the one opportunity that allowed him to show a firm hand was unlikely to enhance his standing. Boris Johnson held several different jobs, serving as MP for Henley, as the party's spokesman on the media, culture and sport, and as editor of the *Spectator*. An editorial in the *Spectator* had accused Liverpudlians of 'mawkish sentimentality' and wallowing in 'victim status' over the death of Ken Bigley, a British hostage who had just been murdered in Iraq. It also claimed that Liverpool supporters had contributed to ninety-six deaths in the Hillsborough football stadium disaster in 1989 by their drunkenness.[45] Howard was horrified. He described the article as 'nonsense from beginning to end', and he ordered Johnson to go up to Liverpool and apologise publicly.[46] Some saw Howard's move as a heavy-handed infringement of press freedom, although it was as much a sign that combining high-level politics and magazine editorship would inevitably generate conflicts of interest. Johnson had to comply if he hoped to keep his place on the front bench. Howard was partly motivated by his own personal affection for Merseyside, and his long-standing view that Liverpool fans had been unfairly vilified over Hillsborough in the past, but there was also a political calculation involved. While many existing Conservatives might agree with the thrust of the *Spectator* editorial, he knew that Liverpool was another example of the kind of conurbation where the party had to start winning seats again.

Two weeks later Johnson was back in trouble when two Sunday newspapers exposed his long-standing relationship with his deputy editor Petronella Wyatt. A few days later, when presenting the *Spectator* parliamentary awards, Howard mocked Johnson with obvious references to the affair:

> There is nothing like the *Spectator* for stirring up and stimulating political controversy. Indeed, in all senses of the word, it could best be described as 'political Viagra' . . . In recent days you've hardly been able to keep out of the pages of the newspapers. It's an absolute triumph. So all I can say, Boris, is you're doing your front-bench job absolutely superbly. Keep it up.[47]

Howard almost seemed to be giving a nod of approval to Johnson's affair. But that weekend, only two days after the awards lunch, it was revealed that Johnson had even paid for Wyatt to have two abortions. Howard promptly sacked the MP from the front bench, though he was quick to stress that Johnson had not lost his job because of his adultery – that would have opened him to charges of hypocrisy, given the way that Howard had wooed Sandra away from her third husband. Johnson was dismissed for having been less than frank when questioned about the reports by Howard's press secretary, Guy Black.

Boris Johnson, who was never reluctant to express an opinion or to do so colourfully, was always likely to be a loose cannon. Since the death of Alan Clark and the disgrace of Jeffrey Archer, he had become by far the most popular Conservative politician with the general public, and one of the most recognised following his regular TV appearances on programmes such as *Have I Got News For You?* Johnson was probably the only Conservative to generate much affection among young people, and, although Howard's decision to sack him was understandable, it did nothing to make the Tories more popular with younger voters.

Affairs at the *Spectator* were a dominant theme at the end of 2004, as Johnson's boss on the magazine, its American publisher Kimberly Quinn, was exposed as having enjoyed a long-standing extramarital relationship with the Home Secretary, David Blunkett. Once again Howard was careful not to be critical of the affair itself, and the Conservatives were even cautious about exploiting allegations – which eventually forced Blunkett to resign – that the Home Secretary had misused his position to secure a visa for Quinn's nanny. Howard left the issue largely to his home-affairs spokesman, David Davis (whom he now trusted much more than twelve months earlier), but the Tory leader was quick to exploit an approved biography of Blunkett by the journalist Stephen Pollard, in which the Home Secretary voiced strong criticisms of several Cabinet colleagues. In successive weeks at PMQs Howard taunted Tony Blair over the Blunkett quotes (which could not be denied, since they had been taped by Pollard). The Home Secretary and his colleagues had to squirm on the government bench as Howard quoted Blunkett liberally:

> I shall tell the Prime Minister what his Home Secretary thinks about the current Foreign Secretary's time at the Home Office. (*Laughter.*) Wait for it. He says: 'It was worse than any of us had imagined possible. God alone knows what Jack [Straw] did for four years. I am simply unable to comprehend how he could have left it as it was. It was a giant mess.' He does not stop there. He thinks that the Secretary of State for Culture, Media and Sport [Tessa Jowell] is weak; the Secretary of State for Trade and Industry [Patricia Hewitt] does not think strategically; and the Secretary of State for

Education and Skills [Charles Clarke] has not developed as expected. He also says that the Prime Minister does not like being told the truth and – as no doubt the Prime Minister will agree – that the Chancellor is a bully.[48]

A week later, once Pollard's book was actually available, Howard threw a copy to Blair across the table of the House as 'holiday reading'. But Blair was well prepared this time, hitting back with an 1991 extract from Woodrow Wyatt's diaries in which Howard was quoted as saying 'unemployment never matters', even if Blair had taken the words out of context.[49]

In the new year Michael Howard would exploit another new biography at PMQs – Robert Peston's book on Gordon Brown, in which the Chancellor was quoted as having said to Blair, 'There is nothing that you could ever say to me now that I could ever believe.' Blair insisted the quote was 'wrong', but didn't refute Peston's claim that he had promised Brown he would step down as Prime Minister before the next election, even though Howard twice pressed him on this.[50]

As Britain prepared for a general election which was widely expected in May 2005, the Blunkett affair and the Brown dispute supplied Michael Howard with considerable fuel for attacks in the House of Commons, but neither episode did much to improve the Conservatives' poor standing in the opinion polls. For years the Tories had been what the experts call 'flatlining' – their line on the polling graphs refused to move upward. Statistically they were no better off under Michael Howard than they had been in the final months of Iain Duncan Smith – if anything, the figures had even got a little worse. The thirteen opinion polls taken during IDS's last three months as leader in 2003 gave Labour an average lead of just under 5 per cent, whereas the seventeen polls taken in the final three months of 2004 showed that the gap had widened fractionally, to around 6 per cent. By mid-January 2005, of fifty-five opinion polls taken since Michael Howard had been elected leader, only four surveys had even put the Conservatives in front – the best of them by only 4 per cent, which, given the big distortions of the electoral system, was not enough even for the party to win more seats than Labour.[51]

Much of Michael Howard's problem stemmed from his failure to advance a clear, coherent position which was fundamentally different from that of Tony Blair. A possible opportunity came over the government plan to introduce identity cards. Many voters were unhappy with the idea – including many Tories, among them the party's home-affairs spokesman, David Davis. Michael Howard initially insisted, however, that his MPs should back the plans as a significant measure against crime, terrorism, illegal immigration, social-security fraud and abuse of the NHS by patients from overseas. Howard was in a no-win position, of course, having been a big champion of ID cards during his days as Home Secretary. But his stance could not very easily be squared with his 'I Believe' statement, in which he had said that people should be 'masters of their own lives . . . not nannied or over-governed', that 'the state should be small', and that 'armies of interferers don't contribute to human happiness'.[52]

Michael Howard was working extremely hard for a man in his early sixties, and by January 2005 he had visited almost all the Tories' 160 target seats. Then came a big blow when the MP for Wantage, Robert Jackson, who had been one of his junior colleagues at Employment, announced that he was defecting to Labour (though he had already announced his retirement from the Commons). His reasons were particularly directed at his former boss. 'The whole Conservative Party have deserved better leadership,' he said. A Howard government would mean 'certain harm' for Britain. The Tories had 'dangerous' and 'damaging' views on Europe; they had 'wobbled' on Iraq; they had been guilty of 'opportunism' on university fees; and the party was 'incoherent' on public services. 'I think that Michael is privately a nice man,' Jackson said. But 'There is a disparity between the private and the public image. Privately he is humorous and relaxed. Publicly he only has two registers. One is scorn and the other is anger and that is too limited a range.'[53]

Jackson's defection seemed to have been timed with the Labour whips to cause as much damage as possible, coming on the weekend

when Howard was due to announce on the *Breakfast with Frost* programme the outcome of the inquiry by David James into scope for
government savings, with his party's plans for cutting waste and low-
ering taxes. The Tories promised to save £35 billion from reduced
waste, which, in comparison with what Labour already intended, left
£12 billion for extra investment and tax cuts. But the impact was
spoilt when Robert Jackson declared that the programme wasn't credible.

At the end of January, in the week in which the world marked the
sixtieth anniversary of the liberation of Auschwitz, Michael Howard
placed immigration and asylum firmly back on the election agenda by
taking a full-page newspaper advertisement with a statement over his
signature. 'Britain has reached a turning point,' he declared. 'Our
communities cannot absorb newcomers at today's pace.' The
Conservatives would introduce annual limits on both the numbers of
economic migrants admitted to Britain and the number of asylum
seekers. There would be twenty-four hour security at British ports,
and an annual points system for work permits, similar to that in
Australia. A Howard government would also withdraw from the 1951
UN Convention on Refugees, which would make it easier to remove
people with unfounded claims for asylum, and he would establish
reception centres overseas to process future asylum cases.

But Howard didn't avoid the personal issue in his ad: 'Britain has
always offered a home to genuine refugees and to families who want
to work hard. I know – my family was one of them. We are a more
successful country as a result.'[54] His words seemed ambiguous (as well
as rather immodest). Did he mean that his family had wanted to work
hard, or that they had been refugees (which was questionable at least
in his father's case)? Several media outlets wrongly took this to mean
that both his parents had been Romanian refugees, and Howard was
now questioned about his family background more closely than ever
before. 'Would your proposals have prevented your own parents –
Jewish refugees from Romania – from entering Britain if they'd
applied for asylum here after your quota had been met?' asked Victoria
Derbyshire on Radio 5 Live. 'Well, I think they would have been *more*

likely to have been able to come in,' Howard replied without correcting her, 'because our plans will allow more genuine refugees to come into the country.'[55]

While Howard could never be accused of being racist, his initiative was likely to appeal to many racists. Opinion polls showed a significant shift in opinion towards the Conservatives, and within a fortnight the new Home Secretary, Charles Clarke, suddenly announced tougher immigration controls and the adoption of the Australian points system.

Meanwhile, Labour was accused of anti-Semitism when it unveiled a couple of proposed election ads on its party website. One denounced Conservative spending plans by depicting Howard and his Shadow Chancellor, Oliver Letwin, who is also Jewish, as flying pigs; the other portrayed Howard as a Shylock-type figure trying to conduct hypnosis with a swinging watch. It was also revealed that Labour had used powers given by the new Freedom of Information Act to seek out government documents on several controversial episodes from Howard's ministerial career, such as the Derek Lewis affair, the question of whether he helped Petronella Wyatt get a new passport, and the decision to release the Liverpool gangsters Haase and Bennett. Howard visited the Home Office in person to read many of the relevant files and then demanded that they be released immediately. Meanwhile the Metropolitan Police announced that they were investigating the background to Howard's royal pardons for Haase and Bennett, though it was made clear that Howard himself was not a suspect.

The 2005 election looked like being one of the nastiest in modern times, not just involving personal attacks, but also with race and immigration expected to play a bigger role than in any contest since the days of Enoch Powell, in the late 1960s.

EPILOGUE

Most football fans pledge allegiance to one club. Michael Howard, in contrast, supports five. Apart from Liverpool, he still retains an affection for the local teams he watched in his childhood, Llanelli and Swansea, and nowadays, as a Kent MP, he regularly watches Folkestone Invicta and another non-League club in his constituency, Hythe Town.

Howard's personal ancestry is equally confusing. His father came from a Ukrainian community in an area of Romania which has often belonged to Hungary; his mother from a Russian town which was later part of the Soviet Union and is now in Ukraine. He was born with a German surname, though his family later adopted an English one; he was brought up in Wales (whose international football team he supports), but has spent most of his life in England. Several of his orthodox Jewish cousins emigrated to Israel, while he himself has long enjoyed a love affair with the United States of America.

Michael Howard often shows himself to be uneasy with this complicated ancestry. His accounts of how his father came to this country are vague and slightly contradictory. He has no interest in retracing his family roots in eastern Europe, despite his enthusiasm as Employment Secretary to help former members of the Soviet bloc and to encourage free-market economies beyond the former Iron Curtain. It is difficult to imagine him presenting the kind of television programme made by his former colleague Michael Portillo, who explored his father's republican and socialist roots in pre-war Spain. To some extent, of course, this may stem from an understandable desire to draw a veil over the horrors which befell those relatives whom Howard's father and grandfather left behind in Romania: it cannot have been easy to spend his childhood with an aunt who had suffered so horribly in Auschwitz and who still bore the scars, both physical and psychological. Since leaving home at the age of eighteen, Howard has treated his Judaism as a private matter; so far as I am aware he has never revealed publicly – or even to many close friends – whether he believes in God (though Sandra confirmed in February 2005 that he does). Many of his acquaintances from his early adult life were surprised to learn later, when he was becoming known as a politician, that he was Jewish. He seems to have perceived his Jewishness as a handicap to his political career, and, sadly, he was probably right about this.

Howard's obvious concern about his foreign origins is an important key to understanding his character. Like many first- and second-generation immigrants, he seems driven by the need to succeed in this country. In part, of course, he is genuinely grateful that the UK accepted his parents, and, whatever the precise details of how they arrived, the Hechts and the Kurshions would probably have been murdered by the Nazis had they not come to Britain. Michael Howard's intense ambition to succeed in British politics, and forget the past, also reflects an immigrant's desire to integrate: there's no better mark of acceptance than the winning of democratic elections. Equally, Howard's super-patriotism on the issues of Europe and immigration may also reflect his consciousness of his foreign antecedents. He needs to prove he is truly British, one of us, a great defender of our rights. This attitude is probably encouraged both by being the MP for Folkestone – effectively a border constituency – and by the pro-British, anti-foreigner drift of the Conservative Party since the advent of Margaret Thatcher.

Yet it is not a simple picture. Howard was not always so ostentatiously patriotic in the days when he enthusiastically endorsed entry to the Common Market and championed the rights of East African Asians.

In politics, as in his football, Michael Howard is difficult to pigeonhole. He cannot be painted simply as an ideological Thatcherite. In his passion for America he seems more comfortable with Democrats than with Republicans – the Kennedys, Lyndon Johnson and, at the personal level, Bill Clinton's former Treasury Secretary Bob Rubin. He admired Ronald Reagan for his role in ending the Cold War, and he backed the 2003 Iraq War, but he has fallen out with the White House of Bush the Younger. He certainly does not regard himself as an American-style 'neo-Conservative' of the type who surround George W. Bush.

The Conservative leader who pressed support for ID cards on to his reluctant Shadow Cabinet, and pursued rate-capping and budget-capping as an Environment minister, is the same politician who says the state is too big and should stop interfering. The man who revelled in the 'swinging sixties', and whose favourite videos – *Darling* and *Brideshead Revisited* – involve loose sexual lifestyles (both heterosexual and homosexual), and who won over somebody else's wife, sits uneasily with the Michael Howard who did so much to introduce Section 28. Howard's admission that the poll tax was a mistake, and his declaration that he would now keep Labour's minimum wage, would look more convincing *mea culpas* if his earlier positions on these policies had not been pursued with such partisan ferocity. Howard the quick-witted barrister could no doubt reconcile all this, but it doesn't convince voters seeking a clear message.

By the start of 2005 the Michael Howard of October 2003 seemed a fading memory. In his Saatchi Gallery speech, in which he declared himself a candidate for his party's leadership, and subsequent statements up to the spring of 2004 we seemed to be witnessing a man who had genuinely changed, who had accepted the modernisers' argument that the Conservative Party needed to show more tolerance and understand how much Britain had changed. In the autumn of 2003 Howard had extolled a party 'broad in appeal and generous in outlook – a party capable of representing all Britain and all Britons'; he had promised 'a new kind of politics', and said, 'we must look forward not back' (very similar to the slogan that Labour chose – or stole – in 2005, 'Britain Forward Not Back').[1] Yet after the spring of 2004, with successive Conservative failures in various elections and the political threat from UKIP on the right, Howard seemed to return to his guise as Home Secretary, with increasing emphasis on crime and immigration. This was clearly encouraged by the party's new campaign manager, Lynton Crosby, whose election successes for John Howard in Australia, particularly in 2001, were partly achieved through a tough line on immigration. The *Sunday Telegraph* columnist Matthew D'Ancona pointed out how the different Michael Howards of October 2003 and early 2005 have even used the same phrase about refusing to accept 'no-go areas'.[2] At the Saatchi Gallery Howard employed it to mean that the Tories should reach out to every part of the electorate and especially the provincial cities which, he said, had become 'Conservative deserts'. Yet in 2005 Howard was arguing that immigration should not be a 'no-go area' in policy terms, and seemed ready to risk a loss of support from ethnic minorities and liberal-minded people in the quest for gains among the wider electorate.

Michael Howard revealed more of himself than perhaps he intended with his choice of book for *Desert Island Discs*. Robert Caro's biography of Lyndon Johnson is about power, not policy or philosophy. Howard is not a politician of ideas. It is unusual for anyone who takes charge of a major British party to have given so little indication of his own vision beforehand, and to have delivered so few personal policy pronouncements. There's not even a substantial pamphlet to Howard's name, let alone a credo book of the kind written by colleagues such as Michael Heseltine and John Redwood. In almost forty years in public life, Howard's published output of ideas extends to only three slim Bow Group tracts written with other people, and a handful of unremarkable speeches for the Centre for Policy Studies and the Conservative Political Centre. Howard once stated that politicians could seldom 'lay claim to original ideas'; instead, they should choose the best ideas from people outside active politics.[3] As leader, however, he has also failed to recruit academics or political thinkers to do this intellectual work for him, or clever writers ready to bring coherence and clarity to what he says.

For all these reasons it is difficult even to start defining Howardism.

For a man who has so many passions outside politics, it is surprising how few genuine political passions he seems to have. Europe and law-and-order are the only issues on which he seems to hold really strong views. Over the last twenty years Howard has been most clearly identified by what he is against – initially it was opposition to the closed shop and a minimum wage; then to the Social Chapter and the single currency; nowadays to crime and immigration. Yet most pollsters and political strategists believe that it is hard for a leader to succeed in a modern democracy without offering some kind of positive, optimistic vision of the kind of society to which he would like to take us.

Michael Howard is a politician of undoubted abilities – a formidable intellect, a powerful debater and speaker, with a reputation for devouring detail and relentless hard work. Yet during his political life – from the presidency of the Cambridge Union, through the chairmanship of the Bow Group, to becoming an MP and ultimately party leader – he, like many of the Cambridge Mafia, has given the impression of being interested more in 'being there' than in 'doing something'. There's an obvious contrast with another Conservative politician from South Wales. Michael Heseltine was probably even more ambitious than Howard, though he never made it to the leadership. Hezza could be just as partisan and opportunistic in attacking Labour. But we always had a far clearer idea of what a Heseltine government would entail.

Michael Howard's best attempt at the 'vision thing' was his 'British Dream' speech of February 2004; it was a powerful, convincing effort, but he has made little attempt to repeat or expand on it since. In his defence, there's been a genuine paucity of ideas on the British Right since Margaret Thatcher's day: no other Tory seems to be bubbling with new policies or ready with winning messages. Nor is it easy to expound new ideas when Tony Blair has moved in on so much Conservative territory and Labour shamelessly plunders any policy initiatives which take its fancy.

Michael Howard might get away with this deficiency in ideas if he didn't have even bigger problems as a personality. Howard's sixteen-year struggle to find a safe seat and his humiliation by parliamentary colleagues in the leadership contest of 1997 reflected the same character flaws which have handicapped him an as effective Leader of the Opposition. It's not just his failure to rid himself of the image first suggested by Ann Widdecombe – as a blood-sucking vampire, a forbidding, dark undertaker figure. Even if he could project his more relaxed side – Howard the human being, the committed husband, father and stepfather, and Howard the film-going, sports-loving, sentimental romantic – he cannot overcome other features such as his slightly odd way of speaking (a relic of his early Welsh accent), his grey appearance, and his notoriously short fuse. He also lacks another important ingredient. Most successful politicians – Tony Blair, Michael Heseltine, Michael Portillo, Bill Clinton – inspire and excite, or at least interest, the public. 'What's he like?' people ask about them. 'Tell me more? What makes him tick?' It's what one former member of the Shadow Cabinet calls the 'tingle factor'. Even if Howard and his advisers could develop a forceful, clear message, even if he could create public amnesia about his record and reputation, not even the best political spin doctor or image-maker can manufacture this form of charisma. You either have it or you don't. The nearest Michael Howard has to a 'tingle factor' is his glamorous wife, Sandra.

The greatest political stars usually attract a significant personal following among MPs, but there has never been an identifiable body of Howard disciples. Ever since Llanelli Grammar School, Michael Howard has always been a loner. Had he not been, and had there been a group of Howardites, inside or outside Parliament, it might have been easier for him to establish a more coherent message and body of thought. The effect works both ways, of course: people are unlikely to flock behind a politician if they have little idea of what he stands for.

History should not assess Michael Howard just on his brief record as Conservative leader. To a large extent he is just another victim of his party's decline, which now stretches back almost two decades, and which his immediate predecessors could do little to halt. As a government minister for twelve years, Howard was undoubtedly more successful than many of his colleagues. His role in the run-up to the Rio summit, his work on housing, and his success in cutting crime rates while at the Home Office would be recognised even by many opponents. And even in more controversial areas of policy one has to acknowledge his success in carrying out the tasks he has set himself, or, in the case of the poll tax and water privatisation, the agenda set by others. Even if one disagrees with much of what he did at the Home Office, one must concede his courage in pressing on with his programme despite strenuous vilification by pressure groups and the media, and with the extra distraction and pressure of the Harry Landy affair. Most men would have found it an impossible load.

At the time of writing, five weeks into 2005, Michael Howard seems to be leading his party to another calamitous defeat in the impending election. True, he has imposed much tighter discipline on the Conservatives than John Major, William Hague or Iain Duncan Smith ever managed, though in reality the infighting and bickering haven't ceased; they're just less visible. And, even though Howard's ability to match Tony Blair in the House of Commons did restore some party morale, there is a serious possibility that the number of Conservative seats will fall further when Britain votes.

If, however, Howard makes significant inroads into Labour's majority he may try to stay and fight the subsequent election, due perhaps in 2009 or 2010, when he will be almost seventy. The Conservatives' chances may be better at the end of a third Labour term, when memories of the Thatcher and Major years will have receded further and people may be even more disillusioned with Labour. Boundary reorganisation will also ensure a fairer contest. Howard would be much more confident if Gordon Brown were to succeed Tony Blair (though Howard and Brown are alike in many of their character traits). Howard has long recognised the Labour leader's appeal to Conservative voters, ever since the time he invited the Blairs to dinner out of curiosity as to why Blair wasn't a Tory. Brown is a less attractive figure to middle-class voters in England.

Don't underestimate Michael Howard's resilience. Weaker figures would have given up politics in the late 1970s, when he couldn't find a seat, or in 1997, when his leadership ambitions seemed for ever dashed. One must admire his persistence and his commitment to continuing in public life, especially when so many colleagues from the

Thatcher/Major years have quit the battlefield in favour of well-remunerated semi-retirement jobs and seats in the Lords. And Howard might be a wealthier man today had he abandoned politics.

Howard is not revered or even regarded with much affection by his Westminster colleagues, merely accepted as leader in the depressing absence of a better choice. In 1997 and 2001 the Conservative jungle was still stalked by big beasts who enjoyed respect and even admiration among the public – Michael Heseltine, Ken Clarke and even Michael Portillo. Rarely in history can the main opposition party have been so bereft of convincing potential prime ministers as now. Neither of Howard's two most likely senior successors – David Davis and Malcolm Rifkind (who is set to return as an MP) – would be an obvious improvement. Davis lacks the confidence of Tory MPs, while Rifkind, though experienced and able, would be another reminder of the past.

Even if the Conservatives lose badly in 2005, Howard has made it clear that he hopes to stay on for at least a couple of years. He thought John Major and William Hague were wrong to resign so promptly after the 1997 and 2001 defeats, and staying in place would give him a crack at what he would see as the significant consolation prize of a 'No' vote in the forthcoming referendum on the new European constitution, due in 2006. The extra time would also allow a younger successor to establish himself, such as one of Howard's apparent favourites, David Cameron and George Osborne, who were only thirty-eight and thirty-three, respectively, at the start of 2005. Both, however, are handicapped by upper-class public-school backgrounds, and it's now more than forty years since the Conservatives chose a leader with such a high-level pedigree.

The downside to retaining Howard as a caretaker leader is that it would inevitably postpone the radical programme of modernisation which the Conservative Party probably needs to make itself re-electable. One cannot see Howard agreeing to a change of name, for instance, major innovations in policy, or catching up with the modern world with a dramatic overhaul of the party's outlook, image and culture. Pragmatist though he is, it's not Michael Howard.

NOTES

Key to Interviewers

MLC – Michael Crick
MAG – Mark Garnett
MWBG – Miles Goslett
TL – Tom Lumley

CHAPTER 1: THE HECHTS OF TRANSYLVANIA

1. *Sunday Times*, 25 Jan. 2004.
2. B. Hecht file, HO Aliens Dept, Nat. Arch. HO405/20669, immigration officers' report, 21 Mar. 1937.
3. Ibid.
4. Ibid., letter, J. H. Hall to J. Simon, 23 Mar. 1937.
5. Ibid., minutes.
6. Ibid., letter, Advisory Cttee for the Admission of Jewish Ecclesiastical Officers to Home Office, 7 May 1937.
7. See R. Skidelsky, *Oswald Mosley*, Papermac, 1975, pp. 393–410.
8. B. Hecht file, letter, ACAJEO to Home Office, 12 Aug. 1937.
9. See L. London, *Whitehall and the Jews 1933–1948*, Cambridge University Press, 2000, p. 11.
10. Birth-registration book, Ruscova village hall, Romania.
11. G. Sava, interview with MLC.
12. M. Hecht, interview with MLC.
13. Ibid.
14. *Universal Jewish Encyclopedia*, vol. 9, 1943, p. 259.
15. M. Hecht interview.
16. See Keith Hitchins, *Romania 1866–1947*, Oxford University Press, 1994.
17. M. and Josef Hecht, M. Morgan, and J. Jones, all interviews with MLC; and Jacob Hecht, *Mail on Sunday*, 2 Nov. 2003.
18. M. Howard speech, 30 Oct. 2003, http://conservatives.com.
19. *Desert Island Discs*, BBC Radio 4, 4 July 2004.
20. *Times*, 14 Feb. 2004.
21. *Breakfast with Frost*, BBC1, 10 Dec. 1995.
22. M. Hecht interview.
23. Josef Hecht, interview with MLC.
24. Sava interview.

25. Josef Hecht interview.
26. M. Hecht interview.
27. Sava interview.
28. Ibid.
29. O. Gheorghe, interview with MLC.
30. *Mail on Sunday*, 2 Nov. 2003.
31. M. Hecht interview.
32. M. Gilbert, *The Dent Atlas of the Holocaust*, Dent, 1993, p. 197.
33. *Mail on Sunday*, 2 Nov. 2003.
34. *Daily Mail*, 12 Feb. 2005.
35. M. Hecht interview.
36. Ibid.
37. Ibid.
38. Ibid.
39. Ibid.
40. Ibid.
41. Ibid.
42. Josef Hecht interview.
43. M. Hecht interview.
44. *Mail on Sunday*, 2 Nov. 2003.
45. R. Hercz (Hecht) file, Nat. Arch., HO405/23635, Carmarthenshire constab. report, 12 Aug. 1954.
46. M. Hecht interview.
47. Josef Hecht interview.
48. *Mail on Sunday*, 9 Nov. 2003.

CHAPTER 2: THE LANDYS OF LLANELLI

1. B. Hecht file, HO Aliens Dept, Nat. Arch. HO405/20669, Carmarthenshire constab. report, 13 Oct. 1947.
2. David Griffiths, *The Chartered Borough of Llanelli 1913–1988*, Llanelli Borough Council, 1989, p. 2.
3. U. Henriques, *The Jews of South Wales*, University of Wales Press, 1993, p. 6.
4. *Encyclopaedia Judaica*, vol. 10, Kater Publishing, 1971, col. 1388.
5. Hyman Landy quoted in *Llanelli Star*, 20 July 1974.
6. *Llanelly and County Guardian*, 20 May 1909.
7. *South Wales Press*, 30 June 1915.
8. Ibid., 14 July 1915.
9. *Llanelly Mercury*, 12 Aug. 1915.
10. R. Stratton, interview with MLC.
11. V. Haebe, interview with MLC.
12. J. Kurshion file, Nat. Arch. HO405/26756, Carmarthenshire constab. report, 13 May 1935.
13. T. Harries, interview with MLC.
14. Hansard, 18 June 1940, col. 61.
15. M. Hecht, interview with MLC.
16. B. Hecht file, Carmarthenshire constab. report, 13 Oct. 1947.
17. Ibid.

18. H. Davies, *Looking Round Llanelli*, ed. G. Hughes, Llanelli Town Council, 1985, p. 203.
19. B. Hecht file, Carmarthenshire constab. report, 13 Oct. 1947.
20. B. Ross, conversation with TL.
21. R. Hercz (Hecht) file, Nat. Arch., HO405/23635, Home Office letter to Carmarthenshire chief const., 30 July 1954.
22. Ibid., Home Office minute, 2 Sept 1954.
23. *Daily Mail*, 12 Feb 2005.

CHAPTER 3: SCHOOLBOY REBEL

1. *The Real Michael Howard*, BBC Radio 5 Live, 27 Dec. 2003.
2. J. Pugh, interview with MLC.
3. E. Rees, interview with MLC.
4. G. Williams, interview with MLC.
5. H. Griffiths, interview with MLC.
6. Ibid.
7. Ibid.
8. *Llanelli Star*, 6 Dec. 1962.
9. Ibid., 22 Mar. 1958.
10. Ibid., 12 Dec. 1959.
11. M. Morgan, interview with MLC.
12. *South Wales Evening Post*, 31 Oct. 2003.
13. J. Jones, interview with MLC.
14. J. Thomas, interview with MLC.
15. *Desert Island Discs*, BBC Radio 4, 4 July 2004.
16. Ibid.
17. *Daily Mail*, 12 Feb. 2005.
18. Morgan interview.
19. Entrance exam to grammar schools, Carmarthenshire Educ. Cttee, 1952.
20. *Evening Standard*, 16 Jan. 1996.
21. Ibid.
22. Report by HM Inspectors on Llanelli GS, Feb. 1953, pp. 13, 9, 12.
23. J. Hopkins, interview with MLC.
24. E. Phillips, interview with MLC.
25. Ibid.
26. *Evening Standard*, 16 Jan. 1996.
27. G. Ballard, interview with MLC.
28. *Times*, 10 Dec. 2003.
29. J. Davies, interview with MLC.
30. *The Report*, Graig School, 1993.
31. BBC News website, 6 Nov. 2003.
32. Ballard interview.
33. R. Woolf, interview with MLC.
34. *Evening Standard*, 16 Jan. 1996.
35. *Financial Times*, 15 Mar. 1986.
36. Morgan interview.
37. *Evening Standard*, 16 Jan. 1996.

38. D. Smith, interview with MLC.
39. *The Real Michael Howard.*
40. *In Conversation with Leslie Griffiths*, BBC Radio Wales, 2 Oct. 2000.
41. *The Real Michael Howard.*
42. *Evening Standard*, 16 Jan. 1996; *Times Educational Supplement*, 29 Oct. 2004.
43. K. Marshall, interview with MLC.
44. V. Jones interview.
45. *Evening Standard*, 16 Jan. 1996.
46. Woolf interview.
47. Marshall interview.
48. *Evening Standard*, 16 Jan. 1996.
49. E. John, interview with MLC.
50. Marshall interview.
51. *Evening Standard*, 16 Jan. 1996.
52. V. Jones interview.
53. Marshall interview.
54. Llanelli GS school magazine, 1958.
55. Hopkins interview.
56. Marshall interview.
57. A. Thomas, interview with MLC.
58. J. Bowen, interview with MLC.
59. Smith interview.
60. G. Evans, interview with MLC.
61. A. Sims, interview with MLC.
62. *In Conversation with Leslie Griffiths*, 2 Oct. 2000.
63. Ibid.
64. *Desert Island Discs*, 4 July 2004.

CHAPTER 4: CAMBRIDGE MAFIOSO

1. *Sunday Times*, 25 Jan. 2004.
2. *Daily Telegraph*, 21 June 2004.
3. See M. Gove, *Michael Portillo*, Fourth Estate, 1995, pp. 39–60.
4. P. Hill, interview with MLC.
5. J. Gummer, interview with M. Balen, 1993.
6. *Varsity Handbook*, Varsity Publications, 1960, pp. 73–4.
7. Ibid., 1961, p. 95.
8. Gummer interview.
9. *Varsity*, 20 May 1961.
10. P. Temple-Morris, interview with MLC.
11. D. Hacking, interview with MLC.
12. *Desert Island Discs*, BBC Radio 4, 4 July 2004.
13. H. Wilson, interview with MLC.
14. L. Brittan, interview with MLC.
15. Temple-Morris interview.
16. CUCA term card, Michaelmas 1960.
17. *Varsity*, 25 Feb. 1961.
18. *In Conversation with Leslie Griffiths*, BBC Radio Wales, 2 Oct. 2000.

19. N. Fowler, *Ministers Decide*, Chapmans, 1991, p. 26.
20. Ibid., p. 27.
21. J. Barnes, interview with MLC.
22. O. Weaver, interview with MLC.
23. J. Dunn, email to MAG.
24. C. Renfrew, interview with MAG.
25. M. Latham, interview with MLC.
26. N. Lamont, interview with MAG.
27. Hacking interview.
28. P. Fullerton, interview with MLC.
29. Temple-Morris interview.
30. Cambridge Union debate minute book, CU Library.
31. *Varsity*, 4 Mar. 1961.
32. Brittan interview.
33. M. Balen, *Kenneth Clarke*, Fourth Estate, 1994, p. 34.
34. *Varsity*, 18 Nov. 1961.
35. Ibid., 11 Nov. 1961.
36. Ibid., 18 Nov. 1961.
37. J. Barnes, interview with M. Balen, *c.* 1993.
38. Balen, *Kenneth Clarke*, p. 36.
39. *Varsity*, 11 Nov. 1961.
40. Ibid., 2 Dec. 1961.
41. Ibid., 18 Nov. 1961.
42. J. Barnes, interview with MLC.
43. Temple-Morris interview.
44. *Varsity*, 25 Nov. 1961.
45. K. Clarke, interview with M. Balen, 1993.
46. Balen, *Kenneth Clarke*, p. 41.
47. A. McSmith, *Kenneth Clarke*, Verso, 1994, p. 18.
48. *Varsity*, 2 Dec. 1961.
49. Ibid.
50. McSmith, *Kenneth Clarke*, 1994, p. 19.
51. *Varsity*, 27 Jan. 1962.
52. Ibid., 28 Apr. 1962.
53. Ibid., 10 Mar. 1962.
54. *Llanelli Star*, 24 Mar. 1962.
55. *Varsity*, 5 May 1962.
56. Ibid., 26 May 1962.
57. Ibid.
58. Ibid., 16 June 1962.
59. *Daily Telegraph*, 1 Nov. 2003.
60. O. Walston, interview with MLC.
61. *Varsity*, 9 Feb. 1963.
62. C. Haddon, interview with MLC.
63. C. Haddon, *The Limits of Sex*, Corgi, 1983.
64. K. Clarke, interview with MAG.
65. B. Davies, interview with MLC.
66. Brittan interview.

67. *Varsity*, 9 Feb. 1963.
68. Ibid., 16 Feb. 1963.
69. Lamont interview.
70. W. Rodgers, interview with MLC.
71. Walston interview.
72. *Varsity*, 9 Mar. 1963.
73. R. Strange, email to MLC.

CHAPTER 5: A TALE OF THREE CITIES

1. MH, raw interview for *When The World Was Young*, BBC Radio 4, 15 Nov. 2003.
2. Ibid.
3. Ibid.
4. CU ESU debating-team report, 1963.
5. J. Toulmin, interview with MLC.
6. CU ESU debating-team report, 1963.
7. Toulmin interview.
8. J. Toulmin letter to parents, dated 9 Oct. 1963 but must be later.
9. *Colombia Missourian*, 27 Oct. 1963.
10. Toulmin interview.
11. MH, raw interview for *When The World Was Young*.
12. Toulmin interview.
13. *Colorado Daily*, 4 Dec. 1963.
14. CU ESU debating-team report, 1963.
15. *Sunday Telegraph* magazine, 28 Nov. 1999.
16. J. Entwistle, interview with MLC.
17. Leroi Jones (Amiri Baraka), 'The Acceptance of Monk', in *The Thelonious Monk Reader*, ed. Rob van der Bliek, Oxford University Press, 2001, p. 166.
18. J. Zarr, interview with MLC.
19. *Desert Island Discs*, BBC Radio 4, 4 July 2004.
20. Entwistle interview.
21. Zarr interview.
22. Ibid.
23. Ibid.
24. J. Gladstone, emails to MLC.
25. CU ESU debating-team biographical notes, 1963.
26. S. Flather, interview with MLC.
27. *Radio Times* (Welsh edn), 15 July 1965.
28. N. Lamont, interview with MLC.
29. R. Somerset-Ward, interview with MLC.
30. J. Entwistle, email to MAG.
31. J. Prescott-Thomas, interview with MLC.
32. Somerset-Ward interview.
33. Prescott-Thomas interview.
34. Lamont interview.
35. *The Real Michael Howard*, BBC Radio 5 Live, 27 Dec. 2003.
36. Prescott-Thomas interview.

37. Entwistle email.
38. *Desert Island Discs*, 4 July 2004.
39. J. Bosworth, letter to MLC; Entwistle email.
40. Lamont interview.
41. *Liverpool Daily Post*, 9 June 1970.
42. Entwistle interview.
43. Bosworth letter.
44. *Liverpool Echo*, 26 Mar. 1966.
45. Ibid., 17 Mar. 1966.
46. *Liverpool Daily Post*, 23 Mar. 1966.
47. Ibid.
48. *Liverpool Echo*, 31 Mar. 1966.
49. *Times*, 2 Jan. 2004.

CHAPTER 6: LOUD PROTESTS AND THUMPING

1. *Guardian*, 29 May 1993.
2. Minutes of Archway Inquiry Proceedings, 18 May 1977, p. 16.
3. *Desert Island Discs*, BBC Radio 4, 4 July 2004.
4. C. Haddon, interview with MLC.
5. E. Cooper, interview with MLC.
6. S. Laufer, interview with MLC.
7. G. Flather, interview with MLC.
8. *All England Law Reports*, 1976, Butterworths, p. 454.
9. *Marshall* v. *BBC*, WLR, 1979.
10. *Guardian*, 29 May 1993.
11. J. Adams, interview with MWBG.
12. P. Levin, interview with MWBG.
13. Minutes of Archway Inquiry Proceedings, 18 May 1977, p. 11.
14. G. Stern, interview with MWBG.
15. Minutes of Archway Inquiry Proceedings, 10 May 1977.
16. Ibid., 18 May 1977, p. 16.
17. N. Tuckman, interview with MWBG.
18. *Evening News*, 19 May 1977.
19. Minutes of Archway Inquiry Proceedings, 20 May 1977.
20. Unpublished interview of MH by N. Tuckman, May 1993.
21. *Evening News*, 21 May 1977.
22. *Evening Standard*, 23 Jan. 2000.
23. Ibid., 28 Mar. 1978.
24. L. Read, interview with MLC.
25. D. Woolley, interview with MWBG.
26. G. Dobry, interview with MLC.
27. C. Symons, interview with MLC.
28. L. Charles, interview with MLC.
29. Dobry interview.
30. S. Graham, interview with MLC.
31. Dobry interview.
32. J. Entwistle, interview with MLC.

33. Graham interview.
34. C. Lockhart-Mummery, interview with MLC.
35. Graham interview.
36. A. Seifert, interview with MLC.

CHAPTER 7: THE LOVE OF HIS LIFE

1. H. Fielding, *Bridget Jones's Diary*, Picador, 1996, p. 235.
2. *Times*, 6 Nov. 2003.
3. *This Morning*, ITV, 6 July 2004.
4. *Daily Mail* weekend supplement, 21 Feb. 2004.
5. *The Real Michael Howard*, BBC Radio 5 Live, 27 Dec. 2003.
6. *Daily Mail* weekend supplement, 21 Feb. 2004.
7. C. Haddon, interview with MLC.
8. *The Real Michael Howard*.
9. L. Seifert (now Goldstone), interview with MLC.
10. J. Entwistle, interview with MLC.
11. R. Somerset-Ward, interview with MLC.
12. A. Mallalieu, interview with MLC.
13. N. Lamont, interview with MAG.
14. Haddon interview.
15. Lamont interview.
16. R. Compton Miller, interview with MLC.
17. *Times* magazine, 30 Oct. 2004.
18. *Harper's Bazaar*, July–Aug. 1968.
19. *Times* magazine, 30 Oct. 2004.
20. Ibid.
21. *Daily Express*, 30 Mar. 1959.
22. *Sunday Express*, 10 Mar. 1963.
23. *Daily Mail* weekend supplement, 21 Feb. 2004.
24. *Daily Express*, 30 Mar. 1959.
25. *Daily Mail*, 1 Apr. 1993.
26. T. Mallett (now Radcliffe), interview with MWBG.
27. *Evening Standard*, 31 Oct. 2003.
28. *News of the World*, 30 Jan. 1977.
29. *Scotsman*, 10 July 1959.
30. *Times* magazine, 30 Oct. 2004.
31. D. Wynne-Morgan, interview with MWBG.
32. *Whicker's World*, BBC2, 22 Apr. 1967.
33. *Daily Mail*, 30 Mar. 1959.
34. *Times* magazine, 30 Oct. 2004.
35. *News of the World*, 5 Feb. 1977.
36. N. Botham, *Margaret: The Untold Story*, Blake, 1995, p. 217.
37. R. Douglas-Home, *Sinatra*, Michael Joseph, 1962.
38. S. Howard, raw interview for *When The World Was Young*, BBC Radio 4, 15 Nov. 2003.
39. *Queen*, Feb. 1967.
40. *Daily Express*, 30 Mar. 1959.

41. *Daily Mail*, 27 Nov. 1962.
42. *Times* magazine, 30 Oct. 2004.
43. P. Hanson, interview with MWBG.
44. Ibid.
45. *Daily Sketch*, 26 Mar. 1965.
46. *Times* magazine, 30 Oct. 2004.
47. *Whicker's World*, 22 Apr. 1967.
48. Ibid.
49. Ibid.
50. Ibid.
51. E. Harrison, *Love, Honour and Dismay*, W. H. Allen, 1976, p. 93.
52. *Queen*, Feb. 1963; *News of the World*, 5, 12, 19 Mar. 1967; *Washington Post*, 12, 13 Feb. 1967.
53. A. Whicker, *Within Whicker's World*, Elm Tree Books, 1982, p. 208.
54. *Whicker's World*, 22 Apr. 1967.
55. Whicker, *Within Whicker's World*, p. 209.
56. *Whicker's World*, 22 Apr. 1967.
57. *News of the World*, 30 Jan. 1977.
58. *Daily Mail*, 16 Oct. 1968.
59. *Times* magazine, 30 Oct. 2004.
60. *News of the World*, 5 Feb. 1977.
61. R. Douglas-Home, *When the Sweet Talking's Done*, Leslie Frewin, 1968. His first novel was *Hot For Certainties*, Longman, 1964.
62. R. Douglas-Home, *The Faint Aroma of Performing Seals*, Leslie Frewin, 1971.
63. S. Douglas-Home, interview with MLC.
64. *La Repubblica*, Venerdi supp., 19 May 2000.
65. Douglas-Home interview.
66. D. Bond, interview with MWBG.
67. Ibid.
68. P. Junor, *Home Truths: Life Around My Father*, HarperCollins, 2002, p. 113.
69. Wynne-Morgan interview.
70. Ibid.
71. Ibid.
72. Bond interview.
73. *Sun*, 5 Feb. 1974.
74. *Sunday Express*, 21 Feb. 1974.
75. *Daily Express*, 8 Apr. 2004.
76. *Times*, 20 Nov. 2004.

CHAPTER 8: SOMEWHERE TO SIT

1. A. Clark, *Diaries: Into Politics*, Jonathan Cape, 2000, p. 18.
2. M. Latham, interview with MLC.
3. D. Walder, *The Short List*, Hutchinson, 1964, p. 10.
4. J. Barr, *The Bow Group: A History*, Politico's, 2001, p. 116.
5. J. Entwistle, interview with MLC.
6. M. Howard et. al., *The Greatest Claim*, Bow Group, 1970, p. 5.
7. *Daily Telegraph*, 26 Feb. 1971.

8. J. Critchley and M. Howard, *A Tax on Inflation*, Bow Group, 1971, p. 3.
9. Ibid., pp. 2–4.
10. *Times*, 5 Oct. 1970.
11. Barr, *The Bow Group*, p. 118.
12. *Daily Telegraph*, 5 Oct. 1970.
13. Cons. Conference Report 1970, p. 31.
14. Barr, *The Bow Group*, pp. 120–23.
15. N. Lamont, interview with MAG.
16. J. Butcher, interview with MLC.
17. Ibid.
18. *Crossbow*, Jan.–Mar. 1971.
19. E. Koops, interview with MLC.
20. N. Lamont, interview with MLC.
21. *Crossbow*, July–Sept. 1971.
22. D. Weeks, interview with MLC.
23. P. Dyas, interview with MLC.
24. *Crossbow*, July–Sept. 1971.
25. Clark, *Diaries*, pp. 6–7.
26. *Wembley Observer*, 16 Feb. 1973.
27. Minutes as read to MLC by R. Bullock.
28. S. Douglas-Home, interview with MLC.
29. *Mail on Sunday*, 2 Nov. 2003.
30. Douglas-Home interview.
31. Ibid.
32. *Guardian*, 29 May 1993.
33. Ibid.
34. M. Parris, *Chance Witness*, Penguin, 2003, pp. 221–2.
35. *The Real Michael Howard*, BBC Radio 5 Live, 27 Dec. 2003.
36. Koops interview.
37. *Daily Telegraph*, 10 June 1996.
38. Butcher interview.
39. P. Thurnham, interview with MWBG.
40. C. Parkinson, interview with MAG.
41. Ibid.
42. P. Rees, interview with MLC.
43. G. Bunting, interview with MWBG.
44. D. Crowthorn, interview with MWBG.
45. J. Palmer, interview with MWBG.
46. Crowthorn interview.
47. E. Bailey, interview with MWBG.
48. Bunting interview.
49. C. Bland, interview with MLC.

CHAPTER 9: IN AT LAST

1. B. Gould, *Goodbye to All That*, HarperCollins, 1995, p. 170.
2. V. Gover, interview with MWBG.
3. *Sunday Telegraph*, 14 Mar. 1999.

4. R. King, interview with MAG.
5. R. Hayward, interview with MLC.
6. Hansard, 29 June 1983, cols. 633–5.
7. Ibid.
8. Ibid., 8 Nov. 1983, cols. 207–10.
9. Ibid., col. 217.
10. See A. Seldon, *Blair*, Simon & Schuster, 2004, p. 34; *In Conversation with Leslie Griffiths*, BBC Radio Wales, 2 Oct. 2000.
11. J. Rentoul, *Tony Blair: Prime Minister*, Little, Brown, 2001, p. 161; N. Lamont and R. Lamont, interviews with MLC.
12. N. Lamont, *In Office*, Little, Brown, 1999, p. 414.
13. S. Douglas-Home, interview with MLC.
14. Hansard, 18 Nov. 1983, col. 1141.
15. Ibid., 19 Dec. 1984, col. 323.
16. Ibid., 27 Feb. 1984, cols. 94–6.
17. P. Mayhew, interview with MLC.
18. R. Caro, *The Years of Lyndon Johnson*, vol. 1: *The Path to Power*, Knopf, 1982.
19. R. Caro, interview with MLC.
20. *Desert Island Discs*, BBC Radio 4, 4 July 2004.
21. C. Katkowski, interview with MLC.
22. *Mail on Sunday*, 26 May 1985.
23. I. Dale (ed.), *Memories of Maggie: A Portrait of Margaret Thatcher*, Politico's, 2000, p. 296.
24. D. Hacking interview with MLC.
25. *Folkestone Herald*, 17 Jan. 1986.
26. *Times*, 27 Oct. 1986.
27. Hansard, 18 Dec. 1985, col. 471.
28. *Times*, 12 Dec. 1985.
29. *Financial Times*, 13 Sept. 1985.
30. Hansard, Standing Cttee E, 28 Jan. 1986, cols. 13–14.
31. *Observer*, 7 Dec. 1986.
32. Gould, *Goodbye to All That*, p. 170.
33. *Financial Times*, 15 Mar. 1986.
34. Hayward interview.
35. Gould, *Goodbye to All That*, p. 170.
36. *Times*, 27 Oct. 1986.
37. N. Lawson, *The View from No. 11*, Bantam, 1992, p. 401.
38. *Observer*, 7 Dec. 1986.
39. W. Wyatt, *Journals of Woodrow Wyatt*, vol. 1, Macmillan, 1998, pp. 250–51 (17 Dec. 1986).
40. *Observer*, 18 Jan. 1987.
41. D. Mellor, interview with MLC.
42. M. Baker, interview with MLC.
43. C. Haddon, interview with MLC.
44. Wyatt, *Journals*, vol. 1, p. 257 (29 Dec. 1986).
45. *Times*, 8 Apr. 1987.
46. *Sun*, 9 Apr. 1987.
47. *Folkestone Herald*, 15 Feb. 1985.

48. D. Gemmell, interview with MWBG.
49. *Folkestone Herald*, 15 July 1983; 9 Aug. 1985.
50. Ibid., 8 Mar. 1985.
51. Howard election address, Folkestone and Hythe, 1983.
52. *Folkestone Herald*, 15 July 1983.
53. D. Gemmell interview.
54. Ibid.
55. *Independent on Sunday*, 7 Nov. 1993.
56. Howard election address, Folkestone and Hythe, 1987.
57. J. Grugeon, interview with MLC.
58. S. Ridley-Day, interview with MWBG.
59. P. Carter, interview with MWBG.
60. D. Crowthorn, interview with MWBG.
61. J. Sloggett, interview with MWBG.
62. G. Pepper, interview with MWBG.
63. D. Gemmell interview.
64. V. Gemmell, interview with MWBG.
65. *Folkestone Herald*, 26 Apr. 1985.
66. *Romney Marsh Herald*, 19 June 1987.

CHAPTER 10: MR POLL TAX

1. Untransmitted material from BBC interview, 2004.
2. *Daily Express*, 22 July 1987.
3. *Sun*, 25 June 1987; 14 Sept. 1987.
4. *Daily Express*, 22 July 1987.
5. *Sunday Times*, 26 July 1987.
6. *Daily Express*, 22 July 1987.
7. See M. Crick and A. Van Klaveren, 'Mrs Thatcher's Greatest Blunder?', *Journal of Contemporary British History*, winter 1991, pp. 397–416.
8. *Sunday Times*, 26 July 1987.
9. *Daily Express*, 22 July 1987.
10. Cons. Party conference press release, 8 Oct. 1987.
11. *Times*, 11 Jan. 1988.
12. *Mail on Sunday*, 19 July 1988.
13. R. King, interview with MAG.
14. *Guardian*, 19 July 1991.
15. N. Ridley, *My Style of Government*, Hutchinson, 1991, p. 126.
16. M. Thatcher, *Downing Street Years*, HarperCollins, 1993, p. 651.
17. N. Lawson, *The View from No. 11*, Bantam, 1992, p. 579.
18. Thatcher, *Downing Street Years*, p. 652.
19. *Guardian*, 28 July 1987.
20. *Sunday Times*, 10 Jan. 1988.
21. *Observer*, 2 Aug. 1987.
22. Hansard, Standing Cttee E, 26 Jan. 1988, col. 133.
23. King interview.
24. K. Baker, *The Turbulent Years: My Life in Politics*, Faber, 1989, p. 140.
25. Hansard, 18 Apr. 1988, col. 623.

26. Ibid., 25 Apr. 1988, col. 148.
27. D. Osborn, interview with MLC.
28. Ibid.
29. Cons. Party conference press release, 8 Oct. 1987.
30. S. Jeffery-Poulter, *Peers, Queers and Commons: The Struggle for Gay Law Reform from 1950 to the Present*, Routledge, 1991, p. 211.
31. Hansard, Standing Cttee A, 8 Dec. 1987, col. 1199.
32. D. Wilshire, interview with MLC.
33. Hansard, Commons Standing Cttee A, 8 Dec. 1987, cols. 1209, 1221.
34. Ibid., col. 864.
35. Ibid., cols. 1209, 1208.
36. Ibid., col. 1230.
37. Ibid., col. 1220.
38. Ibid., col. 1230.
39. Jeffery-Poulter, *Peers, Queers and Commons*, p. 221.
40. *Observer*, 31 Jan. 1988.
41. R. Hayward, interview with MLC.
42. *Times*, 25 Jan. 1988.
43. Baker, *The Turbulent Years*, p. 155.
44. *Times*, 21 Nov. 1988.
45. *Mail on Sunday*, 26 Feb. 1989.
46. *Six O'Clock News*, BBC1, 15 Mar. 1989.
47. Ibid.
48. *Nine O'Clock News*, BBC1, 15 Mar. 1989.
49. L. Price, email to MLC.
50. B. Ingham, *Kill the Messenger*, HarperCollins, 1991, p. 331.
51. *Daily Telegraph*, 6 Mar. 1989.
52. *Six O'Clock News*, BBC1, 15 Mar. 1989.
53. J. Penycate, interview with MLC.
54. *Today*, 7 June 1989.
55. *Sun*, 9 Oct. 1989; *Folkestone Herald*, 13 Oct. 1989.
56. *Times*, 7 Dec. 1989.
57. *Guardian*, 12 Dec. 1989.
58. N. Hardwick, interview with MLC.

CHAPTER 11: ME AND MY SHADOW

1. *No More Mr Nasty*, BBC2, 12 Feb. 2005.
2. *Times*, 25 July 1991.
3. N. Fowler, interview with MLC.
4. *Folkestone Herald*, 12 Jan. 1990.
5. *Times*, 14 Feb. 1980; Hansard, 29 June 1983, cols. 633–5.
6. R. King, interview with MAG.
7. Hansard, 16 Jan. 1990, col. 148.
8. Ibid., 29 Jan. 1990, col. 58.
9. *New Statesman*, 30 Aug. 1991.
10. *Guardian*, 7 Oct. 1991.
11. *Sun*, 9 Oct. 1991.

12. G. Shephard, interview with MLC.
13. *Financial Times*, 13 May 1991.
14. B. Sutlieff, interview with MLC.
15. R. Jackson, interview with MAG.
16. C. Parkinson, interview with MAG.
17. B. Anderson, *John Major: The Making of the Prime Minister*, Fourth Estate, 1991, pp. 143–4.
18. M. Thatcher, *Downing Street Years*, HarperCollins, 1993, p. 852.
19. *Economist*, 24 Nov. 1990.
20. Jackson and King interviews.
21. J. Major, *The Autobiography*, HarperCollins, 1999, p. 191.
22. *Guardian*, 1 Dec. 1990.
23. M. Howard, *Consistency and Change: The Conservative Challenge in the 1990s*, Conservative Political Centre, 1991, pp. 5–7.
24. W. Wyatt, *Journals of Woodrow Wyatt*, vol. 2, Macmillan, 1999, p. 480 (19 Mar. 1991).
25. *House Magazine*, 20 May 1991.
26. *Sunday Correspondent*, 17 June 1990.
27. *Guardian*, 14 Dec. 1990.
28. Sutlieff interview.
29. *Daily Mail*, 12 Feb. 2005.
30. Sutlieff interview.
31. *Times*, 17 Jan. 1991.
32. *Financial Times*, 9 Dec. 1991.
33. *Sun*, 4 Dec. 1991.
34. S. Hogg and J. Hill, *Too Close to Call: Power and Politics – John Major in No. 10*, Little, Brown 1995, p. 155.
35. Major, *Autobiography*, p. 285.
36. *Daily Telegraph*, 10 Mar. 1999.
37. A. Seldon, *Major: A Political Life*, Weidenfeld & Nicolson, 1997, p. 247.
38. H. Young, *This Blessed Plot*, Papermac, 1999, p. 431.
39. *Financial Times*, 12 Dec. 1991.
40. *Guardian*, 19 Sept. 1991.
41. Ibid., 3 Feb. 1992.
42. *Today*, 20 Jan. 1992.
43. J. Rentoul, *Tony Blair*, Little, Brown, 1995, pp. 241–2.
44. Ibid., pp. 243–4.
45. *Mail on Sunday*, 14 June 1991.
46. *Sunday Times*, 21 July 1991.
47. *Independent*, 8 Sept. 1991; *Guardian*, 7 Sept. 1991.
48. *Evening Standard*, 4 Sept. 1991.
49. *Times*, 29 Jan. 1992.
50. *Financial Times*, 16 July 1991.
51. *Times*, 12 Feb. 1992.
52. *Guardian*, 12 Feb. 1992.
53. *Folkestone Herald*, 13 Sept. 1991.
54. J. Birt, *The Harder Path*, Time Warner, 2002, pp. 288–9.
55. N. Jones, *Campaign 1997*, Indigo, 1997, p. 68.

56. Ibid., p. 66.
57. *Today*, BBC Radio 4, 2 Mar. 1992.
58. *Times*, 3 Mar. 1992; *Sun*, 13 Mar. 1992.
59. Jones, *Campaign 1997*, 1997, p. 71.
60. Wyatt, *Journals*, vol. 2, Macmillan, p. 481 (19 Mar. 1991).

CHAPTER 12: GREEN HOWARD

1. *Sunday Telegraph*, 14 Mar. 1999.
2. N. Lamont, *In Office*, Little, Brown, 1999, p. 255.
3. N. Lamont, interview with MAG.
4. *Times*, 14 Apr. 1993.
5. *Guardian*, 15 May 1992.
6. *Sun*, 3 Dec. 1992.
7. *Times*, 17 Sept. 1992.
8. M. Portillo, interview with MLC.
9. *Daily Telegraph*, 30 July 1992.
10. T. Burke, interview with MLC.
11. D. Osborn, interview with MLC.
12. e.g. Cons. Party website, www.conservatives.com, Nov. 2004.
13. *Sunday Telegraph*, 14 Mar. 1999.
14. C. Meyer, interview with MLC.
15. *Guardian*, 11 May 1992.
16. Hansard, 3 June 1992, col. 858.
17. Burke interview.
18. *Observer*, 14 June 1992.
19. *Guardian*, 8 June 1992.
20. Burke interview.
21. J. Major, *The Autobiography*, HarperCollins, 1999, p. 511.
22. *Times*, 14 Apr. 1993.
23. Lamont, *In Office*, p. 348.
24. Ibid., p. 272.
25. *Sunday Times*, 27 Sept. 1992.
26. *Independent*, 3 Nov. 1992.
27. G. Brandreth, *Breaking the Code: Westminster Diaries*, Weidenfeld & Nicolson, 1999, p. 121; *Breakfast with Frost*, BBC1, 28 Feb. 1993.
28. Cons. Party press release, 6 Mar. 1993.
29. M. Rifkind, interview with MAG.
30. *Sunday Telegraph*, 7 Feb. 1993.
31. Lamont interview.
32. *Folkestone Herald*, 25 Sept. 1992.
33. D. Cameron, interview with MLC.
34. W. Wyatt, *Journals of Woodrow Wyatt*, vol. 3, Macmillan, 2000, p. 155 (2 Jan. 1993).
35. *Sunday Telegraph*, 7 Feb. 1993.
36. *Folkestone Herald*, 27 May 1993.
37. B. Walker, interview with MAG.
38. T. Gorman, *No, Prime Minister!* John Blake, 2001, p. 317.
39. *Times*, 5 Mar. 1993.

40. J. Zitron, *Transfer of Affections*, Fabian Society, 2004, pp. 5–6.
41. Burke interview.
42. Ibid.
43. P. Thurnham, interview with MWBG.
44. Ibid.
45. N. Crickhowell, *Westminster, Wales and Water*, University of Wales Press, 1999, p. 167.
46. Lamont interview.

CHAPTER 13: CRIME MINISTER

1. Conference coverage, BBC2, 6 Oct. 1993.
2. *Sun*, 17 June 1993.
3. Ibid., 26 July 1993.
4. J. Rentoul, *Tony Blair*, Little, Brown, 1995, p. 264.
5. *Independent*, 24 Jan. 2000.
6. A. King et al., *Britain at the Polls 1992*, Chatham House, 1993, p. 209.
7. *Sunday Times*, 4 July 1993.
8. *Times*, 20 Mar. 1994.
9. Transcript of raw interview with M. Cockerell for *How to be Home Secretary*, BBC2, 24 Jan. 1999.
10. D. Lewis, *Hidden Agendas*, Hamish Hamilton, 1997, p. 102.
11. Transcript of raw interview with M. Cockerell for *How to be Home Secretary*.
12. Ibid.
13. G. Brandreth, *Breaking the Code: Westminster Diaries*, Weidenfeld & Nicolson, 1999, p. 466 (24 Feb. 1997).
14. L. Brittan, interview with MLC.
15. N. Cohen, *Pretty Straight Guys*, Faber, 2003, p. 10.
16. D. Lewis, interview with MLC.
17. Lewis, *Hidden Agendas*, pp. 122–3.
18. Ibid., p. 124.
19. *Sun*, 30 Aug. 1993.
20. *Guardian*, 2 June 1993.
21. Transcript of raw interview with M. Cockerell for *How to be Home Secretary*.
22. *Sunday Times*, 4 July 1993.
23. *Independent on Sunday*, 3 Oct. 1993.
24. *News of the World*, 3 Oct. 1993.
25. Press release of speech to CPC, 5 Oct. 1993.
26. *Daily Telegraph*, 7 Oct. 1993.
27. Ibid.
28. *Guardian*, 13 Oct. 1993.
29. *Sun*, 7 Oct. 1993.
30. *Daily Telegraph*, 7 Oct. 1993.
31. *Times*, 9 Oct. 1993.
32. *Guardian*, 12 Nov. 1993.
33. *Private Eye*, 3 Dec. 1993.
34. *Sun*, 4 Nov. 1993.
35. M. Portillo, interview with MLC.

36. Hansard, 11 Jan. 1994, cols. 21, 30, 39.
37. Hansard, (Lords), 18 Jan. 1994, col. 482.
38. *Sunday Telegraph*, 23 Jan. 1994.
39. *Guardian*, 2 Mar. 1994.
40. Ibid., 28 Mar. 1994.
41. Lewis, *Hidden Agendas*, p. 120.
42. Hansard, 9 Mar. 1994, col. 292.
43. M. McDonagh, interview with MLC.
44. B. Thomas, interview with MLC.
45. N. Jones, *Campaign 1997*, Indigo, 1997, pp. 65–6.
46. Ibid., p. 66.
47. *Cry Wolf* (Wolverhampton University), Feb. 1995.
48. B. Stewart, interview with MWBG.
49. *Cry Wolf*, Feb. 1995.
50. N. Hardwick, interview with MLC.
51. *Times*, 13 Apr. 1994.
52. Brandreth, *Breaking the Code*, p. 241 (17 Mar. 1994).
53. *Observer*, 20 Feb. 1994.
54. *Sunday Times*, 17 Apr. 1994.
55. *Sun*, 31 Mar. 1994.
56. Hansard, 26 Apr. 1994, cols. 122–4.

CHAPTER 14: ESCAPES AND SCAPEGOATS

1. K. Clarke, interview with MAG.
2. *Observer*, 22 Aug. 1993.
3. *Sunday Express*, 29 Aug. 1993.
4. D. Lewis, *Hidden Agendas*, Hamish Hamilton, 1997, p. 103.
5. *Private Eye*, 13 Aug. 1993.
6. D. Lewis, interview with MLC.
7. Lewis, *Hidden Agendas*, pp. 103–4.
8. *Daily Telegraph*, 7 Sept. 1993.
9. Lewis, *Hidden Agendas*, p. 98.
10. *Times*, 15 Oct. 1993.
11. *Observer*, 17 Oct. 1993.
12. *Independent*, 15 Oct. 1993.
13. Lewis, *Hidden Agendas*, p. 111.
14. Ibid., p. 113.
15. *Daily Telegraph*, 25 Jan. 1994.
16. *Evening Standard*, 17 Feb. 1994.
17. Ibid., 18 Feb. 1994.
18. Lewis interview.
19. *Observer*, 25 Sept. 1994.
20. Transcript of raw interview with M. Cockerell for *How to be Home Secretary*, BBC2, 24 Jan. 1999.
21. *Guardian*, 13 Oct. 1994.
22. *Sunday Times*, 25 Sept. 1994.
23. *Daily Telegraph*, 14 Oct. 1994.

24. G. Brandreth, *Breaking the Code: Westminster Diaries*, Weidenfeld & Nicolson, 1999, pp. 317–18.
25. *Independent*, 20 Dec. 1994.
26. Transcript of raw interview with M. Cockerell for *How to be Home Secretary*.
27. Hansard, 24 Oct. 1983, cols. 23–4.
28. *Evening Standard*, 4 Jan. 1995.
29. Lewis, *Hidden Agendas*, p. 169.
30. Hansard, 19 May 1997, col. 464.
31. Lewis, *Hidden Agendas*, pp. 169–70.
32. *Times*, 20 May 1997.
33. Lewis, *Hidden Agendas*, pp. 171–2.
34. Hansard, 19 Oct. 1995, col. 521.
35. Hansard, Home Affairs Cttee, 18 Jan. 1995, pp. 15–16.
36. N. Kochan, *Ann Widdecombe*, Politico's, 2000, p. 170.
37. *Daily Telegraph*; *Daily Mail*, 28 Sept. 1995.
38. Kochan, *Ann Widdecombe*, p. 177.
39. Ibid., p. 178.
40. Ibid., p. 181.
41. Ibid., p. 186.
42. *The Real Michael Howard*, Meridian TV, ITV, 27 Apr. 2004.
43. Kochan, *Ann Widdecombe*, p. 186.
44. Transcript of raw interview with M. Cockerell for *How to be Home Secretary*.
45. Hansard, 16 Oct. 1995, cols. 32–3.
46. *Newsnight*, BBC2, 16 Oct. 1995.
47. *Independent*, 17 Oct. 1995.
48. *Daily Telegraph*, 18 Oct. 1995.
49. Kochan, *Ann Widdecombe*, p. 187.
50. Brandreth, *Breaking the Code*, p. 343 (19 Oct. 1995).
51. Hansard, 19 Oct. 1995, col. 504.
52. Brandreth, *Breaking the Code*, p. 343 (19 Oct. 1995).
53. Hansard, 19 Oct. 1995, col. 516.
54. Hansard, Home Affairs Cttee, 18 Jan. 1995, p. 15.
55. Hansard, 19 Oct. 1995, col. 517.
56. Ibid., col. 528.
57. Brandreth, *Breaking the Code*, p. 344 (19 Oct. 1995).
58. Transcript of raw interview with M. Cockerell for *How to be Home Secretary*.
59. Kochan, *Ann Widdecombe*, p. 188.
60. Ibid., p. 190.
61. Hansard, 19 May 1997, p. 408.
62. *Observer*, 22 Oct. 1995.
63. *Sunday Times*, 22 Oct. 1995.
64. Hansard, Public Service Cttee, 22 May 1996, p. 104.
65. *Sun*, 30 Mar. 1996.
66. *World In Action*, Granada TV, ITV, 24 Feb. 1997.
67. Lewis interview.
68. *Daily Telegraph*, 14 Sept. 2002.
69. Hansard, 21 Feb. 1994, col. 45.
70. *Independent*, 30 Mar. 1994.

71. *Private Eye*, 24 Sept. 1993.
72. Hansard, 19 Oct. 1995, col. 520.
73. *World In Action*, 24 Feb. 1997.
74. Kochan, *Ann Widdecombe*, p. 183.

CHAPTER 15: THE FOURTH BASTARD

1. M. Portillo, interview with MLC.
2. Ibid.
3. A. Seldon, *John Major: A Political Life*, Weidenfeld & Nicolson, 1997, p. 390.
4. J. Major, *The Autobiography*, HarperCollins, 1999, pp. 343–4.
5. Hansard, 9 June 1993, col. 285.
6. *Breakfast with Frost*, BBC1, 13 June 1993.
7. N. Lamont, *In Office*, Little, Brown, 1999, p. 420.
8. *Breakfast with Frost*, BBC1, 27 Nov. 1994.
9. H. Williams, *Guilty Men*, Aurum Press, 1998, pp. 87, 51.
10. I. Lang, *Blue Remembered Years*, Politico's, 2000, p. 217.
11. Major, *Autobiography*, p. 646.
12. Raw interview for *The Major Years*, BBC1, Oct. 1999.
13. *Breakfast with Frost*, BBC1, 6 Mar. 1994.
14. *Observer*, 1 May 1994.
15. *Daily Telegraph*, 4 June 1994.
16. Raw interview for *The Major Years*.
17. *Daily Mail*, 5 May 1995.
18. W. Wyatt, *Journals of Woodrow Wyatt*, vol. 3, Macmillan, 2000, pp. 471–2 (31 Jan. 1995), p. 670 (30 Sept. 1996), p. 415 (29 Sept. 1994), p. 531 n. (4 July 1995).
19. Ibid., p. 655 (25 July 1996).
20. *Guardian*, 13 Oct. 1995.
21. *Daily Telegraph*, 13 Oct. 1995.
22. Ibid.
23. Ibid., 10 Nov. 1995.
24. *Evening Standard*, 6 June 1996.
25. *Independent*, 13 Oct. 1995.
26. *Sunday Times*, 4 Feb. 1996.
27. *Times*, 10 May 1996.
28. *Guardian*, 4 Apr. 1996.
29. *Sunday Times*, 25 Feb. 1996.
30. *Daily Telegraph*, 10 June 1996.
31. *Times*, 15 July 1994.
32. *Economist*, 15 Feb. 1997.
33. *Independent*, 8 Feb. 1997.
34. N. Lamont, interview with MAG.
35. Hansard, 4 May 1996, col. 934.
36. *Sun*, 18 Oct. 1996.
37. D. Mellor, interview with MLC.
38. *Guardian*, 5 Dec. 1996.
39. *Times*, 17 Mar. 1997.

40. *Financial Times*, 14 Oct. 1996.

41. Press release of speech to Cons. Party conference, 8 Oct. 1996.

42. *Daily Mail*, 24 May 1994.

43. Hansard, 11 Dec. 1995, col. 700.

44. J. Dimbleby, *The Last Governor*, Little, Brown, 1997, pp. 313, 321.

45. *Independent on Sunday*, 19 Nov. 1995; *Jewish Quarterly*, Dec. 1995.

46. *Breakfast with Frost*, BBC1, 10 Dec. 1995.

47. See D. Woodhouse, 'Politicians and the Judges', *Parliamentary Affairs*, July 1996.

48. *Daily Mail*, 10 Apr. 1995.

49. *Independent*, 2 Nov. 1995.

50. Ibid., 24 Jan. 1994.

51. *Times*, 5 Mar. 1997.

52. *Manchester Evening News*, 29 Feb. 1996.

53. *Sunday Telegraph*, 22 Dec. 1996.

54. *Times*, 14 Jan. 1997.

55. N. Bonsor, interview with MLC.

56. C. Gill, *Whips' Nightmare*, Memoir Club, 2003, p. 104.

57. K. Clarke, interview with MAG.

58. Portillo interview.

59. A. Clark, *The Last Diaries*, Weidenfeld & Nicolson, 2002, p. 208 (9 Jan. 1997).

60. Major, *Autobiography*, p. 699.

61. *Sun*, 23 Dec. 1996.

62. *Daily Mail*, 21 Apr. 1997.

63. Raw interview for *The Major Years*.

64. G. Brandreth, *Breaking the Code: Westminster Diaries*, Weidenfeld & Nicolson, 1999, p. 496 (24 Apr. 1997).

CHAPTER 16: CRIMINAL COUSINS

1. *Independent*, 23 Nov. 1999.

2. H. Brooke and H. Aldous, *House of Fraser Holdings plc*, HMSO, 1988, p. 13.

3. *Guardian*, 26 July 1979.

4. Commons Notices of Questions and Motions, EDM 719, 13 Apr. 1989.

5. Ibid., EDM 720, 13 Apr. 1989.

6. Hansard, WPQ, 13 Apr. 1989, col. 641.

7. F. Pollard, letter to M. Howard, 21 June 1989.

8. Ibid., 30 Jan. 1990.

9. F. Pollard, *20 Things You Ought to Know about Michael Howard MP*, c. 1990.

10. *Kentish Express*, 22 Feb. 1990.

11. Hansard, 4 June 1997, col. 308.

12. C. Wardle, interview with MLC and MAG.

13. Wardle interview.

14. Hansard, 4 June 1997, col. 309.

15. Ibid., col. 318.

16. T. Bower, *Fayed: The Unauthorised Biography*, Macmillan, 1998, p. 331.

17. Commons Cttee on Standards and Privileges, 4th report, 1996–7, p. 11.

18. Ibid.

19. Ibid.

20. Ibid., p. 39.
21. *Sunday Telegraph*, 14 Dec. 1997.
22. *Today*, 25 Oct. 1994; Bower, *Fayed*, p. 354.
23. *Guardian*, 21 Oct. 1994.
24. *Mail on Sunday*, 23 Oct. 1994.
25. Hansard, 4 June 1997, col. 309.
26. *Financial Times*, 25 Oct. 1994.
27. Ibid.
28. J. Major, *The Autobiography*, HarperCollins, 1999, p. 568.
29. D. Owen, interview with MLC.
30. Hansard, WPQ, 25 Oct. 1994, col. 524.
31. *Times*, 22 Oct. 1994.
32. Commons Cttee on Standards and Privileges, 4th report, 1996–7, p. 5.
33. Unpublished transcript of M. Fayed testimony before G. Downey, 17 Dec. 1996.
34. Commons Cttee on Standards and Privileges, 4th report, 1996–7, p. 17.
35. Ibid., pp. 97, 21–2.
36. Ibid., p. 23.
37. Ibid., pp. 44, 7, 41.
38. Ibid., p. 42.
39. Ibid., pp. 73, 41.
40. Ibid., pp. 43, 44.
41. *Times*, 14 Nov. 1996.
42. *Guardian*, 14 Nov. 1996.
43. *The Herald* (Glasgow), 23 Aug. 1995.
44. *Daily Telegraph*, 13 Oct. 1995.
45. P. Kilfoyle, interview with MLC.
46. Hansard, 7 Mar. 2001, col. 392.
47. P. Connew, interview with MLC.
48. *Sunday Mirror*, 1 Sept. 1996.
49. *Guardian*, 2 Sept. 1996.
50. *Observer*, 2 Nov. 2003.
51. Ibid.
52. *Independent*, 28 Feb. 2001.
53. P. Ferris with R. McKay, *The Ferris Conspiracy*, Mainstream, 2001, pp. 218–19.
54. *Observer*, 9 Nov. 2003.
55. G. Johnson, *Powder Wars*, Mainstream, 2004, p. 157.
56. Hansard, 7 Mar. 2001, col. 393.
57. Ibid., col. 396.
58. Letter, J. Straw to M. Howard, 5 Mar. 2001.
59. Hansard, 21 May 2004, col. 1279; *Sunday Mirror*, 8 June 1997.
60. *Sunday Mirror*, 25 May 1997.
61. Ibid.
62. *Observer*, 9 Nov. 2003.
63. Hansard, 21 May 2004, col. 1280.

CHAPTER 17: SOMETHING OF A NIGHTMARE

1. *Times*, 16 May 1997.

2. B. Cathcart, *Were You Still Up for Portillo?*, Penguin, 1997, pp. 142–3.
3. *Observer*, 27 Apr. 1997.
4. P. Doherty, interview with MWBG.
5. D. Laws, interview with MLC.
6. J.-A. Nadler, *William Hague*, Politico's, 2000, p. 11.
7. M. Mowlam, *Momentum*, Hodder, 2002, p. 129.
8. N. Lamont, interview with MAG.
9. A. Duncan, interview with MLC.
10. B. Newmark, interview with MLC.
11. Ibid.
12. Ibid.
13. *Daily Telegraph*, 7 May 1997.
14. Nadler, *William Hague*, p. 15.
15. N. Morgan, interview with MLC.
16. A. Hagdrup, interview with MLC.
17. J. Hanson interview with MLC.
18. *Sunday Telegraph*, 4 May 1997.
19. Ibid.
20. M. Howard, *The Future of Europe*, CPS, 1997.
21. *Sun*, 19 May 1997.
22. *Daily Telegraph*, 30 May 1997.
23. *Daily Mirror*, 21 May 1997.
24. *Sunday Times*, 11 May 1997.
25. A. Jay (ed.), *Oxford Dictionary of Political Quotations*, Oxford University Press, 2004, p. 383.
26. *Spectator*, 17 May 1997.
27. *Daily Mail*, 13 May 1997.
28. *Times*, 14 May 1997.
29. *Newsnight*, BBC2, 13 May 1997.
30. *Newsnight at 20*, BBC2, 29 Jan. 2000.
31. *Newsnight*, BBC2, 13 May 1997.
32. N. Kochan, *Ann Widdecombe*, Politico's, 2000, p. 226.
33. *Newsnight at 20*.
34. *Economist*, 17 May 1997.
35. S. Douglas-Home, interview with MLC.
36. *Daily Mirror*, 21 May 1997.
37. *Sunday Telegraph*, 18 May 1997.
38. Hansard, 19 May 1997, cols. 398–9, 405–6.
39. Ibid., col. 406.
40. *Times*, 20 May 1997.
41. Hansard, 19 May 1997, cols. 464–5.
42. Ibid., col. 463.
43. Ibid., col. 466.
44. *Sun*, 20 May 1997.
45. Ibid., 19 May 1997.
46. Hansard, 19 May 1997, col. 408.
47. Ibid., 21 May 1997, col. 732.
48. *Sunday Mirror*, 25 May 1997.

49. A. Clark, *The Last Diaries*, Weidenfeld & Nicolson, 2002, pp. 226–7 (27, 30 May 1997).
50. J. Critchley and M. Halcrow, *Collapse of Stout Party*, Gollancz, 1997, p. 250.
51. *Daily Mail*, 9 May 1997.
52. *Independent on Sunday*, 18 May 1997.
53. Hansard, 4 June 1997, cols. 307–8.
54. Ibid., col. 315.
55. Ibid., col. 318.
56. Clark, *The Last Diaries*, p. 228 (6 June 1997).
57. *Evening Standard*, 9 June 1997.
58. *Times*, 10 June 1997.
59. *Observer*, 8 June 1997; *Guardian*, 10 June 1997; *Independent*, 6 June 1997.
60. *Daily Express*, 26 June 1997.
61. Kochan, *Ann Widdecombe*, p. 232.
62. *Talking Politics*, winter 1997–8.
63. Ibid.

CHAPTER 18: IN THE SHADOWS

1. *New Statesman*, 19 June 1998.
2. N. Lamont, interview with MLC.
3. *Times*, 8 Jan. 1998.
4. *Desert Island Discs*, BBC Radio 4, 4 July 2004.
5. *Daily Express*, 26 June 1997.
6. *New Statesman*, 19 June 1998.
7. *Spectator*, 14 Mar. 1998.
8. *Daily Mail*, 31 Oct. 1996.
9. *Daily Express*, 11 Nov. 1996.
10. *Times* magazine, 30 Oct. 2004.
11. *Cherwell*, 13 Feb. 1998.
12. Ibid.
13. Ibid., 20 Feb. 1998.
14. S. Boteach, interview with MWBG.
15. Ibid.
16. S. Douglas-Home, interview with MLC.
17. J.-A. Nadler, *William Hague*, Politico's, 2000, p. 238.
18. *Sunday Times*, 5 Oct. 1997.
19. *Daily Telegraph*, 9 Oct. 1997.
20. *Sunday Times*, 5 Oct. 1997.
21. *Evening Standard*, 4 Feb. 1998.
22. A. Rawnsley, *Servants of the People*, Hamish Hamilton, 2000, p. 180.
23. Hansard, 27 July 1998, col. 24.
24. Lamont interview.
25. Hansard, 27 Nov. 1998, col. 453.
26. *Daily Mail*, 11 May 1999.
27. *Crossbow*, summer 1999.
28. *Daily Telegraph*, 12 May 1999.
29. *Times*, 19 May 1999.

30. Ibid., 8 Jan. 1998.
31. *Express*, 3 Mar. 1998.
32. Lamont interview.
33. *Sun*, 26 Jan. 1999.
34. *Mail on Sunday*, 25 Nov. 2001.
35. *Times*, 11 Oct. 1999.
36. See P. Cowley, *Revolts and Rebellions*, Politico's, 2002, pp. 191–3.
37. *Folkestone Herald*, 29 Apr. 1999.
38. Lamont interview.
39. *Mail on Sunday*, 28 Nov. 1999.
40. *Daily Telegraph*, 10 Sept. 1999.
41. Douglas-Home interview.
42. J. Archer, *Prison Diary*, vol. 3, Macmillan, 2003, pp. 228.
43. C. Powell, interview with MLC.
44. *Guardian*, 23 Apr. 2001.
45. Ibid., 16 Apr. 2001.
46. *Sunday Telegraph*, 22 July 2001.
47. *Guardian*, 14 Sept. 2001.
48. T. Bower, *Gordon Brown*, HarperCollins, 2004, p. 69.
49. Lamont interview.
50. Hansard, 27 Nov. 2001, col. 839.
51. Ibid., 3 Dec. 2001, col. 97.
52. *Independent*, 15 Sept. 2001.
53. *Times*, 8 Oct. 2001.
54. *Guardian*, 27 Nov. 2001.
55. *Mail on Sunday*, 25 Nov. 2001.
56. *Guardian*, 24 Dec. 2002.
57. *Daily Mail*, 22 Jan. 2004.
58. Hansard, 27 Nov. 2002, col. 327.
59. *Guardian*, 28 Nov. 2002.
60. Hansard, 9 June 2003, col. 416.
61. *Times*, 22 Mar. 2003.
62. *Daily Telegraph*, 9 Apr. 2003.
63. *Breakfast with Frost*, BBC1, 6 Apr. 2003.
64. Commons Notices of Questions and Motions, EDM 922, 4 Mar. 2002.
65. *Breakfast with Frost*, BBC1, 10 Aug. 2003.
66. N. Lamont, interview with MAG.

CHAPTER 19: THE COUP

1. M. Howard speech, 30 Oct. 2003, http://conservatives.com.
2. *Daily Telegraph*, 10 Oct. 2003.
3. *Daily Mail*, 22 Jan. 2004.
4. *Sunday Telegraph*, 26 Oct. 2003.
5. Commons Cttee on Standards and Privileges, 4th report, vol. 3, 2003–2004, pp. 298–9.
6. Mawer, vol. 2, p. 36.
7. T. Renton, *Chief Whip*, Politico's, 2004, p. 331.

8. *Daily Telegraph*, 10 Oct. 2003.
9. R. Syms, interview with MLC.
10. A. Widdecombe, interview with MLC.
11. N. Kochan, *Ann Widdecombe*, pbk edn, Politico's, 2004, p. 311.
12. Widdecombe interview.
13. *Sunday Telegraph*, 2 Nov. 2003.
14. S. Pollard, *David Blunkett*, Hodder, 2004, p. 269.
15. *Sunday Telegraph*, 2 Nov. 2003.
16. Ibid.
17. *Guardian*, 31 Oct. 2003.
18. Howard speech, 30 Oct. 2003.
19. Ibid.
20. Ibid.
21. Ibid.
22. *Sunday Telegraph*, 2 Nov. 2002.
23. K. Clarke, interview with MAG.
24. *Sunday Mirror*, 2 Nov. 2003; *Observer*, 2 Nov. 2003.

CHAPTER 20: LEADING QUESTIONS

1. *Desert Island Discs*, BBC Radio 4, 4 July 2004.
2. M. Portillo, interview with MLC.
3. Ann Widdecombe, interview with MLC.
4. G. Shephard, interview with MLC.
5. *Times*, 2 Jan. 2004.
6. Cons. Party press release, 9 Feb. 2004.
7. *Times*, 10 Feb. 2004.
8. Hansard, 12 Nov. 2003, cols. 279–80.
9. Ibid., 3 Dec. 2003, col. 498.
10. Ibid., 12 Nov. 2003, col. 279.
11. Ibid., 3 Dec., 2003, col. 498.
12. Ibid., 7 Jan. 2004, cols. 249–50.
13. Ibid., 7 Jan. 2004, col. 249.
14. Ibid., 28 Jan. 2004, cols. 343–7.
15. *Times*, 29 Jan. 2004.
16. *Daily Telegraph*, 30 Jan. 2004.
17. M. Howard speech, 12 Feb. 2004, http://conservatives.com.
18. M. Howard speech, 19 Feb. 2004, http://conservatives.com.
19. Ibid.
20. R. Peston, *Brown's Britain*, Short Books, 2005.
21. *Daily Telegraph*, 21 July 2004.
22. BBC Radio 5 Live, 24 Mar. 2004.
23. *Desert Island Discs*, 4 July 2004.
24. *This Morning*, ITV, 6 July 2004.
25. *Guardian*, 7 July 2004.
26. *This Morning*, 6 July 2004.
27. *Times* magazine, 30 Oct. 2004.
28. *Lady*, 30 Nov. 2004.

29. *Times* magazine, 30 Oct. 2004.
30. Ibid.
31. *Scotland on Sunday*, 17 Oct. 2004.
32. GQ, Oct. 2004.
33. *Sunday Times*, 18 July 2004.
34. *Spectator*, 8 Jan. 2005.
35. Hansard, 20 July 2004, col. 203.
36. *Independent*, 21 July 2004.
37. Hansard, 20 July 2004, col. 258.
38. *Sunday Telegraph*, 29 Aug. 2004.
39. Ibid., 7 Nov. 2004.
40. Press release, M. Howard speech, 5 Oct. 2004.
41. Ibid.
42. Author's notes.
43. *Times*, 11 Dec. 2004.
44. *Daily Telegraph*, 14 Dec. 2004.
45. *Spectator*, 16 Oct. 2004.
46. *Times*, 16 Oct. 2004.
47. *No More Mr Nasty*, BBC2, 12 Feb. 2005.
48. Hansard, 8 Dec. 2004, col. 1164.
49. Ibid., 15 Dec. 2004, col. 1662–3.
50. Hansard, 12 Jan. 2005, cols. 291–3.
51. Author's calculations based on BBC compilations of polling data.
52. *Times*, 2 Jan. 2004.
53. *Sunday Telegraph*, 16 Jan. 2005.
54. Ibid., 23 Jan. 2005.
55. BBC Radio 5 Live, 25 Jan. 2005.

EPILOGUE

1. M. Howard speech, 30 Oct. 2003, http://conservatives.com.
2. *Sunday Telegraph*, 30 Jan. 2005.
3. *Financial Times*, 13 May 1991.

INDEX